CANADIAN
E-MARKETING
A STRATEGIC APPROACH

RAMESH VENKAT
Saint Mary's University

McGraw-Hill Ryerson

Toronto Montréal Boston Burr Ridge, IL Dubuque, IA Madison, WI New York
San Francisco St. Louis Bangkok Bogotá Caracas Kuala Lumpur Lisbon London
Madrid Mexico City Milan New Delhi Santiago Seoul Singapore Sydney Taipei

McGraw-Hill
Ryerson Limited

A Subsidiary of The **McGraw·Hill** *Companies*

Canadian E-Marketing
A Strategic Approach

ISBN: 0-07-087857-9

1 2 3 4 5 6 7 8 9 10   TCP   0 9 8 7 6 5 4 3 2 1

Printed and bound in Canada.

Vice President and Editorial Director: Pat Ferrier
Sponsoring Editor: Lenore Gray-Spence
Developmental Editor: Alison Derry
Copy Editor: Valerie Adams
Production Coordinator: Madeleine Harrington
Senior Marketing Manager: Jeff MacLean
Composition: Bookman Typesetting Co.
Cover Design: Dianna Little
Cover Image Credit: Bill Frymire/Masterfile
Interior Design: Deborah Brock
Printing: Transcontinental Printing

Canadian Cataloguing in Publication Data

Venkat, Ramesh, 1962–
    Canadian e-marketing: a strategic approach

Includes index.
ISBN 0-07-087857-9

Internet marketing.   I. Title.

HF5415.1265.V46 2001   658.8'00285'4678   C2001-930328-9

About the Author

Ramesh Venkat is an Associate Professor of Marketing and Director of the Sobey MBA Program at the Frank H. Sobey Faculty of Commerce, Saint Mary's University. He has an MBA in Marketing from Simon Fraser University and a Ph.D. in Marketing from the University of British Columbia.

His training and initial teaching and research interests were in the area of consumer behaviour. He has published extensively on social influences on consumer behaviour. He became interested in the Internet as a commercial medium in 1994. Since then, his teaching, research, and consulting experience have focused on the Internet and E-commerce.

He offered the first graduate-level Canadian MBA course in Internet Marketing in 1995–96. Since then, he has taught this subject at the undergraduate, graduate, and senior executive levels. His research in this area has addressed issues like online advertising effectiveness, the customer relationship online, consumer decision making online, and the impact and challenges in B2B E-commerce. His research projects in E-commerce have been funded by Saint Mary's University, the Purchasing Management Association of Canada, and Industry Canada.

Ramesh is the founder of an E-commerce consulting company called W3Strategy.com, which offers strategic consulting and corporate training in this area. W3Strategy's clients have included small and medium-sized enterprises, as well as various government agencies.

Ramesh shares his life with his wife Manjula in Halifax. His interests include travelling, reading, the Internet, film studies, and creative writing.

Brief Contents

Contents

Preface

What Is Internet Marketing?

Internet marketing is simply the application and extension of marketing concepts to the Internet. The fundamentals of marketing—delivering value to customers, solving their problems, and satisfying their needs—does not change whether one is marketing online or through traditional bricks-and-mortar retail stores. Whereas E-commerce focuses on selling products and services online (including the transaction process and back-end technologies), Internet marketing encompasses everything from product design to post-purchase customer care.

Why Should Marketers Care?

> "In five years every company will be an Internet company or it will it dead."
> —**Andy Grove**, Chairman, *Intel Corporation*, May 1999

That's a rather bold statement, and there are good reasons to believe that Andy Grove is right. The Internet is altering the business landscape. It is forcing old companies to think in new ways. From the procurement of raw materials to the production process, marketing, distribution, and service, the Internet affects every aspect of a business.

The industrial revolution gave us mass production, where all customers were treated alike. Now the information revolution, of which the Internet is a part, is allowing firms to treat each customer as an individual with unique needs. Mass marketing is being replaced by customized marketing. The Internet and advances in information technology allow businesses in a wide range of industries—from clothing to car manufacturing—to customize their offerings.

The Internet allows marketers to engage in one-to-one dialogue with each customer. Auto-makers, for instance, are learning first-hand the preferences of car buyers, as they allow consumers to customize the product online. Previously, the dealers were in charge of negotiating with consumers. Some marketers are now avoiding mass media advertising in favour of more personalized and interactive communication on the Internet. From marketing to segments of consumers, now firms are considering marketing to a segment-of-one consumer at a time.

Direct distribution is replacing lengthy distribution channels, which added cost but no value to the customer. Manufacturers can now sell directly to end-users, bypassing layers of intermediaries. New methods of selling online such as reverse auctions and aggregate buying are putting the consumer in charge of determining the product's price.

There is so much information now easily available on competing products. There are specialized search engines (or shopping assistants) that will find the product/retailer with the lowest price or provide other comparison information on competing products. The availability of information (once very difficult to track down) and the new shopping formats mean increasing downward pressure on prices. The marketer has less control over pricing policy. As online firms reduce prices in an attempt to lure traffic to their sites, there is a danger of brands losing their shine and becoming commoditized. Many experts are questioning the relevance of old-fashioned brand management in this new context.

From product design and communication to determining the price of the product, the consumer plays a crucial role online. In this new environment, the customer is less loyal because there are so many competing offers and one is not limited to buying the brands sold in the local stores. Marketers are scrambling to find ways in which they can encourage repeat buying and loyalty.

Older firms, spanning every sector of the economy, are in the process of reinventing themselves. Meanwhile, newer, more agile firms on the Internet are inventing new business models, from free Internet service to reverse auctions. Small firms find themselves on a more level playing field and some even sell globally, a feat that would not have been possible without the Internet. New technologies that expand the marketer's capabilities are being unveiled at frantic pace. We are just starting to see online shopping and content delivery being extended to palm devices and cellular phones.

Marketing is in a state of turmoil. Some, including Andy Grove, see a paradigm shift, a new way of thinking about and doing business. When you consider the fact that the commercialization of the Internet only began in 1995, the rate of change and the scope of change is astounding. As this book is being written, 300 million people worldwide are online and even small businesses are buying, selling, and advertising online.

As firms scramble to get a piece of the action, many lack strategy. Many are acting first and thinking (or regretting) later. As start-up firms emerge each day and as the old guards embrace E-commerce, businesses are finding that there are not enough people with the necessary skills to market in this new, dynamic environment.

This book was written to provide a strategy guide to marketers, seasoned pros, and students alike. It first lays out the scope and magnitude of change forced by the Internet. The market opportunities are described next. Then, a series of chapters present the tools, concepts, strategic insights, and tactics. The central theme is the focus on customers and the customer relationship.

Why Study Internet Marketing?

First, from reading this Preface so far, it must be evident that the field of Internet marketing is an exciting one—filled with new opportunities and challenges as well as advances in technologies that are changing the landscape of marketing. Marketers have to think differently now.

Second, from the Fortune 500 firms to the new start-up firms, businesses cannot avoid the Internet. Even the so-called "old economy" businesses such as retailing (e.g., Wal-Mart) and automobile manufacturing (e.g., GM) are embracing the Internet. No matter what sector you work in or plan to, it is likely that the Internet will play a big role in the future of your business. It's better to get ready now.

Third, there is a growing demand for those who are knowledgeable in this area. The number of new start-ups and the E-commerce extensions of older firms are increasing by the day. For those who will be in the job market soon and for those seeking a career change, knowledge of Internet marketing and E-commerce will be immensely useful. There is likely to be a shortage of talent in this area for the foreseeable future.

Who Should Read This Book?

This book is primarily written for undergraduate and graduate students in business or allied fields. Basic knowledge of marketing concepts will be useful. This course should ideally follow an introductory course in marketing. Practical experience in the marketing area can also provide the basic knowledge needed. Some experience on the Web (using search engines and visiting Web sites) will also come in handy. The book is written in a style that will not be intimidating to someone new to the field of marketing or the Internet.

In addition to students and faculty in universities and colleges, professionals in marketing or E-commerce as well as entrepreneurs will also find this book very useful.

How Is This Book Different?

First, this book takes a strategic perspective on Internet marketing. It is not a simple "how to" book or a book on Web site design. The book looks at marketing, not in isolation but as part of a series of value-adding functions within an organization. At times, the book crosses functional area boundaries to enable marketers to understand the organizational impact of certain issues. A separate chapter is devoted to marketing organization and strategy, but strategic concepts are incorporated throughout the book.

Second, this book covers topics that often have received little or no coverage in other books. Channel management, business-to-business E-commerce, and security issues (which are critical to the growth of commerce online) are addressed in depth. For marketers, the Internet has two primary roles—as a communication medium and a distribution channel (especially for software and other digital goods). Each of these areas is covered in depth by devoting two chapters.

Third, this book uses current knowledge in marketing, consumer behaviour, and strategy to provide frameworks for understanding marketing on the Internet. Familiar concepts such as the value chain and the consumer decision process model are applied to the Internet context.

Fourth, a global approach is taken throughout the book. The Internet is a global medium. Global trends, statistics and examples are presented in several chapters. This is important because the Internet eliminates national boundaries. In order to standardize currency references from country to country, all dollars are referred to in US dollar values.

Fifth, the book has a companion Web site that is intended for students and faculty. Even as the book was being written, some of the statistics and examples were becoming dated. Internet time is on a much faster clock. The Web site provides updates where required. It also provides additional examples, exercises, links to resources, and separate bulletin boards for students and faculty. The intent is to create a community of Internet marketers.

Lastly, this book is the result of over five years of teaching experience in Internet marketing to undergraduate, MBA, and EMBA students, as well as corporate executives. Student feedback over the years has played a role in how the material is presented. The presentation is non-technical and filled with examples and short cases. The book is written in a style that is, hopefully, easy to read and comprehend.

A Note to Instructors

The book is written in an easy-to-read style. The chapters are filled with examples and short cases (Vignettes and iMarket Demos), which can stimulate class discussion. The book covers areas often neglected by others. It uses a traditional marketing approach by covering markets and marketing mix. Students will be able to relate the concepts to what they have learned in previous courses.

The book takes the view that integration of offline and online marketing is critical. This approach is supported by many experts in this area and by a growing number of case studies. This book is oriented to Canadian academic users.

Instructors will be pleased to note that this book is supported with an Instructor's Manual with Test Bank, and PowerPoint slides. In addition, the companion Web site offers up-to-date resources and the ability to communicate directly with the author.

A Note to Students

Internet marketing is an exciting subject that is rapidly changing. This book is written for readers with varying degrees of familiarity in this subject. Both experts and novices will find the material interesting. Here are some of the highlights:

- Each chapter begins with a Vignette that focuses on one more key issues in the chapter.
- Short cases called iMarket Demos are included in each chapter. These real-life examples will enrich your learning.
- The topics in the chapter and the presentation of material are linked to the learning objectives specified at the beginning of the chapter.
- Summaries at the end of each chapter will help you review the important points quickly.
- Review and Discussion Questions at the end of the chapter help you test your understanding of the chapter's main concepts.
- Internet Exercises at the end of each chapter provide hands-on learning experience.
- The Web site offers updates, links to Web sites, and resources that will support and add to your learning experience.

How Is This Book Organized?

The book is divided into four parts. There are fourteen chapters and five appendices.

Part 1: Introduction to E-Markets

The emphasis of the first part is to introduce the reader to Internet marketing concepts and to provide a thorough understanding of the market opportunities online. The first two chapters provide the foundation, and the next two focus on online markets—the consumer and business markets.

Chapter 1: Introduction. This chapter provides a background and context for commerce on the Internet. The chapter introduces students to Internet marketing through a case study of the automobile industry. Students can see the impact of the Internet on marketing activities—from product management to distribution. An overview of Internet marketing is presented with a brief discussion of two areas of E-commerce—business-to-consumer and businesses-to-business. Market opportunities in each of these areas are considered. The economic and social impact of E-commerce and Internet marketing are also discussed to provide readers with a bigger picture.

Chapter 2: Economics of the Web and Business Models. This chapter focuses on three key areas—value creation, costs, and revenues. Marketers need to understand how to create value, how to control costs, and how to generate revenue. The concept of the value chain is extended to the Internet, and the impact of the Internet on the value chain is discussed in detail. The chapter outlines how the Internet can reduce a firm's cost structure across the entire value chain. After a discussion of costs, different methods of generating revenue (i.e., business models) are presented.

Chapter 3: The Business-to-Consumer Market. The demographic and usage characteristics of the business-to-consumer market are presented in this chapter. Factors that facilitate and hinder consumer adoption of the Internet are discussed. Even the most successful online firms in the business-to-consumer arena are not profitable. Most are struggling to turn one-time consumers into loyal consumers. This dismal performance underscores the need to understand consumer behaviour. The chapter also provides a detailed discussion of consumer behaviour and the consumer decision-making process.

Chapter 4: The Business Market. The business-to-business market is several times larger than the consumer market. Most Internet marketing books do not cover this topic at all. The main focus of this chapter is business-to-business E-commerce (i.e., buying and selling products and services online). Procurement of supplies and trading online are important aspects of B2B E-commerce. Businesses also use the Internet in a variety of other ways. In addition to E-commerce, attention is devoted to other online applications such as salesforce automation.

Part 2: Information and Strategy

Firms that truly understand their customers' needs and can foresee their competitors' moves will be hard to beat. The first chapter in Part 2 focuses on intelligence gathering—understanding consumers and competitors. The second chapter focuses on developing strategies using the information.

Chapter 5: Market Research and Business Intelligence. Just as the Internet empowers consumers with more information, it also allows marketers to gather very detailed information about consumers and competitors. Marketers can adjust their online advertising in real time, in response to the needs or behaviour of each consumer. The Internet is a vast source of information for everything one wants to know about competitors. Annual reports, press releases, patent filings, and product and price information can all be found very easily. The relatively low cost of gathering data online allows even smaller firms to benefit from the technological advances. This chapter presents the different forms of data collection, including primary and secondary research, along with the limitations of online market research. Ethical dilemmas in online research are also highlighted.

Chapter 6: Marketing Organization and Strategy. Consumer and competitive intelligence are crucial to developing a winning strategy. This chapter focuses on strategy and Internet marketing plan development. The marketing organization may have to undergo some changes to function effectively in the Internet environment. Organizational issues such as departmental roles, culture, human resources, and the changing function of the salesforce are addressed in this chapter. Organizational commitment and readiness is crucial for success in Internet marketing. This chapter lays the foundation for Part 3. Issues that are covered in detail in Part 3 are briefly presented in this chapter.

Part 3: Marketing Strategy Implementation

This is where the action is. This part starts with the recognition that the consumer is the central figure in the marketing process. Then, each element of marketing is introduced, while maintaining a focus on the consumer.

Chapter 7: Community and Customer Relationship Management. The Internet provides consumers with more choices and reduces the costs associated with brand switching, thus leading to diminished consumer loyalty. At the same time, customer acquisition costs are high. This chapter focuses on strategies that can stop this vicious circle. To explain the process of customer relationship building, a model is presented. From marketing to large segments of consumers, the chapter focuses on marketing to a segment-of-one consumer. The use of online databases and customer tracking methods and their application in relationship management are described, along with the roles of customization and consumer communities. As firms embrace the notion of customer relationship management, marketing elements such as product, price, and promotion will reflect that philosophy.

Chapter 8: Product Management and Pricing. Product development on the Internet takes on a new dimension with virtual product development teams and continuous feedback from consumers. The Internet is also diminishing the importance of brands in some ways. The ability to compare prices easily and the growing popularity of auction and aggregate buying formats are resulting in greater consumer attention on prices. This makes brands less important. The value of brand marketing on the Internet is discussed, and various online branding strategies are reviewed. Flexible pricing approaches (such as auction, reverse auction, and aggregate buying), which can give the consumer a greater say on prices, and flexible pricing and micro-pricing (unbundling products and selling them at low dollar values) are also described. Online and offline pricing strategies are compared and alternative online pricing strategies are presented.

Chapter 9: The Internet as a Communication Medium. Traditional mass media are one-way, non-interactive, passive media. The Internet is a two-way, interactive, and personalized communication medium. Old notions in mass communications theory have to be discarded if one aspires to market successfully online. This chapter compares the Internet with other media. It provides the reader with a sense of the capabilities of the Internet as a communication medium.

Chapter 10: Advertising and Promotion Online. This chapter builds on the previous chapter and discusses specific methods of online advertising and promotion. Advertising online can take many forms—from the ubiquitous banner advertisement to the microsite. The Internet allows marketers to measure the effectiveness of each ad placement on a Web site. In addition to advertising, various forms of sales promotion such as sweepstakes and online coupons are being used. The effectiveness of these tools is also considered in this chapter.

Chapter 11: The Internet as a Distribution Channel. Not all products will be suitable for direct distribution online. Some will benefit from having direct as well as the traditional indirect channels. Integrating the Internet with other channels and managing channel conflict are important considerations. As some businesses take to direct distribution, existing channels will disappear (or be disintermediated). At the same time, new online intermediaries called cybermediaries are emerging. These two themes are addressed in detail. While business-to-consumer E-commerce focuses mainly on the demand chain (firm-to-consumer), businesses-to-business E-commerce focuses mainly on the supply chain (supplier-to-firm). Channel issues in the B2B and B2C contexts are considered in this chapter.

Chapter 12: Online Retailing. Selling online is a significant part of Internet marketing. This involves setting up an online storefront with appropriate transaction-processing and security systems. Online retailing, or *e-tailing*, is not just about selling products to consumers.

It's about providing value and a superior online experience, which are critical to developing a long-term relationship. This chapter discusses all the issues to be considered while setting up an online storefront. Different business models for online retailing are considered, along with the challenges and opportunities for pure-play Internet firms (such as Amazon.com) and "bricks-and-clicks" firms (such as Wal-Mart, which has bricks-and-mortar and online operations). Concepts from the retailing literature are integrated into the discussion.

Part 4: Technical, Social, and Legal Issues

Chapter 13: Security, Privacy, and Legal Issues. If one can think of three significant barriers to E-commerce, they would be lack of online security, lack of consumer privacy, and a flawed or incomplete legal framework. This chapter addresses these three important areas. Security and privacy breaches online can reduce consumer confidence in online firms. A non-technical, but detailed, presentation of online security issues and solutions is provided. Consumer profiling and other techniques used by online firms have been a cause of concern for consumer protection groups. The chapter stresses appropriate and inappropriate uses of customer information. Lastly, new laws are being written and older laws are being rewritten to facilitate the smooth flow of commerce online. Marketers need to be aware of laws in a range of areas, from copyright to taxation.

Chapter 14: Social, Ethical, and Future Issues. The last chapter takes a step away from the benefits of marketing on the Internet to the individual firm and consumer, and focuses attention on macro-marketing issues. The social benefits and costs are reviewed, and issues such as the digital divide (segments of the population not having access to the Internet) and the displacement of workers are considered. The impact of the Internet on delivery of services such as education, healthcare, and government services is considered. The chapter concludes with a presentation of emerging technologies and a discussion of where Internet marketing and E-commerce are headed.

What Pedagogical Features are Included?

The following pedagogical features have been included in the text to enhance learning and a general understanding of e-marketing.

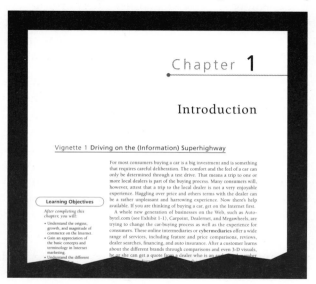

Vignettes. Each chapter begins with a vignette, which can be a case focusing on a specific company or an essay focusing on a specific issue. The vignettes are intended to provide an introduction to the chapter and to provoke discussion in the classroom.

iMarket Demos. In each chapter, boxed illustrations are provided to highlight use of a technology or illustrate an application or a specific issue. These examples can be used as the basis for class discussion. Most of them end with a question, which is intended to make the student think.

End-of-Chapter Features. The material at the end of each chapter is designed to assist the student in understanding and applying the concepts. These features include:

Summary. Each chapter concludes with a one- or two-page summary of the chapter's main points.

Key Terms. A list of key terms is provided at the end of each chapter. These terms are presented in colour in the chapters where they appear. Definitions for the key terms are provided in Appendix A at the end of the book.

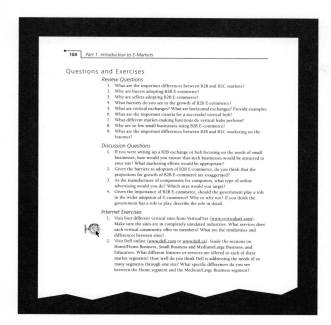

Questions and Exercises. There are three types of questions at the end of each chapter:

- *Review Questions* are intended to enable the students to test their understanding of the concepts presented in the chapter. Most often the answers can be found in the chapter.
- *Discussion Questions* require more thought and additional reading or research.
- *Internet Exercises* are practical applications that will require the student to spend some time on the Internet. Often the student must visit multiple Web sites to complete the exercise.

Appendices. The book has five appendices, which can be used separately or in conjunction with specific chapters.

A. *Glossary of Internet Marketing Terms.* The glossary explains the key terms in each chapter.

B. *An Internet Marketing Planning Guide.* This appendix can be useful to students when doing a course term project. The guide can also be used as a companion for Chapter 6.

C. *Internet Marketing Plan Outline.* This appendix can be used as a companion to Chapters 9 and 10. Appendix C is located online at www.mcgrawhill.ca/college/venkat.

D. *ESOMAR (European Society for Opinion and Marketing Research) Guidelines for Conducting Marketing and Opinion Research Using the Internet.* This appendix can be used in conjunction with Chapter 5.

E. *American Marketing Code of Ethics for Marketing on the Internet.* This appendix can be used with Chapter 14 and throughout the course.

What Teaching Aid Materials are Included?

Instructors' Manual. The Instructor's Manual consists of sample course outlines, suggestions for term projects, project guidelines, teaching tips for each chapter, additional examples for each chapter, and a test bank.

PowerPoint Slides. A set of PowerPoint masters are provided to instructors. Tables, charts, and examples from each chapter are included in the package. Additional data and screen shots are provided, where appropriate.

Web Site. The Web site is intended to be a resource for students and faculty. It contains links to all references cited in each chapter, links to new examples and resource sites, additional

Internet exercises, and bulletin boards. There will be separate discussion forums or bulletin boards for students and faculty. Faculty members can share ideas with each other and interact with the author.

Acknowledgements

I would like to offer sincere thanks to my mentor and former professor Stan Shapiro for providing me with the opportunity to write the Internet Insites in his *Basic Marketing* book. That venture led me to the belief that an in-depth treatment of Internet marketing in the academic context was long overdue. The feedback from Stan and other colleagues gave me the confidence that I could deliver a good product for the Canadian market.

Lenore Gray Spence, the Sponsoring Editor for this book, deserves my deep gratitude for taking my somewhat vague proposal and shaping it into a product that I am proud of. At every stage in this long process of writing this book, she showed immense patience, a willingness to see things from my perspective, and the desire to help me.

The team that she and McGraw-Hill Ryerson provided to support the book was incredible. Alison Derry, the Developmental Editor, was a real pleasure to work with. She had the difficult job of making sure that I met my deadlines. She was cheerful and helpful throughout the process. I also thank Daphne Scriabin, who took on the role of the Developmental Editor towards the final stages.

I am also very thankful to Kelly Dickson, who oversaw the design and production process with great skill. Valerie Adams deserves special thanks for making sure my writing was readable. Last but not least, I would like to thank all the Canadian and US reviewers who provided invaluable input and constructive ideas to improve the book. I, of course, take full responsibility for any remaining errors or omissions.

Writing this book was enjoyable process. But it required an incredible amount of time away from my family. This book would not have been completed without the unflinching support of my dear wife Manjula. She still loves me, even though I ignored her for the better part of a year. Words cannot express my gratitude and love for her. My mother, who has been my inspiration and guiding light, took on the editor's role at times, making sure I was meeting my deadlines. Her love and support mean everything me.

Ramesh Venkat
January 2001

Chapter 1

Introduction

Vignette 1 **Driving on the (Information) Superhighway**

Learning Objectives

After completing this chapter, you will:

- Understand the origins, growth, and magnitude of commerce on the Internet.
- Gain an appreciation of the basic concepts and terminology in Internet marketing.
- Understand the different types of market opportunities available on the Internet.
- Appreciate the difference between business-to-consumer and business-to-business markets.

For most consumers buying a car is a big investment and is something that requires careful deliberation. The comfort and the feel of a car can only be determined through a test drive. That means a trip to one or more local dealers is part of the buying process. Many consumers will, however, attest that a trip to the local dealer is not a very enjoyable experience. Haggling over price and others terms with the dealer can be a rather unpleasant and harrowing experience. Now there's help available. If you are thinking of buying a car, get on the Internet first.

A whole new generation of businesses on the Web, such as Autobytel.com (see Exhibit 1-1), Carpoint, Dealernet, and Megawheels, are trying to change the car-buying process as well as the experience for consumers. These online intermediaries or **cybermediaries** offer a wide range of services, including feature and price comparisons, reviews, dealer searches, financing, and auto insurance. After a customer learns about the different brands through comparisons and even 3-D visuals, he or she can get a quote from a dealer who is an authorized member of the cybermediary. Autobytel.com is then paid a subscription fee for this referral service.

CarCostCanada.com goes a step further and reveals the dealer's invoice price to consumers. Up until now, consumers in Canada knew only the manufacturer's suggested retail price (MSRP). Now they can find out the price that the dealer paid to get the car from a manufacturer. The dealer's cost is very transparent. This information puts consumers in a stronger bargaining position.

According to a study by the Polk Company, only 3 percent of new car buyers in 1999 purchased through an Internet-based service like Autobytel or Carpoint. However, for the same year, a survey of car buyers showed that 40 percent of them used the Web as a main informa-

Exhibit 1-1 Autobytel Sweepstakes Banner Advertisement

tion source. Ninety-three percent of prospective car buyers also said they would use the Web in the future to do their homework before buying their next set of wheels. These data suggest that the Web will play a key role in the purchase process even if the actual purchase transaction is not done online.

In the past, car dealers were an important source of information for consumers. If the cybermediaries can provide many of the services that a dealer can, what happens to the dealer then? Is the dealer in danger of being displaced or **disinteremediated**? Well, not entirely. At least in Canada, that is unlikely for now. There is a law in Canada that requires all new car purchases to be transacted through a dealer. If consumers, however, can get all their information online, they can walk into the dealership being better informed. While the car dealer cannot be entirely avoided, the online services are certain to force many dealers to rethink their roles in the distribution channel.

How efficient are these Web-based intermediaries? Jeremy Cato, a Canadian journalist who covers the auto industry, decided to test the efficiency of the auto-referral Web sites in Canada. He submitted purchase request forms to eight Web sites, including Autobytel.ca, Megawheels.com, Autoweb.ca, and Canadacar.com. His experience was less than satisfactory, as he got price quotes from only two of the eight car dealerships he contacted. This may be one person's experience, but the results are not entirely surprising.

Dealers have generally been slow to adopt the Internet. Only 63 percent of auto dealers in Canada have their own Web sites, and only 40 percent regularly update their Web sites. Most dealers, while benefiting from referral services, have not developed a strategy for utilizing the Internet. To survive in this new arena where consumers have many new options, older businesses, whether car dealers or other retailers, will have to think anew.

Not to be outdone by the cybermediaries, automobile companies themselves are investing heavily in their Web sites. At GM's Buy Power (www.gmbuypower.com), you can "build your exact vehicle, find it at a nearby dealer, view third-party comparisons, get incentive information, request the dealer's best price, and even apply for financing."

Mercedes and Saturn (a GM subsidiary) are among the auto-makers that allow buyers to customize their cars online.

Auto-makers are also using the Web as a component of their advertising strategy, to complement their brand advertising in the mass media. Honda Civic, a popular car with college and university students, placed its ads on Lexis-Nexis, an online information service frequented by students. Cadillac, which targets the high-end luxury car market, placed its "Caddy Up" campaign ads on the financial sections of the CNN and *Wall Street Journal* sites, as well on the golfing site iGolf. Toyota, one of the largest advertisers online, wanted to capitalize on the growing number of women online and placed its ads on Women.com, a portal targeting women, with very good results. The Web allows marketers to precisely target their messages.

Once a potential buyer is drawn to the Web site, technology then allows the company to bring the Web pages to life. Microsoft's Carpoint.com allows 360-degree rotation of images of cars. You can rotate and zoom in and out as you view the interior and exterior of a car. Manufacturers like Toyota offer similar 3-D viewing. Mercedes uses Internet telephony and allows potential customers to speak directly with a service agent at a call centre, while the customer is still on the Web site. As the customer views pictures and specifications of a product on the Web, the service agent can resolve doubts and answer questions. In the past, the car dealers were the ones who had direct interaction with customers. Now, on the Web, manufacturers can interact directly with customers. They can also customize their product and message for each individual buyer.

Exhibit 1-2 Mercedes's "Internet Car"

In the very near future, the Internet will not only be a tool used in the automobile buying process, but it will also likely enhance the automobile itself. Mercedes is among several auto-makers that are planning to bring Internet technology into the car itself. Passengers can surf the Web and the driver can get navigational assistance through an online mapping program (see Exhibit 1-2).

Thanks to the Internet, the car buying experience is changing for consumers. The marketing of automobiles is also radically changing. Soon, consumers will drive their cars on the highway, while surfing on the Information Superhighway at the same time.

Sources: Auto Shoppers Increase Internet Use, *CyberAtlas*, April 19, 2000; Hunting for Wheels Online, *CyberAtlas*, July 14, 1999; Jeremy Cato, "Clicking for Cars," *The Globe and Mail*, April 15, 2000, N1; Robert Cribb, "Web Site Gives Dealers' Car Costs," *The Toronto Star*, December 17, 1999; Tony Van Alphen, "Internet Won't Cripple Dealers, Auto Group Told," *The Toronto Star*, February 17, 2000.

Introduction

Andy Grove, Chairman and CEO of Intel, said, "In five years' time there won't be any Internet companies. All companies will be Internet companies or they will be dead."[1] That was in May of 1999. While some would argue that the impact of the Internet on businesses is industry specific, many would contend that the statement is not without merit. Businesses in industries such as automobiles, computers, financial services, travel, and many others are indeed undergoing a major transformation. The Internet is adding new capabilities as a communication medium and as a distribution channel. It is making communication across the supply chain more efficient, and it's enabling businesses of all types to forge closer ties with their customers. On the Internet everything is 24/7. That means customers can access product information, place orders, or get online support any time of the day.

Author Don Tapscott calls the Internet "the new infrastructure for business."[2] Andy Grove sees the changes ushered in by the Internet as being so far-reaching that he calls it a "strategic inflection point," which occurs when change is so powerful that it fundamentally alters the way business is done.[3] The Internet makes many of the old business paradigms obsolete. As we saw in Vignette 1, we are witnessing a paradigm shift—a new way of thinking about and managing businesses.

A typical manufacturing firm performs a series of value-added functions that culminates in the fulfillment of a consumer need or solution to a consumer's problem. The series of value-added functions, called the value chain, usually includes procurement of raw materials, design and production, distribution, marketing, sales, and after-sales support. Let us continue to use the auto industry example and see how the Internet alters the basic functions of a firm.

On the procurement side, GM, Ford, and other car-makers have joined forces and decided to purchase all their supplies, collectively worth over $250 billion, through a jointly owned online venture. All parts and materials suppliers to the major auto manufacturers will now have to sell through this Web site. A manually drafted purchase order can cost the auto manufacturers $80 to $125. By automating the purchase process, businesses can save ordering time and costs, as well as reduce errors in the ordering process. Vendors can now monitor inventory levels and automatically replenish items as required. This seamless procurement process will save GM, Ford, and other participants in this online supply exchange millions of dollars in ordering and inventory costs.

When it comes to design and production of vehicles, many manufacturers now allow consumers to customize their cars online. This is a significant departure from the days of Henry Ford, who once said that the customer could have any colour he wanted—"so long as it's black." During that era, the desire to lower costs and manage complex production processes led to mass production. In later years, we saw a more flexible incarnation of the mass production concept, where the consumer could select a few options. Now, thanks to the information technology revolution and the recent advent of the Web, businesses such as Saturn and Dell are able to offer the consumer greater flexibility and choice in the configuration of the product. We have come a long way from such rigid mass production to the realization that fulfilling the needs of each individual consumer is the key to success in this new economy.

In the past, automobile manufacturers rarely had direct contact with end-users. The dealers, who were on the frontline, dealt with consumers. Now manufacturers are trying to build direct relationships with customers online. Brand-oriented Web sites encourage repeat visits and have become a means of forging closer ties with customers (see www.toyota.com and www.mbusa.com). As consumers go online to customize their cars, manufacturers can now get first-hand information on the needs and preferences of consumers who buy their products. This also means that companies like Ford and GM have to listen to the needs of each individual consumer. A new approach to design, production, and marketing is required.

On the marketing and distribution side, manufacturers can use the Web to communicate and interact with their customers. Many of the functions performed by car dealers, such as providing information about brands, is now being done more efficiently by manufacturers or new online intermediaries. It is possible for consumers to custom order the car directly from the manufacturer's site and get the financing approved through a cybermediary (such as Autobytel.com). The car dealer then simply becomes a test drive and delivery depot. As the dealers look ahead, they must wonder how they can redefine their roles. Aggressive push selling at the dealership has given way to a consumer pull-driven marketing model.

Clearly, every stage of the value chain is affected when a firm goes online. It is evident that the Internet allows firms to make radical changes to their mode of operation. We will discuss the value chain in greater detail in Chapter 2.

As we examine the dramatic changes engulfing many industries, including the auto industry, it looks like the winner in all this is likely to be the consumer. In the pre-Web era, intermediaries (dealers, travel agents, and retailers) controlled a lot of information. Consumers often made decisions with incomplete and imperfect information. In the post-Web era, this information asymmetry has been substantially reduced. Consumers literally have access to full information about all brands at their fingertips. Now consumers can make well-informed choices. The Web also offers consumers other advantages.

Consumers can benefit from the increased choice available online. This is especially true for those living in smaller communities. One is not restricted to shopping in the local stores. The Internet allows consumers to shop from the privacy of their homes, whenever they want and from wherever they want. Notions of time and space have collapsed now. Time zones and geographic locations do not matter in cyberspace. Chapter 3 will further elaborate on the impact of the Internet on consumers and consumer behaviour.

Even to the casual observer, it must be evident now that the Internet is not a fad. Technology companies like Intel and Cisco conduct 50 to 80 percent of their business online. But the Internet is not limited to technology companies. Airlines are using the Web to directly sell tickets to millions of customers, allowing them to bypass the traditional distribution channel of travel agents. Media organizations like CNN can add value by offering interactive chat, video-on-demand, and instant updates of news stories. From prescription drugs to home grocery delivery, we are seeing new ideas born on the Internet.

For some businesses, the Internet may offer a new distribution channel (for example, software and publishing companies). For others, it may provide a richer and interactive communication environment in which to present their products to consumers (such as automobile companies). For businesses in the less glamorous business-to-business area, the Internet allows them to streamline their procurement and selling processes, leading to significant cost savings.

There is so much excitement surrounding the Internet because we have not seen a technology or set of technologies with such a profound impact on businesses and on our lives. By going online, businesses have the opportunity to reach new markets across the globe, reduce costs, and build closer relationships with their customers. For most businesses the road ahead is likely to be filled with opportunities as well as challenges.

The rest of this book will address these opportunities and challenges. You are unlikely to find all the answers here. You will be challenged to think. New technologies that improve the capabilities of business on the Web are being introduced every day. New businesses and new products are being unveiled on Internet time, where a month is often equivalent to a year. The Internet challenges traditional notions—whether the method of communication, distribution of a product, or the relationship between manufacturers and consumers. It is hard to predict what the future will be even three years from now. Marketing in this dynamic and turbulent time requires us to embrace new ideas. This makes the study of marketing on the Internet an exciting endeavour. Hope you enjoy it!

The Internet and the Web: A Brief Background

The Internet is not just a network of computers, but a network of networks. The idea behind the Internet is attributed to J.C.R. Licklider of MIT, who proposed the concept of a "Galactic Network" in 1962. He envisioned a globally interconnected set of computers that would allow for quickly accessing data and programs from any site.[4] Licklider's vision eventually gave birth to ARPANET in 1969, when four host computers were connected together. From this humble beginning grew the Internet, which today is a vast, complicated network of networks, connecting millions of computers around the world.

The motivation behind ARPANET was to connect military research centres and to create a protection against nuclear attacks. Today the Internet is a continually expanding global network connecting more than 70 million host computers and over 300 million people.[5] For a historical timeline of the evolution of the Internet and the Web, see www.pbs.org/internet/timeline.

The Internet has become the mechanism for instantaneously disseminating information worldwide, a medium for communication and collaboration at work or home, and a medium capable of delivering video or audio on demand. Earlier inventions like the telegraph, telephone, radio, and television each had a single capability. The Internet represents an integration of these capabilities and more. The Internet is composed of many parts, including e-mail, Usenet newsgroups, File Transfer Protocol, and, perhaps the most significant part, the World Wide Web.

E-mail allows for exchange of messages between designated individuals, whereas Usenet messages are posted in a public forum that literally anyone can read. E-mail has revolutionized the way we communicate and is truly a "killer application." File Transfer Protocol (FTP) is another capability that the Internet offers, allowing for downloading or transferring files between different computers. Usenet groups are bulletin boards organized by topics, where people can interact with like-minded individuals. The most recent application on the Internet, the World Wide Web, has been the catalyst for the E-commerce revolution we are witnessing now.

The World Wide Web

Tim Berners-Lee invented the World Wide Web in 1989 at CERN, the European Laboratory for Particle Physics.[6] The Web allows for linking documents and others types of files (such as images, sound, and video) within the same computer as well as between computers anywhere in the world. Users can click on the links, called **hyperlinks**, and will be able to jump from one document or file to another. Hyperlinks can be text or even images, and are usually highlighted. Web pages are written using a language called HyperText Markup Language or HTML.

At the beginning, HTML or Web pages were text pages. A graphical Web browser was invented at the University of Illinois called Mosaic, which allowed for displaying pictures and other multimedia files. Mosaic was the precursor to the popular browser Netscape. Browsers like Netscape and Internet Explorer use **plug-ins** (software applications that run in conjunction with the browser) and allow users to experience video, audio, animation, and interactivity. These features also enhance business Web sites on the Internet.

The Size and Growth of the Internet and the Web

The growth of Internet usage is currently being fuelled by commercial activity on the Web. Commercial use of the Internet started around 1995. The Internet has grown from a user base of less than 30 million in 1996 to over 300 million at the beginning of 2000 (see Exhibit 1-3). The projections for Internet usage in the next few years look quite promising. By the year 2005, one billion people are expected to be online.[7]

Currently, over 40 percent of all Internet users are in North America, but Internet usage in many parts of Asia, Europe, and South America is expected to grow rapidly (see Exhibit 1-4). At the same time, Internet usage is likely to saturate in North America. The growth in the non-English user segment will add to the diversity on the Internet.

The Internet is a global medium (see Table 1-1 and Exhibit 1-5 on page 10). This does create opportunities for smaller firms that could not otherwise engage in global trade. It is easy to find buyers for your product or potential suppliers on bulletin boards, or online trading sites such as Tradingfloor.net.

While the Internet itself is a global medium, so far the evidence shows that very few businesses are fully exploiting the global reach of this medium.[8] According to Forrester Research, an Internet research firm, a significant proportion of orders placed online from overseas went unfulfilled in 1999 due to process failures, meaning businesses were not organized to ship the goods overseas. Take the largest retailer in the world—Wal-Mart. While Wal-Mart has stores in ten countries, its Web site (www.wal-mart.com) is produced by and for Americans only.[9]

Exhibit 1-3 Growth in Consumer Access and Shopping

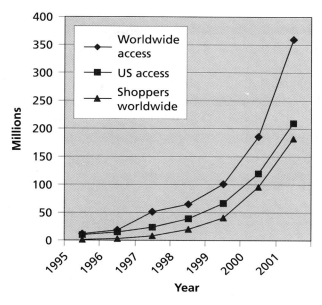

Source: "The Real Numbers Behind Net Profits," ActivMedia, Inc.

Exhibit 1-4 Internet Usage: Projection for 2001

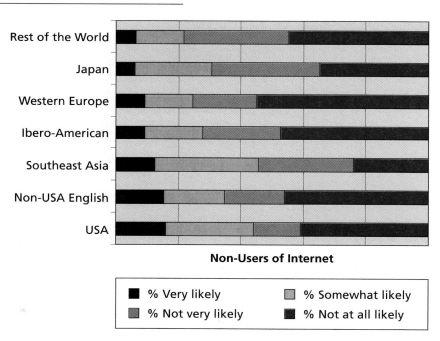

Source: "Face of the Web," Angus Reid Group, 2000.

Table 1-1 Global Internet Users

Region	Users (millions)
Africa	2.58
Asia/Pacific	68.9
Europe	83.35
Middle East	1.9
Canada/US	136.36
South America	10.74
World Total	304.36

Source: Nua Internet Surveys, March 2000.

Exhibit 1-5 Internet Users: Penetration in Top 15 Countries

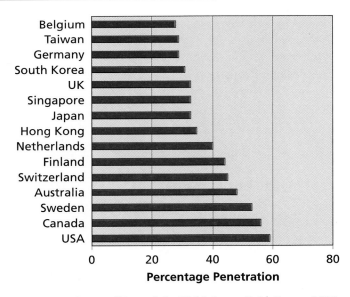

Source: "Face of the Web" Angus Reid Group, 2000.

An Introduction to E-commerce and Internet Marketing

Some of the capabilities of the Internet were discussed at the beginning of this chapter. We have also seen how rapidly the Internet is expanding across the globe. Let's now look at the nature of commercial activity on the Internet in some more detail.

The term E-commerce (electronic commerce or EC) encompasses a wide variety of activities. The most common definition of E-commerce is that it "consists of buying and selling goods and services over the Internet and other electronic networks." It also includes integration of businesses with their suppliers and customers.[10] Some experts suggest a broader definition of E-commerce that includes applications that facilitate the automation of business processes and workflows.[11]

The term **Internet marketing** refers to conducting marketing activities via the Internet or the Web. As you will see throughout this book, the basic marketing principles do not change, whether marketing online or offline, but marketing on the Internet does require knowledge of new concepts and tools.

There are two major, not entirely unrelated, categories of E-commerce: business-to-business (buying and selling or trade between businesses) and business-to-consumer (selling goods or services to individual or household consumers). A third category, sometimes subsumed in one of the above categories, is consumer-to-consumer E-commerce. Marketing activities can occur in any of these categories. Let's briefly consider each of these categories and understand the nature of activities within each category.

Business-to-Consumer (B2C)

The online sale of consumer products (such as books, CDs, clothes, software, news, and gifts) and services (such as financial services, news, and entertainment) is currently worth at least $60 billion. By 2003, the consumer market will be worth an estimated $380 billion worldwide. While this is still less than 1 percent of worldwide retailing, most e-tailers, as well as traditional retailers like Wal-Mart, Kmart, and Sears, are focusing on the future potential. As consumers become comfortable with shopping online and get used the convenience and as online stores iron out the wrinkles in their order-processing and delivery systems, online shopping will become commonplace.

It is not just tangible products that are bought and sold online. Financial services such as online banking and stock trading have gone beyond the novelty stage and are beginning to attract large numbers of consumers. Online stock brokerages such as E*TRADE and Ameritrade have become recognizable names. Banks, such as the Royal Bank of Canada, are encouraging their consumers to migrate online. Other services, including travel (e.g., Expedia.com), career services (e.g., Wetfeet.com and Workopolis.com), medical services (e.g., WebMD.com), and education (e.g., Lansbridge.com and Athabasca University), also have a growing presence online. Many of these services use a multiple channel strategy (such as a bank with both a physical branch and an online presence), thus providing consumers with additional delivery options.

The introduction of non-computing Web-enabled devices is also likely to contribute to the growth of online shopping. One does not have to be a computer user any longer to be able to shop online. WebTV is perhaps the best known of such non-computing Net devices. It allows consumers to access various Internet applications like e-mail and the Web using a regular television set. Cellular phones and other palm devices are also now capable of providing Web access. These new technologies are likely to have a profound effect in accelerating the growth of the Internet.

Developing countries like Brazil, China, and India, which have huge market potential, have limited or outdated telecommunications infrastructure. Such infrastructure is expensive to acquire. Mobile phone technology, on the other hand, is a lot cheaper and faster to deploy, thus having the potential of bringing the benefits of the Internet and E-commerce to developing economies.

Consumers are taking to Internet shopping for a variety of reasons. Convenience and saving time are the foremost reasons why consumers like shopping on the Internet (see Table 1-2). Consumers often find that the prices on the Web are somewhat lower than prices in

Table 1-2 Comparison of Shopping Channels

Reason	Internet	Catalogues	Stores
Offers most competitive price	21%	10%	13%
Everything from one source	12%	7%	13%
Convenience	59%	49%	12%
Saves time	62%	33%	3%

Source: Anderson Consulting.

regular stores. The Web also allows manufacturers to sell directly to end-users, thereby eliminating some of the costs associated with traditional distribution (see iMarket Demo 1-1 for an example in the movie industry).

Each year we see more consumers going online. Consumers use the Internet for a variety of reasons, including

- Searching for product information;
- Purchasing products and services;
- Participating in chat and bulletin boards;
- E-mail;
- Reading news;
- Entertainment, such as games, music, and video-on-demand;
- Online banking and bill payment; and
- Stock trading.

E-mail is the largest application on the Web. As new applications become available, consumers will have more reasons for using the Web. When thinking of the consumer market online, it is important to think beyond shopping. Marketers have many opportunities online besides selling products and services.

Bricks vs. Clicks. Well-known e-tailers like Amazon.com and Buy.com are considered to be virtual or **pure-play** Internet companies. These companies do not have physical stores. On the other hand, companies like Wal-Mart, Future Shop, and Chapters were originally physical or **bricks-and-mortar** retail stores, which have now added a Web presence. From bricks-and-mortar, these retailers have evolved to **clicks-and-mortar** operations, with both a physical and an online presence. As the pure-plays try to acquire physical assets (such as warehouses), traditional retailers are trying to establish their brands online.

E-tail vs. Portal. Consumer sites will typically fall under two categories—e-tail or portal—although we will see in the next chapter that a great variety of online businesses exist now. **E-tail** sites are sites that sell products or services online. **Portal** sites, which may or may not provide online shopping, often act as entry points or gateways to the Web. Portals can also be content sites that carry news, weather, sports, and current financial information. Futureshop.ca is a good example of an e-tail site, while Canada.com is an excellent portal site.

iMarket Demo 1-1 Marketing Movies on the Web

The Blair Witch Project, a movie that barely cost a few thousand dollars to make and less than $1 million to market, was one of the biggest box office hits of 1999. In the third week of release, the movie grossed a record $28.5 million. Some would argue that the fact that many moviegoers assumed the story to be true may have contributed to the success of this movie. Others would point to the clever marketing tactics employed on the Web.

The marketing communications strategy for the movie involved use of word-of-mouth in college campuses (through students who were hired by the film company to act as opinion leaders) as well as use of the Web. Artisan Entertainment, the company that marketed the movie, created a very interactive Web site that ideally complemented the movie. The site filled in the story behind the plot, complete with timelines, photographs of crime scenes, historical documents, interviews, and artifacts. The target audience, mainly university students in the 17 to 22 age group, could be reached easily via the Web.

The publicity was so effective that fans created their own sites for the movie. The rather realistic horror movie created a cult-like following among a younger audience. There are over one thousand fan sites dedicated to this movie (see, for example, *Blair Witch* fanatic's guide at tbwp.freeservers. com/), and these have led to a great deal of online word-of-mouth promoting at no cost to the film's producers.

Media reviews of the movie recognized the marketing efforts. *The Pittsburgh Post-Gazette* (July 30, 1999) said, "*Blair Witch Project* isn't just a movie, it's a meta-media endeavor." The venerable *Boston Globe* (July 30, 1999) declared, "The film is a landmark in movie marketing, the first sensation created almost exclusively on line."

The success of *The Blair Witch Project* demonstrates how the Web can be used to target the audience (in this case students). The Web site was used to augment and complement the product. The movie Web site offered viewers and fans additional content and entertainment. Lastly, knowingly or unknowingly, the marketers of the movie exploited one of the characteristics of the Web—it is essentially a community, where people interact with each other. Word-of-mouth communication spreads rapidly online. Whether you "enjoyed" the movie or not, you have to give kudos to the marketing effort. If you need a "how-to" manual for online marketing of movies, just look at what Artisan Entertainment did with *The Blair Witch Project*.

Sources: James Surowiecki, "Blair Witch's Lessons for Hollywood," *Slate.com*, Aug. 9, 1999; Glen Berry, "Film Festival Strategy: Internet Film Distribution," *FilmFestivals.com*; "Bewitching Movie Marketing Casts Spell Over Web," *PR Week* (www.carma.com/ PRWeek/Witch.htm); Patti Hartigan, "The Mythmakers Behind The 'Blair' Buzz," *The Boston Globe*, July 30, 1999.

Experts believe that in the next few years, the B2C space will see a lot of turmoil and change—with consolidations and mergers being the order of the day. Even the best-known B2C sites (such as Amazon.com) have not made a profit as of the beginning of 2000. The pressure from investors is likely to force smaller players out of the market. This means that to survive in a fiercely competitive online marketspace, firms must understand and practise sound marketing and business principles. Forrester Research has predicted a major shake-out in the B2C space, which may see a wave of consolidations and mergers. Many smaller companies may disappear. See Chapter 3 for a more complete discussion of the business-to-consumer market.

Business-to-Business (B2B)

Business-to-business E-commerce includes the buying and selling of goods and services between businesses and also the interaction of businesses with their suppliers and customers across the industry supply chain. Global B2B E-commerce was estimated at $68 billion in 1998.[12] While there are varying estimates on the growth of B2B E-commerce, according to the technology research firm Gartner Group, in the year 2000 the B2B sector will grow to $403 billion and by the end of 2003 it will reach a mind-boggling $3.95 trillion.[13] Experts predict such a rapid growth in the B2B sector because businesses see several tangible benefits of going online, including:

- *Cost savings*. Inventory and transaction costs will be lower.
- *Efficiencies*. Automating areas like customer service through online delivery of such services.
- *Access to suppliers*. Smaller companies can now source for products from virtually any supplier in the world.
- *Connecting employees*. Large organizations with a national or international network of offices can use the Internet and corporate **Intranets** to connect their employees to share information or provide online training.
- *Communication*. The Internet allows companies to provide technical information in as much detail as necessary.
- *New markets*. The Internet affords a global reach and opens new markets for many businesses.

The business-to-business arena on the Web consists of a variety of businesses. We can classify B2B Web sites as seller-controlled, buyer-controlled, and neutral sites.[14]

Seller-controlled sites are established by businesses, which may or may not have online selling (E-commerce) capability. For instance, the IMP Group (www.impgroup.com), a Canadian conglomerate with interests in aerospace, petroleum, marine, and medical equipment, has a site that offers product information but no direct online sales. This type of site is also called **brochureware** because it is simply an online sales brochure for a company's products and services. Companies that sell complex products that are not suited for direct selling on the Internet are likely to have such an information site.

Boeing (www.boeing.com), on the other hand, has the Boeing PART Page, which allows Boeing's customers to directly purchase aircraft spare parts and track their orders online. Dell is another company that sells to other businesses directly online. Businesses and other institutional buyers can customize their products and manage their customer accounts through Dell's site (www.dell.ca).

Buyer-controlled sites are set up by one or more buyers to shift value and power from suppliers to buyers. The auto industry B2B portal, discussed earlier, has the potential to become one of the largest business-to-business entities since these large auto-makers collectively purchase more than $300 billion worth of supplies and parts per year. Officecoop.com is another example of a buyer-controlled site. Officecoop.com is an aggregator that enables small businesses to join together to make large-volume purchases at lower prices.

Neutral sites include auctions as well as vertical portal sites. eBay.com has a section called Business Exchange, where small businesses can buy and sell through business-to-business auctions. Vertical portals or **vortals** are sites that cater to the needs of specific industries. Chemdex.com brings together buyers and sellers in the chemical industry, while Plastics.net brings together buyers and vendors in the plastics industry.

We will explore the different facets of the business-to-business market in more detail in Chapter 4.

Consumer-to-Consumer (C2C)

The third category of E-commerce is consumer-to-consumer E-commerce. Auction is the most popular format of C2C E-commerce. eBay, Onsale, and the Canadian firm Bid.com (also known as Internetliquidators.com) are some of the firms in this category. Auction sites merely facilitate trade between two parties. Auctions can take different formats, such as Dutch auctions (where prices drop with time), which are popular with those who sell perishable items. See the United Flower Grower's Cooperative Association (www.ufgca.com), a Canadian entity, for an example. Priceline.com made reverse auctions, where sellers bid for the buyer's business, popular. At Priceline, you can purchase airline tickets, hotel accommodations, car rentals, and even home financing and groceries through the reverse auction method.

Lastly, online classified ads also allow consumers to sell used or new items. These sites are no different from the classified sections of newspapers. In fact, your local newspaper most likely has an online edition that carries classified ads. There are also specialists on the Web, such as Epage (www.ep.com) and Excite Classifieds (classifieds.excite.com), who carry thousands of ads each day. Online classifieds allow sellers access to a potentially bigger market, as the Web has a global reach. Buyers also benefit from the wider choice.

Why Study Internet Marketing?

The basis of marketing is to provide value to the consumer, thereby creating satisfaction and loyalty. This fundamental principle holds true whether you're marketing online or offline. Marketing on the Internet, however, does present some new opportunities and challenges to marketers, and marketers need to understand new concepts, tools, and business models.

Advertising and Communication

The Web is an interactive medium that allows for personalized communication. Content on Web pages can be customized based on individual preferences (see CNN.com or Yahoo!). The Web site can also give the consumer an interactive two-way communication experience. A simple example is the opportunity to fill out an online feedback form. Further, with the consumer's permission, personalized e-mail advertising can be delivered. Advertisers online are beginning to understand that the Web is not a mass medium.

The are newer forms of advertising and promotion on the Web. Banner ads can be used to promote brands, and electronic coupons can be used to encourage immediate consumer response. Marketers also need to understand newer advertising effectiveness measures on the Web, such as the clickthrough rate (measure of how many times viewers click on a banner ad) and pageviews (number of times a page is downloaded). It is possible to track consumer preferences on the Web, which then enables the marketer to personalize content or advertising messages. Chapters 9 and 10 will explore advertising and promotion issues in greater detail. It suffices to say here that new communication tools available on the Internet call for a detailed study.

Product and Product Presentation

The Internet allows marketers to customize products to suit the needs of each individual consumer. From auto manufacturers like Saturn (www.saturn.com) to clothing manufacturers like IC3D (www.ic3d.com), companies are moving from mass marketing to personalized marketing by catering to the needs of individual consumers. The Internet makes it possible to offer this kind of customization cost-effectively.

The consumer cannot touch, feel, or taste the product on the Internet. In this regard, the Internet is very similar to a print catalogue. However, the marketer can take advantage of the multimedia capabilities of the Web, including newly emerging 3-D technologies, to present the product in more innovative ways. When a consumer cannot physically examine the product, the online experience on the Web site assumes greater importance. A rich and satisfying consumer experience on the Web site is a must. Marketers need to understand the techniques and tools available for effective online product presentation. We will address product and retailing issues in Chapters 9 and 14.

Pricing

On the Internet, marketers have to contend with new forms of pricing not usually seen in the physical marketplace. Reverse auction sites like Priceline.com allow buyers to set prices. Aggregators like Mercata.com allow individuals to join together to drive down prices through volume purchasing. Technology on the Internet allows marketers to unbundle products like newspapers and sell each article for prices as low as five cents! This is not feasible in the physical world, were the cost of processing the transaction would make it unprofitable to sell such low-value items. On the Web, pricing is not always "cost plus." Pricing can be demand-driven, meaning the consumer can set the price. Pricing issues are discussed further in Chapter 10.

Consumer Behaviour

As we will see in Chapter 3, consumer decision making on the Internet is somewhat different from the decision making process in a retail store environment. Consumers have access to more information now than ever before. It is easy to do comparison shopping through sites like mySimon.com or through the shopping channels of search sites like Lycos. Consumers are less dependent on the marketer now for information. Consumers also make decisions without physically touching or trying the product (except in the case of digital products like music or software). Shopping online is more of a personal than social experience, even though eBay, Amazon, and other community sites do provide a somewhat social experience. Marketers need to understand the factors that influence online consumer behaviour to ensure the effectiveness of their marketing programs.

Marketplace vs. Marketspace: A Paradigm Shift

As we move from the physical **marketplace** (the bricks-and-mortar stores) to the virtual **marketspace** (the online stores), there is a need for a new business philosophy. In the online world, information is instantaneously available. Shopping and service can happen 24/7. Consumers can easily compare prices. Using the auction and aggregate buying formats, consumers can dictate prices. All this means that when a firm goes online, simply adding a Web site to existing operations is not sufficient. Every aspect of the business needs rethinking.

As we saw earlier, the Internet is bringing manufacturers and consumers in close contact. For some businesses it offers the opportunity to sell directly to end-users, bypassing the many layers of intermediaries. It offers businesses the opportunity to communicate directly and one-to-one with each consumer. This allows even large firms to build closer relationships with their consumers. The Internet is fundamentally altering the way many businesses view and manage their operations. Shedding the old ways is not easy. Employees need to be retrained. It requires education to understand and use the capabilities of the Internet.

Even to casual observers it must be evident that the Internet presents a dynamic and rapidly changing environment. New businesses are being created and new business models are being introduced at a frenzied pace. New technologies such as Web-enabled cellular phones are opening exciting possibilities. As "old economy" companies add online capabilities and as new pure-play companies grow, those who understand how to market effectively in the marketspace will be in demand. These are some good reasons for business students to take an in-depth look at marketing on the Internet.

Economic Impact of the Internet

The economic impact of E-commerce can be felt at different levels. Let's consider the key areas of economic impact.

Economy and Jobs

The new economy is credited with fuelling the longest economic expansion in the United States and Canada. Many new categories of jobs, which did not exist a few years ago (such as Web developers), have been created. In fact, the number of start-up ventures related to E-commerce is in the thousands, creating many new, well-paying jobs.

As businesses go online, there is also the likelihood that some jobs will be lost. For instance, banks in Canada are closing some of their physical branches as they encourage more consumers to migrate to online banking. Workers in many industries will have to learn new skills as more jobs become knowledge-based. The infusion of information technology and the Internet is changing the way many jobs are performed, from selling to order processing to customer service.

In 1998, the total revenues attributable to the Internet economy was $28.5 billion (see Table 1-3). It is anticipated that by 2003, the total revenues in Canada will grow to $156 billion.[15] These figures suggest that the jobs created due to E-commerce and other activities on the Internet will make the Canadian economy richer and more vibrant.

The Boston Consulting Group study referred to in Table 1-3 also highlights the difference between the Canadian and American economies. In the United States, revenues attributed to the different categories in Table 1-3 totalled CDN$414 billion in 1998, with 1.4 million jobs. The NASDAQ stock exchange, where many new high-tech companies are listed, saw a total of 165 initial public offerings (IPOs) of shares, compared to only 4 in the Toronto Stock Exchange (TSE). Canada, however, remains among the top five nations in terms of Internet access. While commercial exploitation of the Internet is somewhat underdeveloped in Canada, compared to the United States, very few experts would disagree that there is vast

Table 1-3 The Internet Economy and Jobs in Canada (1998)

Category	Revenue (CDN$)	Jobs
Electronic Commerce and Intermediaries B2B, B2C, Portals, Brokers	$5.5 billion	17 300
Internet Applications Software, Web Development	$0.8 billion	7 400
Internet Infrastructure Hardware, Network, Internet Access (ISP)	$22.2 billion	70 400

Source: The Boston Consulting Group, 2000.

potential. So far, the US has led the world in innovations and new business models in this area. Asia, Canada, Europe, and South America have vast untapped potential.

Cost Structure

The Internet has the ability to lower costs in different areas. This can allow marketers to retain higher margins or lower prices and attract more consumption of their products. Businesses are using the Web to source supplies, which streamlines their procurement process. This allows businesses to reduce costs by automating much of the procurement process and also reduce inventory levels. Smaller firms now have access to a broader range of suppliers.

Studies show that transactions carried out via the Web cost less because there is more automation and less human resource involved. For instance, the offline transaction cost (the cost of providing information to the customer and the cost of taking the order) for an airline ticket is estimated at $8. The same transaction carried out at the airline's Web site costs less than $1.[16] The Internet has the ability to reduce a firm's cost in three areas: the cost associated with procurement of raw materials and supplies, the cost associated with making and delivering a product, and the cost of executing the sale.[17]

Companies like Cisco and Sun Microsystems use the Web deliver their customer support services, and they have realized significant cost savings as a result. This is because they no longer need to publish and print expensive manuals and can cut the size of their call centres significantly. Cisco, in 1997, is said to have saved over $500 million by delivering its service online.[18] Customers now use a "self-service" model to get customer service via the Web.

Market Opportunities

Businesses now have the opportunity to offer new, innovative services (see iMarket Demo 1-2 for an example), and the Web is allowing entrepreneurs to test new product ideas and innovations. From personalized clothing (IC3D.com), to reverse auctions (Priceline.com), to online stock trading (Etrade.com), consumers now have access to new products and new ways of shopping. The Web also opens new markets. Universities, for instance, are delivering distance courses via the Web, and are not constrained by their physical location.

iMarket Demo 1-2 News on Demand

News on the Web is nothing new. From *The Globe and Mail* and CTV to CNN and *The New York Times*, there are many news outlets on the Web. In April 2000, a news site debuted in the UK with more than the usual media and public attention.

The reason for this undue attention was Ananova. She is a newscaster who delivers news on demand via streaming video. She is also the first virtual newscaster.

Ananova has also been designed with a personality. Her inflections, mood, and facial animations change with the tone of each story. Viewers can personalize the news, by choosing the subject area. The content on this site is no different from what you would find in any other news-oriented site. It's all serious news. The presentation, however, is different.

Exhibit 1-6 **Ananova**

Source: www.ananova.com.

Even as Ananova debuted in April 2000, a formidable, and perhaps more intelligent, rival was being introduced. Meet Mr. Chase Walker, under development at Sprint's Advanced Technology Laboratory. Chase Walker is also an animated, virtual news host who can interact with his user. "Ananova isn't interactive," says Scott Prevost, co-founder and president of Headpedal, which is involved in the creation of Chase. "With Chase, you can interrupt him and get him to tell you different stories at different times in various levels of detail."

While personal newscasting is still a technology under development, Chase and Ananova emphasize the point that the Web is a personal medium. It is also a very interactive medium. You no longer have to wait until 10 or 11 p.m. to watch the evening news or watch news that is not personally relevant. As high-speed Internet connections (such as cable modems) become widely available, on-demand webcasting audiences will reach a critical mass.

If personalized news delivery becomes accessible to everyone, will people bother to tune in to the evening television news broadcasts? Move over Peter Mansbridge and Peter Jennings. Ananova and Chase Walker are taking over.

Sources: CNN.com; IDG.net; and Ananova.com.

Global Reach

At a time when trade barriers are being lowered and market economies are being established in the developing world, the Internet is likely to play a positive role in global trade. Seven percent of all business-to-business transactions globally will be conducted through the Internet by 2003.[19] One billion people across the globe are expected to have access to the Internet by 2005.[20] The Internet allows businesses, small and large, to take advantage of this

Table 1-4 Industries Bracing for Net Change

Industry	E-commerce Revenue (1998)	E-commerce Projection (2003)	E-commerce as Percentage of Total Market
Event tickets	$115 million	$2.6 billion	19
Toys	$68 million	$1.5 billion	5
Apparel	$530 million	$13.5 billion	4
Home electronics	$1.2 million	$21 billion	12
Home appliances	$100 million	$5.7 billion	7
Health & beauty	$213 million	$6.3 billion	5
Computers (B2B)	$19.7 billion	$395 billion	39
Auto parts (B2B)	$3.7 billion	$213 billion	15
Chemicals (B2B)	$4.7 billion	$178 billion	14
Utilities (B2B)	$7.1 billion	$169.5 billion	26

Source: *Business 2.0*, March 1999.

global reach. Smaller firms can now source supplies globally and sell their products globally through online trading communities like Tradingfloor.net, without having to establish a costly physical presence in foreign markets.

Bracing for Change

Several key industry sectors will see the impact of E-commerce soon. Many traditional businesses will shift a significant part of their operations and selling to the Internet. In the next few years, the business-to-business sector will see a bigger impact of E-commerce (see Table 1-4).

Growth in the consumer segment is likely to be slower. Security concerns regarding online transactions and the difficulty of modifying consumer behaviour can explain the slower pace of growth in the business-to-consumer marketspace.

Economics of the Web

E-commerce has a macro-economic as well as micro-economic impact. In the previous section, we saw the impact of the Internet on job creation. We also saw the micro-economic impact on individual firms (i.e., a firm's cost structure). In this section we will examine the micro-economic impact of the Internet and E-commerce in further detail.

Is It a Free Economy?

For physical products, there is a marginal cost attached to producing each additional unit of a product. For digital and information products (such as software, music, content, and news), the marginal cost is close to zero.[21] Digital products have high initial production or development costs, but low reproduction costs.[22]

Companies such as Microsoft and Corel may incur high development costs in creating the first copy of a new software application. Once the software has been developed, however, the cost of making and distributing additional copies is nearly zero. Many software programs can now be downloaded directly through the Web, which eliminates even the costs associated with making, packing, and shipping CDs or diskettes. Similarly, when CDNow allows consumers to download music, the company is not incurring all the variable costs associated with production and distribution of a CD (some costs, such as copyright fees, are still incurred). The same logic applies to content sites like *The Globe and Mail*, which provides free news on its Web site. There is little or no marginal cost involved in providing news to the next customer, unlike there is for the print newspaper.

Even in the case of physical products, by turning a physical and manual customer service delivery to online delivery, companies can benefit by eliminating the marginal cost associated with providing service for each new customer. Companies like Cisco, Dell, and FedEx are proving that high-quality customer service can be delivered online at a fraction of the cost of a physical/manual system. In a nutshell, any product that can be digitized and delivered online will benefit from the **law of digital assets** or marginal costs approaching zero.[23]

If products can be produced and delivered without incurring any marginal cost, how will such products be priced? Traditional economists would say that profit maximization occurs when price equals marginal cost. In that case, the digital products should be given away for free. The argument is a bit more complex than that because you must consider that there is a cost attached to creating the first copy of a software product. After the creator is compensated for the first copy, if additional copies are given away for free the creator does not lose anything.[24] That is because the additional copies do not cost anything to make or distribute.

We do, in fact, see examples of such "free" products in the software industry (such as the Internet Explorer and Netscape browsers, the Linux operating system, and many freeware products), as well as in online content (such as online newspapers and broadcast sites). Some have argued that the Internet economy is like a communal cooking pot, where people voluntarily contribute to cooking the shared meal.[25] Before commercial activity started on the Internet in the mid-1990s, it was largely a free frontier. Ideas were exchanged freely and so were software products and other creations.

Even now, traces of such a non-commercial attitude are evident. Jupiter Communications (www.jup.com), an Internet research firm, found that a vast majority of consumers were unwilling to pay for content/information online.[26] *USA Today* started its online version as a subscription-based site, but soon switched to a free (advertising-supported) model when subscriptions could not be sold. Microsoft's online magazine, *Slate* (www.slate.com), also suffered a similar fate and had to reverse its initial strategy. The Jupiter Communications study did, however, find that consumers were willing to pay for very specialized, value-added niche content that was not available elsewhere.

There may be some merit to the argument that digital products without marginal cost should be free. Not everyone, however, would agree with this point of view. While examples of free products are not hard to find, most digital products are not being given away for free. Why is that? One can argue that products are not really priced at the marginal cost, but rather priced according to the value that consumers attach to the products. In other words, even if an extra copy of software costs nothing to produce, consumers may be willing to pay a price for it if it delivers value to them. The product should be priced at zero only if consumer thinks it is of no value.

Also, the notion of marginal cost may be relevant in the mass production scenario. As digital products are likely to be highly customized (such as CDs and content Web sites), marginal cost may play a less important role in the electronic marketspace. As products are customized, multiple copies are not made, and therefore each product is priced separately. Thus, one could argue that marginal cost-based pricing is not relevant in the electronic marketspace.

Is It a Frictionless Economy?

If it is not a free economy, is it a *frictionless economy*? In other words, is the Internet a "perfectly competitive" market with full information and no entry barriers? It has been argued that the Internet could represent a perfect market for several reasons.[27]

First, let's consider information. Information flows more freely on the Internet. Search engines, company and competitor Web sites, and online shopping assistants (such as mySimon.com and other comparison-shopping sites) put information literally at the consumer's fingertips. Before the emergence of this electronic marketspace, consumers never had full access to information on various competing products. Manufacturers and intermediaries in the channel controlled the information flow. Now this imbalance or **information asymmetry** has been reduced to some extent. Armed with more thorough information about suppliers and their products, consumers can make the best choices.

Second, as consumers directly communicate with manufacturers, they not only can learn more about the products they buy, but can often benefit from lower prices. We have also seen how the Internet allows manufacturers and producers to reach consumers directly, bypassing layers of intermediaries. Intermediaries who are adding cost without adding value will be eliminated.

Third, as consumers buy directly via the Web, transaction costs will drop significantly. As value chains are compressed and become more efficient, operating costs will also decline. Fourth, e-businesses require less capital than bricks-and-mortar operations. This could lower entry barriers and invite more competitors into the market.

Free flow of information, a direct relationship between manufacturers and consumers, efficient supply chain management, low transaction or buying costs, and a highly competitive marketspace—some would argue that these are signs of a frictionless, perfectly competitive economy.

Well, is the Internet then really a frictionless, perfect economy? Let us consider the implications and evidence that would contradict the notion of a frictionless market.

In a perfectly competitive market, suppliers can only charge a price that equals the marginal cost. In other words, there will not be any profit. The low entry barriers would make it easy for new competitors to enter the market and copy the ideas of early entrants. This means there is no room for innovation. Innovators would only recover their costs and not profit from their efforts.[28]

Even as the stock prices of Internet companies have declined in the second quarter of 2000, pioneers such as Amazon, eBay, and Yahoo! are still valued much higher than followers. The financial market definitely does not seem to believe that pioneers and innovators will not be rewarded in the Internet economy. We do see several cases where market pioneers or early entrants hold a significant proportion of online traffic and market share. Books (such as Amazon.com), search engines (such as Yahoo!), business-to-business trading communities (such as VerticalNet.com), and online brokerage firms (such as E*trade) are just a few of the categories where market leaders hold a dominant position.

Forrester Research (www.forrester.com) has predicted that several sectors of the Internet economy will see a spate of business failures as well as mergers and acquisitions.[29] This will leave a few strong category leaders and some niche players in each sector. What we may eventually have sounds more like oligopoly or monopolistic competition, not pure competition.

In conclusion, the Internet does make information widely available at negligible or no cost to consumers. It does require lower start-up costs, which levels the playing field somewhat for smaller firms. However, from an economic standpoint, it is far from being a frictionless market.

Internet firms are spending a lot more money than most initially imagined. Top-notch E-commerce sites can be expensive to produce and even more expensive to maintain (due to human resources, customer service, site updates, and other costs). In addition, heavy marketing expenditures are required to create awareness and generate site traffic. So, in theory, entry barriers may seem low. But to be competitive online, significant financial resources are required.

As a market, the Internet does offer more efficiency than the physical marketplace. Lower transaction costs, easier information access to consumers, and supply chain integration are the prime advantages. The notion of a frictionless, perfectly competitive market, however, seems to be mostly a myth.

Social Impact of the Internet

Digital Divide

As we discuss the global impact of the Internet, our enthusiasm should be tempered by the fact that half of the world's population has never even made a phone call. Even in developed countries like Canada and the United States, many are concerned that there is a growing **digital divide**. Studies in the US show that Internet access and computer ownership among minorities, people in rural areas, and people without college education is very low.[30] There is a raging debate going on about the role of governments and private organizations in bridging the gap between technology "haves" and "have-nots." As we move from the old economy to a knowledge- and information-based economy, it would be expensive and illogical to leave vast numbers of people behind. Digital divide and possible solutions are addressed in more detail in Chapter 14.

Connecting People

The Internet gives new meaning to the term "global village." Yes, there are vast numbers of people who will never see the benefits of all this technology. They will never be "wired." At the same time, the Internet connects people from all over the world. An example of this global connection was shown on the *Oprah* show. A couple in China had posted a desperate cry of help for their son, who was suffering from a rare disease. A generous woman in the United States saw the message on an Internet bulletin board, and she responded and spread the message to others via e-mail. Soon there were many volunteers and donors who helped bring the couple and their son to the United States for treatment. Without the Internet, it would be hard to imagine such events happening.

Bulletin boards, chat rooms, and Usenet groups bring people from different cultures together. It is now easy to learn about other countries, and the Internet provides us with a tool to communicate with and understand each other. It is up to individuals to use it wisely.

Education and Skills

The new economy requires new skills. Basic computer skills are a given now. Those who are entering the job market need to understand how businesses operate in this information technology and Internet era. Businesses value those who can understand and use the technology effectively. Schools, colleges, and universities will have to ensure their graduates have the requisite skills to secure jobs and perform successfully in this new economy.

In Canada and the United States, a significant shortage of Internet-savvy employees is being predicted.[31] Businesses have to provide skills training to their older employees, and universities and colleges are moving fast to establish courses in E-commerce and related areas. Educational institutions are also learning to use the technology to deliver courses via the Web. Just as businesses are being challenged by the Internet to reinvent themselves, so are educational institutions. The bottom line is that a nation's competitive edge depends on its Internet infrastructure and technology skills of its citizens.

See iMarket Demo 1-3 for more on the social implications of Internet usage.

iMarket Demo 1-3 Cocooning in Cyberspace

Imagine living your life via the Internet. From shopping to socializing, what if we did everything through the Internet? To most of us it may seem like a weird idea. But that is precisely what a 26-year-old former UPS employee attempted to do on January 1, 2000. His mission was to live an entire year of his life without leaving his home. That meant doing everything on-line—shopping, chatting and socializing, reading news, getting entertained, and so on. He would do all this while the world was watching his every move through 24 strategically placed digital video cameras that would facilitate live webcasting.

The young man assumed the rather befitting name "Dotcomguy" before opening his life to the public. If he survived the whole year, with or without his sanity intact, he would gain $98 000 for his troubles. Sponsors, including UPS and Peapod, signed on to support his cause. Dotcomguy's experiment may seem like a publicity stunt, but he has professed that his mission is to prove that the Internet can add great convenience and simplify one's

life. The Internet can save the weekly trips to the local mall or supermarket—and that time can be spent in pursuit of other personal interests or with one's family, he contended.

One can argue the merits of the Dotcomguy's mission. However, it does raise some important social issues. Faith Popcorn, a futurist known for her predictions of consumer and market trends, talked about *cocooning* a few years ago. Cocooning refers to people's desire to withdraw from the harshness of an unpredictable life and live a very private, secluded life. The growing violence and other problems in big cities is a cause of this trend. Visible symbols of cocooning include the growth of gated communities in North America and increasing sales of expensive home theatre systems. Some have suggested that the Internet is a perfect ally for cocooners.

The Internet can bring everything—products, services, news, entertainment, and even social contact—to your home. You can buy books, clothes, groceries, and airline tickets without leaving your home and with minimal human contact. While it may encourage cocooning, it also adds a new dimension to how we communicate and socialize with others.

In a society where there is time poverty, the time saving offered by the Internet will be alluring to many. The convenience offered by Internet shopping (stores are open 24/7 and there's no need to drive to the mall in busy traffic) is bound to alter at least some of our shopping behaviour. This does not, however, necessarily mean complete isolation from the rest of society.

Consider the fact that chat sites are among the most popular destinations on the Web. Community sites such as iVillage.com, which allow people with common interests to meet and interact, have grown at astonishing rates. Contrary to what some people fear, the Internet will only increase social interaction. A survey of Internet users by the Quebec-based organization RISQ found that while a small percentage (20 percent) said they had less time for their family and social life because of the time they spend online, over 70 percent of users agreed that the Internet has enhanced their social life by helping them meet new people to share their interests.

Less than a quarter of Canadians are online shoppers, and even those who shop online are spending only a small fraction of their annual shopping dollars online. It may be too soon to judge the impact of the Internet on our time use and lifestyle changes. The RISQ survey of Internet users suggests that time devoted to television viewing declined among 71 percent of users and time devoted to sports and hobbies declined among 32 percent of Internet users.

It is obvious that the Internet is here to stay. We are already seeing signs of how Internet usage can alter our time use and lifestyle. Yet, as with any other technology, there's bound to be a negative impact if it takes over one's life. It is up to each individual to find the right balance.

Sources: Annemarie Hodgson, "The Growing Presence of Chat on the Web," *PC Magazine* (Middle & Near East), 10 March 1999. (www.pcmag-mideast.com/html/ic0697.html); Dotcomguy (www.dotcomguy.com); Faith Popcorn's Web site (www.brainreserve.com); RISQ (www.risq.qc.ca); GVU 10th WWW User Survey (www.cc.gatech.edu/user_surveys/).

Summary

The Internet has grown from a technology available to the research community to one that is influencing the average person's life today. Consumers turn to the Internet for news, entertainment, shopping, medical advice, and so many other things. Small firms now have the ability to reach global markets, and larger firms have the ability to lower costs.

There are three major categories of E-commerce—business-to-business, business-to-consumer, and consumer-to-consumer. In each of these categories, tremendous revenue growth is projected in the next three to five years. Entrepreneurs are introducing new business models as well as innovative products and services. The B2B sector is much larger than the B2C sector. Businesses are embracing E-commerce to lower costs, reach new markets, and to ensure they do not lose their competitive edge.

Consumer adoption of the Internet has been comparatively slower. Among those who use the Internet for shopping, convenience and time saving are the main reasons for online shopping. The variety of products available to consumers is ever expanding, and the Internet is also allowing consumers to shop in new ways, such as auctions, reverse auctions, and aggregate buying formats. In addition to shopping, new services in areas like news and entertainment delivery, online education, and online banking are now available to individuals.

There are already signs of the strong impact of the Internet on our economy. New ventures and job creation attributable to the Internet are growing. As we look forward, universities and businesses must address the projected shortage of skilled employees with Internet skills.

The benefits of the Internet are apparent at many levels. As we move from the old manufacturing economy to the new knowledge and information economy, we cannot afford to leave anyone behind. To benefit economically, social issues must be addressed. Canada's global competitiveness depends on ensuring that all Canadians have the skills to compete and excel in this new economy.

Key Terms

Bricks-and-mortar, 12

Brochureware, 14

Clicks-and-mortar, 12

Cybermediaries, 1

Digital divide, 23

Disintermediation, 3

E-commerce, 10

E-tail, 12

HTML, 8

Hyperlinks, 8

Information asymmetry, 22

Internet marketing, 11

Intranets, 14

Law of digital assets, 21

Marketplace, 16

Marketspace, 16

Plug-ins, 8

Portals, 12

Pure-play, 12

Vortals, 15

Questions and Exercises

Review Questions

1. What are the main reasons why businesses use the Internet?
2. What factors do you think motivate consumers to shop online?
3. What are the differences between the Internet and the World Wide Web?
4. What are the three types of business-to-business Web sites? Provide examples.
5. What are online communities? Provide examples.
6. Identify three reasons for studying Internet marketing.
7. What are three possible areas where the Internet is likely to have a positive economic impact?

Discussion Questions

1. Discuss the economic impact of the Internet. How do you think Canada, as a nation, will benefit from the Internet?
2. What are the negative and positive social consequences of the Internet? What steps would you take to address the negative consequences?
3. What do you see as the critical areas that marketers need to consider to market effectively on the Internet?
4. If manufacturers and consumers forge closer ties, as we see happening in the automobile industry, what will happen to intermediaries like car dealers? How can they ensure their survival?

Internet Exercises

1. Visit the Web sites of the following companies:
   a. Nike (www.nike.com)
   b. Procter & Gamble (www.pg.com)
   c. Kraft Foods (www.kraftfoods.com)

   Is the site an "E-commerce" site or an information-only site? Evaluate the sites in terms of content, usefulness of information, ease of use, fun, and "interesting" features. Evaluate each aspect on a five-point scale (5 = excellent; 1 = poor). Is each site targeted to a specific audience?

2. Collect print ads of at least three automobile companies of your choice. Write down your impressions of the ads in terms of target audience, type of message (visual, informational), and brand image conveyed in the ad. Now go to the same companies' Web sites (use search engines to find the sites). Are the Web sites consistent with the print ads? Do you find similar themes, colours, symbols, and messages? Are the Web sites targeted to the same audience as the print ads?

3. Visit the following two aircraft manufacturing company sites: Boeing (www.boeing.com) and Bombardier (www.bombardier.com). What are the similarities and differences between the two sites? How do these two B2B sites differ from the sites for Nike and Kraft Foods (see Internet Exercise 1)?

4. Take two local small businesses (such as restaurants, video stores, beauty salons, and so on). Do a search on the Internet (using Yahoo, Infoseek, Excite, or Lycos) in that product category. Review some of the sites. Write a brief report on how you think the Internet will affect these local businesses.

Chapter 2

Economics of the Web and Business Models

Vignette 2 **It's Free for All!**

The future of electronic commerce on the business-to-consumer side depends on more people having access to the Internet. Currently, there are about 300 million Internet users worldwide, but even in the economically advanced countries, Internet penetration has yet to reach 50 percent. The Internet can become a technology for the masses only if the cost of equipment (PCs or other Web-enabled devices like WebTV and mobile phones) and the cost of Internet access decrease further. A new generation of businesses on the Internet is trying to accomplish this goal.

Even as leading economists discuss how to price Internet access, which is not an unlimited resource, new ventures on the Internet are now giving away Internet access for "free." Yes, that's right, unlimited Internet access at no cost to the consumer. Sound too good to be true? In the US, NetZero (www.netzero.com) and Freeinet (www.freeinet.com), as well as established players such as Juno.com, Exite@Home, and AltaVista, are among several free Internet service providers. A free ISP venture funded by Kmart, called Bluelight.com (see Exhibit 2-1), has signed up over a million users, while NetZero with 3 million members is the largest free ISP in the United States.

Why would a retailer like Kmart provide free Internet service? Internet penetration at the end of 1999 was still limited mostly to households with over $50 000 in annual income. Kmart's target market primarily consists of middle- to lower-income consumers. Free Internet access is a way to bring this large segment of the population online. This is also a certain way to ensure that most of these consumers shop at Kmart's online store. Free online access also ties in with Kmart's strategy to reposition itself as a new economy retailer.

Exhibit 2-1 Kmart's Free Internet Service

Source: www.bluelight.com.

The concept of free access is also spreading in other parts of the world. In Brazil, a country ravaged by many years of hyperinflation, banks are highly automated, which was necessary to lower costs. Now a leading Brazilian bank, Bradesco, offers free Internet access to all of its clients. What's in it for Bradesco? If Bradesco can get more of its clients to go online to do their banking transactions, there is no need to operate so many expensive branches that occupy prime real estate. Bradesco will retain its clients and the volume of transactions, while simultaneously reducing its overhead. The cost of a face-to-face banking transaction is estimated at $1.08, while each online transaction costs less than $0.13, a savings of 89 percent. The Royal Bank of Canada is also betting that the future of banking lies online. They have already sold several of their expensive downtown real estate properties.

Kmart and Bradesco can use the free Internet access to lure consumers to their traditional businesses (retailing and banking), but how can free ISPs like NetZero make money? If the telephone companies and the cable companies don't provide free access to their basic services, how can these ISPs offer free access?

The so-called free ISPs get revenue through advertising (see Exhibit 2-2). Here's how it works. When you sign-up for a NetZero account, you are required to reveal a great deal of personal information such as age, gender, income, shopping habits, and so on. This information is used to target advertising to each user according to his or her profile. Some call this **value exchange**—that is, the consumer gets something of value, in exchange for giving up something of value to the marketer. Others would call this intrusive and an invasion of privacy.

The free ISPs not only get detailed demographic and shopping information when you sign up, they also have the ability to track

Exhibit 2-2 NetZero Sweepstake Ad

Source: www.netzero.com.

your online browsing behaviour. If you have a NetZero account, they can, for example, show you a Barnes & Noble advertisement on part of your screen, if you are browsing through Amazon.com. Barnes & Noble can, thus, target a potential consumer with a tempting offer, while he or she is browsing through a competitor's site. NetZero calls these advertisements "ad missiles." In addition to these ads, a part of your computer screen is always taken up by an advertisement (which matches your demographic and Internet use profile), thus reducing the screen size. The Internet connection on free ISPs can often be very slow, since you are not likely to be the only freeloader. A new venture called FreeDSL (www.freedsl.com) now offers high-bandwidth (roughly 2.5 times the speed of a 56K modem) connection for free, in exchange for personal information. If you cannot stand the ads any longer, FreeDSL will turn off the pesky ads for a monthly fee of $9.95.

Do consumers benefit from all these in-your-face ads that so closely match their Web viewing habits? NetZero would contend that by matching ads with one's preferences consumers are served well. Consumers, however, are reduced to a pair of eyeballs and every move they make online is monitored. If you think consumers would be outraged at such tracking methods, think again. By the first quarter of 2000, 8 percent of Internet users in the US were using free ISPs, a figure that is expected to increase to 13 percent by 2003, according to the Internet research firm Jupiter Communications (www.jup.com). Studies show that consumers are willing to give up some of their privacy if in return they can get services that offer value.

Many industry experts believe that Internet service will be essentially free in the future. Under this scenario, retailers, banks, entertainment companies, and other businesses that benefit from bringing consumers online will pay for Internet access. More Internet users mean more revenue for firms that do business online.

Free Internet access will encourage more consumers to try it and, therefore, more consumers to shop online. At the end of 1999, roughly 12 percent of Canadians and about 25 percent of Americans had shopped online at least once. There is a vast untapped market for online stores. By eliminating the cost of Internet access, businesses may be able to encourage more consumers to try online shopping. Studies show that as consumers spend more time online, they become more comfortable with the idea of shopping online.

While Kmart and Bradesco are trying to take their established consumers online, the ISPs that depend on advertising revenue may have a difficult time. Consumers may grow tired of all the advertising shown on their little computer screens. The long-term viability of the free ISP *business model* has yet to be established.

Sources: "A Deal with the Devil," *Time Digital*, (www.time.com/time/digital/reports/free/isp.html); Liz Logan (2000), "Trying the Free ISPs," *Time Digital*, (www.time.com/time/digital/daily/0,2822,39394,00.html); Lynn Margherio, Dave Henry, Sandra Cook, and Sabrina Montes (1998), "The Emerging Digital Economy," US Department of Commerce, Washington, DC (www.ecommerce.gov), April; Greg Sandoval (2000), "BlueLight.com signs on 1 million customers," *CNET News.com*, March 22 (news.cnet.com/category/0-1007-200-1581313.html).

Introduction

As we saw in Chapter 1, businesses can reap immense benefits by going online. There are opportunities for reaching new markets as well as reducing the cost of operations. At the same time, unless a critical mass of consumers goes online, online businesses cannot be profitable. Vignette 2 highlights several interesting aspects of marketing and commerce on the Internet.

First, banks and retailers who see an opportunity to lower their costs are playing a proactive role in encouraging new consumers to go online. Consumers do not pay when they "window shop" in a local bricks-and-mortar mall. Why should they pay to window shop online? If retailers can bring consumers—free of cost—to their Web sites and show their wares to consumers, wouldn't more people shop online? The management at Kmart believes they will.

Second, as businesses go online, they are not only eliminating unnecessary costs, but they are instead focusing on activities that offer value to their customers. Banks, for instance, can deliver the same services (such as deposits, withdrawals, bill payment, money transfers, and investments) at lower cost and greater speed. Third, many new and innovative business models exist on the Internet. Selling products or services to end-users is not the only method of generating revenue online. Advertising-supported services are among the most popular on the Internet because the consumer gets them free of cost.

Businesses must deliver value to their customers in order to succeed. At the same time, a business cannot become profitable just by delivering value to customers. It also requires controlling costs and developing revenue-enhancing strategies. This chapter will focus on these three areas—value, costs, and revenue. We will build on the concept of virtual value chains, as introduced in Chapter 1, and examine the value creation process online. As we shift from the physical to the online, the impact on a firm's cost structure across the entire value chain will become apparent. Following the discussion of costs, various types of online businesses and revenue-generating opportunities will be presented.

Value Creation Online

Businesses perform a series of actions resulting in a final product or service that offers a certain benefit to consumers or end-users. In manufacturing as well as service organizations, typically the steps start from procurement of raw materials (or inputs) and end with the distribution of the product or service and after-sales service. In between, there are of course design, production of product or service, and marketing activities. The sequence of steps, where value is added at each step, is called the value chain (see Exhibit 2-3).[1]

The primary activities (at the top) are supported by the secondary or support activities, such as human resources and firm infrastructure. Michael Porter, a Harvard professor,

Exhibit 2-3 Traditional or Physical Value Chain

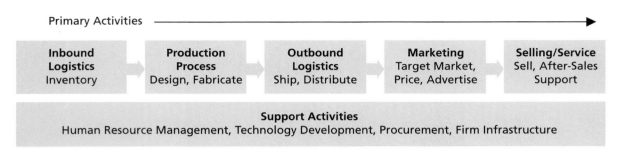

Primary Activities ⟶

| Inbound Logistics Inventory | Production Process Design, Fabricate | Outbound Logistics Ship, Distribute | Marketing Target Market, Price, Advertise | Selling/Service Sell, After-Sales Support |

Support Activities
Human Resource Management, Technology Development, Procurement, Firm Infrastructure

developed the concept of value chain.[2] He professed that by studying the various activities a firm performs in producing and selling a product or service, and by improving the efficiency of these activities, a firm can achieve superiority over its competitors—or competitive advantage.

In the value chain model, information systems (a support activity, which is part of the firm infrastructure) is used at each stage of the value chain to gather critical information that can be used to improve internal processes. For example, information systems can be used in the inventory control process to reduce costs associated with inbound logistics or eliminate bottlenecks in the production process. MIS can also be useful in the marketing stage by gathering vital information about customers and their purchase or product usage behaviour, which can be used in targeting and advertising. Every modern organization uses information systems that underlie its value chain to enhance the efficiency of its operations.

Today, many organizations are not only making physical goods that move through a **physical value chain**, but are also involved in creating and delivering **information goods** via the Internet or other networks. Organizations make physical products for competing in the marketplace as well as the **marketspace**.[3] The physical value chain (PVC), as shown in Exhibit 2-3, does not capture the value creation process in the marketspace or the virtual realm, where E-commerce takes place.

Let's now consider some examples that will help illustrate the differences between the marketplace and the marketspace. Columbia House markets CDs via print and online catalogues. Members get a certain number of CDs at no cost and are then required to buy a specified number of CDs at full price. Columbia House creates value by offering deep discounts and delivering the product to the consumer. This value creation takes place in the physical marketplace—the marketing materials and the goods have to move through a physical chain. CDNow, on the other hand, allows consumers to customize their song selections and also download the songs via the Internet (see Exhibit 2-4). The production, marketing, and selling activities take place virtually in the marketspace. Thus, Columbia House is in the marketplace, while a competitor, CDNow, is in the marketspace.

You no longer have to buy a standard CD where you listen to only three or four songs. In the marketplace model, often 50 percent of the product offers no value to the consumer. By allowing consumers to customize their song selections (a process made simpler by the Web), CDNow provides a superior value proposition compared to Columbia House.

Other companies try to reach consumers through physical as well as virtual channels. The Royal Bank of Canada, for instance, operates bricks-and-mortar branches to serve their

Exhibit 2-4 CDNow: Online Music Download

TODAY'S PICKS

Kenny Rogers
"Buy Me A Rose"
Song Download
Add to Cart
$1.99
Save to Wish List

One of the biggest stars in Country music, Kenny Rogers is known for his orignality and versatile style. Not swaying away from his reputation, Rogers has made his latest album available for download in it's entirety. Available here is the hit single "Buy Me A Rose", Download it now!

All free downloads require Liquid Player and take approximately 12-14 minutes to download on a 28.8k modem, 6-8 minutes on a 56k.

FOR MORE FREE DOWNLOADS **CLICK HERE**.

Peter Frampton: Download "All I Wanna Be (Is By Your Side)"

A Perfect Circle: Download "4-Song Compilation"

Toby Keith: Download "How Do You Like Me Now?!"

Source: www.cdnow.com

clients and also offers online banking. Similarly, airlines that sell tickets in paper form via travel agents also sell electronic tickets online. Online operations in these industries offer value by enabling consumers to complete transactions at any time, as well as by eliminating travel and waiting time. These companies are no longer bricks-and-mortar operations, they are now clicks-and-mortar operations, maintaining a presence in the marketplace as well as the marketspace.

As firms deliver products and services in the physical as well as the virtual realm, they must understand the value creation process in each case. The **virtual value chain**, while similar to the physical value chain (recall Exhibit 2-3), is not the same.

In the physical value chain, information systems are used as a tool to improve the efficiency and effectiveness of processes in each stage of the value chain. Information itself is not used to create value.[4] In the marketspace, companies use their databases and information systems not only to improve physical processes, but also to create value itself.

Let's now consider some examples that illustrate how information that lies within an organization can be turned into something of value to consumers. Federal Express, in an attempt to lower its call centre costs and improve customer service, opened its internal package tracking database to its customers. Now FedEx allows its customers to directly track the status of their shipment. Previously, information regarding the status of a shipment was tracked internally by the FedEx management information system. When that information was thrown open to the customers, FedEx was able to provide additional value to its customers. FedEx still performs all the value-adding functions in the physical marketplace (from pick-up to delivery of packages), but it's now also using the Internet to turn internal information into customer value.

Other firms like Cisco and Dell Computers are also using the Internet to deliver customer service. Previously, customers had to call a toll-free number and wait for their turn. Now a detailed online knowledge base allows consumers to find answers to most of their problems much faster, whenever they want. By sharing the company's expertise (as well as the content of voluminous user manuals) with customers, these companies are creating virtual value.

The basis of competition is changing. In the long term, sustainable competitive advantage in the Internet economy will result from fundamentally transforming the entire value chain. Firms can no longer achieve a competitive advantage just by managing the physical chain; they also need to manage the virtual value chain.[5]

Impact of the Internet on the Value Chain

In Chapter 1 we saw how the Web is transforming the automobile industry. The Internet could potentially impact every stage of the value chain. In addition to creating value in the physical marketplace, firms can also focus on creating value in the virtual marketspace. The value-adding steps in the marketspace are *virtual* in that they are performed through and with information. Exhibit 2-5 demonstrates the value creation process.

Inbound Logistics. Organizations are increasingly using the Internet to procure raw materials and supplies online. The current information technology and the Internet allow organizations to open their inventory positions to their suppliers. Suppliers can automatically replenish inventory as the materials move through the value chain in the buying organization. Purchase orders are generated electronically, with minimal manual work, resulting in increased efficiency.

Electronic commerce can reduce the cost of procurement. Businesses can spend $80 to $125 to draft and process each purchase order, which can sometimes be higher than the cost of the item being purchased.[6] Manually drafted purchase orders are error-prone (for example, an item ordered by the purchasing department may not match the needs of the end-user) and can be time-consuming. The US General Service Administration, a government agency, has reportedly cut in half the time needed to complete a purchase by adopting E-commerce for its procurement.[7]

As the time required to make a purchase declines, so does the need to carry inventory of supplies and materials. Dell Online, a pioneer in the direct delivery model in the PC indus-

Exhibit 2-5 Impact of the Internet on the Value Chain

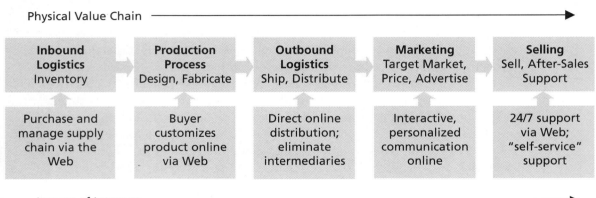

try, carries no more than a week's inventory. Components are literally ordered after receiving a purchase order from the customer. In industries where technology changes rapidly (such as personal computers) or where large numbers of new products are frequently introduced (such as books or CDs), carrying excess inventory can be costly due to rapid obsolescence.

Operations. Mass production, a by-product of the industrial revolution, is now being replaced by mass customization, an offshoot of the information revolution.[8] Consumers are becoming increasingly discriminating and are no longer satisfied with off-the-shelf products that do not fully meet their needs. As consumer needs become more diverse, customization becomes a key competitive strategy.[9]

Historically, manufacturers had to trade off between product volume and product customization. If they desired to have high sales volume, then customization was not feasible. The information technology revolution of the 1990s (especially database technology) and the capabilities of the Web, have changed the equation now.[10]

Companies that allow customization use their existing databases and information technology infrastructure as well as the Internet to accomplish the task. At Motorola's factory, for example, orders are directly received from the notebook computers of field salespeople through the Internet. A flexible, computer-aided production process allows Motorola to make, in theory, as many as 29 million styles of pagers. Style changes can be made in the production line without having to stop production or retool the production line.[11]

Customization is not just a trend in manufacturing companies. We see examples of customized online services in insurance, airlines, stock brokerage, and other service sectors. Contrary to the earlier belief that the Internet may not play a big role in the insurance industry because of the need for customization and its tradition in personal selling, firms like Geico Direct (www.geico.com) use the Web to offer customized quotes.

As you can see from Exhibit 2-6, the Web enables firms to provide a user-friendly interface, where each customer can configure products or services from a menu of choices. In the

Exhibit 2-6 Interactive Custom Clothes Company

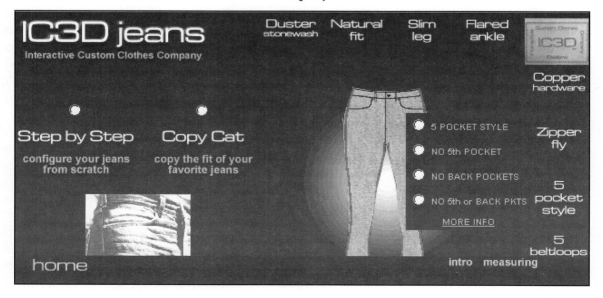

Source: www.ic3d.com.

customization process, the consumer plays a role in the pre-production (design) stage. This blurring of the gap between producers and consumers is referred to as **prosumption**.[12]

We see the Internet playing a role in customization in such diverse industries as automobiles (e.g., Saturn.com), computers (e.g., Dell.com), clothing (IC3D.com), CDs (e.g., CDnow.com), content services (e.g., myYahoo and myCNN), and entertainment (e.g., online video on demand). Without the Internet, it would be hard to imagine customization taking place in such a broad array of industries.

It must be pointed out that customization may not be appropriate or feasible in every case. Customization does require that the organization think differently and organize its processes differently. The emphasis moves away from economies of scale to satisfying each customer and building loyalty.

Outbound Logistics. As companies establish direct channels, disintermediation will occur in some industries. Intermediaries, such as wholesalers and agents, will be eliminated or replaced by more efficient online intermediaries. In Chapter 1, we saw how the auto dealers were facing the threat of disintermediation. That having been said, it must be pointed out that in many industries existing channel members will continue to add value and play a useful role.

Digital product industries, such as music, software and information, are the ones that are already seeing significant disintermediation. In the computer industry, Compaq and Hewlett-Packard are trying to emulate the direct distribution model of their more profitable rival Dell Computers. Non-digital manufactured products, such as cars, are more likely to see the continued use of direct as well as indirect channels.

The direct distribution model can allow manufacturers to retain higher margins (wholesalers and retailers often add 50 percent or more in margins). However, organizations that want to adopt this model need to invest in the physical infrastructure (warehouses, order fulfillment, and delivery systems).

Marketing. The traditional approach to marketing revolved around targeting large market segments and using mass media advertising to reach the audience. The product, price, and promotion (advertising) were typically the same for all consumers. As we saw in the discussion of production processes, however, mass production has now given way to mass customization. In addition to product customization, thanks to the Web, communication and advertising can also be personalized and very precisely targeted. Web sites can track the preferences of users and make offers or suggestions based on past behaviour. For example, Amazon.com tracks the book-buying habits of its customers. Then when they enter the site, book recommendations based on previous purchases are provided.

Canadian Tire (www.canadiantire.com) uses **permission marketing** and sends targeted e-flyers to consumers based on their preferences. Consumers can sign up to receive these e-mail flyers. A consumer interested in promotional offers in gardening supplies or sporting equipment can ask to receive information only in these categories. Rather than sending bulky print flyers to people who never read them, Canadian Tire can send customized messages to those who want such information.

Communication online is a two-way process, unlike mass media communication, which is unidirectional. Furthermore, online communication can also be interactive, allowing consumers to participate in bulletin boards sponsored by companies or fill out feedback forms or instant online surveys. The Internet allows marketers to move away from mass marketing and mass communication to personalized marketing and customized communication. As marketers address the needs of each consumer, there is a greater likelihood of a more favourable consumer response.

Selling. Barnes & Noble, the most successful bookseller in the United States, requires $2 000 000 to set up one book superstore.[13] While top Web sites do spend millions of dollars in site development costs, they do not need multiple retail outlets, as in the case of bricks-and-mortar stores. Thus, online sellers require less investment than bricks-and-mortar operations.

In addition, the transaction costs in the order-placement process (the costs associated with the product information search, product selection, and filling out order forms) are transferred to the buyer in the case of online stores.[14] As Web sites allow consumers to find the information they want and place the order online, transaction costs will decrease. These days, consumers with access to the Internet often use it for finding information before making major purchase decisions. Salespeople spend less time in closing a sale with consumers who have previously been to the company's Web site than with those who have not.[15]

Service and Customer Care. After-sales service and customer care activities are being automated in many industries. Some companies use the Web to provide technical support, while others (such as Geico Direct) allow customers to manage their accounts and bill payment online, thus eliminating the need to interact with service personnel.

Cisco, a leader in computer networking equipment, saved an estimated $525 million in 1997 by moving from the traditional support service (printed manuals and a large call centre with technically qualified staff) to an online model.[16] FedEx was able to cut back 20 000 new hires by automating its customer service.[17] Forrester Research, an Internet research firm, has estimated that sending a service representative into the field can cost $500 to $700, a phone-based customer service call can cost $15 to $20, and an Internet-based customer service system can cost about $7 per call.[18] These cost savings are bound to tempt more organizations to provide at least some of their customer service online.

Cisco and FedEx were able to reduce their costs because fewer employees are required when operating online as opposed to offline. Companies like Sun Microsystems and Cisco have turned their product manuals, troubleshooting guides, and the technical expertise of their staff into online knowledge bases. When a customer requires service or support, he or she can go online and get the answer. Lengthy waiting times associated with telephone service are eliminated. This "self-service" model works well in many cases, contributing to significant cost savings without reducing customer service levels.

Online firms are, however, finding out that not all consumers want such automated and impersonal service. One of the frequent complaints against e-tailers is that service can be poor to non-existent. Some high-end e-tailers are investing more in human resources now. For example, Mercedes Benz allows users to be directly connected to an agent at the call centre while still browsing the Web page (see www.mbsusa.com), and the company Liveperson.com offers a technology that allows consumers to chat with a salesperson via the company Web site. The conclusion is that it may be too soon to tell if the savings accrued due to online service delivery can be sustained. If consumers are unhappy with service levels, we may see the pendulum swing back towards hiring more support staff. Those who overestimated the Web's cost savings are realizing that even when the value chain is virtual, investment in human resources is needed to maintain high service levels.[19]

Virtual Value Creation Process

The examples we have seen so far demonstrate how companies exploit both the physical and virtual value chain. The integration of the value chain described in Exhibit 2-5 enables the organization to capture information at each stage of the value creation process. Information thus captured allows firms to operate more efficiently and create additional value for their customers. By moving some value-adding activities from the physical to the virtual arena, companies can exploit the virtual value chain. For instance, the performance of customer care activities online could result in more efficient service in some cases. In other cases, however, the physical value chain will not be replaced entirely by the virtual value chain. Most organizations may have to manage two value chains side by side, especially if they sell tangible goods.

Just as the physical value chain involves a series of activities, the virtual value chain can also be visualized as a sequence of value-adding activities: gathering, organizing, selecting, synthesizing, and distributing information.[20] In the physical value creation process, firms take raw materials or inputs and convert them to value-added products or services. In the virtual value chain, firms collect raw information and turn it into something beneficial to the consumers through the sequence of value-adding activities.

The information underlay (denoted by "Information Capture" in Exhibit 2-7) will allow companies to perform value-adding activities that can parallel or mirror the activities in the physical world.[21] A firm can create a matrix of value opportunities by putting in place the virtual value-adding steps. Each stage in the physical world (inbound logistics, operations, outbound logistics, marketing, service, and customer care) allows the firm to extract information, which can be turned into a value-adding opportunity by applying the virtual value-adding steps. It is, thus, possible to construct a matrix of value opportunities.[22]

For instance, product design previously performed in the physical world can now be performed in the virtual world by product development and design teams. A team from different parts of the world can work on the project by collaborating and sharing information in the virtual space. Such a virtual product development team that was not bound by the limitations of geographic time or space built the Ford Contour car. By going virtual, automobile companies can also involve the consumer in the design process and offer customized products.

Exhibit 2-7 Virtual Value Chain Mirroring the Physical Value Chain

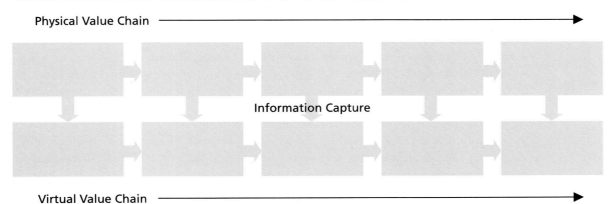

iMarket Demo 2-1 An Old Dog with New Tricks

An encyclopedia is a product that signifies knowledge and enlightenment. The most famous of them all, the *Encyclopedia Britannica*, started in Scotland in 1768. Students, scholars, and historians came to depend on it. Its door-to-door salesmen became famous for their knack of persuading parents that a multi-volume set (costing $1200 or more) was a must in any home with school-age children. Almost 200 years after it was started, sales revenues had reached a record $650 million in 1989, and the firm's sales force had grown to 2300.

In 1993, an unlikely rival named Microsoft introduced a multimedia encyclopedia called Encarta. It included sound and video presentations that brought history and science to life. The product came in a CD-ROM and was pre-installed in most new PCs. Basically, the product was being given away for free. *Britannica* countered by introducing a low-priced CD-ROM of their own, much to the displeasure of their salespeople who saw the CD version undercut their sales of the hard-cover volumes.

And then came the Web. There was so much free content available on every imaginable topic that *Britannica*'s survival was being threatened. *Britannica* responded with a subscription-based site, with regular content updates. Consumers, however, were used to free content on the Web and so the subscription model never really took off.

In October of 1999, *Britannica*'s new owners went a step further and made their site (www.britannica.com) free to users, with revenue coming from advertising. To those who own the hard-cover volumes, it may be shocking to see advertising amidst the content of the venerable encyclopedia. Today, *Britannica* offers free news from many sources, as well as in-depth content that is found in the print or CD editions. It sells CD and hard-cover editions of its encyclopedias, as well as a variety of education and entertainment products for children. There's even free e-mail for users. From a pure publisher, the company has become a portal and a full-fledged E-commerce site.

A company that did business in a certain way (hard-cover books sold by door-to-door salespeople) for over two hundred years has had less than a decade to completely reinvent itself, and *Britannica* didn't mind cannibalizing its own salespeople to save the brand. The new economy requires old firms to embrace change. In fact, *Britannica* was among the first traditional companies to respond to the Internet challenge.

Sources: "We're off to the Online Mall," *The Economist* (Survey E-Commerce), February 26, 2000 (www.economist.co.uk/editorial/freeforall/20000226/su7620.html); Robert Hertzberg (1999), "Oh Britannica," *Internet World*, November 15 (www.iw.com/print/1999/11/15/department/19991115-ednote.html).

Kodak (www.kodak.com) allows consumers to upload, save, edit, manage, and share pictures—all digitally. As photography becomes increasingly digitized, this company's inbound logistics will focus less on chemicals and paper. Kodak is already backing its line of digital cameras with a range of digital services, all performed virtually. As consumers register to take advantage of these services, Kodak also gets to know more about it customers.

Firms must understand the similarities and differences between the physical and the virtual value chains. The physical chain is a linear process, whereas the virtual chain can be non-linear. It is a matrix of opportunities. Some of the rules in the physical world (such as economies of scale) may not apply in the virtual world as businesses focus on customization. From the procurement of inputs to customer service, many activities can be performed more efficiently in the virtual space. Manufacturing companies must still move their products from factories to stores and eventually to the customers. This means that firms must manage the physical as well as the virtual value creation process.

Business Models on the Web

The value chain examines the internal processes within the organization and helps the organization identify opportunities for adding value. Managers or any new online business or existing business going online must be aware of not just the physical and virtual value chains, but also the firm's **business model**.

In very simple terms, a business model describes how firms generate revenue and profits.[23] Business models define the methods of operation. How do firms generate revenue online? Selling products and services online is the most common answer. But as we saw in Vignette 2, NetZero, the company that offers free Internet service, gets its revenues through advertising. There are many different methods of generating revenue on the Internet. In this section we will study the different business models or forms of businesses online. A more thorough definition of the term business model is as follows:

A business model is

- An architecture for the product, service, and information flows, including a description of the various business actors and their roles; and
- A description of potential benefits for various actors; and
- A description of the various sources of revenue.[24]

For most businesses (such as retail stores or real estate agencies), the underlying business models are easy to comprehend. In some cases (such as television broadcast networks), the business model can be harder to grasp because revenue generation and revenue sharing involve multiple actors or parties (for example, the networks, television program producers, advertisers, and so on).

There are several classification schemes of Web business models, but none that is exhaustive. Some online business models are replicas of bricks-and-mortar business models. Innovative entrepreneurs who capitalized on certain capabilities of the Internet have created other models. As most business models are adaptable to B2C and B2B markets, we will present the models without categorizing them into B2C or B2B. If a model is more applicable to one market then it will be noted accordingly.

Selling Online: Sell Side

Sell-side operations are similar to traditional retail or mall operations. Sellers determine the price. The price may or may not reflect the buyer's perceived value of the product.

Online Stores or E-tailing. Products and services are sold online, just as with bricks-and-mortar retail stores. Online retailing or e-tailing operations generate revenue from sales. The primary advantages of online stores include convenient shopping from home at any time of day, a wider selection (consumers are not limited to the choice available in local stores), and lower prices (in some cases, as with books and CDs). E-tailing sites include Indigo.ca, the online bookstore, Futureshop.ca, the online electronic goods store, and Justwhiteshirts.com, a Canadian menswear site.

E-tailers can be pure-play Internet companies without any bricks-and-mortar operations (such as Amazon.com) or what are known as clicks-and-mortar operations, which have physical as well as online stores (such as Chapters). In the latter case, by taking an established brand online it may be easier to attract traffic to the Web site. On the negative side, the online store may cannibalize sales from the bricks-and-mortar store. Some believe that it is better to cannibalize their own sales than to risk losing their sales to a competitor.[25]

Catalogue companies, such as L.L. Bean and Land's End have successfully migrated online. In the B2B area, Grainger, an established print catalogue company that supplies maintenance, repair, and operating (MRO) items to many industries, also has made a successful transition to E-commerce.

Online Malls. There are marketspace concentrators who bring together many different businesses under one umbrella. Online malls (such as iMalls.com) allow smaller firms to establish a Web presence quickly. They will often provide the retail stores in their "premises" with assistance in developing their Web sites, as well as the technology that is required to do online transactions (such as the use of "shopping carts"). Malls usually get a commission on the sales of their tenants and may also charge a monthly fee. When established companies like AltaVista and Yahoo! set up online malls, consumers may be more willing to trust the online stores in those malls.

Bricks-and-mortar malls serve consumers by bringing a broad array of stores under one roof. Malls have become a place for socialization and entertainment. On the Internet, the Web itself is like a huge mall—one can go from one e-tailer to the next with a few keystrokes and mouse clicks. Unlike the physical world, there is very little effort involved in going from one Web site to another. The benefits of online malls, which present several e-tailers in one site, were not clear in the early days of E-commerce.[26] However, with the explosion of E-commerce sites, many consumers (especially those who are new to online shopping) felt lost and frustrated trying to find products on the Internet. Online malls have made a strong revival by aggregating information and making it easier to find products.

According to eMarketer, an Internet market research firm, 15 percent of online business-to-consumer E-commerce revenues in 1998 occurred through online malls or hubs, and by 2003 this figure is expected to reach 40 percent.[27] Established e-tailers will have their own virtual stores but will also have a presence (or a link) in many mall sites, making it easier for consumers to find them. Established companies such as Intel, Yahoo!, and AltaVista are now online mall owners. In the B2B area, sites such as VerticalNet, PlasticsNet, and Hsupply act as malls by presenting a number of vendors on one site.

Virtual malls have the potential to lower information search costs, enhance trust, and offer a consistent shopping experience. Physical malls, however, will continue to play a vital role in the retail sector. They offer consumers the opportunity for a social experience as well as the ability to try products before buying. So far the evidence is that very few consumers are willing to give up the physical experience entirely for the virtual.

Selling Online: Buy Side

Unlike sell-side sites, buy-side sites put the consumer in charge. Consumer demand determines the product price. There are several different forms for buy-side models.

Auctions. This is another offline model that has been extended to the online marketspace. On the Internet, sites such as eBay, Bid.com, and uBid have popularized the auction concept. Previously, participating in an auction required either a physical presence at the auction site or a representative who could take bids via the telephone during the auction. The Internet has removed these time and place constraints. Online auctions are very similar to offline auctions, except that thousands of different products are auctioned daily on sites like eBay. Auction sites get a commission from the seller.

Dutch Auctions. In the traditional auction, the price goes higher with each bid. The bidder with the highest bid at the closing time is the winner. For certain products like flowers, which are perishable commodities, their value is at the highest when they are fresh. With time, their value declines, which should be reflected in a declining price model. This is precisely what happens in a Dutch auction. Auctions start with the highest price and the bids get lower with time. A Vancouver-based flower growers cooperative, United Flower Growers Cooperative Association (www.ugfca.com) allows Dutch auctions and so does eBay. As with traditional auctions, the auctioneer gets a commission here too.

While eBay is a consumer-to-consumer auction site, Jupiter Communications (www.jup.com) has predicted that the future of e-tailing lies in business-to-consumer auctions. Businesses will use the auction format to liquidate excess inventory. Business-to-consumer auctions are expected to reach $3.2 billion in 2002.[28]

Reverse Auctions. At Priceline.com, the customer specifies the price he or she is willing to pay for an airline ticket, hotel room, or a car rental, and sellers bid for the buyer's business. The seller who is at or closest to the buyer's preferred price will be the winner. Buyers must have some knowledge of the price range for a product. This "name your price" reverse auction model is the brainchild of Jay Walker, the founder of Priceline.com.

Why do reverse auctions work? Hotels rooms, airlines seats, and rental cars are like perishable commodities. If a hotel room is vacant tonight or a seat on a flight is empty, that represents revenue lost forever. In such cases, some revenue is better than no revenue. That is why hotels and airlines participate in reverse auctions and often sell below the advertised price. Priceline.com gets its revenue by charging the participating sellers a commission for their service.

Aggregator Sites. In the physical marketplace, Costco is known for its bulk buying discount price model. On the Internet, aggregators represent a similar idea with a twist. As more and more buyers join in to buy a specific product, such as a DVD player or a Camcorder, the price of the product falls. Mercata.com, Mobshop.com (see Exhibit 2-8), and Officecoop.com, which provides volume discounts to small business, are some of the well-known group buying sites.

A consumer who buys just one unit of a product could never think of getting a discount. The group buying sites enable consumers to drive down the price by combining their purchasing power. Aggregator sites usually get a small percentage of each sale as commission from sellers.

Virtual Communities

Community. "Communities of interest" (COINS) are growing rapidly on the Internet. There is a community site for just about every hobby, interest, profession, and lifestyle group. Using bulletin boards and chat rooms, these sites provide user interaction. Other sites encourage members to contribute content on a voluntary basis. Yahoo! and Excite have

Exhibit 2-8 Mobshop: Aggregate Buying Model

Source: www.mobshop.com.

vibrant online communities. Cricinfo.org (a site devoted to the sport of Cricket) is a unique community site. It gets over 180 million page views a year, with volunteers providing live (text commentary) coverage of games from around the world. It is dependent on advertising revenue. AOL is the largest online community in the world—or, rather, it is actually a collection of communities, each with its own interest area.

Some communities are devoted to providing information to the public. Epinions.com and Deja are sites where anyone can post their opinions on different products. These sites are usually advertising-based. Guru.com is a fee-based site, which is a collection of experts in many different subject areas.

Trade Exchange. This is mainly prevalent in the B2B area. Online exchanges, where businesses can buy and sell supplies and materials, are growing fast and are attracting a lot of interest from investors. The seller pays a transaction fee, which can be a percentage of sales. Some trade exchange sites may require an annual membership fee.

Tradingfloor.net is an international community of exporters and importers, which allows real-time, live online trading. Trading exchanges can allow buyers to post requests for quotes (RFQs), sellers to bid, and both parties to negotiate online.

Communities share common interests and tend to be narrowly focused, which makes them an attractive marketing target. Word-of-mouth spreads very quickly in virtual communities. Members tend to trust each other more than they do any paid advertising. The earlier online communities (such as the WELL and Usenet groups) were non-commercial in nature. Now commercial firms sponsor over 75 percent of online communities on the Internet.[29] Communities allow marketers to interact with a vast number of current or potential customers. Hagel and Armstrong, authors of *Net Gain*, profess that marketing will increasingly focus on communities.[30]

Cybermediaries

As some bricks-and-mortar intermediaries—such as travel agents and car dealers—face the threat of disintermediation, new intermediaries are emerging online. A typical intermediary provides information and also delivers products. Cybermediaries, with the exception of digital products such as information or software (which can be delivered via the Internet), are mainly information sources. They play a useful role in product search.[31]

Portals. Portal sites offer a multitude of services and are gateways to the Web. A typical portal site offers a searchable directory of Web sites, news, stock quotes, weather, e-mail, message boards, and so on. Portals allow users to find information easily. Examples of general portals include Yahoo!, Excite, AltaVista, and AOL. Portals make their money mainly through advertising. As portals expand their services—AltaVista offers free Internet access and Yahoo! offers electronic bill payment and auctions—there will be other revenue opportunities (such as user fees).

There are also very specialized portals known as "vertical industry portals," or **vortals**. These portals specialize in a single industry or subject. Women.com and iVillage.com, for example, are vortals offering a variety of services and content for women.

In the B2B sector, vortals focus on specific industries, such as steel (eSteels.com) or plastics (PlasticsNet.com). Specialized portals can get revenue through advertising as well as subscription fees or transaction fees. These B2B vortals act as electronic hubs or eHubs by attracting buyers and suppliers to a common venue.[32]

Infomediaries. Intermediaries in the physical world add value by providing information and products, relative performance, price, and so on. In fragmented markets with many buyers and sellers, consumers are often ignorant of the choices available to them. Hence, there is a need for value-added intermediaries. On the Web, there is a vast array of choices available to consumers, often from vendors of unknown reputation. Consumers can get frustrated looking for information. Infomediaries are online intermediaries who aggregate content and make it easier for buyers to find information. Advertising and tenancy deals, as well as supply-side subscriptions (where vendors pay a fee), are possible sources of revenue in this model.[33]

Portals and vortals can also be considered a form of infomediary. Firms that collect and sell information about consumers (such as NetZero) are a type of infomediary.[34]

Brokers. Not unlike their "real-world" counterparts, brokers also operate on a commission basis. They bring buyers and sellers together and sometimes facilitate transactions. There are two primary forms of brokers: information brokers and transaction brokers.

Information brokers provide information about products, prices, and availability. Even though they sometimes also facilitate transactions, their primary value is the information they provide. Autobytel.ca (an auto referral site that gets a commission from dealers for each referral) is a good example of an information broker.

Transaction brokers provide product and price information, but their main function is to facilitate online transactions. Online stock brokerages such as E*TRADE and Ameritrade are transaction brokers.

Advertising

There are many advertising-supported sites. They usually offer free products or services, thus generating a lot of traffic. As the number of eyeballs (visitors to the site) grows, advertisers are likely to get interested in sponsoring pages or placing banner ads. This is proving to be a difficult model to sustain. There are so many outlets for advertisers on the Web, and as a result, there is more advertising space than demand for such space. The consequence is that there are very few purely advertising-based sites.

Free Services. In addition to advertising-sponsored sites (as described in iMarket Demo 2-2), there are software companies, long-distance services, Internet service providers, entertainment companies, and many others available free of charge. These businesses hope to recoup their costs through advertising.

iMarket Demo 2-2 Something for Nothing?

You can get almost anything for "free" on the Internet if you are willing to reveal some personal details. We saw examples of free Internet service earlier, and there are more vendors joining this free economy.

If you're looking for some extra disk-space for your music and other space-guzzling files, you can go to Netdrive.com, Driveway.com, or iDisk.com to get more megabytes of free hard-disk space. Or you can store your files online and retrieve them when you want. This works well if you have a high-speed connection (cable model or DSL), so that you're not waiting forever to upload and download files.

If you are tired of paying your long distance bills, don't worry. A technology known as voice-over-IP telephony will enable to you make long distance calls through your Internet service provider, so that a call anywhere costs no more than your local access to your ISP (which can be free!). Hotcaller, an Ontario-based company, offers Internet calling to several foreign countries. There is a little catch, however. You not only have to tell your life history, but you also need watch some specified number of ads to earn points, which are then redeemed when you make phone calls. A six-minute call from Canada to the United States, for example, may require watching three online ads.

If you want to be entertained for free, you can watch free movies (mostly short films) at Atomfilms.com, Dfilms.com, iFilms.com, or Reelshort.com. To get a good viewing experience you need a high-speed Internet access.

Free software (freeware) can be found in sites like Download.com and TuCows.com. There are even sites that help you find freebies. Check out Free.com and Freeshop.com.

As everything from encyclopedias to entertainment is offered free on the Web, the traditional method of revenue generation (selling real goods and services) seems a rarity. So far, a good number of consumers have also bought into the **value exchange** concept, where consumers give personal information in exchange for something valuable.

The "free" sites have to generate a lot of traffic to get big advertisers interested. If there is a lot of advertising on these free sites, wouldn't that advertising cost be eventually passed on to consumers in the form of higher prices for other products? Only time will tell if this business model is fundamentally sound. In the meantime, let's go on a free ride!

Discount E-tailers. A discount e-tailer, such as Buy.com, sells products at very low prices. Low prices attract traffic, which in turn attract advertisers. Buy.com and other discount e-tailers hope to make up for their low margins through advertising revenue.

Content Sites. Content sites such as CNN, *The Globe and Mail*, and *Wired* magazine are among the thousands of free content sites. These are advertising-supported sites. Some content sites may require registration. Registered users may also get additional services (see, for example, *The Economist* at www.economist.co.uk). Information collected in the registration process is often used to target mailings or advertising.

Search Engines and Portals. As we saw earlier, search engines and portals, which can also be classified as content sites, are dependent on advertising revenue.

Promotion and Incentives

The main purpose of a promotion or incentive site is to direct traffic to a destination site. There are many different forms of incentive sites on the Web. Netcentives.com, for example, offers loyalty or reward programs that allow consumers to collect points when they shop at online stores. The points can then be redeemed when they make other purchases. Yoyodyne (part of Yahoo!) uses a subscription-based newsletter to entice members to participate in online promotions, such as sweepstakes and games. There are also coupon sites, such as Coolsavings.com and Couponnetwork.ca, that allow users to download electronic coupons that can be redeemed at specified online (and in some cases, offline) stores. Promotion sites direct traffic to the site that is doing the promotion. These sites charge participating merchants a flat fee or a commission.

Affiliate Sites. One method of attracting traffic to a site is through affiliate sites. Many leading sites, such as Amazon.com, Pets.com, eBay, and Chapters.ca, offer affiliate programs. Affiliate sites are usually small businesses that provide a link or a small banner ad and direct traffic to these larger sites. Affiliate sites are mostly paid a commission based on results. If a consumer clicks the Amazon.com link on an affiliate site and then buys a product a Amazon, the affiliate site would get a percentage of the sales revenue. Smaller sites use affiliate programs to augment their revenue. The affiliate model is a pay-for-performance model.[35]

There are thousands affiliate programs with business opportunities ranging from videos (Reel.com), books (Amazon.com, Chapters.ca), garden supplies (Garden.com), pet supplies (Pets.com), and banking services (LendingTree.com). As you can see in Exhibit 2-9, E-commerce sites are willing to pay for traffic delivered to their site.

Is There a Right Model?

As evident from the discussion of business models, there is a vast array of models. We have covered only the most common ones. Very few online businesses nicely fit into one model. As described in iMarket Demo 2-3 on page 48, Amazon.com is an e-tailer, auctioneer, and an online mall. Yahoo! is a portal, mall, auctioneer, and a content provider. Businesses are struggling to find the right business model. They seem to be experimenting with different models.[36] Once a site is established and gains brand recognition, the Internet facilitates the easy incorporation of different business models in a single site. Hybrid business models are definitely here to stay.

Business models seem to evolve and some have a limited shelf life. The pure advertising model, for instance, is now considered a difficult model to sustain. Unless, of course, you are a prestigious brand name site such as CNN, *The New York Times*, or *The Globe and Mail*.

Exhibit 2-9 Top-Rated Affiliate Program at Garden.com

Garden.com	`tell a friend`

Description: Garden.com offers more than 20,000 products that include plants, bulbs, seeds, tools, furniture, garden-inspired gifts, and lots more! You will earn $10 CASH for every referral who becomes a member and who makes a purchase at garden.com. You will also earn between 5% and 10% commission on every sale! The folks at Garden.com would love to see you grow, join now!

[Bulletin Board]

Launch Date: 01-Oct-99

No. of Affiliates: 10000 as of 01-Mar-97

Fee: $10 cash for referrals + 5% to 10% commission

Categories: E-Commerce, Home/Garden

Source: www.refer-it.com.

AOL used to charge its members based on connection time, and the revenue was shared with content providers who were responsible for drawing viewers. Now in North America, ISPs do not usually charge based on connection time. Almost all provide unlimited connection time and some do not even charge a monthly fee (recall Vignette 2). AOL's old revenue model no longer works in this new environment.[37]

Even the big E-commerce players, both in B2B and B2C, are pursuing multiple revenue opportunities. It seems that at least some of them are hedging their bets. The flexibility of the Web allows online firms to pursue multiple avenues—from auctions and direct selling to advertising. We're also likely to see some business models being discarded or made obsolete by new innovations.

Costs, Revenues, and Profits

From costs and revenue models, let's move on to profits. At the outset of this chapter, we discussed the cost-saving potential of the Internet and E-commerce across the entire value chain. But if there's so much potential for cost savings online, why are so few e-tailers profitable? Even the best-known B2C e-tailer, Amazon.com, has yet to make a profit as of the end of the third quarter of 2000.

Some experts contend that the answer lies in understanding the **cost of customer acquisition**.[38] In some industries, the customer acquisition costs online are much lower than they are offline. For instance, the cost of selling a car through referral sites, such as Carpoint and Autobytel, is lower than the cost incurred in traditional media. While there is evidence that the Internet may lower customer acquisition costs for automobile dealers, in many industries online customer acquisition costs are still very high. Average online customer acquisition costs can be as high as $250 per customer, and most consumers rarely purchase items valued at more than $50. This means that online firms must achieve a high degree of customer loyalty in order for the initial acquisition cost to pay for itself. Even established retailers such as Amazon.com find that customer loyalty is very low online.

iMarket Demo 2-3 What Business Are We In?

When Amazon.com started in 1995, it was known as the "Earth's largest bookstore." Somewhere along the line, Amazon has evolved into the "Earth's largest selection." What began as a virtual bookstore has evolved into an online megastore. Some products are shipped directly from the Amazon warehouse in Seattle, while others come from strategic partners such as Drugstore.com.

Amazon is no longer a strict e-tailer. It is an amalgamation of different business models. In addition to directly selling, Amazon is a major auction site and a host to a number of small, independent businesses that sell under the banner zShops.

Yahoo!, another well-known portal site, has similarly evolved over time. From being a directory and search engine, Yahoo now offers a host of services, including free e-mail (and free Internet service through its business partner Bluelight.com), financial services (such as stock quotes and online bill payment), an array of brand name stores under the Yahoo! mall, online auctions, and so on. New value-added services are being added by the day.

Amazon and Yahoo! are among many e-businesses that combine multiple business models. They are also two of the most recognized brands on the Internet. The temptation to leverage the brand in every direction must be irresistible. But is that the right thing to do? Amazon's marketing costs are so high that despite achieving revenues of over $1.64 billion in 1999, the company has yet to make a profit.

Amazon claims to have 17 million customers in over 150 countries. Founder Jeff Bezos thinks Amazon is a leading E-commerce platform, which can be extended to many products and services. One of his stated goals for the year 2000 is, in fact, to expand Amazon's offerings. The company claims that by focusing on customer experience, service, selection, and low prices, it is building customer loyalty, which will pay off eventually. Critics would argue that the company is losing focus by straying from its original business model. What do you think?

Sources: Jeffry F. Rayport (1999), "The Truth About Internet Business Models," *Journal of Strategy and Business*, Third Quarter; Amazon.com, Annual Report, 1999 (www.amazon.com/exec/obidos/subst/misc/investor-relations/1999annual_report.html/104-1407340-8279925).

Chuck Davis, Disney Online's senior vice president for electronic commerce, had estimated that Disney's online store was equivalent to having eight bricks-and-mortar stores selling Disney products.[39] That was in 1998. As consumers become more familiar with E-commerce and comfortable with online shopping, the same online store could become the equivalent of fifty or more bricks-and-mortar stores. That is when the high initial investment in technology and customer acquisition will pay off for Disney.

Most E-commerce entities are still building the customer base. In addition, very few customers they acquire become repeat customers. High customer loyalty can lower costs dramatically. The problem is how can online marketers build loyalty when consumers have so many choices. With heavy discounting and free offers, the emphasis has shifted from brands to prices. As consumers start focusing on prices, they are likely to be less loyal, and there is already proof that online customer loyalty is low. Unless online firms can turn one-time buyers into loyal customers, profits will continue to elude them.[40]

Most online firms are obsessed with building traffic and repeat visits. The "free service" model and heavy discounting of prices (such as with Amazon.com. and Chapters.ca) are used to attract traffic. If consumers get used to free products and discounted prices, will they ever pay the full price again? The big conundrum in Internet marketing circles now is how to "monetize the traffic." In simple words, it means how do we get the customers who visit the site (window shoppers) to actually buy something. Only about 5 percent of consumers who visit E-commerce sites actually buy a product. This figure combined with high customer acquisition costs underscores the importance of repeat purchasing and customer loyalty.

The pressure from investors and the experience of many famous flops (such as boo.com, the luxury apparel e-tailer) is forcing many companies to rethink their strategies. As established bricks-and-mortar firms (with reputed brands and excellent physical infrastructure) go online (such as Wal-Mart), pure-play Internet companies will face further competitive pressures.

The Web allows marketers to customize their products and advertising messages. If a company gets it right, it should be able to first establish a dialogue with the customer (to understand customer needs) and then eventually build a relationship with the customer.[41] In the end, marketing on the Internet is not very different from marketing offline. It's all about satisfying the customer.

Summary

The Internet allows firms to reduce costs across the entire value chain. It also enables firms to create and deliver value virtually, by leveraging internal information resources. A firm that operates in the physical marketplace may have to compete with a firm that operates virtually, leading many bricks-and-mortar companies to embrace the Internet.

There are many different business models on the Web, but very few have stood the test of time. Most firms seem to be hedging their bets by adopting multiple business models. As new models emerge, the old ones fall out of favour. The pure advertising-supported model has given way to hybrid models. Well-known Internet companies such as Amazon and Yahoo! are pursuing multiple revenue opportunities. In general, Internet companies are preoccupied with diversification, partnerships, and traffic building.

In spite of the tremendous cost savings offered by the Internet, so far there are very few E-commerce companies who are actually making a profit. Part of the reason is that these companies are spending a fortune on advertising and promotion aimed at building traffic and customer loyalty. Many companies are also realizing that if they do not provide good customer service (which requires human resources), customer loyalty cannot be obtained.

Key Terms

Business model, 40

Brokers, 44

Cost of customer, acquisition, 47

Infomediaries, 44

Information brokers, 44

Information goods, 32

Marketspace, 32

Permission marketing, 36

Physical value chain, 32

Prosumption, 36

Transaction brokers, 44

Value exchange, 29

Virtual value chain, 33

Vortals, 44

Questions and Exercises

Review Questions

1. What is a value chain?
2. What is a virtual value chain?
3. How is the marketspace different from the marketplace? Provide an example of two competitors—one who is in the marketplace and one who is in the marketspace.
4. Identify any four opportunities that the Internet offers to businesses for lowering costs along the value chain.
5. Explain how the Internet can lower marketing and selling costs.
6. Explain the following business models: (a) infomediary, (b) advertising. In each case, describe how firms generate their revenue. Provide examples.
7. Why do firms use multiple business models?
8. If the Internet affords cost savings in every aspect of a business, why are so few online firms profitable?

Discussion Questions

1. Discuss the concept of the virtual value chain. Find examples on the Internet that illustrate this concept.
2. Amazon.com had revenues of $1.64 billion in 1999, but still no profits. Develop a plan that will take Amazon to profitability in two years. Review the Amazon.com site before you develop your plan.
3. Do you think firms like Amazon and Yahoo! are doing the right thing by expanding into many different services and offerings? Do you think such rapid diversification is unique to online businesses?
4. Many "free" products and services, supported by online advertising, are now available to consumers. Do you think this business model is viable in the long term? Why or why not?

Internet Exercises

1. Visit Yellowpages.com. Carefully study all the features and services.
   a. Develop a value chain model.
   b. Compare Yellowpages.com with your print version of the yellow pages from the local telephone company. How does Yellowpages.com differ from the print version? What new benefits (value) do customers get online?
   c. What is the business model in each case?
2. Visit the Canada Post site (www.canadapost.ca). Study the different services offered on the site.

   a. Who is the target of the Canada Post site?
   b. How would you describe the online business model?
   c. Has the Web changed Canada Post's original business model? If so, how?
   d. Is Canada Post using the concept of the virtual value chain?
   e. Suggest some new services that can be offered online, that are consistent with Canada Post's business model.
3. Visit Kodak (www.kodak.com). What transformations are obvious to you in this company as a result of the Internet? Focus on markets, products,

customers, and the company's processes. How do you think this company's future will differ from its past? Consider the value chain and business model.

4. Consider one of your local stores (such as Futureshop.ca or Chapters.ca) with offline (brick) and online (click) operations. Visit the local store and the Web site and compare the offline and online operations on the following dimensions.

Factor	Brick Store	Click Store
Target market(s)		
Compare product range (number/depth)		
Are prices the same?		
Promotions or sale offers		
Advantage of brick over click store		
Advantage of click over brick store		
Which store offers greater value to consumers in your opinion?		
Describe each business model		

Chapter 3

The Business-to-Consumer Market

Vignette 3 **Doctor on the Net**

The Internet may not be a magic pill, but it is demonstrating an important role in healthcare delivery. A study by Cyber Dialogue found that over 23 million Americans used the Internet in 1998 as a source of health and medical information. This figure is expected to grow to over 30 million in 2000.

Where is the growing demand for online healthcare services coming from? In Canada, according to A.C. Nielsen Canada, the over-55 age group is the fastest expanding segment of online users, even though in 1998 they constituted only 4 percent of the online population. Similar trends are evident in the United States. There are also more women online now. Thirty-eight percent of women are online as of the first quarter of 2000, compared to only 16.5 percent in 1999. It is these two segments—older and female consumers—that are driving the demand for healthcare information and related online services.

Statistics show that women are more likely to visit health information sites than men are. Health ads were rated third among 15 categories of ads that Internet users found useful, with 38 percent of women and 20 percent of men rating them as useful. Older Internet users are much more likely to search for health information. While consumers over the age of 50 look for information on diseases and diet, those under 25 are more concerned with fitness information. Clearly, there is room for target marketing here.

Why are the health sites growing in popularity? The demand for health information online could be the result of growing health-consciousness in our society. According to a study by Cyber Dialogue,

Table 3-1 Top Health Sites by Traffic

Web Site	Unique Visitors (000s)	Percentage
Onhealth.com	3 119	38%
DrKoop.com	2 558	28%
WebMD.com	1 682	18%

Source: Media Metrix.

adults who use health sites feel that the "Internet empowers them to make better choices." The popularity of these so-called do-it-yourself (DIY) health sites seems to coincide with increasing dissatisfaction with service provided by doctors.

The top health sites (see Table 3-1) have name recognition and are backed by big investors. Dr. C. Everett Koop, the former United States surgeon general, founded DrKoop.com (See Exhibit 3-1). Healtheon/ WebMD, valued at $20 billion in 1999, is the first end-to-end Internet healthcare company connecting physicians and consumers to the entire healthcare industry.

It is not just health information sites that are flourishing on the Internet. Pharmaceutical companies have also realized that the Web can be used for targeted advertising to important segments, such as women and older consumers. Table 3-2 lists the top pharmaceutical advertisers on the Web.

Consumers can get over-the-counter and prescription drugs from online pharmacies like drugstore.com (see Exhibit 3-2) and plan-etrx.com. For people who frequent drug stores or for those who lack mobility, shopping online is a convenient alternative.

Exhibit 3-1 DrKoop.com: One of the Many Health Resource Sites on the Web

Table 3-2 Top Pharmaceutical Company Advertisers on the Web

Company	Impressions (000s)	Share of Voice
Schering	22 000	33.6%
Hoechst Marion Roussel	8 900	13.6%
Lifescript.com	3 400	5.6%
McNeil-PPC	3 400	5.2%
Merck	3 300	5.0%

Source: AdRelevance.

Exhibit 3-2 Drugstore.com Ad on Yahoo! When Searching for "Drugs"

Online healthcare is not entirely an American phenomenon. In Canada, for instance, which has a government-funded healthcare system, there are exciting innovations happening in telemedicine. Medbroadcast.com, a Canadian Web site, uses Flash animation and streaming video to educate consumers (see Exhibit 3-3). The site also has an extensive information database. The multimedia content makes this site unique and user-friendly.

Exhibit 3-3 Medbroadcast Animation

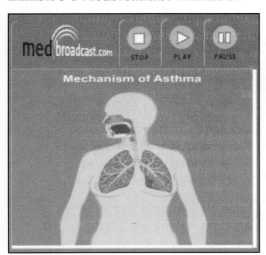

The proliferation of do-it-yourself health sites and the easy access to some drugs online is indeed a cause for concern among medical professionals. Are consumers less likely to get professional advice when they have such easy access to information and drugs? There is also a growing concern about privacy among consumer groups that many of these sites require users to divulge personal information about one's medical history. Some would argue that the loss of privacy is a small price to pay for the convenience offered by these online services. What do you think?

Sources: "The Health Care Industry in Transition," www.cyberdialogue.com; "Gender Gap Impacts E-Commerce," www.cyberatlas.com; "Internet Fact Book," www.acnielsen.ca.

Introduction

For the layperson, E-commerce has become synonymous with selling products to consumers over the Internet. In this chapter we will devote our attention to the consumer market. The nature of products and services targeted at consumers, the demographics and growth of the business-to-consumer market, consumer adoption issues, and online consumer behaviour will be addressed in this chapter.

The Business-to-Consumer Market

Vignette 3 illustrates how the growing diversity of Web users is creating new market opportunities. There are opportunities for selling healthcare products and providing information services. There are also opportunities for marketing to different target markets, such as seniors and young adults, who have differing health needs.

The business-to-consumer market encompasses a variety of business models—ranging from *pure-play* online retailers or e-tailers (such as Amazon.com) to *clicks-and-mortar* retailers (such as Futureshop.com and Chapters.ca). This sector of E-commerce also includes services such as online trading (for example, E*Trade and eSchwab), news and information sites (such as CNN.com and Globeandmail.com), and entertainment sites like Atomfilms.com, which delivers short and animated films via the Web.

As of the year 2000, less than five years since the inception of World Wide Web, it is now possible to purchase virtually everything from real estate and expensive luxury cars to one-of-a-kind antique items on the Internet. It should be pointed out that although consumer adoption of the Internet as a shopping avenue has been growing, earlier projections about the demise of neighbourhood bricks-and-mortar stores seem a bit far-fetched at this stage.

Top Items on the Internet

While the range of products available online is ever expanding, with categories such as clothing, groceries, and prescription medication showing promise, the list of top-selling items (see Table 3-3) has not changed much since 1998.[1]

Some products seem to be more suitable for online buying. Consumers may feel comfortable purchasing these products without physically inspecting them. Other products, such as

Table 3-3 Top 5 Items Purchased Online

Item	Percentage of Online Shoppers
Books	26%
CDs	24%
Software	21%
Computer hardware	13%
Airline tickets	12%

Source: Greenfield Online, CyberAtlas, August 1999.

automobiles, are seldom purchased directly online. However, the Internet does play an important role as an information source in the case of products not actually purchased online.

Growth of the Consumer Market

The growth of E-commerce has been phenomenal. In 1998, total global business-to-consumer E-commerce was estimated at $13 billion. The Christmas season of 1999 produced over $6 billion worth of online sales in the United States alone. The worldwide business-to-consumer E-commerce is expected to expand to $380 billion by 2003.[2] However, online sales in 1999 were estimated at only 0.5 percent of total retail sales.[3] Although this is still a small percentage of total global retailing, the growth rate does look attractive.

The revenue projections are based on the fact that a growing number of users are joining the Net each day. Reduced cost of Internet access and the growth of locally based online merchants are expected to drive the growth of e-tailing. Internet demographics worldwide are rapidly changing as more people go online. There is some concern that in the US, the Internet usage growth rate may be slowing down or even levelling off.[4] Countries in Asia and Europe, however, are expected to be the high growth markets in the next few years.

Global Demographics of the Consumer Market

Internet usage in Europe, Asia, and Latin America is growing. According to the study, "The Face of the Web," by the Angus Reid group (www.angusreid.com), there are already 300 million users on the Web and another 150 million are expected to go online by the end of 2000. The study, based on surveys in 34 countries, predicts that Internet usage will exceed one billion in 2005.[5] Table 3-4 shows top ten countries in terms of Internet usage.

Table 3-4 Top 10 Countries in Internet Use

Country	Users as of End of 1999 (000s)
United States	110 825
Japan	18 156
UK	13 975
Canada	13 277
Germany	12 285
Australia	6 837
Brazil	6 790
China	6 308
France	5 696
South Korea	5 688

Source: Computer Industry Almanac.

The emerging markets for Internet usage and E-commerce are some of the developing countries in Asia and Latin America, according to a Inter@ctive Week.[6] In a report on the "emerging 20," Inter@ctive Week states that South America (Argentina and Brazil), Eastern Europe (Russia), and Asia (China, India, Thailand, Malaysia, and Indonesia) are the markets that will drive global E-commerce growth. Latin America is expected to have 30 millions users by 2003, according to a study by IDC.[7] Brazil led in the number of Internet users for 1999 with 41 percent of users in Latin America, followed by Mexico at 21 percent, and Argentina with 10 percent. India is expected to have over 30 million users by 2004. The Internet is finally showing signs of fulfilling the promise of a "connected world."

Consumer Adoption of the Web

The Web adoption rate has been phenomenal. Earlier inventions such as the telephone and television took a lot longer to diffuse into the society. As a comparison, the telephone took over 20 years to reach 10 percent market penetration in the United States, while the Web has achieved over 40 percent penetration in less than seven years.[8]

The Web has gained rapid acceptance, but there are still vast numbers of people who are untouched by this innovation. Even in North America, as of the beginning of the year 2000, less than 50 percent of the population can be considered regular Internet users. Globally, only a fraction of the population is online. Terms like "digital divide" and "information apartheid" have been used to describe the fact that the Internet has yet to touch the lives of underprivileged people, certain ethnic minorities, and those in rural areas. Government and private sector initiatives are beginning to address this problem.

Roger Everett's Theory of Diffusion of Innovations is widely used by marketers to study the pattern and rate at which new innovations gain acceptance in the marketplace.[9] This theory (see Exhibit 3-4) divides the population into five categories based on how soon they adopt an innovation. Generally, the first adopters of an innovation, aptly called *innovators*, tend to educated, upwardly mobile, younger, and more willing to take risks. These people like to be different and march to their own beat. Later adopters tend to seek more social acceptance, want to be part of the crowd, and are less risk-tolerant. Most innovations, whether the telephone, DVD, or the Web, will never be adopted by some, who are called *laggards*.

The adoption process consists of five stages: awareness, interest, evaluation, trial, and adoption. A consumer adopting the Internet may go through all of these stages.[10] Awareness can be created by many sources, such as friends, colleagues, or the media. Once the consumer is interested in the Internet or the Web, a trial usage may occur. When the consumer is convinced that the benefits outweigh the costs, adoption or the purchase decision will then follow.

Among the people who are online, some have been on the Internet even before the World Wide Web came into existence in 1994. College professors, researchers, software professionals, and students are most likely to fit into this group. The World Wide Web (which provides a point-and-click interface through browsers such as Netscape and Internet Explorer) has played a crucial role in getting the benefits of the Internet to the masses. Even with the World Wide Web, there was a first wave of users in 1994–96, and then a second wave in 1996–98, when the Internet received extensive media coverage.

As of the third quarter of 2000, statistics show that in North America nearly 50 percent of citizens have access to the Internet. That means, in terms of diffusion of innovation stages, Internet usage is at the end of the *early majority* stage. As we will see in the rest of this chapter,

Exhibit 3-4 Diffusion of Innovations Curve

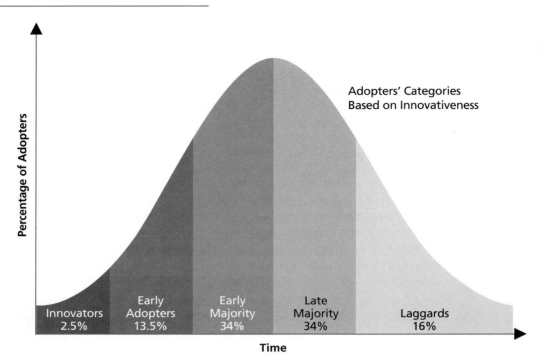

only a small proportion of consumers with access to the Internet are currently purchasing online. Many consumers try online shopping once or twice, but do not engage in online shopping on a regular basis. Among those with Internet access, online shopping is at about 20 percent in Canada, and is at 33 to 40 percent in the United States. So in terms of adoption of online shopping, Canada is still in the early stages of the *early majority*, while the market is more mature in the United States and is likely reaching the end of the *early majority* stage.

It would not be right to place all Internet users in one category. The time that they went online is probably a reflection of their comfort level with the technology. It is also a function of income level and other demographic factors, such as age and education.

Drivers of Internet Adoption

The Internet offers several benefits, such as access to information, shopping, communication tools, and entertainment. Against these benefits one has the weigh the monetary and non-monetary costs.

Lowering Costs. The falling cost of computer hardware and Internet connections will make it easy for many in the lower-income categories to take advantage of the Web. It is possible now to buy a brand name Internet-enabled PC for less than $1000 and to get a basic Internet connection for less than $15 per month.

Convenience. The convenience of shopping at any time of day, and the convenience of not having to leave home to make a purchase is likely to motivate more and more people to accept this technology. In particular, the Web offers older consumers, those with disabilities, and those in remote areas access to information and services that were unavailable before.

Offerings. Each month, there are new services and product offerings online. There is something for everyone. Whether you're an investor looking for stock tips and online trading, a new parent wishing to chat with other parents and purchase baby products, a pet lover looking for pet supplies, or a teenager looking to connect with other teens, the Web does not disappoint.

Barriers for Internet Adoption

Cost and Access. There are clearly huge gaps in the adoption rates of rich versus poor, whites versus ethnic minorities, and urban versus rural. The so-called **digital divide** does exist.[11] Even though the cost of Internet access is dropping, it's still too high for some segments of the population, and there's a genuine concern about this technology not being accessible to everyone.

Technophobia. To go online, one must be reasonably adept at using a computer. For many consumers there is a technology barrier, in addition to the cost barrier. User-friendly Web-enabled devices such as WebTV and Netpliance's i-opener may be the answer for these people (see Exhibit 3-5). Netpliance's i-opener provides access to e-mail, Web browsing, and shopping channels for $99 and a monthly user fee. Many palm-held devices are also on the market now, but it's still too soon to predict if these devices will play a significant role in the diffusion of the Web.

Privacy. Among the people who are using the Internet, many have not migrated to online shopping, which means these consumers are not yet taking advantage of all the capabilities of the Web. In Canada, only 20–25 percent of those with access to the Internet have actually made an online purchase.

Many users are concerned about online privacy.[12] Most sites require users to set up personal accounts and provide a lot of personal information. E-commerce sites routinely ask consumers to allow **cookies**, which are text files stored in the user's computer that contain information on the user's Web surfing patterns, preference settings on Web sites, and more. Consumers are concerned about how this information is used. Prominent firms like Real.com and Doubleclick have been at the receiving end of strong criticism for how they use or collect consumer information. While credible sites do display their "privacy policy," often it is coated in legal language that the layperson may find difficult to understand.

Exhibit 3-5 Netpliance: A Low-Cost Internet Device

Security. Security remains the number one concern among Internet users, and thus, it remains a barrier to complete adoption of the Web.[13] Security concerns appear to be stronger predictors of online purchasing than any other factor, including Internet experience. A study sponsored by the Better Business Bureaus Online found that over 80 percent of users had some concern about credit card security online. Women seem to be more concerned about security online. While 43 percent of men who are online have made online purchases, only 28 percent of women who are online have done so. In Canada, 67 percent of Internet users are concerned about online security according to the research firm Angus Reid Group.

Given this public perception, news about hacker attacks on Web sites does little to change this perception. Unless the majority of consumers feel assured that online shopping is safe, the growth of business-to-consumer E-commerce will be hampered.

Market Segments

The Internet is no longer a homogenous market of high-tech, male professionals with high incomes. The consumer mix on the Internet is now starting to resemble the traditional offline marketplace. While the average income of Internet users is still over $50 000, 44 percent of users have incomes below $39 000.[14] Some refer to this trend as evidence of the "mainstreaming" of the Web. This is not to say that all segments of the population are well represented online. There is, however, a growing opportunity for marketers to target their messages at specific segments, just as they would in the physical marketplace.

Gender

The gender gap is narrowing on the Net. Ninety-four percent of the respondents of the first GVU WWW User Survey conducted in 1994 were male. The tenth survey, in 1998, had 66 percent male and 34 percent female respondents. The "Internet User Trends" study by the Strategis Group suggested that in the United States, 46 percent of males and 38 percent of females are Internet users. In Canada, the gender gap is almost non-existent. According to A.C. Neilsen Canada, while 40 percent of Canadians are online, 51 percent of users are male and 49 percent are female.[15]

The narrowing of the gender gap is evident in other countries as well. In Japan, even though women constituted only 21 percent of Internet users by the end of 1998, 40 percent of all newcomers to the Internet are women. Similarly, in the United Kingdom, 60 percent of all Internet users were men as of the end of 1999, down from 66 percent the previous year.

As the gender gap narrows, the range of products being demanded on the Internet has increased. Women and men seem to want different products and services. Females outnumber males by 4:1 in purchasing clothing items, whereas males outnumber females by 3:1 in purchasing computer software (see Table 3-5). A study by the Strategis Group found that females were twice as likely to be "light Internet users" both at work and at home.

There is also evidence suggesting that women are more likely to use health information sites like WebMD. This is not surprising, since mothers are still seen as the "nurturers" in our society.

Table 3-5 Gender Gap in Online Shopping Habits

	Percentage of Internet Shoppers			
	Computer Software	Clothing	Computer Hardware	Electronics
Males	28.6%	6.6%	18.7%	7.7%
Females	9.7%	26.4%	8.3%	1.4%

Source: The Strategis Group.

Exhibit 3-6 An Ad Targeting Women at iVillage.com

The gender differences in Web usage and online shopping preferences do suggest that gender could be a useful segmentation variable. Sites frequented by women seem to carry specifically targeted ads for baby products, beauty supplies, and health aids (for example, see Exhibit 3-6).

Targeting by Gender. The so-called gender gap in Internet usage is narrowing in North America, but is still significant in Europe and Asia. Table 3-5 suggests that there are differences in online buying habits. Sites targeting men and women must address gender-based differences, if they are relevant to the product category.

In addition to differences in online shopping, the fact that women tend to be "lighter" users of the Internet must also be taken into consideration. This means traditional media, such as magazines and television, are still quite useful in reaching the female market.

In terms of Internet usage, women seem to gravitate towards sites that offer chat, bulletin boards, and other opportunities to meet and interact with people. Sites such as iVillage.com and Women.com have built a loyal following by capitalizing on women's need for socializing.

As more women take up technical and professional jobs, specialized sites catering to these sub-segments are evolving. For women who want to invest in stocks and bonds, a site called Women's Financial Network (www.wfn.com) provides guidance and advice. GirlGeeks (www.girlgeeks.com) targets women who are in technology jobs, such as software, by providing an online community forum, articles, job postings, and a mentoring program. The health sites described in the Vignette 3 also draw a significant female audience, who tend to be young mothers or older women. As the gender divide disappears online and as more women become adept at using the Internet, we may see more specialized sites targeting women.

Many sites also target men. General sports sites (such as ESPN.com and TSN.ca) and specialized sites like the WWF site (www.wwf.com) tend to draw a predominantly, but not exclusively, young male audience. Other sites such as Playboy.com clearly target males. Dating sites (such as Friendfinder and Matchmaker.com) tend to target both men and women in specific age groups or with specific lifestyles.

Age Cohorts

Internet user surveys between 1994 and 1996 generally revealed that typical users were in their mid- to late 20s, with the average age in the early 30s. Now there are more consumers in the older as well as younger age categories joining the online world.

Seniors. The senior segment is the fastest growing online user group. In Canada, Internet penetration in the 55 to 64 age group virtually doubled from 18 percent in 1997 to 34 percent in 1999.[16] There was a similar doubling of the penetration rate in the over-65 age group from 9 percent to 20 percent during the same period. In the United States, seniors represent about 17 percent of all Internet users. Twenty-seven percent of seniors who are online have made a purchase online.[17]

While seniors tend buy more prescription and over-the-counter drugs than other age groups, books and computer software rank as the leading online purchase categories for this group. It is important to note that seniors usually have the time and resources to be online. For seniors with limited mobility, Internet shopping may be a great convenience.

Kids and Teens. The presence of kids and teenagers online is also rapidly increasing. In Canada, Internet penetration in the 12 to 18 age group has risen from 55 percent in 1997 to 74 percent in 1999.[18] In the UK, over 3 million kids are online, which is roughly 50 percent market penetration. In addition, 46 percent of these kids say they have purchased something online. In the United States, the number of children (aged 5 to 12) and teens (aged 13 to 18) combined will increase from 17 million users in 1998 to 38 million users in 2002, well over a 100 percent increase in penetration.[19]

More kids are online because more schools are being wired to the Internet. In homes with PCs, kids tend to be the biggest users. Kids and teens are not just using the Internet to chat and do their school research projects; they're also emerging as a sizable online shopping segment. The National Retail Federation found that over 14 percent of parents with school-age children plan to use the Internet for back-to-school shopping. Teen spending online is expected to climb to over $1.4 billion in 2002.[20]

The younger consumers seem to be less sensitive to brand names on the Internet. Forrester Technographics' study found that the best-known offline brands had no online value among young consumers in the 16 to 22 age group.[21] The generation that is growing up digital (see iMarket Demo 3-1) is rapidly integrating the Internet into multiple aspects of their lives—studying, socializing, communicating, entertaining, and shopping.[22]

Targeting Age Cohorts. The senior market online is currently small. The average age of Internet users is still in the mid-30s. However, there are signs of the senior market growing in Canada. Canada has an aging population, and many new retirees have high incomes, plenty of leisure time, and are computer literate. This market is too important to be ignored.

Site design should take into account the needs of senior consumers. There are studies that show that people over the age of 60 may slow down in terms of information processing ability. Sites that are very complex with too many links and a very busy look may turn off some senior consumers.

Compared to the senior market, the youth market is more volatile and unpredictable in its tastes and preferences. New trends emerge and spread very quickly in this market, so sites targeting youth must stay in touch with these trends. Youth-oriented sites often employ a very young staff that understands this audience. Kids are now introduced to computers at the same time they are being introduced to reading. While the youth market may have limited buying power, marketers who look to the future tend to cater to this market.

The market for young consumers must be further broken down by age groups (for example, under 6, 7–12, 13–15, and 16–19). Interests, hobbies, ability to comprehend material, and purchasing power will vary according to the age group. Disney.com caters to children and families. Online stores such as eToys.com target parents with small children. Kidscom.com caters to children in the 4 to 15 age group with online games and activities.

Just as in the case of the senior market, Web sites targeting children must be designed with the audience in mind. Sites for kids tend to be more colourful and playful in terms of visuals. The use of cartoon characters is quite common. Technical terms and jargon must be avoided. Parental control and supervision is often an issue at kids' sites. Some sites, for example, require parents to sign up and authorize their children to use the site. Parents can also use filtering programs such as NetNanny to ensure that their children do not get exposed to offensive, damaging, and unauthorized content.

iMarket Demo 3-1 Marketing to Gen Y

Generation Y, or the cyber generation, is *growing up digital*. Not long ago, malls across North America were shooing away teenagers. They were perceived as "trouble" by storeowners. But now there's a change in that attitude. E-tailers invite teens to hang out on their sites, in chat and game areas, and shop online. How can kids shop online without a credit card?

Exhibit 3-7 Ad Targeted at Seniors to Encourage Teenage Shopping

The answer is simple—"e-wallets" and other forms of parent-controlled digital cash accounts. Doughnet.com, icanbuy.com and Rocketcash.com (see Exhibit 3-7), are among the sites that allow kids to shop online even if they don't have a credit card. Rocketcash.com requires parents to put money into the kids' Rocketcash account, which the kids can spend on approved vendor sites. Sites like icanbuy.com allow parents to decide where and how much kids can spend in online shopping. Popular product categories are CDs, comics and magazines, video games, and toys. Amazon.com and CDnow are particularly popular sites with Gen Y shoppers.

Gen Y consumers are Internet savvy. In a few years, they'll become big spending consumers like their parents. So why not encourage them to get a taste of online shopping now? "Catch 'em young" is the mantra of successful brand marketing.

Ethnicity

Targeting ethnic communities has never been easier. Ethnic communities share interests in music, food, and culture, as well as news from their countries of origin. Marketers are creating sites targeting different ethnic groups. Advertisers are also advertising on Web sites that draw specific ethnic groups.

In the United States, there are an estimated 4.9 million African-Americans online. According to Cyber Dialogue, about 28 percent of adult African-American and Hispanic American populations were online as of the end of 1999.[23] Netnoir is a site devoted African-American music, culture, and shopping. Periscopio, a Spanish portal owned by Star Media, is among a growing number of sites targeting Hispanics in the United States.

Another large ethnic community on the Internet is the Indian expatriate community in North America. Indians in America tend to be highly educated and maintain strong ties with their roots in India. Among the sites aimed at this group are Bharath.com, a site that features a huge collection of Indian music in RealAudio format, and Namaste.com, a shopping site in the United States founded by two Northwestern MBA graduates, which specializes in Indian foods, music, and other Indian products.

In Canada, the differences between French and English Canadian consumers have been well documented. Compared to English Canadians, French Canadians tend to under-consume certain products such as tea, beer, certain cosmetic products, and sports such as golf. In comparison to English Canadians, they seem to consume more of other products like wine, cigarettes, and life insurance. These differences can be used in identifying opportunities in the English and French Canadian markets.

Some online marketers have addressed these differences, to some extent, by creating sites both in English and French. Staples, a company that sells office products, simultaneously launched its Canadian E-commerce site Staples.ca in both English and French. Interestingly, Chapters.ca, the largest Canadian business-to-consumer site, does not have a French version so far, even though the company does have bricks-and-mortar stores in the mainly French-speaking province of Quebec. Canoe, a Canadian portal site, started with an English-only site, but has added a site catering to consumers in Quebec (www.canoe.qc.ca).

Targeting Ethnic Consumers. Ethnic consumers who are first-generation immigrants tend to consume products from their country of origin. As these consumers become acculturated (or absorb the cultural norms, attitudes, and consumption habits of their adopted country), there may be a decline in the consumption of ethnic products. Children of immigrants born in the adopted country tend to exhibit more mainstream consumption habits.

Having said this, as we have seen in the case of French and English Canadians, certain cultural differences exist for several generations and may never completely disappear. If the particular ethnic or linguistic group has a very small presence in the adopted country, there is a greater likelihood of faster acculturation or assimilation. As ethnic groups grow in population, we tend to see stores, magazines, radio programs, and now Web sites catering to these groups.

Online targeting of ethnic groups is similar to what is done in the offline marketplace, but there is one important cautionary note. Studies show that while certain ethnic groups, such as people of Asian origin, are more likely to have Internet access than the general population, other ethnic groups (especially African Americans/Canadians and American Hispanics) are underrepresented in Internet usage. There are signs that this gap is narrowing. In general, marketers must consider Internet access rates and Internet usage habits of ethnic groups before developing targeted sites.

Language and Culture

As the World Wide Web grows globally, different linguistic groups will begin to establish their presence online. It would be a mistake on the part of North American marketers to assume that English will be the preferred language of communication for all Web surfers. While English remains the most commonly spoken language among Internet users worldwide (see Table 3-6), non-English speakers will soon outnumber English speakers on the Internet.

Even though the Internet is still very much English-centric, content in other languages is growing. As browsers and Web development tools start supporting different languages, non-English content will flourish.

Targeting Overseas Consumers. Firms that target foreign consumers are increasingly developing multilingual Web sites. Portals such as Yahoo! have a presence in many countries, with local content often presented in the local language. Yahoo!'s foreign presence

Table 3-6 Internet Usage by Language

Language	Number (millions)
English	150
All non-English	128
Spanish	17
French	11
Italian	10
All Scandinavian	8
Portuguese	5
Japanese	21
Chinese	15
Korean	10

Source: Global Reach.

includes more than 20 countries, with sites presented in Chinese, Korean, Japanese, Portuguese, Spanish, and other languages. CDNow also has multilingual sites in Spanish, Portuguese, Japanese, and other languages.

 Smaller firms that wish to get a foothold in an overseas market are also resorting to tailored presentation to suit the needs of potential overseas customers. The Canadian Dream (www.candream.com), a company that attracts European tourists to Atlantic Canada for ecotourism, presents its site in both English and French.

Whether marketing online or offline, marketers must be sensitive to foreign cultures, customs, and habits. The standard technique of translation and back-translation (where the text translated from, say, English to a foreign language is then translated back to English by an another translator) must be used. In addition, colours, symbols, and numbers have culturally embedded meanings in some cases (for example, white is the colour of mourning in some countries, while it symbolizes purity in others). Marketers must take into consideration these differences, where appropriate.

Lifestyles

Portal sites such as Yahoo!, Excite, and Canoe.com have several lifestyle-based categories in their searchable databases. The Internet is a very community-oriented environment, and it's easy for people with common interests and lifestyles to have their own Web sites. One can find sites targeting very specific interest groups on the Internet—from fly-fishing to snowboarding. Web communities in sites like iVillage.com are based on commonality of interests, hobbies, and activities—which are indicators of one's lifestyle. The low cost of online publishing is encouraging the growth of lifestyle and special interest sites, and lifestyle segmentation has never been easier for marketers.

SRI International pioneered a lifestyle segmentation scheme based on *values and lifestyle profiles* or *VALS*. VALS uses two dimensions, *self-orientation* (principle-oriented, status-oriented, and action-oriented groups) and *resource availability* (abundant versus minimal) to classify people into one of eight value-lifestyle categories (see future.sri.com for details). *Self-orientation* is a motivational variable and *resource availability* includes monetary and non-monetary resources. The three self-orientation groups are further classified into those with minimal versus abundant resources, creating six groups. In addition, consumers with very high (actualizers) and very low resources (strugglers) are classified without regard to their self-orientations, thus providing a total of eight value and lifestyle groups. VALS has been applied in product positioning, segmentation, advertising, and other applications.

In the mid-1990s, SRI created a segmentation scheme for the Internet called iVALS to capture the unique nature of Internet users at that time. Many of the users at that stage were sophisticated computer users who fell under one specific VALS category called *actualizers*. These are usually "successful, sophisticated, active, take-charge people with high self-esteem and abundant resources." Other types of people were underrepresented on the Internet in the mid-1990s. Since this was the predominant group (consisting of university professors, researchers, software professionals, and executives), SRI created iVALS to study this group in detail.

With the expansion of Internet demographics, which now more closely mirrors the mainstream society, iVALS was no longer deemed necessary. The broader classification offered by VALS, according to SRI, is now capable of capturing lifestyle and value orientations on the Internet. According to SRI, the VALS segmentation scheme is being used in developing and targeting online advertisements.[24]

The importance of lifestyle as a predictor of Internet shopping behaviour is further underscored by a study from the Wharton Business School Forum on Electronic Commerce. According to this study, which is based on a consumer panel, convenience is the main reason for shopping online. For example, one predictor of whether someone will buy music online is travel time to the nearest music store. It is the lack of time, a "wired" lifestyle, and *not* other demographic factors, which emerge as the strongest predictors of online shopping.[25]

A typical online consumer has a *wired lifestyle*. Usually, those who buy online tend to be more experienced Internet users, who also tend to use the Internet at work. The Internet also has an impact on other aspects of their lives, such as daily communication (e-mail) and as a source of daily news. Further, the amount of money spent online is also affected by this wired lifestyle and the extent of time starvation in one's life.[26] This suggests that those who are very busy are more likely to purchase online.

The lifestyle profile of online shoppers is a very active, diverse one. More than half of all e-shoppers have taken a trip abroad in the last year, and 37 percent belong to a frequent-flyer program. These are not necessarily people who spend all their time at work. Their lifestyle activities include photography (34 percent of Web users), biking (40 percent of Web users), and swimming (52 percent of Web users).[27]

Targeting Lifestyle Segments. The Internet is both a blessing and curse when it comes to targeting lifestyle groups. Portals and search sites such as Yahoo!, AltaVista, Canoe.com, and Canada.com offer links to a vast number of lifestyle-oriented sites. Lifestyle sites can focus on activities and interests, sports, entertainment, home and gardening, money and investing, specific types of products (e.g., luxury goods), particular communities, religions or philosophies, and so on.

It is easy for anyone with a specific lifestyle orientation to create a Web site and announce the existence of the site to the world by registering the site in search engines. The fact that a basic Web site is relatively inexpensive to create and maintain has led to a staggering number of sites that can be classified as lifestyle sites. This means that markets based on lifestyle segmentation are likely to be somewhat fragmented and consumers have an incredible amount of choice on the Internet.

Established brands that convey a certain lifestyle (such as ESPN or TSN for sports enthusiasts) do have an online presence, and some of them have been able to create a loyal online customer base. The WWF site offers an online community forum for wrestling fans, which includes chat, news, shopping, and webcasts of WWF programs. This site is clearly not targeted at the Bay Street or Wall Street yuppie.

While some branded lifestyle sites are successful, the great variety of choice in every possible lifestyle category does make it hard to get the marketing message across to the intended audience. There is no simple solution to tackle such fragmentation. We do see lifestyle-oriented TV programs and magazines using multiple media to reach their target markets.

Martha Stewart has extended her brand (which is also her name) to several media, including TV, print, radio, and most recently the Web through the site MarthaStewart.com. The site, part of Martha Stewart Living Omnimedia Inc., offers in-depth content in many categories, as well as online shopping. The Martha Stewart example points to the fact that consumers today and in the future will be more complex in terms of their media habits. They will get their news and entertainment, as well as do their shopping, through a variety of outlets. In most cases, marketers may have to use multiple media and shopping channels to reach specific lifestyle groups. The Web can be an important component of such a strategy.

Consumer Behaviour on the Web

Consumers use the Internet for a variety of reasons, shopping being one of them. Even those who do not directly purchase products online, often use the Web for an information search. Table 3-7 identifies the major uses of the Web.

Table 3-7 Primary Uses of the Web

Use	Percentage
Entertainment	60
Shopping	52
Education	61
Work	66
Communication	35
Personal information	74
Time wasting	37
Other	8

Source: GVU 9th WWW User Survey.

While consumers are embracing online shopping faster than many anticipated, some products are difficult to buy online. Human beings tend to use all five senses in forming beliefs and preferences towards various products. On the Internet, only three of these senses can be used. How will consumers, for instance, buy items like clothing without feeling the fabric? Can online retailers make up for the information deficit caused by the lack of some of the sensory cues?

Fragrancestore.com overcomes the sensory limitation of the Internet by focusing on price and convenience. The discounted prices may appeal to younger consumers as well as those who are purchasing a familiar perfume that does not require fragrance testing.

Land's End (www.landsend.com), offers the consumer the chance to create a model on their Web site, who shares the consumer's body proportions and some physical characteristics. Then, the consumer can try different clothes on this online model. While this is not the same as actually trying on a dress or a jacket, it does enhance the online shopping experience. They even allow the consumer to bring a buddy. You can shop together and chat online with your friend while you browse the site.

In the early days of E-commerce, many pundits assumed that the Web would be suitable only for selling search goods—products that do not require physical inspection or trial. If a consumer had to inspect the product or try on the product (as with clothing), it was assumed that the consumer would prefer to shop at a bricks-and-mortar store. While this is still true for most consumers, it is interesting to note that apparel sales online exceeded $1 billion in 1999 and accounted for almost 7 percent of all online sales at the end of the second quarter of 1999. Apparel is now the fastest growing category online.[28] It is not surprising that this trend coincides with the increasing numbers of women online.

Consumers now purchase a wide range or products online—cosmetics, clothing, books, computer hardware and software, CDs, collectibles, and so on. Auction sites such as eBay and Bid.com reveal the true breadth of product categories that are purchased and sold online. Even in the case of big-ticket items, such as cars, the Internet plays a very important role as an information source.

Consumer behaviour is not easy to change. Shopping online and, in some cases, consuming products and services online, does require some behaviour modification on the part of consumers. Entrenched behaviour patterns have to be altered if a large number of consumers are to shop online. The advantages of shopping online have to be overwhelming and the shopping experience should be exciting. Land's End provides convenience and selection, while trying to mimic the social experience of shopping in a bricks-and-mortar mall.

See iMarket Demo 3-2 for a look at how electronic books will affect consumers' purchase of printed books.

Consumer Decision Process and Influencing Factors

Consumer researchers have developed a sound body of knowledge on consumer decision-making processes in the physical marketplace. Online buyer behaviour is a new and growing area of research. As researchers try to understand how consumers make decisions online (see Exhibit 3-8 on page 70), let's examine what is currently known about online consumer decision-making.

Web Site Characteristics. It is known the that characteristics of the e-tail environment, just like the physical environment and ambiance in a physical store, affect consumers' perceptions about the store, as well their decision of whether or not to buy. Consumer researchers have long known that peripheral cues, such as colour and music, affect consumer decision-making. In a study using a consumer panel, researchers at Wharton found

iMarket Demo 3-2 Stephen King Online: Will Consumers Follow?

Fans of Stephen King, the famed novelist, were in for a unique experience on March 14, 2000. King went online with a short story called *Riding the Bullet*.

Amazon.com and Barnes & Noble.com were swamped by such high demand that downloading became a nightmare for many fans of the horror story master. The e-book was listed at $2.50, but was available free of charge at leading online bookstores.

"Stephen King's decision to publish his new short story in electronic format is a concrete declaration that the e-book format has arrived," says Steve Riggio, vice chairman of Barnes & Noble.com, as quoted by AP. King's novel could only be read on a computer screen or a little palm device called a Rocket *e-book*. The e-book cannot be printed due to encryption technology used.

Is this just a fad or will consumers change their behaviour? King himself says that while the Internet holds great promise, "I don't think anything will replace the printed word and the bound book." What do you think? Will consumers change their behaviour and take to reading novels on a computer screen or a palm device?

Source: Martin Stove, "Stephen King Online Swamps Servers," *Newsbytes.com*.

---

that characteristics of a Web page, including background pictures and colours, influenced consumer perception and ultimately their product choice.[29]

This means by manipulating the look and feel of a site, marketers may be able to influence consumer behaviour. This does not, however, mean that content and value are unimportant to the consumer.

Web sites' characteristics may affect the consumer reaction to the site and the brand (see Table 3-8 on page 71). In particular, brand name and prior shopping experience stand out as the most important factors.

Product Characteristics. Some products, such as software, CDs, books, and airline tickets, are considered more appropriate for online shopping. These products are generally easy to evaluate based on specific product features, and are referred to as "search" goods. On the other hand, "experience goods" (such as clothing), which require trial or sampling before making a purchase decision, are deemed less suitable for online shopping. While categories such as clothing are showing signs of promise, products that do not require physical inspection or whose quality can be verified online seem to be the ones that are currently leading in online sales. The use of virtual reality, multimedia, and 3-D technologies may make it easier for consumers to shop for experience goods online.[30]

It is also conceivable that higher-involvement goods are also less likely to be purchased online. According to a study by the Better Business Bureaus Online, items involving higher dollar amounts or greater risk, such as financial services, are deemed less suitable for online shopping by consumers. The average annual purchase online is less than $1000, which is a small fraction of the amount a typical family spends on all purchases annually.

Exhibit 3-8 Influences on Online Consumer Decision Process

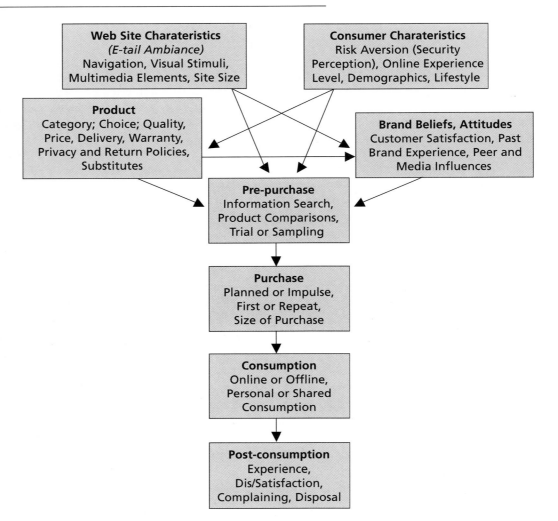

Consumer Characteristics. There are few studies on Internet shoppers and their characteristics. There is evidence, however, that those who have shopped through catalogues are likely to be much more comfortable with Internet shopping.

There is also some evidence that Internet shopping is generally not based on demographic factors like age or income, but on certain lifestyle factors.[31] Convenience is one of the most important reasons for online shopping.[32] Busy professionals and couples, as well those with limited mobility, are most likely to find online shopping attractive.

One demographic factor that does seem to suggest differences in online shopping behaviour is gender. As we saw in Table 3-5, women and men seem to purchase different products online. Women also seem to have greater security concerns than men do. In a few years, as online shopping becomes commonplace, some of the individual differences may diminish.

Beliefs and Attitudes. Consumer attitudes towards security are a major determinant of online shopping. From the consumer behaviour literature, it is known that beliefs and atti-

Table 3-8 Factors Influencing Visits to Sites (Apparel)

Factors	Percent
Familiarity with the brand	15%
Prior shopping experience	13%
Historically low price	8%
Recommendation from friends	6%
Online ads	6%
Radio/TV commercials	3%
Print ads/billboards	3%

Source: PC Data Online.

tudes towards brands affect one's response as a consumer. On the Internet, there are numerous brands, most of them new and unknown to consumers. There is some evidence, at least for now, that consumers do not have very high brand recall of pure-play Internet companies.[33] This suggests that established brands with which consumers have had offline experience and have formed certain beliefs and attitudes, are likely to have an advantage. Given the widespread security and privacy concerns, brand names that denote trust are likely to have greater success in winning over consumers.

Web site, product, and consumer characteristics, along with consumers' brand beliefs and attitudes, are the major factors that are likely to determine online buyer behaviour. Let's now focus on the three stages of the consumer decision process.

Pre-Purchase Stage. The Internet has become the primary source of product information for many consumers. In a study of automobile buyers, it was found that over 40 percent of consumers who purchased an automobile in 1999 had used the Internet as a source of information.[34] In the automobile category, sites such as Autobytel.ca and Dealnet.com have become the first point of contact for many prospective car buyers.

In another survey, 93 percent of American Internet users said that they planned to go online in search of information before making certain purchases.[35] The GVU World Wide Web User Survey (see Exhibit 3-9) shows that the Internet is becoming the primary source of pre-purchase information across many product categories. Even when consumers do not actually make the purchase online, the Internet is used as an important source of information in the decision process, as evident from Exhibit 3-10.

In addition to visiting different company Web sites and using keyword searches in search engines, consumers can easily compare brands through sites like mySimon.com, Buybuddy.com, and Productopia.com. Expert opinions on different products and experiences of other consumers can be found in different usenet groups and sites like Epinions.com.

Consumers searching for information before highly involving and major purchases tend to look for sources that are credible and offer detailed information. In a comparison of the Web with other sources such as television ads, print ads, and salespeople, the Web was rated

Exhibit 3-9 Internet and Other Media as Information Sources

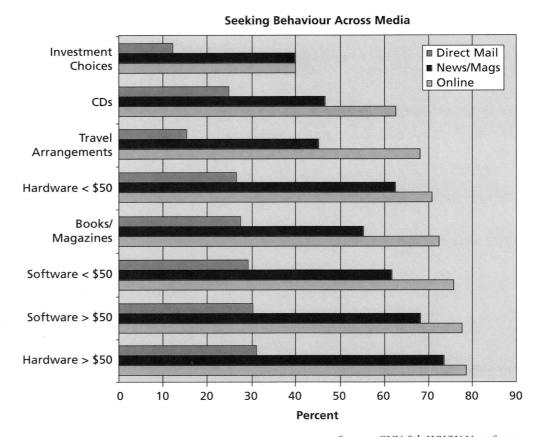

Source: GVU 9th WWW User Survey.

as most informative. The Web was also seen as more credible than television advertising or salespeople.[36] Many see the Web as a medium where the consumer has greater control, as compared to mass media where the information is thrust on the consumer.[37] This data may encourage consumers to use the Web as an information source in the pre-purchase stage.

Purchase Stage. Consumers seem to be shifting their dollars from bricks-and-mortar to online stores, but they're not necessarily spending more money. Less than 10 percent of online e-tail sales are expected to be incremental in 2002.[38] This means the Internet is not generating new sales, but in most cases is stealing from bricks-and-mortar stores.

Do consumers make mostly planned purchases on the Internet or does the online environment facilitate impulse buying? Some would argue that the lack of physical in-store stimuli, as well as the delay between the purchase decision and actual consumption (sometimes several days or weeks), is likely to reduce the possibility of impulse buying.[39] There is, however, evidence that some impulse buying does occur on the Internet.[40] The advent of digital wallets, which eliminate the need to provide credit card information each time a purchase is made, is supposed to boost impulse buying on the net. Digital wallets can automatically fill out order forms, thus reducing the time required to make an order. This faster check-out process may

Exhibit 3-10 Information Seeking vs. Purchasing Online

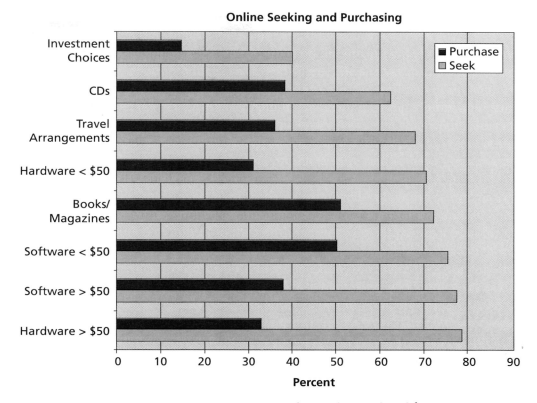

Online Seeking and Purchasing

Legend: ■ Purchase □ Seek

Categories (top to bottom): Investment Choices, CDs, Travel Arrangements, Hardware < $50, Books/Magazines, Software < $50, Software > $50, Hardware > $50

X-axis: Percent (0, 10, 20, 30, 40, 50, 60, 70, 80, 90)

Source: Source: GVU 9th WWW User Survey.

induce more impulse buying, but there are currently very few major e-tailers who accept digital wallets. For examples of digital wallets, see www.gator.com and www.brodia.com.

To encourage impulse shopping, online marketers can use digital coupons (see Exhibit 3-11). These coupons pop up on the screen as the consumer is browsing a Web site. Standard online coupons can be delivered to all consumers, or their delivery can be linked to a specific consumer action. For instance, if a consumer just selected a shirt in an online apparel store, a coupon for a tie can be presented before the consumer checks out. The ability to instantly save money could induce some consumers to engage in impulse buying.

In addition to the planning of the decision, the size of the purchase is also important. The level of online experience seems to affect the magnitude of a purchase on the Internet. There is evidence that more experienced shoppers are willing to make bigger purchases online.

In terms of the process, purchasing on the Internet is not unlike catalogue shopping. One can browse through different Web sites or sections of a Web site before making a choice. The experience is, however, different from shopping in bricks-and-mortar stores. The consumer cannot touch or feel the product, and there are no salespeople to influence the customer.

Newer technologies will make the actual purchase process easier and more enjoyable for consumers. Land's End allows online consumers to chat with other online consumers as they browse the Web site—almost mimicking the experience of shopping in a mall with friends.

Exhibit 3-11 Instant Digital Coupons Encourage Impulse Buying

Source: www.selfcare.com.

Buybuddy.com is among many stores that now offer "live salesperson" support. The salesperson can answer questions or walk a customer through the shopping process.

Consumption and Post-Consumption Stage. Except for digital products that are downloadable, the consumer has to wait for at least a day to experience the product purchased online. This delayed consumption or delayed gratification is similar to the catalogue shopping experience. Digital products—whether news stories, financial information, software, music, or video-on-demand—can be consumed online. Other tangible products require physical delivery of the product, and hence a delay in consumption.

After consuming the product, a consumer usually forms an opinion regarding the quality of the product—or a satisfaction judgment. Dissatisfied consumers often choose not to take any further steps because of the time and cost involved. Some consumers may complain or take other measures against the marketer. On the Internet, there are sites where consumers can voice their displeasure about a product or service. The Better Business Bureaus Online is one such outlet. Another specialized site that acts as a liaison between dissatisfied consumers and manufacturers is Ecomplaints.com. This site allows consumers to voice their complaints and seek recompense from the company. Consumers can also engage in the post-consumption disposal of used products at auction sites like eBay or barter sites like uBarter.com.

Opportunities and Challenges in the Business-to-Consumer Market

Opportunities in the Consumer Market

Selling Online. Some of the prominent business-to-consumer sites that sell online include Amazon.com, CDnow, Chapters.ca, eBay, and Buy.com. Each of these was a start-up company not too long ago. This is good news for entrepreneurs and small businesses.

New Products and Services. The Internet has spurred the growth of many new products and services, and it is forcing companies innovate. The technology is allowing companies to do things that were not possible before. From sites that offer customizable CDs and downloadable music in MP3 format to sites that offer real-time stock quotes and direct stock trading capability, we are constantly seeing new ideas flourish on the Internet.

iMarket Demo 3-3 Personal Shopping Assistants

There's never been so much information about so many products literally at the consumer's fingertips. If the problem earlier was lack of information, now with the Internet some consumers complain that there is too much information. The ease of publishing online has led to this information overload, and not every source is reliable or trustworthy. How can consumers sift through so much information and make the right choice?

Consumer Reports and other online consumer guides are a good starting point. You can also turn to sites like ePinions.com, where average consumers and some self-proclaimed experts post their opinions on various products and brands. Personalized content delivery offered by Netsanity.com is another means of minimizing the consumer's search cost and time on the Web. Netsanity delivers content to the user's desktop along with targeted ads (based on user opt-in) without the user having to wade through the Web.

Finding the right deal on the Internet is a lot easier than finding the proverbial needle in the haystack. If you want comparison information on different brands and want to know which online or offline store has the best deals, mySimon.com (see Exhibit 3-12) could be your friend. This site, as well as others like GoTo (shop.goto.com/) and Lycos (shop.lycos.com), offer comparison-shopping features, which allow you to compare multiple brands in a category and find a retailer who will sell the item at the lowest price. MySimon.com has prices from over 2000 stores in many product categories.

Finally, there is of course Priceline.com. Here you can name your price for items such as airline tickets, hotel accommodations, cars, and home financing. Priceline's search agent then goes to work for you and will come back with names of suppliers who can offer the service or product at or near your preferred price.

These so-called "intelligent agents" or "bots," which are second-generation search engines, have received mixed reviews. The intelligent agents go out and search multiple Web sites based on keywords and can report the results in an indexed format. However, agents such as mySimon and Junglee may not be able to search all the sites. It is possible to prevent the entry of such bots into a site, if a merchant decides not to provide information for such products or price comparisons. Also, while the bots can tell you who is charging the lowest price on a given item, shipping costs and other hidden costs are often not included.

The consumer should definitely read the fine print. While there is help out there for those who want to search for information more efficiently, the buyer should always beware.

Sources: Tim J. Mullaney, "New Services Claim to Do More than Regular 'Bots.' How Good Are They?" *Business Week*, December 13, 1999, (www.businessweek.com/1999/99_50/b3659033.htm); Tracey Stanley, "Intelligent Searching Agents on the Web," (www.ariadne.ac.uk/issue7/search-engines/).

Exhibit 3-12
mySimon.com

Reaching New Segments and Markets. According to a study by the Canadian Internet Advertising Bureau, only 14 percent of Canadian firms were selling online at the beginning of year 2000. For smaller firms, the Internet opens the global marketplace.

Take the case of East Coast Model Company (www.ecmc.com). This is a small company in Prince Edward Island, a province inhabited by less than half a million people. They offer kits, parts, and various supplies for making model toys—from airplanes and helicopters to ships. Now this firm sells it products to hobbyists all over the world.

As you will see later in this chapter, the Internet also allows firms to precisely target their advertising to different market segments. Portal Web sites as well as the growing number of lifestyle Web sites allow marketers to reach the right audience.

Personalized Marketing. The Internet offers an incredible ability to customize and personalize product or service offerings. Content sites like Yahoo! and CNN allow individuals to create accounts and set their own preferences. Each user will receive customized content when they log in. Those who sell tangible products, such as the jeans manufacturer IC3D.com, allow users to customize the product online by giving them control over a wide variety of options and parameters. Even car manufacturer Saturn allows customers to customize the automobile.

The notion of permission marketing, which is discussed in Chapters 10, is based on the view that creating a marketing message and a product offering that is unique to each individual is likely to be more fruitful than mass marketing. The Internet facilitates *marketing to a segment of one* consumer.

Reinforcing Current Marketing Efforts. Even for firms that do not directly sell online, the Internet can play a vital role in their business strategy. It is a communication medium that can reinforce other forms of communication. It facilitates building relationships with customers. Detailed product and usage information can be presented vividly on the Internet, and customer service and troubleshooting can be delivered online, saving consumers time and money. Whether or not a firm is selling online, the Internet is likely to play a key role in its overall business strategy.

Challenges in the Consumer Market

Digital Divide. Over 80 percent of Canadian companies are online as of the beginning of the year 2000, but only 45 percent of consumers have access to the Internet. The picture is not very different in the United States. Studies in the United States show that there is indeed a real **digital divide**. In a study commissioned by the US Department of Commerce, it was found that African-American and Hispanic households were approximately one-third as likely as those of Asia/Pacific Islander descent, and roughly 40 percent as likely as white households to have Internet access at home.[41]

Income level is still a strong predictor of Internet usage, with households earning more than $75 000 being more than 20 times as likely to have access to the Internet as those at the lowest incomes. However, rural dwellers, irrespective of income levels, are less likely to have Internet access than residents of cities. Age-based gaps in Internet usage are also evident. Lack of Internet skills among many in the baby boom and older generations is often cited as a reason for the age-oriented "digital divide."[42]

In Canada, the federal government has acknowledged the existence of the digital divide and is taking proactive measures to address the problem. The Canadian government's strategy is to make Canada the most "connected" country in the world. Through government funding as well as partnerships, Connecting Canadians, a community-focused program, aims to provide greater Internet access to rural areas and public libraries. Digital divide and possible solutions to this vexing issue are discussed further in Chapter 14.

Privacy. Consumer concerns about privacy continue to be at the forefront. According to a study by Forrester (www.forrester.com), based on a panel of 100 000 American and Canadian ~~nsumers~~, concern over the privacy of information passed over the Internet is ~~amount of time and money people spend online.~~[43] According to this report, ~~ent~~ of consumers want greater control over their personal information on the ~~notion~~ of **value exchange**, where consumers provide personal information and ~~r~~ interests or shopping habits in exchange for free services is becoming preva- ~~consumers~~ are becoming increasingly comfortable sharing some personal ~~in~~ exchange for valuable services, net privacy does remain a serious concern. ~~are~~ addressed in greater detail in Chapter 13.

~~inesses~~, financial institutions, and credit card companies have to address secu- ~~to~~ the satisfaction of consumers. Even if online security breaches are very rare, ~~onsumers~~ see this as problem, marketers must deal with it proactively. ~~for~~ instance, clearly states that if credit card fraud is committed on their site, ~~will~~ have no liability at all. Businesses have to put in place proper security ~~communicate~~ their security policies clearly to consumers. Security issues are ~~greater~~ detail in Chapter 13.

~~perience~~. We are likely to see more e-tailers devote attention to enhancing ~~experience~~ of consumers. The basic online catalogues that we see on sites are ~~ough~~ to entice consumers. In a physical store, consumers can touch, feel, and ~~product~~. The next generation of business-to-consumer sites will feature more ~~ements~~. Use of 3-D and virtual reality technologies can provide consumers ~~shopping~~ experience.[45] Cycore.com and Metacreations.com are among the ~~eloping~~ 3-D technologies. Cycore's Cult3D allows consumers to rotate products ~~ally~~ "use" some of the products.[46] JVC, Palm, Toyota, Lego, and even CBC.ca ~~this~~ 3-D technology on their sites, and consumers are reacting favourably to ~~nce-oriented~~" shopping environments.

~~roach~~ to improving the shopping experience is to offer "live salesperson" sup- ~~on.com~~ is a company that provides the technology for enhancing online sales ~~port~~ by enabling the consumer to speak directly to another person via the Web.

~~me vs. Profits~~. As companies invest heavily in new technologies and mar- ~~hey~~ are unlikely to realize profits in the short run. Forrester research predicts ~~e-play~~ Internet retailers will have a short life span.[47] Companies without ~~entals~~ in terms of earnings and market position will not survive. CDnow, a ~~iler~~, is among those in trouble, with stock prices plummeting to less than $3 per share in the first quarter of 2000.

Marketing expenditures of most e-tailers are so excessive that Forrester and GartnerGroup are predicting that many e-tailers will cease to exist by 2002. In many sectors, increased competition and spiraling marketing costs are likely to force consolidations and mergers, leaving fewer well-managed companies.

On the Internet, most vendors are unknown and consumers would not have had an experience with these vendors in the physical marketplace. Hence, gaining consumer credibility and trust becomes important. The cost of acquiring a customer online is not cheap. It is repeated purchasing and referrals, which lowers customer acquisition costs, that drives profitability online, and many e-tailers are struggling to transform one-time visitors into loyal customers.

Summary

The growth of the online consumer market has been phenomenal. Globally, nearly 300 million users were online at the beginning of the year 2000, and by 2005 the figure is expected to cross the one billion mark. New and innovative business models—from Priceline and Mercata to Medbroadcast.com—have emerged. The business-to-consumer e-tail figures, while minuscule compared to the size of the total retail industry in North America, are projected to exceed $380 billion by 2003. That is not small change.

Marketers focusing on the business-to-consumer market must understand the differences between online and offline buyer behaviour. The decision-making process online and the factors that influence the decision-making process have to be understood. Many e-tailers are trying to make the online shopping environment richer and more experiential—live customer support, three-dimensional rotating product images, and chat-while-you-shop features are just some of the innovations.

Security and privacy concerns clearly dominate the discussion when it comes to impediments for online commerce. Consumer perceptions regarding security must be addressed. Sites that clearly display their policies in simple language are likely to reassure the consumer.

While the online marketspace is growing, there is concern about certain segments of the population being left out of this revolution. A "digital divide" clearly does exist. Those in lower economic groups and in rural areas are less likely to be online. If our society as a whole is to benefit from the opportunities offered by the Internet, improved access to this technology must be addressed.

Key Terms

Cookie, 59	Search goods, 68	Value exchange, 77
Digital divide, 59		

Questions and Exercises

Review Questions

1. What are the different stages of the consumer adoption process on the Internet?
2. What are the barriers to consumer adoption of the Internet?
3. Name three business-to-consumer business models. Describe and provide examples for each model.
4. Which regions of the world are likely to fuel the growth of global E-commerce?
5. What are the different factors that affect online buyer behaviour?
6. How can a Web site's features affect consumer shopping or browsing behaviour?
7. What are some of the challenges facing the business-to-consumer market?
8. What opportunities do small businesses have in the business-to-consumer market?

Discussion Questions

1. How can online marketers effectively market to the teenage segment? What are the challenges in marketing to teenagers online?

2. How is the shopping experience online different from shopping in a physical retail store? What do these differences mean for e-tailers who are encouraging consumers to shop online?

3. Consider a CD or an article of clothing such as a jacket. How is consumer decision making online different from consumer decision making in the physical marketplace for these products?

4. How can some of the barriers to consumer adoption of Internet shopping be overcome? What are online marketers currently doing to encourage greater adoption?

5. The Internet allows for personalized marketing (marketing to a segment of one). Is this more or less effective than traditional target marketing? Why?

Internet Exercises

1. Visit the following sites targeting women: www.iVillage.com, www.women.com, www.webgrrls.com, and www.girlgeeks.com. What specific female segments are targeted by each of these sites? How do Webgrrls and Girlgeeks differ from the first two sites? Visit the Women's Financial Network (www.wfn.com). Is gender-based segmentation of financial services effective?

2. Identify some sites targeting senior citizens. If you were to design a site targeted at senior citizens, what features would that site include? How would you make the sites "user-friendly"? How would you encourage older Internet users to frequent your site?

3. Kellogg's and Kraft are two well-known brands. Visit www.kelloggs.com and www.kraftfoods.com. Evaluate their segmentation and targeting strategies. How is each brand utilizing the features of the Web? What role can the Web play in the marketing of frequently purchased, packaged food products?

4. Assume you wish to buy a DVD player. Search for information online and select one brand based on criteria that you consider important (such as price, features, and delivery time). Visit relevant search engines and E-commerce sites to gather information. Document each step of your search process. Prepare a brief report.

Chapter 4

The Business Market

Vignette 4 **Joining Forces with Competitors**

Learning Objectives

After completing this chapter, you will:

- Understand what B2B E-commerce means.
- Understand the differences between the online consumer and business markets.
- Appreciate the factors that contribute to or deter the growth of B2B E-commerce.
- Understand the different types of B2B marketplaces on the Internet and the specific functions they play.
- Be able to apply the concepts of B2B E-commerce to analyzing a specific industry.

The world of business-to-business E-commerce is redefining competitor relations in many industries. Companies often derive competitive advantage from their business processes. Internal processes have been closely guarded secrets, but that's now changing to some extent. In a range of industries, such as automobiles, computers, grocery stores, and retailing, there are alliances being formed by competing firms. The goals of these alliances are simply to streamline procurement of materials and supplies, to reduce costs, and to boost operational efficiency. Let's look at how competitors in four different industries are working together to achieve these goals.

In the automobile industry, GM, Ford, and Daimler-Chrysler have joined together to set up Convisint (www.convisint.com). This is an online exchange that will handle the entire procurement processes of the three companies. All suppliers to these three big auto manufacturers will have to deal with Convisint. GM, Ford, and Daimler-Chrysler have eliminated their individual procurement and supply management solutions for a common solution.

Sears and Europe's Carrefour have joined forces to set up GlobalNet Xchange (www.globalnetxchange.com), a B2B exchange for the retail industry (see Exhibit 4-1). This site will handle the combined $80 billion in purchases of the two retail giants. These two retailers purchase from over 50 000 suppliers worldwide, who will now be forced to supply through GlobalNetXchange. This B2B exchange is also open to other retailers.

In the grocery sector, the Grocery Manufacturer's Association of America (GMA), the world's largest association of food and beverage manufacturers, successfully pilot-tested an Internet-based system that is intended to streamline how manufacturers deliver products to retail-

Exhibit 4-1 **GlobalNetXchange**

Source: www.globalnetxchange.com.

ers. The system allows retailers and suppliers to synchronize pricing, promotions, inventories, invoices, and other data via the Internet, while eliminating price mismatches. Many in the grocery industry believe this pilot test will lead to a full-fledged industry-wide B2B E-commerce system.

In the computer industry, Dell has had an advantage over rivals such as Compaq because of its build-to-order and just-in-time inventory model. Compaq, Hewlett-Packard, Gateway, Samsung, Hitachi, and others have united to create an independent company that will serve as a B2B supply exchange for computing and electronics manufacturers. The founding companies estimate that a staggering $600 billion in parts and components will be sold via this online exchange in the next few years. The key benefit that these companies anticipate from this exchange is the reduction of supply chain costs. The founding companies anticipate savings of 5 to 7 percent.

Buyers in several industries are realizing that by pooling their purchasing power, they can realize better bargains. Cooperation among competitors, or *coopetition*, is reaching new levels as firms realize they can save more by working together.

Where does this leave the suppliers in these industries? As buyers in every major industry pool their purchasing power, there is more pressure on suppliers to lower costs and offer just-in-time inventory. Some suppliers are countering the buyer-oriented exchange with their own exchanges. It is too early to declare winners and losers, but B2B supply exchanges clearly hold a lot of promise. We will know in a few years if they can deliver on the efficiencies and cost savings they promise.

Sources: Jerry Dubrowski (2000), "GM Retools for Cyberspace," CNNFn (www.cnn.com), August 24, 2000; Michelle Dennehy (2000), "Sears, Carrefour Form Retail B2B," AuctionWatch.Com, February 29, 2000; "Food Manufacturers Take First Step Toward 'Real B2B E-Commerce' For Grocery Industry," Grocery Manufacturers of America (GMA) (www.gmabrands.com), Press Release, August 3, 2000; Dan Briody (2000), "Compaq, HP, and Others Team Up on Internet Exchange Company," Infoworld.com, May 1, 2000.

Introduction

Business-to-consumer E-commerce has garnered a lot of media coverage. Even consumers who are not online have likely heard of Amazon, eBay, Priceline, and E*Trade. At the same time, even most consumers who *are* online would be hard-pressed to name one or two business-to-business E-commerce sites. Business-to-business (B2B) E-commerce deals with businesses selling products or services to other businesses. B2B E-commerce may be the unglamorous cousin of B2C E-commerce, but this is where we are already seeing a significant economic impact.

From $145 billion in 1999, B2B E-commerce is expected to top $2 trillion by 2003. Contrast this with B2C revenues of about $13 billion in 1998 and worldwide projections of about $380 billion in 2003. Behind the numbers is the real story of B2B E-commerce. Businesses are flocking to the Web to reduce costs, streamline their processes, and make their supply chain management more efficient. B2B E-commerce is not just about adding a Web site to a company's current operations. It also requires organizations to transform many of their internal processes. B2B E-commerce connects suppliers and buyers, creating efficient markets.

In this chapter, we will explore the different dimensions of the business market—its size and scope, the various business models in the B2B space, and the nature of B2B marketing on the Internet.

Drivers of the B2B Marketspace

Estimated projections of B2B E-commerce vary widely depending on the source of information. The consistent factor is that B2B is expected to outpace the B2C growth by several times. According to the research firm Gartner Group, the B2B marketspace is estimated to be roughly $400 billion worldwide in 2000. By 2002, this market is expected to soar to $2.18 trillion, and at the end of 2003 worldwide B2B revenue is projected to reach $3.95 trillion. In 2004, B2B E-commerce is expected to represent 7 percent of the forecasted $105 trillion total global sales transactions.[1]

One-fourth of all B2B purchasing in the United States is expected to be done over the Internet by 2004, according to the Boston Consulting Group.[2] North America leads the world in B2B E-commerce, but the rest of the world is expected to catch up quickly in the next few years. By 2003, $1.8 trillion worth of B2B transactions are expected to take place outside North America. A global survey of CIOs from large companies revealed that 70 percent of them will have adopted Internet applications linking their company to another—most likely suppliers and/or customers.[3]

Why is the business market so much bigger than the consumer market? Why is it growing at a much faster rate? Let's examine why buyers and sellers are drawn to E-commerce.

The Evolution of B2B E-Commerce

B2B E-commerce predates the Web. It has gone through an evolution over the past two decades, and there are four distinct phases in this evolutionary process.[4]

EDI. In the 1980s and early 1990s, E-commerce was conducted through **electronic data interchange (EDI)**, "which is computer-to-computer transfer of business transaction information (such as invoices and purchase orders) using standard, industry-accepted message formats."[5] Experts consider this to be the first phase of E-commerce, even though it was not conducted over the Internet.

EDI was conducted over proprietary networks or value-added networks (VANs), which required significant capital investment. The investment was required to obtain private lines connecting buyer and seller computers, as well complex software required to allow the computers to exchange and read documents. The huge upfront investment put EDI beyond the reach of smaller companies. Another limitation was that EDI was batch-oriented and not a real-time application. That meant delays and the inability to price products dynamically in response to market conditions.

Direct Selling. The second phase is **direct selling**, or basic E-commerce, where the products are sold directly from the seller's Web site to the buyer. There is no intermediary in this process.[6] Dell still sells directly from its Web site. In the early days of the commercial Internet, the direct selling business model was easy to implement. Companies like Dell and Cisco are in the technology industry, selling to other technology companies. This made the direct selling model a natural choice for these companies. Direct sellers display catalogues on their Web sites and accept online orders and payment. Dell, however, has now gone beyond a static catalogue by allowing customization of products.

B2B Exchanges. The third phase is the **B2B exchange** phase or the **community commerce** phase. Here many buyers and sellers congregate on one site. Exchanges can support catalogue sales, auctions, and bid/ask transactions (where buyers can post RFQs and sellers can bid). Exchanges make it easy to source suppliers, and they provide suppliers a venue for selling off excess inventory for the best price.

The Next Generation. The newly emerging phase, referred to as next generation E-commerce or collaborative commerce, is one where there is true collaboration between suppliers and buyers. Supply chains and demand chains are linked together. Suppliers and buyers will have access to each other's databases. Buyers' inventory position will be visible to suppliers, who can then automatically replenish the inventory at the right time. Suppliers will also be able to see through buyers' demand chains.

The Buy Side

In this section, we will look at the benefits of business-to-business E-commerce (see Table 4-1 for a summary of the benefits).

Table 4-1 Top Benefits of E-Commerce for Buyers

Benefits

- Streamlines processes; greater efficiency

- Reduction in transaction and administrative costs

- Speed (reduction in processing time)

- Greater access to suppliers; global sourcing

- Better communication; information flow

- Focus is on strategic issues (instead of tactical matters)

Source: Ramesh Venkat (2000).

The e-Procurement Process. Companies, large and small, are taking to online procurement because it offers several distinct advantages over the traditional paper-based process. Online purchasing is much simpler than the traditional method. Some steps in the process are automated and redundancies are eliminated. The streamlined process is an attractive reason for many firms to adopt online procurement.

Suppose an employee wants to buy a particular piece of equipment. The online procurement process can allow the employee to select an item from an online supplier catalogue (which can be hosted within a corporate *intranet*, which is an internal password-protected Web site for employees). The requisition form can be automatically generated and sent electronically to a manager for approval. Once the request is electronically approved (by appending a *digital signature*, see Chapter 13 for a complete discussion of digital signatures), the purchase order can be electronically generated. This ensures that there will be no data-entry errors. The purchase order can be transmitted to the supplier via the Internet. Once the item is received, the necessary accounting entries are made and payment can then be released electronically.

Such a buying process is decentralized, allowing end-users in different departments to initiate the buying process without having to go through layers of bureaucracy. It reduces order cycle time. A study by the Aberdeen Group found that the purchase and fulfillment cycle fell from 7.3 days in the traditional/manual buying process to a mere two days in the Internet procurement process.

Contrast this with a manual buying process, where authorization happens after a purchase order has been cut. Sometimes the manager may not authorize a purchase, which means the effort involved in product search, vendor selection, and purchase order preparation are wasted. In an electronic format, even if authorization is declined, very little time and effort are actually wasted.

Cost Savings. The cost of processing a purchase order manually can be as high as $125 to $175. Online procurement can reduce this cost to about $10 to $15 per order.[7] The savings in time due to automation and the reduction in follow-up faxes and telephone calls account for this dramatic savings. Consider the fact that some industries operate on a margin of less than 5 percent. A cost reduction of even 1 percent can make a significant difference to the company's fortunes. Even for small firms, over a period of time such savings can make a significant impact on the bottom line.

In a recent study of national purchasing managers in Canada, it was found that the average transaction cost savings were significant at 5.8 percent. In addition, purchasing managers estimated a savings of inventory-carrying costs to the tune of 2.3 percent.[8] Cost savings are a tangible benefit that draws businesses to E-commerce.

Transparency. E-commerce enables firms to easily track orders and analyze trends in purchasing behaviour. Whether it's an errant business unit that fails to follow procedures or a poorly performing supplier who does not meet delivery schedules, mistakes will be clearly documented. The procurement process from initiation of the purchase order to fulfillment and payment becomes very transparent. Thus, management can have greater control and accountability.

In addition to the process, on the Internet companies can source for supplies globally. That creates availability transparency.[9] It is easy to verify the availability of products, and the need for accumulating inventory is diminished.

Prices also become transparent. In many industries, prices are individually negotiated. The growing number of B2B exchanges (see Vignette 4 for examples) creates price transparency. Internet auction pricing models can reveal the supplier's floor and ceiling prices. See Chapter 8 for further discussion on price transparency.

Real Time. The auction format creates a dynamic interplay between demand and supply. Many B2B sites allow live trading, where prices change in real-time. Some B2B exchanges allow buyers and sellers to negotiate online in private. Information flows smoothly between buyers and sellers.

Technology Standards. In the mid-1990s, the technology standards were not clear. Now, **XML (eXtensible Markup Language)** has become the standard for B2B sites (see iMarket Demo 4-1). Security encryption systems and online payment methods are much more advanced now. As industry-wide standards are established, more firms are likely to adopt E-commerce.

Supply Chain Management. For buyers the ultimate goal is more efficient supply chain management. Supply chain management is defined "as a process for designing, developing, optimizing, and managing the internal and external components of the supply system, including material supply, transforming materials and distributing finished products or services to customers, that is consistent with overall objectives and strategies."[10] By managing the supply chain, firms try to lower procurement and inventory costs, ensure an uninterrupted supply of materials, and use the expertise of the supply partners in areas such as quality improvement. The Internet allows suppliers and buyers to share information and develop the kind of integration required for efficient supply chain management.

The Sell Side

Suppliers are concerned that as large buyers join together, there will be a severe cost squeeze, drastically cutting into suppliers' margins. There is also the fear that B2B exchanges that bring together a large number of suppliers will commoditize many products (recall Vignette 4). In spite of these misgivings, suppliers have several good reasons for being part of the emerging Internet markets.

iMarket Demo 4-1 XML 101

If you are familiar with HTML (HyperText Markup Language), which is used to create Web pages, you can learn XML (eXtensible Markup Language), which has quickly emerged as the standard for creating business-to-business sites. The term "markup" is used to identify anything put within a document which either adds or provides special meaning (for example, **bold** text).

HTML uses tags to tell the Web browser (Netscape or Internet Explorer) how to display the page. For instance the tags "<u>" and </u>, when placed before and after a word respectively, will display that word in an underlined format. HTML "marks up" text or data. See www.w3.org/MarkUp/Guide/ for an introduction to HTML.

XML also marks up text and data, but in addition it also allows for "defining" data. The major difference between XML and HTML lies in the fact that while the latter has predefined tags for everything (underline, centre, bold, paragraph, tables, and so on), the former has no predefined tags. Users create their own tags. XML tags define the meta-information (information about information). Here is an example of a document written using XML:

```
<?xml version="1.0"?>
<basket>A Fruit Basket
<oranges>navel</oranges>
<apples>granny smith</apples>
<peaches>red haven</peaches>
<grapes>concord</grapes>
</basket>
```

In the above example, all words contained within the angled brackets "<..>" are tags. They carry the smallest unit of meaning. In addition, all tags must be paired so that they have a start <basket> and an end </basket>. Tags combined with data form elements. An element consists of a starting and ending tag, with content in between the two tags. For instance, the following is an element:

```
<basket>A Fruit Basket</basket>
```

Elements are organized in a nested fashion. In the above example, <basket> is a parent of <oranges>, <apples>, <peaches>, and <grapes>, which are siblings. The siblings can also be parents of sub-elements where defined for each.

How does XML really benefit business? First, it affords far greater flexibility than HTML as a Web development platform. Unlike HTML, in XML it is possible to define the content of a document separately from its formatting. Second, this ability to define content allows buyers and suppliers to exchange business data easily. In the above example, if a large grocery chain were to use a Web-based B2B E-commerce application to deal with a large fruit and vegetable distributor, XML can allow computer systems at the two firms to talk to each other effortlessly. Third, while HTML pages can be formatted (underline, italics, bold, centre, fonts, styles, and so on), the content created cannot be reused. With XML, using appropriate supporting applications, a user can extract data from a Web page and then use it in another application later. For example, pricing and product specification data on a Web page can be easily extracted into a database program for competitive comparisons.

The latest version of Netscape and Internet Explorer support XML to varying degrees. While some Web developers may be wondering why they need to learn another language, many in the E-commerce community are convinced that the savior has arrived.

Sources: XML Tutorial, GE Global eXchange Services; Extensible Markup Language (XML), W3C (www.w3.org/XML/).

Costs. Just as the buyers can lower their order costs, sellers too have the chance to lower their costs by adopting E-commerce. Online exchanges draw many buyers, making the task of marketing a lot simpler. VerticalNet (www.verticalnet.com), which operates several B2B exchanges or communities, brings together many buyers and sellers in each of these communities. Sellers can reach many buyers through one site, and this lowers the customer acquisition costs. The salesperson need not make as many cold calls, but instead can focus on prospects who have shown an initial interest, perhaps through an online inquiry.

Selling costs can be lowered also by eliminating mistakes. It is estimated that up to 40 percent of all orders have to be reworked because of errors.[11] Online order processing eliminates the need for duplication of data entry and consequently can lower costs.

Different Selling Options. Suppliers can respond to requests for quotes (RFQs) for customized items, they can take standard orders through their Web sites, and they can even auction off excess inventory. VerticalNet allows suppliers to participate in auctions anonymously. Thus, a competitor or a buyer will not know that a particular supplier has excess inventory.

Margins. In addition to lowering costs, sellers can get the best price by using different selling formats. Studies show that in reverse auctions (where the sellers bid for a buyer's order), buyers do not necessarily choose the lowest price bid. In the standard auction format (where buyers bid), when it is a unique item or an item in demand, the seller has the best chance of getting the highest possible price.

Closer Ties with Buyers. While there is some fear that the online marketplaces may drive prices down and commoditize all products, there are also reasons to believe that the Internet will, in fact, enable closer ties between buyers and sellers. Many firms are trying to replicate the Dell model, which lowers inventory costs by ordering components only after receiving an order for their product. Such a just-in-time model requires a closer link with the suppliers.

As buyers see the benefit of supply chain management, the flip side is that it will lead to closer link with suppliers. **Extranets**, a secure Internet link between two firms (see iMarket Demo 4-2), are used in sharing data and building a collaborative buyer-seller relationship.

Differences Between B2B and B2C Markets

Business-to-business E-commerce is already much bigger than business-to-consumer E-commerce. It is also projected to grow at a much faster pace. Apart from the size and scope, there are other important differences between these two types of E-commerce. Table 4-2 on page 89 summarizes the major differences.

iMarket Demo 4-2 Intranets, Corporate Portals, and Extranets

The Internet is an open network, which allows everyone to gain access to documents without a lot of security. Businesses often want to limit access to documents and other resources to their employees and/or their suppliers, customers, and partners.

An **intranet** is a private network within the enterprise. Usually it contains a gateway to the outside Internet. Intranets are essentially Web spaces that only company employees can access. This is ideal as a sales force application. Printed materials may get dated, but the travelling salesperson can always have the latest price, inventory, and market information on a secure Web site. Intranets also play an important role in knowledge management. As businesses pool the expertise, experience, and knowledge their employees have, intranets can be used to share the knowledge. Intranets can also provide a cost-effective solution to certain sales training needs.

Most large companies use intranets. Sun Microsystems has internal sites on more than 600 servers spread across every major functional area. Over 80 000 employees use Ford's intranet worldwide, while Hewlett-Packard's intranet is hosted on over 200 servers catering to over 10 000 employees.

Many large companies are now thinking in terms of "corporate portals." Companies are realizing that it is often the employees who do not read the marketing brochures. Corporate portals can take information from many different applications, locations, and databases and present them in one place that is secure and easy to access. Employees can learn about products and work being done in other parts of the company, or clarify some doubts regarding their HR policy or benefits package. Corporate portals, like the commercial ones, can be personalized and they can offer newsletters, contests, and interactivity through bulletin boards. The corporate portals can also be E-commerce enabled. This form of E-commerce has been labelled business-to-employee (B2E) commerce. Right from this internal site, employees can purchase certain products for office use (thus decentralizing some of the procurement within the corporation), book and pay for airline tickets, and so on.

Corporate portals and B2E commerce puts a great deal of information at the employee's fingertips. When used properly, it should lead to greater productivity and efficiency.

Extranets are somewhat similar to intranets in that they are also private communities. Extranets, however, link the company with other firms in the supply chain, or with customers or partners. Extranets also use the Transmission Control Protocol/Internet Protocol (TCP/IP) and HTML (HyperText Markup Language) to display Web pages. An extranet can be seen as part of a company's intranet that is extended to users outside the company. Password-protected pages are a simple way of implementing extranets. In order to facilitate the transfer of vital business data, extranets must have security and privacy. Typically, firewalls, encryption systems, and digital certificates are used to ensure that only authorized people are allowed entry (see Chapter 13 for further discussion of security issues).

Extranets allow companies to share product catalogues with buyers or distributors, share inventory information with suppliers, manage joint programs with other companies, provide exclusive access of one company's products or services to another company's employees, and so on.

Many organizations have invested in intranets and extranets without a clearly defined strategy. Now many are carefully examining the return on investment (ROI)

of these ventures. Companies are realizing that intranets and extranets can play an important strategic role.

Sources: "Sun Microsystems' Internal Web Usage," CIO.com (www.cio.com); Tobias Arndt, "B2E: Business-to-Employee," Spotlight, Electronic Commerce, InfoNet (www.ecin.de/spotlight/1-2000/000315-spotlight.html); Epicentric: Calculating B2E Portal ROI (www.epicentric.com); Mark Rankin and Theresa Mogavero, "Business-to-Employee Commerce: The Hidden Market," *Perspectives on Business Innovation*, Issue 3, (www.business innovation.ey.com/journal/issue3/features/bustoemp/loader.html).

Table 4-2 Differences Between B2B and B2C E-Commerce

Issue	B2B	B2C
Average order size	$50 000–$75 000	$50–$100
Pricing	Negotiated, long-term contracts, auctions, and catalogue pricing	Mainly catalogue pricing, fixed prices, and some auction pricing
Payment and credit	Credit cards, purchasing cards, and bank credit lines (electronic funds transfer)	Credit cards
Decision maker	Buying committee for complex decisions; approvals required for purchases	Single decision maker; sometimes family members participate in the decision process
Decision criteria	Value, cost, delivery, quality, and service	Brand, word-of-mouth, advertising, and price
Delivery and fulfillment	Critical; delivery schedules must be maintained	Lenient; more likely to wait

Source: Collaborative Commerce, Morgan Stanley Dean Witter, April 2000.

Infrastructure

The infrastructure required to start a B2C business is relatively easy to acquire, at least at the low end. A very inexpensive online store can be built for under $10 000—including an online catalogue with pictures, a shopping cart, and secure credit card transactions. A sophisticated B2C site can be built for well under a million dollars. B2B marketplaces involve expensive technology and extensive database integration. In addition, compatibility with the systems in buying organizations may have to be considered. According to an estimate by Morgan Stanley Dean Witter, for a B2B exchange that brings buyers and sellers together, basic market-making functions will have a start-up cost of $12 to $50 million. (For examples of market-making functions, see the section "What Do Vertical Hubs Do?" on page 94). When marketing and operating costs are added to this, it becomes obvious that a significant investment is required in the case of B2B marketplaces.

Process

B2B transactions are much more complex than B2C transactions. An individual often makes B2C purchase decisions, and such purchase decisions may or may not be carefully deliberated. Businesses, on the other hand, make their purchase decisions based on more objective criteria. Business purchases can involve a group or committee decision. This is especially true for the purchase of capital equipment or other expensive items. Credit cards are generally used to pay for consumer purchases on the Internet. B2B purchases require a greater variety of payment methods, such as credit cards, purchasing cards, and electronic funds transfer (EFT).

Buyer Power

Large buyers in a range of industries are flexing their muscles by forming their own B2B sites. As we saw earlier, auto-makers, retailers, and computer and electronics stores are some examples. These are industries where a few large buyers wield substantial buying power. It would be very difficult for a supplier not to participate in such buyer-controlled marketplaces.

Branding and Marketing

Branding is a bigger issue in the consumer market than in the B2B market. Consumers respond to recognized brand names. Just look at the advertising and marketing budgets of consumer-oriented companies like Amazon, and the importance of advertising and branding become obvious. Even though more B2B firms are advertising now (see Exhibit 4-5 on page 99), B2B purchases are based not on "brand image," but on more objective criteria such as technical specifications, delivery, and service.

Seller's Expertise

In the B2C area, while expertise in the product category or specific product market can be very useful, it is not always essential. In the B2B market, it is harder to transfer knowledge from one vertical industry, such as steel-making, to another, such as software. In-depth understanding of the market, products, and the needs of various buyers is crucial to success. VerticalNet, which operates several vertical portals, or "vortals," uses experts in each industry to design the content for a specific vortal.

Relationship with Customers

In the consumer market, the biggest challenge right now is retaining customers. Most online consumers make one or two purchases, never to return to the same vendor again. Business-to-business purchasing requires a long-term commitment. A business cannot buy from one supplier today and from another tomorrow. Components and parts have to match exact technical specifications, and delivery times must be accurately predictable to ensure uninterrupted production. Business-to-business marketing is based on long-term relationships between buyers and sellers.

Value Proposition

B2C is a one-way network, where one seller sells to many buyers. In the B2C market, the benefit to an individual customer does not depend on whether there are 50 customers or 5 million customers purchasing from a site. In either case, the customer derives the same benefit.[12]

B2B hubs are two-way hubs, where buyers can choose from many sellers and sellers can find many buyers. Buyers benefit from more choice, and sellers benefit from having access to more potential customers. Sellers can reduce their marketing and customer acquisition costs; buyers can reduce their search and transaction-processing costs, while having access to greater number of suppliers.[13]

B2B Business Models

In Chapter 2, we saw mainly the B2C business models. In this section we will examine the different B2B business models.

There are different classification schemes of B2B business models. Table 4-3 offers one classification based on ownership and control.[14] The **seller-controlled sites** are typically Web sites of specific companies that simply provide information (also known as brochure-

---

Table 4-3 Classification of Business-to-Business Sites

Seller Controlled

- Information-only vendor Web sites
- Vendor Web sites with online-ordering

Buyer Controlled

- Web site procurement posting
- Purchasing agents
- Purchasing aggregators

Neutral

- Industry or product specific search engines
- Business malls (multiple vendor store-fronts)
- Auction spaces

Source: Berryman, Harrington, Layton-Rodin, and Rorelle (1998), "Electronic Commerce: Three Emerging Strategies," *The McKinsey Quarterly*, Number 1, 152–159.

ware, because these sites are like an online version of a print brochure) or directly sell products online to end-users. IMP Group (www.impgroup.com), a Canadian conglomerate with interests in aerospace, petroleum, and medical equipment, has a site that offers product information but no direct online sales. Companies that sell complex products that are not suited for direct selling on the Internet are likely to have information sites. Dell Online (www.dell.com or www.dell.ca), on the other hand, is an example of a vendor site with ordering capability. Businesses and other institutional buyers can customize the products they buy and manage their customer accounts with Dell through the Web site. Cisco apparently generates over 70 percent of its revenue through direct sales from its Web site.

In addition to the direct sell model, large suppliers are setting up B2B marketplaces. In the healthcare industry, for example, suppliers including Johnson & Johnson, GE Medical Systems, and Abbott Laboratories have joined together to form their own B2B exchange. In the automobile industry, major suppliers including Delphi Automotive Systems, Motorola, and Dana are said to be considering such a joint supplier-driven exchange. Some see this as a defensive move because these large suppliers do not really like the buyer-controlled marketplaces that are being established in several industries.

Buyer-controlled sites are set up by one or more buyers. Convisint, a joint venture between General Motors, Ford, and Daimler-Chrysler, is a buyer-controlled site that allows these three automobile manufacturers to source supplies online. Broadlane, which is partly owned by Tenant Healthcare, is another buyer-driven B2B marketplace that caters to the high-volume hospital and medical supplies market.

Buyer-controlled marketplaces shift the power from sellers to buyers. Buyer-controlled sites are generally established by large buyers, as in the case of Convisint (auto industry) and GlobalNetXchange (retail).

Another form of buyer-controlled site is the aggregator. Here companies pool their purchasing power to get lower prices. Works.com is an aggregator, or buyers' cooperative, that enables small businesses to join together to make large volume purchases at lower prices.

Buyer-driven marketplaces are being set up mostly as joint ventures, separate from the parent companies. The emphasis is on eliminating inefficiencies in the supply chains of founding and member companies. Transaction fees and (sometimes) advertising are the sources of revenue for these exchanges.

Independent third parties run the **neutral sites**. These sites may provide a variety of services, ranging from market-making functions (matching buyers and sellers), to facilitating online auctions or purchasing, all the way to managing integrated supply chains. Many of these neutral sites are labelled vertical portals or vortals because they cater to specific industries. For example, Chemdex.com brings together buyers and sellers in the chemical industry, Plastics.net brings together buyers and vendors in the plastics industry, and Hsupply.com caters to the hospitality industry.

B2B Hubs

B2B sites are called hubs because like the hub in wheel that brings the spokes together, these sites bring buyers and sellers together. Hubs are neutral Internet-based intermediaries that focus on a specific industry (or set of products) and offer various types of transactions between buyers and sellers.

Business-to-business selling requires in-depth knowledge of the industry. The chemical industry is entirely different from the electronic components industry. Industry structure, nature of demand and supply, nature of products, manufacturing processes, and end uses differ widely across industries. Such varying demand across industries has necessitated and spurred the growth of what are known as **vertical hubs**. Vertical hubs are designed to meet the needs of a specific industry, such as automobiles, retailing, or computers.

For certain products, such as MRO (maintenance, repair, and operating) and office supplies, which are purchased by companies in different industries, **horizontal hubs** can provide a good service. Horizontal sites are also called functional sites. Examples include Grainger.com, Ariba Network, CommerceOne's Marketsite.com, and EmployEase.

Horizontal and vertical hubs can simply connect buyers and sellers by acting as match makers or as intermediaries who facilitate the transaction. They can range in complexity—from simple sales lead generation all the way to extranets and supply chain management. Exhibit 4-2 presents an example of a horizontal B2B site that brings together exporters and importers of many different products from different parts of the world.

Vertical B2B Hubs and Exchanges

Vortexes, eHubs, and Net **market makers** are some of the names used to describe sites that facilitate B2B commerce within a specific industry by providing the necessary technology and infrastructure. The hubs play a vital role by bringing together buyers and sellers in an industry.

As is evident from Table 4-4, there has been a proliferation of B2B hubs. Some analysts think that not all of these hubs will survive. Buyers will not pay transaction fees to purchase from vendors they already know or do business with. So business models based primarily

Exhibit 4-2 Bidmix.com, a Global B2B Site

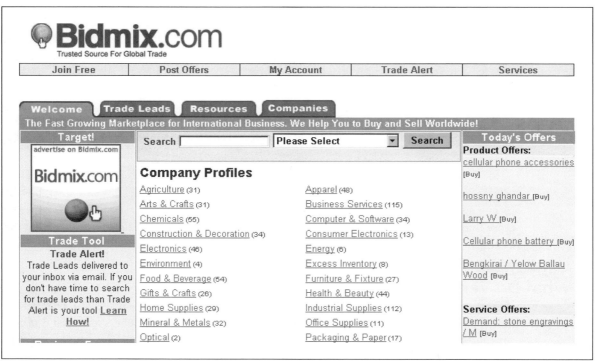

Source: www.bidmix.com.

Table 4-4 Selected Vertical Hubs and Exchanges

Industry	Company	Site
Agriculture	AgWeb	www.agweb.com
Automobiles	Convisint	www.convisint.com
Construction	ContractorHub	www.contractorhub.com
Chemicals	ChemConnect	www.chemconnect.com
Computers	BizBuyer	www.bizbuyer.com
Electronic parts	FastParts	www.fastparts.com
Employment	Ants.com	www.ants.com
	HireAbility	www.hireability.com
Healthcare and life science	Healtheon/WebMD	www.healtheon.com
	Chemdex	www.chemdex.com
Hotels/hospitality	Hsupply.com	www.hsupply.com
Metals	MetalSite	www.metalsite.com
	e-steel	www.e-steel.com
Paper	PaperExchange	www.paperexchange.com
Plastics	PlasticsNet	www.plasticsnet.com
Retail	GlobalNetXchange	www.globalnetxchange.com
Telecom	Arbinet	www.arbinet.com

Sources: Company Web Sites, "Collaborative Commerce," Morgan Stanley Dean Witter, April 2000, and "B2B eCommerce," Legg Mason Wood Walker, Inc., Spring 2000.

on transaction fees may be in trouble. In some industries, such as plastics and steel, buying from a few big suppliers is essential to make any neutral B2B hub successful. Sites that offer more than just vendor identification have a better chance of succeeding. Some sites offer the ability to buy directly from suppliers, as well the opportunity to participate in auctions, reverse auctions, aggregate buying, and posting RFPs.

What Do Vertical Hubs Do?

Hubs can employ a variety of market-making and trading mechanisms.[15] The transaction model allows buyers to find sellers, places the order online, and pockets a transaction fee. This model is suited to catalogue items that are standard with fixed prices. MRO items and other low-value, high-frequency items are best suited for the catalogue model.

The auction model allows for dynamic pricing based on demand and supply. It is better suited to nonstandard, unique items, where the seller is trying to find the best price. At times, it can be used to get rid of excess inventory of standard items. VerticalNet, for example, allows suppliers to auction excess inventory anonymously. This means that competitors and customers will not know that a particular supplier has excess inventory.

The exchange model works well for commodities, where demand and prices fluctuate frequently. Exchanges allow for real-time trading, which allows for demand and supply management. E-steel, ChemConnect, and PaperExchange are some examples.

Lastly, the barter model can also be part of hubs. The Web is giving a new lease on life to this old concept. Barter exchanges are usually considered part of underdeveloped economies, but according to the International Reciprocal Trade Association, in the United States $16 billion worth of B2B barter transactions take place each year. Bigvine.com is one of the players in this category. The key for the barter model is to have a large number of buyers and sellers who can offer a variety of products and services that will interest the participants.

Hubs can combine any of these four models or other models. Some vertical hubs also have partnerships with functional or horizontal hubs to ensure that their members can do all of their direct and indirect material purchases on one site.

Criteria for Successful Vertical Hubs

There are several criteria that determine if a product or sector is suited to vertical B2B exchanges. The chief ones among them are discussed below.

Fragmented Market. A fragmented market, with a low concentration of buyers and a high number of geographically dispersed suppliers, elevates the need for a neutral market maker. Markets with few buyers and sellers will generally not need the services of a third-party market maker.

Nature of the Product. Standardized products that can be purchased via online catalogues and products where the brand name is not important are good candidates for vertical marketplaces.

Decision Criteria. Direct and indirect materials that are frequently purchased and require a fairly routine decision process are ones that can succeed in vertical exchanges. New buys or specialized one-time purchases may require closer interaction with the supplier and may not be suited to an automated process. If the products are purchased based on availability, delivery, and price, and not based on supplier-buyer relationship, then vertical exchanges may be appropriate. If the relationship with the supplier is an important consideration, buyers are unlikely to switch suppliers. This makes participation in an online exchange less likely.

Most vertical hubs do not have great entry barriers to prevent competition. Anyone with the capital to invest can enter the fray. In some industries dominated by few large buyers, if the major buyers are locked into one hub, the competition can be virtually shut out. The competitive landscape in many of the vertical markets is still emerging. We will know the winners and casualties in a year or two.

Classification of B2B Hubs

B2B hubs or e-hubs have been classified into four categories based on two dimensions: how businesses buy (spot vs. systematic) and what businesses buy (operating supplies vs. manufacturing inputs).[16] Exhibit 4-3 presents the classification of B2B hubs.

MRO hubs deal in maintenance, repair, and operating supplies. These items are routinely purchased by organizations. MRO hubs can increase efficiencies in purchasing. These hubs

Exhibit 4-3 Classification of B2B Hubs

	What businesses buy	
How businesses buy	operating inputs	manufacturing inputs
systematic sourcing	**MRO Hubs** Ariba W.W. Grainger MRO.com BizBuyer.com	**Catalogue Hubs** Chemdex SciQuest.com PlasticsNet.com
spot sourcing	**Yield Managers** Employease Adauction.com CapacityWeb.com	**Exchanges** e-Steel PaperExchange.com Altra Energy IMX Exchange

Source: Steven Kaplan and Mohanbir Sawhney, "E-Hubs: The New B2B Marketplaces," *Harvard Business Review*, 78 (3) May/June 2000, pp. 97–103.

cater to wide variety of industries and are "horizontal" in nature. They have the potential to cause disintermediation by taking on the function of traditional middlemen.

Yield managers cater to spot buying of operating inputs such as human resources (Employease.com), manufacturing capacity (CapacityWeb.com), and capital equipment (iMark.com). They help businesses deal with volatility in demand and supply. A company in need of additional manufacturing capacity can source the needed capacity through CapacityWeb. By matching buyers and sellers in areas where demand is somewhat unpredictable, yield managers allow firms to scale their operations up or down at short notice. Yield managers tend to be horizontal rather than vertically focused.

Catalogue hubs streamline procurement within specific vertical industries. While MRO hubs are horizontal in nature, catalogue hubs are vertical in nature. They carry routinely purchased items for specific industries, thus having a great deal of depth and limited breadth in their product range. Just like MRO hubs, catalogue hubs can also lower the cost of purchasing by enabling firms to automate routine purchases.

Lastly, **exchanges**, as described in the previous section, create spot markets for commodities such as paper and steel. Similar to yield managers, exchanges also smooth out demand and supply. Many online exchanges allow real-time trading. Exchanges mediate the relationship between buyers and sellers.

MRO and catalogue hubs tend to play an *aggregation* function.[17] They can offer products from many manufacturers at one site. They bring a large number of buyers and sellers together and allow both parties to lower their transaction costs. The spot sourcing hubs (yield managers and exchanges), on the other hand, create value by playing a *market matching* function.[18] They allow buyers and sellers to negotiate prices and trade on a real-time basis.

B2B and Small Businesses

A lot of what is happening in the B2B world may seem oriented toward big business. By 1999, only 7.5 percent of small businesses in the United States were engaged in E-commerce, while the corresponding figure for medium and large enterprises was 35 percent. This gap is expected to vanish by 2002, when roughly 70 to 80 percent of all firms, irrespective of their size, will be engaged in E-commerce.[19]

Small businesses have found it harder to get into the B2B E-commerce mindset. High initial costs and lack of services aimed at small business needs are among the major stumbling blocks. A study by Cyber Dialogue found that customer service is woefully lacking in many B2B sites aimed at small businesses.

At the same time, small businesses are realizing that the Internet can level the playing field for them and are fighting to overcome these constraints. In the first quarter of 2000, small business B2B spending increased by 138 percent in the United States.[20] In both Canada and the United States, it is a known fact that more jobs are being created by small businesses and start-ups than large corporations. A growing number of small businesses are expected to use the Internet to sell and buy products. A study by IDC (www.idc.com) predicts that 30 percent of worldwide Internet commerce revenue will be generated by small businesses by the year 2003, up from 17 percent in 1997.

Many B2B companies are rushing to fill the needs of small business that are online. These include marketing services (such as SmartAge), Web development and E-commerce (such as ECBuilder, BigStep, and Workz), one-stop consulting portals (such as AllBusiness and bizzed, shown in Exhibit 4-4), and procurement services (such as BizBuyer and Onvia). The old EDI based on private networks was beyond the reach of small businesses. Now GE offers a Web-based EDI for small businesses (www.getradeweb.com).

Marketing in the B2B Arena

Business-to-business marketing differs from consumer marketing in many ways. In the B2B arena, delivery at the precise time is often an important requirement: unless components and parts are delivered on time, production scheduling will be in disarray. To ensure that products meet specifications and quality, and a smooth delivery is guaranteed, businesses often develop partnerships and alliances with suppliers. Thus, buyer-seller relationships have greater longevity than they do in the consumer market. Industrial purchases can often be very technical, customized, and expensive. As a result, there is a need for personal selling through knowledgeable sales staff.

Businesses rarely make their decisions on the basis of brand name or other emotional criteria. Cost, technical superiority, delivery, and other terms are carefully scrutinized. Unlike consumer buying, where an individual may be the sole decision maker, business purchases tend to be group decisions. End-users, the finance department, and the purchasing department may be some of the parties to the buying decision, and multiple levels of approval may be required for complex and expensive purchases.

Whether marketing online or offline, these characteristics of the business-to-business market must be addressed. Marketing strategies and tactics have to be tailored to meet the

Exhibit 4-4 Bizzed, Citibank's Small Business Services Portal

Source: www.bizzed.com.

expectations of businesses. The different decision processes must be considered while developing a marketing program aimed at the business customer.

Advertising and personal selling are used by B2B entities to attract customers, but advertising tends to play a secondary role to personal selling. The specialized nature of the products, the complexity of the decision process, and the need for extensive support and training make personal contact very important in the B2B selling process.

Advertising in the B2B Market

While companies like Amazon, Priceline.com, and E*Trade rank as the top companies in terms of advertising expenditures, other B2B companies are increasingly making their presence felt online. A study by AdRelevance found that online ads were increasingly taking a B2B bias. In the four-month period from October 1999 to February 2000, B2B ads on the Internet grew by 58 percent from the previous four-month period. During this same time, B2C ads grew by only 4 percent.[21] As the number of businesses online increases, the use of the Internet to find new business customers is also increasing.

B2B advertising is targeted at Internet users at work. As a result, B2B ads are more common on business sites, computer/technology sites, business portals, and search engines. The AdRelevance study also found that 62 percent of all business ads feature services such as Web design, E-commerce security, and technology products. Exhibit 4-5 shows some examples of B2B banner ads.

Exhibit 4-5 B2B Banner Ads

Personal Selling and Sales Force Automation

While advertising creates awareness, businesses often require detailed presentations and negotiation during the purchase process. Once advertising generates interest and a sales lead, personal selling takes over. While routine procurement of supplies and standard items can be fully automated on the Internet, complex and customized products require the personal touch. The Internet can also assist the salesperson in this case.

The salesperson can use the Internet to generate sales leads. Companies such as Hoover's (www.hoovers.com) and Thomas Register (www.thomasregister.com) allow the sales staff to search for leads and identify prospective buyers.

Sales force automation (SFA) software applications typically offer contact management and the ability to track leads. Sophisticated applications offer the ability to configure and price the products instantly. For instance, a medical equipment salesperson selling an MRI scanner to a hospital can use information on room dimensions to instantly configure the product and determine its price. SFA applications also allow for instant updates of pricing and inventory information from the company Web site.

Perhaps the most significant benefit of such software applications is that they enable the salespeople—nationally or even globally—to share information. It is possible to share sales leads, vital competitive intelligence, or other knowledge across the entire sales force. SFA can ensure that a geographically dispersed sales force has access to current information and strategies via the Web and their laptops.

Often major purchases involve more than one individual decision maker. If there is a buying committee involved, SFA applications can allow for tracking and communicating with different participants. The Internet can be used synchronize information regarding a prospect across multiple computers. This will enable a salesperson working with an operations manager in Nova Scotia to track the progress of a fellow salesperson working with the controller at the prospect's headquarters.[22]

See Goldmine (www.frontrange.com) for examples of sales force automation and contact management products. Internet Sales Management (www.avv.com) is a sales lead and contact management system for the automotive industry. In addition, prospect and lead generation can be outsourced on the Internet to companies like ProspectBuilder (www.prospectbuilder.com) and Lead to Sales (www.leadtosales.com).

Web Sites

The Web site is a critical component of business-to-business marketing efforts. In a study of European B2B Web sites in 16 countries, it was found that only 11 percent offered the option to register as a member or for a newsletter, 11 percent offered the possibility of purchasing online, and only 3 percent had a secure area dedicated to clients or dealers. Product brochures and catalogues are the most common applications found on B2B sites.[23]

Marketing Challenges

Customer Care. The B2B exchanges and net markets do attempt to automate the routine aspects of the procurement process. Businesses often require customer service, support, and training. There is some concern that the Web may make the purchase and post-purchase process very impersonal. Small businesses in particular have been ill served by many of the B2B sites. Unless the B2B exchanges invest in customer support (call centres and Web-based support), many buyers will soon be turned off.

The Chicken-and-Egg Dilemma. B2B sites cannot assume that if "we build it, they will come." Many neutral B2B marketplaces have the twin task of attracting buyers and sellers at the same time. Unless several large suppliers are present, buyers may not be interested in joining an e-procurement site. Suppliers are also likely to be reluctant to join a site unless a large number of buyers are on board. Marketing and personal selling efforts have to be directed at both sides simultaneously. Anyone thinking of starting a B2B vertical or horizontal hub must be willing to invest in marketing initially.

Market Entry Timing. The above dilemma leads to another interesting issue. When should a hub open its doors to buyers and sellers? Ideally, buyers and sellers in an industry must be ready to participate in a hub. If there are too few buyers or two few sellers, the other side will not realize significant benefits. VerticalNet, a company that hosts over 50 vertical hubs, followed an interesting strategy. At the beginning, the hubs were vertical communities filled with content that allowed buyers and sellers to find each other. Gradually E-commerce functionality was added, and now the site generates over 50 percent of its revenues from E-commerce transactions.

The Road Ahead: Challenges and Opportunities

On the one hand, there are astonishing predictions regarding the growth of B2B E-commerce. On the other hand, there is the sobering reality. A study by the National Association of Manufacturers (www.nam.org) in the United States found that 68 percent of responding manufacturing companies said they were not using B2B E-commerce.[24] "No one questions the benefits of B2B E-commerce, yet relatively few manufacturers are participating in it," said NAM President, Jerry Jasinowski.[25] A study of purchasing managers across Canada sponsored by the Purchasing Management Association of Canada (PMAC) lends support to this statement. It revealed that 58 percent of the firms did not use the Internet for purchasing.[26]

The Canadian study also found that only 3.25 percent of all business-to-business purchasing can be classified as Internet purchasing or e-procurement. Canadian firms use the Internet more as an information source to "search for potential vendors" (86 percent), post RFQs (39.5 percent), and access suppliers' online catalogues (76 percent). When it comes to actually carrying out the purchase transaction online, most firms have not taken that big step.[27]

The Canadian study and the NAM study show that the gap in E-commerce usage is quite significant between smaller firms and large firms. Industry leaders have generally adopted E-commerce in most industries—whether manufacturing, retailing, hospitality, healthcare, or transportation. Among the firms using E-commerce in North America, the most popular B2B uses of the Internet include searching for vendors and shopping for prices, product searches in online catalogues, and posting requests for quotes or proposals.

From a diffusion of innovation perspective, B2B E-commerce is still in the early stages of adoption, with only a small fraction of firms taking full advantage of capabilities of the Internet from procurement to supply chain management. Why is the adoption rate so low at present? What barriers need to be overcome to ensure more organizations are benefiting from the technology? Some of the barriers and issues raised by purchasing managers are presented in Table 4-5.

Security is the overriding concern among those firms considering the adoption of B2B E-commerce. Smaller firms are concerned about cost. The National Association of Manufacturers study revealed that 53 percent of smaller firms do not have internal IT staff. For smaller firms the technology issues are more challenging to overcome. B2B solution providers must address these concerns to ensure wider adoption of B2B E-commerce.

There is good news for those who have invested in B2B technology companies. As the NAM president said, businesses do realize that B2B E-commerce can offer several benefits. The most commonly mentioned benefits found in the purchasing managers study are shown in Table 4-6.

If the benefits of an innovation or new product are visible, diffusion of innovation theory would suggest that that product or innovation has a good future. In the case of B2B E-com-

Table 4-5 Barriers to B2B E-Commerce Adoption

Issue	Percentage
Security (transaction and data security)	41.5%
Cost (systems and training)	11.2%
Technology (implementation and integration with legacy systems, standards)	11.2%
Training and human resources	10.1%

Source: Ramesh Venkat (2000).

merce, there are several visible benefits, but there are also some nagging concerns. The extent to which B2B technology providers quickly address these concerns will determine the rate of adoption of B2B E-commerce.

Industry associations such as the National Association of Manufacturers, National Retail Federation (www.nrf.com), the Grocery Manufacturers of America (GMA), the National Association of Purchasing Managers (NAPM), and its Canadian counterpart Purchasing Managers Association of Canada (PMAC) have programs and initiatives to address B2B E-commerce adoption in their areas. Such industry-wide efforts will help in the adoption of E-commerce.

Among the Canadian firms that have adopted B2B E-commerce, senior management commitment to E-commerce was an important driver. In these organizations, generally there was a comprehensive E-commerce strategy.[28] In organizations that were lagging behind, the PMAC-sponsored study found that senior management commitment and a comprehensive strategy were lacking.

Table 4-6 Benefits of B2B E-Commerce

Benefit	Percentage
Streamline processes	27.5%
Reduction in administrative and transaction costs	26.7%
Speed and efficient use of time	22.2%
Greater access to suppliers, global sourcing	12%
Better communication with suppliers	12%
Focus can be shifted to strategic issues	10%

Source: Ramesh Venkat (2000).

B2B E-commerce often requires changes in business processes. Automated purchasing and online real-time purchasing will have significant implications for how firms interact with and manage relationships with their suppliers. E-commerce has the potential to turn suppliers into closely networked partners, and this may be a new paradigm in many organizations. It also requires employees to learn new skills. E-commerce can lead to decentralized purchasing, where end-users in departments can directly order products from approved online vendor catalogues, bypassing layers of bureaucracy. While some workers may be empowered by such change, others may feel threatened. In some organizations there could be resistance to this kind of change.

Organizations that do not see the benefits of E-commerce outweighing the costs are unlikely to make the necessary commitment. The cost savings, the ability to source globally, greater efficiency, and the ability to focus more on strategic issues (see Table 4-6) are potential benefits of adopting B2B E-commerce from the buying organization's perspective. It is not an exaggeration to say that the competitiveness of most organizations will be influenced by their ability to effectively manage their supply chains and reap the benefits of B2B E-commerce.

Summary

B2B E-commerce is much bigger than B2C E-commerce. According to some projections it will grow to $3.95 trillion by 2003. Buyers are flocking to E-commerce because it lowers their search and transaction costs, has the potential to lower inventory costs, eliminates redundancies, and streamlines their procurement process. Sellers can reduce their marketing and customer acquisition costs, develop closer links with buyers, and get the best price for their products using the auction format.

While the benefits are clear, there are also some concerns that impede the adoption of E-commerce among businesses. Security is the primary concern. Technology standards and compatibility of E-commerce systems with existing IT infrastructure, cost, and the need for skilled employees (or training existing ones) are some other barriers to adopting E-commerce. The adoption of E-commerce is especially low among smaller companies.

Business-to-consumer E-commerce is less expensive. The emphasis is on branding and providing personalized experience for consumers. Consumers often make purchase decisions based on brand image or other subjective criteria. Businesses buy on the basis of more objective criteria such as technical specifications, delivery, and service. Businesses also tend to prefer long-term relationships with suppliers.

These differences must be taken into account as organizations develop marketing programs for B2B sites. Some advertising in business sites and trade publications may be appropriate. The emphasis, however, is on personal selling and making the task of the salesperson more efficient though sales force automation applications and the use of intranets.

Key Terms

B2B exchanges, 83
Buyer-controlled sites, 92
Catalogue hubs, 96
Community commerce, 83
Direct selling, 83
Electronic data interchange (EDI), 83

Exchanges, 96
Extranets, 87
Horizontal hubs, 93
Intranets, 88
Market makers, 93
MRO hubs, 95
Neutral sites, 92

Sales force automation, 100
Seller-controlled sites, 91
Vertical hubs, 93
XML (eXtensible Markup Language), 85
Yield managers, 96

Questions and Exercises

Review Questions

1. What are the important differences between B2B and B2C markets?
2. Why are buyers adopting B2B E-commerce?
3. Why are sellers adopting B2B E-commerce?
4. What barriers do you see to the growth of B2B E-commerce?
5. What are vertical exchanges? What are horizontal exchanges? Provide examples.
6. What are the important criteria for a successful vertical hub?
7. What different market-making functions do vertical hubs perform?
8. Why are so few small businesses using B2B E-commerce?
9. What are the important differences between B2B and B2C marketing on the Internet?

Discussion Questions

1. If you were setting up a B2B exchange or hub focusing on the needs of small businesses, how would you ensure that such businesses would be attracted to your site? What marketing efforts would be appropriate?
2. Given the barriers to adoption of B2B E-commerce, do you think that the projections for growth of B2B E-commerce are exaggerated?
3. As the manufacturer of components for computers, what type of online advertising would you do? Which sites would you target?
4. Given the importance of B2B E-commerce, should the government play a role in the wider adoption of E-commerce? Why or why not? If you think the government has a role to play, describe the role in detail.

Internet Exercises

1. Visit four different vertical sites from VerticalNet (www.verticalnet.com). Make sure the sites are in completely unrelated industries. What services does each vertical community offer its members? What are the similarities and differences between sites?
2. Visit Dell online (www.dell.com or www.dell.ca). Study the sections on Home/Home Business, Small Business and Medium/Large Business, and Education. What different features or services are offered to each of these market segments? How well do you think Dell is addressing the needs of so many segments through one site? What specific differences do you see between the Home segment and the Medium/Large Business segment?

Chapter 5

Market Research and Business Intelligence

Vignette 5 **The Electronic Trail**

Learning Objectives

After reading this chapter, you will:

- Understand the process of market research on the Internet.
- Understand the different methods of collecting online data about consumers, competitors, and the market environment.
- Appreciate the strengths and weaknesses of different online market research techniques.
- Be able to choose the appropriate online research method for a given problem.

Consumers leave an electronic fingerprint wherever they go on the Web. Marketers can find out a lot about consumer behaviour on the Web with relative ease. Sophisticated tracking software programs can provide the online marketer with a great deal of information. When a user visits a site, it is possible to detect the operating system of the user's computer, the type of browser (Netscape or Internet Explorer), the Web site seen before the current one, any pages seen in the current Web site, the exit site (did the visitor go to a competitor's site?), and much more. Such information is collected unobtrusively in the background.

Online advertising networks (such as DoubleClick, Flycast, and ValueClick) track consumers on the Web to identify their surfing habits and preferences. DoubleClick, the largest online advertising network, has over 11 500 sites on its system. When a user visits one of these sites, DoubleClick sends a "cookie" (a small text file, which is like an ID number) to the user's computer. The cookie files can contain data regarding user preferences, previous purchases, Web sites visited, pages visited, frequency of visits, and banner ads seen or clicked.

The cookie files allow DoubleClick to recognize that computer when it visits the same site again or another site. Such recognition enables online publishers and advertisers to customize content and advertisements based on a user's prior visits.

Most E-commerce sites send cookie files and some sites (such as Indigo.ca) require the user to allow cookie files in order to shop in their site. (Cookies are described in detail later in this chapter.) Customers who want to personalize the content of Web pages (for example, using My Yahoo!) or those who want free services (such as Hotmail) may be required to allow tracking through cookies in exchange for the free services.

In addition Web tracking data, it is also possible develop "inferential" or "psychographic" data based on Web surfing habits. For instance, if someone frequently visits a sports site or a financial information site, a lifestyle profile of the user can be developed based on this information.

DoubleClick found itself in hot water when it announced that it was taking consumer tracking a step further and was going to match online tracking data with users' personal information such as address, age, gender, income, credit card, and shopping information. In other words, DoubleClick would not only know the users preferences and shopping habits, it would actually know who the user was. That means there is simply no anonymity online. How can DoubleClick know such personal information about Web surfers?

DoubleClick acquired a company called Abacus Direct Corp., a direct-marketing services company that maintains a database of names, addresses, and retail purchasing habits of virtually all American households. This database provides DoubleClick with the ability to match personal information with cookies. Here is how the matching process roughly works. Assume you buy a product from an online store. While you are on that site, DoubleClick will send a cookie with a unique ID number to your computer and send the same ID number to the site that you are on. That site (which is part of the DoubleClick network) will immediately send DoubleClick information about you (perhaps your address or phone number), which can be used to identify you in the Abacus database.

While consumer groups such as the Center for Democratic Technology (www.cdt.org) were outraged by DoubleClick's action, DoubleClick defended its action saying that it allowed for better personalization of Web sites and advertising, which would benefit consumers. Consumer activists, however, were getting ready to take this issue to the US Federal Trade Commission. A dozen Web sites were reported to be participating in DoubleClick's new tracking method by sharing information about online shoppers with DoubleClick. Many of DoubleClick's advertising partners have not signed on, perhaps due to the adverse consumer reaction.

Advertising networks like DoubleClick, 24/7 Media, Flycast, Adknowledge, and Real Media were proposing self-policing through an industry association. Flycast, one of DoubleClick's competitors, had proposed that it be in charge of a clearinghouse of personal consumer information. Such information would be shared among consortium members. Flycast's proposal would enable the tracking of consumers from one site to another. Competitors were not very enthused with the idea of sharing information. DoubleClick, an industry heavyweight, seems to be pursuing its own strategy.

The DoubleClick case shows two sides of the Web. In some ways the Web is a market researcher's dream come true. From the moment someone logs on to an Internet service provider, advertisers can track which banner ads that person clicks on (and if that click leads to a purchase). They can compile a profile of Web viewing habits on each user. However, so far all of this was being done while respecting consumers' privacy. When a marketer learns about the needs, preferences, and habits of consumers, it can result in more tailored and better quality service.

Now by removing the veil of anonymity, DoubleClick's approach does raise several questions. Does the marketer *need* to know such personal information about consumers? Just because the technology allows marketers to capture such information, should it be used? And how can consumers' privacy rights be guarded while allowing businesses to market more efficiently?

Sources: Will Rodger (1999), "Online profiling firms to police themselves," USATO-DAY.COM, November 23; Will Rodger, "Activists charge DoubleClick double cross," USATODAY.com, June 7, 2000; "CDT Empowers Consumers to Reject DoubleClick's Double-Cross," CDT POLICY POST (www.cdt.org), Vol. 6, Number 3, February 1, 2000; Whit Andrews (1997), "Consumer Profiling Firefly Proposes Clearinghouse for Sharing Information on Users," Web Week, Vol. 3 (5), March 3; Cookiecentral.com.

Introduction

In Chapter 2 we saw how information can be used to enhance the value delivered to consumers. Online marketers can obtain vast amounts of personal information about consumers unobtrusively. Such personal information can be used for personalized delivery of content or services based on user preferences and past behaviour. Unfortunately, there is also the danger of such information being abused. Responsible and ethical market research can benefit the consumer and the marketer alike.

Regardless of your opinion on DoubleClick's methods, it should be apparent that businesses have great access to information because of the Internet. In addition to consumer information, the Internet is a rich mine of information about competitors and industry and business trends. Government and private databases, competitors' Web sites, and stock quote sites can provide vital information about competitive trends.

Businesses are realizing that intimate knowledge about their customers, competitors, technologies, and processes can lead to better decisions and eventually superior performance. Intellectual capital within organizations is cited as a source of competitive advantage.[1] As Peter Drucker said, "Knowledge has become the key economic resource and the dominant—perhaps the only—source of comparative (competitive) advantage."[2] This chapter should be read in this context.

The notion of managing intellectual capital or knowledge within organizations requires a systematic process for

- generating knowledge (about consumers, competitors, new technology, etc.),
- empowering decision makers with relevant knowledge,

- embedding knowledge in organizational processes, products or services (refer to the discussion on mass customization in Chapter 2, for instance), and
- measuring the value or impact of such a knowledge management process.[3]

Marketing research, at least in the traditional sense, has been associated with discrete projects conducted at sporadic intervals. The Internet allows organizations easier, faster, and richer access to information about markets, consumers, competitors, and changes in the external environment. While traditional approaches to market research are still valid, in this new economy firms require a **business intelligence** approach, which goes beyond occasional marketing research projects. It is a systematic and ongoing monitoring of all internal and external facets of a business, which results in knowledge creation. The Internet plays a vital role in any firm's strategy to leverage its intellectual capital.

As users of research and research organizations realize the potential of the Internet as a tool for market research and business intelligence, it is important to understand how the Internet and the Web can be used for research. This chapter will discuss different methods of gathering information about consumers, competitors, and the external business environment. The following are just some of the questions that a firm may want answered about its consumers:

- Who are our customers—current and potential? What is their profile?
- How do they make their purchase decisions? What factors influence their decisions?
- Why do consumers buy our product (or our competitor's product)?
- What percentage of visitors to our site are actually buying our products?
- Are they satisfied with what they buy?
- Are they loyal? What can we do to make them loyal to our product?

Market research can help a business find answers to these questions. The result can be improvement in product offering, better targeting of messages, or simply an improved overall marketing effort.

It is not sufficient to understand who the consumers are and what their motivations are. Information about competitors can be crucial as well. By getting advance warning about a competitor's action or by studying the flaws in a competitor's product or strategy, a firm can strengthen its own market position. **Competitive intelligence**, which is a subset of business intelligence, is a systematic program for gathering and analyzing information about competitors to further the company's goal.[4] This chapter will examine the use of the Internet in competitive intelligence gathering.

There is evidence that the Internet will play a vital role in business research in the coming years. Marketing research is a $6 billion industry in North America. In 1999, an estimated $72 million was spent in the United States on online market research, and most of this money was shifted from traditional research to online research.[5] However, a survey of Fortune 2000 executives by the Council of American Survey Research Organizations showed that 87 percent of the respondents had a favourable view of online research, and over 80 percent expected to use the same or a greater amount of online research in the next year.[6] Online research firms are also gearing up for this growth market. Many, such as Angus Reid, NFO, Harris, CF Group, and Greenfield, have started interactive research divisions.

Marketers interested in understanding variables such as consumer demographics, lifestyles, purchase behaviour, and Web usage patterns can obtain information through many different methods such as online publications and databases, e-mail or Web surveys, online focus groups, and content analysis of consumer e-mail or newsgroup postings. Competitive and market information can be obtained from government and syndicated data sources, by studying competitors' Web sites, and by examining consumer feedback and newsgroup postings. The different methods are described in the remainder of this chapter.

Marketing Research Process

Marketing research can provide answers to particular problems or address a knowledge gap a company may have through a specifically designed research project. It can also serve the purpose of intelligence gathering, discussed later in this chapter, where information about customers and competitors is collected on a routine basis. There are many methods of collecting data. Sometimes, previously published data or reports can provide the answers. This type of research is called secondary research. Other times, a problem or question may require a specifically commissioned research study. This type of research is called primary research. But regardless of the nature of the study, a systematic and thorough approach is required to ensure that the results are usable. Internet market researchers can use the following steps as guidelines for organizing research projects:

- *Problem definition and research objectives*. What is the question or problem the company needs to answer or solve? If the company needs research to address a specific question (for example, "Why are so few customers returning to our Web site for repeat purchases?"), then that question has to be defined clearly.
- *Research methodology*. Can the research problem be addressed through secondary research or does it require primary research or a combination of the two? If primary research is required, is it appropriate to conduct qualitative or quantitative research (discussed later in this chapter) or both?
- *Sampling frame and sample design*. For primary research, specifically survey research, the population from which the sample of respondents or participants will be drawn must be defined. In this step, the research must address a number of questions. Who are the participants in the study? How do we ensure the sample is representative of the population and that sampling biases will not affect the study's conclusions? How many participants (sample size) are required to provide a statistically reliable result? How do we solicit participation in the study?
- *Instrument design and testing*. If data collection is to be done by the survey method, a detailed questionnaire has to be developed. Online research lends itself well to conducting structured survey research, where respondents check off responses from multiple choices. If the data collection is done through qualitative research techniques such as a focus group or in-depth interview, a general guide with open-ended questions should be developed. In either case, the data-collection instrument must be tested with a small sample of subjects taken from the same population as intended for the final data collection.
- *Data collection*. The researcher must choose between online and offline data collection. The method of data collection and the data collection protocol must be defined. The data collection method may depend on the nature of the study and the appropriateness of using the Internet for such a study. On the Internet, surveys can be posted on a Web site or implemented as pop-up surveys (where a short survey appears on a new window while a person is viewing a Web page). Surveys can also be e-mailed to a selected group or posted in relevant newsgroups. Each method has its strengths and weak-

nesses, which will be discussed later in this chapter. In addition to choosing the method of online data collection, the data collection protocol must be decided. How will participants be recruited for the study, what is the duration of the study, and what reminders will be sent to participants are some of the issues that need to be addressed at this stage.

- *Analysis and presentation.* Finally, the statistical tools that will be used to analyze the data, and the presentation and publication format must be decided. The presentation of results can also be accompanied by a list of recommendations, if appropriate.

Whether the entire research is done online or offline, the researcher must follow this process. In the remainder of this chapter, we will look at different online data collection methods in detail.

Secondary Research

Secondary research is based on previously published data or information. It involves information not gathered specifically for the purpose of the study at hand but for some other purpose.[7] Government as well as private databases on the Internet can be vital sources of information. Government sources generally tend to provide free information, while private or syndicated research companies may charge a subscription or usage fee for accessing their online databases. Secondary data can come from a wide variety of sources on the Internet, including university or academic sites, government departmental sites, commercial research sites, industry association or trade publication sites, and news and information sites.

Search engines like AltaVista, Excite, Northernlight, and Yahoo! make it easier to find information. In addition to these search engines, the portal sites devoted to business, finance, and technology issues offer the ability to search their archives and databases. A researcher looking for secondary data can save time by using meta-search engines (see iMarket Demo 5-1 on page 115).

Free Secondary Sources: Government and Public Sites

There are a vast number of free information sources on the Internet. Businesses file various types of reports with government agencies and may be required to disclose financial information. Universities and industry associations can also be sources of free online information.

If a business wants to find out the potential for marketing a product in a foreign country, the *CIA World Fact Book* (www.cia.gov/cia/publications/factbook/index.html) can be a good starting point. It provides detailed information about the economic and political environment in all countries. Online encyclopedias such as Britannica (www.britannica.com) and Encarta (www.encarta.msn.com) are also valuable sources for conducting a broad survey of a potential foreign market, including cultural and geographic issues. See Table 5-1 for a selection of online secondary information sources.

Governments the world over have realized the importance of information and *knowledge management*. In most advanced countries and some developing countries, government departmental sites and online databases are the best source of free information. Industry Canada's Strategis (see Exhibit 5-1 on page 113) as well as the US Commerce Department's National Trade Data Bank (www.stat-usa.gov) are rich sources of information that cover a wide range of topic areas in great depth. They include domestic and foreign trade data as well as industry-specific data.

Table 5-1 Selected Online Secondary Information Sources

Type of Information	Sources
Demographics and population (online and offline)	US Census Bureau (www.uscensus.gov) Statistics Canada (www.statcan.ca) GVU WWW Survey (www.cc.gatech.edu/gvu/user_surveys) Angus Reid Group (www.angusreid.com)
Internet growth usage, segments, industry projections and performance	CyberAtlas (cyberatlas.com) Nua (www.nua.com) Forrester Research (www.forrester.com) Jupiter Communications (www.jup.com) Gartner Group (www.gartner.com) eMarketer (www.emarketer.com)
Foreign and domestic trade data, economic and business information	Department of Commerce (www.stat-usa.gov), see NTDB Industry Canada—Strategis (www.strategis.ic.gc.ca)
Competitive information	Lexis-Nexis (www.lexis-nexis.com) SEC's Edgar database (www.sec.gov/)
Patents	US Patent Office (www.uspto.gov) PATSCAN (www.library.ubc.ca/patscan/services.html) Canadian Intellectual Property Office (www.cipo.gc.ca)
Legal	International Trade Law (www.itl.uit.no/trade_law/) LEXum (www.lexum.umontreal.ca/index_en.html)
International business	ExportNet (www.exporttoday.com) International Chamber of Commerce (www.iccwbo.org) I-TRADE (www.i-trade.com) NAFTAnet (www.naftanet.com)
Industry-specific information	Dialog (www.dialog.com) Dun & Bradstreet (www.dnb.com)
Financial information	Edgar Database (www.sec.gov/edgarhp.htm) Dow Jones Interactive (www.djnr.com)
Financial news (daily)	CNNfn (www.cnnfn.com) CNBC (www.cnbc.com) Financial Post (www.financialpost.com)

(continued)

Table 5-1 (continued)

Type of Information	Sources
Sales and business leads	Hoover's (www.hoovers.com) Thomas Register (www.thomasregister.com)
Advertising and marketing	Advertising Age (www.adage.com) AdWeek (www.adweek.com) BrandWeek (www.brandweek.com) MediaWeek (www.mediaweek.com)

Note: This list includes free and commercial sources.

Commercial or Subscription Information Sources

In addition to free information, there are a number of commercial research companies that offer detailed, competitive, and market information based on subscription or usage fees. Commercial sources such as Dun & Bradstreet (www.dnb.com), Lexis-Nexis (www.lexis-nexis), Dow Jones Interactive (www.djnr.com), the US Commerce Department's National Trade Data Bank (www.stat-usa.com/tradtest.nsf), and Dialog (www.dialog.com) offer access to information and databases for a fee or subscription.

Exhibit 5-1 Strategis Site by Industry Canada

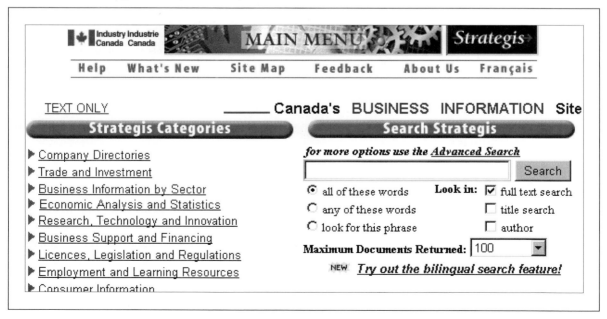

Source: www.strategis.ic.gc.ca.

Advantages Online Secondary Research

Amount of Information. Compared to what we had a few years ago, the Internet is a vast gold mine of information. Information on countries, products, patents filed by other companies, and the financial performance of competitors can all be found online easily.

Time and Cost. The traditional method of collecting secondary data from books, microfilms, and other sources can be expensive and time consuming. On the Internet, information sites generally provide search engines, which make information retrieval very easy. Information can be found fast and often at no cost.

Currency of Information. Government and private fee-based online databases are updated frequently or even daily. Unlike with print publications, you can obtain very recent information online.

Ease of Data Collection. Search engines make it easy to identify information on the Internet. Meta-search engines can search multiple directories or search engines. Intelligent search engines can offer more precision in search results (see iMarket Demo 5-1 for examples). As more databases and full-text online library sources become available, secondary research can be done entirely online.

Disadvantages of Online Secondary Research

Online secondary research does have some limitations, and you must be cognizant of these before drawing conclusions from secondary data.

Authenticity of Information. The cost of publishing on the Web is very low, and that has resulted in a plethora sites that claim to provide authentic information. For such sites, you must check the date on which it was last updated, who owns or operates it, and if the site has any external accreditation.

Reliability and Bias. Many free content sites are supported by advertising or have sponsors. Researchers must check to see if the site is providing a slanted version of events or data. Is the site biased towards its sponsors? Or is it objective in the presentation of information?

 Methodologies. When it comes to Internet growth, Web usage, and online shopping statistics, major research companies like Forrester Research (www.forrester.com), Jupiter Communications (www.jup.com), Nua (www.nua.com), and the Gartner Group (www.gartner.com) provide projections using different methodologies, so there are often inconsistencies in their conclusions.

Primary Research

The collection of data that previously did not exist is known as **primary research**. Primary research is initiated for studying a specific problem at hand.[8] Questions or problems that are specific to a particular organization require primary research. Primary research can answer questions such as what is the company's customer profile, why are sales declining, is the advertising campaign effective, and so on.

The traditional methods of undertaking primary research include surveys (administered by telephone, mail, or in person), focus groups, and experiments. On the Internet, it is possible to conduct surveys (via the Web or e-mail), focus groups, and experiments. The Internet also allows businesses to capture a great deal of consumer behaviour data based

iMarket Demo 5-1 Searching with Intelligence

No one knows the precise number of documents and pages on the Web. According to research firm Cyveillance, however, there were 2.1 billion Web pages as of July 2000. With roughly 7 million new Websites being registered each day, the volume of information on the Web will continue to grow at a phenomenal rate. The sheer volume of information makes it difficult for market researchers or competitive intelligence researchers to find what they want. Search engines are helpful to some extent, but often a search based on keywords can return thousands of pages from most major search engines.

Meta-search engines like AskJeeves, Metacrawler, Ixquick, and Chubba search several other search engines and report the results. Meta-search engines do not maintain their own databases or directories; instead they search other search engines like AltaVista, Lycos, and Infoseek. Meta-search engines can make secondary research more efficient by eliminating the need for searching several individual directories or search engines.

Some meta-search engines can eliminate duplicate listings and can aggregate results in one ranked list. Copernic and Web-Ferret are two downloadable meta-search engines that can be run from the user's computer. Most meta-search engines search only a small proportion of the sites listed in the various search engines. They may not all have the capability to handle complex searches. Some meta-search engines allow complex searches using Boolean operators (that is, they use the words AND, NOT, and OR to include or exclude items), as well as operators like opening and closing quotation marks to refine the search.

Intelligent search agents are somewhat more complex and more sophisticated than meta-search engines. Intelligent search agents are automated search intermediaries. The user can give specific commands to "target a particular location," or "go to certain directories," and "retrieve particular files." When launched, the agent travels along the Internet or other networks (Web sites, online databases, and so on), identifies the required files, and returns the files to the user's computer. It can then compare the retrieved files against the user's information needs (queries) and sort the files for relevance. Natural language queries and complex searches can be done. Some intelligent search agents offer extensive search and reporting features. Two examples are Intelliseek's Bullseye (www.intelliseek.com) and Satyam Computer Services' Searchpad (www.searchpad.com).

The average search engine may return thousands of pages for a search, but most of them are not relevant to the user's needs. With the advanced search tools, however, market researchers and competitive intelligence professionals who spend a lot of time searching for information can perform precisely targeted searches without wasting time.

Sources: J. Bourseton (2000), "Using Intelligent Agents for Competitive Intelligence," *Competitive Intelligence Magazine*, January–March, Vol. 3 (1); Meta Search Engines, April 2000, www.lib.berkeley.edu; Steve Collins (1997), "Seek and Ye Shall Find," *.net*, 27, January, pp. 50–66.

on Web surfing habits and online shopping preferences. Such data can also provide valuable insights.

Qualitative Research

Qualitative research involves gathering detailed information, mostly through conversation with participants in a study, using open-ended questions. This type of research is generally conducted in person using focus groups or in-depth interviewing techniques. The researcher may try to find patterns and common themes in the responses of different participants. This type of data, however, does not lend itself well to statistical analysis. Qualitative research, therefore, is generally used as exploratory research when the researcher does not have a full grasp of the problem.[9] In such cases, a qualitative study may be followed by a quantitative study (such as a survey or an experiment). Qualitative research may also be used as conclusive research, without further follow-up studies.

Qualitative research is very useful online for a number of marketing research applications. Product concept testing can be done via online focus groups, which is described in detail later in this section. Consumer evaluation of Web sites or online ads can also be done using focus groups.

Focus groups are used extensively in commercial market research. Focus group studies involve carefully selected small samples of eight to twelve individuals who are generally homogenous with respect to demographics, lifestyle, or some other important attribute.

Focus Groups on the Internet. Focus group research brings together a small group of consumers who are carefully selected. Often the researcher may want the participants to be homogenous in terms of demographics (such as age, gender, income), lifestyle characteristics, or purchase and consumption habits. The group is assembled in a room, where an independent moderator leads the discussion by asking questions. Representatives of the client firm can observe the discussion from an adjacent room via a one-way mirror. The transcript of the discussion is analyzed, based on the specific recommendations made to the client. This type of research is used extensively in product concept testing and ad copy testing.

Technology has made it possible to conduct focus groups without the need for a face-to-face setting. Using interactive, real-time chat applications, it is now possible to conduct an **online focus group** where participants can be anywhere in the world. Angus Reid, a leading Canadian market research firm, offers such an online focus group service to its clients (see Exhibit 5-2).

An online focus group discussion is similar to real-time (synchronous) chat on the Internet. Participants can be recruited from anywhere in the world (as long they have Internet access). They do not need to be in the same room, as is the case with a traditional focus group. Just as in the case of a face-to-face focus group, here too the moderator can control the discussion and ask probing questions. Participants may come from an online consumer panel or may be recruited specifically for a study.

The software application used to conduct online focus groups (see Exhibit 5-2) will allow the participants to type their comments and will also allow participants to see each other's comments. The space above the comment area is called a "white board," where the moderator can display pictures or play a video clip or even show a Web site. In a product testing study, the white board can be used to show a video demonstration of the product prototype.

Online focus groups have several advantages. First, the elimination of a face-to-face setting lowers the cost of conducting focus groups. Second, participants can be recruited from all over the world. Third, the Internet demographics at present are still skewed towards the

Exhibit 5-2 Angus Reid: Online Focus Group

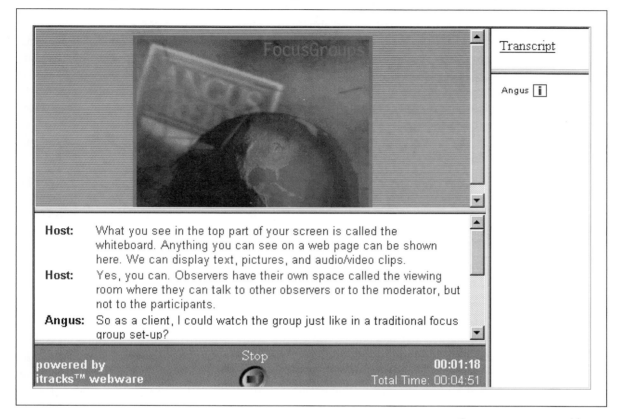

Host:	What you see in the top part of your screen is called the whiteboard. Anything you can see on a web page can be shown here. We can display text, pictures, and audio/video clips.
Host:	Yes, you can. Observers have their own space called the viewing room where they can talk to other observers or to the moderator, but not to the participants.
Angus:	So as a client, I could watch the group just like in a traditional focus group set-up?

Source: www.angusreid.com.

higher socio-economic segment (higher education and income). These consumers are generally trendsetters and early adopters of products. Their views on new products can be obtained via online focus groups. Fourth, the online environment offers anonymity to the participants.[10] They are not facing other participants or the moderator. Emboldened by this anonymity, participants may be willing to reveal their true feelings, leading to better results.[11]

The online focus group also changes the nature of group dynamics that occur in a discussion group. Groupthink (where individuals surrender their individuality), attitude polarization (where group opinions polarize towards extreme opinions held by some group members), and domination of the discussion by some participants are common occurrences in group situations.[12] Online focus groups may allow more equal participation.

On the Internet, communication apprehension (CA), which is the fear or anxiety associated with communication with others, may be reduced for some individuals.[13] There is some evidence that individuals may be less worried about what other people think and be more outspoken when communicating in a computer-mediated environment, such as the Internet.[14]

Critics, however, charge that online focus groups lack the richness and subtleties of the face-to-face environment.[15] Body language and facial expressions, which convey a lot of meaning in face-to-face conversation, are lost online. Some focus group moderators may encourage online participants to use **emoticons**, where certain characters are typed on the screen to denote certain facial expressions (for instance, the symbol :-) means the writer is joking or making a light-hearted comment).

Even though traditionalists discount such attempts to simulate face-to-face interaction, the real issue is whether online focus groups can provide ideas and insights that are comparable to face-to-face encounters. This is an area where more work is required from market researchers and social psychologists. Supporters of focus group research contend that it offers better results for topics like online ad testing and in the case of sensitive topics.[16] As bandwidth (the speed of data transmission on the Internet) increases through more widespread use of cable modems and DSL (a technology used by telephone companies), we may soon see the use of Internet video-conferencing for online focus groups. Windows NetMeeting software provides a glimpse of the possibilities.

Observational Research. Observing consumer behaviour through hidden cameras or by using in-store personnel is an old technique.[17] Just by observing consumers while they are shopping, researchers can get valuable clues on the consumer decision process. The Internet takes **observational research** to a new level. Web site tracking and the use of cookies, as discussed earlier, provide market researchers the opportunity to monitor consumer behaviour from behind the scenes. In a physical store, observational data can be obtained through hidden cameras or by in-store sales personnel. On the Internet, the technology allows for monitoring people's Web-viewing habits and preferences.

E-mail Newsgroup and Content Analysis. Companies like NetCurrents can provide valuable data on what consumers are saying about a company or its products in public forums like newsgroups. Online businesses can sponsor newsgroups or bulletin boards, thus allowing them to closely monitor consumer feedback. NetObjects, a software company, sponsors its own newsgroups where consumers talk about NetObjects' products (go to www.netobjects.com/), and help each other with problems. It also gives company staff firsthand knowledge of how customers use the product. Postings in bulletin boards and newsgroups can be analyzed to understand consumer perceptions, level of satisfaction, and more. Table 5-2 lists several market research organizations in Canada.

Quantitative Research

Quantitative research typically involves the use of surveys or experiments, which enable the researcher to gather data using structured questionnaires. The data collected are analyzed using statistical programs. Quantitative research is appropriate when the researcher has a fairly solid understanding of the problem and the specific variables that need to be measured. Two common approaches to quantitative research are surveys and experiments. Data collected through either approach can be analyzed using statistical programs or spreadsheets.

Surveys on the Internet. The Internet allows market researchers to implement surveys in two main forms: web-based surveys and e-mail surveys.

Web-Based Surveys. Participants can be recruited in different ways (see the section entitled "Recruiting Participants for Online Research" on page 121). **Web-based surveys** can be implemented using the form capabilities in HTML (which is the language used to construct Web pages). They can have various types of questions, such as check boxes (appropriate when the participant can check multiple responses to a question), radio buttons (appropriate when only a single response must be checked), drop-down menus, and open-ended questions. After the participant completes the survey, the survey can be submitted by clicking on

Table 5-2 Selected Canadian Online Market Research Firms

Firm	URL
Angus Reid Interactive	www.angusreid.com
iTracks	www.itracks.com
Clearpicture	www.clearpicture.com
SurveySite	www.surveysite.com
Manta	www.mantacorp.com
CF Group (Canadian Facts, Burke, ARC)	www.cfgroup.ca

a "submit" button. Forms are processed using a program called a CGI (common gateway interface) script. The script may be written in languages such as Perl. Interactive forms can also be designed using Java, a more robust programming language.

Even as researchers are becoming familiar with Computer Assisted Telephone Interviewing (CATI), Computer Assisted Web Interviewing (CAWI) is beginning to make an impact.[18] Web-based surveys can provide the researcher flexibility in designing the questionnaire, as well as a good degree of control over the data collection process. Table 5-3 lists several online survey companies.

Table 5-3 Selected Online Survey Solution Providers

Company	Feature
SurveySite	Best known for pop-up surveys, which open in a new window when the consumer is browsing through a Web site. The consumer is given the choice to respond or decline the offer. URL: www.surveysite.com
ClearPicture	Survey results are displayed immediately after respondent fills out the survey. Results are shown graphically. URL: www.clearpicture.ca
WebSurveyor	Will host online surveys for free and will send the data file to the researcher. URL: www.websurveyor.com
Perseus	Award-winning Web survey product, Survey Solutions. URL: www.perseus.com
Marketing Masters	Survey Said software can be implemented online or in a local area network (LAN); Java or HTML format. URL: www.surveysaid.com

E-mail Surveys. Unlike Web surveys, which are posted on a Web site and where participants are invited to complete the survey, e-mail surveys are sent to participants via e-mail. These surveys are easy to implement. Armed with an e-mail list of qualified participants, even a researcher with a small budget can collect data quickly. E-mail surveys do not require a very high level of computer skill. Thus, they have the potential of reaching participants all over the world and, in most cases, generating a very quick response.[19]

E-mail survey presentation is not as elegant as the Web-based survey. The survey appears in a text file (ASCII) format. This may make it harder to fill out than a Web survey. E-mail programs may also restrict the width of each line. If the survey exceeds this width, it may appear jumbled on the user's screen.[20]

There is some evidence that electronic surveys may provide a superior quality of response.[21] This may, however, be dependent on the nature of the topic and whether respondents opt to participate or if the survey is an unsolicited e-mail survey.

The increase in unsolicited e-mail surveys, which are perceived to be *spam* (or junk e-mail), is leading to lower response rates.[22] If the survey is sent to a panel (where members have agreed to participate in regular surveys) or a group of customers who have given permission to be e-mailed, then the response rate is likely to be higher.

Whether one chooses the Web-based survey or the e-mail option, questionnaire construction should be done according to accepted procedures. A multi-step process that includes defining the domain of the study, development of sample items, and pre-testing of sample items is recommended by experts.[23] The validity of the items in the questionnaire or scale (that is, are items measuring what they purport to measure?) and the reliability of the scales (that is, are they internally consistent and do they produce the same results over repeated administrations of the survey?) are important considerations.[24]

Experiments. Experimental research examines the cause-and-effect relationship between two or more variables.[25] The Web can be turned into a laboratory for testing various marketing stimuli (such as advertising) with real customers. For instance, a researcher who wants to find out the best design and layout for a site can do a controlled online experiment. It is possible to send visitors randomly to different versions of the homepage. Variables such as time spent on the site, navigational path, and purchases or other forms of interaction by the customer can be measured using tracking programs.

Similarly, ad copies can be tested online in, perhaps, one or two sites, before the full launch of the campaign. Again ads can be rotated randomly on the main page of a site, ensuring that a certain number of individuals see each version of the ad. Click-through and other responses can also be measured. As the respondent leaves the site, a pop-up questionnaire can be used to measure recall, attitude, purchase intent, and so on.

From site colour to price, every variable can be tested for optimal effect, and academic researchers are beginning to make use of the flexibility the Internet affords as an experimental laboratory.

Sampling Bias and Representativeness

Internet penetration has reached about 50 percent of the population in North America, but in other parts of the world adoption rates are much lower. For this reason, any study that requires a nationally representative sample should not be conducted online until the Internet reach is about 80 percent.

The typical Internet user is likely to have at least college education and is likely to be in a well-paid professional job. These consumers are likely to be innovators and more willing to try new products. Studies that require the opinions of trendsetters could be done on the Internet. On the other hand, in a given country if only 15 percent of users are women, online research would not be the best way to find out why women are not using the Internet. Similarly, a study with the objective of projecting or generalizing the results to the whole nation (such as a study on the attitudes of Canadians towards smoking) will have limited external validity or generalizability if it is conducted online.

Experts such as Andy Kohut, director of the Pew Research Center, point out that entire demographic groups are missed by Internet surveys. Offering an analogy, he says, "If I went down to K Street in Washington and interviewed people and adjusted the data, it wouldn't make them look like America."[26] Survey researchers often make corrections for **sampling bias**, but these tend to be corrections for small imbalances in the sample. When entire segments of the population are omitted, as in the case of the Internet where large groups of people have no chance of being selected for a survey, it is hard to correct such an imbalance. Kohut argues, as others have, that Internet surveys will be a lot more useful when Internet usage hits the 80 percent range from the present 40 to 50 percent penetration.

Telephone and mail surveys are typically based on a **random sampling** method, which ensures that each person in a known population has an equal chance of being selected to participate in the study. It is easy to draw a random sample in the case of telephone surveys since the listings in all the telephone directories combined are equal to the entire population. In the case of Internet surveys, however, no such national registry of e-mail addresses exists.

Researchers try to simulate random sampling online in a variety of ways. Content and E-commerce sites frequently do intercept surveys, where every nth visitor is randomly selected as they hit designated Web pages. Others randomly draw e-mail addresses from an opt-in database of clients. Pop-up surveys also allow for random sampling of visitors to a Web site. In this case, a small window pops up on the computer screen while the visitor is a viewing a Web page, with a request to participate in a study (see Exhibit 5-3). The visitor then has the option of participating or declining.

Since the Internet has a limited reach, many market research companies augment Internet data with data from traditional methods such as telephone or mail surveys. Each method of data collection has its own error rate and sampling bias. Researchers must ensure that the specific method of data collection (directly talking to a person in the case of telephone survey, or anonymously filling out a survey in the case of a Web survey) does not cause a bias in responses to the survey, and it is important to be cognizant of such issues while pooling data from different sources.

Recruiting Participants for Online Research

There are many methods of recruiting participants over the Internet. Web-based surveys have a self-selection problem.[27] Only those people who are online will have access to the survey. Out of these, only those who know that a survey has been posted on a Web site and are willing to take the time to fill out the survey will participate. In order to ensure that a vast number of people have the opportunity to participate in a survey, links or ads announcing the survey can be posted on high-traffic sites and portal sites. This may be expensive. The GVU WWW User Surveys at Georgia Tech University have successfully used this recruitment method (www.cc.gatech.edu/gvu/user_surveys/).

Another method is to use e-mail solicitations, where messages announcing the survey (and perhaps an incentive for participation) are mailed to a list of people or posted in relevant newsgroups. This approach should be used cautiously. Some research companies gather

Exhibit 5-3 Pop-up Survey by Survey Site

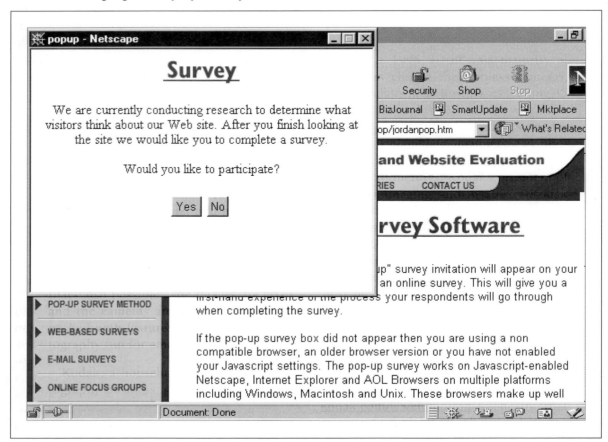

Source: www.surveysite.com.

e-mail addresses from the over 50 000 newsgroups, which represents the largest congregation of Internet users. Since a wide variety of discussion groups are available, it is possible to draw a fairly heterogeneous e-mail list.

Some market research companies are very successful in recruiting participants by telephone. A short telephone call can be useful in verifying a person's eligibility to participate. Upon such verification, the person can then be recruited to participate on a voluntary basis. Of course, all participants must have access to the Internet. Initial telephone screening will ensure that the final sample has the characteristics desired by the researcher.

Research companies such as Harris, Greenfield, NFO, and AC Nielsen use online panels to ensure high participation rates and quality of data. In Canada, Angus Reid and CF Group Inc. (which is part of NFO), two leading market research companies, use online panels. Panel research allows the research company to screen participants at the time of admission to the panel. A broad range of participants can be included on the panel. Panel members can be selected on the basis of a number of demographic and psychographic variables, as well as Internet usage behaviour. NFO Interactive, a leading market research firm, has an online panel of over 750 000 individuals in the United States. Angus Reid Worldwide has an online panel of over 60 000 individuals.

Panels allow research firms access to a qualified pool of participants. High response rates to surveys can often be achieved, whereas non-panel surveys rarely achieve more than a 20 percent response. Panel members are recruited through incentives and other awards. Tracking panels, such as the one used by AC Nielsen/Net Ratings to study Web site audience size, allow the research firms to track everything they do on the Internet. These are voluntary participants who willingly submit to tracking, and provide high-quality data.

The nature of the study, the budget, the timeframe of the project, and the type and depth of questions may dictate the sample and the recruitment method.

Online Market Research Applications

Online market research can be used for a variety of applications, including product concept testing and advertising copy testing. Web sites are using pop-up surveys to track consumer satisfaction with the site's design and content or products and services.

Site evaluation can be outsourced to companies like Site Survey. Through their InSite-Survey solution, they try to gauge what visitors like and dislike about a site, why they came to the site, and what they would like to see changed. Instead of relying on cookies and site log analysis exclusively to understand consumer behaviour, this approach allows online marketers to uncover the mindsets and motives of consumers.

BizRate.com offers independent exit surveys on many popular e-tail sites. After the customer has placed an order, a short survey may pop up in a new window. Satisfaction with price and other attributes is then captured, and the ratings are displayed publicly on BizRate's site. In another example of the Internet's openness, ratings of competing companies are displayed in product or industry groupings. This increases the pressure on businesses to perform. E-tailers can also implement their own customer satisfaction surveys, so listening to the customer is now more important than ever.

Businesses can also listen to their employees more easily now. Web-based employee satisfaction surveys are very inexpensive to implement. In a marketing application, the national sales force can be surveyed to gather market feedback and measure various aspects of job satisfaction.

Advantages of Online Primary Research

Cost. Surveys and focus groups can be done on the Internet at a fraction of the cost of conventional approaches. Compared to telephone and mail surveys, Web surveys are very inexpensive (see Exhibit 5-4 for a comparison of Web and telephone surveys). There are no long-distance charges or postage and photocopying charges. Online focus groups are also less expensive because participants can participate directly from their homes.

Time. Online surveys and focus groups can be done very quickly, compared to the traditional methods. Often, surveys posted on the Internet can get responses on the same day. The ease of filling out an online survey results in more prompt responses.

Interactivity. Surveys can be interactive. Based on the response provided by the participant to a question, a specific follow-up question may then be asked. This will allow for capturing more detailed information.

Consistency Checks. Since the Web-based survey is essentially a software application on the computer, it is easy to build in consistency checks in the form-processing program. If the responses to different questions are inconsistent, the program can display an error message on the screen.

Exhibit 5-4 Time and Cost in Web vs. Telephone Survey

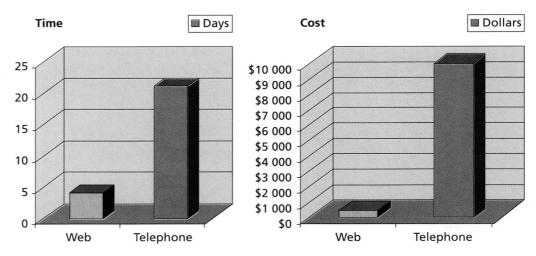

Source: Perseus Development Corporation (www.perseus.com).

Automated Data Entry. This applies to Web surveys. Since the survey is posted on a Web site using the "form" capabilities of HMTL, the data can be directly sent to a database. As each respondent fills out the survey and submits it, one more record will be added to the database. This eliminates the need for manual data entry, which can be costly and time consuming and is prone to error.

Ability to Target Innovators. Internet users tend to be highly educated with above-average incomes. These consumers tend to be the first buyers (innovators) of new products and services. Online surveys and focus groups can solicit the opinions of this very important consumer group.

Disadvantages of Online Primary Research

Representativeness. As discussed earlier, while the Internet demographics at this stage may allow researchers to target innovators and trendsetters, there are serious concerns about the representativeness of any sample drawn from Internet users. As more citizens have access to the Internet, any sample drawn from the Internet will start resembling the general population. We may reach this point in the next three to five years.

Authenticity of Responses. The same respondent may send multiple responses from different computers. The anonymity offered by Web surveys may prompt some to provide inaccurate responses. It is known that a large number of users who register for free e-mail services do not provide full and complete information as sought in the registration questionnaire. It must be noted that other methods of data collection are also susceptible to such problems.

The researcher must design the questionnaire with adequate cross-validation checks so that blatantly inaccurate information can be detected. Interactive Web surveys can offer some validation while the respondent is filling out the survey.

Length of Questionnaire. Most experts agree that online surveys cannot be very long.[28] A survey that takes more than ten minutes to fill out is likely to suffer from a poor response rate. Again, panel surveys can be more detailed because the panelists have agreed to submit information on a regular basis in exchange for incentives or rewards.

Online focus groups also tend to be a bit shorter than face-to-face focus groups. Some people may find it strenuous to type quickly and to stare at the computer screen for a long time.

Security Issues. Some survey software applications have the ability to instantly add the material to a database as the participant submits the online survey. The data must be backed up and stored securely to avoid break-ins or hacker attacks. It is not just the data that needs to be safeguarded, but also the personal information submitted by respondents. In the case of online focus groups, the research firm has to ensure that the participant is actually the person he or she claims to be. Proper verification and authentication procedures must be used.

Conduct in Online Focus Groups. Those who are familiar with newsgroups will know that "flaming" (the use of abusive language in response to another person's posting) can quickly lead to deterioration in the signal-to-noise ratio and bring down the quality of discussion or debate. Focus groups are not immune from this. Anonymity, which can at times be a strength, can also lead people to use abusive language or other forms of inappropriate communication. One market researcher referred to this behaviour as the "animal house" effect in online focus groups. Moderators have to know how to control the discussion, and eject any participant who does not follow the rules.

Non-PC Internet Devices. Consumers are beginning to access the Internet (for e-mail, news, and stock quotes, as well as shopping) through the use of handheld devices like cell phones and PalmPilots. Online surveys and focus groups can be conducted with great efficiency as long as consumers use their personal computers to connect to the Internet. As more and more consumers start using non-PC Internet devices, which is a highly likely scenario in the next few years, the current technologies used for online primary research will not work. Online researchers may have to find new ways of reaching consumers as new Internet devices gain consumer acceptance.

Consumer Tracking and Data Mining

In Vignette 5 we saw some aspects of consumer behaviour tracking on the Web. When used properly and ethically, such tracking can benefit consumers who seek more personalized and targeted services. Software programs can be used to track and store information including ad exposures or clicks, product searches, purchases in online stores, and personal preferences for customized services. In iMarket Demo 5-2 some of terminology used in consumer tracking is described.

By tracking consumer behaviour on the Web, marketers can profile consumers. **Consumer profiling** can involve the use of online surfing patterns, online purchase history, and even demographic data. Consumer profiling can allow marketers to target their products and messages to match the needs of each consumer. Customization of products and personalization of online experience does require the gathering of personal information.

Profiling is a controversial subject. Consumers fear that marketers may observe and collect personal information without authorization. As we saw in Vignette 5, there are ethical issues pertaining to the use of online consumer data that marketers must address.

In this section we will examine several consumer tracking methods, including the use of cookies and Web site logs. When a large site like Chapters.ca or GlobeandMail.ca attracts hundreds of thousands of consumers each day, tracking and analyzing behavioural data from these consumers is not an easy task.

iMarket Demo 5-2 Web Metrics and the Net Ratings War

Consumer tracking has now risen to a new level because of the Web. There are so many different metrics to gauge consumer behaviour. Advertisers who are looking for effectiveness measures now have so many options to choose from. Each measure, however, does have its limitations. But when used judiciously, the online marketer can learn a great deal about how consumers use the Web. Here is a review of some of the common Web metrics:

- *Click rate:* The number of times an Internet user clicks a mouse to link to another page or Web site, including advertisements. Click rates have dropped to below 1 percent and may be in the 3–10 percent range for very precisely targeted ads. Higher click rates may not lead to higher sales. Advertising is sold on the basis of click rates.

- *Hits:* The number of times a user visits a single file on the Web. Each Web page is made up of many files, including graphics and photographs. When a viewer visits a page, it may result in 20 or 30 hits, depending on how many image files are on that page. This is an ineffective and inaccurate way of measuring a site's popularity.

- *Eyeballs:* Number of people viewing a site.

- *Impressions:* The number of times a person is exposed to a Web page with a specific advertisement. It is the basic unit for selling advertising space online.

- *Page views:* The number of times a person sees a page of content.

- *Reach:* The percentage of all Web users within a given demographic group (Americans, women, teenagers) viewing a particular site.

- *Stickiness:* A casual term denoting the time people spend at a Web site and the number of repeat visits they make.

- *Unique visitors:* The number of different people who visit a Web site, excluding repeat visitors.

- *Unique pages per visitor per day/month:* The average number of different page requests made per day or month by people visiting a specific site or category.

- *Usage days per visitor:* Average number of days in the month a person visits a site.

In addition to these more common measures, some experts suggest that online marketers should be tracking several leading indicators or early warning signs. This can help in nipping a problem in the bud. It may lead to concrete solutions or strategies aimed at curbing the problem. Some of the measures include the following:

- *Number of visits per sale and browsers-to-buyers* (how many people merely view the site and how many actually buy). These measures tell if a large proportion of visitors to a site never buy a product. Studies show that typically only 5 percent of the visitors to an E-commerce site actually buy a product there. Marketers have to figure out how to "monetize" the traffic. The number of visits per sale can be monitored over time to see if visitors are being converted to buyers faster.

- *Number of days between visits* (frequency of repeat visits) and *number of return visits to the site*. These are indicators of loyalty. Given the high cost of marketing on the Web (discussed in Chapter 2), loyalty is crucial to building a successful online business.

Comparison of customers and non-customers, number of visits for customers versus non-customers, number of pages visited for customers versus non-customers, and the time spent on the site for customers versus non-customers. These measures can help determine how to convert non-customers into paying customers.

Many sites depending on advertising revenue are desperate to show high page views and high unique visitors. Hence, these metrics are taken very seriously. AC Neilsen, the company that does television ratings, also provides ratings of Web sites. Web traffic can also be monitored through other independent entities.

As many dot-com companies are strapped for cash, the leading indicator measures become very important. These metrics can say a lot about when and if a company will become profitable. As pressure from investors grows, dot-coms will be paying more attention to these metrics.

Sources: Hillary Appleman (2000), "Ratings That Know What You're Looking at, and When," *New York Times on the Web*, Special Section E-commerce, June 7; Cliff Allen (1999), "Leading Indicators of the Future," Clickz.com, October 12.

Data mining (also known as knowledge discovery in databases) techniques are employed in the analysis of the data described in this section. Data mining is defined as "the nontrivial extraction of implicit, previously unknown, and potentially useful information from data."[29] Statistical techniques, artificial intelligence tools, and graphic or visualization techniques are used to convert raw data into knowledge that is meaningful to people.

Cookies. When a user visits a site, the site's server (computer on which the Web site resides) requests a unique ID from the user's browser. If this browser does not have such an ID, the server sends an ID. This information is contained in a small text file called a cookie file, which is stored on the user's computer hard disk. The next time the user visits the same site, the browser can send the unique ID to the server. This will enable that Web site to recognize the user's computer. The information contained in a cookie file may not make sense to the average Internet user (see Exhibit 5-5), but cookies do have several useful applications.

Easy Shopping. Sites like Amazon.com may use cookies to make shopping online easier. If a consumer orders a book and places it in the shopping cart, that information may be stored in the form of a cookie. This would enable the consumer to browse other sections of the Web and perhaps add some more items to the shopping cart. Since the cookie keeps track of orders, when the consumer is ready to checkout, all the correct items would be displayed on the order form. The Canadian book-seller Indigo.ca requires the use of cookies when customers purchase products on that site.

Exhibit 5-5 **Inside a Cookie File**

```
# Netscape HTTP Cookie File
# http://www.netscape.com/newsref/std/cookie_spec.html
# This is a generated file!  Do not edit.

kcookie.netscape.com      FALSE   /       FALSE   4294967295        kcookie  <s
www.credit-suisse.com     FALSE   /home   FALSE   963119981         performanc
.go.com TRUE      /       FALSE   1924991981        InfoseekUserId 9ECF013161
.ama.org          TRUE    /       FALSE   2051222878        SITESERVER       ID
.doubleclick.net          TRUE    /       FALSE   1920499140        id        80
.amazon.com       TRUE    /       FALSE   2082787183        ubid-main        07
www.thestandard.com       FALSE   /       FALSE   963589120         survey2000
.chapters.ca      TRUE    /       FALSE   1262321747        mscssid BVA3UTPC83
www.chapters.ca FALSE     /       FALSE   1262322372        ShopperManager%2F
.excite.com       TRUE    /       FALSE   1061159024        UID      3AFEE548DF
.excite.com       TRUE    /       FALSE   1061159024        registered       no
www.redherring.com        FALSE   /       FALSE   1293839969        AnalysisUs
ads.admonitor.net         FALSE   /       FALSE   1293837159        ID        20
.verticalnet.com          TRUE    /       FALSE   2051222074        SITESERVER
.foodingredientsonline.com        TRUE    /       FALSE   1262303692        SI
.mysimon.com      TRUE    /       FALSE   1276548417        a        2D32313432
..tdbank.ca       TRUE    /       FALSE   1293839938        RMID     c8be101239
.altavista.com TRUE       /       FALSE   1388491175        AV_USERKEY       AV
.harrisinteractive.com    TRUE    /       FALSE   2051222376        SITESERVER
.bizrate.com      TRUE    /       FALSE   1276698822        br       9613388484
.northernlight.com        TRUE    /       FALSE   1592099530        nltr      B-
.canada.com       TRUE    /       FALSE   2051222896        SITESERVER       ID
```

Serving Targeted Ads. Assume a frequent visitor to GlobeandMail.ca reads the financial news every time. Using cookies, a pattern of usage can be established. This would allow GlobeandMail.ca to serve targeted ads that focus on online trading, insurance, or other financial services.

Cookies can also be used to track how many times a user has been exposed to a specific ad copy. This will enable advertising networks such as DoubleClick and Flycast, which control online ad placement, to serve new copies at appropriate times. This will eliminate "banner burnout" from overexposure to the same ad.

Personalized Content. The most significant application of cookies is the ability they offer online content and service providers to personalize or customize the content. For instance, My Yahoo! is a customized service provided by Yahoo!. Users can choose the look and feel of their Yahoo! page and also choose what categories or news topics they want displayed on their personalized Yahoo! pages. In order to deliver such personalized services, Yahoo! must to be able to identify a user each time he or she logs on to the Yahoo! account.

Effective Selling. If a consumer had a pair of slacks from LL Bean in her shopping cart and this shopping cart was written as a cookie file, LL Bean could read the cookie file and offer a complementary product such as a shirt or belt with a price discount. The implication and extent of cross-selling is unlimited.

Limitations of Cookies. Cookies do, however, have several limitations. First, cookies track "computers" not "consumers." This was true until DoubleClick started associated demographic data with online tracking data. In general, if more than one individual uses the same computer, cookies cannot differentiate one user from the other. Second, cookies can be turned off in Netscape and Internet Explorer browsers. In Netscape, a user can go to the Advanced option under Preferences (in the Edit tab) and then choose "Disable Cookies." This would ensure that no cookie files are sent back to the user's computer. This would prevent sites from tracking shopping or Web browsing information about the user, but would also prevent the user from shopping in some sites.

Second, there are programs such as Buzof, Cookie Monster, and Cookie Pal, which allow users to manage cookies. They can remove cookie files from their computer, thus preventing companies from tracking their online behaviour. Users can also routinely delete their cookie files, thus preventing businesses from establishing a pattern of user behaviour.

Third, non-computing Web-enabled devices such as WebTV and mobile phones are read-only devices where cookie files cannot be written. However, we may see new forms of tracking for such devices in the future.

Last but not least, consumers are also very wary of the fact that their online behaviour is being tracked. Consumers are raising genuine privacy concerns, and businesses must be sensitive to these concerns.

Web Site Logs. It is possible to learn a great deal about an Internet user by using tracking or site log programs. Web site log analysis programs come in many forms with a wide price range.[30] Site log programs will capture information such as the page from which someone came to the site (the referring page), the IP address of the user's computer (which is a unique address or numerical code given to each computer connected to the Internet), pages seen inside the site, the amount of time spent in the site, repeat visits, key terms used in search engines, the user's computer operating system and type and version of browser (Netscape or Internet Explorer), and much more.

Site logs can, for instance, indicate if a site where your business is advertising is actually sending traffic to your site. By capturing information about the user's computer system and type of browser, businesses can design sites that most consumers can see. By knowing the type of browser and the version (Netscape Navigator 3.0 or Netscape Communicator 6.0), Web designers will know how technically sophisticated a site can be. Examples of site log analysis can be found in many sites on the Internet (see www.ussailing.org/reports/).

Site log analysis, while useful, does have a number of limitations.[31] First, for sites that have a lot of pages and attract a lot of traffic, site logs can become very voluminous. A powerful computer has to be devoted to capturing the visitor information. In addition to the routine reports produced by site log programs, statistical analysis may be required to deduce usage patterns.

Second, when a user goes to a Web site, the contents of the pages visited may be stored in the cache memory of the user's computer. On a subsequent visit to that same Web site, the pages may be served from the cache rather than the Web server that is hosting the site. This would result in the site log program missing or undercounting some page views. Third, site logs cannot perform activities such as FTP downloads or streaming content downloads (through RealPlayer, for example) that occur from non-HTML servers.

In spite of these limitations, Web site log analysis is a useful way of keeping track of usage patterns and studying peak time and slack time usage volumes. Sites that require very basic analysis can use free services such as NedStat (www.nedstat.com). There is a vast array of software tools from a few hundred to a few thousand dollars in price. Web Trends, Hot List Pro, Aria, Market Focus, Sitescope, and Surf Report are some of the commercial programs.

The advanced packages can provide real-time reports and three-dimensional graphical presentations of data. They can also allow the webmaster to export the site log data into statistical or spreadsheet programs.

Online firms can do their own site traffic analysis with the help of one of the commercial programs, or outsource this service to entities like NedStat.com or WebSiteTrafficReport.com. Outsourcing will be a cost-effective solution for smaller companies that do not have the financial or technical resources.

Online Shopping Data. In bricks-and-mortar stores it is rather difficult to collect shopping data on consumers. What products does a consumer buy regularly? If a marketer knows the answer to this question, then sales promotions and coupons can be targeted to match the purchasing habits of each consumer. In the past, only retailers who required a membership, such as Costco and Columbia House, could track shopping behaviour with consistency. The Internet, however, has made it very easy to capture this kind of shopping data on individuals and create a customer database.

Amazon.com, for instance, tracks purchasing as well as browsing behaviour to make recommendations to customers. If a customer has previously purchased a book on European modern art, that person may receive recommendations on several new titles in the same area on his or her next visit to Amazon.com. Amazon.com also sends book recommendations, based on previous purchases, via e-mail.

On the Internet, most E-commerce companies require consumers to provide detailed personal information at the time of ordering. Information collected while setting up an account/membership or while processing an order can include name, address, credit card, phone, e-mail, preferences with respect to other products, and so on. Postal code and street address data can be used with programs like MapInfo (www.mapinfo.com) or other Geographic Information System applications to conduct further demographic or market segmentation analysis.

E-mail and Newsgroup Messages. E-mail messages and postings in **Usenet newsgroups** can be a vital source of information. Postings in public chat rooms, bulletin boards, and Usenet groups can reveal consumer attitudes toward a company or its products. There are over 50 000 newsgroups and literally hundreds of thousands of bulletin boards. These are public forums that marketers cannot control. At these venues, there are likely to be both positive and negative comments posted. Newgroups can reach a worldwide audience, so negative information posted on these sites can be very damaging to the company's reputation.

NetCurrents.com is among several online research companies that will monitor newsgroups and bulletin boards on behalf of other companies. Companies can use this service to contain negative word-of-mouth and the spreading of false rumors, and also to learn about consumers' opinions. NetCurrents' CyberFacts program tracks a targeted universe of message boards, e-publications, newsgroups, and Internet locations. NetCurrents identifies comments as positive, negative, or neutral and uses this data for statistical tracking, online perception measurement, reporting, and making strategic recommendations.

Deja.com (see Exhibit 5-6) is one of many sites through which Internet users can access over 35 000 Usenet newsgroups. Deja.com allows for searching the content of these newsgroups using keywords. In addition to Deja.com, meta-search engines like Chubba (www.chubba.com) can also be used to search for Usenet newsgroup content.

Newsgroups allow for free-flowing, usually unmoderated discussion. Usenet newsgroups are not limited to discussions about products and companies. They cover thousands of top-

Exhibit 5-6 **Deja.com: Search Usenet Newsgroups**

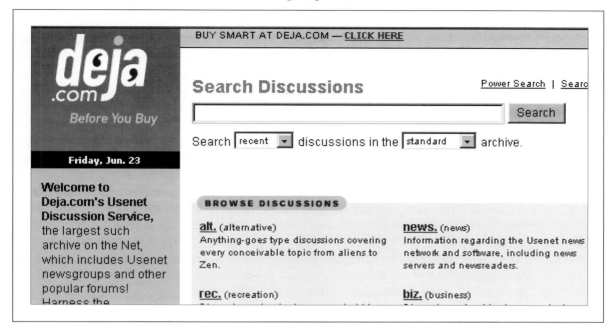

Source: www.deja.com/usenet.

ics and are rather unwieldy. Sites like Epinions.com offer a more structured environment for consumers to post their opinions. Epinions.com offers the opinions of individual consumers and self-proclaimed product experts on over 100 000 products. Before the Internet, word-of-mouth was limited to a few friends and family members. Now individuals can share their views literally with the world.

Monitoring relevant bulletin boards, chat rooms, and newsgroups can provide companies with insight into consumers' real opinions and feelings. It is important to note that postings in these forums are not in response to a questionnaire. Marketers can find more revealing insights when consumers are sharing their feelings and experiences informally with other consumers.

Site logs, cookies, and online shopping data can reveal some aspects of consumer behaviour. These methods, however, cannot reveal what motivates consumers or what they think and feel.[32] Getting this sort of information requires other forms of primary research, using qualitative and quantitative research methods.

Competitive Intelligence Online

Competitive intelligence (CI) is not a one-time or sporadic effort to understand the competition. It is an ongoing process and a systematic approach to studying the competition. By establishing a CI program, a company can avoid mistakes by learning from the competitors, anticipate competitive threats before they affect the company, and on the whole make better decisions.[33]

Even as firms embark on establishing online CI, they need to realize that their competitors may do the same. The Internet makes some aspects of a business's operations transparent and makes every firm susceptible. Creating extranets or password-protected pages for clients or other external partners is one way of shielding sensitive information from public exposure. CI has gained significant momentum as a discipline since the advent of the Web.[34]

Table 5-1 (see page 112) lists a small sample of sites and online databases that can provide valuable competitive information. From patent filings of competitors (which can tell you what new products they may unveil) to financial information (through filings on stock exchanges) and competitors' job vacancies (which may reveal their growth strategy), the Internet makes it easier to develop detailed profiles on each competitor.

A company that wishes to establish a CI program has to start by subscribing to several of the leading online databases. The online component of a CI program should also involve the monitoring of competitors' Web sites. Most firms post their press releases and annual reports. Many even provide archives of such material. These documents can help in developing a detailed history. In addition, detailed product and price information, as well information on their strategies, can be gathered from regularly visiting competing businesses' sites. Some firms even send online mystery shoppers to competing sites to document the online experience.

CI, while heavily dependent on secondary research, is not limited to such research. Newsgroup postings can reveal the problems consumers may have with a competitor's product or if they are satisfied with the service experience provided by a competitor. Online focus groups and surveys can also help in understanding how consumers or channel partners perceive competitors.

Searching on the Internet is an important activity in competitive intelligence gathering. This means that efficiency and accuracy in searching is important. Some of the tools available for improving search efficiency and accuracy are described in iMarket Demo 5-1 (page 115). In particular, meta-search engines and intelligent agents are essential for anyone who does secondary research on the Internet.

While a complete discussion of CI is beyond the scope of this book, it must be emphasized that the Internet is simply one of the many ways of gathering intelligence. Internet research does not eliminate the need for other forms of research. For instance, talking to former employees of competitors and gleaning news from the mass media can also provide very useful insights on competitors.

As the inimitable Yogi Berra once said, "You can see a lot by just watching." The Internet allows marketers to learn a lot—if only they will care to look.

Ethics in Online Research

At the beginning of this chapter we saw some examples of ethical dilemmas facing online marketers and researchers. No other technology has had this ability to track and monitor consumers as the Internet does. Overzealous marketers can intentionally or unintentionally violate consumer privacy and confidentiality rights.

Professional market research associations, such as PMRS (Professional Market Research Society) and ESOMAR (World Association of Research Professionals) also have guidelines for conducting research ethically (see the ESOMAR guideline for Internet research is included in Appendix D). These guidelines cover seven broad areas, including voluntary participation by the respondents, respondents' right to anonymity, ensuring data security, and securing adult permission when interviewing minors.

While traditional market research firms subscribe to the guidelines of ESOMAR or other professional bodies, E-commerce companies are not bound by any such guidelines. Online advertising networks and others who collect consumer information on the Web have proposed self-policing. An industry association, Network Advertising Initiative or NAI (www.networkadvertising.org), has been proposed to police consumer tracking.[35] Part of the proposal is to allow consumers to "opt-out," whereby they can use special Internet cookies that will prevent companies from gathering data about them.

NAI's stance against critics of the online advertising industry is simply that online advertising is essential to provide all the free services and content that consumers enjoy on the Internet. In order for this business model to work, consumers have to share some information with advertisers, who can then better target their communication and create more personalized services.

The Internet has made businesses recognize the power of information and knowledge. As we have seen throughout this chapter, it also gives businesses access to an incredible amount of information about consumers. With such access comes the responsibility of ensuring consumer privacy and undertaking ethical research, and we must remember that what is legal is not always ethical.

TRUSTe (www.TRUSTe.com) is an independent online organization that has laid down a protocol for consumer privacy protection. Sites that carry the TRUSTe symbol are expected to adhere to their standards (see Chapter 13 for a more detailed discussion). While the symbol itself may provide some assurance, consumers must read the privacy policy of each company and take adequate precautions if they are concerned about online privacy. Toysmart, an online toy store owned by Disney, was in court when it went bankrupt and tried to sell its customer database. The company had promised its customers that the information they provided would not be shared with or sold to any third party.

While ethical companies will adhere to good business practices whether offline or online, with or without the TRUSTe seal, there are too many others who will not. Online market research has a lot of benefits, as we have seen in this chapter. However, its potential may not be fully realized if consumers do not trust online market researchers and e-tailers who gather consumer data.

Summary

The Internet has created access to information and knowledge that was previously very difficult or expensive to obtain. From a business intelligence perspective, it allows organizations to monitor competition, consumers, and market trends on an ongoing basis without having to incur huge outlays.

Secondary research on the Internet can provide market researchers and competitive intelligence professionals with detailed information about competing firms. Much of this information is publicly available and easily accessible from government sites and online databases. There are a vast number of information brokers who are collecting, packaging, and reselling valuable business information. These services often provide access based on subscriptions or user fees. Secondary research has become easier due to the availability of meta-search engines and intelligent search agents, which can handle very refined searches and queries.

Online firms employ various continuous tracking programs, including cookies and site logs. These programs allow businesses to develop a user profile and customize services to meet the tastes of each user. They allow businesses to cross-sell, up-sell, and improve their online marketing efforts.

Primary data collection on the Internet includes both qualitative and quantitative methods. Online focus groups are now common in the market research community. Online surveys can be implemented via the Web or through e-mail. Online data collection through primary research methods is relatively inexpensive, it has the potential of reaching participants worldwide, and it can be completed speedily.

Both primary and secondary research methods online can be used to study consumers as well as competitors. Each research method described in this chapter has its strengths and weaknesses, so the researcher should carefully select the method based on the nature of the problem being studied.

Gathering personal information about consumers on the Internet and aggressive competitive intelligence gathering have led to concerns about the ethics of online research. Ethical research practices require market researchers to abide by consumer privacy rights. Ethical standards set by professional organizations such as the PMRS and ESOMAR should also be rigorously followed.

Key Terms

Business intelligence, 109
Competitive intelligence, 109
Consumer profiling, 125
Cookies, 127
Data mining, 127
E-mail surveys, 120

Emoticons, 117
Observational research, 118
Online focus groups, 116
Primary research, 114
Random sampling, 121

Sampling bias, 121
Secondary research, 111
Usenet newsgroups, 130
Web-based surveys, 118
Web site logs, 129

Questions and Exercises

Review Questions

1. Describe the process of conducting marketing research.
2. What is the difference between primary and secondary research?
3. What are the strengths and weaknesses of online focus groups?
4. What are the strengths and weaknesses of Web-based surveys?
5. What are the different methods of recruiting participants for online primary research?
6. How useful are cookies as a means of tracking online consumer behaviour? Provide examples.
7. How can the Web be used for gathering information about competitors?
8. Identify at least five methods of measuring online marketing effectiveness.

Discussion Questions

1. An online advertiser is interested in finding out if that company's online ads are effective. First, select one or more effectiveness measures that you consider appropriate for this context. Then, suggest one or more research methods (qualitative or quantitative) that can be used to study the effectiveness of online advertising. Outline the steps involved in conducting this research project.
2. An online content and E-commerce site has found out through member registrations that the vast majority of its regular visitors are young adults (aged 19 to 23 years). The site's owners are keen on expanding the usage to other age cohorts, especially those over age 30, who have more purchasing power.

What research method would be appropriate in determining: (a) whether consumers over age 30 would be interested in the content and products offered by this site, and (b) why these consumers are currently not visiting the site.

3. How can consumer privacy be protected and guaranteed, while allowing online marketers to enhance their marketing effectiveness?

Internet Exercises

1. Assume you are representing a PC manufacturer (such as Dell or Compaq). Your task is to gather competitive intelligence on one of your main rivals (of your choice). Prepare a basic competitive intelligence report by using online secondary research. Use the company site as well as third party sites. List all references at the end of the report. The report should cover the following: (a) names of senior managers; (b) countries where the product is marketed; (c) product range, brands, and prices; (d) financial performance in the last two years—revenue, net profits, retained earnings, earnings per share (EPS); (e) current share price, with 52-week high and low; and (f) major strategic initiatives and any new products or business alliances introduced in the past 12 months.

2. Browse through the GVU WWW User Survey site (www.cc.gatech.edu/gvu/user_surveys/). Study the General Demographics section from the 3rd through the 10th surveys. Prepare a table showing the demographic changes and trends for the following variables: (a) gender, (b) average age, (c) median income, (d) location, (e) marital status, and (f) occupation. What conclusions can you draw from the trends found in your table? What are the managerial implications for online marketers?

Chapter 6

Marketing Organization and Strategy

Vignette 6 **Boo Is Back**

After completing this chapter, you will:

- Understand organizational issues involved in designing an online business.
- Appreciate the fundamentals of designing an effective online strategy.
- Gain an understanding of a framework that can be effective in the strategy development process.
- Become familiar with the elements of an online marketing plan.
- Be able to apply this knowledge to critique the actions of a firm or to formulate a strategy for a firm.

Many Internet companies that were once the darling of Wall Street and investors are falling by the wayside like balloons without air. The casualties include some high-profile companies like Toysmart (majority owned by Disney), Pop.com (started by movie mogul Steven Speilberg), Brandwise (backed by the Hearst Corp.), and Boo.com (with an estimated $135 million investment). So what's going on? Why are so many companies struggling or failing? At least some of what's happening can be explained if we look at the companies' strategies or lack thereof.

Boo.com, perhaps the most expensive casualty, has emerged as a case that business schools may use for some time. The company was started by Swedish 28-year-olds, Kajsa Leander and Ernst Malmsten, who readily admit they were not knowledgeable about the Internet. They had a vision—to create the first truly global Internet company selling fashion products. Investors such as J.P. Morgan and Bain Capital backed the company. Some of the best-known names in fashion, such as Louis Vuitton and Benetton, were also behind this venture.

The founders' dream was to create a "cool" and "hip" site that would be the ultimate in Web shopping. The products ranged from casual to athletic wear, and the site allowed users to rotate clothes on display to see the product from different angles. There were even virtual mannequins that could be used to try on clothes. Consumers could search for products by brand, clothing type, or even the nature of the sporting activity.

The site was designed in six languages and consumers could choose 35 different countries as their country of origin. Payment was accepted in many local currencies, not just US dollars. As part of its global strategy, the company had offices in London, Paris, Munich, Stockholm, and New York. The company, at one time, had over 300 employees.

The name "boo" was deliberately chosen to be vague with a mystic appeal. The phrase "Miss Boo" apparently meant "a little girl." Miss Boo, a 3-D shopping assistant featured on the site, provided answers to questions about products, sizes, and so on. The site was technology-heavy.

Boo.com's advertising budget ran into the millions of dollars, with the ad agency DDB Needham in charge of creating a funny and somewhat shocking series of ads. The image was a site where fantasies came true. The premium pricing on the site was intended to create a high-quality image. In fact, some products were said to have gross margins over 100 percent.

The huge investment, backing from well-known investors, partnerships with leading fashion brands, a global presence, and an image intended to appeal to the youth market were all part of a plan for creating a truly global E-commerce site. Boo.com thought that such massive entry strategy would to some extent inoculate the company from direct competition. Founder Ernst Malmsten was quoted as saying, almost arrogantly, "Who is going to be our competition?"

It turned out that Boo.com didn't need a rival. The company was its own worst enemy. In less than a year, the company collapsed. First, the site was too technology-heavy and slow to download. While the site was slick and appealing to its intended target market, the heavy use of Java and Flash animation made surfing the site a painful experience for the vast majority of home Internet users, who had slow modems. The users' comfort didn't seem to be the primary concern of those who designed the site. Some of Boo's pages were four to six times the size of a typical Web page, and there weren't enough young users with high-speed Internet access in late 1999. Second, the high prices were not sustainable in all the countries.

Third, the two founders had absolutely no experience managing a multi-million-dollar global company. The company spent lavishly on advertising and corporate parties. Some experts claim the company could have been run out of one office, rather than six, and with just 20 percent of the staff.

Lastly, there didn't seem to be a great demand for such a global fashion site. While the Boo.com name became popular, the underlying concept of selling international brands to international consumers on the Web simply failed to capture the imagination of the intended audience.

The site launch was delayed several times due to various glitches. In the meantime, it benefited from huge publicity and media stories even before it was launched. That led to very high expectations. Boo.com was supposed to do for clothing and fashion sales online what Amazon.com has done for book sales. In terms of the image and

Exhibit 6-1 The New Boo

Source: www.boo.com.

execution, Boo.com and Amazon.com were polar opposites. Boo, unlike Amazon, sacrificed efficiency for style and slickness.

Now the old Boo.com is no more. The company closed up shop in less than year after its much-publicized launch. Creditors, including ad agencies, were owed millions of dollars. Fashionmall bought the brand and the site domain name (www.boo.com) for throwaway prices, and the back-end technology, which apparently cost millions to develop, was sold for less than $400 000.

Now Boo has been re-launched under new management and with a new philosophy. The new Boo.com (see Exhibit 6-1) may look similar to the old one at first sight. But the new Boo doesn't carry inventory as the old one did. When consumers click on a product, they are taken directly to the brand manufacturer's site or an authorized retailer's site. The new Boo is sort of a fashion portal, a gateway for finding the latest fashion apparel. Will the new Boo survive? Let's wait and see.

Sources: James Ledbetter (1999), "Boo.com's Bold Fashion Statement," *The Standard* (www.thestandard.com/article/display/0,1151,4525,00.html), May 10, 1999; "Boo Crystallizes the Dot Com Stock Rot," *IT-ANALYSIS.com* (www.it-analysis.com), May 22, 2000; "Boo.com: Is It the Start of the End?" *IT-ANALYSIS.com* (www.it-analysis.com), May 19, 2000; "US Fashion Portal Buys Boo Name," *BBC News* (news.bbc.co.uk), June 1, 2000; Carol Sliwa (2000), "Boo.com to Get New Life Under Fashionmall.com Label," *ComputerWorld* (www.computerworld.com), August 2, 2000.

Introduction

Gone are the days when investors threw money at every dot-com venture. The dwindling stock prices and the growing failure rate has focused attention on two key elements necessary for any successful business—a sound strategy and excellent execution. The vignette highlights this fact. Boo's concept was indeed innovative. They got so carried away by the technology and the image of a "global site," which led to their eventual downfall.

It is also evident from Vignette 6 that the reputation of the investors and the amount of money invested in a new online venture are not very good predictors of success. Online firms must get back to the basics—develop a sound business strategy and execute it well. The organizational structure and internal processes are critical to effective execution of strategy.

This chapter first presents a discussion of organizational issues that e-businesses must deal with, including organizational structure and culture. Following that, we will look at a framework for Internet marketing strategy, and finally, we will address important considerations in the Internet marketing strategy development process.

Organizational Issues in E-Business

The Internet, as we have seen in earlier chapters, is fundamentally altering business practices in many areas. It is also forcing companies to examine how they are organized internally. Boo.com is a case of a bloated organization with too many employees and too many global offices. Some see the flawed organizational structure as one of the reasons for Boo's failure.

The Internet has also forced many older companies, such as *Encyclopedia Britannica* (see iMarket Demo 2-1 on page 39), to reorganize rapidly. Even large companies like General Electric have decided that they have to embrace **e-business**, which not only includes E-commerce but also other processes like supply chain management and customer relationship management that leverage the Internet. While some companies have transformed themselves, others have seen the Internet as an appendage, meaning their internal processes and structures have changed little.

As we saw in the case of Boo.com, a worthwhile idea cannot succeed if the organizational structure is burdensome. The online marketspace is one that is fast-paced. The landscape changes rapidly. New technologies allow competitors to offer innovative services. Companies can forge relationships online with suppliers, customers, and partners in a manner that was not possible without the Internet. In such an environment, a company must be structured to allow for agility and innovation.

In the rest of this section, we will examine various organizational challenges and organizational structure issues. Emerging organizational models are also discussed. The organizational structure must be aligned with the strategy in order to effectively implement the strategy. This section looks at the organization as a whole, rather than focusing on just the marketing organization. This approach, explained in the rest of this section, is based on the idea that as companies embrace the Internet and gradually expand the nature of their activities online (from brochureware to E-commerce to customer relationship management, and so on), organization-wide processes will have to be changed (for older companies). In the end, effective Internet marketing will depend on having the right organizational structure in place.

Organizational Challenges

In the early days of online commerce, the term "going online" meant that a company was launching a Web site. Soon, many companies realized that adding a Web site could have far-reaching implications. It is not the same as launching a new print brochure. Volvo was one of the early companies to learn this lesson.

Integration of the Front End and Back End. Volvo was the first car manufacturer to go online. The site, launched in 1994, was intended to enhance brand image, be a selling tool, and create some loyalty. The site's only interactive feature, e-mail feedback, had rather unintended consequences. While Volvo anticipated laudatory messages from loyal consumers, what they got instead was a great deal of complaints.[1] In those early days of online commerce when Web sites were still a novelty, Volvo did not have qualified customer service people to support the site. As consumer complaints went unanswered or inadequately answered, customer dissatisfaction grew.

Volvo's experience stresses the point that organizations must fully understand the impact of their site and how consumers will use the site, and they must have the appropriate organizational structures and resources in place. Even now, many companies fall short of consumer expectations when it comes to customer service. A study by the Gartner Group found that even by the end of the second quarter of 2000, none of the top 50 sites received an "excellent" or "good" rating from consumers for their customer service.[2] Online companies as well as clicks-and-mortar operations are realizing that investment in customer service is essential for customer retention.

The Culture: Old vs. New. Many of the so-called "old economy" companies were simply unprepared for the Internet revolution. While they had the financial and human resources, as well as the physical infrastructure (such as warehouses), they were unsure of the potential scope of the Internet. As a result, there was a great deal of lethargy in their online activities. Examples include such giants as Wal-Mart and the Bay.

Wal-Mart has shown a reluctance to merge its offline and online operations into a seamless experience for consumers. Wal-Mart.com has been set up as a separate company with its own board and management team.[3] It is almost as if they do not want the old to burden the new. The problem is that when a consumer buys a product at Wal-Mart.com, he or she may expect to be able to return it at a local Wal-Mart store if necessary. The twin-organizations approach makes it harder to achieve the integration that consumers expect.

Many large organizations like Wal-Mart, Kmart, Safeway, and P&G have invested in online spin-off ventures. The bureaucracy in some of the older companies can stifle innovation and may not be conducive to a fast, real-time response that is essential for online enterprises. Creating a separate new venture may allow the company to unleash its potential, but complexity will increase greatly when the new venture and the old start speaking to each other. Managing customer expectations, maintaining a high level of service on delivery modes (online or offline), and integrating different delivery modes so that consumers can choose their preferred method of delivery are difficult challenges.

On the other hand, new start-up companies, armed with venture capital, have been much bolder and willing to experiment. While Internet pure-plays like CDNow allow consumers to customize products, the sites of older companies like Columbia House and BMG are less innovative.

Clearly, old companies have a bigger challenge as they try to leverage the assets of the traditional business with the opportunities online to create an online competitive advantage. There is bound to be tension between the two operations if the Internet operation is perceived as getting preferential treatment. At the same time, older companies will have assets, from brand name to an existing sales force, which can be leveraged online.

Senior Management's Role. When old companies take the first step towards going online, there is often confusion regarding who is responsible for the online presence. In many cases, the Information Technology or MIS department have been assigned the responsibility of managing the online presence and operations. As we saw in Chapter 2, the Internet has the ability to significantly alter a firm's value chain—end to end. That means that the decision to launch a site or to take a company online must be a strategic decision, and senior management's vision and participation are essential. It cannot be a decision for the technical staff alone.

In one study on the adoption of business-to-business E-commerce, it was found that companies that had senior management support and vision were far ahead of companies that lacked such support.[4] Jack Welsh, the venerable CEO of General Electric, is credited with the vision for the transformation GE is still undergoing. The giant conglomerate, which includes a diverse array of businesses from network and cable television to airplane engines, now sees itself as an e-business. As part of a multi-pronged strategy that included elements such as globalization, service focus, and superior quality, Jack Welsh required all GE divisions to have an E-commerce and e-business strategy. To focus the business units' attention on the urgency of the e-business strategy, he created a "destroy-your-business-dot-com" initiative within each business unit.[5] This strategy not only provided new growth opportunities for many of GE's mature businesses, but it also led to a superior financial performance in 1999.[6] This senior management vision, commitment, and support is critical to turning old economy companies to new economy successes.

Challenging the Legacy Mindset. The previous two sections on culture and senior management responsibility lead to a more basic, but related issue in older companies. Getting employees to think in new ways and getting them to shed the legacy (traditional) mindset is not easy. Some old companies are bringing in new outside managers, who are Internet savvy, to manage the online ventures or the transition from the old to the new. The belief is that fresh leadership with new ideas is necessary to shake things up. At the same time, it is important that people familiar with the traditional business have a stake in the new online operations. These are people with in-depth knowledge of the business and industry and are a valuable resource to the organization.

Wal-Mart.com seems to have achieved the delicate balance between the old and the new. The board of the new venture includes the Chairman and the COO of Wal-Mart Stores, Inc., the parent company.[7] At the same time, operations of the new venture are in the hands of a new management team.

The other area where E-commerce ventures require different thinking is with respect to performance measures. Internet ventures typically invest heavily up front in marketing efforts to lure customers to their site and to build the brand.[8] The payoffs, if traditional measures such as return on investment (ROI) are used, are unlikely to materialize in the short term. Even Amazon.com, the largest B2C site, has yet to make a profit as of the end of the third quarter of 2000. This is not to suggest that profitability measures should be ignored. They are critical. A company that wants to maximize short-term profits, however, is likely to underfund the marketing initiatives necessary to build the brand, create traffic, and motivate consumer loyalty. While keeping an eye on financial performance, Internet ventures, at least at this relatively early stage of online commerce, require a more flexible investment strategy with a long-term horizon.

Financial and Human Resources. New Internet companies, especially in the United States, did not have a lot of trouble getting venture capital funding and other strategic partnerships until 1999. The many high-profile dot-com failures since then (see Vignette 6 for example) have led to a cooling-off period. Many venture capitalists and angel investors are wary of business-to-consumer start-ups. The outstanding ideas will likely still find investors, but investors are more selective now than they were in 1998.

Old-economy companies, especially the larger ones like GE and Wal-Mart, have lots of internal resources. As these companies move forward with their E-commerce strategies, they are likely to have certain advantages. Unlike Internet pure-plays, which start with a Web site and then gradually acquire the expensive physical infrastructure (office building, warehouses, fulfillment operations, and so on), older companies already have the infrastructure in place. They also have the advantage of recognized brands that consumers trust.

Wal-Mart is a case in point. After waiting on the sidelines for many years, the retail giant has made a big move online. Wal-Mart.com offers over 600 000 products and a wide array of services, such as travel reservations.[9] Even as Amazon.com was being labelled the "Wal-Mart of the Internet," Wal-Mart has made its intentions clear by making a significant online presence. The company also has a joint venture in Europe with AOL, intended to establish the Wal-Mart brand in Europe.[10]

In addition to the financial resources, pure-plays and old-economy companies must find talented people to manage the business. Technical as well as managerial expertise is at a high premium. There is a projected shortfall of skilled workers with IT and software expertise in the US, Canada, and Europe. New companies have been attracting senior executives from older companies. The excitement of doing something cutting-edge and the stock options are incentives used to attract both managerial and technical talent.

As we saw in the case of Boo.com, if a company's workforce grows too quickly and outpaces revenue growth, that could spell trouble. In the first two quarters of 2000, several dot-coms have laid off workers and downsized their operations. Whether an organization is an old-economy company going online or a new company, a proper strategy for recruiting and retaining employees must be put in place.

Developing and Designing the Internet Organization

Once a grasp of the organizational challenges is gained, a firm must plan its organizational structure. Pure-plays and old-economy companies, including bricks-and-mortar companies that go online, have different challenges here. In this section we will consider issues surrounding the selection of organizational structure.

From Brick to Click or Click to Brick

New Internet start-ups and online spin-off ventures of old companies that operate only in the online marketspace, and not in the physical marketplace, are considered pure-plays. Most bricks-and-mortar companies, which operate in the physical marketplace, no longer question whether the Internet is important or if it will change their business. They are transforming themselves into clicks-and-mortar companies, with a presence in the marketplace as well as the marketspace.

Older companies in the bricks-and-mortar world clearly have an important decision to make with respect to organizational form. One of the first issues confronting older companies is the degree of autonomy and integration that the online business will have with the offline business. In Wal-Mart's case, even though Wal-Mart.com draws upon the resources of the parent company, it has been given a great deal of autonomy. Traditional companies can thus set up online ventures that benefit from both autonomy and speed that only smaller organizations can exhibit, as well as the ability to draw from the assets and resources of the parent company.

The alternative is to create an organization that embraces the old and the new, or the clicks-and-mortar (or clicks-and-bricks). These companies use the Web as an additional communication medium and/or distribution channel. The physical and virtual are intended to complement each other. For instance, consumers can search for product information online and then purchase the product in a physical store. They can then go back online after the purchase for customer support.

In reality, achieving such integration is difficult. Take Amazon.com's partnership with Toys R Us. After the initial failure of Toysrus.com, the company decided to team up with Amazon, presumably to benefit from Amazon's huge traffic flow and customer base. The joint venture, however, does not allow consumers to return merchandize bought online to a Toys R Us store in a local mall. At least, not yet.

In most cases, clicks-and-mortar companies seem to gradually evolve from modest experimental beginnings to a more formalized structure, where the organization is taking full advantage of the Internet. A four-stage model of evolution from bricks to clicks has been proposed (see Table 6-1).[11]

General Motors had 160 different Web sites in the grassroots stage, with every division and brand pursuing its own projects. Now the company has eliminated many and consolidated others. In the focal point stage, companies need a leader who can give direction and develop a cohesive strategy for the myriad of Web projects. Often an outside leader with some Internet experience will play a key role in this second stage.

The third stage involves establishing a formal organizational structure for the emerging e-businesses. From incubators some of the ideas may be established as independent

Table 6-1 From Bricks to Clicks: The Four Stages of E-volution

Stage 1 Grassroots	Stage 2 Focal Point	Stage 3 Structure and Deployment	Stage 4 Endgame
• Different initiatives underway without coordination. • Allow Internet initiatives to propagate throughout the company with minimal direction.	• A lead executive is in charge of all E-commerce efforts. • Devise cohesive Internet business strategy and develop Internet awareness throughout the firm.	• Structure (embedded, independent, joint venture) is determined; e-business group sets priorities. • Act on the promising opportunities by allocating resources.	• Risky ideas weeded out and opportunities are translated into products and services; the endgame is not static—it evolves. • Formalize the structure and translate promise into performance.

Source: Adapted from Jim Albrinck, Gil Irwin, Gary Neilson, and Diann Sasina, "From Bricks to Clicks: The Four Stages of E-volution," *Strategy & Business*, 20 (2000), p. 62-72.

companies. Others could be embedded within the existing parent company, and still others may be candidates for partnerships or joint ventures.

Lastly, the emphasis turns to consolidation and making sure the new operations are producing the desired results. Skills such as business development, partnership management, content management, project management, and marketing are required to turn promise into performance. Poor ideas must be effectively weeded out in the earlier stages for the endgame to have the desired results.

The sequential process described in Table 6-1 captures the journey that many firms take. Very few traditional firms delve into the Internet with all their resources straight away. Charles Schwab, for instance, did not become an online trading company in one step. A task force worked on the idea for a while before eSchwab was created and tested. Gradually the distinctions between the online and offline operations have blurred, bringing the online and the offline together.[12]

Others have sent trial balloons off into the virtual space before deciding to continue or abandon certain initiatives. Some companies do dive into the Internet with both feet, often with disastrous results. Citibank's Citi f/i, an Internet-only bank and financial portal service, was abandoned after a few short months. Similarly, in a much publicized example of how-not-to, the Bank of Montreal folded its Internet-only bank called mbanx and merged it into its main online banking service (www.bmo.com).

Internet pure-plays have a different challenge. Many Internet pure-plays have realized that they must acquire expensive physical infrastructure to deliver a high-quality service to customers. Many e-tialers (such as HomeGrocer and Amazon.com) have invested millions in warehouse and order-fulfillment facilities. For pure-plays, partnership with bricks-and-mortar stores may be an easier route to acquiring the assets they lack. Many organizational challenges, such as the fit between the cultures of two companies or the processes of two companies, must be overcome to make such joint ventures work.

The Vertical vs. the Networked Organization

The era of mass production saw many large companies vertically integrating to gain control of their supply and distribution networks. In this age of information and networks, businesses are focusing on their core competencies rather than trying to take everything on. There is a trend toward networked organizational structures.

Marketing literature, somewhat independent of the developments on the Internet, has seen a healthy debate on the concept of **networked organizations**.[13] Networks were born out of the need for efficiency and cost reduction in some cases. Companies started outsourcing many activities previously performed in-house—from market research to recruitment and IT services. Networks were also the result of the relationship marketing concept, which was a response to a changing and uncertain customer environment, including declining loyalty and a greater number of choices.[14]

Some of the key features of a networked organization include:

- smaller size;
- vertically disaggregated;
- flexibility for individual units, while maintaining loose organization-wide coordination;
- knowledge-based;
- team-based; and
- partnerships.

The concept of the networked organization was an interesting one when it was first proposed in the marketing literature in the early 1990s. Today, the Internet has made this concept a reality. Tapscott describes the **internetworked organization** as a virtual corporation, one that leverages the technology.[15] The Internet makes it possible for businesses to develop such a networked organizational structure (see Exhibit 6-2). We saw in Chapter 4 how the Internet allows businesses to forge closer ties with their suppliers, and we'll look at forming closer ties with customers in Chapter 7.

Tapscott and his colleagues have extended the concept of the networked organization further in their proposal of business webs or **b-webs**. B-webs are described as "distinct systems of suppliers, distributors, commerce service providers, infrastructure providers and customers that use the Internet for their primary business communication and transactions."[16] The emergence of b-webs can be seen through examples such as the Ariba Network (specializing in operating resources and supplies) and VerticalNet, which brings together buyers and sellers on a global basis.

Traditional bricks-and-mortar organizations may take longer to shed their legacy systems and slim down, as required by the network structure. The nature of the industry is likely to dictate whether such a networked structure is appropriate or not. It is conceivable that most organizations in the next few years will have at least some network relationships and participate in b-webs even if they do not become full-fledged network organizations.

Ownership and Control

Another important decision facing companies embarking upon online operations is the nature of ownership and control they desire. In the case of older companies, joint ventures (such as Wal-Mart's alliance with AOL in Europe) can be an easy route to acquiring skills and market access. There are also examples of Internet ventures being fully owned ventures. Many old-economy companies have also made strategic investments in Internet start-ups, such as Safeway's investment in GroceryWorks.com, an online grocery delivery company.

Some organizations choose to have their Internet ventures embedded within their existing business. This allows the firms to fully utilize any synergies between the online and offline operations. Customers can benefit if a seamless integration is achieved. Other

Exhibit 6-2 Networked Organization on the Internet

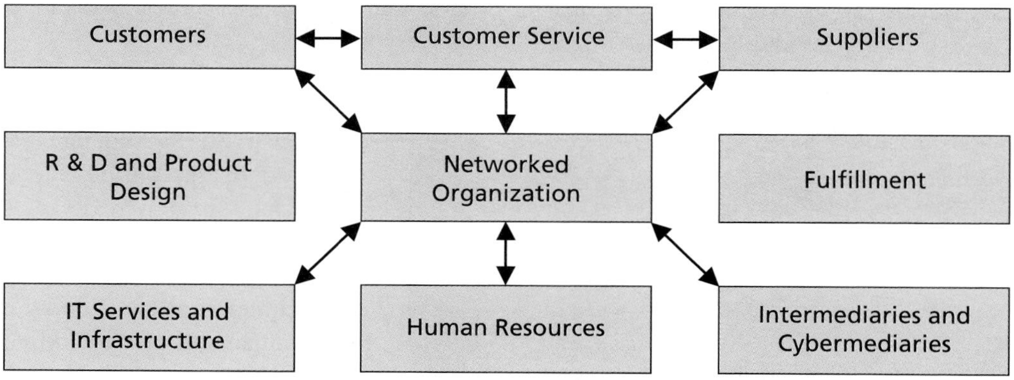

Note: This is a simplified example. Other complex linkages are also possible.

companies decide to have their Internet ventures operate at arms length in a laissez-faire model. This, as we saw earlier, allows the new venture to innovate freely without being burdened by the bureaucracy and legacy thinking in the parent organization.

The Bank of Montreal's mbanx and many of the Microsoft ventures (such as Expedia and Carpoint) fall under this category. If the new venture is related to the traditional business (as in the cases of Citibank's Citi f/i, Bank of Montreal's mbanx, and Wal-Mart's online store), some synergies will be compromised to give the new venture its needed freedom. Management's preferences will play a role in determining the ownership and control structure.

The preceding discussion on organizational issues stresses the importance of having a process in place for dealing with "internetization" of a business. At the end of the process, only viable ideas must be left on the table. An organizational structure, with priorities, people, and performance measures must be ready.

The development of a strategy and the evolution of the organizational structure often happen side-by-side. The structure should be there to serve the overall business strategy. It must make the implementation of the strategy easier.

Some Key Issues Facing Internet Companies

Stories about teenagers becoming overnight dot-com millionaires are now being replaced by stories about business failures. In most cases, the lack of a proper strategy and the lack of understanding of the online market seem to be the causes of these failures. When well-funded ventures like Boo.com and Pop.com collapse, that should make current and potential online companies examine their own businesses carefully. In some cases, good ideas fail because of poor execution. Currently, many online businesses suffer from a number of problems that threaten their positions.

High Marketing and Customer Acquisition Costs

The need for creating brand awareness, trust, and initial trial lead to high marketing and customer acquisition costs. A study by the consulting company McKinsey found that the average customer acquisition cost was at $250 in 1999. The average online purchase was usually in the $50–75 range. That means that a company generally does not make a profit on a customer until he or she makes four or five purchases. Companies will lose money if customers turn out to be one-time shoppers. They must find a way to entice customers to come back. **Sales and marketing expense ratio (SMR)** as a percentage of total revenues was as high as 149 percent in the first quarter of 1998 and was at 61 percent in the first quarter of 2000 (see Exhibit 6-3).

Exhibit 6-3 Sales and Marketing Expense Ratio for Net Firms

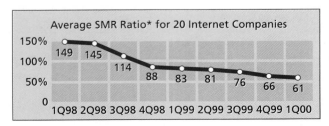

Source: *The Standard* (www.thestandard.com).

Low Loyalty

While everyone talks about building one-to-one relationships online, there is ample evidence that online loyalty is still very low. Clearly, given the high customer acquisition costs, loyalty is the key to profitability. The variety of choices online, the ease of product and price comparison, and the infrequent nature of online shopping (which describes the behaviour of most consumers currently) all contribute to lower loyalty.

How can online marketers create loyalty? They must go back to the basics. Creation of superior value including the ability to customize the product, superior online experience, competitive pricing and excellent customer service are some of the elements likely to influence customer loyalty.

Getting and keeping customers for the long term is the main challenge that Internet companies face. There are many competitors and aggressive price-cutting. Brands seem to be less important in some cases (see Chapter 8 for a discussion of branding online). No longer can marketers assume loyalty toward a brand and charge premium prices.

Difficulty in Sustaining Competitive Advantages

Often new features and processes embedded in a Web site can be easily copied or adapted by competitors. It is difficult to acquire a sustainable long-term competitive advantage. In the old economy, firms looked to the physical value chain to achieve a competitive advantage—by performing certain functions within the value chain in a manner that was superior to competitors. Now firms must turn to the virtual value chain, where information is turned into value (see Chapter 2). While some firms, such as FedEx, have been able to take advantage of the virtual value chain, their advantage has been short lived. FedEx was the first courier company to allow customers to track their shipments from pickup to delivery. Now, rival UPS (see "Track" in www.ups.com) and even Canada Post (see "Delivery Confirmation" in www.canadapost.ca) offer the same features.

The Internet makes product features and some processes very transparent. This does not mean that firms will not be able to develop competitive advantages. It simply means that it's now more of a challenge. Some companies have resorted to seeking patent protection for their business models and processes to prevent competitors from copying them (see iMarket Demo 6-1). As many of these cases have ended up in the courts, the results of such tactics are not yet clear.

Volatile Markets

From 1995 to 1999, a record number of new ventures were funded in the United States. In 1999, 165 initial public offering (IPO) deals were completed on the NASDAQ stock exchange. Such enthusiasm has now withered, as of the end of the year 2000. The stocks of leading Internet companies in e-tail as well as other online services have plummeted to their all-time lows. Still, the market may go up again.

In the meantime, many firms are realizing that they need to become profitable quickly or at least show strong revenue growth in the short term to keep the investors' faith. Strategic alliances and mergers are becoming commonplace, as many Internet start-ups find out that they cannot do it by themselves. Internet pure-plays are establishing ties with older land-based firms (as with Amazon.com's alliance with Toys R Us). The online company's brand and site traffic combined with the offline company's physical infrastructure may turn out to be a potent formula. It is too early to judge if these partnerships will prove beneficial in the long run. In the short term, Internet firms may focus excessively on profits to please the financial markets, at the cost of long-term customer loyalty and brand building. Focusing on short-term results, especially for new firms, may prove to be detrimental in the long term.

The Planning Horizon

Online marketing strategy will still draw from traditional concepts in strategy. As we have seen, there are some challenges strategists must confront.

iMarket Demo 6-1 Patenting Web Technologies and Business Models

In the old days, companies that had unique processes, expertise, or products were able to gain a competitive advantage. The Internet makes a business's operations very transparent. That means competitors can easily copy or modify processes or products. The battle to maintain control over original methods, names, processes, and products is heating up on the Web.

Companies like Amazon.com, Priceline.com, Open Market, and DoubleClick have filed for patent rights over E-commerce business models and business processes. These patents, called E-commerce method patents, are used to scare off competitors. Priceline, for example, sued Microsoft over the use of the "reverse auction" business model in the Microsoft Expedia travel site. E-commerce companies are watching this case with great interest, as it might affect the future of the online competitive landscape.

Open Market owns a patent for "a method of buying and paying for goods online" (the electronic shopping-cart concept) and Netcentives Inc. received a patent for its online frequent-buyer program. Do such "discoveries" deserve patent protection?

Amazon.com won a case against its main rival Barnes & Noble, preventing them from using the "one-click ordering" process. Amazon owns a patent for this process. Many consumers and experts were outraged by Amazon's actions. Amazon was also claiming a patent for the use of "affiliate programs," where affiliate sites get paid for sending referrals to Amazon (see Chapter 2). Affiliate programs have now become widespread. Many experts fear that such patents will stifle innovation and competition. Critics, including Prof. Tom Novak at Vanderbilt University, have charged the company with being a bad Web citizen.

The US Patent Office even granted several patents to a computer scientist named Allan Konrad for "making use of a Web site that provides interactive database operations." Most large E-commerce sites integrate databases with their Web operations. Konrad has filed a case against several large companies for infringing on the patent rights.

Another case involves GeoWorks, which claims to have a patent over Wireless Application Protocol (WAP), which is an essential technology for delivering Internet content via cellular phones. This patent is also in dispute.

Is it fair to patent basic business processes such as reverse auctions? Some experts believe that these patents may not hold up in court. So far, both Priceline and Amazon have won the first round in their legal battles.

Sources: Ellen Messmer (2000), "New Web Technology: Patently Unfair?" *CNN.com*, July 5; Mark Gimein (1999), "Jay Walker's Patent Mania," *Salon.com*, August 27; Julia King (1999), "Net Patents Stir Debate," *IDG.net*, August 24; Prof. Tom Novak's letter to Amazon.com, (www2000.ogsm.vanderbilt.edu/novak/amazon_2_28_00.htm).

If marketing is underfunded, a good idea may never take off. If, on the other hand, marketing and sales expenses skyrocket while loyalty and repeat buying are low, the company will soon run out of cash. Striking a balance is a difficult task. While the degree of risk tolerance within an organization may dictate how a company will approach this issue, it does underscore the importance of screening ideas thoroughly in the early stages.

Strategy planning for online business requires more flexibility. The dynamic nature of the online market, with new technologies and competitors emerging unpredictably, makes longer-term planning quite difficult. If companies were getting comfortable designing their sites for personal computers, now they will have to learn how to deliver content and shopping experience for small handheld devices. Voice-based Web devices also present opportunities and challenges. When there is a significant new technology emerging two or three times a year, the planning horizon does become shorter.

On the Internet, planners must deal with moving targets. In addition to changing technology, the rules of the market are still under debate and evolving in some cases (such as E-commerce taxation, privacy issues, and consumer protection). Consumer adoption of online shopping is still in the early stages. While businesses are more eager to embrace online purchasing, there is vast untapped market potential in B2B markets as well. Competitors can reconfigure themselves quickly, and portal sites can suddenly become financial service providers or ISPs.

Some experts call for real-time planning. The firm must have a longer-term focus, but monitor its plan, and modify it as necessary, on an ongoing basis. Regardless of the planning horizon, a good place to start when developing a strategic plan is to define the business clearly—its mission, objectives, activities, products or services, markets, and so on.

E-Business Strategy Development Framework

Success factors are likely to vary across industries and sectors, but there are some factors that have already or will likely emerge as critical. This section presents an eight-factor model to guide online business strategists (see Exhibit 6-4).

This model can provide a sense of where a business is in its online evolution. In the most basic form, a firm can be a simple online promotional site with some content. At the complex

Exhibit 6-4 Eight Cs for a Successful E-Business Strategy

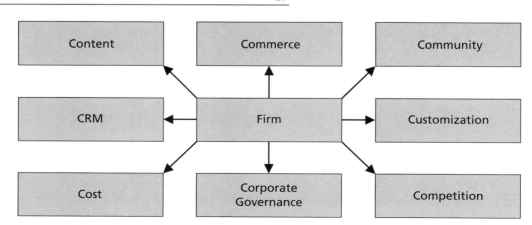

end would be a business that uses the Internet for customer relationship management (CRM), which can require significant coordination among various departments and changes to business processes.

Content

Content is critical no matter the nature of the site. Content is not something that only online publishing or news sites worry about. Even e-tailers who offer nothing more than an online catalogue must create content that is current, exciting, and visually appealing (where possible), and that has editorial integrity.

Most companies that made a gradual transition to the Internet may have started with an electronic brochure. As the business evolves, the company can migrate to selling products or services online—the commerce stage.

Content can play a vital role in creating repeat visits. Amazon.com, for instance, offers professional reviews and customers' reviews of books. For certain books, excerpts are provided. A mere online catalogue with book titles and cover pictures would be boring in comparison. Amazon's focus on content shows that the company understands the medium. The experience is, therefore, richer because the consumer can make an informed choice.

Commerce

For most people, the Internet is synonymous with E-commerce. This may not be appropriate for all sites. For instance, Boeing's Web site (www.boeing.com) offers a great deal of product information, but not E-commerce. B2B sites (such as Boeing) that do not directly sell online may use the Web to support their sales staff. One can expect most sites to migrate from pure content to include commerce. Portal sites such as Yahoo! and AltaVista are now E-commerce sites, offering a lot more than just content.

We have seen the first generation of E-commerce, which has been similar to buying from print catalogues. The second generation will focus more on the consumer experience. These sites will leverage the technology to a greater extent. The experience could be animated, multimedia, and three-dimensional. Some examples are already emerging in sites like Landsend.com. We will simultaneously see the emergence of the third generation that will focus on M-commerce (or mobile commerce) and T-commerce (or interactive TV commerce).

The evolution to the commerce stage from the content stage is not just a matter of adding an online catalogue with shopping-cart software. Companies that excel in online commerce pay attention to customer experience.

Community

In addition to the use of technology, the focus on user experience is leading some sites (such as Amazon.com and eBay) to focus on the social experience online. Amazon's customers post reviews that others read. These reviews act as a social influence on purchase decisions. eBay has created one of the largest online community sites by facilitating interaction among ordinary consumers who wish to buy and sell things.

Other companies use online communities to build stronger relationships with their customers (e.g., Shell, Kraft, Pentax, Heineken, Wine.com, and NetObjects). By providing an online forum for customers to post their opinions and interact with each other, marketers can understand their customers more intimately. These online bulletin boards often reveal how people use the products (sometimes in ways unintended by the marketer), their likes and dislikes, and even their views of competitors' products.

The move from commerce to community requires a lot more interaction between the marketer and the customers. While the online community can be a great source of information and can promote goodwill among customers, it does require investment of resources to be effective.

Customers (in B2C and more so in B2B) are increasingly organizing themselves into online communities. Marketers who dismiss the idea of online communities may be losing out on valuable opportunities. Details of community formation and the benefits of online communities are discussed in Chapter 7.

Customization

This step, again, may or may not be appropriate for every organization. We do see a vast array of products (cars, computers, CDs, clothing, and so on) and services (news and financial services) being customized by using the Web as the interface between the company and the customers.

Customization is a major strategic decision. Customization does not just mean allowing customers to select features from a list of options—it goes far beyond that. Manufacturing processes must be configured to produce individual items to unique specifications. Rather than emphasizing economies of scale, the emphasis is on creating superior value for each customer that is served. Imagine buying a CD with 10 songs for $10, where you listen to only three songs. Seventy percent of that product offers no value to you. On the other hand, for the same price, a site that allows a customer to custom build a CD (such as CDNow) with even six or seven songs significantly enhances the value proposition for the consumer.

As customization of certain products becomes widely prevalent, consumers may expect more personalized products and services in other categories. The marketer now has to market to a segment of one. In this case, however, there is a greater chance of building a lasting relationship with the customers. Customization requires a different business philosophy. Dell Computers was built on the philosophy of flexible manufacturing and customized products. Companies that have no experience in the build-to-order model may have to re-engineer their processes. This decision can have far-reaching implications throughout the organization. If competitors make the first move they may gain a significant advantage (as in the case of Dell vs. Compaq).

Customer Relationship Management

The importance of customer service was stressed earlier in this chapter. **Customer relationship management (CRM)** calls for a "consistent, unified customer interaction across all communication channels, all applications, and all business functions."[17] That means a firm that markets through the Web, retail stores, and catalogues must speak to the consumer with the same voice. The customer must be able to seamlessly go from one channel to another. A book purchased online should be accepted for return or exchange in the retail store. A customer who made an offline purchase should be able to get customer service online in real-time.

Imagine an airline that not only calls you and informs you that your flight is late, but is also able to reschedule your hotel and rental car bookings! To deliver such a level of service the company must have intimate knowledge of each customer. That is the first part of CRM—developing a comprehensive database with detailed profiles of consumers. CRM may incorporate some elements of direct marketing, but it is a concept that goes beyond marketing. It calls for organization-wide effort to focus on serving the customer. A lasting customer relationship is built by exceeding consumer expectations and by rewarding loyal customers. See Chapter 7 for further discussion of CRM.

While the first five components of the model (Exhibit 6-4) discussed so far represent an evolution of the firm from a content site to full-fledged e-business (where the Internet is being used to manage relationships with important stakeholders), the last three components of the model play in the background. Competition is an external variable, while the other two—corporate governance and cost are internal variables.

Competition

Competition on the Internet is fierce in most product categories. In many cases, entry barriers are minimal, leading to a multitude of new entrants. Only the fittest of these firms will survive.

Competition online can also take a global perspective. This is especially true in B2B exchange sites, which draw buyers and sellers worldwide. Geographical or locational advantages do not count for much now.

In the early days of E-commerce, most online companies were funded by venture capitalists and private investors. Now several large, so-called old-economy companies are online. In retailing, companies such as Wal-Mart, Kmart, Sears, and JC Penney are online. These firms have established brand names and vast resources. They compete directly with smaller online e-tailers.

Rapid technological changes and innovations can often dethrone market leaders. At the same time, rivalry in many product categories (books, CDs, clothing) and service categories (airline tickets, financial services, online vocational education) is leading to competitive pricing and better services.

Given the dynamism of the online marketspace and the constantly changing competitive landscape, firms must monitor the actions of present and potential competitors closely.

Corporate Governance

Many organizational challenges and organizational structure issues were discussed earlier. Some of the key points are worth repeating here.

We saw that the options for governance structures ranged from independent spin-offs to completely embedding the Internet business within an existing business.[18] Companies such as Wal-Mart, Microsoft (Expedia), NBC (NBCi), and Nordstrom have pursued the first path. This approach works only when the spin-off has the autonomy to innovate, attract talent, and draw investors on its own. In cases where it is hard to distinguish the online from the offline business, the embedded or integrated structure may be more appropriate.

If there is a greater potential to unlock shareholder value or minimal similarities to existing offerings (for example, Microsoft's Expedia, a travel site, is unrelated to the company's core software business), the need for a different culture or for entirely different business processes can be good arguments for establishing a spin-off. On the other hand, if the value is in improving the current business and its operations by taking it online and the e-business opportunity has an organization-wide impact and not just a local effect on one business unit, one could make sound arguments for keeping the Internet operation within the existing business. Of course, for pure-play start-up companies, the decision regarding the governance is somewhat simpler. They do not have to contend with an existing business. Governance structure is of paramount importance because it can affect a number of areas that have a direct bearing on performance—ranging from speed of response and speed of innovation.

Cost

As we saw earlier, marketing costs are skyrocketing while loyalty rates are plummeting. Many online businesses are spending more on customer acquisition than the revenues they get. While this may be fine in the short run, it is clearly an untenable situation in the long run.

Cost management has not been very popular with Internet executives so far, and the stock market is taking notice. We see stocks of some of the best-known Internet companies like Priceline, CDNow, and even Amazon.com trading at all-time lows (as of October 2000). The message is clear. Financial performance is critical for long-term survival. The honeymoon for dot-coms is over.

Internet companies must not only continue to focus on customer acquisition, but also on retention and loyalty through a variety of efforts, including customization and CRM techniques. At the same time, they cannot allow the costs to get out of control as some have done in the past.

This balance is hard to achieve. It calls for a prudent growth strategy—one that will not place undue burden on resources. A company that consistently achieves positive cash flows and has adequate cash reserves, even if there are no profits in the short run, is likely to have a better chance of succeeding in the long run.

The online market is still young, with vast untapped potential. Yet, we can no longer use this as a reason for a spending spree (with the promise of profits sometime in the future). The reaction of investors and the dramatic failures of well-funded dot-coms stress the importance of prudent financial management.

Steps in Developing an Internet Marketing Strategy

In this section, the steps in developing a strategy are presented. It must be emphasized that while the major areas that apply to most firms are considered here, other factors may have to be considered depending on the type of business.

Defining the Business—Nature and Scope

Objectives and Business Model. The objectives of the Internet venture and the nature of the business model must be spelled out. Lack of clarity at this stage can lead to trouble later. Start-up ventures usually have a higher burden because they must convince investors to take on the risk. Traditional companies that decide to invest in their own Internet venture would also benefit from developing a comprehensive business plan and business case analysis.

This does not mean that the objectives and the business model are cast in stone. We do see examples of companies adding to and modifying their model as new opportunities arise. Digitization has changed the face of many industries such as books, music, and photography. In the last category, Kodak has seen its business go through a major transformation (see iMarket Demo 6-2). Old companies like Kodak have to find new ways of creating value when their old products become obsolete. Companies like Encyclopedia Britannica and Kodak are redefining their objectives and business models.

Amazon.com, another example of an evolving business, is very different today from the online book-seller it was at its inception. Now it's a **megamediary** that sponsors other smaller "stores," called zShops, and offers auction sales. While recognizing that businesses do evolve, it is still important to have a clear vision at the beginning.

Ideas that sound good on paper often may not be viable. Pop.com, an online venture designed to deliver video-on-demand started by director Steven Speilberg, had a short life because the timing and technology were not right. Video-on-demand requires high bandwidth (DSL, cable modems, or ISDN), which very few households in North America have at this time. While the concept was interesting, it was ahead of its time as the current technology proved to be a limiting factor. The technical, financial, and market viability of the business model must be thoroughly analyzed.

iMarket Demo 6-2 Kodak's Internet Strategy

The microprocessor and digitization have transformed many product categories. One of the categories significantly influenced by digitization is photography. While professionals still use film to shoot, amateurs have been wooed by small and sleek digital cameras, priced from under $200 to over $1000. The benefits are significant—no film is needed, images can be downloaded onto a computer and manipulated using software applications such as Adobe PhotoShop, and images can be shared with others by posting on Web sites or through e-mail. And if you want to a print copy, that's also possible. The images are crisp, and the cameras are easy to handle and packed with features that can make photography fun for amateurs.

Kodak, a household name in the photography business, saw this trend coming

as early as 1996. If the vast majority of consumers choose the filmless cameras, one of Kodak's main businesses (selling 35 mm film through retail stores) will be in jeopardy. Realizing this, Kodak started a service in 1997 to let consumers view photos they have taken, order reprints, and send e-mail pictures. Kodak's president of consumer imaging said in 1997, "Kodak believes the day is approaching where virtually every picture will be digitized and delivered electronically." The company has tried to stay at the cutting-edge of this digital revolution, rather than be swept away by it.

For business customers, such as film companies that buy motion picture film, Kodak allows online ordering. The Kodak Web site also contains a variety of other information of value to filmmakers (see www. kodak.com/US/en/motion/). The Internet can benefit Kodak in the B2B market.

Consumers can go to the Kodak Web site (www.kodak.com) to learn about photography, upload and save pictures online for others to see, edit the pictures, and even create electronic postcards. Other interactive features include a discussion board and a live chat with the "expert" (see Exhibit 6-5). Kodak's rival, Fuji (www. fujifilm.com) also offers several interactive features online. Kodak offers these features at no cost to consumers. The revenue potential of building such relationships with customers must be assessed. Will the company charge a fee for these services? Or will the loyalty created through the value-added features online lead to purchase of other Kodak products like digital cameras and photo printing paper? Also, several private Internet firms like Clubphoto.com

Exhibit 6-5 Kodak's Web Site

Source: www.kodak.com.

and Photofun.com offer some of the same services. Can Kodak stay ahead of these smaller, but perhaps nimbler, competitors?

In the B2B market, Kodak may still be able to sell its traditional products (film for motion pictures, X-rays, processing chemicals, and so on) for the foreseeable future. But in the consumer market, conventional film is on its way out. Instead, Kodak is focusing on digital print fulfillment. Even when consumers take pictures using digital cameras and send them to loved ones through e-mail, there is still a desire to see the pictures in print.

Kodak has made an equity investment in PhotoAlley.com. Kodak will provide PhotoAlley with exclusive processing, scanning, and uploading services through its Print@Kodak operation. PhotoAlley is to become Kodak's e-dealer, with full rights to sell Kodak's digital products on its site. Kodak also has a Shop@Kodak online shopping centre on its site for consumers who wish to buy directly from Kodak. In Britain, Kodak has a partnership with Freeserve, the largest Internet service provider in that country, for a co-branded Web site.

Kodak has made its intentions regarding the Internet very clear. The company uses interactive features on the site to make sure customers spend time on the site and revisit often. Kodak has been aggressive in direct sales of products in both B2B and B2C markets. Forming partnerships and joint ventures with other Internet firms is another way of ensuring that Kodak stays ahead of its rivals. Just as *Encyclopedia Britannica* did (see Chapter 2), Kodak has had to change its business model. From physical value creation (through film and printing), now the firm is creating virtual value (through the ability to save, edit, and send pictures digitally online).

The transition from the analogue to the digital world seems to have taken a bit of a toll on Kodak's stock prices. From a 52-week high of about $67, the shares were down at about $42 at the end of November 2000. As the company moves ahead, it must watch out for potential channel conflicts that may arise from its direct online sales operation. Smaller rivals that also offer services to digital photographers must be watched carefully. In an industry going through its greatest change since the introduction of the Kodak Brownie camera (cost $1) in 1900, Kodak seems to be making all the right moves. Will Kodak's strategy pay off in the future?

Sources: "Kodak to Link Customers, Photo Labs on the Internet," *Bloomberg Business News*, February 21, 1997; "Kodak Demonstrates Ordering by Internet at Showbix Expo," Kodak Press Release (www.kodak.com), Beth Cox (2000), "Kodak Ups its Internet Ante," *InterntetNews.com*, October 10.

The Business Form and Structure. The discussion in the preceding section on organizational issues stresses the importance of addressing questions pertaining to ownership and desired organizational form. While start-up ventures can make a clean start, bricks-and-mortars must try to leverage the assets of the existing operations and at the same time minimize conflicts between the old and the new.

Net Readiness. Related to the previous point is the assessment of the firm's Net readiness. This is critical for older companies migrating online. Several aspects of a firm must be assessed to see if the firm is ready to succeed online. Net readiness can be defined as the combination of four drivers (leadership, organizational structure and governance, competence/skills, and technology) that enable enterprises to deploy high-impact Web-enabled business processes that are focused, accountable, and measurable.[19] Leadership refers to the ability to identify and capture opportunities earlier than competitors. It also refers to senior management's vision, as discussed in the previous section. Organizational structure issues were also discussed in detail in the previous section. Competence refers to the organization's ability to manage change, innovate, and develop business partnerships essential for success on the Internet. Technology, the fourth driver, refers to the ability of the organization to leverage technology to achieve its goals and have technology that is scalable as the organization grows. While technology can be acquired if the firm lacks it, the other three drivers are harder to acquire.

Global vs. Local. Just like the business model decision, the global versus local choice may also be an evolving decision in some cases. An organization that starts as a local/national venture can evolve into a global operation (such as Yahoo!). However, global operations online require a specific set of skills and capabilities. This is not a decision to be local or global, but is a strategic one that cannot be taken lightly. Even though Wal-Mart operates stores in 10 countries and has an online joint venture in Europe with AOL (in a comparison shopping site called ShopSmart), Wal-Mart.com is still a US-only operation. This may change in the future. It is, however, worth noting that even a company as large as Wal-Mart, with a great deal of global experience, is not taking the globalization decision lightly. Boo.com's grandiose global plans and its subsequent failure provide important lessons for other firms.

There is a temptation to think that one's market is global in scope because one is online. This is not always true. While a Web site can be accessed from anywhere in the world, the market may not necessarily be global. Local services and local news by definition have a local market. Other products, such as paper and packaging materials, may have a limited geographic market because overseas shipping costs can exceed the value of the product.

If the decision is made to pursue certain global markets, the firm must pay attention to several additional considerations:

- *Business model*. Not all business models can be transported across national boundaries.[20] While information services (such as Yahoo!) and some online retailers (such as Amazon.com) have had little difficulty going global, businesses such as financial services (for example, E*Trade) or digital music (such as MP3.com) have a bigger barrier. Regulatory environments in foreign countries must be supportive of such business models.
- *Markets*. If the business model is transportable, then suitable foreign markets must be identified. Economy, regulation, culture, language, and availability of skilled workers are some of the considerations. A thorough market analysis and market entry strategy must be developed. Internet usage trends and regulations with respect to online commerce in those markets must be studied. Many developing markets with great export potential are still in the early stages of going online.
- *Culture and communication*. The Web offers users the ability to tailor communication to the needs of the audience. A growing number of global E-commerce sites are considering the use of multilingual presentation on their Web sites (see Exhibit 6-6). This may be appropriate when the bulk of export revenues come from a specific country or region. Cultural differences in terms of colours and symbols as well as interpretation of words must be carefully considered. Many sites seem to follow the approach of "think global, but act local." For example, Yahoo! has sites in many countries and

Exhibit 6-6 CDNow: Multilingual Presentation

CDNOW Europe

For faster, less expensive delivery to <u>Europe and the Middle East</u> selected items will be shipped from our European shipping center.

日本語　<u>Deutsch</u>　<u>Español</u>　<u>Français</u>　<u>Italiano</u>　<u>Nederlands</u>　<u>Português</u>

Source: www.cdnow.com.

languages, each catering to the local population. The brand name, the services, and Yahoo!'s marketing power have been transported globally.

- *Content*. The site should be designed with the consumer in mind. What information is critical to the consumer decision process? Even such information as the local time zone or long-distance calling codes and mailing address may be useful to international customers.
- *Currency*. Companies using the Internet for international business must consider the most convenient currency for potential consumers. Boo.com went to an extreme by accepting many currencies.
- *Technology*. In Europe, Asia, and South America, consumers pay for Internet connectivity based on the duration of usage, unlike North America where most Internet service providers offer unlimited access for a very affordable monthly fee. The Web site should be designed keeping in mind the constraints of end-users.
- *Fulfillment and customer service*. Foreign orders require special order fulfillment procedures. A firm may wish to outsource the fulfillment services. Online customer service, especially when real-time interactive technologies are used (such as Liveperson.com), can play an effective role in global customer service.
- *Regulation*. In the area of privacy, for instance, the United States and Canada have generally allowed Internet companies to self-regulate their behaviour. In Europe, there are stringent regulations protecting consumer privacy. The laws there also bar companies from exchanging personal consumer data with firms located in countries that do not adequately protect the privacy of that information.[21] One must be aware of regulations with respect to privacy, security, taxation, and liabilities in the foreign markets before venturing into global E-commerce.

Internal Analysis

The issues raised in the previous sections (business model, global vs. local, net readiness, and organizational structure) can form part of an internal analysis. The internal analysis must focus on the strengths and weaknesses of the firm. The organizational issues addressed at the outset of this chapter must be considered in detail. Is the organizational form and culture conducive to competing and succeeding in the new marketspace?

Bricks-and-mortar firms that go online will generally have significant physical infrastructure, brand equity, and financial resources to make a strong online entry. Several traditional retailers such as Wal-Mart, Sears, and JC Penney have demonstrated this. At the same time, these firms may not possess the same degree of awareness of the Internet as a market that some of the new entrepreneurs might possess. The traditional mindset may be a barrier.

Bricks-and-mortar firms must also change some of their processes and learn to interact more closely with customers online. As we saw earlier, they face the additional challenge of integrating their offline and online operations so that consumers can have a seamless, high-quality experience in every channel.

Pure-play companies often start with innovative business models (for example, Priceline, eBay, and Pop.com). The models are untested and their viability unknown. As we have seen, many of them spend a great deal on advertising to build brand awareness and traffic. High initial marketing expenditures, combined with low online customer loyalty, has put a question mark on the future of many online start-up ventures.

On the positive side, online start-ups have been more daring and innovative than their traditional bricks-and-mortar rivals. Even if business failures are high, the really good companies may reap significant benefits in the long run. Clearly, sound management is needed. Companies that grow too fast, rather than managing their growth, are likely to pay the price, as we saw with Boo.com in Vignette 6.

The internal analysis should address the organizational issues, strengths of the business model, sources of competitive advantage, resources, skills of managers, brand strength, market position (leadership or follower), and financial performance. Bricks-and-mortar firms going online and pure-play companies must address issues that are unique to their case.

External Analysis

Once the basic issues pertaining to organizational objectives and scope of operations are defined, a thorough market analysis must be undertaken.

The Market and Customers. Specific issues pertaining to the B2C and B2B markets were analyzed in Chapters 3 and 4. Whether a company is in the B2B or B2C space, the size and nature of customers, the market growth rate, buyer characteristics, barriers, and facilitators of online buying/usage are some important considerations.

In both B2C and B2B markets, there is a significant growth in new online purchasing each year. This global trend is expected to continue for the next three to five years. Security issues still hamper Internet usage and online purchasing in both markets, while convenience, savings, and increased choice are some of the drivers.

Each company must address issues that may be unique to that industry. Online banking or stock trading is different from buying books online. The decision process and the factors influencing the decision may vary greatly in each case. A generic customer analysis will, therefore, not suffice.

The use of focus groups or surveys with existing clients can provide insights into why they will or will not migrate online. Rather than making decisions based on generic research reports, some primary research may be essential to capture the unique issues that each industry or organization faces.

Competition. The competitive landscape on the Internet is very dynamic. First, there is greater potential for foreign competition. Second, competition is not limited to only those who are online. In the online grocery business, companies such as Webvan, NetGrocer, and Peach Tree must consider the traditional grocery stores, such as Safeway, as competitors. The traditional bricks-and-mortars who are not online now are likely to have the resources to make a big online entry.

The Internet is also seeing a degree of cooperation among competitors that is relatively new. In the automobile industry, rivals GM, Ford, and Daimler-Chrysler have joined together to combine their purchasing power and do all of their procurement through a common Web site called Covisint.com. The computer, grocery, and retail industries are also experiencing similar cooperative efforts. Mergers of rival firms are also becoming increasingly common online. While the rival firms still compete for market share and consumers' mind share, coopetition in certain areas can produce a win-win situation for everyone.

Competitive analysis for Internet firms must consider:

- Current online competitors—domestic and foreign,
- Potential future competitors, especially the larger bricks-and-mortars, and
- Potential avenues for coopetition.

Strengths and weaknesses of competitors must be analyzed. Their brand, quality of product or service, markets served, and financial and human assets are some of the factors that must be studied.

From a competitive strategy standpoint, first entry and leadership position are very much related. But we also see examples of first entrants failing or floundering because of mismanagement or miscalculations. Amazon.com, which entered the online music business much later than its pioneering rival CDNow, quickly achieved market dominance in that category. Amazon's bigger and more loyal customer base and stronger brand franchise played a key role.

Firms currently online or intending to go online must constantly monitor the competitive environment. The Internet has made it easier for firms to engage in competitive intelligence (see Chapter 5), and firms specializing in online business intelligence can be hired to provide ongoing intelligence on competitors.

Firms online tend to respond much faster. Price cuts are matched instantly, and unique features on one Web site are adopted quickly by others. Some companies like Amazon.com have tried to protect their unique business processes and models through patents. In spite of such attempts, maintaining a competitive advantage online is a big challenge.

Product Market and Growth Strategies

The preceding analysis should lead to consideration of appropriate strategic alternatives. As companies develop products for the Internet, they must have strategic direction. Just as in the physical marketplace, online marketers have several product strategies available to them. The generic product/market matrix (see Exhibit 6-7) is a useful way to begin the exploration of opportunities.

Smaller product markets, known as *niche markets*, can provide some protection against bigger competitors who may consider these markets too small. For instance, specialized wineries have online stores that appeal to specific segments. A search in Yahoo! for "wineries" will reveal numerous small, specialized regional and local wineries that cater to niche markets. The Internet has made their market size bigger. Barnes & Noble (www.bn.com) is still known as the largest bookstore in the United States. The company also has a share in Chapters.ca, the largest Canadian online and offline bookstore. While Barnes & Noble has expanded to some categories beyond books, such as software and music, it's still mostly a *single mass marketer*, true to its original roots.

Amazon.com, on the other hand, started with the slogan "Earth's Biggest BookStore" and has now evolved to the "Earth's Largest Selection." It wants to be the Wal-Mart of the

Exhibit 6-7 Generic Product/Market Strategy Matrix

		Market Segment Size	
		Small	Large
Segment Targeted	One	Single Niche	Single Mass Market
	Several	Multi Niche Market	Multi Mass Market

Internet, before the real Wal-Mart establishes a strong online presence. Amazon is a good example of a *multi mass marketer*. Yahoo!, similarly, has evolved from an online search directory service to a complete portal that offers e-mail, news, the most popular financial discussion forums, financial services such as electronic bill payment, free Internet service, and more. In each case, Yahoo! needs to reach a mass market to achieve success.

When considering product-market strategies, it is important to consider whether to sell the same product to every consumer or to provide mass customization. This is an important issue for both niche and mass-market players. The Internet has turned everything from newspapers, computers, CDs, and clothing into customizable offerings. It is not just the size of the product market—whether a small niche or a global market—that should be of concern. Will all consumers get the same offering or will each consumer be able to choose a tailored offering from a menu of choices? The traditional 2×2 generic product-market matrix should now be viewed along with a third dimension, namely, mass customization.

Many new companies that dominate the online landscape offer new products to new markets. Take the case of the controversial music file sharing facilitator, Napster. This is an innovative idea that works because of the Internet. We also see examples of existing products being modified and repositioned into existing markets (see Exhibit 6-8). Verizon (formed by the merger of GTE and Bell Atlantic) offers Superpages.com, which combines yellow

Exhibit 6-8 Generic Diversification Strategies for Internet Companies

		Product	
		New	Existing
Market	New	Unrelated Diversification	Related Diversification
	Existing	Related Diversification	Penetration

pages and white pages and adds online shopping capability. Verizon is reaching its current customers with a new and enhanced service online.

As Amazon expanded from books to CDs to drugs to toys to home improvement products, each expansion was aimed at existing customers, as well as new customers not currently shopping at Amazon. Amazon wants to expand not just its product line, but also its customer base.

When catalogue companies like Grainger.com or LLBean.com offer their products online, they are simply taking their paper catalogue online, thereby trying to reach new markets. The foundation of their business model has not changed. The Internet has added interactive capability and eliminated catalogue printing and mailing costs. These catalogue companies now tap into new foreign markets due to the global reach of the Internet.

Other companies have had to significantly alter their product or business model when they went online. In Chapter 2, we saw how *Encyclopedia Britannica* has evolved from a book publisher to a free online content service. As in the case of the catalogue companies, Britannica Online is still reaching its traditional customers—families with school-age children. It is also reaching new markets in foreign countries. As companies move from the marketplace to the marketspace, or from one marketspace to another, they may have to redefine their core business model.

Defining the Key Success Factors

It is harder to define the *key success factors* (KSFs) online than it is offline. The rapid changes in technology allow companies to do things that were unimaginable just a few years ago. Some differences do set the online world apart from the offline. These include:[22]

- One-to-one relationships (less emphasis on scale)
- Cannibalization (through use of multiple channels)
- Experimentation
- Real-time execution (as opposed to long-term planning)
- Alliances and partnerships
- Greater risks (prospect of failure) and (long-term) rewards

While both offline and online businesses may exhibit these traits, each of these is more likely online than offline. Some of these, including alliances and one-to-one relationships, are often critical to success online.

Clearly, the KSFs will vary from industry to industry. Portals and content sites may have different KSFs from e-tailers and online banks. It is paramount that these be defined to the extent possible at an early stage.

As the online marketspace matures and in many cases online and offline operations are integrated, the distinction between online and offline success factors may diminish. Having said that, it must also be emphasized that new technologies and maturing online customers can place new demands. Take the case of customer service. In the early days of E-commerce, some companies were under the mistaken impression that consumers would shop online merely for the convenience and efficiency and would care less about customer service. That has been proven to be an incorrect assumption.

Some companies like Volvo paid the price for not understanding consumer behaviour online. Other companies like Cisco and Sun Microsystems have saved millions of dollars by automating their customer service, and showed how superior online customer service can be delivered.

While the cry for online customer service was not very audible in the period from 1995 to 1998, customers now expect the same or a higher level of service online as they get offline. This means that what was once considered to be a minor factor has now become a major factor. Companies are investing in back-end support and technologies that facilitate customer support (such as live chat from Liveperson.com and integration of Web and call centre technologies from Connectivity.ca).

From the preceding discussion, some generic KSFs can be deduced:

- Front-end systems facing the customers and the back-end systems with which they interact (customer management systems) must be designed with the customer's needs in mind.
- Integrating core business operations. For instance, the online ordering system integrated with the inventory system can tell the customer which items are in stock (and thus save the frustration of finding out later that an item selected is not available).
- Scalability. Reliable technology that can serve a growing customer base is essential.
- Customer service and superior online experience.
- The ability to move quickly through a site (for example, windows should open quickly, and download times should be minimal).
- Business vision. Firms must understand that success online is not about technology (recall Vignette 6), but about exceeding customer expectations.

Resource Allocation

The analysis should lead to defining the strategic direction as well as competencies (or KSFs) required to succeed in the chosen market. Next, the firm should allocate sufficient resources—financial and human—to implement the plan. Often, promising new ventures die prematurely because they are underfunded. As we saw earlier, unbridled marketing expenditures are not the answer either. Companies that spend more money and at a faster rate than they can generate through sales are likely to be short lived too.

On the financial side, the budget must cover the cost of establishing the site and managing the site. If the site has a lot of database integration (inventory, customer accounts, and so on, linked to the Web site) and many interactive features (such as an online community site or live service support), the cost of developing and maintaining the site could be high. In addition to budgeting for creation and maintenance, there should be funds available for promotion and traffic building. For new firms this is crucial. Large operations (such as Amazon.com) have very powerful computer systems. The technology and technology support people can cost a lot of money depending on the size of operation.

On the human side, there is an increasing realization that customer service is the key to gaining customer loyalty. That means trained professionals must staff the back-end operations. Most Internet firms will have a team of technical personnel to manage the site and the technology. Marketing and business development professionals are needed to secure new business and develop partnerships. As the company grows, other functional and staff positions must be created to support this growth.

With Internet stocks going down, stock options may not be the most attractive incentive to many talented professionals. Many leave secure jobs in older companies and join start-ups because of the excitement and the chance to create something new. Hiring the right talent is a challenge that should not be minimized.

Implementation and Control

The firm must have an proper implementation plan. A strategy is only as good as the implementation. If service staff is untrained, if the fulfillment and delivery are inefficient, or if the Web site crashes frequently, the result is not likely to be positive. The technology, the people, and the resources all play a role in ensuring the success of the strategy.

Measurement and metrics must be developed or specified to ensure that performance is on track. Unique visitors, time spent on the site, number of pages seen, repeat visits, purchases, purchase size, repeat purchases, and referrals are some measures used to gauge the performance of a site. Conventional measures such as market share and ROI must also be used. Brand awareness, attitude toward the brand, and customer satisfaction are other indices that may be insightful. A systematic way of gathering data (see Chapter 5) and analyzing the data must also be put in place. The Internet provides real-time information, so consumers are no longer willing to wait for answers. Firms must develop measurement and control systems that can respond with speed.

Putting It Together: The Marketing Plan

The discussions above provide an overview of the issues that managers and strategic planners must analyze in the strategy development process. A detailed outline for an Internet marketing plan is also provided in Appendix B.

It must be stressed that the **marketing plan** is a document that is produced after a detailed strategic planning exercise is undertaken. The issues described in this chapter can provide inputs to the marketing plan. A marketing plan can be developed for a number of reasons, including seeking external funding (if the plan is part of a larger business plan), providing the management and the frontline staff a sense of direction, and serving as a benchmark for judging performance.

A marketing planning exercise should enable the firm to do the following:

- Identify suitable opportunities,
- Select the right products and markets,
- Determine the goals to be achieved,
- Design a plan of action for achieving the goals, including tactical areas such as the marketing mix,
- Specify the resources and organizational support needed to achieve the goals,
- Develop performance measures to monitor and improve performance, and
- Propose contingency plans.

In its basic structure, the Internet marketing plan is not very different from any traditional marketing plan. Details can vary and some new issues have to be addressed.

The main body of the marketing plan consists of the following:

- A description of the target market (Chapters 3, 4, and 7 cover topics related to markets).
- The marketing mix:
  - Products (including a look at branding and customization are discussed in Chapter 8).
  - Pricing (including flexible pricing methods such as auctions are also discussed in Chapter 8).
  - Promotion (Chapters 9 and 10 provide a detailed discussion of online communication including permission marketing and customized advertising).
  - Channel and distribution (Chapters 11 and 12 cover issues related to setting up Internet distribution, channel management, and setting up an online storefront).

The emphasis in subsequent chapters is often on integrating online and offline efforts. While such integration is more crucial to the so-called clicks-and-mortar firms, with online and offline operations, Internet pure-plays must also develop an integrated strategy as they advertise in mass media or develop partnerships with land-based firms.

While this chapter has laid the groundwork for understanding the strategy formulation process, Part 3 of this book provides the substance needed to develop a comprehensive marketing plan.

Summary

Organizational variables such as culture, governance structure, and people directly affect the performance of a company. Traditional firms that venture online must resolve issues regarding organizational form and structure before a detailed strategy can be developed. Pure-play start-ups have a slightly simpler task since they are not tied to an existing parent company.

The strategy development process for Internet firms follows very much the traditional approach, with a few nuances. It is obvious that many firms venture online with a poorly developed strategy or mismanage their operations, thus leading to a premature demise. It is critical that the senior management and owners develop a detailed strategy. Given the speed with which changes happen online, Internet firms must, however, be flexible enough to modify their plans if the situation demands.

An eight-factor model was proposed as a guide for those seeking to develop an Internet business or marketing strategy. The first five factors represent an evolution in the sophistication of the organization (even though some factors can occur concurrently and some may be omitted, if irrelevant). These include content, commerce, community, customization, and customer relationship management. The next variable—competition—is an external variable that must be monitored on an ongoing basis. The last two variables are internal to the firm: corporate governance and cost. The framework allows firms to visualize the evolution of the business, while also emphasizing the need to monitor internal and external variables. Understanding the organizational issues and the strategy development process and applying the eight Cs framework will lead to a more thorough marketing plan.

Key Terms

B-webs, 145	E-business, 139	Marketing plan, 163
Corporate governance, 152	Internetworked	Megamediary, 153
Customer relationship	organization, 145	Sales and marketing
management (CRM), 151	Networked organization, 144	expense ratio (SMR), 146

Questions and Exercises

Review Questions

1. What are the organizational challenges involved in setting up e-businesses? Discuss them briefly.
2. What issues must be considered when an organization moves from the bricks-and-mortar world to the online world?
3. Why are many Internet companies incurring losses or failing?
4. What are some of the key success factors for online companies?

5. What challenges do business strategists face with respect to Internet firms?
6. What are the eight Cs that must be considered during the strategy formulation process?
7. What are the key areas addressed by an Internet marketing plan?

Discussion Questions

1. Discuss the importance of having the right governance structure for an Internet company? When would you recommend an "embedded" versus a "spin-off" model?
2. What are some of the challenges a bricks-and-mortar company is likely to face as it moves from the old world to the new? How can it avoid pitfalls? Use real examples in your discussion.
3. Discuss the validity of the eight Cs framework. What additional factors would you consider if you were doing a strategic analysis of a firm?

Internet Exercises

1. Visit the new Boo.com (www.boo.com) and go through the site thoroughly. Answer the following questions:
   a. What is the business model of this site?
   b. What is the role of Miss Boo?
   c. Who is the intended target audience?
   d. What is the strategy for attracting and retaining the target market?
   e. What threats or dangers do you see ahead for this firm?
   f. Evaluate Boo.com using the eight Cs framework (ignore factors where information is not available).

Chapter 7

Community and Customer Relationship Management

Vignette 7 Build Your Home ... and Your Community

The Internet makes the world a global village of sorts. People with similar interests, professions, and lifestyles can congregate together. Advertisers and marketers love such online communities that bring together like-minded individuals. These communities, which come in several different forms, make it easier to target advertising messages.

The Web publishing sites offer a **community** model where individuals build their homepages. Not too long ago, Web sites that allowed users to build their own free homepages were considered the next big thing. The early leaders in this category were Tripod and Geocities. Others like TheGlobe.com and Xoom.com were also making waves.

The business model is quite simple. With free space and easy-to-use tools, even non-technical users were able to build Web pages. The Internet allows any individual to become a publisher. People can share their creative talents, hobbies, and professional interests with the rest of the world. Tripod and Geocities, as early pioneers in this space, captured a sizable following.

People who design the pages are likely to visit these pages and invite others to visit them. That translates to a lot of traffic, loyalty, and stickiness (time spent on the site). All of this should be attractive to advertisers and even open the door for some E-commerce opportunities later.

Individual Web pages are organized into topic areas for easy search and access. Tripod then arranges the Web pages into zones, called "pods," based on the interest or the topic of the page. Geocities uses the term "communities" for the collection of its user pages.

The portals, which were engaged in a battle for customer loyalty and advertising dollars, saw the concept of free personal homepages as a way of driving repeat visits and loyalty. Lycos acquired Tripod in 1998 for a stock deal worth $58 million. A year later, Yahoo! paid a whopping $4.65 billion for Geocities and its user base of about 19 million. At the height of the Internet stock frenzy, TheGlobe.com had a very successful initial public offering (IPO), which saw its shares skyrocket by an astonishing 606 percent at the end of the first day of trading.

Consumers who want free homepages have so many choices now, including most Internet service providers. The homepage community sites are now struggling to maintain their revenues. It is becoming evident that a pure Web publishing community business model is not viable. Geocities and Tripod are now part of larger portal sites that offer a variety of features. TheGlobe.com saw its shares drop in value by 88 percent and were trading at around $1 per share in September 2000. They are now tweaking their business model by licensing their community-building tools to other sites. Xoom.com is now part of NBCi.

Apart from the Web publishing model, there are other online community models as well. One such model, offered by eGroups.com, is a Web-based e-mail list. Members of a community can keep in touch via e-mail. Yahoo! Clubs is one of many Web-based bulletin boards where each community has its own homepage. Anexa.com (see Exhibit 7-1) similarly offers a homepage for each community, along with collaborative tools such as bulletin boards, chat rooms, calendars, and user

Exhibit 7-1 Anexa.com: A Free Online Community Provider

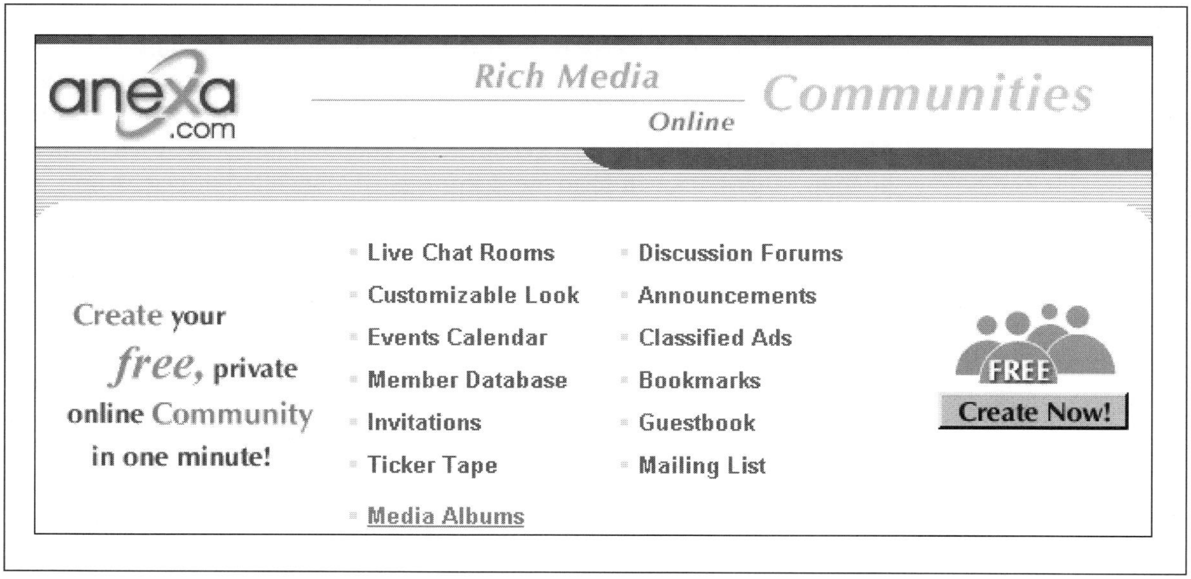

Source: www.anexa.com.

profiles. There is a bit of turmoil in the consumer community space, and it is unclear which types of community model will survive.

Many companies are shifting the focus from social communities to work groups in business settings. Intranets.com is a company that allows businesses as well as individuals to create a community or a portal that is for members only. They also provide different collaborative tools that encourage interaction and file sharing. Other companies in the intranet space include Centrinity (which makes the Firstclass software) and eRoom.com. These companies are betting that once they invest in a technology, businesses are likely to be less fickle than individual consumers. Work-based communities can enhance productivity and encourage collaborative work. Project teams within an organization, as well as buyers and sellers (e.g., VerticalNet communities), can be brought together using these collaborative tools. Even those who hate online communities may soon join one at work.

Sources: "Lycos Acquires Yahoo!," CNN, February 3, 1998; "Yahoo! Buys GeoCities: Growth Without Bounds in a Virtual World," Zona Research (www.zonaresearch.com), January 28, 1999; "You Are Not a Community Site?" Red Herring, (www.redherring.com/insider/1999/0325/inv-community.html), March 25, 1999.

Introduction

The concept of online communities has important implications for marketers. Some experts lament the fact that marketers have not made full use of online communities.[1] At the same time, as we saw in Vignette 7, there has been an overemphasis on community-based business models on the Web, with many of them proving to be unsustainable.

While sites like GeoCities and TheGlobe offer tools that enable users to build their own communities, there are other ways that marketers can use online communities. In this chapter, we will explore the use of virtual brand communities, which are sites that bring consumers and other stakeholders of a brand together. These communities, when used properly, can become an integral part of an effort to build stronger relationships with customers.

The concept of **lifetime customer value (LCV)** and the notion of relationship marketing, where the marketer aims to build a mutually beneficial long-term relationship with the customer, have gained new significance on the Web. Low customer loyalty has been the cause of many a "dot-com" failure. As we saw in the earlier chapters, the Internet allows marketers to interact closely with end-users inexpensively. We now see consumer product companies, automobile manufacturers, and airlines taking advantage of the technology. Increased competition and the increasing cost of customer acquisition, however, mean that businesses must concentrate more on improving customer retention rates.

The central theme of this chapter is customer relationship management, which is a customer-centric approach that focuses on the needs of individual customers. Such an approach requires ongoing interaction with customers. Brand communities can play a vital role in providing this interaction and act as live "focus groups." A community of consumers can provide valuable feedback and ideas for improving products and service.

Online Community

An online or virtual community is any place where groups of people can communicate with each other—such as mailing lists, newsgroups, multi-user domains (MUDs), chat rooms, or Web sites. Collaborative online workspaces, such as the ones promoted by Intranets.com, can also be described as virtual communities. The common thread among these different models is that they bring together people who have similar interests or common goals.

The concept of communities has been at the centre of the Internet since its inception.[2] Commercial exploitation of the Internet was strictly looked down upon by the early pioneers. The culture on the Internet in the early days can be characterized as anti-commerce. Even now, some old-timers on the Net hold such an attitude.[3] The Well, an online community started in 1985, epitomized the online culture of the era—thousands of participants discussing hundreds of topics in an open and free forum.[4] Other commercial online services like AOL and Prodigy, however, marched to different drummer.

The infamous Canter and Siegel case in 1994, where two immigration lawyers in the United States posted an advertisement for their services across more than 6000 newsgroups, perhaps represented a rude awakening to the then non-commercial Internet community.[5] This might have been the first mass advertising attempt on the Internet. Those less charitable would label this unethical *spamming* (sending unsolicited e-mail messages to a large number of people or newsgroups; for more on spamming and other etiquette issues, see iMarket Demo 7-1).

This case also represented a clash of cultures at that time. The Internet represented a society where everything was free, there were no barriers, and people came online for a free exchange of ideas. Canter and Siegel came with a profit motive, thus violating the norms of the Net society. They may have unwittingly contributed to the change, for better or worse, in the nature of the Internet forever—from a non-commercial environment to a commercial environment.

Why Online Communities?

A community site can be a home away from home. When people are passionate about something—whether a hobby or a profession—community sites allow them to connect with those who share the same passion. Sites like Parent Soup, for example, attract parents who seek answers to questions and wish to share their experiences. The best community sites depend on user-generated content. A new breed of sites offers a vast array of services (news, free e-mail, content, expert interviews, and shopping), while also enabling users to interact with each other. A successful community site depends on a sizable number of participants who actively participate in the online community.

According to a *Business Week*/Harris Poll, 57 percent of those of Net users frequent the same sites, instead of wandering to new sites each time they go online. Of the 89 percent of Net users who use e-mail, a third claim that they are part of an online community.[6]

The surge in online communities is partly attributable to the fact that there are more people over the age of 40 joining the Net. There are also more women who are online now. In a society where most people are time-impoverished, online communities provide an alternate way of meeting people and making friends.

Types of Online Communities[7]

The two principal types of online communities are consumer-oriented communities and business-oriented communities. Each of these categories can then be divided into several subcategories.

iMarket Demo 7-1 Etiquette for Online Communities and E-mail

Old-timers on the Internet have developed a set of norms for behaviour in newsgroups, chat rooms, and e-mail messages. Those who are new to these ways of communication would do well to take the time to understand these unwritten rules. Newbies (those who are new to the online world) often become the target of ridicule because they ask the most basic questions or violate an established norm. Here are some basic do's and don'ts.

Be Brief. People generally do not like to read long messages. Bulletin boards are usually not the place to show off one's essay-writing skills. You can be witty and write interestingly, while still being concise. There's a greater chance of someone reading your message if you adhere to this simple rule.

Quotes. When replying to someone's message, you don't have to reproduce the entire message written by the original poster. You can selectively quote parts of the original message to which you are responding. This will keep the reply short.

Threads—Read and Don't Just Respond. If you respond without carefully reading the original message and the replies to that message, there's the danger of completely missing the point. When a series of messages use the same "subject" heading, they become a thread. When replying to a message in a thread, don't change the subject heading (which will create a new thread), unless absolutely necessary.

Don't Shout. Shouting on the Internet is when someone uses all upper-case letters. It is visually irritating to read an entire message, especially a long one, when it is written all in capitals.

Don't Start Flame Wars. A flame is basically an electronic verbal attack. Messages that strongly criticize other members, at times for minor offences like poor spelling, can lead to back-and-forth exchanges of heated words. It simply increases the noise level in a discussion forum and will turn off people who want intelligent and interesting discussion.

Don't Spam. The Web may be a commercial space, but most newsgroups and bulletin boards do not approve of blatant commercial messages, especially spam. Spamming occurs when unsolicited advertisements are sent to multiple unrelated newsgroups or e-mail addresses.

Avoid Personal Information. While using your real identity is appropriate, you should avoid giving out personal information such as your phone number or address.

These are some of the basics that might make your adventure into online forums more enjoyable. Going online into a chat room or a bulletin board the first time can be intimidating for novices. Strange acronyms such as ROTFL and indecipherable symbols like ;-) and :-> may punctuate the messages found on online community sites. The uninitiated may feel at a loss.

Communication through the Internet (at least the way it is currently done) does not allow you to show facial expressions. Body language, which can often say more than words, is also absent. Smilies or emoticons are symbols that are used as visual cues that convey some additional meaning about the sender of a message and his or her mood. The list of such symbols is always growing. You need to know the most common ones and the appropriate way to use them. Smilies have gained universal acceptance and at times can make cross-cultural communication in some of the newsgroups a bit easier.

:-) Your basic smiley. This says that the message sender is making a sarcastic or joking statement. Some people may use this to mean they are in a happy mood.

;-) A wink. User just made a flirtatious and/or sarcastic remark. It's a sort of "don't hit me for what I just said" smiley.

:-(Frowning smiley. User did not like that last statement or is upset or depressed about something.

:-I Indifferent smiley. Better than a :-(but not quite as good as a :-).

:-> A really biting sarcastic remark, which is worse than a ;-).

>:-> User just made a really devilish remark.

>;-> A very lewd remark—a combination of a wink and a devilish remark.

(-: User is left-handed.

%-) User has been staring at a green screen for 15 hours straight.

:*) User is drunk.

[:] User is a robot.

8-) User is wearing sunglasses.

In addition to mastering these symbols, you must also master some abbreviations, most of which are not common in the English language. These abbreviations save some keystrokes. For newbies they are often a source of confusion. Here is a sample of such abbreviations:

BCNU: be seeing you
BTW: by the way
FWIW: for what it's worth
FYI: for your information
IMHO: in my humble opinion
OBO: or best offer
ROTFL: rolling on the floor laughing
RTFM: read the funny manual
TNSTAAFL: there's no such thing as a free lunch
TTFN: ta ta for now
TTYL: talk to you later

Lastly, remember that there is no such thing as privacy when you post messages on bulletin boards. Your employer can monitor every message you send out using your computer at work. There are also those who collect e-mail addresses from messages posted on bulletin boards and in newsgroups, with the intent of creating and selling e-mail lists.

Now that you've mastered Online Etiquette 101, are you ready to try an online community or two?

Consumer-Oriented Communities.

Demographic. A vast number of community sites aimed at individual users are organized according to demographics. Community-oriented sites such as iVillage and Women.com target women. Seniors.com, Seniornet.com, and Adultlivingchannel.com are among several community sites that cater to senior citizens. Parent Soup and Pampers.com target mothers. Teenage girls have a variety of sites to choose from, including bolt.com, go-girl.com,

Exhibit 7-2 A Community Site for African Americans

Source: www.blackvoices.com.

sweet16.com, and iTurf.com. There are also community sites for specific ethnic groups, such as NetNoir and BlackVoices (see Exhibit 7-2), which target African Americans.

Activities and Interests. In addition to the demographic focus, there are several lifestyle and interest sites that bring people together. The Women's Financial Network (www.wfn.com) and the Motley Fool (www.fool.com) target those with an interest in personal financial management. The Usenet newsgroups in the "rec." category are organized according to activities and interests.

Geographic. While the Internet is global in its reach, sites that cater to local needs tend to draw a lot of traffic. People living in the same city or town share a lot in common, and an online community is a natural extension of their physical community. Some of the geographically based sites cater to tourists (e.g., NewYork.com) and others have a stronger local community focus. InsiteBlackHouston.com not only has a local focus, but it also focuses on a specific demographic group. The Usenet newsgroups in the "soc.culture" category are similarly geographically based, focusing on people with an interest in specific countries or cultures.

Business-Oriented Communities. Just as in the case of consumer communities, the business-oriented communities can also have a national, international, or specific geographic focus. They can focus on specific industries or functions that cater to a wide range of industries.

Vertical Communities. Participants within specific industries—suppliers, manufacturers, and intermediaries—have a good reason to participate in online communities. Online communities of this sort are known as **vertical communities**. VerticalNet offers over 50 different B2B community sites, which promote buyer-seller interaction, while also enabling E-commerce. Other examples include Physicians' Online (www.po.com), a community site for practising physicians, and Agriculture Online (www.agricultureonline.com), a community for agriculturists. These sites offer communication tools for members to interact with each other. They also offer content, news, and other value-added services.

Trading Communities. These communities can be seen as a combination of the B2B hubs and exchanges discussed in Chapter 4. Trading communities support two basic functions of E-commerce—dynamic product catalogues and order processing (buying, selling, auction/bid, and payment). VerticalNet communities offer such capability. These communities are beginning to play a vital role in supply chain management. They allow buyers to source supplies worldwide and get the best prices. Sellers can also reach a global market. Both parties can lower their transaction costs. One of the features of trading communities is the value-added services that offer greater efficiency and cost savings, such as logistics planning and support. Some logistics planning and support providers are moving towards multi-firm logistics planning, where efficiencies in distribution and delivery can be achieved by pooling multi-firm product flow.

Category Communities. A site aimed at small businesses or exporters would be a category-based community. Let's Talk Business Network (or LTBN at www.ltbn.com) is a face-to-face network of entrepreneurs that acts as a support and resource group. LTBN has chapters in different North American cities, and its Web site is intended to complement its offline efforts.

Differences Between Consumer and Business Communities

Social vs. Formal. Consumer communities tend to have more of a social purpose. They bring like-minded people together. Some communities may even act as a social support system. While most community sites have some rules and norms, there is often a great degree of flexibility. Except in moderated groups, where someone is policing the discussion, it is hard to enforce strict rules of conduct. Business communities, on the other hand, tend to have a more formal agenda. Information gathering, searching for buyers or sellers, and trading products are some of the activities in business communities. There are often stricter rules for participation. For example, many actions (such as an offer to buy) can have legal implications.

Entry and Exit. Consumer communities are easier to enter and exit, and there is usually no cost attached to quitting a group. Businesses that join an online trading community may have to make significant changes to their purchasing process. As a result, there is a cost attached to entering and exiting a community.

Creation. Consumer communities are easy to start. The software and technology required is even available free of cost. Business communities that provide multiple vendor catalogues, live trading, auctions, electronic payment, logistics support, and other features can cost millions of dollars to build. Further, the founders of B2B communities must attract a large number of firms to make the operation viable and profitable. Consumer communities also need a good traffic flow to make them viable, but this is usually a much lower threshold than what business communities face.

Business Model. Most consumer sites are free. Sites that generate sizable traffic (such as Yahoo! and iVillage) can generate revenue through advertising. Community sites often expand into commerce opportunities by partnering with e-tailers (as with iVillage). In this case, the sites act as an online mall and generate commissions or a fee. B2B communities also have a variety of revenue streams, including advertising, commissions, transaction fees, membership or subscription fees, fees for hosting Web pages, and so on. In both consumer and business communities a variety of business models are possible.

Building Online Communities

"If we build it, they will come" is not likely to be true for most online communities. The community must capture a need for people—whether individuals or businesses—to get together. When community sites are built around shared interests, hobbies, or professions, there is a greater likelihood of success. The competition among community sites is intense, meaning some will end up as casualties. For example, there are at least 10 community sites targeting teenage girls.

A community site must be able to attract a large enough number of users. If the site caters to a broad segment as well as sub-segments, it may attract a lot of traffic. If there are too few participants, there will be too few messages, and this will fail to attract newcomers. A site that obtains a critical mass of members rapidly has a better chance of succeeding. Hagel and Armstrong recommend a four-stage process for developing the membership of such a site.[8]

Step 1: Attract Members. The content of a community site must be appealing to the audience. Incentives and free membership can be used to lure consumers. Advertising in mass media outlets and other related content Web sites can also be effective in creating awareness. Job sites such as Monster.com and HotJobs, which are communities of job seekers and employers, have used advertising effectively to draw in a critical mass of the two target groups.

Step 2: Build Membership. The key to building a successful community site is to ensure a steady flow of member-generated content. Articles, homepages, bulletin board postings, and chat are some of the ways members can interact with each other.

While member-generated content is important, giving members special access to other content or live interviews with guests can also encourage participation in the site. Women's community site iVillage.com has partnered with several other sites such as Parent Soup. If members are passive and do not post messages, a community site cannot thrive. While a large number of members may be passive (or "lurkers"), it is vital to ensure that different opinions are presented on the bulletin boards and in the chat rooms. The style and look of the site should match the audience and the topic.

Step 3: Customize and Create Loyalty. Members build relationships with other members as well as with the site host. The vast number of content and community sites on the Internet makes it difficult to win the loyalty of users. Customized online experience, trustworthiness, ease of use, and current and relevant content are some of the attributes that can lead to loyalty.

Step 4: Provide Value and Add Commerce. Community and commerce can interact once there is a loyal membership. Most community sites add shopping channels (as on iVillage, NetNoir, and iTurf) by partnering with reputed online stores or malls. For example, iTurf.com, which targets teenage girls, has partnered with Fashionmall, while iVillage has Planterx.com as a partner.

As the membership becomes loyal, the stickiness of the site is also likely to increase. This will lead to targeted advertising and permission marketing opportunities. For instance, members who are loyal and trust the site may agree to receive targeted one-to-one advertising messages. Such advertising can be an important source of revenue.

Online Brand Communities

The personalized and interactive nature of Internet communication is something that caught most brand managers by surprise. Few were prepared to take advantage of the technology. Some brand marketers who have dared to integrate the Internet into their brand marketing plans have ventured to create **online brand communities**, which are centred specifically on the brand. If a marketer can get consumers to talk to each other about the brand and their experiences with the brand, under the watchful eyes of the company staff, it's like having a live focus group all the time.

According to one study of the more than 300 000 topic-based discussion boards on the Internet, some 85 percent are operated by commercial organizations.[9] Forrester Research reported in 1998 that 60 percent of brand marketers had or planned to offer community-building features such as chat, message boards, and member-only areas.[10]

The Case for Brand Communities

Studies show that a typical visitor to a Web site spends less than two minutes, while visitors to community sites like iVillage and AOL tend to devote more than half an hour or more each day. This sort of stickiness is very appealing to brand managers. If consumers spend time in a branded environment on a Web site, that can help foster a closer relationship between the marketer and consumers. Active community sites can tell a marketer a lot about how consumers use the product and how they perceive the product. Vital market research information can be collected without the artificiality of focus group settings. Brand communities can also promote goodwill by showing that the marketer cares about the views of consumers and is responsive to feedback.

The Case Against Brand Communities

One school of thought on brand communities is that they're simply a pipedream that brand managers must abandon.[11] Analysts at Forrester Research make the argument that creating a site for consumers of a brand to talk to each other about is not likely to be a fruitful endeavour.[12]

Some experts have argued that unless a brand has an almost cult-like following (such as Harley Davidson or the VW Beetle) or the product has a high level of significance or involvement (such as Pentax cameras for hobbyists and professionals), it will be difficult to get people excited enough to go online to chat about the product. Tampax (www.tampax.com) and Radio Shack (www.radioshack.com) were not very successful in their community-building efforts. Radio Shack now sponsors community sections at the MSN network.

Kraft Foods (www.kraft.com) features a message board called "Wisdom of Moms Exchange," where mothers can share ideas on everything from nutrition to Halloween costumes. The only problem is that there are just a handful of messages, suggesting a lack of consumer involvement. Labatt Breweries also features a bulletin board with very few postings (see Blue Lounge at www.labatt.com). The messages typically are very favourable to the brand and completely uncontroversial. Are such highly sanitized forums worth anything? A casual visitor to these bulletin boards does not learn anything new and will find no reason to visit again. The company is also unlikely to get any new insight on consumer behaviour.

Wine.com (formerly VirtualVineyard.com), on the other hand, offers message boards with some free-flowing discussion, as well as a message board to create interaction between consumers and Wine.com's staff. In this section, the "Cork Dork" answers a broad variety of questions about wine from consumers. Creating such interaction between consumers and the sales/service staff is not easy. Wine.com has a product category where the average consumer is not very knowledgeable and hence such interactivity is somewhat easier to create.

While some of Procter & Gamble's sites do have bulletin boards, the trend is not towards creating consumer-to-consumer interaction, but to create marketer-to-consumer interaction. Customized e-mail, interactive product selection tools, and customized products or services are some of the ways in which such interaction can be enhanced.

Managerial Issues in Online Brand Communities

Before deciding to establish an online brand community, which is a costly decision, several issues must be addressed.

Goals of the Community. While some community sites are successful, many have failed. Brand communities do not seem to create a lot of excitement and participation, with a few exceptions. Before creating a brand-centred community, the goals of the community must be clearly delineated. For instance, is the community intended to serve as a customer feedback forum or is it a part of customer support system?

Nature of the Product and Usage Experience. Some products lend themselves to online community building. Brands that have a unique social image or brands that are highly involving (have a high degree of personal relevance) for the consumers seem to have a better chance of developing a successful brand community. It is unlikely that consumers will want to chat about toothpaste or house cleaning products. Consumers are not going to take the time to participate in communities for all the brands they consume. The brand should mean something substantial to them to justify the time and effort involved in participation. Few brands can pass such a test.

Disney's Family.com is among the exceptions. The site offers message boards on a variety of topics and tends to draw a large number of parents. The power of the Disney brand and its strong association with children and families explains the success of this site. While this is a brand-sponsored site, the discussion does not focus on the brand.

Consumer- vs. Marketer-Created Communities. Unlike the community sites that cater to people with different interests, the online brand communities are intended to bring consumers of the brand together. Companies create brand communities to foster interaction among users as well as to get feedback from the users of the product. Pentax offers a community on its site for hobbyists and professionals (www.pentax.com/discussion.html).

Some brand communities are consumer-created. For instance, there are several Harley Davidson communities or clubs created by bike owners or enthusiasts (see www.excite.com/communities/). Some of these communities are rated as "adult" content by Excite, the portal that hosts the communities. Such communities along with the image of bikers created by groups like the Hell's Angels can damage the brand image.

Harley Davidson has countered such private clubs with their own official community called Harley Owner's Group (www.hog.com). The Harley Davidson case shows the difficulty of controlling and protecting a brand's image online.

Moderated vs. Unmoderated Communities. Most brand communities are moderated to some degree to ensure that messages that are very damaging to the brand are not posted. Procter & Gamble's Always (www.always.com) even specifies a topic for discussion each month. Such sanitized communities will not promote free-flowing discussions, nor will they enable the brand manager to know the consumers' true feelings and experiences with the brand.

Exhibit 7-3 Messages from Shell's Bulletin Board

> **Date:** July 10, 1999 03:55 PM
> **Author:** Fiona Lough (_lough368E@btinternet.com_)
> **Subject:** clean up money or cover up money?
>
> I read recently in NI (July 1999) that Shell has spent $32 million on PR cleaning up it's image after the Nigeria fiasco.
>
> What I want to know is why does shell spend this money cleaning up its image. Why not spend this money cleaning up Nigeria and helping local people there?
>
> Fiona Lough
>
> . . . .
>
> **Date:** February 05, 2000 02:03 AM
> **Author:** Kerri Bowes (_kerribowes@hotmail.com_)
> **Subject:** cover up or clean up? neither!
>
> Cover up or Clean up? How clever since you obviously have not cleaned up Southeast Nigeria. Also, your cover up, which compromises a large portion of this site, is weak and many people are seeing through it.

Source: www.shell.com.

Shell, on the other hand, allows users to post messages that may be very critical of the company's record in areas like the environment and social issues (see Exhibit 7-3). By facing the critics directly, Shell may be able to soften the impact of negative word-of-mouth. Such a forum also gives Shell a chance to set the record straight if a particular viewpoint is wrong. Clearly, it is a risky strategy. But Shell has decided that it is a risk worth taking.

Establishing Community Norms and Rules. Just like any other group setting, such as a place of work, a classroom, or social club, online communities also have their own set of norms and rules. For a community to thrive, participants must adhere to some rules.[13] Some of the areas where policy may be required include the use of appropriate language, identity (whether members should use their actual names or assume a different identity), flaming, and message content (should discussion focus on a specific issue, as in the case of Always.com, or can the topics and threads evolve according to users' interest).

eBay, the best-known community site, which brings millions of individual buyers and sellers together, asked a court in Chicago to ban a user for using foul language and violating its rules. Responding to concerns regarding copyright violation, eBay also had to ban auctions of certain music and software products. In addition, the company has had to ban other illegal auctions of body parts. eBay polices the postings on its sites closely to ensure that illegal activity does not take place on its site.

 Technology and Nature of Interaction. There are many different software tools available for online community building (for examples, see <u>thinkofit.com/webconf/index.htm</u>). Some chat programs are graphically based (such as <u>www.worlds.net</u> and <u>www.chatpoint.com</u>), thus allowing individuals to assume a visual image called an avatar (such as a person, animal, or some object). Heineken's bulletin board called the Heineken Lounge uses ChatPoint and offers a visual chat environment (see Exhibit 7-4).

Brand Communities and Marketing Relationships

The key benefit of brand communities is that they can foster a closer relationship between the company and different stakeholders. While Shell's community section draws strong criticism from environmentalists and others, it also provides the company an opportunity to understand the concerns of different groups. Brand communities can be an integral part of a company's relationship marketing and customer relationship management efforts.

 Community sites not only allow marketers to know their customers better, but they also create consumer-to-consumer interaction. This online word-of-mouth can be quite powerful and can play a useful role. NetObjects (<u>www.netobjects.com</u>), a company that makes Web development software products, has a team of volunteer users, called Team NetObjects, answering questions on several of the NetObjects newsgroups. In these newsgroups, users share experiences and experts help novices. The newsgroups are unmoderated, meaning

Exhibit 7-4 Heineken Lounge

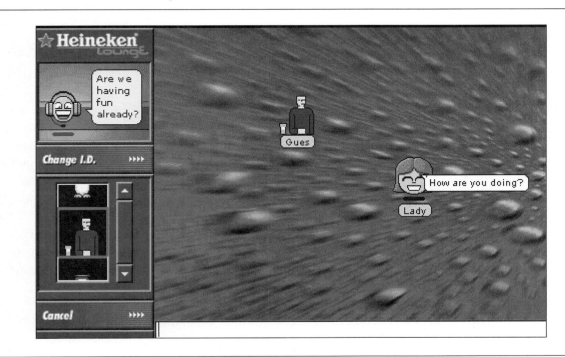

Source: www.heineken.com.

Exhibit 7-5 Marketing Relationships on Online Brand Communities

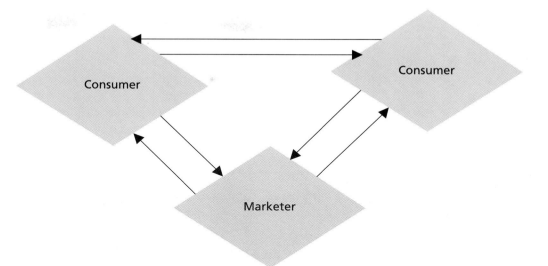

negative comments about NetObjects are allowed. The consumer-to-consumer interaction substitutes for expensive customer care and support personnel.

Since community sites like these can foster both marketer-customer relationships and consumer-consumer relationships, marketers must understand the dynamics of such a three-way interaction (see Exhibit 7-5). By promoting a relationship among users of a brand, the company may be able to influence word-of-mouth communication. In the NetObjects newsgroups, some expert users often act as opinion leaders. Their views seem to carry a lot of weight. If the opinion leaders are favourably disposed toward the brand, the brand can benefit from the influence they exert among their followers.

Customer Relationship Management

Even before the advent of the Web and Internet commerce, businesses were beginning to realize that building long-term relationships with their most valued customers will significantly impact financial performance. We see several trends online that will accelerate the move towards a relationship-based marketing approach.

First, the Internet provides many choices for consumers. Only 10 to 15 percent of visitors to a site return and exhibit some degree of loyalty.[14] Low loyalty leads to greater customer acquisition costs. The average customer acquisition cost for Internet pure-plays was $82 in 1999, and it is not uncommon to see companies spend in excess of $200 per customer acquired.[15] Online firms also spent an unsustainable 119 percent of their revenues on marketing in 1999, as they struggled to establish their brands.[16] Internet pure-plays in some sectors, such as apparel, can spend 20 to 40 percent more in customer acquisition costs, as compared to stores that have both a physical and online presence. The combination of low loyalty and high customer acquisition costs can be devastating for new companies.

Second, consumers have also become more discriminating and are increasingly demanding products that are personalized to suit their individual needs. To meet such expectations, marketers must engage in an ongoing dialogue with each customer. The move from mass

iMarket Demo 7-2 Instant Messaging: The Way to Connect Online

We live in world of instant communication, where even a short wait for someone to respond to an e-mail or message on an answering machine may seem like eternity—and it's definitely unfashionable. Thanks to instant messaging, we no longer have to wait. Instant messengers are like pagers, with a slight difference. They work online and can give us instant access to anyone we want, as long as they are also online.

The applications in business are endless. In BancorpSouth's operations centre in Mississippi, employees use instant messengers to give technical support to customers. Credit Suisse First Boston custom-developed an instant messaging tool called Global Talk to let 1500 bond traders, analysts, and salespeople in offices worldwide exchange time-sensitive trading information. In this business, information has to travel in real time (like telephone) and hence the conventional e-mail will not work.

Some organizations are not sure if instant messaging is a valuable business tool or if employees will use it engage in private chat. BancorpSouth, so far, does not have a strategy for using it organization-wide, even though some employees are using it voluntarily. At Minneapolis-based Behavioral Health, 150 of the 2000 desktop computers have instant messaging, but the organization is still evaluating this tool.

In a survey done by *ComputerWorld* magazine, 17 percent of IT managers said that their organizations used instant messaging, while an overwhelming 78 percent felt that it was unnecessary because existing e-mail and other communication tools do the job fine. While questions may remain about businesses adopting this technology, there is no doubt that consumers are beginning to use instant messaging in huge numbers. Currently, an estimated 80 million people use instant messaging, with AOL catering to roughly half of the market. MSN and ICQ are two other messaging services with substantial adoption rates.

The latest generation of instant messaging services are not just text-based or person-to-person. They include multi-party chat, buddy-to-buddy voice communication (via the Internet), and even instant-messaging-to-cell-phones (ICQ allows instant messages to be forwarded to cell phones).

The most common instant messenger applications are ICQ, AOL Instant Messenger (AIM), MSN Messenger, Yahoo Messenger, and Tribal Voice PowWow. There are also several other instant messaging services. Currently there's a battle between AOL and other companies because AOL does not allow other messaging services access to its members. This is like Sprint telephone customers not being able to call AT&T's customers. This lack of interoperability is frustrating for consumers because they cannot connect with friends or co-workers who are on a rival messaging service.

In the not-too-distant future, instant messaging is likely to be part of regular e-mail and Web browser software. As technologies converge, the ability to initiate the message in one medium (instant messenger, e-mail, cell phone, or fax) and receive it another medium will become commonplace. The instant messaging applications can definitely play role in marketer-customer communication.

Sources: Dominique Deckmyn (1999), "Instant Messaging: Tool or Temptation?" *ComputerWorld*, July 12, 1999; Gregg Keizer (2000), "CNET Reviews Top Instant Messengers," *CNET* (www.cnet.com), April 4, 2000; Christa Degnan (1999), "Instant Messaging Salvos Hit Users," *eWorld* (www.zdnet.com/eworld), August 22, 1999.

marketing to **mass customization**, which is evident in many industries (such as computers, automobiles, clothing, and online content services), will bring the marketer and the consumer closer to each other.

Third, the Internet makes even small local companies compete in a global market. The intense competition is driving companies to invest in strategies that will increase customer retention rates. Increasing retention rates by 5 percent can increase profits by 25 to 50 percent.[17]

Lastly, a customer contributes a lot more to profits when he or she makes repeated purchases and exhibits brand loyalty. Studies of lifetime customer value and customer life-cycle economics are showing that customers, especially in the case of e-tail companies, tend to be unprofitable in the initial few purchases, when customer acquisition costs are higher than the contribution from the customer to company profits. As a customer is retained, not only does the average purchase size and the frequency of purchases increase, but so does the profit-per-customer metric.[18] A study by Bain & Company showed that in different product categories like books, groceries, and apparel, online retailers lose anywhere from $25 to $85 per customer in the first year. By the third year, the company can make $15 to $85 in profit per customer if it retains the customers.[19]

The economic reality is that unless Internet companies develop customer loyalty, which means engaging in a long-term relationship-building strategy, profitability will remain a distant dream. Unfortunately, many companies pay lip service to customer relationships, but fail to implement the systems and strategies needed to succeed. For instance, when consumers make purchases online they provide a lot of personal information, including address, e-mail, and product preferences. Very few marketers take advantage such customer data. In fact, only 4 percent of firms sent a personalized follow-up message following a purchase, 47 did not ask customers if they would like additional related information sent, only 25 percent recognized repeat buyers, and 40 percent of e-mail messages were unanswered.[20] In the following sections, the advantages of customer relationship management, its components, and key managerial issues are addressed.

Relationship Marketing Online

Relationship marketing (RM) has been extensively studied since the 1980s. Relationship marketing has been defined as "attracting, maintaining, and in multi-service organizations, enhancing customer relationships."[21] In the business-to-business marketing literature, relationship marketing is defined as "marketing oriented toward strong, lasting relationships with individual accounts."[22] A discussed earlier, establishing a long-term relationship with customers can lower the cost of marketing and reduce transaction costs for the firm. For the customers, the decision process is simplified and so is the cost of making the decision.[23] As firms shift their emphasis from customer acquisition to customer retention, the notion of building a life-long relationship with customers has gained significance.

In the last few years, the advent of the Internet as a communication medium and a marketing channel has suddenly enhanced the marketer's ability to engage in relationship marketing.[24] The Internet, due to its interactive nature and global reach, is adding new dimensions to relationship marketing. The Internet has been hailed as the ultimate medium for relationship marketing. It allows real-time interaction between the customer and marketer—and at much lower costs when compared to the traditional channels.

On the Internet, relationship marketing approaches can include customized e-mail and Web pages, online communities (chat, bulletin boards), customized products, and customized technical services. Dell, for example, offers a Premier Page for larger customers, which is a dedicated Web space that includes a customized store and technical support services, order status, and tracking services.

In contrast, the traditional communication methods (mail, phone, fax) tend to limit the extent of interaction and offer less flexibility and opportunities for customization. The Internet allows the marketer to learn more about the consumer and provide a fast, customized response to customer needs. Table 7-1 highlights some of the differences between Internet-based and traditional relationship marketing methods.

While it is important to understand the differences, businesses should aim to integrate the Internet with other modes of communication. This ensures multiple contact points for the consumer, allowing him or her to choose the best means of interacting with the business.

From Relationship Marketing to Customer Relationship Management

Some may argue that the term **customer relationship management** (CRM or eCRM) is just a new buzzword for the well-known concept of relationship marketing. While the concepts are not entirely different, CRM takes a view that goes beyond marketing. CRM calls for a "consistent, unified customer interaction across all communication channels, all applications, and all business functions."[25] Such an integrated approach is essential to satisfy and retain customers.

CRM is not just a marketing effort, it is an organization-wide strategic effort, with the "end-goal of having a real impact on the way the company competes in the market."[26] CRM is about managing the **total customer experience** (TCE) from the initial information seeking to post-purchase customer care. This means a firm that has an offline store and an online store should be able to sell products online and accept returns in the physical stores. The consumer is guaranteed consistent, high-quality service, regardless of the channel of communication and transaction.

Amazon.com has a strategic partnership with Toys R Us, which allows Amazon.com to sell toys online, but the logistics of returning the products to a physical Toys R Us store have not been implemented so far. Other firms, which have dual channels, such as Sears and Wal-Mart (which are both offline and online) are not doing any better. When a customer buys a product online, a lot of personal information is recorded. If the customer shops in the physical store later, the retailer should be able to effectively use the customer profile gathered online. Some e-tailers, such as Wal-Mart, are operating their online ventures separately from their offline stores, which can lead to a less-than-satisfactory experience for the customers who use both channels.

CRM is about ensuring a superior total customer experience with the entire organization:[27]

Table 7-1 Traditional vs. Internet-Based Relationship Marketing

Criteria	Relationship Marketing— Traditional Method	Internet-Based Relationship Marketing
Degree of customization	Focus on mass market segments, not customization	Enhanced ability to customize content and products *Consequence*: Higher satisfaction
Response time	Delayed response; complaints and queries often fail to get timely response	Ability to provide real-time response using online communication; online customer service using intelligent e-mail software *Consequence*: Higher satisfaction
Frequency of customer-marketer interaction	Infrequent interaction; high cost of interaction	Frequent interaction; low cost of interaction *Consequence*: Greater trust and understanding
Nature of customer marketer interaction	Superficial	More in-depth *Consequence*: Greater mutual understanding
Knowledge base	Difficulty in capturing customer data; high cost	Customer data can be captured easily at relatively low cost *Consequence*: Marketer more aware of customer needs

Source: Ramesh Venkat (1999).[28]

- Across all touch points (call centre, Web, kiosks, sales reps, service personnel)
- Across all company divisions or departments (sales, marketing, accounting, operations, distribution and logistics, support services)
- Across all experiential elements (pre-sales activity, product selection, design/customization, purchase/ordering process, post-sales customer care).

Investment in Technology. Such coordination requires a well-defined strategic direction and substantial investment in technology. In many large organizations, customer data is collected by different departments (sales, marketing, accounts, shipping, and so on) and through different channels (call centres, sales reps, Web site, store, and so on). CRM requires significant IT infrastructure that would streamline customer data gathering and dissemination.

 According to research by the International Data Corporation (www.idc.com), the CRM software application market was worth $3.3 billion in 1999 and is expected to reach

$12.1 billion by 2004.[29] CRM software applications fall into three categories: sales automation, marketing automation, and customer support and call centre software. A detailed discussion of the technology is beyond the scope of this book. It is, however, evident that marketing is becoming highly aligned with sales and customer service.

Strategic Direction. The desired end-state or CRM vision must have buy-in at all levels of the organization. PriceWaterhouseCoopers had identified three critical success factors for CRM: (1) unique understanding of the customer, their habits, likes, and dislikes; (2) knowledge of the organization, its preparedness to meet customer needs, and its resources and capabilities; and (3) a commitment to continuous quality improvement, including gaps in quality and process for monitoring and improving quality.[30]

Steps in CRM. Understanding and responding to customer needs is at the heart of any CRM strategy. The CRM process essentially begins with the identification of customers, followed by the differentiation of customers based on their needs and their value to the company. Not every customer needs the same treatment—those who buy more frequently may need more attention. The ability to differentiate among the customers requires a rich customer database filled with information on demographic information and behavioural data such as usage patterns. After gaining an understanding of the customers, the market must create an ongoing method of interacting and communicating with customers in a cost-effective manner. E-mail, Web-enabled call centres, and other tools can be used together to customize the communication for each customer. Lastly, the result of the deep customer knowledge and personalized communication should lead to customization of some aspect of the product or service.[31]

Enterprise Perspective. The heavy investment in information technology has led to the misguided notion that CRM is the responsibility of the IT department. Nothing could be further from the truth. CRM requires an enterprise-wide view and commitment. Dell, for example, allows the consumer to configure and customize the product, track the progress of the order online, and get personalized technical support. This requires the commitment of not just the marketing department—operations, logistics, accounts, and customer service must also function with the common objective of providing a superior total consumer experience.

In North America, Nissan has 1100 Nissan and 152 Infiniti dealerships. Nissan decided that it was not enough to have a simple customer database. Nissan wanted a integrated system that would enable them to "access consumer information, analyze data or demographics, profile buyers, segment them, do data mining, predict response to campaigns, and generate outbound campaigns."[32] Nissan's plan is to take a "holistic view of customer relationship." Rather than focus on single channels, the company plans to integrate the Web, the call centre, and the fulfillment departments with the dealers in the frontline. The intent is to respond to customers in a manner that will encourage loyalty.

The Result. A company that is customer-centric and has an efficient CRM system in place will consistently perform at or above consumer expectations. Assume, for example, that a frequent airline traveller has had a flight delay. A call from the airline is a rarity. A customer-centric airline with a CRM system in place is likely to respond differently.

A customer-centric airline would link flight information to a customer notification system. When there is a flight delay, the scheduling system would automatically notify the passengers and designated contacts using the preferred mode of communication previously specified. The airline's internal system then might send an e-mail to the traveller's assistant, place a phone call to the traveller's spouse, call the traveller's cell phone, and issue an update to the reservation systems of the hotel and car rental companies. The messages would be created and sent automatically, without human intervention, based on agreements made beforehand between the airline and its customers.[33]

Tapscott and his colleagues refer to the business web or b-web as the force that creates "relationship capital" and shifts power away from the marketer for a new marketer-customer relationship.[34] As businesses focus on loyalty and lifetime customer value, customer relationships become assets. Two-way communication, and not the mass marketing one-way communication, is the new rule. B-webs are nerve centres where the consumer and the marketer communicate with each other. Such communication becomes the vital ingredient in building a relationship. Imagine a b-web at Volvo or any other car manufacturer, who (just like the efficient, customer-centric airline) not only sells cars (customized, of course), but also offers a range of services. The car-maker, having sold a customized product, takes care of the insurance and financing, picks up the car for regular service and upgrades, and using the Internet-enabled car can provide plans for long road trips and even call 911 when the owner has been in an accident.[35]

While some may see such an extended service taking the company away from its core business, we already have the technology to create such a relationship between the consumer and the marketer. As competitors offer similar technologies, features, and product quality, customer relationship building will increasingly focus on service elements.

Customization and Customer Relationship

The Internet is gradually, but surely, changing the one-way producer-consumer model, where producers "pushed" their products down the channel and consumers bought them because there was no other choice. The Internet allows the producer to understand the needs of each consumer and provides a cost-effective interface through which consumers can design the products and services they want. The distinction between consumers and producers is being blurred in some cases, and consumers are becoming "prosumers."[36]

Customization of products and personalization of online experiences is the mantra now. Advances in computer-aided production methods have allowed businesses to follow flexible manufacturing methods. The Web allows businesses a cost-effective interface where consumers can configure the product to their liking. We see examples of customization in such industries as apparel (Levis and IC3D.com), automobiles (Saturn, Toyota, Volvo, and Mercedes, see Exhibit 7-6), and computers (Dell, Gateway, and HP). Digital products such as music (CDNow) and news (CNN, Yahoo!) are also personalized.

Why Customization? In an era when competitors have the capability to offer similar features and quality, product differentiation is not visible in most industries. All offerings look the same to the consumer. Increased choices through the Internet and a growing emphasis on price (see Chapter 8 for a discussion of this topic) have reduced loyalty significantly. Customization is seen as a way to build one-on-one relationships with customers. The consumer engages in a value exchange by sharing personal details and product preferences in exchange for a customized product.[37] The success of early pioneers in customization (such as Dell) has encouraged others to follow.

For consumers, the value proposition is likely to be far superior in the case of customized products. When a consumer pays $10 for a CD with 10 songs, where he or she is only interested in three songs, 70 percent of that product delivers no value to the consumer. If, on the other hand, the customer could custom-build a CD with 10 favourite songs, that

Exhibit 7-6 Mercedes Allows Customization

See your ideal luxury vehicle take shape before your eyes as you build your own Mercedes-Benz.

MBUSA.com's Build Your Own allows you to custom-design your C320 by choosing the colors, accessories, packages and options you desire.

Building your own Mercedes-Benz not only ensures that your new vehicle suits your tastes and fits your lifestyle. It also allows your Mercedes-Benz retailer to more quickly fulfill your order, finalize pricing and get you into your new Mercedes-Benz.

Source: www.mbusa.com.

product offers three times the value. A satisfied customer has a greater chance of being a loyal customer.

How Do You Customize? There are different approaches to mass customization. The four basic approaches to customization are transparent, adaptive, collaborative, and cosmetic customization (see Exhibit 7-7).

Cosmetic customization is simply changing the presentation of the product. With consumer packaged goods manufacturers may allow different types of retailers (supermarkets, convenience stores, and warehouse clubs) to purchase different package sizes with different labelling. The product is the same, but the presentation is different. Collaborative cus-

Exhibit 7-7 The Four Approaches to Customization

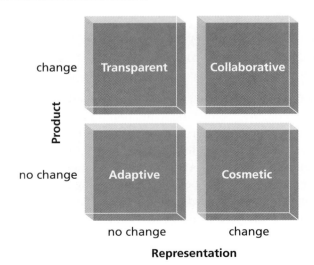

Source: Gilmore and Pine II (1997).[38]

tomization requires the customers to articulate their needs and have a dialogue with the marketer. Products that require a personal fit, such as eyeglasses, apparel, and shoes, are good candidates for such customization.

Adaptive customization is when the same product is delivered to all customers, with the customer having the ability to tailor or modify the product for different uses. Dell's online support and knowledge base is a standard offering, where each consumer can use different queries to find answers to specific questions. Standard computer monitors sold to different consumers can be adjusted for colour, brightness, and hue to suit individual preferences. Lastly, transparent customization occurs when the personalized product or service is delivered without the consumer being aware of it. Web sites that use collaborative filtering (such as Amazon.com, which tracks purchases) can make recommendations for new products based on past behaviour. Web sites that use cookies and other tracking devices can deliver different pages or ads to different consumers, based on historical preferences.

Not all products and services will be good candidates for customization. Consumers may never want to customize certain products, and the nature of customization may differ from what we have seen so far.

Planning for Customization. Customization for the sake of customization is an ill-advised move. There are several planning questions must be answered before an organization can effectively implement online customization:[39]

- Does the firm need customization? Will customization provide a competitive advantage and add value to customers?
- What are the objectives of customization? Is the goal to generate sales or traffic? Measures for judging the effectiveness of the strategy must also be specified.
- The target market for customization must be defined. Will customization be available to all consumers or only to members or subscribers?
- What are the rules for customization? What features will be offered on a customized basis? What technology is required to implement customization? There are several companies that offer the required database and customization software solutions. These must be tested and evaluated.
- Will collaborative filtering (see iMarket Demo 7-3), a methodology that allows firms to make individualized product recommendations, be used?
- Is the firm collecting the appropriate consumer data (user profile, preferences, shopping history, and so on) and are the firm's data organized appropriately to enable customization? For instance, can the customization program recognize that a person who buys skis will also need bindings?
- How will the firm ensure privacy and security of consumer data?
- Does the firm have a plan for pilot testing customization? Yahoo!, for instance, tested its personalization service (myYahoo) with a subset of its market before a full-scale launch. Potential problems can be avoided by offering customization in just one area of the Web site or carrying out a test with a sample of customers.
- What are the resource requirements? Programming costs, maintenance, and support, as well as the cost to scale upward as the site grows, must be considered.

Challenges in Customization. Case studies show that mass customization requires a flexible manufacturing process, which does not require huge inventories, as Dell has successfully demonstrated. Such as process requires a new way of operating—build-to-order and

iMarket Demo 7-3 Collaborative Filtering: Linking Community and Customization

Consumers buy many products on the basis of subjective judgments. These products may be complex and sometimes difficult to evaluate on concrete attributes. They may include everything from books to movies and stereo systems. What if there was a way for consumers to share their experiences with each other and make recommendations to each other? If you know that Consumer A reads the same kind of books as you do, wouldn't you be interested in a recommendation she has for a new book? Wouldn't such recommendations from people with similar interests make your decision-making process easier, especially when faced with information overload?

Sites such as Amazon.com allow consumers not only to review products, but also to make recommendations to each other. Amazon also tracks the purchases of "like-minded" customers and when you search for a book title, it also provides additional recommendations under the heading, "Customers who bought this book also bought." Thus, Amazon creates a sort of customized store for each customer by providing a list of recommendations.

Filtering is simply the process of selecting the most valuable and interesting information when there is a vast amount of information available. **Collaborative filtering**, the process that companies like Amazon use to make recommendations, is filtering based on evaluations, recommendations, or purchases made by other people.

The premise behind collaborative filtering is that consumers looking for information should be able to make use of what others have already found and evaluated, without having to reinvent the wheel.

Collaborative filtering on the Web takes advantage of the ability to track consumer behaviour online. By tracking a community of consumers, similarities in purchasing behaviour and preferences can be used as the basis for making recommendations. In other words, it is automated word-of-mouth. Some sites merely make product recommendations, which is similar to *cross-selling* (selling a related product) or *up-selling* (selling a more expensive product).

Much of the personalization and customization efforts on the Web are based on collaborative filtering. The Firefly Network (acquired by Microsoft in 1998) was a pioneer in this area. Firefly's flagship product, called Firefly Passport, collected user preferences anonymously, recommended Internet content, and sent out targeted advertising. Other companies like Engage (www.engage.com) and Net Perceptions (www.netperceptions.com) also offer personalization and filtering technologies. Collaborative filtering depends on data mining. Vast amounts of user preference data must be converted into meaningful sets of recommendations

Collaborative filtering tools have been used in Usenet newsgroups, where millions of messages are posted each day, to make recommendations on messages to read based on the popularity of messages in a newsgroup. Large organizations that generate lots of reports and documents can also use collaborative filtering to enable employees to make recommendations to each other on what is useful and what is not.

A critical step in building customer relationships is to gather data about customers' purchases and preferences and utilize this information in creating customized experiences. The collaborative filtering methodology enables online marketers to effectively utilize information from individuals as well as online communities of consumers to generate customized recommendations for each customer.

Sources: "Filtering and Collaborative Filtering," *Notes from the DELOS Workshop*, Budapest, Hungary, November 1997; David Maltz and Kate Ehrlich (1995), "Pointing the Way: Active Collaborative Filtering," *Proceedings of the ACM SIGCHI Conference* (www.cs.cmu.edu/~dmaltz/ACF95-draft8.txt); John Fraim (1998), "Collaborative Filtering, Engage & Webmining ... The Internet Store Moves Closer to Reality," *Insights*, The C. G. Jung Page, November (www.cgjungpage.org/articles/insights3.html).

not build-to-stock. Going from mass production, which attempts to drive costs down through repetitious tasks, to mass customization, which calls for a flexible system that responds quickly to customer needs, is not an easy task. Investment in technology and training, as well as a sound strategy, are essential.

Nissan reportedly had 87 different steering wheel models. Consumers did not want to choose from so many options.[40] Understanding what product consumers want to customize and what attributes or features of the product are important is vital. It is wasteful to offer many options when the consumer is not looking any.

Amdahl offered customization of mainframe computers by maintaining high levels of inventory for all components, but the company soon learned that this was not a profitable approach. Successful customizers like Dell have a rationalized supply chain where parts are ordered only when they are needed. Such a supply chain management strategy will take time and effort to develop.

CRM: Promise vs. Performance

One-to-one marketing and customer relationship management suggest that the emphasis should not be on market share building, but on building sustained relationships with top customers. In theory, customer relationship management, mass customization, and one-to-one marketing sound good, but do the results measure up?

A study by Anderson Consulting that examined 250 companies in six industries, found that CRM and one-to-one marketing capability can significantly affect profits.[41] The study examined the impact of different CRM capabilities, such as having customer insight (turning information into insight, customer acquisition and retention), customer offerings (strong value proposition, brand management), customer interactions (customer service and key account management), high-performance organization (motivating and rewarding people, building service culture), and enterprise integration. The conclusion was that when an organization moves from an average to a high-performance company on these capabilities, the impact on profits is significant.

While these results suggest that the arduous path to building customer relationships is worth the trouble, there is also evidence questioning the impact of relationship management efforts. On the Web, for every success story there are innumerable failures.

According to Peppers and Rogers, authors of several books on one-to-one marketing, successful one-to-one marketing requires the integration of customer data from different departments and the use of this data to satisfy the needs of the customer.[42] Such integration can be expensive and is a stumbling block in large organizations.

Companies that go overboard with the technology will end up with a system that does not offer a human interface. Case studies show that in business-to-business settings, CRM systems that offer little flexibility for price negotiation and interaction with sales/technical staff may meet with consumer resistance or rejection. While CRM has become a technology-driven process, the lack of person-to-person communication is seen as a flaw.[43]

The promise of consumer profiling is that technology will allow Web sites to study the behaviour of each consumer and then modify the offerings, ads, or pages accordingly. Such customization does require detailed customer data, which has raised privacy concerns among consumers. Marketers must earn the trust of consumers in order to succeed in their CRM efforts.[44] Consumers should be partners in the effort, not adversaries.

Many marketers have shown an inability to transform from a mass marketer to a one-to-one marketer. Marketers at times make excessive demands on customers who want a personalized approach. They are bombarded with e-mail messages, many of which are not really customized. Companies have also shown that they do not always reward loyalty. The focus on "top customers" can make other loyal customers feel unappreciated.[45] Going from mass marketing to CRM or one-to-one marketing not only requires investment in technology, but also a change in business philosophy.

If the technology challenges, implementation problems, and privacy issues can be addressed, then the promise of customer relationship management looks very inviting. Marketing will not just be the "4 Ps" controlled by the marketer. Marketing will be based on a relationship with the customer, where the customer plays a role in designing the product and even dictates the price of the product. This means that traditional marketers will have to rethink the way they function.

Summary

Online communities are still a big draw on the Internet. Contrary to the expectations of many that the Internet will reduce interaction and communication among people, the thriving bulletin boards and chat rooms are showing that people will learn to use these new tools to socialize with each other.

As marketers move away from mass marketing to more individualized marketing and communication, many have tried to build online brand communities. These communities are intended to foster interactivity on the site, as well develop frequent and meaningful communication between the marketer and customers. In reality, however, very few brands have had the power to create strong online communities. The concept of brand communities could still be part of a larger customer relationship management effort.

The Web is a personalized medium. The advent of the Web coincided with developments in mass customization in the early 1990s. We now see a wide range of products and services being customized. Marketers are making efforts to move from impersonal mass marketing to a more personalized one-to-one marketing. The customer is not seen as a transaction, but as someone worthy of a long-term relationship.

Customer relationship management strategies are being implemented in many large organizations. The process requires the integration of data from diverse departments and a coordinated and consistent response to the consumer's needs, regardless of the channel of contact—offline or online. In reality, CRM efforts have been successful in some organizations, but have failed in others. The mistakes range from poor understanding of the CRM process to unworkable technology. In spite of these setbacks, most experts agree that CRM and one-to-one marketing will be a big part of the future.

Key Terms

Collaborative filtering, 188
Community, 166
Customer relationship
  management (CRM), 182

Instant messaging, 180
Lifetime customer value, 168
Mass customization, 181
One-to-one marketing, 189

Online brand community, 175
Total consumer
  experience, 182
Vertical communities, 172

Questions and Exercises

Review Questions

1. What is an online community?
2. What are the different types of consumer and business-oriented communities?
3. What steps should one follow in building an online community?
4. Describe an online brand community. Provide examples.
5. What are the arguments for and against establishing online brand communities?
6. Define relationship marketing.
7. What is customer relationship management?
8. Why have some companies failed in their efforts to implement CRM?
9. Why is mass customization gaining popularity? What are the four different methods of customization?

Discussion Questions

1. Do you think that CRM will lead to a situation where face-to-face interactions become very rare? Would you recommend that companies offer face-to-face interaction even when they implement CRM?
2. How can governments (local, state/provincial, or federal) use the concepts discussed in this chapter—community, customization, and customer relationship?
3. Do you think customization is just a fad or is it here to stay? Substantiate your point of view.

Internet Exercises

1. Visit the site for either Yahoo! or CNN on at least two successive days. Record your impressions of the sites. Then personalize the site (go to myYahoo and myCNN). Now use the site for at least two successive days. Record your impressions of the personalized site. Compare it with your earlier experience.
2. Visit the following auto-makers: Mercedes (www.mbusa.com), Saturn (www.saturn.com), and Toyota (www.toyota.com). Explore the custom-building features on these sites. How different is the experience from buying a car from a dealer (where you have some flexibility in choosing options)? Which of the three companies does a better job in terms of customization? What recommendations would you make to each site to improve their customer relationship efforts?
3. Visit an online brand community, such as www.shell.com or www.pentax.com (go to USA). Follow some of the messages and threads. What are your views regarding the value of the community for the brand?

Chapter **8**

Product Management
and Pricing

Vignette 8 **Old Economy Brands in the New Economy**

Learning Objectives

After completing this chapter, you will:

- Understand how the Internet facilitates product development.
- Understand the impact of the Internet on brand management.
- Appreciate the challenges involved in online branding.
- Appreciate how the pricing function is affected by online marketing.
- Be able to apply concepts in online branding and pricing to real-life decisions.

Companies like Procter & Gamble (P&G), Unilever, and General Mills are dubbed "old economy" companies because they produce mundane fast-moving consumer goods (FMCGs) that are routine, low-involvement purchases in bricks-and-mortar supermarkets and drug stores. These products are not considered part of the technology revolution that defines the new economy.

That may be so, but you cannot ignore the fact that P&G alone spends an estimated $3 billion a year on advertising. Companies like P&G, Unilever, Colgate, Coca Cola, and General Mills have collectively poured tens of billions of dollars into brand marketing campaigns, using mass media such as television. An interesting question for product and brand managers is how these consumer products will be marketed in the coming years, given the presence and impact of the Web as a communication medium.

For example, a study by AOL and Roper Starch Worldwide, a research firm, showed that people's media habits are changing due to the Internet. In that study, 43 percent of those surveyed said they viewed less television after they began using the Internet. In another indication of the Web's growing importance in delivering timely news, 50 percent of those surveyed said that they expected to get more of their news online in the next two years. If consumers are watching less television, the only way marketers can reach them is if they follow them to the Internet. In the two years since the AOL/Roper Starch study was released, we have seen ample evidence of this happening.

The consumer product giants are indeed getting ready to harness the power of the Internet. While consumers may not yet associate these famous names with the online marketspace, that may be changing soon. Let's consider some examples of FCMG brand sites on the Internet and see what they are doing.

Procter & Gamble has sites devoted to each of its major brands—from Folgers coffee to Vidal Sassoon hair-care products to Crest toothpaste. The emphasis seems to be on building sites that do more than "sell" the brand, and there is ample content, community, and interaction.

On the Folgers site, consumers can find coffee brewing and grinding tips, product information, and an archive of Folgers radio and TV commercials. Vidal Sassoon offers an interactive hairstyle guide, where hairstyling options are provided based on one's facial and hair characteristics. The Crest site offers detailed dental care information and has a specialized section for dentists and dental students. It also has a special site named "Sparkle City" for kids (see Exhibit 8-1). Here there is music, colouring, games, and lots of other entertainment, which can be useful in educating kids about dental care.

Unilever, one of P&G's rivals, has sites for its popular brands such as Ragu pasta sauce and Lipton tea products, among many others. Ragu was among the first FMCG brands to go online in 1995. Its site maintains an Italian theme, where consumers can talk to Mama, who is the

Exhibit 8-1 Sparkle City: A Crest Brand Site

Source: www.sparkle-city.com (owned by Procter & Gamble, www.pg.com).

Ragu brand persona. There are also recipes, health guides, a Q&A with Mama area, sweepstakes, and more.

Becel, Unilever's margarine brand (see Exhibit 8-2), has a site that targets a dual audience—consumers and healthcare professionals. The site assumes the authoritative title of "Heart Health Information Bureau." This health-oriented approach may deflect any criticism of the product by those who perceive it as not very wholesome. The site includes an interactive meal planner, recipes, and tips on shopping. It also has a special health information section for healthcare professionals.

P&G calls its Pampers site "Pampers Parenting Institute," which is an online community and content site for parents. The site is rich in content on a wide range of topics of interest to parents. Articles by experts cover topics such as "helping a child cope with loss and grief," behaviour matters, child development, and health issues. Always, a feminine hygiene product by P&G, hosts a content and community site for mothers and teenage girls.

Virtually every consumer product company is now trying to utilize the Internet in some way. Hershey's, for example, has over 15 Web sites

Exhibit 8-2 Becel®: Unilever's Margarine Brand

Source: www.becelcanada.com.

®Becel is a registered trademark of Unilever Canada.

devoted to its various brands. Coca Cola, another big advertiser, also has an interesting online presence. The company sells Coke memorabilia and features an application (using a plug-in) that allows consumers to listen to several international radio stations. This may be an attempt to link the brand with the kind of music that appeals to its target market.

These are just some examples of what FMCGs are doing online. It is obvious the consumer product giants realize that the Internet is as much about relationship marketing as letting the consumer build a relationship with the brand. P&G's Frederic Colas, the associate director of interactive marketing in Europe, shows that the consumer product giant is willing to learn some new tricks. As he says, "The Internet is a totally different medium … potentially big mistakes [can be] made by transferring mass market advertising to the Internet." P&G has made various pronouncements indicating that it will shift a big part of its media budget to Web advertising. One report suggested that P&G may shift as much as 80 percent of its advertising budget to the Web by 2003.

Established B2B brands are also active on the Internet. Given the larger size of the B2B market online, this is not surprising. W.W. Grainger, an established name in the MRO (maintenance, repair, and operating items) supplies business, had successful retail and catalogue operations. Now the firm has established a strong online presence with a dynamic multi-vendor product catalogue and the ability to buy directly online.

B2B firms have realized that the Web is ideal for building relationships with their customers (see Chapter 7). At the same time, the Web also makes many of these older firms vulnerable to new forms of competition. Grainger now has new online rivals such as MRO.com. Older firms often have greater brand recognition and consumer trust. Unless they take advantage of these strengths quickly online, the newer Internet-savvy rivals could pose a major threat.

We see many B2B firms—from computers (Dell and IBM), to consulting services (Anderson Consulting and Booz Allen and Hamilton), to material supplies (Grainger)—establishing leadership roles online. Unlike many B2B start-ups, these firms have the advantage of an established customer base.

While the battle between the old and new brands, both B2B and B2C, is far from over, it is already evident that we shouldn't write off the older brands in this new economy. Their presence in the physical and virtual worlds seems to be working in their favour. Ultimately, it may not be the new-economy brands, but the old-economy brands that prove to be the real winners.

Sources: "Internet Becoming Necessity to Users," *CyberAtlas* (cyberatlas.internet.com/ big_picture/demographics/article/0,1323,5931_151821,00.html), December 3, 1998;

Ben Rosier (1999), "The Future of FMCG.Com," *Marketing Focus* (www.marketing. haynet.com/feature99/1021/index.htm); Peter Galuszka (1998), "Net Advertising: P&G's Push to Figure It Out," *Business Week Online* (www.businessweek.com/ bwdaily/dnflash/aug1998/nf80819d.htm), August 18; "Global Online Ad Spending: $33 Billion by 2004," *CyberAtlas*, August 12, 1999, (cyberatlas.com/big_picture/ demographics/article/0,1323,5941_181901,00.html).

Introduction

It is not just the so-called "virtual" companies like Amazon and eBay that can take advantage of the Web's capabilities. The Internet is not a medium that is limited to technology products either. As we just saw in Vignette 8, consumer product companies are also establishing a Web presence.

In this chapter we will explore how the Internet affects product development, product and brand management, and pricing decisions. When new products are introduced in the B2B or B2C market, brand management is crucial to the success. Pricing decisions are very much linked to the branding strategy. This is especially so in the case of the Internet, where the market can play a significant role in determining prices (for example, through auctions) and consumers have easy access to competitive price information through price-comparison sites. Strong brands, which had often charged a premium price, now have a harder time justifying price premiums. As we will see in this chapter, firms that employ effective branding strategies can not only defend successfully against competitors—but also from downward slides in prices.

Innovations and the Internet

The Internet has spurred a tremendous amount of innovation in many different industries and product categories—not just new online digital services and products. A growing number of tangible products are also beginning to acquire Internet capability. The Internet, one can justifiably say, is the catalyst for a growing amount of R&D and innovation in a range of industries.

Businesses have realized that many products and services can be delivered via the Web. In the consumer products area, free Web-based e-mail with worldwide access (such as Hotmail), online digital radio (such as Broadcast.com), and virtual photo albums (such as Photopoint.com) are just a handful of the new and innovative product ideas that were made possible by the Internet. In each of these cases, the product or service is delivered via the Internet.

We have also seen the invention of tangible products, which can be categorized as non-computing Internet-enabled devices, that are designed to take advantage of the Internet's capabilities. Some of these interesting innovations include WebTV and wireless Internet-enabled phone devices.

We may soon see Internet capability also being embedded into mundane household products. Ceiva is a digital picture frame capable of displaying several pictures. The product does not require any knowledge of personal computers. One can simply post an album of pictures on the Ceiva Web site and then allow family and friends to see the photos via a specially designed Internet-enabled photo frame (see Exhibit 8-3). There is also talk of an Internet-enabled refrigerator that can be linked to an online grocery store, which will trigger purchase orders resulting in automatic replenishment of the inventory as needed. We already have automobiles with Web capability.

Exhibit 8-3 Ceiva Virtual Picture Frame (Left) and Kerbango Internet Radio (Right)

Source: Ceiva (www.ceiva.com) and Kerbango (www.kerbango.com).

Netpliance's i-Opener and Intel's Dot.Station are two products that allow users to browse the Web, send and receive e-mail, chat, and shop. These products are priced well below $500 and are likely to make the Internet accessible to many young and low-income consumers.

Product Categories for the Online Marketspace

Marketing textbooks categorize consumer products into convenience goods (magazines, detergent), shopping goods (appliances), specialty goods (luxury items), and unsought goods (insurance, dental services). Industrial products are classified into materials, repair and maintenance items (MRO), capital items, supplies, and services. We see the entire range of product categories being sold online.

As discussed in Chapter 3, the Web does not offer the ability to feel the fabric or smell the perfume. It does not even offer customers the opportunity of trying out the product, unless the product can be sampled digitally (as with music or software). That makes it challenging for some product categories to do well online. Selected product categories still dominate consumer purchases online. Table 8-1 shows PricewaterhouseCoopers' study of the top Web product categories. In the study, clothing is, perhaps, the biggest surprise. Those who buy standard sizes from catalogues have easily migrated online. Those who need custom-tailored clothes also find many options online. That may explain the prominence of this product category online.

Computer hardware and electronic products are two other fast-moving categories in the adult market. Other product categories that require "experience" or consumption to judge their quality do not rank well. However, categories such as perfume and wines are growing online because of replacement sales. If a consumer has used a brand of perfume or wine (and knows the fragrance or taste), online purchasing can be very convenient. Among services,

Table 8-1 Top-Selling Product Categories Online

Teenagers	Adults
CDs and cassettes	Books
Clothing	CDs and cassettes
Books	Computer software
Computer software	Toys
Toys	Clothing

Source: PricewaterhouseCoopers.

travel, tickets (airline tickets and event tickets), banking, and online stock trading are categories that have captured consumers' attention.

As consumers gain confidence in online shopping and as technology improves, we are likely to see more product categories being purchased online. We now see automobile sites, from Toyota to Mercedes, offering 3-D views of their products. Real estate agents can also use this technology, thus enabling potential homebuyers to get an intimate virtual tour of the property. Land's End allows shoppers to try the clothes on a "virtual model" who can be turned at various angles. As marketers move from just selling a product to providing an online experience, products that once did not seem like good candidates for the online market may become the winners.

Product Development and the Internet

Developing Products in Internet Time

Even before the advent of the World Wide Web, technological advances in micro-chip design were beginning to fundamentally alter existing products, and it became possible to introduce new ones. Consumer electronic products have become more "intelligent" and compact, and are bundled with more features than ever before. Technological advances in the last two decades have had some significant effects on businesses:

- *Shorter product life cycles.* The black-and-white television enjoyed nearly a thirty-year reign before being replaced by the colour television. Today, products have a much shorter life span. New technologies make old ones obsolete very fast.
- *Greater importance of innovation.* In a range of industries from computers to automobiles to consumer electronics, competing firms are able to provide very similar offerings in terms of quality and features. It is increasingly difficult to hold on to any competitive advantage. That means companies have to constantly offer cutting-edge products to stay where they are.
- *Speed.* It is not just innovation, but rapid innovation that is the order of the day.

Compaq, a company started in the 1980s, has become the biggest PC manufacturer. Its success against IBM, which was once the leading PC manufacturer, can be attributed to its faster product development cycle. Companies are very aware that in addition to faster product development, the cost of development should also be kept low. As product life cycles shrink, they offer a limited scope for becoming long-term cash cows.

What does all this mean in the context of the Internet? The Internet has become an important tool in the product development process. Initially, this was true for software companies. Now hardware manufacturers, automobile manufacturers, and engineering companies use the Internet to achieve the twin objectives of lowering product development costs and accelerating the speed of innovation. By enabling the formation of worldwide product development teams and more efficient communication, the Internet has become a vital part of product development for many companies.

The traditional product development process started with the complete definition of the concept. The concept would not undergo any modifications once it was "frozen." The Internet allows firms to engage in flexible product development, where the product goes through modifications and improvements even in the implementation stage.[1] Flexible product development is not limited to online products. Industries where technology, competition, and consumer needs change quickly are now forced to adopt a more flexible approach to product development.

When one company drastically reduces the "time-to-market," as Compaq did, there is increasing pressure on everyone in the industry to reduce the product development cycle. Companies are now competing on **Internet time**, which signifies the telescoping of the normal phases of business development into amazingly short time spans[2] (see iMarket Demo 8-1). This calls for a flexible product development process, which allows for ongoing feedback from consumers.

Netscape introduced Navigator 2.0 in January of 1996, and immediately began work on Navigator 3.0, which was released in August of the same year. Talk about a short product life cycle! But that's what Internet time is all about—rapid deployment of new products and rapid movement into new markets.

Cusumano and Yoffee, authors of *Competing in Internet Time*, caution that success in this environment does not depend on just speed and rapid development. It requires companies to be willing to change their strategies, processes, and even organizational structures.

There are some important prerequisites for competing on Internet time.[3] First, companies that compete on Internet time have to be willing to forge external partnerships. Netscape did this by using a large pool of volunteer consumers to "beta test" the product before the final version was released.[4] Consumers not only were able to identify "bugs" in the software, but they even suggested additional features that could be added. In the early days of E-commerce, beta testers played an important role in testing browser security features. Now, many software companies routinely release beta versions and solicit feedback from end-users.

Second, even as companies are working on implementing a product design, they need to start developing the next product. Competition may leapfrog the current technology. This requires continuous product development, as demonstrated by Netscape. One could call this forced obsolescence of the old product.

Third, even as companies deploy new products that short-circuit the life of older products, they need to ensure that consumers do not postpone their purchases by waiting for the better, cheaper technology to arrive. These days as soon as a consumer buys a top-of-the-line computer or a digital camera, he or she can rest assured that there will be something better on the market the next day. How can companies encourage consumers not to postpone their purchases? Lowering the price is one way to do it. Cusumano and Yoffee argue

iMarket Demo 8-1 What's the (Internet) Time?

Swiss watchmaker Swatch would like to do away with all the time zones and has created a new unit of time that is appropriate for the Internet. This new universal unit of time is called Swatch Internet Time (SIT). It recognizes the fact that the Internet has eliminated time and geographical boundaries.

Exhibit 8-4 Net-Time: Swatch's Internet Time Watch

Source: www.swatch.com.

How long is a Swatch beat? The virtual/real day is divided into 1000 "beats." One Swatch beat is the equivalent of 1 minute 26.4 seconds, meaning 12 noon in the old time system is the equivalent of 500 Swatch beats. This new time zone is still "unofficial" and has not received the approval of the world's nations.

Swatch has a small downloadable Internet time converter that can run from your computer and tell you the Internet time given the standard time and vice-versa. They even have a series of colourful wristwatches (aptly named Webmaster, Net-Time, Net-Surfer, and so on) that display Internet time.

In an era of global, virtual product development teams and 24/7 shopping from anywhere in the world, a single time zone might make sense to a lot of people. Cynics may see this as Swatch just trying to cash in on the Internet. Is this concept ready for acceptance or is it ahead of its time? Or it is fundamentally flawed? What do you think?

Sources: Mark Gibbs (1998), "Internet Time: Old Wines, New Bottles," *Network World*, November 16; Swatch Web Site (www.swatch.com).

that on the Internet, long-term arrives very shortly, and hence companies need to focus on building marketing share, customer loyalty, and relationships. They chide Netscape for not lowering the price of the browser quickly (when faced with Microsoft's free giveaway of its competing Internet Explorer) and instead focusing on short-term profits.[5]

Fourth, product development is no longer done just at an organization's headquarters. Multinational companies take advantage of their globally dispersed expertise in the design and development process. Companies are also involving suppliers and other strategic partners in the development process, so that they can tap into the expertise of these firms. This approach to product development requires inter-enterprise and cross-enterprise integration (this sort of integration is discussed in greater detail later in the chapter).

The Internet is forcing technology and software companies to compete in a more dynamic environment. Some fundamentals, however, remain the same even now. Superior product quality, creating entry barriers for the competition, and customer lock-in (through higher switching costs and relationship programs) are still vital.[6]

Virtual Product Development

Product development is a team-based activity that draws expertise from engineering and design, R&D, materials management, marketing, and operations. Traditional product development required the team to work together in the same physical space. Computer-aided design (CAD) technology has been in use for many years, but the development process has been rigidly sequential in the past. Product development was a lengthy process, with concept-to-market time of about three to five years for many products. This was particularly true in the automobile industry.

Now, from software to automobiles, global companies are realizing there is a more efficient, faster, and cheaper way to innovate and develop products: **virtual product development**. There is no reason why in this Internet age, global companies cannot tap on their globally dispersed expertise. Cross-functional product development teams can be set up with different team members working in different countries and across many time zones.

Texas Instruments uses the global software development model by assembling product development teams in Dallas, Texas, and Bangalore, India. As the product development team in Dallas finishes the day's work, they hand over the project to the team in Bangalore. The process continues until the development is completed. The time difference becomes an advantage. It allows companies to engage in virtually non-stop development, dramatically cutting the time it takes to get a product on the market.

Ford developed intranet-supported technology and tool sets called C3P, which unite computer-aided design tool sets in three areas—design, manufacturing, and engineering.[7] An intranet (which is an Internet site that is available only to employees) can help in information sharing. Ford also abandoned its traditional country-specific product development teams and decided to incorporate the best design team by drawing from a worldwide Ford employee talent pool. The best engineers, designers, and marketers from around the world were then brought together.

Using collaborative software tools and intranet-supported CAD/CAM (computer aided design and computer aided manufacturing) technology, Ford built its first "global car."[8] The product was called Contour in North America. Ford has also used virtual prototyping, where prototypes are virtually, not physically, created and tested using simulations.[9] Boeing, similarly, used virtual design technology to develop and test prototypes of the 737 airframe.[10] This process dramatically lowers costs.

Collaborative software tools such as Microsoft NetMeeting, Netscape Conference, CU-SeeMe, and Internet Conference Professional can be used for a variety of real-time, synchronous applications. All of them have Internet phone, whiteboard (where engineering drawings, images, and text can be displayed), chat, and file transfer between participants. NetMeeting and CU-SeeMe allow video-conferencing. NetMeeting also allows users to share documents and software applications. In addition to these collaborative tools, solutions such as MesaVista (www.mesasys.com), a product development portal for engineering design teams, allow engineers to share data during the process of designing and developing products.

Collaborative team-based product development used to be a novelty, but it's now emerging as the norm in many industries.

Brand Management Online

When new products are launched, in the B2B or B2C market, brand management begins. **Branding** has been an integral part of product strategy for many decades now. A brand is a name, term, sign, symbol, or a combination of these that allows companies to differentiate their offerings from competitors' products.[11] Brand marketing strategies involve heavy investment in brand awareness and brand image creation. Brands that are remembered and are associated with positive feelings or benefits will likely be purchased. A well-recognized brand name may denote superior quality or a known level of quality in the minds consumers. In fact, the brand name is often used as the basis for making a purchase decision.

Challenges in Online Brand Building

Brands such as Campbell, Coca Cola, and Mercedes have been elevated to the status of cultural icons. These brands are said to have high brand equity. Brand equity is based on factors such as brand awareness, brand loyalty, perceived quality, and brand associations.[12] Building strong brands is not just a concern of offline marketers, but also Internet pure-plays. Online companies have been pouring money into establishing their online brand identities.

Inability to Convey Emotions. There is a raging debate in the advertising and marketing community about the value of Internet advertising as a means of brand building. Internet advertising is considered by many to be inappropriate for brand building. Banner ads, especially, offer a very small space for communicating a message and cannot convey the emotions that television commercials so effectively do. Allen Rosenshine, Chairman of BBDO, a leading advertising agency, has been one of the most vocal critics of Internet advertising. He has declared it unsuitable for brand advertising. Experts from this school of thought argue that it is very difficult, almost impossible, to build emotion into online advertising.

A study on Internet advertising in 1999 showed that major consumer brands such as Wal-Mart, Pepsi, Coke, Burger King, Nabisco, and Nike might be heeding Rosenshine's advice. They were absent from the top 50 Web sites.[13] Some experts have argued that online brand building will not work for every brand. For low-involvement consumer products, it is difficult to create the need for online interaction. It is, therefore, not surprising that there is some evidence suggesting that Internet advertising is focused on E-commerce (that is, selling) and not on building brands.[14]

Limited Reach. Critics also point to the limited reach that even the best-known content Web sites enjoy today. An ad during the Super Bowl or a popular TV show such as *Friends* can reach tens of millions of consumers at the same time. Even Yahoo! does not have this ability to instantaneously reach such a large number of consumers in a specific demographic segment. Thus, the Internet may not be appropriate for creating wide brand awareness. Some argue, however, that what you lose in quantity, you gain in quality. The Internet does allow for precise targeting of advertising, delivering ads instantaneously based on what a consumer is doing online at any given moment, and measuring the response to ads.

Creative Constraints. Internet advertising, as defined by banners, may be inadequate for many reasons. Some ad industry experts consider ad banners too small to do anything other than send out a call for action. Ad banners that offer contests, sweepstakes, or free products receive the most attention. Most ad banners are about 468 × 60 pixels, which provides limited creative room. Brand advertising has historically been based on building an emotional aura around the brand. Marketers have used TV advertising to imbue emotion into everything from fabric softener to cold remedies. Banner ads do not have the capability to convey emotions. Complicating matters further, consumers have also learned to ignore banner ads, thus rendering them ineffective.

Price Transparency on the Internet. Branding creates a perception in the consumer's mind that the branded product is of a superior quality. Top brand names, such as IBM and Nike, can charge higher prices than their rivals because of this perception. In an imperfect market, where consumers do not have full information or have to incur expenses (time and money) to gather information about competing products, consumers often make decisions based on limited information. In such cases, consumers may depend on cues such as brand name or price to decide if a product is of superior quality.

On the Internet, the seller's costs and prices become very transparent. Auction sites, reverse auctions, online negotiating, and aggregate buying sites, which are among the most popular B2C (and C2C) sites, take the emphasis away from the brand and put the focus on price. Reverse auctions (such as Priceline) and aggregate buying sites (such as Mobshop and Mercata) reveal the seller's price floor. Consumers who buy at Mercata, NexTag, or Priceline focus on prices, and such a focus detracts from the brand manager's ability to build an image or charge a premium price.

Complicating matters further, the Internet makes it easy to compare prices. Sites like mySimon, PriceScan, and BigCompare allow consumers to search across retailers and find feature- and price-comparison information. Easy price comparison and the emergence of auction and reverse-auction sites, which emphasize price, are likely to make it difficult to justify premium pricing.

Price transparency is not just happening in consumer product categories. In business-to-business markets, such as steel, price has been historically negotiated between producers, traders, and consumers. The launch of electronic steel trading sites has led to more price transparency.[15]

Some marketers worry that once consumers find out that competing brands offer similar features, the emphasis will turn to price. There is also a growing feeling that brands will be commoditized by the increased salience of price in the consumer decision process. While there is evidence that specific groups of consumers (such as teens) do not pay attention to brand names on the Internet, there is no overwhelming evidence yet suggesting that brand marketing will not work online.

Online Brand Building Strategies

As Vignette 8 points out, the Web could be a potentially powerful medium for building brands. Yet firms should not rely on banner ads exclusively to accomplish that mission. Traditional consumer product companies are using other creative ways, besides banners, to build brands on the Web. The emphasis is on trying to engage the consumer in the brand Web site. By providing a lot of useful content, online community and message boards, interactive games, sweepstakes, and opportunities to win prizes, these marketers believe that they can create a "relationship" between the brand and the consumer.

Traditional mass media advertisers, such as P&G, are looking to the future. Their online advertising expenditures may currently be very small, but as bandwidth expands (through wider availability of high-speed cable modems, DSL, and satellite), Internet ads will start to resemble TV ads. Denis F. Beasejour, P&G's vice-president of worldwide advertising says,

"Eventually, this medium is going to hit us. It is critical that we be in this space, experimenting, trying to develop our own business models."[16]

For others, the Internet may already be paying off in terms of brand building. This is especially true for traditional retailers who see the Internet as another additional channel. "It is clear the Internet presence is extending our brand to shoppers we were not reaching with our stores," says Kent Anderson, president of Macys.com. "To us, that's classic brand building."[17] General Motors revamped its Saturn site to be more user-friendly, adding features like a lease-price calculator, an interactive design shop for customizing the car, and an online order form. The site has seen its visitor statistics skyrocket, generating over 80 percent of its customer leads.[18] This, GM would argue, is also a classic case of brand building. These firms have gone beyond the hype and have realized that it is time to produce results online.

The Domain Name. The domain name (or URL or Web address) is an important part of a firm's online branding strategy. This applies for B2B and B2C companies. Many leading companies own hundreds of domain names—including names of future products and misspellings of current brand names. Protecting the company and brand names online is very important. Parody sites, which are often critical of a brand or company, can have a negative impact on the brand image. If a company does not register domain names for all of its brands, someone else might to do it, perhaps with the intent to selling it back to company for a huge profit (see iMarket Demo 8-2).

iMarket Demo 8-2 Get Ready for the Web Warriors

If you search for a major brand like Nike or Calvin Klein on one of the popular search engines like Yahoo!, don't be surprised if the first site that comes up is an anti-Nike or anti-CK site. Gone are the days when only large companies with big media budgets could communicate via mass media. The Web allows, in many cases for free, anyone to set up a Web site to voice their opinion. Their audience is not just friends and neighbours, but literally the rest of the world.

Brand managers, strategists, and ad agencies meticulously craft the image they want to portray with a brand. A dissatisfied consumer or a consumer activist who disagrees with the corporate practices can easily set up a Web site to air that dissatisfaction. If you type "Nike" on any of the popular search engines, you are likely to find anti-Nike sites like Nike-Watch (www.caa.org.au/campaigns/nike/index.html), Just Do It! Boycott Nike! (www.geocities.com/Athens/Acropolis/5232/), and Clean Clothes Campaign (www.cleanclothes.org/companies/nike.htm). Yahoo! has even created a subcategory for anti-Nike Web sites. Calvin Klein is another popular brand that has motivated the creation of several negative sites.

Even the Internet's best-known brand, Amazon.com, has not been spared (see Exhibit 8-5). Irked by Amazon's patenting of its "one click" shopping system, noAmazon.com contains articles attacking Amazon, as well as a call for action.

While free speech rights protect such parody and public expression of dissatisfaction or criticism, there are some who cross the line and violate trademarks or copyrights. Brand names must be protected against such violation.

Cyber-squatting is another problem that can affect brands. This refers to individuals using the names of companies and brands to register site domain names, before the companies themselves do it. Recently, a court in the United States ruled in favour of Gary Kasparov, the famed chess champion, when someone had registered a site by the name Kasparov.com. Kasparov had registered his name as a trademark and was able to convince the court that only he is entitled to Kasparov.com. In another landmark ruling, an arbitrator determined that a Canadian resident who registered protest monikers such as Wal-MartCanadaSucks.com and Wal-Mart-PuertoRicoSucks.com, does not have the rights to those names, and has determined they belong to the department store giant Wal-Mart Stores, Inc. Courts in the US are ruling against cyber-squatters when the plaintiff has an established trademark.

On the Internet, the site domain name (such as www.xyz.com) represents the brand. It must not only be carefully chosen, but it must also be protected. Often companies register the name in multiple ways (with .com, .net, and .org). The consequence of not doing this can be quite damaging (for example, Amazon.org is a lesbian/bisexual women's site). By mistake, the brand may give the wrong impression in some people's minds.

In addition to creating anti-brand sites or parody sites (e.g., www.gwbush.com is a parody site that pokes fun at George W. Bush), information can be disseminated on the Web via bulletin boards, chat rooms, and newsgroups. Often rumours can spread like wildfire. How can you monitor or take action to curb such information flow that may be damaging to a brand? Companies like CyberAlert (www.cyberalert.com), NetCurrents (www.netcurrents.com), and eWatch (www.ewatch.com) track the information that is appearing on the Web and in bulletin boards and newsgroups regarding brands. NetCurrents will advise their clients about possible damage and even initiate action to curb incorrect information. It is obvious marketers have to get used to a new communication environment, where information flows both ways. Consumers have the ability to express their views, which may not always coincide with the marketer's best interests.

Exhibit 8-5 An Anti-Amazon.com Site

Source: Casey Muratori, www.noamazon.com.

Sources: Matthew Reed, "Wide Open to the Web Warriors," (www.marketing.haynet.com); Robert Thompson (2000), "Monitoring Web Misinformation," *E-Business Journal*, May 8; Dimitry Elias Leger (2000), "Monitoring Your Online Reputation," *Fortune*, May 16; Claire Barliant (2000), "Domain Name Disputes Settle Quickly Online," *law.com*, July 5; Steve Bonisteel (2000), "Wal-Mart Sucks Name Away From Domain Claim Jumper," *ComputerUser.com*, August 3.

The domain name must be easy to remember and consistent with the brand name. When last checked, both Procterandgamble.com and Proctorandgamble.com (note the different spelling) were owned by someone other than Procter & Gamble, the consumer product company. The URL www.p&g.com does not take you to the company site either. The Web address for Procter & Gamble is www.pg.com, which many consumers may not know.

A domain name is an important asset. Names should be carefully chosen to reflect the brand. All the good names with the common ".com" extension have been taken. New extensions such as ".tv" are now available. Others like ".shop" and ".firm" may soon be available. See the Internet Corporation for Assigned Names and Numbers (www.icann.org), the organization in charge of determining new top-level domain names, for further information. Domain names for ".com," ".net," and ".org" can be registered at many sites including Networksolutions.com and Dotster.com.

Interactivity and Consumer Involvement. The challenge for marketers is to understand this new medium and take advantage of the opportunities it provides. The Internet is a medium that really requires the interaction and participation of consumers. Unlike television, which is a passive medium, the Web can allow consumers to participate in a variety of ways. Posting messages on online bulletin boards, providing feedback, voting in online polls, answering pop-up surveys, downloading files, or playing streaming audio and video files are some ways in which marketers can get consumers to interact with the company in a branded environment. The conventional method of communication, which is one-sided, one-size-fits-all, mass communication, does not work on the Web. There is opportunity for personalizing the content and the message.

Consumer researchers have long held that interaction and experience with the product will lead to stronger brand perceptions or attitudes than merely advertising-induced attitudes. The Internet provides an environment where consumers can interact with the brand. This is especially true if the products are of a digital or informational nature or if they are high-involvement products. Terms like "rational marketing" and "experiential marketing" are used to describe the brand attitude development process on the Internet.[19] Rather than rely solely on an emotion-laden 15- or 30-second ad spot, the online environment allows the consumer to learn about the product in greater detail. This approach is consistent with the brand community and relationship-building approaches discussed in Chapter 7.

This new approach to brand building, rather than the passive method used in television advertising, requires the active participation of the consumer. In other words, the consumer has to participate in the marketing efforts.[20] Even low-involvement, packaged goods manufacturers (recall Exhibits 8-1 and 8-2 on pages 193 and 194) are trying to provide their consumers with a unique online brand experience. Yet this is not as easy as it sounds.

Companies such as Coca Cola, P&G, and Unilever, which are powerhouses when it comes to mass media advertising, generally market low-involvement products where consumers may not be thinking in terms of "having a relationship" with the brand. Even though the Web can engage the consumers, provide entertainment, and allow for consumer participation, the million dollar question is: Will consumers be interested in interactive experiences with a brand of toothpaste or margarine or feminine hygiene product? Even these marketers are unsure. In the meantime, they are pouring money into experimental sites that allow them to learn about communication on the Web, hoping they will see tangible results down the road.

Using Offline Media to Build Online Brands. Much of Amazon's advertising is done online, but there is also a strong television component as the company tries to expand its customer base.[21] GM's television commercial featuring a student shopping for a Saturn car online was intended to bring the offline customer base online. The Christmas season of 1999 saw a big surge in mass media spending on pure Internet companies. In the first three quarters of 1999, expenditures grew by 291 percent, compared to the same period in the previous year, with advertising spending totalling $1.4 billion.[22] Online brands such as Amazon, eBay, and Yahoo! are among the best examples of the power of online branding. They are testimonies to the fact that brand marketing is still alive.

As we saw in Vignette 8 at the beginning of the chapter, consumer products can indeed use the Web in their brand-building efforts. The debate on the capability of the Web as a brand-building medium has focused mistakenly on the issue of whether the Web can replace television. It is more appropriate that the Web be seen as part of a larger media mix. In the future, the Internet may resemble television through greater availability of multimedia content and video-on-demand. Then, perhaps, the mass media's role will require a serious examination.

It is also important to understand why branding may be important on the Internet. As consumers deal with e-tailers who have no physical presence or online firms they have no prior experience with, they are likely to look for cues that will indicate quality, reliability, and trustworthiness. In other words, a recognizable brand name may make it easier to shop online. Needless to add that once a customer makes the commitment to buy, superior online experience and service are essential to bring the customer back again. A recognizable brand can attract traffic, but sales growth depends on providing customer satisfaction.

Thus, mass media may still be the best way to attract traffic or create brand awareness—if you can afford it. Once the mass media attracts traffic, the marketer can use the Web to deliver a more personalized message and experience. While mass media, by its nature, requires uniformity, the Web allows for interaction and customization. In theory, as consumers interact with the brand and personalize their online experience, they should have more favourable feelings towards the brand.

Co-Branding. One of the trends online is **co-branding**. This occurs when two brands jointly promote a product or service, which carries the names of both brands. Co-branding is an effective strategy if the two brands are complementary and both have strong reputations. One can frequently see portal sites entering into co-branding agreements with online content sites. Portal sites need new and current content to encourage repeat visits, and content sites benefit because the portals can expose more consumers to their content. Netscape (which is now a portal site) and CNET.com (which includes News.com), which provides current technology and E-commerce news articles and technology product reviews, have such a partnership.

Online Brand Strategies for B2B Firms

Branding is not just an issue for consumer products. Business-to-business brands are also now engaged in branding strategies. Even for B2B firms, in industries ranging from steel to chemicals and computer parts, online price transparency is a serious threat. One consequence of such transparency could be the commoditization of brands (i.e., all brands in a category being perceived as having similar attributes).

Why Do B2B Branding? First, a strong brand can provide a defence against commoditization. In many B2B categories (such as Boeing in aircrafts, Cisco and Nortel in networking, Oracle in databases, and McKinsey in consulting services), strong brands exist. The products and services these companies offer are considered to be superior. That differentiation in the minds of customers can protect the brand in the online marketspace.

Second, just as in the case of consumer products, for businesses branding can break through the clutter and simplify the decision-making process. While it is unlikely that high-value B2B transactions will be made purely on the basis of a brand name, the name and reputation of the firm can provide assurance of quality and trust.

Third, business-to-business sales are often based on derived demand. Intel's branding of the Pentium processor was partly aimed at computer manufacturers but was more targeted to consumers. The "Intel inside" sticker has become a symbol of a superior product in consumers' minds. Such a strategy has given Intel some protection against competitors. VerticalNet, a company that operates over 50 B2B community sites, was quick to establish a "leader" image on the Web. The company has now expanded the brand presence across a vast array of industries.

Fourth, competition is fierce on the Internet. Pure-play firms that offer online procurement and supply chain management capabilities (such as the VerticalNet sites, MRO.com, and hsupply.com) can be a threat to traditional suppliers and distributors.

At the same time, consumer-oriented Web sites are entering the B2B space. Yahoo!'s B2B Marketplace (b2b.yahoo.com) and eBay's Business Exchange are two examples. These companies are leveraging their strong brand names in their expansion strategy. This suggests that firms that build strong online brands will not only have a defence against competition and price wars, but may also have new opportunities available to them.

Online B2B Branding. Businesses and other large organizations like universities, hospitals, and governments base their purchase decisions more on rational criteria. The Internet offers B2B firms the ability to build long-term relationships with their customers. As part of an online brand-building strategy, B2B firms can pursue various approaches:

- *Offer personalized and customized services.* Dell offers a "premium page" feature for its business and institutional customers, which allows the firms to track their orders and manage their accounts. B2B firms can use extranets to link with their customers. Extranets can provide a secure method of sharing data and offering customized services. The Internet offers a great ability to capture customer data (usage, preferences, previous history, and so on). Data mining techniques must be employed to effectively employ customization strategies.

- *Offer consistently superior experience and value.* Success in the B2B space depends on the ability to deliver value, lower cost, improve efficiency, or demonstrate other tangible benefits. Unlike some low-involvement B2C categories, where brand image and awareness may often lead to purchase, businesses are less likely to be swayed by image alone. Cisco and Sun Microsystems saved millions of dollars by providing online customer service, while simultaneously enhancing customer value. Now firms are offering "live" online customer support.

- *Focus on two-way communication.* The Internet is ideal for soliciting feedback from customers. Online community and other feedback options should be used to enable customers to communicate with the firm. The Web site, more than a print catalogue or advertisement in mass media, can be a rich source of information for customers. Use of product demo videos and the ability to search online catalogues can be effective tools.

- *Develop an integrated strategy.* Online and offline strategies must be integrated. In every channel, offline or online, the customer must get the same superior and customized service. This means, as described in Chapter 7, an enterprise-wide customer relationship management strategy is required.

While the nature and substance of a branding strategy in a B2B context may be different from the B2C context, such a strategy is no less important for B2B firms.

Web Brands vs. Traditional Brands

Some Web brands, such as Yahoo!, Amazon, and eBay, have already become mega-brands (Table 8-2 lists the ten best-known online brands). Even consumers who are not online recognize these brands. The first two brands have already been leveraged and extended far beyond their original raison d'être. These brands defy the notion that brands will not be valuable online. Trust with online vendors is still an issue in the consumers' minds. Branding can provide the necessary inoculation against security and privacy concerns (which affect trustworthiness). Consumers are likely to feel safer dealing with a familiar brand name. It is no wonder that companies like Priceline, E*Trade, and AutobyTel have invested heavily in advertising to develop familiarity.

There is evidence that brand recognition pays off online, but there is also good news for lesser-known brands. In terms of information search behaviour on the Web, about 18 percent of consumers go directly to a branded Web site before doing a broader search. When looking for a specific product category, 38 percent go directly to the site of a brand they are familiar with. The majority of consumers, however, start with a broader search, using a search engine, before visiting a specific brand site.[23]

Traditional brands and online brands have different challenges. The challenge for pure-play Internet brands is to create brand recognition and build credibility. The challenge for

Table 8-2 Top Ten Web Brands (August 1999)

Rank	Brand	Percent Awareness	People (millions)
1	Amazon.com	60.1	117.8
2	Priceline.com	55.4	108.6
3	eBay	46.4	90.9
4	E*Trade	43.8	85.8
5	eToys	26.2	51.3
6	HotJobs	26	50.9
7	Monster.com	24.1	47.2
8	AutobyTel	22.6	44.3
9	CDNow	20.2	39.6
10	Reel.com	19.4	38.0

Source: ORC International (www.opinionresearch.com).

traditional, offline brands is to figure out the role the Web should play in their communication and brand marketing strategy.

Positioning: Branding and Price

Positioning refers to how consumers perceive a brand in relation to an ideal product and/or competitive offerings. There may be a rational component to this perception based on brand features and benefits. There may also be an emotional component created through advertising, where the brand evokes certain feelings.

Positioning strategy is key to placing the brand in the consumer's mind vis-à-vis the competition. In addition to using price, brand features are used to create differentiation in the consumer's mind. Take the case of the very competitive online stock trading business. Charles Schwab maintains a premium image through a higher price of $29.95, compared to rivals E*Trade ($14.95–$19.95), TD Waterhouse ($12.00), Ameritrade ($13.00), and Datek ($9.99). Charles Schwab has been able to justify the higher price and hold its own by providing online investors additional value through research tools, the ability to interact with brokers by phone, and access to preferred IPOs. The competitors, who have all positioned themselves as discount brokers, are in a tight competitive space.

Often a high price may denote high quality, in the absence of other information. Branding and pricing are two sides of the same coin. Pricing is discussed in detail in the next section. Many Internet brands use an aggressive penetration strategy as a means to achieve scale economies quickly. Low prices at the introductory stage can lead to a low-cost brand image. It may be harder to raise prices or reverse that image later. We have seen the dilemma some online content sites have faced. Slate.com started as a free online publication. When Slate tried to get its users to pay a subscription fee, it faced consumer resistance. Slate had to quickly abandon the subscription model to prevent losing its audience.

While some marketers are concerned about brands becoming commodities online, there are those who reject that point of view. In a study of brands, consulting company Booz, Allen & Hamilton found that even in industries that are usually regarded as commodities (such as steel, airlines, and home mortgages), it is possible to create strong brands. The key is intense focus on creating true economic value for customers and a brand strategy based on product quality, delivery, and service.[24] Jay Walker, CEO and founder of Priceline, a pioneer in differentiated pricing, believes that brands that provide a false distinction and pretend to be superior or differentiated will be stripped of that distinction and will be commoditized. On the other hand, brands that offer genuinely superior value—whether through delivery or after-sales support—will continue to be successful brands.[25]

Recognized brands offer the consumer some degree of comfort. While many brands will lose their shine due to intense focus on prices on the Internet, it would be premature to conclude that brand marketing is an outdated concept. What the Internet does is, it truly raises the stakes. Brands have to prove they are worthy of the prices they demand.

Pricing Policy

We saw in Chapter 2 how the Internet affects a firm's activities across the entire value chain. It is evident that the Internet offers certain efficiencies in operations that can lower costs. The Internet also allows manufacturers to bypass intermediaries and reach the consumer directly. By eliminating the margins added by intermediaries, the manufacturer gains more flexibility in pricing the product. Increased efficiencies and shorter distribution channels should allow firms to enjoy higher profit margins or compete more effectively on price through lower prices. Whether a firm chooses to retain its margins or lower its prices is a strategic decision that online marketers have to make.

Price is an important variable in a firm's overall marketing strategy. High price may signal quality and a lower price may be used to scare off smaller competitors who cannot afford lower margins. Not too long ago, marketers had a great deal of control over pricing policy. Consumers have traditionally been price-takers, who do not have much say over pricing. What we had, and still do in most industries, is a sell-side model where the sellers set the price. There is little room for negotiation.

There may be deviations from a product's price based on different factors, including volume or frequent use or specific use (such as academic use of a software) discounts. Price discrimination (charging different prices for different consumers) has been a practice in many industries. Discounts are often given to seniors or based on time of usage (such as cheaper movie tickets on some days of the week).

Yet even these variations in price are seller determined. Consumers have had little say in the prices they pay. On the one hand, increased internal efficiencies and more efficient channels may offer a marketer higher margins. However, we have also seen examples of how the Internet takes this total control away from the marketer. In the case of auctions, reverse auctions, and aggregate buying models, price is determined by the direct interaction of demand and supply. Market forces determine the price.

While marketers may be losing some control over pricing, it would be wrong to conclude that marketers would lose control over pricing because of the Internet. Pricing remains a strategically important variable, whether marketing online or offline. Let's now consider some pricing strategies available to online firms.

Factors Influencing Online Prices

There are numerous factors that affect prices online. Some factors may exert an upward influence on prices and others a downward influence.

Efficiency. As we saw in Chapter 2, the Internet offers companies the ability to streamline operations, eliminate printing costs, and automate order processing and even some of the customer service. It may take a while for startups to achieve the scale where they begin to realize these efficiencies. As organizations use the Internet to build closer links with suppliers and customers, bringing the supply and demand chains together, there is potential for lowering operating costs. This should result in lower prices in the long term.

Consumer Price Sensitivity. Online consumers expect lower prices. As layers of intermediaries are eliminated, consumers expect marketers to pass on some of the savings to them. It is questionable if this is happening in reality. Just as in the physical marketplace, products in the virtual marketspace also have to be priced according to the consumer's willingness to pay.

Competition. The online environment is fiercely competitive, and the competition is worldwide, not just with the neighbourhood stores. The ease with which consumers can compare prices adds to the competitive pressure. Dealtime, PriceScan, BigCompare, mySimon, and BottomDollar are some of the comparison search engines that can compare features and/or prices. These days, consumers take parity on quality and features as a given. Price, service, and support often tend to be the differentiating elements. As price becomes a more significant part of the consumer decision process, it will become increasingly difficult to justify higher prices.

Traffic and Brand Building. The need to attract traffic and build brand recognition is forcing many e-tailers to offer low prices. Many are betting that once the volume increases, they will be able to compensate for the razor-thin margins. Well-known e-tailers such as Amazon, Outpost, Buy.com, Futureshop, and Chapters are among those adopting a penetration pricing strategy, which calls for low prices to attract the mass market. Top sites were being judged on metrics such as total unique visitors. As investors start focusing more on the bottom line, however, there may be upward pressure on prices.

Costs. Initially, selling online was perceived to be a cheaper alternative to setting up bricks-and-mortar establishments. Now, many entrepreneurs are realizing that this is not necessarily true. According to NetB2B (www.netb2b.com), a site that monitors Web site development costs, a site that requires database integration (for linking order-processing and inventory systems or linking a customer database to the Web to allow personalization) may cost upwards of $500 000. Top sites spend over $2 million in development and maintenance costs each year. In addition, e-tailers are realizing that online selling cannot be a completely automated process. Customer service personnel are still needed. Live chat with customer service staff (see www.liveperson.com, for example) and voice buttons, which link the Web to a call centre, are features that can enhance customer satisfaction. They also add to the cost. Adding to these costs is the significant marketing expenditures that online startups incur. Customer acquisition costs are reportedly over $200. As firms focus their immediate attention on traffic and brand building, prices will remain low and will not fully cover the costs.

Are Internet Prices Lower?

One would expect the increased operational efficiencies, lowering of transaction-processing costs, and elimination of intermediaries who add costs but not value to the end-user would result in tangible benefits to consumers in the form of lower prices. Do consumers really see lower prices on the Internet? The answer at this stage seems to be—yes and no.

There is evidence indicating that there has been some lowering of commissions charged by online stock brokerages. In other sectors, such as airlines, even though more consumers are benefiting from last-minute purchases through Priceline and other online travel services, there is evidence suggesting that the average cost of air travel has not declined. There is no sign that airlines are passing on some of their savings in travel agent commissions (due to direct online ticket sales to consumers) to consumers.[26] Among the several studies on online pricing (see Table 8-3), each with its own methodological limitations, only one study emphatically reported a decline in prices.

One could argue that these studies are a few years old and we need more recent data. Even though the studies may have some flaws, they do provide some insight into pricing strategies at a macro level. As we will see in the next section, many online vendors do aggressively discount prices to attract more consumers. The OECD report, however, suggests that on average, across different types of industries, there is no evidence of a general decline in prices for consumers.

Online Pricing Strategies

Everyday Low Pricing. Price on the Internet has also become a tool in attracting traffic to a site. Low prices are initially necessary to attract consumers. E-tailers like Buy.com and Egghead.com sell at very low prices, while trying to enhance their operating margins through advertising revenue. Buy.com offers a "low price guarantee" where a consumer who finds a lower price at another store, within 24 hours of ordering from Buy.com, will be

Table 8-3 Impact of E-commerce on Prices

Survey	Coverage	Limitations	Findings
Ernest & Young, 1998	3 online and offline vendors for 32 consumer products (92 prices)	Shipping costs and taxes not included; offline stores were all in one city	Online prices lower for 88%, same as offline for 6%, and greater than offline for 10%
Forrester Research, 1997	150 companies, 12 B2B categories		Lower costs mean higher margins, most of which are currently being retained
Goldman Sachs, 1997	Comparison of 30-item basket of goods sold by Wal-Mart	Only one store, product selection not random	On an average online prices higher than offline by 1%
OECD, 1997	Comparison of 24 000 prices for books, CDs, and software	Shipping costs and taxes not included	Online prices are slightly higher than offline prices

Source: "The Economic and Social Impact of Electronic Commerce: Preliminary Findings and Research Agenda," OECD, 1999.

refunded the difference. New entrants are using low prices as a means to gain a foothold in the market. Dotster (www.dotster.com), which offers domain registration service (to register .com, .org, .net and other new top-level domains), faces a bigger and more established rival in Network Solutions (www.networksolutions.com). Network Solutions had a monopoly over domain name registration for many years before the market was opened for competition. To counter Network Solutions' $35 registration fee, Dotster has made its initial promotional pricing of $15 its permanent price (see Exhibit 8-6).

To win the battle for traffic and customers, online marketers see low prices as the answer. Many analysts are worried that e-tailers who do not achieve sales quickly will fall by the wayside as they operate with little or no margins.

Marginal Cost Pricing. Many online sellers are adopting marginal cost pricing, where the product is sold at the cost incurred in making the last unit. This approach does not allow the firm to generate positive cash flows or profits in the short term. Online bookstores discount their prices heavily, often selling at or below cost. Amazon continues to take a lot of flak for not making a profit for their shareholders. Amazon has so far countered these attacks by saying that it is building a brand and a close relationship with its customers. Amazon used its aggressive discounted pricing strategy even in the case of the *Harry Potter* book

Exhibit 8-6 **Dotster's Low Price Strategy**

From: "Dotster INC." <mailinglist@dotster.com> <u>Save Address</u> - **Block Sender**
To:
Subject: New Low Rates at Dotster
Date: Sat, 06 May 2000 09:55:52 -0700

| Reply | Reply All | Forward | Delete | Previous |

Dotster News: Domain Name Pricing Stays at $15!
Registrar Transfer Fees Reduced to $10!

At Dotster, we think $15 per year for domain name registrations is a fair price. That's why we've decided to make $15 our new standard pricing for all one year domain name registrations! This new pricing extends to multiple year registrations as well: two year registrations are $30, five year registrations are $75, and 10 year registrations are $150. So from now on, you can expect one low price for all your domain name registrations. Visit http://www.dotster.com/

Source: E-mail from Dotster, Inc.

series, where initial demand far exceeded supply. One may recall parents lining up in front of bookstores to get *Harry Potter and the Goblet of Fire*. Such a pricing strategy may defy conventional wisdom, which dictates higher prices when demand exceeds supply (remember "Tickle-Me Elmo"?).

Promotional Pricing. Contrary to everyday low pricing or the marginal cost pricing strategy, which call for lower prices over a longer term, we also see cases of promotional pricing (see Exhibit 8-7). The online marketer may introduce a product at a low price to garner consumer acceptance or to temporarily boost sales. Prices normally return to regular levels once the promotional period is over.

Usage-Based Pricing. Under this pricing scheme, the price depends on the amount of usage. High usage will result in higher charges, but may also be rewarded with discounts or frequent usage points. Internet service pricing, not too long ago, was based on usage. Many ISPs would offer hundreds of hours per month at a low fixed price and then charge a small fee for each additional hour beyond that. Even now, many Web hosting services (which host the Web sites of other companies on their servers) have a usage-based pricing scheme. Hostway (www.hostway.com) and Verio (www.verio.com), two of the popular Web hosting companies, offer a fixed amount of disk space and bandwidth (volume of data or pages that consumers can download from a site) for a flat fee. Additional disk space and bandwidth are charged separately.

In terms of Internet service, usage-based pricing is not popular.[27] It discourages users from being online for a long time. Studies show that consumers who use the Internet more frequently, and are comfortable with the online environment, are more likely to shop online.

Exhibit 8-7 **Promotional Pricing Strategy**

Indigo.ca

Just what the summer ordered...

Sizzling Summer Sale
Save Up To 50%!

With prices like these, why not treat yourself or someone you know?

Source: Indigo.ca's promotional e-mail.

Realizing this, we now see e-tailers offering free Internet service. Free Internet service providers such as NetZero are gaining support from advertisers, who are betting that as consumers spend more time online, they are also likely to spend more dollars online.

Price Discrimination. The practice of selling a product at different prices to different buyers, even though the cost of the product is the same in each case, is called **price discrimination**. Price discrimination among buyers may be based on personal characteristics such as income, or age, or on geographic location. Staples.com (Staples.ca in Canada), for instance, requires users and registered customers to type their zip code or postal code before prices of products are revealed. Thus, Staples can conceal prices charged in one region from customers in another region. This is an example of geographic pricing. We also see examples of discounts offered to specific groups of customers (such as students, faculty, or seniors).

Price discrimination is a likely consequence of the increased mass customization that we see on the Internet. As the product or service is tailored to the needs of each individual consumer, the idea of charging a uniform list price will cease to make sense.

Researchers suggest that the ease of implementing price changes in an online environment, as opposed to the physical store environment, is one factor favouring price discrimination on the Web. Economists have argued that "menu costs" or the costs associated with printing and changing prices in a store are drastically reduced in the online environment. In supermarkets, it costs $0.52 per price change.[28] The Internet offers the ability to change prices on a real-time basis at virtually no cost.

In addition, as we saw in Chapter 5, marketers can study the preferences and price sensitivities of consumers. Some e-tail sites like Amazon and Buy.com require consumers to set up an account, with their name, address, and other information. Many sites require consumers to log on using a password. Cookies and IP tracking also provide insight into personal preferences. Using these methods, a marketer can track the price sensitivities of each consumer. For example, a marketer can track how a consumer responds to regular versus promotional pricing. By capturing price sensitivity (and even the reservation price or maximum price someone is willing to pay) at the individual consumer level, a marketer can dynamically alter the price according to a specified formula or algorithm. Economist Hal Varian and Bill Gates, founder of Microsoft, have both predicted newer forms of price discrimination online.[29] Gates has predicted customized pricing for each consumer, made possible by detailed tracking of online behaviour and purchase history, which will enable the marketer to extract the highest possible price from each consumer.

Even before the advent of the Internet, price discrimination has been prevalent in different industries, including the airline industry. The passenger in the next seat may have paid twice as much—or half as much—as you did. The Internet reduces the costs associated with implementing such a variable pricing system, making it easier to vary prices for different consumers. Each consumer chooses his or her own price based on willingness to pay. The seller, thus, extracts the maximum price from each consumer for the same product.

Micro-Pricing. The difficulty of selling a newspaper article or a song as a separate product has necessitated the bundling of related products. Until recently, it would not have been economically feasible to sell one song or one article or story from a newspaper. Consumers had to buy an entire CD or the entire newspaper, even if they were interested in only a small piece of the product. Technology available on the Internet resolves this problem, thus permitting **micro-pricing**, which allows marketers to sell unbundled low-value items as separate units using **micropayment** methods. Millicent by Compaq/Digital, NetBill by Carnegie Mellon University, and IBM Micro Payment are some of the many micropayment methods available.

In the past, high transaction-processing costs associated with credit card transactions made it uneconomical to accept credit card orders for items below five dollars. Micropayment methods allow for selling products online for just a few cents. Most micropayment methods require an online bank account to which charges are made. It does not require the use of a credit card for each transaction. For a technical discussion of micropayment see <u>www.w3.org/Ecommerce/Micropayments</u>.

Micropayment not only allows marketers, especially online and digital content providers, to unbundle their offerings, but it also allows for charging a usage-based price. For instance, a software vendor can, using micropayment, allow a consumer to use a software application just once and price the single-usage license at anywhere from a few cents to a few dollars.

Supporters of micropayment argue that requiring consumers to subscribe for online magazines or content services is akin to building a wall—it will only keep people out.[30] The experience of USAToday.com and Slate.com (owned by Microsoft) shows that online consumers do not like subscriptions, especially if they can find similar content elsewhere for free. Even the venerable *New York Times* now requires users to merely register, and not subscribe. Micropayment can allow consumers to choose what is of value to them, rather than forcing them to subscribe to or buy the bundled product.

Skeptics argue that any time there is a new electronic payment method, consumer acceptance will be an issue. In the case of micropayment methods, we still do not see widespread usage. Clearly, there is an opportunity for marketers to unbundle their offerings and attract consumers who otherwise may be unwilling to pay the full price. It remains to be seen whether this payment and pricing method will gain widespread acceptance.

Real-Time and Dynamic Pricing. On the Internet we are starting to see a strong emergence of online markets and trading communities where the market, and not the marketer, sets the price of the product. Auctions represent the most popular format for this real-time pricing. There are several variations of the auction pricing model.

The standard auction (or the English auction) starts with the lowest bid price acceptable to the seller. In this format, the seller announces a reserve price or a low opening price. Bidding increases the price progressively, until the winning bid is reached. At this stage, no other bidder is willing to pay a higher price.

The Dutch auction, or the descending price auction, starts with a very high price. The price continues to fall with time until a buyer claims the item by placing a bid. When multiple units are sold, the first bidder may not purchase the entire inventory. In that case, the auction will continue, and the price will continue to decrease with time, allowing subsequent buyers to pay a lower price. The flower growers in Netherlands used this auction format. These perishable products can get the highest price when they are fresh. With passing of time, they lose value, and hence the lowering of the price. Dutch auctions on the Internet can be found at eBay and Bid.com, among other sites.

The reverse auction, pioneered by Priceline, allows consumers to set the price. Consumers name the price they are willing to pay for products such as car rentals, airline tickets, and hotel rooms. Sellers then send quotes and bid for the buyer's business. The Internet makes the implementation of such a concept easy. Why would established airline companies and hotels participate in such an auction format, which might undermine their profits or even brand image? The answer is simple. Hotels, airlines, and car rental companies lose revenue when they do not have full occupancy. A rental car sitting in the car lot or a vacant seat on an airline is revenue lost forever. Reverse auctions allow these firms to get the best price they can from last-minute shoppers.

Priceline, after initial success with airline tickets, has expanded the reverse auction model to new areas like grocery shopping and home mortgage financing. Adauctions.net facilitates auctioning of advertising space in magazines, which must be sold before the deadline. Unsold ad space is lost revenue.

Consumers seem to respond favourably to such auctions. Apart from companies that sell perishable commodities or products, from airline tickets to hotel rooms, big brand names have so far not entered the auction space—most likely because they are concerned about diluting the brand value.

So far, with the exception of reverse-auctions, auctions have been primarily used in a consumer-to-consumer setting. The best known auction site, eBay, is a consumer-to-consumer auction site. Other players such as Egghead.com have entered the business-to-consumer auction space. A study by Jupiter Communications predicts that the future of e-tailing lies in B2C auctions. Businesses that have excess inventory can use the auction format to get the best price for their products.

Sites like eBay, Bid.com, and Egghead.com enable consumers to participate in auctions around the clock, from anywhere in the world. Online auctions have truly democratized the auction process by opening it up to millions of consumers. Before the advent of online auctions, participation in auctions was limited to those who were located near the auction venue. Auctions were seen as a pastime for the wealthy. Now consumers can buy functional items, such as airplane tickets or a cruise vacation, by going to an auction site.

Auction pricing gives the power to the consumer. The consumer decides what price he or she is willing to pay for a product. The price of the product then rises with demand. For conventional marketers, it may be difficult to come to grips with the idea of fluctuating prices and margins. But this may be the way of the future.

Amazon.com experimented with dynamic pricing in the fall of 2000. The prices of 68 DVD titles were randomly manipulated over a five-day period, resulting in discounts ranging from 20 to 40 percent. Thus, different consumers got different prices. The intent of the study was to examine the impact of price on sales. When the story about this experiment broke in the media, Amazon had to do some damage control. They refunded about $3 to nearly 7000 customers who did not receive the lowest prices. While this initial experiment may have been a public relations disaster, it does show the potential for using consumer data (such as previous history, demographics, and so on) in setting customized and dynamic prices. Ethical questions regarding such a pricing strategy cannot be dismissed easily.

Cost Transparency on the Internet

It is evident that both consumers and sellers can benefit from auctions. Sellers must, however, be concerned that auctions do result in **cost transparency**. In addition to various auction formats, which can reveal the seller's floor prices, there are online sources that allow consumers to easily find out the seller's costs. For instance, it is possible to find out the price car dealers pay manufacturers (see www.carcostcanada.com). This has a significant impact on the seller's ability to manipulate the price of the product as part of a strategy.

Let's now consider how the Internet may affect a marketer's pricing strategy.

Impact on Margins. It is obvious that cost transparency will reduce the seller's margins.[31] Armed with product feature and pricing information, as well the information about the experience of other consumers (for example, see www.epionions.com), consumers can verify which brand offers the best value for their dollar. Previously, due to high information search costs, both in time and money, very few consumers engaged in such detailed product comparisons. Now the information is available free, virtually at one's fingertips. It is difficult to justify premium prices, unless it can be demonstrated that the product is sufficiently differentiated and offers superior value.

Impact on Brand Image. Brands that are seen as charging unjustifiably high prices or engaging in price discrimination through dynamic pricing techniques may suffer from negative consumer perceptions.[32] Buy.com's "low price guarantee" seems to be saying that if the consumer finds the price unjustifiably high, Buy.com will lower the price to match any competitor. Price differentiation on a more sophisticated level is already a reality on the Internet. However, sites like Epionions.com and Deja.com, which promote online word-of-mouth communication, make it easy to find out what other consumers paid for a product. Herein lies the danger of dynamic pricing and technology-driven price discrimination. If there are wide variations in prices, can such a practice be legally and ethically defended? One way to overcome potential trouble is by offering other bundled or value-added services that can make the cost less transparent.[32] While the technology allows for customized pricing, each marketer has to decide if that is in the best interest of the brand and the consumer.

Summary

Opening the Internet for commerce has led to a surge of innovative products and services. The Internet, by collapsing time and space, has also changed the way products are designed. Global teams work round the clock, cutting the time it takes to get new products to market. Product development now happens on compressed Internet time. This places pressure on firms to engage in continuous innovation.

Once products go from the design stage to the market, the Internet presents new challenges and opportunities in branding. The cost transparency, easier access to product comparison information, and the consumer's ability to dictate prices through auctions and reverse auctions will make brand management very challenging in the years ahead. At the same time, we have seen online brands such as Amazon, E*Trade, and eBay gaining significant recognition, even among consumers who are not online. Companies like Amazon, which focus intensely on customer value and service, are showing signs of success in their branding strategy. The "also rans" that merely provided glitz without substance, such as boo.com, have fallen by the wayside.

It is evident that the Internet will place downward pressure on prices. Greater operational efficiencies, disintermediation, and lower communication costs may increase consumer expectations about lower prices. At the same time, marketers have to be wary of growing marketing expenditures incurred to build brand recognition and acquire customers. These costs, along with growing Web development, maintenance, and customer support costs are likely to cause many marketers to focus more on their operating margins.

While auctions and aggregate buying may take away some of the marketer's control over price, we're still likely to see new innovations in pricing. Customized pricing, real-time pricing (where price changes occur in response to a consumer action on a Web site), and micro-pricing (where content and digital products can be sold for as low as a penny per use) are some of the pricing innovations on the Internet.

While price discrimination may become easier online, marketers must be wary of consumer response. Widespread variation in prices can cause widespread consumer dissatisfaction. Marketers also need to be aware of the legal framework with respect to price discrimination.

Lastly, pricing and branding go hand in hand. Before setting a price, marketers should think about the brand image they want consumers to hold. Heavy discounting, which is widely prevalent on the Web, may draw some traffic and sales initially. In the long run, however, it may negatively affect the brand perception and the company's bottom line. As with each area of marketing, the Internet will continue to provide new opportunities and challenges in product and pricing decisions.

Key Terms

Branding, 202
Co-branding, 207
Cost transparency, 218
Internet time, 199

Micropayment, 216
Micro-pricing, 216
Positioning, 210
Price discrimination, 215

Real-time pricing, 217
Virtual product
  development, 201

Questions and Exercises

Review Questions

1. How are conventional brands like Crest and Coke using the Internet as part of their brand marketing strategy?
2. What do you understand by the term "Internet time?"
3. How does the Internet alter the product development process?
4. Describe the virtual product development process.
5. What are the challenges brand managers face online? What factors may hinder online brand-building efforts?

6. What are the factors that exert pressure on online prices? List them in terms of whether they exert upward or downward pressure on prices.

7. Discuss three different methods of pricing products on the Internet. When would you use each method?

Discussion Questions

1. How can the interactive and multimedia capability of the Internet be used to build online brands and strengthen offline brands?

2. Do you think that price and cost transparency online will diminish the value of brands and, perhaps, commoditize brands? How can companies defend their online brands?

3. Identify two new product or service opportunities for the online marketspace. Provide a rationale for why you think these products or services will succeed online.

4. Will micro-pricing and micropayment become popular? Even after nearly five years of trials, why have marketers (and consumers) not adopted this pricing approach?

5. If you were in charge of a leading offline brand that wanted to make its foray into the online world, what steps would you take to protect the online brand image. How can the offline and online images be made consistent?

6. Free products (ISPs, Internet phone service, content/news services, and so on), which are mostly advertising supported, and heavily discounted products are widely available on the Internet. There are questions regarding the economic viability of such strategies. Do you see marketers continuing such trends in the foreseeable future? Why or why not?

Internet Exercises

1. Use at least two price comparison sites (such as PriceScan, BottomDollar, BigCompare, and mySimon) and identify the highest and lowest price for the following product categories: notebook computer, DVD player, handheld PDAs (such as Palm III). Make sure your price comparison across vendors is for the same model. What insights did you gather from your search? Did you find the comparison sites useful as a consumer? Report on your findings.

2. a. Go through a newspaper like *The New York Times* (requires registration online) or *The Globe and Mail*. See the print version in your library and then visit the Web site (www.nyt.com, www.globeandmail.com).

   b. Visit a bricks-and-mortar store such as Sears, Wal-Mart, Future Shop, or Chapters. Also visit their Web sites (www.sears.com, www.wal-mart.com, www.futureshop.ca, www.chapters.ca).

   For both (a) and (b), answer the following questions. Is the online brand image similar to the offline brand image? What similarities and differences do you notice in the online and offline presence for this company? How would you compare their online branding strategy with their offline branding strategy?

Chapter **9**

The Internet as a Communication Medium

Vignette 9 American Airlines Takes Its Campaign Online

Learning Objectives

After completing this chapter, you should:

- Understand the differences between the Internet and other media.
- Understand the different communication tools available on the Internet.
- Appreciate the pros and cons of Internet advertising.
- Understand the role of the Internet in an organization's communication mix.

The travel industry has undergone a major revolution since the advent of the World Wide Web. Airlines were very quick to exploit the potential of the Web. American Airlines (AA) is a case in point. After some early experiments with interactive cable, American Airlines gained momentum with the emergence of the Web in 1996. Now, AA's Web site (AA.com) draws both leisure and business travellers. AA's goal initially was to ensure that AA and AAdvantage (frequent flyer) customers managed their travel and frequent flyer account needs through AA.com. The Net SAAver Specials (see the banner ad in Exhibit 9-1) were designed as an ongoing promotion intended to entice the discriminating online consumer.

AA.com's online strategy was based on a specific focus on one target market—the financial sector. The online campaign was referred to as the "Vertical Finance Plan." By comparing general online consumer demographics with their own AAdvantage Program membership database, American Airlines concluded that the finance sector would make an ideal test case. These consumers engaged in large volumes of online trading and were quite comfortable with the notion of online commerce. They also happened to be frequent flyers, were predominately males in the 25 to 54 age bracket, and had an average annual income of over $60 000.

The Vertical Finance Plan was specifically intended to generate awareness of AA.com among these consumers. The campaign was not limited to banner ads, but included sponsorship identification integrated into content sites, portal advertising, a pop-up window at CBSMarketwatch.com, keyword buys, and sponsored e-mailings with special offers.

Exhibit 9-1 AA.com Interactive Banner Ad with Drop-Down Menu

Having defined its target and strategy, AA.com's next step was to create a media strategy. Media buys focused on travel sites such as Travelocity, TravelWeb, and TheTrip.com. Ads were also placed in search engines and portals such as AltaVista, Yahoo!, AOL, Excite, Infoseek, and LookSmart. Additionally, weekly e-mails were sent to two million members in AA.com's "NetSAAvers" program, notifying members of weekly specials.

American Airlines now offers Internet users two types of Net SAAver fares. Both fares include e-mail notification, and one is for immediate weekend travel and the other service is for alerts for travel bargains a week ahead. These fares are also posted on the AA.com Web site.

The campaign's target was to deliver at least 10 million impressions. Since redesigning the site in 1998, pageviews reached 1.7 million per week. In 1999, AA.com expected to gross sales of $500 million. Michael W. Gunn, American's senior vice president of marketing, was quoted as saying that 200 000 new visitors were joining the site each month.

As far the banner ad campaign is concerned, early results show that the ads performed well in travel-related areas, particularly in the frequent flyer and business travel sections of mass audience sites, with AOL and Yahoo! proving to be good media buys. Certain elements of the program, such as the pop-up ads (see Exhibit 9-2), have performed very well—above 10 percent in some weeks. The banner ads performed lower than AA.com's average click-though rates for 1998, which were over 7 percent.

American's experience suggests that the Internet can be an effective communication medium, especially when multiple means of communication are used. AA.com not only offered consumers lower

Exhibit 9-2 AA.com Sweepstakes Pop-up Ad

This pop-up ad appears one time per visit at CBSMarketWatch.com

prices, but also the convenience of a 24/7 online site. The target market was clearly defined and multiple advertising tools (banners, e-mail, sponsorship) were used. Overall, American had a well-defined strategy backed by excellent execution.

Sources: www.channelseven.com; www.aa.com; www.webtravelnews.com.

Introduction

Before the emergence of the World Wide Web in 1993, the Internet had remained well-kept secret for many years. A small percentage of the population was on the Internet. The early participants were mostly computer professionals and academics. E-mail had not yet gained the critical mass to become the "killer application" that it is today. Many online communities were also active during this period. There were about 10 000 newsgroups and bulletin boards by the early 90s, and there were some generally accepted norms or "netiquette" that most people followed when they were in the discussion groups.[1] Other than that, there were few rules governing online communications at this time. The Internet had not become a commercial communication medium yet. In fact, commercial exploitation of the Internet was strictly looked down upon by the early pioneers. Even now, some veteran Internet users still hold such an attitude.[2] The Well, an online community started in 1985, epitomized the online culture of that time—thousands of participants discussing hundreds of topics in an open and free forum.[3] The culture on the Internet then can be characterized as anti-commerce. Other commercial online services like AOL and Prodigy, however, marched to a different drum.

From being an intellectual gathering place that it once was, the Internet has, in a very short span of five years, become the nerve centre of commercial innovation and entrepreneurship. The establishment of the World Wide Web protocol, followed by the development of the graphical interface of the Web browsers, has fuelled the creation of new content and entertainment. The development of Java, a platform-independent programming language, has enabled Web pages to become more interactive, and plug-ins, such as RealPlayer and Shockwave, have brought Web pages to life. The user-friendly technology, the lowering of hardware and Internet access costs, and the availability of content for many segments of the population are all factors that have spurred the growth of the Web all over the world. The Web is now an advertiser's dream come true. Incidentally, the Well (www.well.com) is now part of a commercial enterprise owned by online publisher Salon.com. Times have certainly changed.

The World Wide Web offers businesses a communication medium with many unique benefits. It is a richer communication medium than print because it can deliver audio and video while allowing more in-depth presentation of product information. It is more involving than television because it offers interactivity (Interactive TV is still largely an experiment) and requires the consumer to make conscious navigational choices. By using audio, video, and text, information can be presented to multiple sensory organs. These characteristics make the Web a very attractive marketing communication medium.

From a communication standpoint, there are some disadvantages to this rapid commercial growth. First, the volume of information available online is mind-boggling. The number of pages on the Web is growing at a dramatic rate. There are about 550 to 600 billion Web documents according to one estimate.[4] Second, there are a growing number of abuses, ranging from consumer privacy violation to unsolicited e-mail messages. These factors do detract from the effectiveness of the Web as a communication medium.

This chapter will explore the role of the Web as a communication medium. The strengths and limitations of the Web as a communication medium will also be discussed.

The Critical Mass

Bob Metcalfe, inventor of Ethernet and founder of 3Com, proposed the Metcalfe Law, which states that "the cost of a network expands linearly with increases in network size, but the value of a network increases exponentially." As networks, such as the Internet, expand, they become more cost-effective and useful. Metcalfe's Law underscores the importance of a *critical mass*. The Internet has attained this critical mass.

The Internet reaches an estimated 150 million people in North America and over 300 million worldwide.[5] Estimates of Internet usage growth suggest a doubling of this number each year at least until 2005. By way of comparison, it took radio 38 years to reach 50 million users, 13 years for television, and five years for the Internet to reach the 50 million user mark. AOL's chat services reached the first 50 million users in just 30 months.[6]

Marshall McLuhan, a renowned expert in mass communications, envisioned that technology would make our world a global village.[7] The Internet is already making that vision a reality. The ability of the Internet to link people across the world is unmatched by any other medium.

A few years back, the Internet had a very narrow, upper-income, young male demographic. Now there is a critical mass of women, which enables sites such as iVillage.com to offer content and chat rooms targeting women. Game sites targeting children and teens are also popular. The Internet has something to offer everyone, from online stock traders to retired grandmothers.

The Internet is far from an egalitarian medium. There are, however, signs indicating that the online demographics are expanding. In North America, for instance, the over-55 age group is among the fastest growing Internet user groups.[8] As more consumers go online, more marketers will go chasing after them. Product and service offerings online are increasing by the day, and online advertising expenditures tell the story.

Internet Advertising Expenditures and Estimates

To put things in perspective, let's look at the total volume of Internet advertising at present. In 1998, total Internet advertising in the United States was estimated at $2.1 billion.[9] This is roughly the same amount spent annually on all billboard advertising in the United States. By 2000, Internet advertising expenditures in the US will total between $4.7 billion and $6.5 billion. According Forrester Research, this figure is expected to rise to $22 billion in 2004. Global online advertising spending will swell to $33 billion by 2004.[10] In Canada, Internet advertising expenditures for 1998 totalled $24.5 million. In 1999 expenditures are predicted to be $55.5 million and are projected to reach $109.0 million by 2000.[11] Table 9-1 lists the top ten online advertisers.

According to Forrester Research, consumer goods advertisers will increase their share of Internet media dollars. More than half of marketers surveyed by Forrester said their online ad spending would constitute the highest percentage of their media budget, and 33 percent of marketers surveyed intended to cut their TV budgets in favour of online advertising.[12]

In addition to advertising on the Web, businesses are also devoting attention to their overall Web presence, including the corporate Web site. For large corporations, the cost for a "starter" E-commerce-enabled corporate Web site can be upwards of $300 000, with average

Table 9-1 Top 10 Internet Advertisers (May 2000)

Rank	Advertiser	Impressions (000s)	Reach (%)
1	TRUSTe	2 530 051	38.9
2	Yahoo	816 618	36.4
3	ClassMates	798 068	14.5
4	Yahoo!	600 288	49.0
5	Amazon	578 770	62.9
6	AOL	571 927	44.8
7	eBay	461 574	26.4
8	Microsoft	454 696	45.0
9	NextCard	349 926	33.3
10	SexTracker	336 031	10.5

Source: Nielsen/NetRatings (www.nielsennetratings.com).

Note: These rankings may change each month.

Web development costs estimated at $1 million.[13] It is no longer uncommon for businesses to spend $2 million or more on Web site development. The corporate Web site, after all, has a very important function—to reinforce the corporate and brand image.

The online advertising and Web development expenditures suggest that marketers are taking the Web seriously. The Internet is no longer an experimental medium. Gone are the days when companies had shabby Web sites. The AA.com experience described in Vignette 9 is proof that the Web can indeed deliver results when used appropriately.

The Web as a Communication Medium

The medium is the message.
— Marshall McLuhan

As a communication medium, the Web has several unique characteristics. These include multimedia and hypermedia content, global reach, interactivity, and integration with other applications. The Web is clearly changing the way we communicate and socialize. Chat sites are among the most popular destinations on the Internet.[14] For businesses, it is more than just a new way of reaching consumers. The Internet is ushering in a new era of personalized and customized communication. Let's now examine the characteristics of this medium.

Characteristics of the Web

Multimedia. The Web offers users the ability to communicate through several means—text, audio, video, and animation. News sites such as CNN.com and MSNBC.com offer excellent examples of the Web multimedia capability. CDNow and Sony allow consumers to sample the music before they buy a CD. Brand sites and special promotional sites are often created with multimedia features that bring the Web to life. It is almost like television, only better in some respects because the user can interact with the objects on the Web site. The Crest toothpaste site presented in Exhibit 8-1 on page 193 is an example of such as site. Nestle created a special promotional site for its "Lion" candy bar in Europe. The site features Flash animation, a Quicktime movie clip, and interactive games and contests to entice kids (see Exhibit 9-3).

These are just a few of the examples of multimedia on the Web. Clearly, the multimedia capability makes the Web a richer medium than print, and the ability to provide more in-depth product information at a lower cost makes the Web superior to television. Commercial multimedia applications are still limited because of bandwidth constraints, but as broadband becomes more widespread, communication on the Web will continue to improve.

Hypermedia. On the World Wide Web, documents from a Web site can be linked to other documents in that site or to other sites. It is this linking of documents that makes it a "web." From a communications perspective, there are important implications to such linking of documents.

First, the presentation of information is nonlinear. Rather than reading an article from top to bottom, one can exit the page in the middle, go to another page or article via a link, and then return to the original article. Studies show that too many links on one page can be distraction.

Second, this nonlinear search-and-retrieval process "provides both essentially unlimited freedom of choice and greater control for the consumer, and may be contrasted with the

Exhibit 9-3 Multimedia Brand Promotion Site by Nestle

Source: www.nestle-lion.de.

restrictive navigation options available in traditional media such as television or print."[15] The impact of nonlinear presentation on recall or retention requires serious research.

Global. The Internet is the first truly global medium. Satellite technology has taken North American television programs to a global audience, and the infrastructure required for this global satellite networking is enormous. In comparison, a Web site created by a small business in North Carolina or Nova Scotia can now reach a global audience. The reach of the Web is limited at present. North America accounts for more than two-thirds of Internet usage. By 2002, it is estimated that 66 percent of Internet use and 40 percent of E-commerce revenue will come from outside the US.[16] For retailers like L.L. Bean (www.llbean.com), this means access to new markets. For companies such as Texas Instruments, Lotus, and Microsoft, the Internet offers the ability to engage in globally dispersed software development by hiring the best worldwide workforce.[17] They can communicate and collaborate with colleagues in different time zones. To the average consumer, the global reach of the Internet could mean access to a greater variety of products. For example, international newspapers from countries as far away as Australia or India are just a few mouse-clicks away. From a communications perspective, distance and time are no longer impediments.

Interactive. The Web is an **interactive medium** that allows for audience participation. Interactivity can take many forms. IBM (www.ibm.com) features interactive games on its sites with the intent to generate brand familiarity among teenagers. Nestle also uses an interactive game to create brand awareness.

Another form of interactivity is the online chat. The online chat section of iVillage, a site that targets women, is a major attraction. Portals like AOL and Excite also attract large numbers of participants to their online chat communities. More than 750 million messages are sent each day through AOL's Buddy List® community and the company's ICQ service.[18] Feedback and pop-up online surveys can also give the consumer interactive experiences.

Video-conferencing applications are likely to be integrated into Web sites, allowing consumers to talk directly to suppliers. This is another application that awaits the widespread availability of broadband.

The ability to play audio or video content or an online game is a relatively simple form of interaction, where the customer and employees of the company are not interacting with each other. Filling out an online order form or a feedback form can also be considered a basic form of interaction. Here the customer is likely to expect a response. Often the response can be automated. For example, filling out an order form results in an automatic order acknowledgement e-mail. Special cases (such as an item not available, a problem with the credit card, or a special complaint) must be addressed personally by customer service staff.

Consumer-to-consumer interaction through bulletin boards brings many consumers together and can often bring employees and customers together. Here the company must commit the necessary human resources to monitor, moderate, and respond to queries. Lastly, real-time interaction between customers and employees (such as live online chat-based customer service) or among customers themselves (such as a chat forum) requires two-way "live" participation. Again, the necessary human resources must be committed to implement such interaction effectively.

Virtual Communities. As we saw in Chapter 6, the Internet, at its core, is really a community. It is a global community of users. Virtual communities are a thriving part of the Internet because most people tend to have interests or hobbies and feel the need to connect with other people.[19] In Usenet newsgroups, such as alt.autos.mercedes and alt.cellular, commentary on

iMarket Demo 9-1 Word-of-Mouth Communication Online

Some people see the Internet as an impersonal medium. Others would argue that nothing could be further from the truth. Online communities are a vital part of the Internet and the Web. These communities, many of which are commercially sponsored, draw like-minded people to interact with each other. The Usenet newsgroups, bulletin boards, and chat rooms cover a broad spectrum—intellectual discussion, business talk, romantic encounters, financial advice, and much more. Many go online just to meet new people. Here is an example of an exchange between two consumers taken from the alt.autos.mercedes newsgroup, as posted on December 12, 1999:

Consumer A:

>I just test drove a 1990 350 SD(L)? at a
>dealership today. The car has 125,000
>on the clock, but drove nicely, and ac-
>celerated well. The dealer is asking
>$19900 for the car. Aside from minor
>cosmetic problems (dings and scratches)
>with the paint it looks good. Is this car
>a good deal for the price, or should I
>run away from it as fast as I can?

>TIA for any and all opinions,

>—Duncan (9/11/99)

Consumer B's Response:

The 350 engine is NOT something you want. Apparently, it's a bored out 3.0L engine that's simply not strong enough internally. Connecting rods have bent. Word is that M-B accommodates the ORIGINAL owners of these dogs; subsequent owners are on their own. If you want this vintage M-B buy a gas model not this 3.5L diesel disaster.

- TGL (9/12/99)

Marketers have very little control over such exchanges happening in a public forum. In the old days, the spread of word-of-mouth communication was limited to one's family, friends, and peers. Now consumers can share their experiences, good or bad, with literally the whole world.

Sources: alt.autos.mercedes; Chris Adams, "The 1996 Internet Counterrevolution: Power, Information, and the Mass Media." (www.crim.ca/inet96/).

products and exchange of information on consumption experiences is quite common (see iMarket Demo 9-1). The influence of online word-of-mouth communication on consumer behaviour should not be underestimated. Communication in virtual communities has become very sophisticated. Now Web-based chat rooms or virtual communities allow people to post pictures and audio or video messages (for example, see www.excite.com/communities/directory/), and marketers are now actively encouraging virtual communities centred on their brands.

Integration. The Web can offer the consumer a richer experience, thanks to the IP or Internet Protocol technology that supports the Internet. Customer databases can now be linked to Web sites. For example, Federal Express (www.fedex.com) allows customers to track their shipments on its Web site by using the airway bill number. Dell Computers allows for online customer account management through their Premier pages (www.dell.com). Customer service is taken to new levels because of this integration of databases with the Web. In addition to these characteristics, the nature of information flow on the Internet is different from what we see in traditional mass media. Let's explore some of these differences now.

Web Communication Model

Television and print media are mass media or **one-to-many media** (see Exhibit 9-4). The firm (F) transmits content through a medium to consumers (C). The nature of the content—static (text, image, and graphics) or dynamic (audio, full-motion video, and animation)—depends on the medium (television, print, or billboard). No direct interaction between consumers and firms is present in this model. Customization or individualization of messages is impossible in these media. For example, television carries the same advertising message to millions of consumers. While targeting of advertising is possible by choosing the appropriate magazine or television program, there is little room for varying the message for each reader. The one-to-many model best describes mass media communication.

In this model, the consumer is a passive recipient of information. Television is the best example of such a low-involvement, passive medium. Consumers become a captive audience, lacking control over what is seen.

The Web is a hypermedia *computer-mediated environment* (CME). Hoffman and Novak define a hypermedia CME as "a dynamic distributed network, potentially global in scope, together with associated hardware and software for accessing the network, which allows consumers and firms to (1) provide and interactively access hypermedia content (i.e., machine interaction), and (2) communicate through the medium (i.e., person interaction)."[20] In the distributed hypermedia computer network (that is, the World Wide Web), users access and provide hypermedia content (multimedia content connected across the network with hypertext links).

Communication on the Web or hypermedia CME is described by the **many-to-many model** (see Exhibit 9-5). Here, marketers are not the only ones with messages. Consumers now

Exhibit 9-4 One-to-Many Communication Model

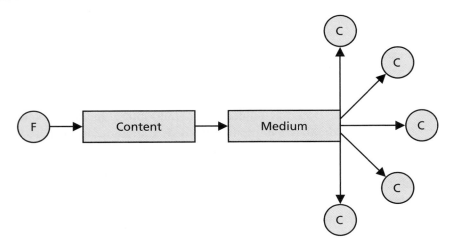

Source: Hoffman and Novak (1996).

Exhibit 9-5 Many-to-Many Communication Model

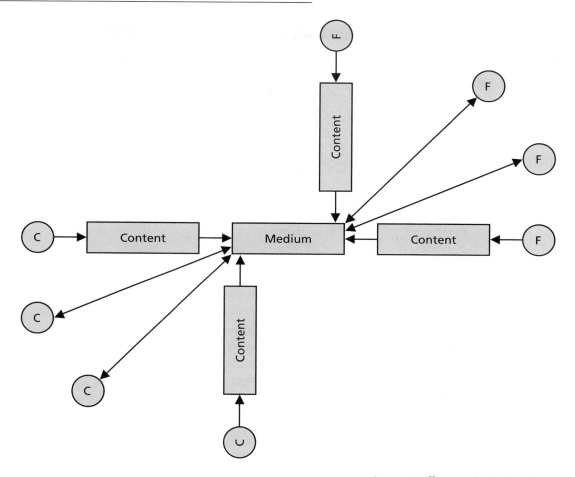

Source: Hoffman and Novak (1996).

 have a medium where they can inexpensively and easily voice their opinions. Take the case of Nike. In addition to the Nike corporate Web site (www.nike.com), consumers have created several Web sites devoted to this brand. A search using the keyword "Nike" on Yahoo! brings up not only the Nike corporate Web site but also dozens of pro- and anti-Nike sites, ostensibly created by consumers (for example, www.cleanclothes.org/companies/nike.htm).

In the many-to-many communication model, unlike mass media, there can be direct interaction between consumers and marketers, as well as among consumers. Table 9-2 presents a comparison of different media in terms of level of interactivity and type of content.

Push vs. Pull Debate. Television is a **push medium**, where advertising messages are pushed to the consumer. While the consumer has the choice of changing channels, he or she does not control the messages delivered. On the Internet, however, the consumer controls what he or she reads or hears. In other words, consumers "pull" the messages that they want to see. Thus, the Internet is a **pull medium**. A consumer has to make deliberate choices by typing the URL (Web site address) or by clicking hypertext links on a page.

Table 9-2 Comparison of Media Characteristics

Media	Interpersonal Model	Machine Interaction	Interaction	Content
Print	One-to-many	No	No	T, I
Billboard	One-to-many	No	No	T, I
TV-Cable	One-to-many	No	No	A, V, T*
Interactive TV	One-to-many	No	Yes	T, I, A, V
Fax	One-to-one	Yes	No	T, I
Telephone	One-to-one	Yes	No	A
Teleconference	Many-to-many	Yes	No	A
WWW**	Many-to-many	Yes	Yes	T, I, A, V

Source: Adapted from Donna Hoffman and Thomas Novak (1996).

Notes: A = Audio, I = Image, T = Text, V = Video.

*Text is quite limited in TV.

**WWW includes forms, Java-based interactive applets.

In the early days of the Web, there was great excitement over making the Web a "push" medium. Push technology requires users to usually install a small software application on their computers. When the users log on to the Internet, preselected information (such as news from selected media outlets, stock quotes, and so on) are automatically sent to the user's computer at periodic intervals. Such information can be displayed on the browser or a small window.

PointCast (www.pointcast.com) was at the forefront of this movement. Consumers, familiar with the way TV works, tried PointCast in large numbers. PointCast may have disappointed Wall Street, but it still has a loyal customer base.

Here is how it works. PointCast aggregates news and information from over 700 sources worldwide and broadcasts it via the Internet or corporate intranets directly to the viewers' desktops. Consumers can choose from a variety of channels, such as National News, Business News, and Lifestyle. Consumers can also decide how frequently they want their news updated.

When the consumer logs on to the Internet, the latest news in the selected channels gleaned from a variety of sources, such as CNN, *The New York Times*, and *The Globe and Mail*, is automatically delivered to the viewer's desktop. All of this is free. The only catch is that the consumer gets some advertisements along with the news. Just like your local TV, advertisers pay for the PointCast broadcast on the Internet.

PointCast's valuation took a tumble since its heady days a few years ago, and it was acquired by LaunchPad Technologies to create a new entity called Entrypoint.com. Entrypoint (now merged with another company called Infogate) combines PointCast's push technology with e-wallet capability (where online order forms are automatically filled out) that makes online shopping easier. It remains to be seen whether PointCast will succeed in its new incarnation.

FreeLoader, one of PointCast's competitors, is no longer in business. Early failures like this seem to suggest that the broadcast or push model on the Web has not caught the consumer's fancy. Perhaps consumers are unwilling to surrender their navigational control or maybe the constant exposure to advertising is annoying. Other online companies have not given up on the push model entirely.

NetSanity is another company that offers a service where content from a variety of sources is delivered to the user's computer, thus reducing the user's need to search for information. In exchange for the free content delivery, the user must be ready to accept targeted advertising messages. NetZero, a free ISP, also pipes ads to the user's desktop and targets the ads based on user demographics and preferences. There are a variety of free services on the Internet, from free phone service to free PCs, that depend on targeted push advertising for revenue (see iMarket Demo 2-2 on page 45).

Will consumers be turned off by the constant exposure to advertising? Or will they see the advertising as an acceptable price for the valuable content, product, or services they get? The jury is still out on such "free" or purely advertising-supported business models.

Push technology eliminates the need to type URLs or search for information. More than anything else, it offers convenience. This technology uses the *narrowcasting* capability of the Internet (as opposed to the broadcasting capability of television) and turns the Web into a personal broadcasting system with individualized programming. The applications of push technology extend beyond consumer services. For example, companies can use this technology to send real-time data to salespeople or supervisors on the production floor. Marimba's (www.marimba.com) Castanet is a push technology product that is aimed at such business applications.

Consumer-to-Company Communication. One of the features of the many-to-many communication model (Exhibit 9-5) is that the Internet allows customers to communicate with the firm. Businesses can use e-mail, online feedback forms, bulletin boards hosted by companies, and live chat to give their customers the ability to provide feedback. Many companies now provide online customer service using live chat. It is likely that the availability of a variety of communication tools will also increase consumer-to-company communication. Use of the Internet for communication may be seen as more convenient and less time-consuming. This means businesses must now engage adequate staff to deal with the flow of information from their customers.

The Online Marketing Communication Mix

There are several means of communication on the Internet. Depending on the communication goals, the means of online communication must be carefully chosen. In this section, an introduction to online communication mix is presented. In the next chapter, each communication tool will be discussed in greater detail.

Web Sites

The Web site is, perhaps, the most important aspect of the online communication mix. It can be used to effectively convey the brand image. For example, corporate sites usually have a more serious look and typically use white as the background colour. Sites targeted at

iMarket Demo 9-2 Web Sites and Brand Image

The Royal Bank of Canada's site conveys a traditional image by maintaining the corporate colours—blue and yellow. The site has all the seriousness that you would expect from a financial institution. When consumers go to this site, they know they are in a familiar place. Products and services are easy to find. Navigation is functional and efficient.

Contrast this with mbanx, Bank of Montreal's pioneering virtual bank, established in 1996. Among the first Internet banks in the world, mbanx was backed by strong imagery-oriented advertising. While brand recognition was high among Canadians, mbanx is considered a failure. In spite of the new name and different positioning, mbanx heavily cannibalized the Bank of Montreal's customer base.

The bank wanted a new brand name for its online bank. Maybe the decision was guided by the feeling that the name "Bank of Montreal" lacked a global appeal. The mbanx site was unlike any other online bank site. In its early days, the site had a black background, and the traditional Bank of Montreal logo was missing. The site looked very jazzy and featured rock stars like Alanis Morrisette. Some analysts think the site was way "too cool" to be effective.

Could it be that in these early days of Internet banking, consumers are looking for the reassurance of an established name? Should a corporate site resemble its offline counterpart (if there is one)? Does it depend on the target market? When can you make an argument for consistency versus a new online identity?

Incidentally, mbanx was recently decommissioned and its customer accounts merged into the Bank of Montreal site.

Source: "Way, way too cool," *Canadian Business*, August 27, 1999.

hobbyists and kids tend to have a more playful look. The site conveys the brand image and makes a first impression. It is no wonder that large E-commerce sites are spending millions of dollars in Web site development and maintenance costs each year. See iMarket Demo 9-2 for more on brand image and Web sites.

Advertising

There are various advertising opportunities on the Internet. The banner ad, usually a 468-by-60-pixel image file, is the most common format. The banner can comes in various sizes and shapes. It can be animated or static, interactive or non-interactive. Banner ads are placed in content sites where the advertiser's target market can be reached.

Banner ads are only one form of advertising on the Internet. Content or event sponsorship is another method that is growing in popularity. Sponsorship of a section of a content site gives the advertiser a permanent placement on the page, unlike banner ads, which are rotated.

Banner advertising can be precisely targeted at consumers, and ads can be placed in sites that match the customer profile of the advertising company. Ads can also be placed to match keywords when users search for product information on search engines. Technology now

iMarket Demo 9-3 Using Neural Networks to Target Online Ads

Technology allows marketers to target their advertising on a real-time basis. Solutions based on neural networks are being incorporated into ad serving and management operations. Net Perceptions, a developer and supplier of real-time recommendation technologies, launched "Net Perceptions for Ad Targeting" in 1998. According to Steve Larsen, Net Perceptions' vice-president of marketing and business development, the product helps marketers learn the interests and tastes of site visitors. It then places the right ad in front of the visitor in real time. "Targeting gets increasingly personalized as the software continually learns about each visitor's individual interests and tastes."

Another intelligent online ad targeting product in the market comes from Neural Applications Corp. Its technology is available as a plug-in for Microsoft Site Server 3.0. Neural Applications' vice-president Bill Staib said, "the implications don't stop at online advertising. This same profiling and analysis technology can be applied to a broad range of services on the Internet, such as personalizing Web page navigation and optimizing product targeting for e-commerce applications."

These "intelligent" targeting systems monitor variables such as recency and frequency of visit, behavioural information, time of day, demographic information, keywords used in the search engine, and other categorical information. Neural Applications and Net Perceptions claim great improvement in click-through rates, indicating that they are more cost-effective for advertisers.

Sources: "Net Perceptions Launches Ad Targeting Solution," *InternetNews.com*, October 8, 1998; "Neural Applications to Customize Ad Targeting for Site Server 3.0," *InternetNews.com*, March 5, 1998.

exists to monitor and track user preferences while they surf the Web and serve them ads that match their preferences (see iMarket Demo 9-3).

E-mail

Direct mail is a more targeted communication format compared to mass media. The same is true in the case of e-mail marketing. The message can be targeted or tailored to each recipient of the e-mail. Industry analyst reports predict a bright future for e-mail marketing. The major stumbling block seems to be privacy concerns (and how companies address that) and *spamming* (sending unsolicited junk e-mail to a large number of Internet users). Guidelines in these two areas are still evolving.

Promotion

In addition to advertising, online marketers can invest in a variety of response-inducing sales promotional efforts. Electronic coupons can be redeemed in online or offline stores. Sites such as eCoupons.com, Coolsavings.com, and smarts provide a range of coupons that can be used in online or offline stores. Online coupons are particularly effective if the marketing objective is to immediately drive up sales.

Brand Communities

As we saw in Chapter 6, building brand communities is an effective method of reaching a vast number of actual users. If the community is not rigidly moderated, the marketer may be able to observe users in a more relaxed setting where they are talking to each other. It is like a "live" focus group and can be a valuable source of information. The fact that users are in a branded environment does create some exposure to the brand name, which cannot hurt the company. Large companies, from auto-makers to consumer product manufacturers, never had intimate contact with end-users. Consumer surveys and focus groups were done on an ad-hoc basis. Now there are opportunities for ongoing dialogue with consumers via the Web. Some companies using brand communities include Kodak (www.kodak.com) and Shell (www.shell.com).

Communication with Stakeholders

The Internet is not only an appropriate medium for communicating with current and potential customers, but also with other stakeholder groups. Table 9-3 describes some of the possible communication tools available for different stakeholder groups.

Current customers, with whom the firm desires to build one-to-one relationships, can have password-protected extranets, customized e-mail or Web pages specific to their needs, or the opportunity to interact with a "live" person online. Communication with potential customers may be more general. The use of promotional or brand Web sites, targeted e-mail (if they have signed on and provided permission), and online advertising can be effective ways of reaching this group.

Table 9-3 Use of the Internet to Communicate with Multiple Stakeholders

Stakeholder Group	Online Communication Tools
Current customers	Web site, e-mail (permission marketing), live chat with customer service personnel, online brand community, extranet
Potential customers	Web site, banner ads, online promotions, targeted e-mail (permission marketing)
Employees	Intranet, collaborative tools, and e-mail
Suppliers, channel and strategic partners	Extranet, e-mail, EDI
Investors	Web site (annual reports), feedback forms
Media	Online press releases, Web site
Public and interest groups	Web site, e-mail, or bulletin boards
Regulators	Electronic filing of documents

Note: This table describes the most commonly used tools in each case, but does not rule out other possibilities.

Internal marketing refers to directing communication efforts towards employees. Organizations are using the Web (intranets) to deliver training courses and to link salespeople with vital information and databases. Teams within organizations can use intranets to collaborate on projects. Everything from human resource policies, internal job postings, online vendor catalogues, and pension or retirement plan details are now being deployed through intranets. The term business-to-employee (B2E) marketing is used to refer to internal communication within the organization.

Just as intranets are used in internal communication within organizations, extranets are used in communication with those outside the firm, including suppliers and business partners. Extranets also use the Web but provide password-protected access to authorized people. Businesses can share real-time data, avoid the expense and delay involved in phone calls and faxes, and increase the overall efficiency of operations by using the Web to communicate with suppliers and partners.

Companies are also using the Web to post press releases to the media and offer information to investors (such as details on company management or financial statements) and other public interest groups. Shell (www.shell.com) operates an online bulletin board, where environmental activists often participate and express strong opinions against the company. Shell's employees then respond to the criticism.

Challenges for Marketers

The Internet has opened a new communication medium for marketers. It allows for personalized as well as mass communication. Several big advertisers are cautious in their Internet advertising expenditures now. But can any firm afford to leave the Internet out of its media mix?

Myer Berlow, AOL's Senior VP of Interactive Marketing, may be able to convince skeptics with these words:

> *No other medium allows advertisers the opportunity to immediately capture the attention of active and engaged consumers; to provide them with more information about their product or service; and to complete transactions. This is one of online's real competitive strengths over print and television advertising, and one that cannot be duplicated in the offline world.*[21]

Along with the benefits, the Internet also brings some challenges in this area. The largely unregulated nature of the Internet, coupled with the fact that it is an open technology-driven environment, complicates matters at times. Let's now consider some of the challenges that marketers confront online.

Trademark and Copyright Protection

Recent court cases involving Playboy Enterprises highlight the fact that marketers and the legal community need to come to grips with the new reality that is the Internet. Playboy claimed that the portal site Excite sold *meta-tags* linked to keywords such as "playboy" and "playmate" to hardcore pornographic sites. Ads for these sites are likely to be displayed when someone searches for information on "Playboy" in Excite. A US federal judge in Virginia agreed that "Playboy" and "Playmate" are trademarks and ruled in favour of Playboy Enterprises. A judge in California, however, said these words are part of the English language and cannot be controlled by Playboy Enterprises.[22] Several similar suits are now pending before the courts. Estee Lauder has also launched a case against Excite, alleging that competitor ads were displayed at the top of search results when users were searching for Estee Lauder in the Excite search engine.

Portals and search engines link banners to keywords. Advertisers have far greater control in other traditional media. The fact that legal opinion is split on this matter highlights the complexity of the issue. Until a higher court issues a final ruling, online advertisers will closely watch these cases. There is clearly a need to define rules for both search engines and advertisers.

Problems in Ad Traffic Statistics

The click-through rate, which is an important metric especially for advertisers on a pay-per-click program, is susceptible to manipulation. Tech-savvy con artists can inflate click-through numbers. A technical discussion of this topic, however, is beyond the scope of this book. Ad networks such as DoubleClick and ValueClick, which administer the click-through payment programs, include clauses in their contracts prohibiting such hit inflation. Dan Clements, vice-president of Banner Brokers, an ad network firm, estimates that 15 to 20 percent of click-throughs could be spurious or phantom clicks.

This is, indeed, a serious problem for advertisers. Legitimate ad sellers and ad networks also suffer from such unscrupulous actions. The ad networks have formed an industry watchdog association called Ad Cops to combat the hit inflation problem.[23] While the technology allows for detailed measurement of activity on the Internet, it is obvious that it also provides scope for abuse.

Banner Busters

Remember the earlier discussion about how the Internet was a free space in the pioneer days, devoid of commercial activity? The people who want to reclaim the Internet from marketers are now offering ad-blocking software programs. Companies like Webfree (www.webfree.com) and Junkbuster (www.junkbuster.com) are spearheading this campaign. Once installed in a computer, these programs can tune out banner ads and other forms of "intrusive" or unwanted messages. Are such software programs likely to affect advertising on the Internet?

The Association of Canadian Advertisers (ACA) does not seem to be very concerned.[24] The advertising industry is counting on the belief that only an insignificant number of consumers will go to the trouble of installing such software. Since the most common business model on the Web is the advertising-supported model—free content or services in exchange for "eyeballs"—it is likely that consumers who enjoy these benefits will not mind the exposure to commercial messages.

Web Demographics

The reach of the Web is expanding. More women are online now. In North America, the gender gap in Internet usage is insignificant. Younger people have access in schools or at home. Yet, a significant proportion of the population is still not represented online. The problem of "digital have-nots" cannot be dismissed easily. This may be one reason why companies that advertise online are hedging their bets by advertising offline as well. The key question for marketers is whether or not the target market is online.

Consumer Behaviour

Consumers have far greater control on the Internet than they do with television. From an information-processing perspective, marketers do not yet fully know how consumers process information online. How are brand attitudes or brand beliefs formed on the Internet?

Information presentation on the Web is nonlinear. Hyperlinks allow consumers to exit and enter documents at various stages, as opposed to a simple top-down presentation in print media. How consumers make online decisions and how they reconcile information from the online and offline worlds are questions that do not have answers yet.

Competitive Ad Monitoring

On the Internet almost everything is transparent. If you can see your competitor's ads, Web sites, and online strategy—so can they. Monitoring competitors' advertising and media buys is now easier than ever. In the offline world, companies such as Nielsen track advertising placements and costs. These reports often take months to compile. On the Internet, where speed is of the essence, companies like AdRelevance and Leading Web Advertisers (LWA) are providing faster ad monitoring services. LWA provides overnight access to competitive ad information. These companies will monitor anywhere from 200 to 600 leading Web sites, which account for the bulk of advertising activity. They can then provide estimates of ad insertions and ad spending by various competitors. The availability of such information means quicker reaction from competition.

Integrating Promotional Methods and Media

There is a consensus that using a mix of online promotional methods will lead to better results than excessive dependence on any one method. Larger companies with bigger media budgets usually spend heavily on conventional mass media. Television can create awareness, billboards can remind people, and the Web site can create interest in the product. While television can convey humour and other emotions quite well, the Web can deliver cerebral information better than other media. The communication goals of each medium should be clearly defined, but the metrics for each medium may be different. Awareness may be a good measure for TV and radio, while direct response measures may work online.

Given the strengths and weaknesses of each medium, advertisers must define the communication objectives and role of each medium. In fact, offline advertising now accounts for a significant portion of the marketing budgets of leading online firms. Television was used by 75 percent of leading Internet companies, followed by radio (68 percent), consumer magazines and periodicals (53 percent), and newspapers (52 percent).[25] Mass media advertising is especially effective in reaching those who are not online but will be soon. As the Internet still has only about a 50 percent reach in North America, the use of mass media to create awareness is not surprising. Once consumers are online, banner ads can provide interaction and enticement, while Web sites can provide in-depth information, interaction, and personalization.

Netscape is credited with launching the first fully integrated campaign in January 1999. As the company changed its identity to become the portal of choice, consumers had to be made aware that Netscape was more than a company that made a Web browser. The campaign involved TV, print (see Exhibit 9-6), radio, billboards, and of course the Web. TV ads

Exhibit 9-6 Netscape Print Ad

Sources: www.netscape.com, www.channelseven.com.

ran in shows like *60 Minutes* and *The X-Files*. Print ads ran in *Rolling Stone*, *Time*, *Wired*, and other magazines. Online ads were featured in portals and entertainment sites.

Not too long ago, a client had to hire separate agencies to deal with traditional media and interactive media. Now, in the advertising business "full-service" is the buzzword.[26] Clients and agencies have realized that unless a multiple media campaign is truly integrated, there has to be a common agenda. There is evidence of rivalry among different media. The Internet is likely to take away some of the advertising revenue from traditional media, but in the end, each medium will have a defined role to play.[27]

It may not be easy for traditional marketers (especially those in consumer brand marketing) to give up the bias towards mass media and choose the Web, which is an interactive and personal medium. While this may be a challenge for some, companies that see the Internet as part of a larger media mix will also see new opportunities for more effective communication with all their stakeholders.

Ethical Boundaries

Internet advertising has received a lot of flak, perhaps rightfully, for a number of reasons. Consumers still have a great of concern about online privacy. Most commercial sites collect basic consumer data online—pages visited, browser-type, frequency of visits, and so on. Some require consumers to register for their free services, and registration entails providing personal information. In some cases this may require just one's name and e-mail address. In other cases, additional information on hobbies and other demographic variables may be sought.

This so-called **value exchange**, where consumers willingly submit information in exchange for free services, is seen as the way of the future by some experts.[28] Free services—whether news or e-mail—are supported mostly by advertising. Companies collecting consumer profile information use such information to attract advertisers and also to target advertising based on profiles.

While advertising pays for some "free" services that consumers get, what are the legitimate uses of such personal information? Most sites aggregate personal information and use the aggregated demographics or site statistics to attract advertisers. Some sites do sell non-aggregated personal information. When an online purchase is made, the customer's address, e-mail, and credit card information are provided. It is the sale or unauthorized use of such information that really invades the consumer's privacy. Many companies are realizing that they can build consumer trust by having an ethical privacy policy and disclosing the policy. See Exhibit 9-7 for an example.

A study by the Federal Trade Commission in the United States showed that most of the top 100 sites did not have a privacy policy.[29] Responding to consumer concerns, several leading online companies have joined forces with TRUSTe, a non-profit organization, and have created the Privacy Partnership.[30] The aim of this partnership is to educate consumers and online companies about privacy issues. See Chapter 13 for a more complete discussion of this topic.

Summary

The Internet has opened a new communication medium for marketers. It offers many advantages, such as the ability to deliver multimedia content, the ability to engage the consumer

Exhibit 9-7 Privacy Policy at Yahoo!

In our role of delivering targeted advertisements, Yahoo! plays the middleman. Advertisers give us an advertisement and tell us the type of audience they want to reach (for example, males over 35 years old). Yahoo! takes the advertisement and displays it to users meeting that criteria. In this process, the advertiser never has access to individual account information. Only Yahoo! has access to individuals' accounts. This kind of advertisement targeting is done with banner ads as well as promotional email through Yahoo! Delivers. You will only receive special offers via email from Yahoo! if you have indicated in your account preferences that you would like to receive them. You can change your account preferences at any time.

Yahoo! does research on our users' demographics, interests, and behavior based on the information provided to us upon registration, during a promotion, from our server log files or from surveys. We do this to better understand and serve our users. This research is compiled and analyzed on an aggregated basis. Yahoo! may share this aggregated data with advertisers or business partners.

Source: Yahoo! (See www.yahoo.com/info/privacy/ for complete privacy statement).

through interactivity, and the ability to offer more in-depth information. It doubles as an advertising medium and a distribution channel at the same time. Newer forms of advertising, such as interactive banners, can take a consumer straight from exposure to product purchase within seconds.

The Internet is a many-to-many communication medium. Consumers have an active voice and can often create content, whether in newsgroups or on personal Web sites. Unlike TV, the Internet is not a passive medium. The consumer makes active navigational choices and the medium requires greater cognitive involvement. Marketers have to understand these differences in order to communicate effectively on the Internet.

There are many forms of communication possible on the Internet. These include the Web site, banner advertising, sponsorships, e-mail, and promotions. Each has strengths and weaknesses. Rich media advertising and the promise of broadband bode well for the future of Internet advertising. Early experiments in rich media ads show they can be effective. Many advertisers are not fully convinced about the effectiveness of Internet advertising, especially when the objective is to build a brand.

Marketers face some difficult issues as they try to figure out how this new medium works and how effective it is. In particular, they must grapple with issues ranging from escalating costs and unreliable (or even fraudulent) measurement data, to more fundamental questions concerning business ethics.

As marketers wrestle with these issues, there is also excitement in the air. The promise of broadband changes the playing field, and advertisers are now starting to think beyond the banner.

Key Terms

Hypermedia, 227

Interactive medium, 228

Many-to-many medium, 230

Multimedia, 226

One-to-many medium, 230

Pull medium, 231

Push medium, 231

Value exchange, 241

Questions and Exercises

Review Questions

1. How does the Internet differ from other media, such as television and print? What unique benefits does it offer advertisers?
2. Is the Internet suited more for personalized communication or mass communication?
3. What are the key differences between the one-to-many and many-to-many communication models?
4. What are the important characteristics of the Web as a communication model that distinguish it from other mass media, such as television or print?
5. What are the different methods of communicating on the Internet?
6. Are there some products or services that would benefit more from Internet advertising than others?
7. What challenges must marketers, individually and collectively, overcome to take advantage of the communication capabilities of the Internet?

Discussion Questions

1. How can brand marketers, such as Procter & Gamble, who wish to reach millions of households use the Internet effectively as a communication medium? Be specific in your suggestions.
2. Mass media are often described as push media. The Internet allows the user to choose what he or she wants to see, and hence, is called a pull medium. Can push advertising (such as PointCast) succeed on the Internet? Why or why not?
3. Advertiser interest in banner advertising is decreasing. The limited space available for communicating and the low click-through rates are two of the reasons. What alternative forms of online advertising do you see gaining ground in the next few years? Why?
4. As advertisers shift their advertising budgets from mass media to the Internet, they must cut spending in other media. Experts predict that as Internet usage increases (both number of users and time spent online), more advertisers will follow the users to the Internet. Internet advertising is expected to reach $33 billion by 2004. If this prediction comes true, which traditional media do you think will be affected most adversely? Why?

Internet Exercises

1. Go to Yahoo! or AltaVista and do some keyword searches. See what banner ads are displayed. Study the banner copy. Is the banner effective in terms of (a) getting attention, and (b) persuading you to click or take some action? Click on the banner and go to the site behind the banner. Do the site and the banner convey similar images and messages? Are they consistent with each other?

2. Develop an online communication strategy for the following three products: (a) a new brand of fruit juice, (b) a new Internet-based custom clothes designer, and (c) an established luxury watch brand. Assuming each company will use a mix of media, what role should the Internet play? In each case: (1) identify the appropriate demographic group online, (2) identify some themes or concepts for Internet advertising, and (3) develop media strategy— where, when, and how much advertising?

Chapter 10

Advertising and Promotion Online

Vignette 10 **Bridging the Media Divide**

Remember the famous Nike billboard that gave you the feeling that Olympic gold medal winner Carl Lewis was jumping from one billboard to another one across the street? Now Nike has done it again. This time they want the audience to jump from one medium to another.

Nike used commercial spots featuring athlete Marion Jones (see Exhibit 10-1) and baseball star Mark McGwire to launch its new cross-trainer shoes. Celebrity endorsements are nothing new in the shoe business. These TV ads, however, created a cliff-hanger situation, an unresolved ending, with a tag line "continued at whatever.nike.com." Apparently, two of the major TV networks objected to those words and resisted playing the commercial, fearing that their TV audience would stop watching their programming and may go online to see the ending of the commercial. In the end, the campaign ran (without the tag line on two networks and with the tag line on one), and it did draw the television audience online to see the ending.

Once the viewers went online to the whatever.nike.com site, they were given a full brand experience. They could see one of seven possible endings to the commercial, learn more about the product, read about the athletes featured in the ads, and purchase the product online. Nike also ran an online campaign to drive traffic to the whatever.nike.com site using a technology called the SUPERSTITIALS format, developed by a company called Unicast (www.unicast.com). These ads, created using Flash, are fully animated and include audio. They are delivered from Unicast's servers.

A television commercial is a limited experience. By enticing viewers to go online to follow the ending of the commercial, Nike successfully

Exhibit 10-1 Nike Ad Clips Featured in the Promotional Site

Sources: www.nike.com; www.unicast.com.

converted what would have been a 30-second experience, to one that was 10 or 20 minutes long. Apparently, the SUPER-STITIAL ads led to a click-through rate that was 12 times higher than typical banner ads. Sales for this brand increased significantly, according to Mike Wilsky, Nike's vice-president of US marketing.

Nike's campaign succeeded by using a concept that gestalt psychology describes as "closure." Human beings like to see the endings. An incomplete storyline leaves viewers with the feeling that something's missing.

In addition to this clever execution, this may have been the first instance of a campaign that deliberately drew a television audience to the Web. It may not be the last. Advertisers know that each medium has its strengths and weaknesses. The Nike case is an example that blends two media, taking advantage of the action and emotion that TV can deliver with the interactivity and E-commerce the Internet can deliver.

As the number of online consumers grows and as people's media habits change, advertising campaigns must change as well. Rather than taking the "either… or" approach, combining the power of different media, as the Nike case demonstrates, may be the answer.

TNT (Turner Network Television) used a reverse strategy, driving traffic from the Web to a television program. A promotional site was designed for the movie *Pirates of the Silicon Valley* (see Exhibit 10-2). The site contained information on characters, trivia quizzes, and even some interactive 1980s video games that brought back a lot of nostalgic memories. A banner ad campaign was launched to drive traffic to the site and from there to the television program.

In the Summer of 2000, we saw hit television shows such as *Survivor* and *Big Brother* using the Internet to keep their audience engaged and interested, even after each episode was over. We saw in iMarket

Exhibit 10-2 TNT's Movie Promotion Ad

Source: tnt.turner.com.

Demo 1-1 (see page 13) how the movie *Blair Witch Project* was marketed so effectively using the Web.

The Internet is definitely a competitor to television. The 2000 US Democratic and Republican party conventions saw some famous television personalities like Sam Donaldson and Tom Brokaw acknowledging that fact. Webcasting during the conventions gave a more in-depth and interactive look at the events.

At the same time, the Web can also be an ally to the television medium. All major television networks and cable stations offer video on demand on their Web sites, interactive features such as chat, and more in-depth coverage of events. CNN.com is an excellent example.

Both media companies and advertisers will have to learn how to bridge the old media with the new. For some time now, the debate has been framed in terms of the new media versus the old media. Instead, using multiple media—each for a specific communication objective—may be a more productive approach.

Sources: Seth Fineberg (2000), "Choose Your Own Adventure, Swoosh Style," *Channelseven.com*, January 1, 2000; Seth Fineberg (2000), "Nike's "Whatever" Campaign Results Are In," *Channelseven.com*, May 2, 2000; Unicast (www.unicast.com); James Surowiecki, "Blair Witch's Lessons for Hollywood," *Slate.com*, August 9, 1999.

Introduction

Advertising on the Internet is the most visible aspect of the Internet to those who are online. Most people equate Internet advertising with the ubiquitous banners that show up on almost every Web site. But banner advertising is only one component of Internet advertising, and it may become a smaller component of online advertising efforts for many marketers. In this chapter, you will see a variety of other marketing communication tools available to marketers.

As we saw in Vignette 10, marketers now view the Internet as part of a media mix, where each medium can play a specific role. In this chapter, you will see that a similar approach is necessary when considering the different components of Internet advertising. Each component can serve a specific purpose.

To make effective decisions with respect to online communication, marketers must be familiar with measurements of online advertising effectiveness. The Internet offers new ways of paying for advertising, based on performance rather than on just the number of ad impressions. Advertising measurement and payment issues are also addressed in this chapter.

Online Marketing Communications Mix

There are several communication tools available on the Internet. Each has its strengths and weaknesses. In this section, an introduction to each of these tools is provided.

Online Advertising

Banner Advertising. For most people, Internet advertising is synonymous with **banner advertising**. Hotwired (www.hotwired.com) is credited with the "innovation" of the banner ad in 1994. Until then, companies exchanged reciprocal links. No one had thought of charging for the "real estate" on Web sites. A new form of advertising was born. Ad agencies and Web developers had to master the challenges of creating copy for the new medium (See Exhibit 10-3 for banner ads for the major automobile companies).

To make the task of selling ad space easier for advertisers, agencies, and site owners, banner advertising standards had to be established. CASIE or the Coalition for Advertising Supported Information and Entertainment (www.casie.org) and the IAB or Internet Advertising Bureau (www.iab.net), an industry consortium, led the way in establishing these standards. Table 10-1 lists the standard sizes for banner ads.

In the early days there was the static banner—an image with some text. Now most banners came with some animation. The next generation of banners, referred to as "rich media ads," offer sound, video, animation, and text. The narrow bandwidth limits the use of such ads. Very few consumers have access to broadband—cable modems or DSL. But in the next few years, as broadband becomes more widely available, rich media advertising may become commonplace. Internet ads will then look and feel more like television commercials.

Another variant of the banner that is getting a more favourable consumer response is the interactive banner. Consumers could never interact with a message on television or radio. On the Internet, interactive banners can take a consumer from advertising exposure to purchase within seconds. Usually, there is a drop-down menu that allows the consumer to make an instant decision after seeing the banner.

Interstitials. An **interstitial** is a Web page or banner inserted in the normal flow of editorial content for the purpose advertising or promotion. It can be more or less intrusive and the reaction of viewers usually depends on how welcome or entertaining the message is. An interstitial is usually designed to move automatically to the page the user requested after allowing enough time for the message to register or the ad(s) to be read.

These ads appear on the screen as the viewer moves from one Web page to another or from one Web site to another. When you click on a link and are waiting for a page to download, an advertisement usually appears on a page for a few seconds and then disappears. For examples of interstitials see www.blueplatypus.com/advertising/interstitials/.

Table 10-1 IAB/CASIE Advertising Banner Ad Sizes

Size (pixels)	Description
468 × 60	Full Banner
392 × 72	Full Banner with Vertical Navigation Bar
234 × 60	Half Banner
120 × 240	Vertical Banner
120 × 90	Button 1
120 × 60	Button 2
125 × 125	Square Button
88 × 31	Micro Button

Exhibit 10-3 Banner Ads from Top Automotive Brands

Sources: Respective automobile companies.

Webmercials and Superstitials. Webmercials (see www.kmgi.com) and superstitials (see www.unicast.com) are interstitial or splash pages that offer full multimedia commercial presentations. When a viewer clicks on a link to a specific page, a fully animated commercial will be played without the viewer requesting it, just as in the case of television commercials. The requested page will be displayed after the webmercial is played. Webmercials feature animation and sound. They can be banner size or full screen size. Webmercials may require Flash, Shockwave, or other plug-ins and tend to be effective as presentation tools only under high-bandwidth conditions.

Affiliate Advertising. Amazon.com has led the way in using this form of advertising. Amazon will pay the affiliate if a consumer clicks the Amazon banner on the affiliate site and eventually buys a product at Amazon.com. This is a result-oriented advertising method. See Chapter 2 for a more detailed discussion of this topic.

Corporate and Brand Web Sites

The Web site plays an essential role in the branding of a site. For examples, see virtual companies like Yahoo!, eBay, and Amazon.com. Yahoo! is the classic example of online branding. Being a pioneer in the search engine category, Yahoo! is now cashing in its brand equity by expanding into new categories like shopping, auctions, and online bill payment (see Exhibit 10-4). Yahoo! started as a directory service and has now made its foray into financial services. In addition to bill payment, Yahoo! offers co-branded access to leading online stock brokerages such as E*Trade and TD Waterhouse. Yahoo! also has strategic alliances or co-branding agreements with CIBC, a leading Canadian bank, and NetBank, the leading Internet bank in the United States. Yahoo! serves as a classic example of how a powerful brand name can be leveraged effectively on the Internet. Even though most people still think of Yahoo! as a search directory service, it has grown into the largest portal.

Corporate Web Sites. The company Web site is perhaps the most significant aspect of the online communication mix. The Web site can communicate to different audiences and stakeholder groups. Detailed product information and direct selling online are just two of the many possibilities. The Web site can be used to create and maintain relationships with customers (see Chapter 6) and investors. It can also attract potential employees and speak to different local community groups. A corporate Web site should be designed keeping in mind the multiple audiences and their differing interests. At the same time, it should clearly convey the corporate image.

Brand Sites. In addition to corporate sites and portal sites, companies that have multiple brands devote attention to brand-specific sites or promotional sites. Procter & Gamble's Sparkle City site for Crest toothpaste and Unilever's Becel site (see Chapter 8) are brand-

Exhibit 10-4 The Power of Branding

Source: www.yahoo.com.

specific sites. Most of the P&G brand sites seem to emphasize chat, bulletin boards, and other forms of user interaction aimed at forging a closer relationship with the consumer.

The brand sites are a venue to really show off the technology and offer a "rich media" experience for the consumer. These sites typically use Flash, Shockwave, and Java applets to create animation and sound. They may also contain streaming video or audio presentations.

Brand sites should try to reinforce or build a brand image. There are opportunities to do things online that cannot be done through mass media. Presentation of detailed product information and engaging consumers through interactive games, chat, bulletin boards, and other forms of user participation are common features at most brand sites.

Many brand sites are becoming brand communities. As we saw in Chapter 6, these communities can be a good source of consumer feedback and early problem detection. More than advertising, the experiences of another consumer or the words of an online opinion leader may influence buyer behaviour. Brand communities make it easier for brand managers to see what consumers say about their products. Misperceptions can be corrected and false rumours can be nipped in the bud.

The Usenet groups and other public bulletin boards represent non-moderated discussion. Marketers have little control over what is said here. Brand communities, which are bulletin boards or chat areas sponsored by the brand, allow marketers to gain some degree of control over brand-related word-of-mouth communication on the Internet. The key, however, is not to fully moderate the discussion, as this will not help reveal how consumers really feel about the brand.

Brand communities are the environments within which the company and the customer carry out an online relationship. If a company wants to build an online brand community, its own people must be ready and willing to communicate and spend time in developing relationships. By actively participating in virtual brand communities, marketers can gain a better understanding of consumer needs.

Micro-Sites and Promotional Sites. In 1997, JC Penney created a **micro-site**, which was really a "mini-store." An interactive banner ad was created with search capability. When a user would submit a search (for a clothing item), it would spawn a transactional micro-site, which is like a mini online store. Customers could then directly order from the micro-site, which opened in a new window, without any interruption to their online experience.[1] Micro-sites generally run during a specific advertising or promotional campaign. Micro-sites can be placed in high-traffic portals or content sites. They can provide rich information about the brand without having to incur the high cost of a full-fledged Web site.

More generic promotional sites, such as the Nestlé "Lion" candy bar site, have the mission of creating excitement, and perhaps initial product trial. Ford and Sony joined hands to create the co-branded "Mustang Music Lounge," a micro-site hosted within the Sony site (www.sonymusic.com). This site featured animated images of vintage Mustang cars. In addition, users could listen to music, download Mustang screensavers, participate in sweepstakes, and even purchase Sony music products. Rock-and-roll music and cars have gone hand-in-glove for generations of consumers, and the co-branded Mustang Music Lounge rekindled nostalgic images for some consumers, while creating brand awareness in the minds of the younger generation.

JCPenney.com ran a "back to school" promotional campaign on AltaVista. When viewers clicked on the banner ad, a micro-site opened, which offered customers a chance to sign up for a contest and other promotions offered by JC Penney and AltaVista. This is an effective use of an interactive banner with a promotional site.

Both JC Penney and Ford/Sony set out to create their micro-sites with a clearly defined mission and target market in mind. Such campaigns are effective. According to Melisa Vazquez, account director at Giant Step, an ad agency that handles some of P&G's brands, "It never makes sense to build a big, hefty website for packaged goods."[2] Most consumer product brands tend to have micro-sites.

The nature of the site will depend on the product and the market. If the product can be sampled online (such as music), consumed online (such as information or news), or purchased online (such as books or mutual funds), then a destination site filled with content, E-commerce capability (the ability to sell directly), and post-sales support features can be built.

Complex products such as cars and computers are now being mass customized, with Web sites providing the consumer with the ability to customize the product. High-involvement purchases, such as some kinds of clothing and appliances, can benefit from fashionable, animated micro-sites. Micro-sites can be placed in other high-traffic sites, thereby ensuring high exposure to the brand. Once a customer enters the micro-site, various interactive tools, from chat to games, can be used to inform and engage the consumer.

Corporate Web sites, especially for frequently purchased consumer goods, tend not to provide much product information. Unilever and P&G have decent, but by no means extravagant, sites. For consumer products, the resources are often better spent on creative ad campaigns rather than the Web site. Consumers are less likely to seek out a toothpaste site than a car site.

Online Sales Promotion

Promotional Banners. Banner ads can be used to reinforce the brand image or invite immediate response by making an offer. Promotional banners are very much like any other banner ad, except that they include a specific sales promotional offer (see Exhibit 10-5). Such banners are effective in stimulating initial trial.

E-coupons. The Web offers direct marketers a great venue. Marketers are increasingly using **electronic coupons** and other sales promotional tools. Couponnetwork (www.coupon network.ca), Coupongenie (www.coupongenie.com), Valupage (www.valupage.com), eSmarts (www.esmarts.com), MyPoints (www.mypoints.com), eCentives (www.ecentives.com), Coolsavings (www.coolsavings.com), and eCoupons (www.ecoupons.com) are some of the sites that offer online and/or offline coupons (see Exhibit 10-6). Typically, these sites allow users to print online coupons, which can be redeemed in local stores. Some online coupon services carry local and national coupons. Some sites like E-centives.com allow users to either print the coupon to use in a local store or redeem the coupon electronically in an online store.

Exhibit 10-5 Promotional Banner from ihomedecor.com

Now save 40% on every purchase.
Type in discount code: FOODFUN during checkout.
Offer expires 8/31/00.

ihomedecor.com

Source: www.ihomedecor.com.

Exhibit 10-6 Online Coupon Site

Source: www.ecoupons.com.

Electronic coupons, according to an industry report, have a high redemption rate in some categories, such as fast food (96 percent), groceries (94 percent), toys (84 percent), and books (83 percent). In terms of electronic coupon usage, groceries (59 percent), books (32 percent), and music (26 percent) are among the top categories.[3] Among coupons users, electronic coupons now account for about 10 percent of all coupon usage. The high redemption rate and growing usage could be attributed to the fact that the coupon user usually has to seek the coupon by going to a Web site or by opting-in for an e-mail delivery of coupons. Unsolicited coupons are likely to have a lower redemption rate.

Sweepstakes. Auto-makers want to ensure that their brand has "top of mind" recall and awareness among graduating college students, who are likely to buy cars. Honda launched a banner ad and sweepstakes micro-site campaign featured solely in the Academic Universe section of Lexis-Nexis (www.lexis-nexis.com).

WinDough.com, Sandbox.com, and iWon.com (a popular search engine, but also a premier sweepstakes site) are among numerous sites devoted to online sweepstakes. Exhibit 10-7 shows a sweepstakes micro-site for Pert Plus, a popular brand of shampoo.

Event or Content Sponsorship

Sponsorship is gaining ground, in some cases, at the cost of banner advertising. If Company X sponsors a section of Company Y's site, that gives Company X a permanent place in Company Y's site. Sponsorship is subtler than banner advertising.

Exhibit 10-7 PertPlus Micro-Site Features Sweepstakes

Source: pertplus.com/pert_index.asp.

Banner ads on a page are rotated. Sponsorship, on the other hand, gives the advertiser a more permanent location on the site, as shown in Exhibit 10-8. At this site, every viewer will see (at least theoretically) the Adobe and Webex logos on the Webmonkey page during the period when the sponsorship is in effect.

Sponsoring content can sometimes be risky. If the content is inappropriate or not well matched with the brand, there could be a detrimental effect on the brand. Before sponsoring content, it would make sense to study the site, its content, editorial policies, and so on.

Event sponsorship is another avenue open to advertisers. Netaid.org, a charity organization, has used webcasting of music to raise money for worthy causes. Companies like Cisco and KPMG are among Netaid's sponsors. Some sites do live webcasting of sporting events and others do live interviews with celebrities. Such events also provide sponsorship opportunities.

There are also independently published newsletters and discussion forums that draw people with specific interests or demographics. There are literally hundreds of these newsletters to choose from. Media buying services such as Lot21 and Modem Media can place ads in e-mail newsletters. As we saw in Chapter 6, Web communities or discussion forums draw large numbers of users. Two such communities offering sponsorship and advertising

Exhibit 10-8 Web Content Sponsorship

Sources: www.hotwired.com (left) and www.clickz.com (right).

opportunities are eGroups and eCircles. In eCircles, an advertiser can even send a birthday reminder message to members, which may be appropriate for gift products.

E-mail Marketing (or eDirect Marketing)

An estimated 85 percent of home users and 75 percent of workplace computer users conduct personal and business correspondence via the Internet.[4] E-mail, in fact, ranks as the most common reason for using the Internet (see Exhibit 10-9). With virtually everyone on the Internet having access to e-mail, there is little wonder that marketers see a big future for direct marketing via e-mail.

Advantages of E-mail Marketing. In addition to the access it offers, there are some additional benefits to using e-mail as a tool for marketing communications. First, e-mail communication is much cheaper than direct marketing through standard mail or telemarketing services. Targeted e-mail addresses are often sold at $0.20 or less per address. The high cost of direct mail and the broad-based nature of television and print media have forced marketers to examine customer acquisition costs closely.[5] E-mail changes the economics of direct marketing by eliminating printing and postage costs associated with direct mail campaigns.

Second, it is possible to reach a vast number of recipients within a matter of minutes. Changes to prices or new product announcements can be communicated in real-time.

Third, the latest generation of e-mail programs (such as Outlook, Eudora, and Netscape, as well any Web-based e-mail application like Hotmail) allow for receiving HMTL

Exhibit 10-9 Top Reasons for Using the Internet

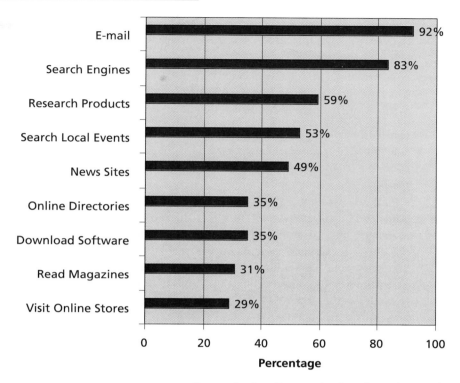

Source: Jupiter Communications (www.jup.com).

e-mail. The user can simply click on the link to a special offer and can then be taken to the marketer's Web site from the e-mail. This makes it easy for the consumer to respond to an offer.

Fourth, current e-mail programs are also capable of handling pictures as well as audio and video attachments. Direct marketing via e-mail need not be bland text messages. They can be colourful and entertaining.

Finally, e-mail ads can be personalized to the needs of each consumer. Reputed e-mail marketers first get the consumer's permission to send messages. They also find out what the consumer likes and dislikes. The greater the relevancy of the messages, the better the response will be. **Click-through rates**, one of the indices for effectiveness of online advertisements, are very low for banner advertising (less than 1 percent). For e-mail ads, however, click-through rates tend to be much higher, in the 5 to 20 percent range.[6]

Concerns with E-mail Marketing. There are at least three major concerns with e-mail marketing: spamming, consumer privacy, and consent.

Spamming. Not too long ago, e-mail was hailed as the "killer app" that has revolutionized communication. E-mail is unfortunately frequently abused and maligned. Many in the industry worry that the "killer app" may itself be killed. People who do not respect the privacy rights of others continue to send out unsolicited messages, very much like the junk mail we find in our mailboxes. Such junk e-mail, or spam, may be the biggest threat to the legitimate use of e-mail marketing.

Consumer Privacy. Then there is the question of consumer privacy. In order to target e-mail messages to match each consumer's interests, the marketer first has to collect detailed data, which may include demographics, psychographics, and shopping behaviour. There are serious concerns about who has access to this information. A study by Forrester Research found that privacy concerns are a major impediment to online shopping and the growth of E-commerce. While women are more concerned than men, privacy concerns cut across demographic lines.[7]

Consent. Legitimate e-mail marketers do get the consumer's consent before sending e-mail. This is called "opting-in," where the consumer chooses to receive e-mail messages or advertisements that are tailored to his or her needs. There are those who follow the "opt-out" method, where unsolicited e-mail is sent first and the recipient then has to send a return e-mail requesting to be deleted from the e-mail list (see Exhibit 10-10). Very often people who send unsolicited e-mail, however, do so using e-mail systems that can only send e-mail messages, but not receive messages. So the hapless consumer has no way of opting out!

Those who sell junk e-mail collect e-mail addresses from Usenet groups, bulletin boards, and Web sites. These advertisers believe that any attention from consumers, even if they incur the wrath of annoyed consumers, is a good thing. There is now proposed legislation that would offer more protection to consumers.

A non-profit organization called Mail Abuse Prevention System (MAPS) is fighting spammers (mail-abuse.org). Those who send unsolicited e-mail messages or otherwise violate consumer privacy are placed in a "real-time blackhole" list. MAPS is hoping that by publicly shaming these organizations, their behaviour can be changed.

Exhibit 10-10 Excerpt from Junk E-mail Selling "Junk E-mail Service"

```
=> 1,000,000 E-mails Delivered for Only $500 (Normally $999)

=> 2 Free Mths Bulk Friendly Web-Hosting & 5,000,000 e-mails delivered
for
Only $2,199  (Normally would cost $5,800)

Try working smarter, not harder and let us put Technology to work for
you Today!

Call Now to place your order or to get more information:


*********************************************************************
REMOVAL INSTRUCTIONS:

If for some reason you would like to opt-out from our Newsletter and
E-zine, then
simply send an e-mail to the e-mail address below and put "Opt-Out" in
the subject
field.
```

In the meantime, the Coalition Against Unsolicited Commercial Email, a US-based organization with worldwide membership, is pushing for legislation to curb e-mail abuse. Currently, legislation is pending before the US Congress.

Permission Marketing. Permission marketing is built around the "opt-in" model of direct marketing. First, if a consumer expresses a desire to receive information, there is a greater likelihood that the consumer will pay more attention to the message. Any form of unsolicited advertising, whether e-mail or paper mail, does not receive the same degree of attention. Second, as the consumers give their consent, there is an opportunity to gather data about their backgrounds and interests. This allows the marketer to precisely target each consumer. In other words, permission marketing moves away from mass e-mail and operates in the realm of one-to-one marketing. Permission marketing is not limited to e-mail marketing, but is often discussed in this context.

Seth Godin, who is credited with the development of the permission marketing concept, has argued that mass media communication is "interruptive."[8] Television commercials, for example, interrupt viewers' enjoyment of television programs. In addition, mass media advertising suffers from clutter that reduces advertising effectiveness. As consumers are bombarded with advertising messages, they simply tune out. With permission marketing, the consumer has given the marketer an invitation to enter his or her private space.

A consumer may give permission for any number of things. The permission may be for receiving a periodical newsletter, information about product updates, or information on sale offers. The marketer must respect the consumer's wishes and use the permission only as intended by the consumer.

Canadian Tire, the national hardware chain store, has been very successful with its e-flyers program (www.canadiantire.ca/eflyer/e/index.html). This program allows Canadian Tire to customize the information delivered to each customer, based on product preferences. Someone not interested auto parts is not bombarded with such information. Since consumers opt in to the program, there is a greater likelihood that they will respond to the message.

Proponents of permission marketing argue that this method has a better chance of succeeding in today's media-saturated marketplace. In order for e-mail marketing to succeed, the following issues must be considered.

Tailored Messages. Demographic characteristics and user preference data are used to ensure e-mail advertising is relevant to the recipient. When consumers opt in, they can be surveyed on their preferences and what information they would like to receive. Rather than doing one mass mail-out, each e-mail can be tailored to each recipient.

Consumer Control. Consumers must have the ability to opt in and opt out of the e-mail delivery service.[9] Many e-mail marketing programs use an opt-out model, where e-mail addresses captured from online purchase order forms, bulletin boards, and newsgroups are used to send out mass mailings. The recipient has not opted to be on the mailing list, but is given the chance to opt out. Such e-mail campaigns can be very annoying to consumers. By giving the consumer the chance to opt in or out, the marketer is demonstrating respect for consumers' privacy.

Rewards and Reinforcement. Consumers must be given a good reason to opt in. They also need positive reinforcement from time to time. Seth Godin recommends incentives to get people into such a direct marketing program and further incentives (such as coupons, rebates, and freebies) to maintain their interest.

Presentation. E-mail advertising is getting rather sophisticated these days. E-mail can be delivered in HTML format with images and even multimedia features. It does not have to be done through dull and drab ASCII format messages.[10] By sending rich media e-mail messages to those who have the right technology, response rates can be increased. Table 10-2 shows the response rate for different types of e-mail advertising.

Brand Strength. E-mail marketing should strengthen the brand, not detract from the brand image in any way. Many consumers consider e-mail advertising to be junk e-mail and a nuisance. For every relevant e-mail message, it is not uncommon to receive ten unsolicited, irrelevant messages. Since there are so many disreputable organizations selling e-mail addresses, e-mail marketing can, unfortunately, put even good brands in bad company. Privacy, control, and rewards can help protect the brand.

Future of E-mail Marketing. A report by Forrester Research predicts that by 2004, the e-mail marketing industry will be worth $4.8 billion. Marketers are expected to send more than 200 billion e-mails.[11] Companies are expected to outsource strategic and technical aspects of e-mail marketing, which will fuel the growth in this new industry.

Viral Marketing

Viral marketing, which is essentially a combination of e-mail marketing and word-of-mouth (or word-of-mouse) communication, can be defined as any advertising that propagates itself the way viruses do—through e-mail messages that are forwarded from one user to another.

When users of Hotmail e-mail service send e-mail messages, there is a tagline at the end of the message, which is a free advertisement for Hotmail. Hotmail apparently spent less that $500 000 in marketing and promotion from its launch until it reached 12 million users. This compares with the over $20 million its rival Juno spent for a fraction of Hotmail's membership. Hotmail now has over 50 million users worldwide, a customer base that was mostly built through viral marketing. Viral marketing depends on word-of-mouth and referrals.

Among the viral marketing success stories is Flooz.com, a company that offers an electronic currency called Flooz, which it defines as "online gift currency." Flooz.com's challenge was to acquire more consumers, which in turn would entice more online merchants to accept the Flooz currency, thus leading to more consumers. Flooz started a program called "Flooz-Your-Friends," which offered each Flooz customer $3 for each referral account opened. New members got $10 worth of Flooz for opening an account and could also make money by making referrals. Flooz.com sent e-mail to its 400 000 members to announce the referral program.

Table 10-2 E-mail Response Rates

Type of E-mail	Click-Through Rate	Cost per Message
Plain text e-mail	3–4%	$0.02
Clickable text e-mail	6–8%	$0.03
HTML e-mail	12–15%	$0.05
Average	10%	$0.04

Source: "The e-Marketing Report," Morgan Stanley Dean Witter (www.msdw.com).

That led to 200 000 new referral addresses and 20 000 actually signing up to become members.[12] Following the success of its first viral marketing campaign, Flooz.com implemented another successful campaign, this time without the financial incentive.

Viral marketing is especially effective when the product itself can be "tasted" or sampled via e-mail. A rich media e-mail campaign created for the popular band *NSYNC was so effective that one girl forwarded the message to 500 "friends." It contained video messages from band members that were exclusive to this ad campaign. MindArrow, the rich media e-mail marketing company that handled *NSYNC's campaign, sent the e-mail message to 250 000 fans who opted in on the band's Web site. However, 60 percent of those who finally saw the message and the video were not part of the original mailing. They received the message forwarded by a friend.[13]

Search Engine Ranking and Placement

Search engines are one of the most commonly used means for finding information online. When consumers use keywords related to a product category to search, those firms listed in the top 10 to 20 are much more likely to be clicked on, compared to low-ranking firms. Top search engine ranking, some experts say, is more potent in delivering traffic to a site than banner advertising. Ranking high on search engines requires a lot of effort. It must, however, be pointed out that the tactics used to accomplish a high ranking are more of an art than a science.

One should distinguish between a *search engine* and a *directory*. Search engines use a spider or a crawler program, which goes to all Web sites and pages on the Internet and then indexes the Web pages automatically (for example, WebCrawler). Directories, on the other hand, depend on humans to compile a listing of sites and pages (for example, Yahoo!). Directories ask for a description of the site, the URL, and the appropriate category where the site should be placed (see "Add URL" or "Suggest a Site" in most directories). Human editors then decide whether the site should be included or not. Webmasters, who manage Web sites, must ensure that sites are registered in all top search engines and directories in the appropriate category. In this book, the terms *search engines* and *directory* are used interchangeably.

When a user types a keyword and searches for information on a topic, search engines and directories go through a huge database and retrieve results that best match the keyword. HyperText Markup Language (HTML) allows the Web site builder to incorporate what is known as a meta tag at the top of each Web page. See Exhibit 10-11 for an example. These tags will not be visible to consumers who view the Web page. Search engines and directories use

Exhibit 10-11 Keywords Used by Sony.com

```
<META HTTP-EQUIV="keywords" CONTENT="Sony, music, Columbia,
Epic, movies, motion picture, Columbia, Tri-Star, home theatre,
electronics, mini-disc, minidisc, walkman, VAIO, vaio, computers,
Playstation, playstation, The Station, station, games, television,
video games, A/V, entertainment, home video, shopping, shop,
mall, buy, products, services, questions, store">
```

Source: www.sony.com.

the keywords listed by the site developer in the ranking process. To see the meta tags for some of the popular Web sites, go to the site and then go to Page Source under the View option in Netscape (or Source under the View option in Internet Explorer).

Different search engines use different methodologies for ranking sites and pages. Some search engines will look for how many times a key word is repeated in a page (more repetitions will result in a higher ranking). Other search engines will want to ensure that the keywords are used at the top of the page text, as well as in the middle and end of the page. Search engines often modify the rules they use for ranking sites and never publish these rules. This keeps webmasters and consultants specializing in ranking services guessing how the ranking process works.

A full discussion of the technical issues involved in Web site development and search engine ranking is beyond the scope of this book. (See SearchEngineWatch.com to learn more about search engine ranking and meta tags. For HTML basics, see www.ncsa.uiuc.edu/General/Internet/WWW/HTMLPrimer.html.) However, a few important managerial considerations must be highlighted.

First, ensure that appropriate keywords are used. The Sony site specifies over 30 keywords (see Exhibit 10-11). One must view the selection of keywords from the consumer's point of view. How are consumers likely to search for a particular product? What keywords are they most likely to use? There is an optimum number of keywords, which can be determined only by trial and error. Use of an excessive number of keywords may lead to penalties from the search engine. Some sites even specify common misspellings of brand names or use both lower- and upper-case letters. The bottom line is that you must choose the keywords strategically.

Second, realize that a high ranking is a temporary achievement. Competitors can study your Web site keywords and search engine submission strategy and copy them easily. If search engines change their ranking rules, a top site may then lose its top position. This means Web site ranking in major search engines must be constantly monitored.

Third, use software applications such as WebPosition Gold (www.webposition.com), Top Dog (www.topdog2000.com), or PositionWeaver (www.positionweaver.com) to analyze Web site rankings and competitive site rankings on major search engines. These tools can help in writing copy (Web page text) that will result in high rankings. WebPosition can point out why a page is ranking low when a keyword search is done. Often the keyword presence in the text must be increased. This means that developing a Web site is not just the work of an ad or Web development agency. An understanding of the ranking process is essential. Keywords must be reflected in the page content. A page that is rich in images with little or no text will generally rank low.

Fourth, when designing pages, avoid the use of frames, which cannot be recognized by many crawler or spidering programs. Also, provide hypertext links to all pages on a site from the main homepage. Do not use just buttons (or image maps) as links to other pages on a site. This will allow spidering programs to access all pages on a site and index them.

Fifth, use different keywords for different pages, as appropriate. Multiple pages on a site can be submitted to most search engines.

Sixth, some search engines like GoTo.com charge a fee, which is similar to a bidding process. The firm that pays the highest fee gets the highest ranking, the second highest bidder gets the second-highest ranking, and so on. In Yahoo! sites can "own" keywords where their ads will be displayed whenever a user types in the keyword. One can pay one's way to the top ranking in some sites.

Lastly, site ranking also requires coordination between creative people in the ad or Web development agency developing the site and technical people, who understand the ranking process. A high site ranking can lead to greater brand awareness and higher site traffic. Since all competitors try to constantly improve and maintain their ranking, site ranking in search engines requires ongoing monitoring.

Media Planning and Media Buying on the Internet

When advertisers realized that the Internet offered very detailed tracking of consumers, many wanted to pay for advertising only if the consumer actually responded to the ad in some fashion. Procter & Gamble, one of the largest advertisers, reportedly insisted on paying only when the consumer clicked on a banner ad. In this model, called cost-per-click or CPC, a site may host several ads. The advertiser will pay a fee only when viewers click on the banner ad and end up in the advertiser's site. Mere exposure to the ad is not sufficient. Some ad networks like eAds.com (www.eads.com) charge as little as $0.10 per click. Valueclick.com (www.valueclick.com) is another ad network that touts itself as the "pay-for-results network" and charges on a cost-per-click model.

Extending the CPC model further, it is possible to pay based on a more specific response beyond a click, such as cost-per-lead, cost-per-enquiry, or cost-per-sale. These cases can be summarized as **cost-per-response** or **CPR**. Affiliate programs follow the cost-per-response model. The affiliate site is paid only when a visitor from an affiliate site actually purchases a product or places an enquiry. Portal sites pay affiliates just for diverting traffic to their site. The affiliate gets a commission based on the response.

The CPR model, which encompasses cost-per-click, may work well for the advertiser, but content sites and publishers would obviously prefer a different model, based on impressions as opposed to responses.

Most Web advertising space is still sold on the basis of the traditional method called **cost-per-thousand-impressions** or **CPM**. Here the media buyer pays a standard fee depending on the number of impressions required. Ad rates are based on the "eyeball" model; that is, how many people see an ad. Thus, the more traffic a site gets, the greater the number of "eyeballs." High-traffic sites like Yahoo! get a big chunk of the ad spending. Sites that focus on a specific demographic or lifestyle segment often seem to have a higher CPM rate. CPM rates can vary from $10 to $100, depending on the reach and targetability of the site. The DoubleClick Canada Network charges $37 CPM for an untargeted banner and up to $43 CPM for unlimited criteria. Most large advertisers will bargain and pay a lot less than the published rates. There is more ad space or inventory available on the Web than demanded by advertisers. The result is dropping CPM rates. Flycast Network (now part of Engage Media) competes on low CPM rates (see Exhibit 10-12).

Exhibit 10-12 Flycast Network Advertises Lower CPM Rates

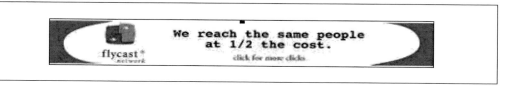

Source: www.flycast.com.

The Industry Standard reports that the average ad-banner CPM rates are continuing to fall—from around $35.13 in December 1998 to $33.75 in December 1999, according to AdKnowledge. The drop is not just a sign of uncertainty about the effectiveness of banners; there's also a flood of available banner inventory. The number of sites seeking to include online ads in their revenue model has skyrocketed since 1998. At the end of that year, about 1400 sites included advertising; by the end of 1999 there were about 3350 ad-supported sites.[14]

Experts believe that the Internet's effective CPM is only about $4, well below all other advertising-supported media (see Exhibit 10-13). However, in spite of the current drop in CPM rates overall, top Web sites may be able to negotiate higher prices by demonstrating ROI (return on investment) benefits of targeted advertising.[15]

Online companies spent an estimated $4.2 billion in advertising online and offline during the period of January to November 1999, but the bad news is that they were only able to sell an estimated $3–4.4 billion in advertising space during the same period.[16] At best, there was no net gain in online advertising revenue.

Selling ad space has become a very competitive business. Ad buyers can shop around to find good buys. Many ad executives think that advertising on the Internet is terribly overpriced. Major advertisers, such as Procter & Gamble, have insisted on much lower prices.

How should advertisers pay for online advertising? Is the traditional CPM model the right one, or should a performance-based method like the pay-per-click model be chosen? It is likely that both methods will continue to exist. The smaller and lesser known sites will use the performance-based method to sell ad spaces on their sites, and the high-traffic sites like Yahoo! and CNET have little unsold ad space. They do not need to take the risks that lesser-

Exhibit 10-13 Comparison of CPM Rates Across Media

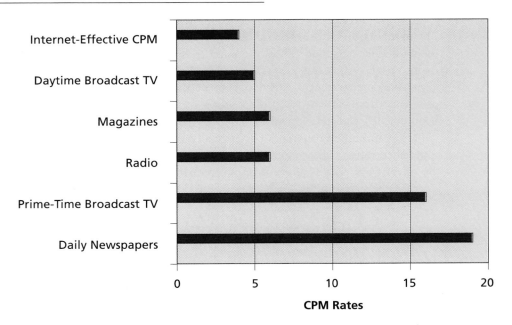

Source: Internet Direct Marketing & Advertising Services, Morgan Stanley Dean Witter (www.msdw.com), May 3, 2000.

known sites do and so they prefer CPM. Forrester Research in a report on online advertising made the argument that online advertisers should come to terms with CPM. They should try to hold the ad agencies (which create the banners) and not the sites (which feature the ads) responsible for the click-through rate.[17] Exhibit 10-13 shows the CPM rates for various media.

CPM rates are based on the popularity of the site and the traffic it draws. In addition, sites that draw a very specific target, offering advertisers the ability to reach the right audience, can attract higher CPM rates. Some of the top Web properties and their audience size are shown in Table 10-3. "Unique visitors" eliminates multiple counting of repeat visitors and is considered a more reliable measure of total customer base.

Not everyone can afford to pay to advertise on the Internet. How can small and home businesses drive traffic to their sites without paying for banner ads? Banner ad exchange services are the answer. Link Exchange, the most popular of such services (now owned by Microsoft), has a membership of over 400 000 sites. Member sites feature each other's ads. The more ads you feature on your site, the more exposure your site gets at other member sites. Members can usually decide where they want their ads featured and what types of ads should or should not appear on their own site. SmartClicks' SmartAge offers a comparable service.

There are numerous media options on the Internet. After going through the various options, the final decision is driven by communication objectives and budget. The media decision on the Internet is very much metric-driven. Media buyers look at pre-buy reports, which provide usage data about each potential site (total traffic, average per day, visit length, and so on), as well as demographic information. They should compare statistics for similar

Table 10-3 Top Ten Digital Media and Web Properties* (July 2000)

Rank	At Home Users	Unique Visitors (000)	At Work Users	Unique Visitors (000)
1	AOL Web Sites	53 051	Yahoo!	21 032
2	Yahoo Sites	47 567	AOL	21 002
3	MSN	35 158	Microsoft	17 964
4	Microsoft	32 750	MSN	17 457
5	Lycos Network	24 175	Lycos	17 457
6	Excite@Home	21 568	Excite@Home	10 948
7	Go Network	18 309	Go Network	9 614
8	About.com	14 334	Alta Vista	8 031
9	Time Warner	14 164	Time Warner	7 959
10	AltaVista	13 243	About.com	7 538

Source: Nielsen/NetRatings (www.nielsennetratings.com).

*Note: A *web property* is one that offers more than one site.

sites to arrive at a good decision. During a campaign, it is imperative to monitor audience response to determine if adjustments need to be made. After the campaign is over, post-buy statistics about how many impressions were delivered, the delivery rate, click-through rates, and other related performance information can be used to judge campaign success.[18]

The Online Advertising Industry

The online advertising industry is made up of many different types of services (see Table 10-4 for an overview). There are media buying companies, both new media and traditional media, who work on behalf of advertisers. The sell-side players sell advertising space on their sites or their members' sites. Some companies specialize in providing online promotional programs, such as coupons and contests. As companies tackle the challenge of personalizing their online services and content, companies like Net Perceptions provide personalization tools. Finally, there are independent audit and measurement companies that can provide third-party verification of site traffic. These companies play an important role because authentic reporting of site statistics is essential in determining advertising rates.

Role of Ad Agencies and Ad Networks

Advertising Agencies. The rapid emergence of the Internet as an advertising medium caught many ad agencies by surprise. Most did not initially have the capability to develop sites or advertising for the new media. Many quickly acquired the capability through acquisitions or alliances because of the need to provide "full service" to their clients. Leo Burnett, for instance, bought a majority stake in a Web developing company called Giant Step (www.gianntstep.com). Some agencies like BBDO Worldwide are still skeptical about the

Table 10-4 Online Advertising Industry

Buy Side	Sell Side	Promotions	Web Tools
New media buyers (Avenue A, Mediaplex)	Portals (Yahoo!, AltaVista)	Providers of loyalty programs (Netcentives, SurfGold, MyPoints)	Audience and ad measurement services (Media Metrix, Nielsen/NetRatings)
Traditional media buyers (Interpublic, Omnicom, True North, Young & Rubicam)	Ad networks (DoubleClick, Engage, 24/7 Media)	Incentives and coupons (BeFree, CyberGold, Coolsavings, eSmarts, eCoupons)	Site-level marketing infrastructure, personalization technologies (Net Perceptions, NextClick, BeFree)
Direct e-mailers (Digital Impact, MessageMedia)	E-mail newsletters (LifeMinders)		

Source: Based on "Internet Direct Marketing and Advertising Services," Morgan Stanley Dean Witter (www.msdw.com), May 3, 2000.

Table 10-5 Comparison of Top Ad Networks

Company	Number of Sites	Number of Advertisers	Rate
DoubleClick	1 600	Over 2 300	$2–60 CPM
24/7 Media	Over 2 600	Over 300	$10–30-plus CPM
Microsoft Link Exchange	Over 400 000	N/A	Free for Link Exchange members; $5–45 for non-members
FlyCast Network	700	350	$6–15 CPM
ValueClick	10 000	60–70	12–15¢ per click

Source: *The Industry Standard* (www.thestandard.com), March 1, 1999, and the companies' Web sites.

Reprinted by permission of *The Industry Standard*.

role of the Internet, while other like J. Walter Thompson and Chiat/Day have embraced the Web more willingly. Some contend that traditional ad agencies, who are used to designing communications for mass media (where getting attention is key), do not yet understand the many-to-many interactive communication model on the Web.[19]

Businesses that want a complete communications solution will prefer one-stop shopping. The Internet should be seen as part of a larger communications mix. The interactive Web site developed by J. Walter Thompson for Nestle's Lion candy bar is an example of how an agency can handle print, television, and the interactive media for a client.

Advertising Networks. In television there are only a handful of networks and local stations where marketers can advertise. In print, there are more options. On the Internet, however, the number of sites offering ad space is staggering—and it's growing continuously. How does a media buyer choose from the plethora of sites available?

Advertising networks such as DoubleClick, 24/7 Media, ValueClick, and FlyCast (now part of engage.com) play a crucial role in matching supply with demand (see Table 10-5 for a comparison of the top ad networks). Ad networks are a one-stop shop for planning, serving, and tracking campaigns across many different sites. Networks use proprietary ad-placement and site-performance software to optimize media buys for the advertiser. Publishing sites use the ad networks to sell advertising on their sites. Each ad network will have thousands of member sites where ads can be placed. An advertiser will have a choice of sites based on demographic or other target market characteristics.

Effectiveness of Internet Advertising

Are online advertisers getting value for their money? There has been a great deal of debate about what form of online advertising is effective and what effectiveness measures are appropriate. In 2000, companies are, however, expected to spend more than $13 billion in various forms of online promotion.[20] This figure is projected to reach $33 billion worldwide by 2004.[21]

Online advertising is now bigger than billboard advertising. As total spending on online advertising increases, questions regarding the effectiveness of such expenditures still linger. In this section, we will look at current evidence on the effectiveness of online advertising.

The Internet Advertising Bureau (IAB) conducted the largest study on banner ad effectiveness, involving 12 leading Web sites and over 16 000 respondents.[22] Some of the findings from this and other studies of online advertising effectiveness are presented below.

Banner Ads Create Awareness

Mere exposure to banner advertising can create brand awareness. This is true even if you don't click on the banner ad. In terms of awareness creation, banner ads have been found to be comparable to other media advertising. The IAB study found that awareness increased by 30 percent as a result of banner ad exposure.

There is no simple, linear relationship between ad spending and "top of mind" brand awareness.[23] A survey by Greenfield Online showed that awareness levels are not necessarily linked to the dollars spent on advertising. Not surprisingly, brands with well-known offline identities, such as Barnes & Noble and the Gap, did well in the online brand awareness test. Many pure-play Internet companies are realizing that a bricks-and-mortar presence can be beneficial. HomeGrocer, an online grocery store, sent out its empty delivery trucks (with the company name displayed on the sides) around the city to create brand awareness.

The Web offers marketers the ability to precision target advertising. However, it has a limited reach compared to television. The Web still does not have the capacity to reach large numbers of people at the same time, as TV does. A new Pepsi commercial during the Super Bowl can reach upwards of 80 million people at the same time. In comparison, the number of viewers drawn at any one time to even the most popular sites is very small. Even though Internet advertising has shown to be effective in creating awareness, if the communication objective is to create mass awareness then television still holds the edge.

Banner Ads Influence Perception

Banner ads can create a positive impression of the brand. In the IAB study, banner ads changed consumer perception regarding the Volvo car. There were significant increases in the belief that Volvo "was a good automobile" and that it "offers something different from other brands." Often banner ads are used as a link to a brand site or micro-site. The findings on brand awareness and brand perception suggest that close attention should be paid to the ad copy.

Relevance of Click-Through Rates

The IAB study did not find any correlation between click-through and brand perceptions, or other staples of brand building. This result calls into question the importance placed on click-through rates. Even when consumers did not click on an ad, exposure to the ad influenced their awareness and brand perceptions.

Other studies have found a link between click-through and other measures of advertising effectiveness. One study found that clicking on banner ads led to more positive attitudes toward the ad and toward the advertised brand.[24] Click-through rates tend to be higher when the consumer is involved in a product category.[25]

Targeting Ads

The Internet offers the ability to target the message to the appropriate audience. For effective targeting of messages, you need to understand the demographic (age, gender, income) and psychographic (lifestyle, attitudes) profile of consumers. Web user surveys from Georgia Tech University and Neilsen/CommerceNet provide a macro view of Internet demographics. Online surveys are now being frequently used to study the demographics of specific sites. Clear Picture (www.clearpicture.com) and Perseus (www.perseus.com) are two companies that offer software products for online surveys. Thanks to these and other data-gathering tools, sites that sell advertising space can provide advertisers with reliable user profiles.

More than television or magazines, the Web offers marketers the ability to target their messages to specific lifestyle groups. The plethora of lifestyle e-zines makes it possible for marketers to precision target their messages. SRI International (future.sri.com/vals/VALSindex.shtml) has extended its famous VALS (Values and Life Styles) segmentation scheme to the Internet (see Chapter 3 for a more thorough discussion).

There is a lot of evidence suggesting that targeted banner ads work better than a random approach. Many advertisers are moving away from banners to more targeted sponsorship deals because they offer greater targeting ability.[26] Targeted ads can be more expensive, but can also be more effective.

Targeting not only means placing the ads in the right Web site, but also matching the ad to keywords in search engines. For instance, if you search for "automobile" on a search engine like AltaVista or Yahoo!, you're likely to see a banner ad for Autobytel or a car manufacturer like Toyota. This type of targeting ensures that someone who is currently interested in that topic sees the ad, and that exposure to the ad occurs when it is most appropriate. By paying to "own" keywords in search engines for a certain length of time, advertisers can ensure that their ads reach consumers who are searching for information in that product category.

Direct Response vs. Brand Advertising

The Internet is very useful in direct response advertising. When a viewer clicks on a banner ad, the viewer can be taken to a Web page where an order can be placed. Interactive banner ads allow the viewer to purchase the product or place an inquiry from the banner ad itself. When the viewer clicks on the banner, a drop-down menu allows the viewer to respond. The banner is typically seen as a weapon suited for direct response. Recent studies challenge this limited view. In one study, static banner ads produced a 40 percent recall, compared to a 41 percent recall for a 30-second TV spot.[27] These results suggest that banner ads could be useful in brand advertising as well.

Some experienced advertising professionals, however, question the use of Internet advertising for brand marketing. Allen Rosenshine, CEO of BBDO Worldwide, raised some eyebrows with his comment that the Web, as an advertising medium, was "hopelessly ineffective."[28] Is the Internet suitable for advertising branded products like soft drinks and sneakers? Some marketers consider the Internet, in its present form, as more suitable for direct marketing or direct response advertising. Television, on the other hand, is seen as the medium that can deliver emotional messages and generate favourable brand feelings. The Morgan Stanley *Report on Advertising* concluded that the Internet, until broadband becomes widespread, is more suited to direct marketing.[29] Others point to high brand recall and awareness created by exposure to banner ads as proof of its worthiness in brand advertising. This debate will not conclude any time soon.

Banner Ad Size and Positioning Effect

There is some evidence suggesting that the position and the size of the banner ad may influence click-through rates. Ads placed in homepages (or first pages) as opposed to inside pages, and larger ads (468 × 60 pixels), as opposed to smaller ads (234 × 60 pixels), are more likely to be clicked.[30]

There is also some evidence suggesting that banner ads placed in the bottom right corner of a page may receive higher click-throughs than ads placed at the top of a page.[31] It must be cautioned, however, that these were experiments with limited sample sizes, where all extraneous variables were not fully controlled.

Banner Burnout

After a certain number of impressions, click-through rates will decline and consumers may even avoid the ad. DoubleClick, a leading online advertising network, suggests that after the fourth exposure, there is a significant drop in response rates. Using different ad copy or controlling the frequency can help reduce banner burnout.

Rich Media Ads

In a study developed to determine the effectiveness of rich media ads in a broadband environment compared to narrowband ads, broadband ads outperformed narrowband ads. Recall, comprehension, shift in imagery, and time spent interacting with the ad improved significantly for broadband ads compared to narrowband ads. AT&T, Bank of America, First USA, Intel Corp., Levi Strauss & Co., and Toys R Us participated in the study.[32] Redsky Interactive (www.redsky.com) and KMGI.com (www.kmgi.com) are two of the new breed of Internet advertising agencies that offer interactive and rich media advertising on the Web.

Beyond the Banner

In the early days of E-commerce, banner advertising was the darling of new media advertising agencies. It still gets a lot of attention. Most advertisers, however, have figured out that they need to look beyond the banner to find different ways of promoting their site and the products they sell online. This is not to say that the banner ad should be discarded. It should be one element in a mix of online promotional methods. ActivMedia Research asked online companies to rate the effectiveness of different promotional methods. The results are presented in Table 10-6. A comparison of click-through and conversion rates is shown in Table 10-7.

Table 10-6 Ratings of Online Promotional Methods

Online Promotional Methods Rated Excellent or Very Good	Percentage
Search engines/directories	48.4
Buttons and links	22.5
Online PR and press releases	17.3
Reciprocal ads and links	16.2
Affiliate programs	9.9
Paid banner ads	6.2

Source: ActivMedia Research (www.activmedia.com).

Table 10-7 Comparison of Click-Through and Conversion Rates

Medium	Click-Through Rate	Conversion of Clickers
Banner	0.5%	1.0%
Direct mail (purchased list)	0.7%	N/A
E-mail (in-house list)	14%	10%

Source: "The e-Marketing Report," Morgan Stanley Dean Witter (www.msdw.com).

Another telling statistic is the comparison of banner and e-mail click-through rates. When consumers opt in for e-mail advertising or when member or customer e-mail lists are used, such direct marketing can yield results that are far superior to banner advertising.

Choosing the Right Metric

The Internet offers marketers the ability to measure audience response at multiple levels. As an advertiser, you can accurately measure the number of click-throughs generated by an ad placed on a particular Web site. If a viewer clicks on a banner, the advertiser can then track that individual's behaviour. Did he or she place a product inquiry, purchase the product, or simply leave the site soon after entering it? These questions can be answered with a high degree of accuracy. Using click-through rates and other performance measures, the best performing Web sites for an ad campaign can be identified.

Given the number of advertising effectiveness measures on the Internet, it is easy for a novice to be confused regarding the appropriate measure. Using multiple metrics, some behavioural (such as click-through or other measurable action) and some psychological (such as attitude, perception, and recall) may be appropriate. The choice of the measure should also depend on the communication objectives. If the ad campaign focuses on brand building, then attitudinal and perceptual measures become important. If the ad is oriented towards selling, then click-through and other response measures may be appropriate. For more on choosing the appropriate metric, see iMarket Demo 10-1.

Developing an Integrated Marketing Communications Plan

Very rarely will it make sense to use the Internet as the sole medium of communication. As we saw in Chapter 9, each medium has its own strengths and weaknesses. The approach suggested here is an **integrated marketing** communications plan. The following steps can be followed in developing such a plan.

Define Communication Objective

The first step would be to define the marketing communications objective. The specific media and the specific Internet tool used for communication will vary based on the objective. Some possible objectives include awareness creation, attitude change, building a brand image, building a one-to-one relationship, and reminding/reinforcement.

Television is effective in creating awareness because of its reach. It is also effective in conveying an emotional message. Both the Internet and television can be used to build brands

iMarket Demo 10-1 Which Metric Is the Right One?

Advertisers can examine several statistics before choosing a site for their ads. In the early days, *hits* were the mostly commonly used metric. A high hit figure was meaningless because hits were based on the number of files downloaded. If a Web page had 25 image files, then each one was counted as a hit. Hits do not convey anything about site traffic.

Pageviews overcome the problem to some extent by simply counting the pages downloaded—not each element or file contained on that page. Pageviews are used in measuring the number of impressions an ad gets. What about multiple exposures to the same individual? Pageviews do not account for the same individual being exposed to an ad multiple times. Using the *unique visitor* metric can help overcome the problem to some extent by avoiding double counting by using the IP address of a computer. Each computer connected to the Internet has a unique Internet Protocol or IP address. The problem arises when several individuals use the same computer—in a family, office, or a computer lab. So we do not live a perfect world—no measure is perfect.

As one critic said, "Television has the Nielsen ratings. Radio has Arbitron. The Web—well, the Web has served up a seemingly endless parade of would-be audience yardsticks that somehow always fall short of describing exactly what advertisers need to know." Every measure has a flaw. *Unique visitors*, for instance, cannot differentiate between a teenager who accidentally stumbles into an online brokerage site and an investment pro looking for some good buys. Clearly, one visitor is more valuable to the site than the other. No measure precisely summarizes audience activity, and the associated revenue-generating potential of a Web site, in one easy-to-understand figure.

Savvy advertisers who refuse to be intimidated by all of these metrics, are turning to the bottom line—return on investment or ROI. Ad buyers can use iterative analysis of Web advertising purchases—and the sales that result from these placements—to buy ads at the sites giving the highest payoff for a marketer's advertising investment.

No single measure will satisfy everyone. Some are now tracking repeat visits and loyalty. For content sites, counting registered users can be a measure of success. However, a measure that works for a portal, such as Yahoo! or Excite, may not be the appropriate one for a direct marketer or an e-tailer.

Sources: Steven Vonder Haar (1999), "Metrics: Go Figure. Too Many Yardsticks, Too Little Time," *Business 2.0*, June 1999.

by emphasizing different aspects—in-depth brand knowledge and interactive experience versus an emotionally appealing message. Radio and billboards are often used for reminder ads. Banner ads could also serve the same purpose, even though some studies show that they are only useful in awareness creation when the audience is online. In short, the choice of the medium should be based on the communication goal.

If the intent is to build one-to-one relationships, then the Web site will assume vital importance in the communication process. Interactive elements, password-protected areas for members or customers (extranets, where they can manage their accounts with the firm), customized Web pages and e-mail, and online brand communities can be used as relationship-building tools. Promotional sites can be effective in supporting the branding strategy. Online incentives such as electronic coupons and sweepstakes can induce immediate action.

The choice of the media (TV, Internet, print, radio, and so on) and the choice of specific communication tools within each medium (such as e-mail, banners, promotional sites, and electronic coupons on the Internet) must be linked to the overall communication objectives. It is possible for different media to play specific roles in different stages of the communication process. For instance, TV and banners for awareness creation, promotional sites and online incentives to induce trial, and a Web site to build relationships and personalized marketing.

Define Target Market and Media Choices

The target market or markets must be defined next. The choice of specific online or offline media will depend on the target. On the Web, depending on the target (e.g., young male sports fans, professional women, techies, wealthy investors, senior citizens), different Web sites may be chosen for advertising. A similar approach is necessary with television and print media as well.

The suitability of each medium for the target market and the defined communication objectives must be considered. With respect to the Internet, the following issues regarding suitability must be addressed before deciding on whether this is an appropriate medium for advertising a given product.

Is the target market online? Does the product have a good "fit" with the medium? Software, computers, financial services, information services, travel, books, some clothing items, and specialty foods are examples of successful online categories. There is generally more advertising in these categories. What are the advertising objectives? If the objective is to create a direct response, the Internet is very likely to be part of the media mix. Is the competition online? If so, a firm may wish to ensure parity with the competitors.

Determine the Budget

While Internet advertising is not cheap, banner ad rates have been declining. Web site development and maintenance costs can be substantial, especially if the site needs a lot of multimedia and interactive communication features. Many firms consider Web sites as part of their capital expenditures (similar to opening a store) rather than as part of their promotional expenditures.

Percentage of sales, competitive parity, and objective task (where the budget is linked to specific objectives) are commonly used methods for setting budgets. Internet firms (especially new pure-play companies) have been spending a vast amount of money on advertising. Creating brand awareness, building traffic, and building loyalty are prime concerns of online firms. Marketing communication is usually geared toward these goals.

Design and Testing

Time and resources should be committed to designing the communication element—e-mail, Web site, banner ads, and so on. The copy and creative elements should be consistent with the overall communication goals. Copy testing is important to ensure that the message has the desired effect on the audience.

In the case of Web sites, testing assumes a technical nature. Large Web sites may take months to develop. The site must be reliable and interactive features must work without any flaws, even when millions of users log on each day. In other words, the site must be scalable. Security and privacy features must also be tested to ensure that there are no compromises.

Media Buy

Advertising networks play an important role in the media buy stage. The ad agency will usually negotiate the prices by working with the ad networks such as DoubleClick and ValueClick. DoubleClick offers a standard 15 percent discount to recognized ad agencies. See DoubleClick's Canadian site (www.doubleclick.net/ca/advertisers/ad_rates/) for a sample of advertising rates. Large advertisers may be able to negotiate much lower prices than the published rates.

Evaluation

Internet advertising, whether banners or promotional sites, can be evaluated using a variety of measures, such as pageviews, click-throughs, or other specific response (such as purchase rate). With television or radio, it is virtually impossible to get that kind of precision in evaluation. Specific evaluation measures must be identified for each medium and each tool. For instance, electronic coupons can be evaluated in terms of redemption rates, while banner ads can be judged in terms of clicks or other response. Offline advertising is often judged in terms of recall, awareness, attitude, and purchase intent. Return on investment (ROI) is increasingly being used as an indication of the overall impact of advertising.

Summary

Advertising and promotion on the Internet have become a vast and rapidly developing field. It is astonishing that the first banner ad was placed only in 1994. In a little more than half a decade, new forms of advertising and multiple measurement and tracking methods have been developed.

Advertisers have many different advertising options on the Internet. The corporate and brand Web site plays a vital role by providing in-depth information. Brand sites and microsites can offer entertainment, interaction, and a personalized touch to communication. Simple static or animated banners and rich media ads, which offer video and audio, are effective in different settings. While ads can create awareness, online sales promotion is effective in driving immediate response. Electronic coupons and online sweepstakes are being used by well-known brands. Online sweepstakes also allow a company to build a mailing list.

E-mail marketing remains controversial because of indiscriminate use by some unethical marketers. When used appropriately, with the consumer's permission, it can be an effective tool for targeting personalized communication.

Advertising space on Web sites is sold according to different models. CPM (cost-per-thousand-impressions) rates are based on delivering a set number of impressions in designated Web sites. The CPR (cost-per-response) rate can be based on click-throughs (how many viewers click on a banner ad) or even actual sales (as in the case of affiliate programs). Advertisers must choose the appropriate method of payment.

The plethora of online communication tools available makes the task of an advertiser quite daunting. An integrated communication strategy that uses some online tools with offline media can produce the best results.

Key Terms

Banner advertising, 246
Advertising networks, 265
Click-through rate, 255
Cost-per-response
  (CPR), 261

Cost-per-thousand-
  impressions (CPM), 261
Electronic coupons, 251
E-mail marketing, 254
Integrated marketing, 269

Interstitials, 247
Micro-site, 250
Permission marketing, 257
Viral marketing, 258

Questions and Exercises

Review Questions

1. What is the difference between a corporate Web site and a brand site?
2. What is a micro-site? Provide examples.
3. What are the strengths and weaknesses of e-mail marketing?
4. Describe how electronic coupons work.
5. What are the essentials of a successful viral marketing campaign?
6. What steps must be taken to ensure a high search engine ranking for a site?
7. Describe the differences between CPM and CPR, two methods of paying for online advertising.
8. What role do advertising networks play in the online advertising industry?
9. Identify four factors that affect the effectiveness of a banner advertising campaign. Discuss each one briefly.
10. What are the steps involved in developing an integrated marketing communications plan?

Discussion Questions

1. There has been a shift in people's media habits. More consumers are now getting their news through the Internet than ever before. Average time spent online is steadily increasing. What are the implications of this trend for the advertising industry? Provide a thorough analysis.
2. Is there too much advertising on the Internet? In your opinion, are consumers tuning out online ads? What can marketers do to maintain the effectiveness of online advertising?
3. Why do you think marketers are shifting their emphasis from banner ads to other forms of advertising, such as sponsorship?
4. Will e-mail marketing survive all the negative publicity it has received? Most consumers think of it as junk mail or spam. How can genuine e-mail marketers, who respect the privacy of consumers, use this tool? Will their image be tarnished if they engage in e-mail marketing?
5. A new product targeting teenage girls and young women is about to be introduced by a large consumer product company. What role should TV and the Web play in the product launch and advertising campaign? Assume the company has a $20 million budget for the campaign.
6. An online financial services company has been affected by a security breach of its computer systems. The company wants to reassure worried investors that the problem has been fixed.
   a. What role can the Web play in getting this message across? Be specific.
   b. What role will other media play in this communication challenge?

7. What advantages do clicks-and-mortar firms (those with offline and online stores) have over pure-play Internet firms when it comes to advertising? Focus on branding issues.

Internet Exercises

1. Identify three sites that would be appropriate for targeting ads to each of the following groups: (a) young women, (b) baby boomers of either gender, and (c) families with school-aged children. Develop a brief description of each site (nine sites in all) and explain why you think it is a good media choice.

2. Go to Yahoo! and AltaVista. Use the following search terms: golf, stocks, music, travel, toys, and books. Note all the ads that are displayed after each keyword search. Are the ads targeted to your search? Which companies advertise in these categories?

3. Visit the following Web sites: Saturn.com and SparkleCity.com (you will need Flash). Thoroughly examine each site. Given the two product categories (cars and toothpaste), how do the sites differ from each other? How well do these sites speak to their audience? What does the SparkleCity site tell you about advertising for low-involvement products?

4. Visit the following search engines or directories: Yahoo!, AltaVista, Excite, Lycos, and GoTo.com. Find out the process each employs for registering new Web sites. Look for a section such as "Add URL" or "Suggest a Site" or something similar to find out the process.

The Internet as a Distribution Channel

Avon, a company founded in the late 1800s, is closely identified with its door-to-door sales representatives or consultants. Avon did not take the traditional route to distributing cosmetics through drugstores and fashionable cosmetic boutiques in department stores. Instead, the company's position as a Fortune 500 business was built on the **direct selling** model. Mary Kay, a company founded in 1963, followed a somewhat similar strategy. Mary Kay cosmetic parties hosted by sales consultants are well known. Mary Kay's success is reflected in the fact that it ranks in the Fortune 500 and has been listed as one the best companies to work for and one of the most admired corporations in America.

Can these two companies continue to succeed using the direct selling method? With the majority of women now working outside the home, door-to-door selling has become more challenging. In an era when not only are more women working, but almost half of all women have access to the Internet, companies that target women have to rethink their marketing strategies. Successful companies do not surrender: they reinvent themselves. They embrace new ideas when required.

The two companies have taken different approaches to integrating the Internet into their strategies. Avon now offers direct sales of cosmetic products from its Web site. It also offers the products through its salespeople. For those who need a personal cosmetic consultant, the Web site allows them to locate a consultant by zip code or postal code. The consultants have their own personal Web pages, which enable them to sell products to their local clients. There is also an "Intranet" section on the Avon site, where sales consultants get product informa-

Learning Objectives

After you complete this chapter, you will:

- Understand the role of the Internet as a distribution channel.
- Appreciate the impact of the Internet on older intermediaries.
- Understand the role of new Internet-based intermediaries.
- Understand how the Internet can be used in conjunction with other channels.
- Be able to assess the channel strategy of online firms.

tion and can place orders. Avon, thus, uses the Web as a sales support tool and as a direct marketing channel.

Avon's Internet strategy seems to be focused on a young, more affluent, and Internet-savvy target. Typically, these women were not part of Avon's original target market. Avon's target in the United States has generally been an older and less educated demographic group. Now, thanks to the Internet, the company has found a way to reach a new demographic group. Avon has also made good use of banner ads to attract targeted consumers to its site.

Mary Kay, on the other hand, offers detailed product information and even has a virtual makeover, which can help customers choose the products necessary to achieve a certain look. The company, however, does not sell directly online. Customers can find a local consultant via the company's Web site (see Exhibit 11-1) and then order the products from the consultant's site. The Web is used as a sales support tool rather than a direct marketing channel.

According to Russell Mack, Executive Vice President of Global Communications at Mary Kay, "Anything we do on the Internet will be aimed at supporting the work of the consultants—not to go around them or take their place. This company is where it is today because of the persistent work of the independent sales force. We will always honor their knowledge and experience and do whatever we can to help them succeed." That statement underscores the Mary Kay Internet strategy.

Exhibit 11-1 Mary Kay's Site

Source: www.marykay.com. Courtesy Mary Kay Inc.

It is striking to note that both Avon and Mary Kay, two companies known for their direct selling success, have not abandoned their independent sales representatives for the Internet. With Internet penetration hovering at around 50 percent in North America, this is not surprising. However, each company is using the Internet differently. Avon uses the Internet as alternative channel, while Mary Kay uses it to support its existing channel.

Sources: "Avon: Invites You To Shop Online..." *ChannelSeven.com*; Coy Barefoot, "The Mary Kay Way" from *Network Marketing Lifestyles Magazine* (www.nmlifestyles.com/reprints/marykay/).

Introduction

In Chapters 9 and 10, we saw the role of the Internet as a communication and advertising medium. For many products, digital and non-digital, the Internet can also be a viable distribution channel. The changes at Avon and Mary Kay underscore how the Internet is revolutionizing the distribution function within organizations. Whether selling computers, cosmetics, digital content, or clothes, companies can use the Internet as a direct distribution channel—either on its own or in conjunction with other traditional channels.

The use of the Internet as a channel offers advantages but also presents organizations with challenges. Notably, when companies use the Internet along with traditional channels, conflict among channel members may arise. Firms that have historically used external channel partners may face additional challenges in establishing the infrastructure required for implementing direct distribution. This chapter will examine the role of the Internet as a distribution channel, and address the challenges and opportunities that organizations face in this area.

Channel Management

Marketing channels—wholesalers, dealers, and retailers—add value by making products available to customers where they need them (place or geographic region) and when they need them. The distribution channel members can also serve consumers by reducing search and information costs. They play a match-making function by identifying needs and matching them with appropriate products. Channel members can carry inventory, thereby reducing the working capital needs of the manufacturer and even end-users. They can also provide manufacturers with vital market information, as they are closer to consumers than the manufacturers, who may be geographically far away from the end-users.

Channel decisions are among the most critical and complex decisions that organizations make. Channel relationships develop over a long period of time, and the partners in these relationships require training and incentives. They also need advertising and promotional support to be effective. An auto manufacturer wishing to set up a dealer network in a new market must examine the dealer's prior experience, financial position, and management strengths. The amount of investment required by the dealer and the nature of the tasks to be performed by the dealer dictate that the auto manufacturer have a long-term relationship with the dealer.

The nature and complexity of the channel depends on the type of products and industry. A direct channel involves the manufacturer selling directly to end-users. Indirect channels, which use intermediaries, can take many forms. There could be one or several intermediaries. Industrial products require channel partners with a high degree of product and technical knowledge, as well as the ability to deliver service.

Typically, firms look at the economic criteria (cost-benefit), degree of control desired (direct channels offer more control than indirect channels), and flexibility in deciding the type of channel.[1] Often **multiple channels** are used to serve different markets or even the same market.

The advent of the Internet as a direct marketing channel is an exciting development. There is an expectation that in many industries the intermediaries will be squeezed out because the Internet now enables manufacturers to directly reach consumers. Yet, this may be easier said than done.

The Internet as a Marketing Channel

The Internet not only offers manufacturers and service firms the ability to reach their final customers directly, but it also helps these firms support the functions of their existing channels. In the case of Avon and Mary Kay, the Web site is also a sales support tool for the sales representatives.

As manufacturers in a variety of industries begin the use the Internet as a direct distribution channel, it has been predicted that intermediaries will face a slow, but sure, demise. The elimination of intermediaries who add more costs than value is referred to as **disintermediation**.

While some intermediaries are being eliminated, there are new intermediaries emerging on the Internet. These so-called **cybermediaries** come in different shapes. The B2B vertical exchanges described in Chapter 4 play an intermediary role by bringing buyers and suppliers together. Some of them play a purely match-making function, while others provide further value-added services.

As a distribution channel, the Web offers several definite advantages.

Distribution Costs. E-commerce allows for lower distribution costs than traditional marketing (see Table 11-1). In the case of digital products like software and music, distribution costs are virtually eliminated. The Internet also enables fast distribution, especially in the case of information goods or digital products.[2]

Table 11-1 Impact of E-Commerce on Distribution Costs (in US$)

Method	Airlines	Banking	Bill Payment	Term Life Insurance	Software
Traditional	8.00	1.08	2.22 to 3.32	400 to 700	15.00
Internet	1.00	0.13	0.65 to 1.10	200 to 350	0.20 to 0.50

Source: "The Economic and Social Impact of Electronic Commerce: Preliminary Findings and Research Agenda," OECD, 1999.

Channel Control. E-commerce offers firms greater control over distribution channels. A study on channel relationships by channel management consultants Frank Lynn Associates (www.franklynn.com) revealed that manufacturers often spend 15 percent of their revenues on channel maintenance costs. With E-commerce, channel monitoring costs will decline and the firms will have greater control over the distribution function.

Channel Conflict. Direct distribution presents no channel conflict if a company is an Internet pure-play. Often manufacturers and channel members have different goals. With each trying to safeguard their position, they may work at odds with each other. Conflict between manufacturers and retailers is known as vertical conflict. Selling directly to the end-user eliminates this conflict.

While these are some advantages that make direct Internet sales attractive, there are also a number of important issues to be considered. These include the expertise required to undertake direct distribution, the cost involved in acquiring the necessary infrastructure, and the ability to reach all present and potential customers through the direct channel. If a substantial segment of the market is not online, as in the case of Avon, abandoning the traditional channel is not a viable option. The use of the Web as a distribution channel also depends on several factors.

Nature of the Product. Is the product conducive to direct distribution? Companies like Procter & Gamble, which sells low-priced items to millions of geographically dispersed consumers, are not in a hurry to embrace the Internet as a distribution channel.

Role of the Channel Partners. If the channel partners are truly adding value, and not just cost, it will be hard to displace them. Some resellers offer products from a variety of vendors, providing consumers a great deal of choice and flexibility. Consumers may prefer to deal with such resellers rather than a single vendor.

Disintermediation: Fact or Fiction?

Several authors and futurists predicted the demise of intermediaries in the early days of E-commerce.[3] After nearly five years of commercialization of the Internet, there are questions about if and to what extent disintermediation has actually taken place. Some have argued that the intermediaries add significant costs to the value chain, which result in higher prices.[4] In the high-quality shirt market, it has been argued that retail prices can be lowered by more than 60 percent by eliminating wholesalers and retailers.[5] It has also been argued that the information technology available today allows companies to perform some of the functions previously performed by intermediaries. By directly linking with suppliers and customers through extranets and electronic data interchange (EDI), a manufacturer can take charge of the information flow across the supply and demand chains. This is likely to make some intermediary functions redundant. Lastly, manufacturers who can eliminate at least some of the intermediaries will be able to retain higher profit margins or be able to compete more aggressively on price. This should also serve as an incentive for manufacturers to engage in disintermediation. Transaction processing costs and distribution costs are significantly lower online for many products and services. The final price may be higher due to shipping costs, but there is room for lower distribution costs in many categories.

The OECD's studies show that in most product categories the intermediaries typically add anywhere from 33 to 45 percent to the final price.[6] If the manufacturer could take on some of the functions of the intermediaries, the potential impact on profits could be significant.

In several categories we see manufacturers or service providers reaching directly to consumers, in some cases bypassing the intermediaries and in other cases augmenting the role of the intermediaries. In the travel category, all major airlines offer direct ticket sales from their Web sites (see Vignette 9 for an example). Jupiter Communications has predicted that by 2002, 62 percent of all airline ticket sales will occur directly via airline Web sites.[7] Auto manufacturers are also reaching out directly to consumers. Many now allow consumers to customize their cars online. They also use their sites to gather vital information about consumers, an area where they were previously dependent on dealers (see Vignette 1 on page 2). In the computer industry, Dell's direct selling model is the envy of its rivals, who are trying to emulate Dell (see iMarket Demo 11-1).

We saw in iMarket Demo 2-1 (see page 39) how *Encyclopedia Britannica* has reinvented itself. *Britannica's* sales force is currently at 10 percent of what it was prior to 1990. The company uses the Internet to directly offer content and other services to consumers. Advertising is an important source of revenue now.

In the music industry, while there is legal cloud hanging over firms like Napster and MP3.com, they have shown that artists can directly reach their fans without the support of the big recording companies. Many smaller artists use the Internet to gain recognition. Authors can also reach readers without the services of publishers. The era of digital books and e-books is here.

Nowhere else is the impact of the Internet on distribution so striking as it is in the B2B space. Many of the vertical hubs (see VerticalNet.com for example) bring suppliers in contact with end-users, eliminating intermediaries. However, resellers and large B2B suppliers have successfully migrated to E-commerce. Resellers who have the financial resources and are able to add value will be hard to disintermediate. For example, W.W. Grainger (Grainger.com) is a large industrial supplier that adds value by offering a vast array of products from hundreds of vendors.

Death of the Salesman and Saleswoman

Technology companies such as IBM and Oracle have something in common with Avon and Mary Kay. They also use a huge number of salespeople. That may be about to change. Oracle, IBM, and SAP already derive a significant percentage of their sales through the Web. Oracle has plans to increase online sales to 80 percent of its total sales.[8] IBM already sells its software products to business partners via its extranet. The fate of the nearly 30 000 salespeople at IBM and about 10 000 salespeople at Oracle is not difficult to predict. Even the company's own sales staff can be disintermediated. Since salespeople can cost upwards of $200 per sales call, selling directly and servicing directly via the Web (backed by a call centre) are attractive options for many companies.

This does not mean that these large B2B companies are radically altering their selling methods by eliminating salespeople. Intermediaries whose selling technique is simply saying "I've got the stock" face the likelihood of being disinteremediated.[9] Whether they're part of the company's sales force or third-party distributors, the intermediary's role in the E-commerce era must go beyond holding inventory or persuading consumers to buy the product.

Sales representatives across industries are being forced to redefine their role and function. Straight selling and price negotiation will not be the focus of their jobs. Their value-adding will come from providing consulting services and solutions to customers and to the firm. Many companies are retraining their salespeople for this new economy. We see travel agents

iMarket Demo 11-1 Selling Computers on the Internet

Dell Computers is credited with making the direct selling model a great success. The Internet allowed Dell to extend the direct selling model by allowing consumers more control. Consumers can customize products and can also manage their accounts with Dell online. Once an order is placed online (or by phone), it can be tracked via Dell's site. Gateway, which has a similar business model, has also had success in the same space. Dell's make-to-order model has allowed the company to carry inventory for just 8 to 12 days. As a result, Dell is more profitable than other computer manufacturers.

Older rival computer companies have been using the traditional channels, where products are built and shipped to retailers. From production to sale, it may take two months or even longer although Compaq direct ships all consumer products in 5-10 days. Eighty percent of a PC's cost is made up from the components, whose prices drop 30 percent a year. Dell is in a better position to take advantage of the dropping prices because it is not carrying inventory for months.

Dell's rivals are realizing that E-commerce, both B2B and B2C, can save costs and drive profits higher. Compaq (see Exhibit 11-2) and HP now offer direct sales through their sites, even though they continue to use the traditional distribution channels.

The trend toward lower-priced PCs is another important reason for the players in this industry to consider direct sales via the Internet. There are several under-$1000 PCs available now, and consumers expect PC prices to drop even further. The margins on low-end computers are not very high. Direct distribution can allow manufacturers to take some of the retailers' and resellers' margins.

Exhibit 11-2 Compaq's Online Store

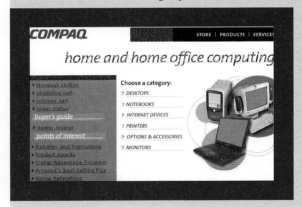

Source: www.compaq.com.

Sources: "The Economic and Social Impact of Electronic Commerce: Preliminary Findings and Research Agenda," OECD, 1999; Mike Hogan (1999), "Internet Becomes Crucial PC Distribution Channel," *PCWorld.com*, January 12.

redefining their function by becoming travel consultants and by focusing on package tours and corporate sales.

The State of Disintermediation

There is some evidence of disintermediation occurring in different industries. However, since revenue from Internet sales is still less than one percent of total retail revenues in North America, it may be too early to judge the economic impact of disintermediation.

Disappearance of intermediaries has been predicted in a variety of areas, from travel and insurance to groceries and retailing, but the disappearance of bricks-and-mortar stores may have been exaggerated.

Many manufacturers who were initially attracted by the prospect of bypassing distribution channels are realizing that they have to invest heavily in warehousing and order-fulfillment systems. In the past, many manufacturers outsourced these tasks to their channel partners.

Even firms that are engaged in online direct sales, from Avon to Oracle, have not eliminated their proven sales channel for something that is new. Now experts think that disintermediation will occur more slowly than initially predicted. In the early days of E-commerce, some experts even anticipated the end of bricks-and-mortar retail stores, but this has not happened. We'll examine this issue later in the chapter (see the section "Managing Multiple Channels" on page 290).

It has also been suggested that the industries that were best suited for disintermediation, because of easy digitization of their products or services (such as banking and education), use relatively few intermediaries.[10] In the case of tangible products like CDs and books, the new e-tailers are not displacing the older bricks-and-mortar retailers, at least not entirely. Amazon still uses the traditional book wholesalers to acquire inventory. In fact, many e-tailers are simply competing with bricks-and-mortar retailers.

Not only has disintermediation been slow in many cases and its effects unclear, but we have also seen the emergence of new intermediaries on the Internet. Cybermediaries and infomediaries are two of many terms used to describe these new online players. Some are market makers and others are simply information brokers. Some are in the B2B space and others provide services to consumers. We will examine this new breed of intermediaries in the next section.

Internet-Based Intermediaries

Contrary to early beliefs that the Internet would simply connect manufacturers and service firms with their end-users and eliminate everyone in the middle, the Internet has actually given birth to new and enhanced forms of intermediation. In some cases, displaced intermediaries are coming back in a new form. In other cases, the Internet is enabling—and even demanding—the presence of new intermediaries.

Reintermediation

Reintermediation is simply the reincarnation of a disintermediated channel player or the emergence of a new intermediary.[11] Publishers who can custom publish books (by taking essays or chapters from different books), real estate brokers who provide their clients with online postings and advertisements with 3-D viewing technology, photos, and other details, and travel agents who focus on value-added services that airlines cannot match will reintermediate themselves.

As E-commerce displaces some intermediaries, it creates others. Take the case of companies like FedEx and UPS that play a vital part now in delivery service. Electronic commerce also requires the guarantee of security and authenticity. Firms like Cybercash, which provides online payment solutions, or Verisign, which provides encryption and Internet security solutions, have emerged as new intermediaries online. We will consider other forms of Internet intermediaries in the section entitled "Cybermediaries."

The Role of Internet Intermediaries

We'll look at the role of Internet intermediaries in terms of seven concepts: access, trust, aggregation, costs, facilitation, matching, and value-adding.[12] Descriptions of these concepts are provided in Table 11-2.

A study spanning three sectors (retail, automotive, and information goods), which examined B2B and B2C cases, found that electronic markets do increase the importance of certain functions performed by the intermediaries. Electronic markets may reduce the need for aggregation services, but they increase the importance of trust (security and authentication services), facilitation (exchange of information), and to some extent the matching function.[13]

Cybermediaries

The term cybermediary simply refers to an Internet-based intermediary.[14] There are many variations of such intermediaries, some of which were examined in Chapter 2's discussion of business models. Cybermediaries can be found in B2B, B2C, and C2C markets. The most common forms of cybermediaries are discussed below.

 Directories and Search Services. General directories such as Yahoo! and commercial directories such as the All Internet Shopping Directory (www.all-internet.com) offer a vital intermediary service by making information searches easier. These directories simplify the task of finding products or companies. Search services such as Infoseek and AltaVista allow

Table 11-2 Internet Intermediary Roles and Functions

Concept	Function
Access	Using the technology, the intermediary can provide access to information and enables online transactions to occur 24/7, throughout the year.
Aggregation	By recruiting many buyers and sellers, the Internet intermediary provides a platform for trading to occur on multiple products from multiple vendors; provides bundled products and single-price packaged solutions.
Costs	Reduces costs by enabling efficient searching of information and lowering transaction-processing costs.
Facilitation	Facilitates information exchange between the two parties. Can track market information and information on buyer preferences, which can be used to deliver better services.
Matching	Enables buyers to locate suppliers easily.
Trust	Internet intermediary can act as a neutral, unbiased mediator between buyer and seller. Can ensure that transactions will be secure and will not fail. Can also play a regulatory role, if required.
Value-adding	Can add value by introducing unique solutions and products.

Source: Based on Chrusciel (2000) and Bailey and Bakos (1997).

users to search using keywords. Unlike Yahoo!, however, they do not allow the user to drill down their database.

Intelligent Agents. These agents are software applications that run from the user's computer and can accomplish complex search tasks. Copernic (www.copernic.com) and BullsEye (www.intelliseek.com) are two examples. Copernic Shopper allows consumers to find reviews and compare prices in many different product categories at over 250 content sites and stores.

Financial Intermediaries. Electronic commerce depends on electronically making and authorizing payments from buyer to seller. The most basic and common payment systems are credit card authorizations by major card-issuing companies like Visa and MasterCard. Other financial cybermediaries include new forms of payments such as electronic cheques (CheckFree) and solutions, which extend physical-world payment methods into the virtual world (eCash) or micro-payment methods like Millicent and NetBill.[15]

Trust Enablers. Verisign, a company that provides technology for secure transactions, and TRUSTe, an organization that enables Web users and Web sites to address consumer privacy, are two examples in this category. Both organizations play a vital role in building consumer trust and confidence in E-commerce. I-Escrow (www.iescrow.com) is a company that offers escrow services for participants in auctions at sites like eBay. The payment is released to the seller by I-Escrow only when the buyer receives the product in satisfactory condition.

Infomediaries. Infomediaries can collect information about consumers and use it to generate advertising revenue (one example is NetZero, a free Internet service provider). Data about consumer behaviour online is a valuable commodity. Infomediaries can also act as information brokers on behalf of consumers, helping them find Web sites and products (for example, Copernic Shopper and Gomez.com).

Online Malls. Online malls, just like their physical counterparts, present many stores at one site. The main benefit is the ability to reach different sellers easily from one point. Malls may also offer other value-added services. Guarantees of security and consumer privacy protection are common. Yahoo Shopping, an example of an online mall, is a collection of brand name stores. It is a gateway to the Web sites of the different stores. Yahoo! also offers a digital wallet, which makes it easy to fill out order forms for regular shoppers.

Buy/Sell Fulfillment. There are several online financial brokerages, which allow consumers to buy and sell securities for a fee. E*Trade and Ameritrade are two examples. The online brokerage model has been extended to other categories such as cars (as with CarsDirect.com).[16]

Market Exchange. This type of cybermediary is found in B2B markets. ChemConnect and MetalSite are examples in this category. Typically, a market exchange firm charges a fee based on the value of the sale.[17]

Trading Communities. VerticalNet has created over 50 online trading communities, each linking buyers and sellers in a specific industry. These communities include product information, directories of suppliers, industry news and articles, job postings, and more. They also enable B2B transactions and auctions.

Auctioneers. Onsale and eBay are examples of online auction houses that bring buyers and sellers together. Priceline, which allows consumers to name their price for airline tickets, hotel rooms, car rentals, and even groceries, follows a reverse auction model, where sellers bid for the buyer's business. The auction sites, regardless of format, provide a venue for the online auction to take place. They bring the buyer and seller together, and they charge a fee or a commission.

There are many other varieties of cybermediaries. Many of them leverage the technology and deliver a new product or service that is required by either the buyer, seller, or both. Others take traditional business models (like the mall or the auction house) and use the Internet to expand the scope and market.

Pure-Play vs. Multi-Channel Marketing

The collapse of the **bricks-and-mortar** economy (comprised of companies that have no online presence, but only a physical presence) was seen imminent not too long ago. E-commerce stores were expected to sweep established old economy companies out of the market. The reality, so far at least, has been a lot different. Yes, e-tailers have had a strong showing in some categories, but they are also shown to be vulnerable if they remain pure-play Internet companies.

A study by the consulting firm McKinsey & Company and Solomon Smith Barney on e-tailing concluded that e-tailers are likely to have a better future if they sell to customers across a number of channels—catalogues, bricks-and-mortar stores, and online. "The notion of pure-play is turning out to be the wrong play," according to Joanna Barsh, a leader in McKinsey's e-tail practice.[18]

Online purchases, especially in B2C, do not account for a significant portion of total spending yet. Only about half the population is online, and consumer behaviour (shifting from retail to online) has been slower than anticipated. Further, e-tailers have not been very discriminating in terms of their targeting. Given low revenues and no profits, they have been willing to take any consumer at any price (usually a heavily discounted price). These factors have made it difficult for e-tailers to break-even. The McKinsey report argues that a multi-channel approach may be the best bet.

Another study, by the Consumer Electronic Manufacturers Association (CEMA), found that nearly 60 percent of shoppers were using both retail stores and Internet stores.[19]

The reasons for this conclusion are not difficult to find. Many consumers use the Web as an information source and then go to the bricks-and-mortar store to buy the product. The CEMA study found that roughly 50 percent of consumers use the Web as an information source and then make a purchase in a retail store. Alternatively, consumers may see the product and examine it or sample it in the bricks-and-mortar store, and then use the convenience of the Internet to purchase the product. In fact, the CEMA study found that 35 percent of consumers did go to the store before buying online. An Internet pure-play, which has only an online presence, does not allow the consumer this option of using dual channels—each for a different stage of the purchase decision process.

The lack of physical stores also hurts some start-up e-tail ventures. Building the awareness, creating the trust, and persuading the consumer to buy—all at the same time—is a difficult task. Firms that have physical stores usually have better brand recognition, which can then be leveraged online. HomeGrocer, a pure-play Internet grocery delivery company, used to send out its empty delivery trucks (with the company logo) to neighbourhoods that were considered potential targets. The signage with the brand logo, buildings, and other physical assets can create a subtle image of a solid company in the consumer's mind.

Buyer Conversion Rate

By October 1998, one-third of all retailers had launched a Web site. Even some late entrants like Wal-Mart have invested heavily in their online presence. Others are already in their second or third generation Web sites. The combination of an established brand name, presence of physical stores (where one can complain or return a defective product), and an online presence is paying off for these e-tailers. A study by Shop.org demonstrated the impact of the multi-channel strategy in terms of buyer conversion rate (see Table 11-3). The fact that multi-channel retailers can communicate with consumers through different media and sell through different channels does contribute to the superior conversion rate.

From Brick to Click

In 1998, e-tailers such as Amazon and eToys dominated Web sales. In 1999, several major retailers entered the online marketspace. By November 1999, 49 percent of the top 100 US retailers had the ability to sell online.[20] The top 50 e-tailers include several major land-based retailers.

The preferred method to enter the Internet seems to be through a separate spin-off. Wal-Mart has formed a stand-alone company to manage Walmart.com. Target Corporation, owner of department store chains Target, Mervyn's, and Dayton's, has also launched a separate online store (www.target.com).[21] Typically, the spin-off involves a venture firm or a technology firm with Internet experience. These big retailers bring their brand, retailing experience, and customer base with the hope that an Internet-savvy partner will assist in establishing an online presence.

Some analysts do caution that this spin-off strategy may have its own risks. First, there is the likelihood of some animosity between the workers in the bricks-and-mortar stores and those in the new e-tail operation. Second, if the Web operation is not in sync with the retail operation, customer frustration and dissatisfaction can quickly result.[22] For instance, if a product purchased online cannot be returned to a local land-based store, customers are bound to be displeased.

Egghead closed all of its retail outlets and became an e-tailer. Egghead did have the name recognition that is likely paying dividends in its online venture. Citibank, on the other hand, killed a "Net only" project.[23] The leading bank toyed with the idea of a pure Internet venture, but it shut down its Internet-only subsidiary, Citi f/i, and merged it with its traditional online banking service. In Canada, the Bank of Montreal, which was a pioneer of sorts in the online banking world, set up mbanx, a separate online bank. After some flawed strate-

Table 11-3 **Pure-Play vs. Multi-Channel Retailers**

	Multi-Channel Retailer	Internet-Only Retailer
Buyer Conversion Rate	6.1%	3.0%
Repeat Buyers as a Percentage of Total Buyers	26%	17%

Source: Shop.org, Survey, November 1998.

gizing, mbanx lost its separate identity. Citibank's Citi f/i, went through some turmoil as well, with frequent changes in management.

In the B2B space, W.W. Grainger, which had established retail and print catalogue operations as an MRO (maintenance, repair, and operating items) supplier, has made a smooth transition online, but has not abandoned its bricks-and-mortar operations. Three new Grainger Web ventures—FindMRO.com, Orderzone.com, and Grainger Auction provide a full range of supply management services in a wide range of products. Grainger reportedly gets 25 percent of its sales online when the company's offices are closed. Online orders average 70 to 80 percent higher than offline orders.[24]

There are some worthwhile lessons to be learned from the experience of these firms. Traditional companies, no matter their industry, have to develop sound strategies for the online market. The parent companies sometimes do not allow the start-up freedom to innovate in the new space. Often the rules of the old economy are applied to the Internet. The technology and the uniqueness of the Internet as a communication medium and channel are not yet fully appreciated.

From Click to Brick

Some Internet-only e-tailers are moving in the other direction, going from "click" to "brick," and opening physical stores. Bluemercury.com, a beauty products e-tailer, has opened physical stores in the Washington, DC, area to offer consumers the opportunity to try the products at the store before purchasing them at the store or online (see Exhibit 11-3).

Gazoontite.com, which offers allergy and asthma relief products, has made a similar move by opening land-based stores in San Francisco, Orange County, Chicago, and New York. Many other e-tailers, including the gift company Redenvelope.com, offer con-

Exhibit 11-3 Bluemercury.com

about bluemercury   the stores   mailing list   our guarantee   email us   1.800.355.600

Yes it's true!
bluemercury operates two retail stores in Washington, D.C. if you'd like to experience the fun of shopping the old-fashioned way!

Store Locations:

Georgetown	DuPont Circle
3059 M Street NW	1745 Connecticut Ave. NW
Washington, DC 20007	Washington, DC 20009
Phone: 202.965.1300	Phone: 202.462.1300

Source: www.bluemercury.com.

sumers the choice of shopping through a print catalogue, which consumers can request at the Web site. Dell Computers continues to use catalogues and call centres to ring in the orders.

These attempts show that Internet start-ups with relatively unknown brand names are taking the multi-channel strategy seriously. When products require trial (such as beauty products) or expert opinion (such as pharmaceutical products), the use of physical stores can augment the online efforts. The print catalogue with a toll-free telephone number may make it easier for some to shop, especially if they are uncomfortable with Web technology or have security concerns.

E-tailers such as Amazon have invested enormous amounts in physical infrastructure, but have not opened actual bricks-and-mortar stores. While some Internet pure-play e-tailers have made the "click to brick" transition, so far none of the major e-tailers have moved in that direction. It is conceivable that some may move in that direction, while others may pursue different approaches.

Strategic Partnerships. Amazon has entered into an agreement with Toys "R" Us, the leader in that category.[25] Toyrus.com's difficulty in securing venture funding and the site's lackluster performance eventually led to Toysrus.com being closed. Now the toy retailer has a co-branding arrangement with Amazon, allowing Amazon to sell its products. Toys "R" Us did not seem to have the expertise in the Internet area required to create a successful e-tail operation. A smaller, but Internet-savvy competitor, eToys.com, did not make life easy for Toysrus.com.

This new arrangement, however, still has some problems. Coordination between the Toys "R" Us retail stores and the Amazon site in such areas as consumer complaints, returns, and product recalls must be worked out in precise detail. Whether the cultures of the two firms will mesh is something that remains to be seen. For Amazon, this is a very significant partnership. While not actually making an entry into the world of bricks-and-mortar, Amazon is clearly making good use of the name of an established bricks-and-mortar retailer with a good product mix and customer base.

E-Commerce to M-Commerce

Even as firms try to come to grips with E-commerce and develop synergies between their brick and click operations, mobile commerce, or **M-commerce**, has arrived. Consumers can now order products, purchase stocks, and receive news and even targeted ads via their cell phones or other handheld devices.

Rather than wait for the consumer to come to the store or the Web site, M-commerce truly enables anytime-anywhere commerce. Access to a PC or a laptop with an Internet connection is no longer required. We are still in the early stages of M-commerce. There are interesting opportunities and challenges, one being the presentation of product information and images on the small screen of a cell phone. Currently, M-commerce is text-based, but future generations of technology can change that.

Experts have argued that the Internet will become ubiquitous. Consumers will be able to access the Net and shop or get information from a variety of devices. In other words, rather than bringing the customer to the Web site, the emphasis will be on getting the message to the customer. A strategy with multiple ways of reaching the consumer is referred to as **contextual marketing**.[26]

Managing Multiple Channels

We see existing companies going online and some Internet pure-plays going offline to reach their customers through a variety of channels. Firms that have an online and an offline presence are referred to as **bricks-and-clicks** or **clicks-and-mortar**. As older firms move online and e-tailers establish physical presence or partnerships with land-based retailers, several interesting challenges and opportunities will arise.

Channel Conflict

Channel conflict arises when two channel partners (a manufacturer and a wholesaler/retailer or even two retailers carrying the same product) differ in their goals, motives, and actions. When one partner feels that the other partner is not contributing as much or if one partner's feels that their efforts have not been adequately rewarded, channel conflicts arise. When a manufacturer decides to go online and sell directly, that is a potential source of conflict with existing distributors or retailers. Still, it's not as if the Internet has introduced "channel conflict" into the marketer's vocabulary. This type of conflict has always been there.[27]

When Sony started selling products directly from its online music store, retailers who had long played an active role in promoting the Sony label and its artists were upset. After dragging its feet for some time, when Merrill Lynch entered the low-cost online trading arena, that distressed 15 000 stock brokers. Earlier, we also saw how IBM and Oracle, along with Avon, may be causing a great deal of concern to their own sales staff. Will these companies end up cannibalizing their current business or will the two channels offer more than the sum of the parts?

Channel conflict, when entering the Internet, may arise from two sources—the ease with which existing businesses and business processes can be transferred online, and the degree of control a firm has over its channel.[28] Companies that have businesses that transfer easily to the Web, but do not have a great deal of control over their channels, are likely to face a high degree of channel conflict. In particular, airlines, insurance, securities trading, and computers are some of the industries where channel conflict is evident now. Generally, firms with greater channel control face less conflict when they migrate online (for example, consulting or other professional firms).

Cooperating with the existing channel, integrating the existing channel with the online channel, and collaborating with the existing channel are all possible solutions to channel conflict.[29] As Oracle retrains its sales staff for a new role, Avon encourages online consumers to meet their local sales staff. The homepage of the Avon site prominently shows a link for "locating" its local representatives. This shows that Avon is not simply bypassing them.

Integration and Analysis

Potential channel conflict should not in itself be a reason for ruling out entry into the online market. The benefits may far outweigh the costs. Ideally, the Internet should be combined with other channels, if they exist. Each channel can then focus on a different target market or region, if possible. Alternatively, each can supplement the other in different ways. It is possible to minimize conflict even if it cannot be completely eliminated.

The goals of the multiple channels must be aligned. Each channel must be rewarded commensurate with its performance. Competition in the E-commerce area, the existing relationships with the channel partners, and future goals of the organization must be factored into the channel decision.

Channel conflict is only one of the issues. Firms must deal with the possibility of cannibalization when they offer products through multiple channels. Many marketers believe that cannibalization is better than losing sales to competitors. The new channel, whether it happens to be the Internet or physical stores, should be economically viable. That means generating positive cash flows and profits.

There was proof that e-tailers were actually taking sales away from retailers. Jupiter Communications revealed that only 10 percent of Internet sales were incremental, and the rest were drawn from bricks-and-mortar stores.[30] Retailers paid attention to this warning. Now all the major retailers are online, and many smaller ones are preparing for entry soon. The multi-channel strategy simply recognizes that not all consumers want the same shopping experience. As marketers move towards providing personalized products and services, some choice in terms of shopping experience seems appropriate.

The Internet allows firms to gather a great deal of information about customers. The information can come from online registrations, online orders, and other Web site traffic-tracking programs. When firms have multiple channels, it would make a great deal of sense to ensure that data on important metrics are being collected in every channel. A firm must be able to answer questions such as:

- Who are our online customers and how are they different from our customers in other channels?
- Is the Internet cannibalizing from other channels or is there an incremental gain in revenue?
- What marketing programs and products are best suited for each channel?
- Are consumers using the different channels in their decision process (such as information gathering on the Web and purchasing in the retail store)?
- How effective are the marketing programs designed for each channel?

Clearly, there are many more interesting and important questions that must be addressed. Such cross-channel analysis can provide early warning, help avoid conflicts, and assist in creating synergy across channels.[31]

Summary

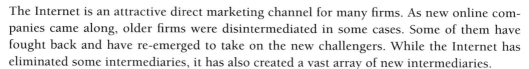

The Internet is an attractive direct marketing channel for many firms. As new online companies came along, older firms were disintermediated in some cases. Some of them have fought back and have re-emerged to take on the new challengers. While the Internet has eliminated some intermediaries, it has also created a vast array of new intermediaries.

These cybermediaries range from malls and auctioneers to companies that facilitate online payment or secure transactions. Online directories and search engines also qualify as cybermediaries.

Businesses, online and offline, have realized that a multiple channel strategy may be more appropriate than a singular focus. Such an approach gives the consumer the option of shopping online or offline. For land-based retailers, it ensures that the new online start-up competitor is not taking sales away from the established business. All the major retailers now have an online presence, and some e-tailers are moving the other way, setting up physical stores or catalogue operations.

While the multiple channel strategy has several advantages, it also raises an old problem—channel conflict. As airlines started selling tickets directly from their sites, they created a conflict with their travel agents. Sometimes companies that sell directly online even create conflict with their own salespeople. There are different ways of minimizing channel conflict. Channel conflict in itself should not prevent a firm from opening a new channel—if the benefits outweigh the costs.

Channel decisions are complex for many reasons. Since channels take a long time and a lot of resources to develop, the decision to go offline or online must be made after thorough analysis. A good channel strategy will help avoid missteps later.

Key Terms

Bricks-and-clicks, 290

Bricks-and-mortar, 286

Channel conflict, 290

Clicks-and-mortar, 290

Contextual marketing, 289

Cybermediary, 279

Direct selling, 276

Disintermediation, 279

M-commerce, 289

Multiple channels, 279

Reintermediation, 283

Questions and Exercises

Review Questions

1. What are the strengths of the Internet as a distribution channel? When is it appropriate to use the Internet as a channel?
2. What are the weaknesses of the Internet as a distribution channel?
3. What is disintermediation? How widely prevalent is it?
4. What is reintermediation? Provide examples.
5. Who are cybermediaries? Name and describe three types of cybermediaries.
6. What are the main functions of the Internet as an intermediary?
7. Why is using multiple channels more effective than using only the Internet as a channel?
8. What are the strengths and weaknesses of a multi-channel strategy?
9. What is channel conflict? Provide three specific examples using Internet companies.
10. How can channel conflict be resolved?
11. What is M-commerce? What products and services are likely to succeed in this channel?

Discussion Questions

1. Why haven't the major e-tailers made an entry into land-based operations? Are the business models, operations, and philosophy for land-based and online operations very different?
2. How can retailers who open online stores avoid channel conflict?
3. Do you think major e-tailers will open physical stores or pursue other channels besides the Internet? Why or why not?
4. Why are cybermediaries essential? Choose one or two types of cybermediary to make your case.
5. Why do multiple channel stores have a higher buyer conversion rate than Internet-only stores?

Internet Exercises

1. Visit the following sites: www.ticketmaster.com, www.benjerry.com, www.supercuts.com. How are these companies using the Internet from a channel perspective?

2. Visit Avon.com and Marykay.com. Examine their strategies from a channel management perspective. How is each firm using the Internet? How are they dealing with channel conflict?

Chapter 12

Online Retailing

Vignette 12 eLuxury—Niche Marketing Online

The average dollar value of a consumer purchase is still less than $100, and very few consumers spend over $500 per year on online purchases. As a percentage of total spending, consumer online spending is well below 10 percent. Given these numbers, is there a market online for luxury goods? Are there consumers out there who are willing to put a set of diamond earrings that cost $42 000 or a golf bag that costs $3000 into their virtual shopping carts? What about an antique bookcase for $300 000 (see Exhibit 12-1)?

Concerns with security, privacy, and trust with online vendors are frequently cited reasons for the slow rate of consumer adoption. Will consumers pay thousands of dollars at an online store for a product they cannot touch and feel?

There is definitely a niche market online for luxury products. In a study of global retailing on the Internet, Ernst & Young predicted that by 2005, 10 percent of the $76 billion luxury goods market would belong to online retailers. Brand name designer clothing, watches and jewellery, art and antiques, cars, and luxury vacations will be sold online to those who can afford these luxuries. In some categories, such as luxury cars, the Internet is expected to have a significant impact on purchase behaviour.

The demographics are there to support the vendors who have dared to enter this space online. People with high incomes often have access to the Internet. Many of the rich and famous also prefer to protect their privacy and like to remain anonymous, which is hard to do in a bricks-and-mortar store. The convenience of online shopping, coupled with the presence of leading brand name luxury stores online, makes it attractive for high-end consumers.

Exhibit 12-1 A $300 000 Antique Bookcase at LuxuryFinder.com

Circline

Gothic Breakfront Bookcase, $300,000

PURCHASE

Height: 9'4", width: 7'10¼", depth (at sides):
23½", (in center): 25¾"
Great Britain, circa 1810-20

After a design by George Smith, in A Collection
of Designs for Household Furniture, 1808.

This magnificent neo-gothic bookcase contains a
full-size desk within the central case section,
complete with numerous secret compartments.

View All Circline
View more gift ideas out of this world

Source: www.luxuryfinder.com.

The field of competitors in this space is getting crowded. Established names like Tiffany, Fortunoff, and Harrods are combining their physical stores with a virtual presence. Tiffany.com offers over 200 products, including $50 silver jewellery for those starting out in the luxury market. As we saw in Chapter 11, by taking an established brand name to the Internet, these bricks-and-clicks stores are benefiting from multiple channels.

A new breed of luxury portals has recently emerged. Luxury Finder.com sells products in different price ranges and categories. It is also a portal site and features an online magazine. Modaitalia.net is a European fashion and luxury goods portal with links to Europe's major fashion houses.

In the United States, Ashford.com, an Internet pure-play, offers a range of luxury products, including watches, writing instruments, leather bags, fragrances, and jewellery. For those who want to pamper themselves occasionally but do not have deep pockets, Ashford also has some affordably priced products like the $298 Burberry fountain pen.

Ashford.com recently entered into two strategic partnerships. One is an alliance with Yahoo! and America Online, which will likely bring more visitors to the site. The other was selling a stake to Amazon.com, which can open the door to Amazon's huge customer base. Ashford targets customers with $1 million in assets and, by the end of 1999, had reportedly sold over $30 million worth of luxury goods online.

In addition to these e-tailers, eBay and other auctioneers like Sotheby's (Sotheby.amazon.com is a joint venture between Amazon and Sotheby's) also offer antiques, collectibles, and luxury items. See the Arts & Antiques section of eBay for high-priced auction items.

The average consumer may see online stores as places to get bargain prices, and the Internet allows easy price comparisons for those seeking bargains. At the same time, we are also seeing the emergence of category leaders in the high-end luxury goods market.

This luxury marketspace has a lot of potential, but there are some interesting challenges too. Those who shop in these online stores are likely to have very high expectations regarding service quality and the shopping experience. The site has to convey a sense of class and elegance. This means site design is a critical element in establishing an online luxury e-tail store. There is also the challenge of dealing with sites that sell counterfeit Gucci and Rolex products. Conveying an image of authenticity, as well as building trust and gaining the confidence of potential consumers, is going to be important.

Sources: "Luxury Goods: All That Glitters is No Easy Capture," in *Global Online Retail Report*, Ernst & Young, LLP, 2000; Kathleen Ohlson (1999), "Amazon, Sotheby's to Launch Joint Online Auction," *Online News*, June 16; "Internet Attracting New Car Buyers in the UK," *CyberAtlas* (cyberatlas.com/big_picture/geographics/print/0,1323,5911_ 209881,00.html), September 30, 1999.

Introduction

E-tailing or retailing on the Internet has matured very quickly. Virtually anything that is available in bricks-and-mortar stores is available online. In fact, there is a greater choice of brands and retailers on the Internet. From bargain hunters to luxury seekers, there are products on the Internet for everyone. From toys for kids to drugs for seniors, the range of products online is complete.

As product choice online has grown, so has the competition. Some weaker players have already fallen by the wayside. The big powerhouses like Wal-Mart and Sears are leveraging their brand equity and are using a multi-channel strategy. The so-called clicks-and-mortar model is a threat to Internet pure-plays like Amazon and eToys.

There are new business models being tested in the world of e-tailing. Personalization, superior customer experience, and customer relationship management are themes that are dominant in online retailing today.

In this chapter, we'll begin by exploring the size and scope of online retailing, then we'll look at what motivates or deters consumers from shopping online, and finally, we'll examine the issues involved in setting up an online store.

Online Retailing: Size and Scope

Business-to-consumer E-commerce is expected to grow rapidly for the next several years. Let's start by examining the current revenues and future projections. There are several predictions regarding the future growth of B2C E-commerce—some cautious and others overly optimistic. Each research organization uses its own proprietary methodology, which leads to discrepancies. There are, however, similarities between various published projections of online commerce. They all suggest growing revenues; the disagreement is in the rate of growth.

Global Perspective

A study by Forrester Research predicts that by 2004, US online retail sales to consumers will grow to $184 billion from $20.2 billion in 1999.[1] According to Dataquest, European B2C revenues are expected to reach $115 billion by 2003 (up from $5.4 billion in 1999), and global revenues are expected to reach $380 billion in 2003 (up from $31.2 billion in 1999).[2]

A study on global Internet retailing by Ernst & Young pegs the average online household expenditure per year at $1200 (up from $230 per year in 1999).[3] Forrester projects a growth in annual household expenditures to $3738 by 2004.[4] As a percentage of annual household expenditures, Internet purchases will still be less than a quarter of total expenditures in most households.

Forty percent of all households globally with access to the Internet have made at least one purchase online.[5]

Online Experience

There is a positive correlation between the number of years a consumer has been online and the average size of online transaction. Those who were online in 1995 or earlier had an average transaction of $388 in 1999, while those who went online only in 1998 or 1999 had an average transaction size of $187. This suggests that comfort level with the technology and online shopping experience can affect shopping behaviour on the Internet.

Demographics

Not surprisingly, those earning more than $100 000 are more likely to have spent more than $500 in online purchases in 1999. Sixty-one percent of this income group also made 10 or more online purchases in 1999, as compared to only 32 percent in the under-$30 000 income group.[6] As we saw in Chapter 3, men and women differ in terms of their major online purchases. Women are more likely to buy clothes, toys, and prescription drugs, and men are more likely to buy electronics and software. Table 12-1 provides demographic buying patterns for six countries.

Table 12-1 Demographics of Online Consumers

	US	Canada	Australia	UK	Italy	France
Age (mean)	41.0	41.7	37.9	36.7	37.7	35.3
Household Income (US$)	$59,000	$50,300	$62,300	$64,600	$36,300	$48,300
Gender (male/female)	50/50	63/38	59/41	69/31	85/15	76/24
Education (% college grad.)	41%	48%	58%	56%	55%	64%

Source: "Global Internet Retailing Report," Ernst & Young, LLP, 2000.

Table 12-2 Top Online Retailers

Rank	Company	Projected Buyers (000s)	Overall Reach (%)	Unique Users (000s)	Buy Rate (%)
1	Amazon	1 810	22.1	18 133	10.0
2	Ticketmaster.com	676	7.2	5 916	11.4
3	Barnesandnoble.com	338	7.2	5 893	5.7
4	Buy.com	310	4.1	3 334	9.3
5	Drugstore.com	293	2.5	2 030	14.4
6	Real.com	223	15.7	12 899	1.7
7	JCPenney.com	218	3.0	2 466	8.9
8	Sears.com	207	3.8	3 093	6.7
9	Pets.com	196	2.5	2 059	9.5
10	CDNow.com	191	7.1	5 829	3.3

Source: PC Data Online (www.pcdataonline.com), July 2000.

Note: These are monthly rankings, which can change each month.

Buy rate refers to the number of users who are converted to actual buyers.

Major Players

Data on online retail sales confirms Amazon as the leading e-tailer. Amazon is in a category of its own, with the largest reach and three times the projected buyers of the next firm. Among the top ten e-tailers (see Table 12-2) are two old players—Sears and JC Penney. Sears made a smooth transition online because of the infrastructure it had for its catalogue business. JC Penney was among the earliest entrants online and has been credited with innovations in online advertising.

As traditional retailers like Sears, Wal-Mart, and Kmart aggressively pursue their online presence while leveraging their established brand names, the e-tailer rankings may change. Some experts suggest that as more women and middle-income consumers go online, they are likely to gravitate towards the traditional and well-known names. Kmart has wisely invested in a free Internet service provider to attract the next wave of online consumers, who are likely to be from slightly lower income groups than the present online demographics.

Some Internet companies have been able to establish a global presence within a few short years. Yahoo! and Amazon are among the top-rated sites in several countries (see Table 12-3). Even though these companies do not have the long history of the traditional retailers, these are now global brands.

Revisiting Consumer Behaviour

Consumers go online for a variety of reasons. E-mail, information search, chat, downloading music or software, playing games, shopping, and reading news are some of the activities

Table 12-3 **Popular Sites on the Internet**

Rank	US	Canada	Australia	UK	Italy	France
1	eBay	eBay	Amazon	Amazon	Virgilio	Yahoo!
2	Amazon	Amazon	Common-Wealth Securities	QXL	Amazon, CHL	Amazon
3	Yahoo!	Chapters	Yahoo!	Yahoo!	Yahoo!	AltaVista

Source: Global Internet Retailing Report, Ernst & Young, LLP, 2000.

consumers perform on the Internet. E-tailers must understand why consumers shop online and how that experience can be made very satisfying for them. They also must understand the perceptions of non-adopters. Why are some consumers, even if they have access to the Internet, not shopping online? How can these consumers be encouraged to shop online?

Reasons for Shopping Online

Online shopping is attractive for a number of reasons. It compares favourably with bricks-and-mortar and catalogue shopping on several important decision criteria (see Table 12-4). Let's look at some of these reasons now.

Convenience. A primary reason for shopping online is that store hours are 24 hours a day, 365 days a year, and customers can shop from the convenience of their own homes. A mouse click can take you from one online store to another. Adding to the convenience is home delivery (see iMarket Demo 12-1).

Selection. A greater variety of products are available on the Internet than in any one single store or mall. Rare items and foreign-made products can be purchased easily, and vendors selling specialty or niche market products have access to bigger markets now.

Comparisons. It is easy to compare prices online. Comparison shopping agents such as mySimon, BigCompare, ValueFind, and BottomDollar make product and feature comparisons

Table 12-4 **Comparison of Shopping Channels**

Criteria	Internet	Catalogue	Stores
Most competitive prices	21%	10%	13%
One-stop shopping	12%	7%	13%
Convenience (24/7, shop from home, etc.)	59%	41%	12%
Saves time	62%	33%	3%

Source: Andersen Consulting (www.andersenconsulting.com).

iMarket Demo 12-1 Online Grocers

This may be a reflection of the fact that this is a wealthy society where there is "time poverty." Most families are two-income families. Even in times of prosperity, people are working longer hours, according to statistics. Home delivery of groceries seems like the perfect remedy for a task that many hate to do—the weekly trip to the grocery store. The concept is simple. For a few extra dollars, groceries ordered via the Internet are delivered to your home. The consumer can now spend the time saved on more important things than a mundane trip to a grocery store.

Market penetration (spending on online groceries versus total groceries) remains minuscule. It is such a tiny proportion that big grocery chains like Safeway have not bothered to have a presence in this space. Matt Meehan, a grocery industry expert, says, "The value proposition for the consumers just isn't there." The firms who have made an entry into this space are betting that even if home shopping captures 15 percent of grocery shopping, that can lead to a $80 billion industry.

That may explain why the online grocery business has become quite competitive in a few short years. The key players include Webvan, HomeGrocer (now part of Webvan), Peapod (the first to go online), NetGrocer, Priceline, and Streamline. There are also several smaller and regional online groceries.

The business models tend to vary greatly. While Webvan and HomeGrocer try to deliver everything that one can find in a bricks-and-mortar grocery store, NetGrocer focuses on non-perishable items. HomeGrocer and Webvan have invested heavily in big state-of-the-art warehouses and fulfillment systems. Peapod relied on grocery stores initially, but has now invested in warehouses. Priceline, as in other categories, allows consumers to "name their price" and gets regular grocery stores to bid. When a store accepts

Exhibit 12-2 HomeGrocer's Online Grocery Store

Source: www.homegrocer.com.

the bid, the consumer can go to the participating store to purchase the items.

The online grocery industry has several challenges it must overcome. First, consumer behaviour when it comes to grocery shopping is fairly set. A behavioural change is required. Will home shopping on a regular, weekly basis appeal to a large enough audience? Second, the infrastructure required to operate in this space is very expensive. Automated warehouses and fulfillment systems do not come cheap. Third, the marketing costs to acquire customers are currently very high. HomeGrocer and Webvan merged recently with the intention of cutting their marketing expenditures. Peapod needed a substantial infusion of cash from the European supermarket heavyweight Royal Ahold to stay afloat. It remains to be seen how many of the online grocery stores will manage to survive.

Sources: "Webvan: Groceries on the Internet," Harvard Business School Case, 9-500-502, May 5, 2000; Tom Monroy (2000), "Online Grocery Shopping: A Way of Life," *Inter@ctive Week*, June 11, 2000.

easier. In the automobile category, sites like Carpoint, Dealernet, Autobytel, and Autoweb allow easy model and feature comparisons.

Price. Consumers perceive online prices to be lower than prices in bricks-and-mortar stores (see Table 12-4). As we saw in Chapter 8, such a perception across all product categories may be unwarranted. It is true, however, that in some areas (such as airline tickets and books) you can find much lower prices on the Internet.

Control. The consumer has greater control over the shopping experience on the Internet. One can shop without being bothered by sales staff. Online browsing, which is somewhat akin to browsing in a physical store, is a consumer-driven process.

There is also another type of control the consumer has on the Internet. In Chapter 8, we saw that auction and aggregate pricing sites are very popular. These sites give the consumer greater control over the final price paid for an item. In the reverse-auction model followed by Priceline, a consumer can name the price and let sellers bid. The consumer can then decide which offer, if any, to choose.

Time Savings. The 1999 holiday shopping season saw the first widespread use of the Internet by shoppers. Many chose to shop online because they did not want to deal with crowded stores and heavy traffic at the height of the holiday shopping frenzy. Whether booking a ticket for an event, purchasing a book, or registering and paying for a course at a university, the Internet saves time.

Reasons for Not Shopping Online

If Internet shopping has so many advantages, why are so few consumers with access to the Internet shopping online? E-tailers must understand the perceptions of non-adopters so that they can address these concerns. As competition online grows, there is a battle to convert casual browsers into shoppers and one-time shoppers into loyal customers. It is, therefore, important that e-tailers understand why the vast majority of consumers still do not shop online. Even among those who have shopped online, only a small percentage actually return. Table 12-5 presents some of the barriers to online purchasing.

Table 12-5 Barriers to Online Purchasing

	US	Canada
Uncomfortable giving credit card information online	50%	72%
Prefer to see product before purchasing	41%	67%
No credit card	37%	27%
Can't get enough information to make decision	22%	13%
Not confident with online merchants	20%	34%
Can't talk to salesperson	17%	36%

Source: "Global Internet Retailing Report," Ernst & Young LLP, 2000.

Trust Issues. We saw in Chapter 3 that trust issues, such as online security and privacy, are major concerns. Safety of credit card and other personal information provided to online vendors is an issue that deters many consumers from purchasing online. Fears regarding security, however, are somewhat exaggerated. Most credit card companies make the cardholder liable for only $50 in the case of a disputed transaction, and some cards even waive that liability. Still, the perception that credit card information transferred via the Internet is not safe continues to persist.

As online retailers attempt to personalize their content and products, personal information about consumer demographics and behaviour will be collected. Many well-known Internet companies, such as DoubleClick, Toysmart (a company partly owned by Disney), and even Amazon, have been in the eye of the privacy storm. Amazon faced the wrath of consumer advocates when it announced that personal customer information will now be made available to third parties as the company deems fit. While there are some widely accepted standards regarding privacy (such as the Privacy Partnership initiative at TRUSTe), there are concerns about how personal information is being collected and used. Chapter 13 will address trust issues in more detail.

Limited Sensory Input. Many consumers are still uneasy with online shopping because they cannot see or touch the product. When buying clothes, most people do like to try them on. While companies like Land's End are trying to mimic the physical world experience through the use of virtual models (see iMarket Demo 12-2) for certain product categories, consumers still have to make decisions based on limited information. Digiscents (www.digitscents.com) tries to bring the sense of smell to Web sites through a device that is attached to consumers' computers.

Fulfillment. Order fulfillment, logistics, and delivery are areas where many online retailers have yet to find consistency in service quality. The 1999 holiday shopping season revealed the poor fulfillment infrastructure at many start-up e-tailers. They were unable to scale up quickly. Even now it is not uncommon to find e-tailers promising delivery in three to four business days, but not meeting that commitment.

iMarket Demo 12-2 It's All About Experience

Customer satisfaction is out. Customer experience is in. At least for now. What exactly is customer experience?

There are different aspects to providing an enjoyable and satisfying online experience. First, there is the Web site design. It must be user-friendly and quick to download, and it must enable the user to find the required information easily and place the order easily. These are usability issues that must be addressed in the site design process.

Reflect.com, a custom beauty products store (backed by Procter & Gamble) requires customers to fill out a multi-screen registration form before they can begin shopping or browsing. A site should welcome visitors— not erect barriers to shopping.

Land's End sells clothes, mainly to women. While women and men have been buying clothes through catalogues for decades, the inability to try the clothes on does complicate the decision process. On their Web site, Land's End allows women to use a virtual model to try clothes on. The model's body and face shape, as well as hairstyle, can be tweaked to resemble the customer's characteristics (see Exhibit 12-3).

Land's End even gives customers the opportunity to shop with a buddy. Two customers from different locations can chat in a window, while shopping at Land's End. They can even drop items into a single shopping basket, just as they would at a bricks-and-mortar department store.

Dell allows customers to personalize the products they buy and also enables them to track the progress from the point of ordering to the point of delivery. Amazon keeps track of purchases made by customers and presents a customized list of recommended books based on previous reading habits.

Customer experience can be enhanced by developing a user-friendly site that offers personalization tools (as Dell and Amazon do), and even gives them a surprise or two (as Land's End does). Experts argue that customer experience is really a strategic issue, not just a Web design or technology issue. It is not about flashy animation or creating a jazzy site. Customers return to sites that give them good products and a good shopping experience. High-end technology is not the answer. Web sites that understand and respond to the customer's thought processes will usually provide a superior customer experience.

Exhibit 12-3 **Personal Model at Land's End**

Source: www.landsend.com.

Sources: "A Deep Understanding of the Customer Experience," *Webword.com*, September 17, 1999 (webword.com/interviews/hurst.html); B.L. Ochman (2000), "Creating Great Customer Experience," *Webreview.com*, June 23, (webreview.com/pub/2000/06/23/feature/index03.html).

In addition to delays, the cost of shipping is another major concern for consumers. A survey by Greenfield Online revealed that 32 percent of consumers surveyed cited high shipping costs as the reason for not shopping online.[7] Often a product may sell at a discount, but when the shipping cost is added in, the consumer may end up paying more than at a local bricks-and-mortar store.

Returns. Difficulty in returning products is a frequently cited reason for consumer dissatisfaction with online retailers. In the Greenfield Online survey, 32 percent of respondents cited the difficulty in returning merchandise as a reason for not shopping online. BizRate.com, a company that measures post-purchase satisfaction with e-tailers, found that in a survey of 9800 consumers, 89 percent said that return policies influence their decision to purchase online.[8] Simply having a return policy may not be enough. Consumer dissatisfaction is also the result of inability to receive a credit (some firms may insist on exchanges only) and a limited time to return the product.

Service. There is overall dissatisfaction with customer service provided by most online retailers. The inability to talk to a salesperson is a concern for some consumers. Older consumers, as well as those who are relatively new to Internet shopping, are more likely to demand a live salesperson.

Planning and Constructing an Online Store

E-tailing has seen a few spectacular failures. Even the most recognized e-tailing brand, Amazon, has not made a profit as of the second quarter of 2000. E-tailers who were once considered category killers, such as CDNow and Peapod, have questionable future prospects. Smaller e-tailers, such as Books.com, have been taken over by larger firms such as Barnes & Noble (www.bn.com). In the first two quarters of 2000, stock valuations of major e-tailers have tumbled dramatically.

All this points to the importance of strategy and good execution. The firms that have succeeded offer lessons for others. In this section, we'll look at the basics of a good online store.

Strategic Considerations

Store vs. Mall. Smaller firms may find it difficult to invest in building a good Web site and in promotional tools that will drive traffic to the site. One option for these firms is to set up shop in an online mall. Many Internet service providers and portal sites now operate online malls. Malls provide the technology required for secure online shopping. Some of them will provide basic Web design or a template that can be used to build a site. The malls will also host the Web site in many cases. The advantage of malls is that for small stores, they may be a good way to attract traffic without having to spend money on promotion. It can also be a way to quickly deploy a site. Malls generally charge a fee for their service.

Having a separate store, however, does have its own advantages. The site need not conform to the sometimes rigid conditions that a mall may impose, and it will not be put in immediate visual proximity with competing stores. Thus, comparisons with other brands will take more effort on the part of consumers. If the company wants to build a strong online brand, then an initial presence in a mall may be not be appropriate.

The online mall vs. the store decision is not an "either-or" decision. Now even bigger brand name stores have a presence in online malls, in addition to operating their own separate store (see "Yahoo! Shopping" in the Yahoo! site). Yahoo! has a co-branded space for its clients, which include famous names such as Macy's and Nordstrom. By registering once with Yahoo!, consumers shop at dozens of stores on the site without the need for separate registration at each store. Stores such as Nordstrom also have their own individual Web sites that consumers can directly access without going through the Yahoo! mall.

The mall gives an additional online presence for an e-tailer who also maintains an independent Web site. The old mantra in retailing—"location, location, location"—is not entirely outdated online. Providing consumers multiple entry points into a store is still very important, so a strategically chosen online mall presence can be a significant advantage in the long run.

Pure-play vs. Bricks-and-Clicks. As we saw in Chapter 11, even pure-play companies are trying to provide consumers with the option of shopping through other channels. Some are going back to print catalogues and toll-free telephone ordering. Others are partnering with or starting their own bricks-and-mortar stores. Online shopping is still minuscule compared to the total size of retailing in North America, and consumers online are not shopping frequently or spending the amount of money that most e-tailers need to break even. A multiple channel strategy, where appropriate, must be seriously considered.

The key issue here is whether the Internet is replacing the existing channels or is an additional channel. A marketer must understand how consumers use the Internet. There is strong evidence that the Internet is being primarily used as an information source. Purchasing online is a secondary and occasional activity for most consumers. If an e-tailer has clicks-and-mortar operations, the Web site could play an informational role, while transactions are completed offline. Those who want to use the Web for direct purchasing will also have that option available.

Partnerships and Alliances. Many e-tailers enter into partnerships with other businesses that offer complementary services, such as fulfillment and delivery, escrow, customization solutions, direct e-marketing solutions (including permission marketing), online content management, customer service, and so on.

Outsourcing jobs that require special expertise can save time and cost. Partners, however, must be carefully chosen. There are many new firms in these supporting service areas, but very few have a proven track record. A customer who is unhappy with the delivery or customer service will most likely express dissatisfaction toward the e-tailer, not the partner who delivered the support service.

Marketing Costs vs. Revenues. Many e-tailers who have expanded too quickly and have failed to manage their growth have fallen by the wayside (recall Boo.com from Chapter 6). It is vital that e-tailers manage their growth. Building traffic, repeat visits, purchases, and repeat purchases are important. Sites that focus on superior customer experience (such as Amazon and Land's End) invest a lot in back-end technology and customer support. It is important to manage the costs carefully. Even if the company is not profitable initially, revenue growth is important.

Marketing and Customer Considerations

Target Market. The store, its contents, merchandize, branding and image, advertising, and pricing will all depend on the target market. The target market must be carefully defined. Some products are more likely to be purchased online than others. First, the marketer must determine whether the product is suitable for online direct selling. Second, the marketer must find out whether the potential target market is already online or will migrate online soon. The size and growth of the market are important considerations even before a firm starts an online store. Third, the marketer must understand the technological sophistication of the potential consumers. The Web site should not be based on technology (such as Flash animation) that most users are unlikely to possess. Finally, the overall image conveyed by the online store will also depend on the target market.

Ashford.com conveys an image of luxury by using appropriate visuals (see Exhibit 12-4). This will appeal to the target market. The "free overnight shipping" is a nice touch that is likely to make the luxury consumer segment feel special.

Product Mix. As in the case of bricks-and-mortar stores, the product mix for an online store must be carefully determined. Online bookstores claim that they carry millions of titles. They do not have each item in inventory, but they should have the ability to get any title quickly from the publisher or wholesaler. The depth and breadth of products to carry must be carefully determined. Amazon offers a wide range of products on its site, from books to health and beauty aids, toys, CDs, and more. Some of these products, such as health and beauty aids, are delivered through Amazon's partner sites (in this case Drugstore.com). In contrast, Barnes&Noble.com (www.bn.com) has a narrower product mix, its main focus being the book business. Recently, however, Barnes&Noble.com entered into joint promotional partnerships with 1800Flowers.com, jcrew.com, and PlanetRx.com.

Customization. Customizability is one of the strengths offered by the Web. Using the Web, consumers can choose what they want. There are many successful examples of customization in a range of categories, including cars (Saturn.com), greeting cards (Hallmark.com), computers (Dell and Gateway), CDs (CDNow), news and content (CNN.com and Yahoo!),

Exhibit 12-4 Ashford.com Features Visuals That Emphasize Brand Image

clothes (IC3D), shoes (Nike), and many others. Amazon tracks a customer's purchases and then provides a customized list of suggested readings when the customer visits again.

Customization not only works in the B2C market, but it can also be effective in business-to-business marketing. Dell offers customized "premier pages" on its site. This is an extranet that is dedicated to each customer, containing details of the client's account.

Interaction. As we have seen in previous chapters, one of the strengths of the Web is its ability to engage the consumer by providing an interactive experience. Interactivity can be achieved in many ways, including online forums, a bulletin board or live chat, and even by using online games. Appropriate interactivity not only brings the site to life—it can also make the consumer experience more enjoyable.

Community. As we saw in Chapter 7, a thriving online community has several benefits. Amazon is not only the largest e-tailer, but is also a vibrant online community. Readers post their reviews on books and others respond to them. By creating consumer-to-consumer interaction, Amazon is increasing the time people spend on their site (known as stickiness). Very few e-tailers have turned their sites into communities, but we do see some community-oriented sites like Yahoo! and iVillage pursuing E-commerce.

Fulfillment. There is evidence that most service failures with e-tailers occur in the fulfillment area. If items delivered do not match the order or if there is a long delay in delivery, consumer dissatisfaction will usually result.

A report by Forrester Research entitled "Mastering Commerce Logistics" provides a grave warning. So far most sites have been selling few products to few customers, with order fulfillment and logistics being done in-house. As E-commerce expands and more consumers join the online market and online stores expand their offerings, a number of problems are likely to arise. Forrester's report suggests that an "expanded selection of products sold online, the need to move a large volume of small parcels, and rising customer expectations—will combine to put new pressures on order fulfillment systems."[9] The Forrester study suggests that companies that put the emphasis on selling, but not fulfillment, will face serious customer retention problems.

In some areas like home grocery delivery, e-tailers promise delivery within a one- or two-hour window. An online grocery store, such as Webvan, has a complex fulfillment task. Quality perceptions regarding perishables like fruits may vary widely. Firms like Webvan must fulfill orders in a fashion that does not degrade service quality or product quality.

Many e-tailers do not have the size to build efficient in-house fulfillment systems and may not be able to afford outsourced solutions. Until an e-tailer reaches a certain size, outsourcing may be an attractive option. FedEx has a logistics division that caters to E-commerce companies. In Canada, the government-owned postal service, Canada Post, has an E-commerce fulfillment service called eParcel (www.canadapost.ca/eparcel/). Other fulfillment specialists offering outsourced solutions include Fingerhut Business Services (www.4fbsi.com/) and Valley Media (www.valley-media.com), which offer fulfillment services for the music and entertainment industry.

Service. Customer service is another area where many e-tailers face criticism. Even when consumers order directly from a site, there may be a need to "talk" to a customer service representative (by phone, e-mail, or live chat). A report by Datamonitor (www.datamonitor.com) found that only 8 percent of the over 60 000 call centres in the United States were Web-enabled. Only 1 percent of Web sites currently offer live customer assistance.[10] According to Forrester Research, nearly two-thirds of shopping carts are abandoned before consumers place the order (for reasons ranging from difficulty in completing the order form, very slow download of pages, or concerns regarding security). Better online customer service should be able to salvage at least some of them. LivePerson.com (www.liveperson.com) offers a Web-based customer service and sales support solution using a real-time chat (see Exhibit 12-5).

Customer support can also be delivered in other ways. The use of a Help or FAQ (frequently asked questions) section can address a lot of customer concerns. If a consumer is unsure about how the shipping is done, when the credit card will be charged, or what happens if one item in a multi-item order in unavailable, the uncertainty could lead to postponement or abandonment of the purchase transaction.

The Help section for eToys provides answers to various questions and also offers "live" toll-free telephone support. As shown in Exhibit 12-6, all the information is neatly arranged in several categories.

Exhibit 12-5 Web-Based Customer Service by LivePerson.com

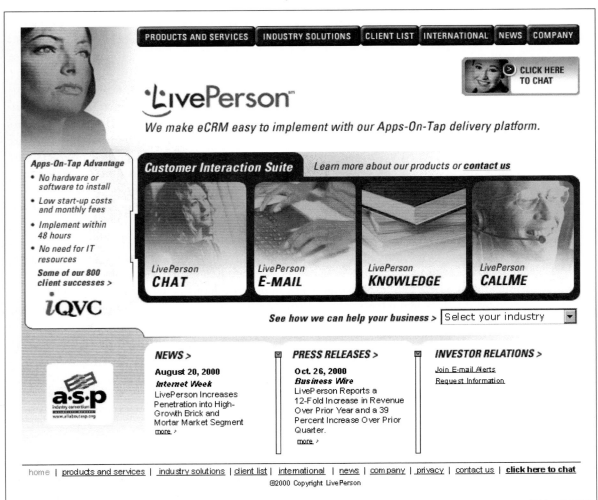

Source: www.liveperson.com.

Exhibit 12-6 Customer Support and Help Online

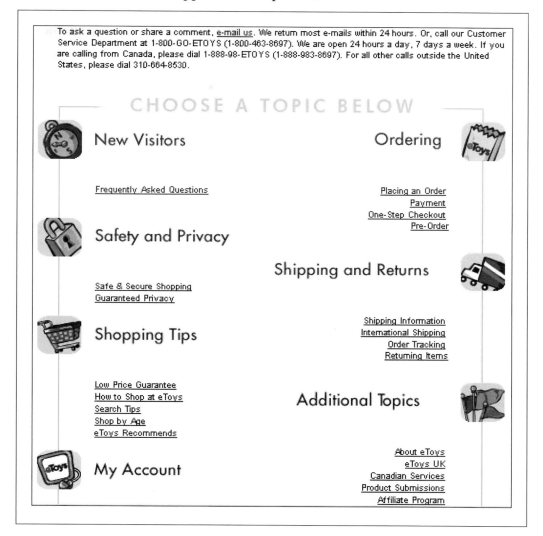

To ask a question or share a comment, e-mail us. We return most e-mails within 24 hours. Or, call our Customer Service Department at 1-800-GO-ETOYS (1-800-463-8697). We are open 24 hours a day, 7 days a week. If you are calling from Canada, please dial 1-888-98-ETOYS (1-888-983-8697). For all other calls outside the United States, please dial 310-664-8530.

CHOOSE A TOPIC BELOW

New Visitors

Frequently Asked Questions

Safety and Privacy

Safe & Secure Shopping
Guaranteed Privacy

Shopping Tips

Low Price Guarantee
How to Shop at eToys
Search Tips
Shop by Age
eToys Recommends

My Account

Ordering

Placing an Order
Payment
One-Step Checkout
Pre-Order

Shipping and Returns

Shipping Information
International Shipping
Order Tracking
Returning Items

Additional Topics

About eToys
eToys UK
Canadian Services
Product Submissions
Affiliate Program

Source: www.etoys.com.

Customer Satisfaction Measurement. Tracking customer satisfaction on an ongoing basis can help e-tailers uncover problem areas before the damage becomes irreparable. Some sites do their own exit surveys (which can be short pop-up surveys) after the ordering process is completed. Most of the well-known e-tailers participate in the BizRate customer rating.

Trust and Process Considerations

Security. Consumer perception regarding security of credit card information is still quite negative (see Table 12-5 on page 302). Security can be compromised due to a variety of reasons, such as Web site break-ins by hackers, denial of service attacks (where a malicious person blocks access to a Web site), human error, and unauthorized access to information (which could lead to modification or abuse of information). Online retailers must address these security concerns directly. The remedies are discussed in detail in Chapter 13.

Privacy. An easy-to-read privacy statement will go a long way in assuaging any misgivings about how a site uses personal information. The policy must adhere to the best standards.

Company Identification. Many small e-tailers provide insufficient or no information about the company, its owners, or where it is located. An "About us" section with information about the company and its history can help create trust. If the company is backed by well-known investors or has reputed senior management staff, customer perceptions are likely to be positive.

Ordering Process. The ordering process must be simple and easy to follow. Some sites ask too many questions at this stage, perhaps due to the belief that this is an opportunity to capture consumer information. A very lengthy questionnaire can lead to the shopping cart being abandoned. Amazon's one-click shopping system allows regular shoppers to purchase as easily as they would at a bricks-and-mortar store.

   Yahoo! uses a "wallet" system to make the ordering process easier. A digital wallet stores credit card and personal information (such as name and address). It is usually stored securely in the user's own computer. The digital wallet can be activated whenever the consumer wants to fill out an order form. The wallet will automatically fill out the required fields, and there is no need to type information (see wallet.yahoo.com/ for an example).

Payment Options. Providing multiple payment methods can increase the number of purchasers. If a site accepts only one type of credit card, those who do not have that card simply do not have the opportunity to make a purchase. Some sites allow consumers to call a toll-free phone line to give credit card information. Other sites allow credit card information to be faxed. These options can ease the fear that consumers experience with respect to transmitting credit card information over the Internet. At the same time, such manual acceptance of credit card information may require additional staffing.

Shipping Options and Costs. Multiple shipping options with varying shipping costs give the consumer more control over the purchase process. Some consumers may be turned off if the only shipping method is an expensive overnight delivery. The shipping information section should also handle questions like: Is there a shipping charge on each item? Is shipping free if the order exceeds a certain amount? In a multiple item order, how is shipping handled if one item is not in stock? Amazon addresses the last question by stating that only one shipping charge is made, even if several different packages are shipped on different days. In addition to the process, information on shipping costs must be displayed prominently. If consumers are charged hidden costs that will cause ill will.

   As discussed earlier, order fulfillment and delivery continue to be the cause of most consumer complaints against e-tailers. Attention and resources committed to this process issue can pay off in terms of higher customer satisfaction.

Site Design Considerations

Image, Look, and Feel. A site must not only make a good first impression, it must also convey an image that is consistent with the brand. The site must be designed to cater to the widest audience possible. That means using technology that most people are likely to use. The same Web site can look a little different in Netscape and Internet Explorer. The technology used in the site must serve a purpose. A site that is filled with Flash animation or Java applets that increase the download time without any real benefit is unlikely find many repeat visitors.

Navigation and Organization. Amazon allows users to search by product categories, and for books, the user can search by author, title, and subject. When the site design is complex and the navigation scheme is unfriendly, the online store is likely to have a low browser-to-buyer ratio. Making the navigational process simple can enhance the chance that a casual browser will become a paying customer. The menu of choices must be easy to understand, and the site should be organized in a manner that makes information easy to find.

Exploiting the Medium. The Web is unlike any other medium. Information can be presented in a non-linear fashion, and does not necessarily have to flow in a top-down format. Users can click links in the middle of a page, go to another page, and then come back to first page.

The Web enables marketers to provide dynamic pages. Using a technology called Active Server Pages (ASP), pages can be created "on the fly." Rather than downloading static pages, a Web server will construct the page based on the user's search criteria. The Web can also offer interactivity through online forums, chat, bulletin boards, interactive games, and so on. If appropriate, the Web site can include animation, sound, and video to enhance the online experience.

Reliability. A study by Anderson Consulting, which involved over 400 online purchases, found that a quarter of the transactions could not be completed because of the site crashing or being otherwise inaccessible. If a site crashes in the middle of a shopping session, that consumer is less likely to shop at that site in the future. A site crash may have particularly damaging consequences in the case of first-time or inexperienced online shoppers. Ensuring the reliability of the Web server and ensuring that the Web site functions well in different user environments are very important. Many sites now offer a simple HTML version for consumers with a slow Internet connection and a Flash or multimedia site for those with faster connections. A slow download time will drive traffic away.

Five Steps to Effective E-tailing

There are five steps to creating an effective online store. The first is to attract customers to the site. The second is to provide an excellent experience and a highly satisfying product or service. When the first visit occurs, the consumer must be left with a very pleasing experience. The third step is to ensure that people spend more time on the site. As consumers spend more time on a site, they are likely to develop an affinity and become more comfortable with the idea of shopping there. This also means that less time spent at a competitor's site. The fourth step is to ensure that people are not just hanging around in the site, but are actually opening their wallets and making purchases. The last step is to ensure repeat visits and purchases. This is a measure of loyalty. A site with more loyal customers can substantially reduce the marketing costs.

Building Awareness and Traffic

Various advertising and promotional methods described in Chapter 10 can be used to build traffic. Firms that do not have large advertising budgets use banner ad exchanges as well as affiliate programs. Many webmasters will vouch that a top placement in a search engine is more effective than paid online advertising. Most consumers start their Web browsing from a search engine. If a Web site can rank in the top 5 or 10 for important key words that describe the product category, there is a high probability that consumers will find the site. Low-ranking sites are seldom visited.

While mass media advertising and online advertising can bring visitors to a site for the first time, to bring them back, the site must provide interesting content that is frequently updated.

Customer Experience

Good products alone are not sufficient for e-tailing success. **Customer experience** on the site is equally important. A site that is cluttered or poorly organized can lead to a frustrating experience. A site that has too many bells and whistles may download very slowly, which may result in loss of visitors. The process of browsing through the online product catalogue, viewing the presentations (images, animated demonstrations, or multimedia content), and ordering the product must be smooth and easy to accomplish.

Amazon filed a patent for its "one-click" shopping system. This procedure greatly simplifies the ordering process. Other sites require the customer to go through several hoops before the product can be ordered or the order can be confirmed.

Stickiness

Stickiness refers to the ability of a Web site to attract repeat visitors and customers and keep them on that site. Advertising space is still sold mainly on the basis of page views. The number of unique visitors is another metric used to measure the effectiveness of a Web site marketing program. Stickiness adds another dimension by measuring the amount of time users spend at a site. Table 12-6 lists the ten stickiest sites on the Web.

This measure is particularly important in the case of sites that generate revenue through advertising. If consumers spend more time on a site, their exposure to advertising will be

Table 12-6 The Ten Stickiest Sites

Site	Hours per Month
AOL	5.5
eBay	2.0
Gamesville	1.5
Hotmail	1.3
Yahoo!	1.0
MoneyCentral	0.8
Excite	0.6
ESPN	0.5
MSN	0.5
Netscape	0.4

Source: MediaMetrix (as reported in *Internet World*, March 29, 1999).

Note: These figures change monthly.

greater. Sites with higher stickiness can attract more advertising. Stickiness can be created through online communities, interesting and regularly updated content, and the use of engaging and interactive tools.

According to Media Metrix, Amazon attracted 1.1 million Canadian consumers to their site. These consumers saw an average of 6.6 pages and spent 5.4 minutes on the site. Chapters, the leading Canadian online bookstore, attracted 655 000 consumers, who saw on an average 13.3 pages and spent 11.8 minutes on their site. It seems as if Canadian consumers are using Amazon to search for product and price information (such as reviews of books), and are then shopping at Chapters.ca.[11] Stickiness alone is not sufficient. E-tailers must ensure that time on their site also eventually translates to money spent at the site.

Buy Rate

Buy rate measures the browsers-to-buyers ratio (recall Table 12-2 on page 298). A low buy rate means that only a small proportion of visitors are actually buying products on that site. Amazon has a low, but higher-than-average, buy rate of about 10 percent. Drugstore.com, which attracts far fewer unique visitors than Amazon, has an even higher buy rate of over 14 percent. There are no clear-cut rules as to what the appropriate conversion rate should be, but obviously marketers should aim to do better than their competitors.

The buy rate can also be seen in terms of "monetizing the traffic." In the early of days of E-commerce, sites would declare success based on hits and number of visitors. Now the emphasis is on financial performance. Even Amazon is able to monetize only 10 percent of its traffic. The challenge is to increase this number to a higher level.

Retention and Loyalty

Customer **loyalty** is a concept that bears some relation to stickiness, but is distinct. Measured in repeat purchases and referrals, loyalty is seen as the key driver of profitability for online businesses. While stickiness looks at repeated visits and time spent, loyalty measures repeated purchasing behaviour. Barnes&Noble.com claims in a press release on its fourth-quarter performance in 1999 that repeat purchases rose from 52 percent in 1998 to 66 percent in 1999. Not surprisingly, during the same period the company saw a decline in marketing costs (as a percentage of sales) from 99 percent to just 38 percent.

Superior product, better-than-expected service, competitive price, efficient order processing and fulfillment, and excellent complaint and returns handling procedures are some of the essential ingredients to building a loyal customer base. E-tailers have not found it easy to develop loyalty. Statistics show that the majority of online customers never return to make a second purchase from the same site.

The five steps described in this section are not necessarily sequential. They may have to be pursued concurrently. Needless to say, other areas like branding and a multi-channel strategy (where the Internet is combined with other channels such as catalogue or bricks-and-mortar stores) are important considerations as well.

Summary

Online retailing is the most visible part of the Internet and E-commerce to the average consumer. There has been a great deal of mass media coverage on some of the big-name e-tailers, as well as the impact of online shopping during the holiday season in 1999.

While consumer spending online is increasing in many categories, business-to-consumer E-commerce has been overshadowed by business-to-business E-commerce. The former is minuscule compared to the latter. Online retailing is currently at less than one percent of total retailing. While consumers like the convenience, choice, and control with online shopping, there are still a number of barriers to the adoption of online shopping. Security and privacy concerns are the most commonly cited barriers.

Marketers must always keep the intended audience in mind when developing an online store. The product mix must suit the intended audience. Customization, interaction, and community can enhance the online experience for customers, and key areas of service failures such as fulfillment and customer support must be addressed. Integrating back-end systems (such as inventory and customer accounts) with the order-processing system will help to make this process easy and seamless.

Once the marketing issues are addressed, the e-tailer must address Web site design issues and methods of enhancing trust and consumer confidence. The site should focus on superior customer experience, but not use high-end technology without any real purpose. Security and privacy issues must be addressed directly and forthrightly.

It is not sufficient to attract traffic to the site. The challenges most e-tailers face today are finding ways of keeping the customers on the site (stickiness) and converting browsers into buyers. The high stock valuations that most pure-play e-tailers had in 1999 may be over permanently. As investors focus on profits, they may not really see a difference between an e-tailer and a bricks-and-mortar store. E-tailers have to find ways to deliver results, not just in terms of revenue, but also profits.

Key Terms

Buy rate, 313	Fulfillment, 302	Navigation, 311
Customer experience, 312	Loyalty, 313	Stickiness, 312

Questions and Exercises

Review Questions

1. What are the main reasons that motivate consumers to shop online?
2. What are the major barriers to online shopping?
3. What is the buy rate?
4. Define the term "customer experience."
5. When a site is being designed, what are the important considerations in "navigation and organization"?
6. Why is it important for e-tailers to build customer trust? What are two or three ways in which trust can be developed?
7. What are the five steps to developing a successful online store?

Discussion Questions

1. Online shopping offers many benefits. Why are so few consumers shopping online? What can e-tailers do (individually and collectively) to increase online shopping?
2. In Table 12-2 (page 298), we see Real.com with over 12 000 unique visitors but a very low buy rate, whereas Drugstore.com has one-sixth the number of visitors as Real, but a buy rate that is over seven times higher. How can you

explain these numbers? What are the factors that contribute to the buy rate? How do you think the buy rate of e-tailers compares with buy rates of bricks-and-mortar stores?

3. What are the essential ingredients to building a successful online store? Discuss strategic issues, site design issues, and tactical issues separately. Provide real examples to substantiate your points.

Internet Exercises

1. Compare Amazon.com with Barnes&Noble.com (www.bn.com) and Chapters.ca (www.chapters.ca). How is the ordering process different in each store? Compare the stores on important attributes discussed in this chapter—look and feel, navigation, security and privacy policy, product mix and selection, special features, and overall user experience.

2. Visit HomeGrocer.com. Explore the site. What are the strengths and weaknesses of this site?

3. Visit the following sites: Sotheby's (www.sothebys.com), Wal-Mart (www.wal-mart.com), Banana Republic (www.bananarepublic.com), and Avon (www.avon.com). Given what you know about the general image of these brands/stores, how are the e-tail operations complementing their operations in their traditional channels? Do you find any differences between online and offline operations in terms of brand image, target market, merchandise, or other attributes?

Chapter 13

Security, Privacy, and Legal Issues

Learning Objectives

After completing this chapter, you will:

- Understand the key issues in establishing online security and privacy policies.
- Appreciate the legal and regulatory challenges presented by the Internet.
- Understand the importance of gaining consumer trust on the Internet, as well as the elements necessary to building consumer trust online.
- Be able to analyze online companies and recommend trust-building strategies, using the proposed consumer trust framework in the chapter.

Governments, businesses, and consumers are worried about crime online or e-crime as some would like to call it. While the Internet enables the formation of communities of consumers, it also enables hate-mongers and terrorists to connect with each other. There are fly-by-night operators whose aim to commit credit card fraud. Then there are those who simply like to cause misery to others by sending virus programs via e-mail, breaking into computer systems, or simply shutting off access to a company's Web site. Governments are worried about espionage online. These are just a sampling of criminal activities online.

To protect citizens and businesses, governments and law enforcement authorities are gearing up to tackle crime on the Internet. Businesses are taking their own steps to address online security issues. The FBI in the United States, the Royal Canadian Mounted Police (RCMP) in Canada, and Scotland Yard in the United Kingdom have all devoted resources to tackling cyber crime. In particular, the FBI has created the Internet Fraud Complaint Center (IFCC).

Some of the law enforcement initiatives have come under heavy criticism from privacy and free speech advocates. One such controversial program is the FBI's Carnivore (www.fbi.gov/programs/carnivore/carnivore.htm). There are those who believe that such surveillance is necessary to prevent criminal behaviour, but there are also those who believe that monitoring online activity is an invasion of privacy and that such powers could be abused.

The FBI itself justifies this program by saying that "the ability of law enforcement agencies to conduct lawful electronic surveillance of the communications of its criminal subjects represents one of the most important capabilities for acquiring evidence to prevent serious criminal behavior." If a case is brought to trail, the FBI can then present hard facts as opposed to conjectures.

When criminal activity is suspected, the FBI will get a court order to undertake online surveillance through Carnivore. It will then seek the cooperation of the Internet service provider. The portion of the traffic or data that emanates from a specific source, where criminal activity is suspected, will be copied and sent to the Carnivore program. Here a filter will be used to sort out the illegal activity from legal activity.

Such surveillance, similar to phone tapping, raises concerns in many quarters. There has been a US Congressional hearing on this subject, and watchdog organizations like the Electronic Privacy Information Center (www.epic.org) and the Center for Technology and Democracy (www.cdt.org) are actively involved in monitoring the development and use of this technology. Internet service providers are also concerned about the use of Carnivore. Veteran users of the Internet are concerned that the free and unmonitored nature of the Internet will be lost if such government surveillance is allowed.

Business losses due to criminal activity can be staggering. Recently, hackers stole source codes for software products under development at Microsoft, which could prove to be very costly to the company. One could argue that the proper role for law enforcement agencies is to help in the prevention of such crimes and the capture of these criminals.

It is not just the law enforcement agencies that may be watching online behaviour. Employee monitoring of e-mails and Web surfing is becoming common. Products like ProxyReport (netrics.com/ProxyReport/index.html) and Stealth Activity Recorder & Reporter (STARR) (www.opus.com) can monitor employee Internet surfing behaviour and provide reports. Many companies are concerned about unproductive use of time on the Internet, as well as the possibility that employees are sharing company secrets with competitors through the Internet. Still, businesses are realizing that implementation of such surveillance devices can lead to problems. So far, there is no universal requirement for companies monitoring employees to notify their employees. Courts, however, have upheld the right of companies to monitor usage of their computer equipment.

Companies are also setting up filtering programs that will prevent employees from viewing certain types of sites. Privacy advocates are opposed to such monitoring, and organizations like Electronic Frontier Canada (www.efc.ca) have lobbied against the use of such technologies. The Child Online Protection Act in the United States, which sought to impose Internet filters on publicly funded institutions such as libraries, also drew protests from civil liberties groups opposed to censorship on the Internet.

Businesses, it seems, can make legitimate claims for monitoring some of their employee behaviour online. The limits of the laws have not been fully tested in this regard. Crime prevention also requires authorized monitoring of suspicious persons. The question is: When will such surveillance be a threat to individual privacy for law-abiding citizens? And to what extent should each of us give up some privacy so that criminal activity or harmful acts online can be curbed?

Sources: Carnivore: Diagnostic Tool, www.fbi.gov; Margaret Johnston, "FBI Still Hunting With Carnivore," *IDG News Service*, October 20, 2000; Steve Bellovin and Matt Blaze (2000), "Open Internet Wiretapping" (www.crypto.com/papers/opentap.html), July 19, 2000; "Right to Monitor Employee E-Mail Upheld" (www.channel2000.com), October 12, 1999; Jennifer Ditchburn (1999), "Canadian Furor Over Net Filters," *Wired* (www.wired.com/news/print/0,1294,20391,00.html), June 24, 1999.

Introduction

In Vignette 13 we saw how security and privacy issues can be intertwined, and emphasis on security can sometimes come at the cost of some privacy. However, without the guarantee of a high level of security, businesses could not function effectively online, and consumers and businesses would not have the confidence to engage in online transactions. The growth of commerce on the Internet can be greatly deterred by concerns about security and consumer privacy.

The existence of proper security systems, privacy protection, and legal framework can build trust and confidence for both consumers and businesses. These three factors can be seen as enablers of E-commerce. This chapter will provide a non-technical introduction to each of these factors, and then address important managerial issues. These issues do not just concern the technical people within organizations. A high level of consumer trust in E-commerce and e-tailers will translate to faster adoption of online shopping and more spending online. Hence, it is vital that marketers also understand the factors that build consumer confidence and trust online.

Security Online

Consumer Perception

As we saw in Chapter 3, consumer concern with online security of financial and personal information is a major stumbling block to the adoption of online purchasing. This is true for both business-to-business and business-to-consumer purchasing. In fact, security concerns appear to be the strongest predictor of online purchasing.[1]

Consumer adoption of online purchasing is still in the growth stage. Yet, while the number of online shoppers is growing, only about 40 percent of those online can be classified as online shoppers. Among those, very few are regular shoppers. A typical online purchase is still usually for an item below $100. Several studies have indicated that consumer perception about online security of credit card information is still quite negative.

While credit card companies maintain that giving a credit card to a waiter in a restaurant (in a face-to-face transaction) is riskier than giving one's credit card number online to a reputable company, consumer perception is quite different. One study reported that 53 percent of Americans were concerned with online security.[2] In the UK, 55 percent of those who are online consider Internet shopping to be risky.[3] In Canada, security and privacy concerns worry almost 73 percent of those who are online.[4] There is also some indication that more women are holding back on online shopping because of security concerns.[5]

While it is true that the percentage of consumers who are uncomfortable with online security is declining, the percentages are still quite high. Credit card issuing companies like Visa and MasterCard play down the significance of online security risks. They claim that fraud rates are no higher in online transactions than in face-to-face transactions. A report by Ernst & Young on online retailing suggests that credit card security is a non-issue as far as retailers are concerned.[6] Technology exists today that can make online transactions as safe as face-to-face transactions. The problem, according to this report, is consumer misperception.[7] That means marketers must educate consumers to change their negative attitudes.

Impact on Businesses

Negative consumer attitudes and lack of trust in Web sites can hurt online companies and slow the growth of E-commerce. On the one hand, businesses must take steps to correct consumer misperceptions, and on the other hand, they must address real security threats.

Businesses can potentially suffer from different forms of online security violations. Consumers, however, are primarily concerned with the safety of the credit card information they provide to Web sites. According to Gartner Group, small and medium-sized enterprises (SMEs) are the most vulnerable to attacks on their computer systems via the Internet.[8] Most companies that are affected by an online security breach through a virus, Web site hacking, or distributed denial of service attacks (DDOS), which prevents Internet users from accessing a Web site, simply react to the event rather than proactively managing the computer network security (see Table 13-1 for a list of online crimes). This is especially true in the case of SMEs, which cannot afford the resources and personnel needed to establish stringent security systems.[9]

Security breaches cost businesses dearly. When there is a credit card fraud, it is the merchant who pays for it. Consumer liability is usually capped at $50 and in some cases even that deductible is waived. Other forms of online security breaches, such as virus attacks, hacking, or breaking into a company Web site also cost businesses a great deal.

While credit card companies maintain that there is no significant difference between offline and online fraud rates, a survey by the Gartner Group found that 12 times more fraud exists on Internet transactions. Credit card issuing companies are charging e-tailers discount rates that are 66 percent higher than traditional retailer fees.[10] A study by *Information Week* estimates that the cost of virus attacks and other disruption caused by online vandalism or crime will be a staggering $1.5 trillion worldwide in the year 2000. The cost for US businesses alone is estimated at $266 billion or 2.5 percent of that nation's GDP.[11]

Businesses online pay a double penalty. If consumers fear there is a lack of online security, they are less likely to shop online. At the same time, businesses pay a heavy price each time a security breach is committed. They also have to invest in security systems (hardware and software) and have the personnel to handle online security.

Businesses must take proactive measures to ensure security of the networks, Web sites, and customer information. In addition, they must convince consumers that online shopping is safe.

Table 13-1 A Sample of E-Crimes

- Impersonation: the use of another person's identity or e-mail
- E-mail pyramid schemes
- Hacker "sniffs" credit card or other personal information and steals such information
- Hacker vandalizes a site by breaking in and changing the information on the site
- Hacker directs users to another site when they type the URL
- Denial of service attack, which prevents access to the site
- Sending viruses that can destroy information on computer networks
- Buyer falsely claims an item is undelivered
- Seller exaggerates the quality of a product, and delivers a substandard item in an auction
- Seller engages in "shilling," where seller bids on his or her own items to drive up the price
- Electronic gambling and lottery frauds
- Posting false and damaging information about a company on bulletin boards

Principles of Online and Transaction Security

Corporate networks connected to the Internet must adhere to strict standards of security. Security risks can take many forms, including virus attacks, denial of service attacks, theft of information stored (such as credit card numbers), and so on. Security systems are comprised of hardware and software designed to prevent such events. A good security system must conform to several basic concepts in security:[12]

- *Privacy*. A secure Internet site must be able to guarantee privacy, which means shielding information from those who are not supposed to have access to it. Personal information about consumers stored in computers must be shielded from unauthorized access.
- *Authenticity*. Authentication is the process of verifying the true sender of the information and also ensuring that the information itself has not been altered.
- *Integrity*. This requires the assurance that information that is transmitted or stored (such as charges on credit card numbers) is not tampered with.
- *Availability*. The Web site and communication services should be available when required and the availability should be predictable. Denial of service attacks, which are aimed at shutting down access to a site, for instance, violate the principle of availability.
- *Blocking*. A site should have the ability block unwanted intrusions (such as denial of service attacks or viruses).
- *Confidentiality*. The system should ensure that information communicated and stored is kept private and can be revealed only to people on an approved access list.
- *Identification*. When required, the system must be capable of verifying that the sender of the message is actually who he or she claims to be.

Security systems must not only protect the corporate networks and Web servers from external attacks, but they must also ensure that data transmitted via the Internet is secure. While it is virtually impossible to divert credit card or other data while in transmission from a consumer to an e-tailer's site, there have been many cases of credit card information being stolen from the computer systems of e-tailers. In March 2000, MSNBC reported that there was a theft of information on 485 000 credit cards from an E-commerce site. The thief apparently stored the massive database secretly in a US government agency Web site.[13] Even though there was no evidence of any actual fraudulent transactions using any of the credit card information, the magnitude of the theft does raise questions about the security systems on E-commerce sites.

Firewall and Network Security

A **firewall** is software and/or hardware that stands between a company's internal computer network and the external network or the Internet.[14] Employees inside the organization usually get full access to the Internet, whereas anyone from outside wishing to access the company's Web site must pass through the firewall. A firewall can limit access to outsiders by requiring user name and password authentication or by Internet IP address or domain name. For instance, access can be denied to anyone with a ".edu" domain name, which is used by universities and educational institutions. In addition to blocking unwanted traffic, firewalls also play the function of providing metered and audited access to the Internet for employees.

While firewalls can protect against external intrusion, they cannot prevent vital information leaking to competitors in other forms. An employee who wants to pass on critical information to a competitor can still do so using fax, telephone, or other forms of communication. Vandals and hackers do find new ways to break into networks that are protected by a firewall. Finally, firewalls do not provide adequate safety against virus attacks, which are primarily sent through e-mail messages. Experts suggest using a separate virus-scanning program throughout the corporate network, rather than using the firewall to detect viruses.

There are different types of firewalls that offer varying levels of security and also impose varying levels of constraints on users. Important managerial considerations involved in the implementation of firewalls include:[15]

- *Objective of the firewall*. Is it intended to prevent unauthorized entry or provide monitored access to people inside the organization?
- *Level of risk and security*. The organization must decide what level of risk is acceptable and what level of security is required. The more complicated the system, the more expensive it is likely to be.
- *Cost*. There are basic personal firewall software applications priced below $50. High-end firewalls used by large organizations can cost upwards of $100 000 with overheads.
- *Technology*. There are many different types of firewalls, each with its own strengths and weaknesses. A suitable technology must be decided.
- *Outsourcing*. Management must also decide whether to outsource computer network security or to establish it and manage it from within.

There are different types of firewall systems. The most common ones are these:

- *Packet filter*. On the Internet, messages (e-mail, HTML files, etc.) are divided into packets and are individually transmitted. Each packet can follow a different (or more efficient) route to the destination, where individual packets are reassembled and presented as a complete message. Packet filter firewalls examine each packet entering or leaving the network, and they either accept or reject the packet based on user-defined rules. A device called a router (from companies like Cisco) is used in the packet filtering process. Packet filtering is fairly effective and transparent to users. However, hackers have been known to have circumvented such filters.

- *Proxy servers and application gateways.* Proxy servers are computers that sit between the Internet and the company's internal network. They monitor and can intercept all incoming and outgoing traffic. Both incoming and outgoing traffic must talk to the proxy server, which in turn will communicate with the appropriate destination. A proxy server could block employees' access to certain Web sites. Application gateways are used in conjunction with proxy servers. They apply security mechanisms to specific applications, such as such as FTP (file transfer), SMTP (e-mail), and telnet (remote login) servers. An outsider wishing to access a specific application server must pass through the application gateway, which may reject unauthorized traffic.

Encryption and Transaction Security

Firewalls provide security to the corporate network. E-commerce also requires security at the transaction level. Transaction processing occurs when consumers fill out online forms, such as order forms. It is important to ensure the integrity, authenticity, privacy, and confidentiality of consumer data.

Even though it is virtually impossible to intercept credit card information transmitted via the Internet, consumer perception towards online transaction security is still quite negative. Even businesses are concerned about the security of financial and other confidential data sent through the Internet.[16] Transaction security is accomplished through the use of encryption.

Encryption. In very basic terms, **encryption** refers to the scrambling or disguising of data at the sender's end and the descrambling of the same data at the receiver's end. Thus, while the data is in transmission via the Internet, even if it is intercepted, it cannot be read. The unencrypted message is referred to as plain text and the encrypted message as cipher text. There are two types of encryption commonly used—**symmetric-key** and **public-key** encryption. A key is a combination of numbers, letters, and symbols, often running to several lines, used in transforming plain text into cipher text.

In symmetric-key encryption, the sender and receiver of the information use the same key. The message is encrypted using this key or code and sent to the receiver, who then decrypts the message using the same key. In this system, both the sender and receiver have access to the same key, which can be used to lock and unlock the message. While the message itself can travel safely, the limitation of symmetric-key encryption is that the sender and receiver must agree on a key without anyone else finding out about it. This method of encryption can work in a small network (such as a corporate network), but when the parties are unknown to each other (such as a customer and a merchant) exchanging the key information presents a challenge. Symmetric-key encryption ensures the privacy of information, but it fails to meet two other important requirements of security online—identification and authentication.

Public-key encryption requires two keys, a private and a public key. Each individual and business will have two keys. If Sarah wants to send a message to Bob, she will use Bob's public key (which is known to everyone) to encrypt the message. Upon receiving the message, Bob will use his private key (which only he knows and has access) to decrypt the message.

RSA, named after its inventors (Rivest, Shamir, and Adleman), is a public-key algorithm that involves the product of two very large prime numbers. The size of the integers, represented as bits, indicates the difficulty of breaking the key or code. For example, a 128-bit algorithm provides greater security than a 40-bit algorithm. The US government controls the exportation of the 128-bit encryption algorithm. Pretty Good Privacy (PGP) is a free and publicly available encryption program that uses public-key cryptography to authenticate messages and maintain confidentiality (see www.pgp.com).

Digital Signature. Similar to a written signature, a **digital signature** is supposed to verify the identity of the person sending a message or placing an order online. If each individual has a uniquely identifiable signature, then such a signature applied to confidential messages should provide an additional layer of security. Digital signatures are based on the private key that is unique to each individual. Digital signatures are created by applying a hashing algorithm to the message. This creates an abbreviated version of the message called the message digest. The message digest is then encrypted using a private key. Only by using that individual's public key can digital signatures be decrypted.

In the summer of 2000, US President Bill Clinton signed a bill into law using a digital signature. This gesture, however, does not mean that the use of digital signatures will become pervasive anytime soon. Experts believe that consumers may first start using digital signatures for big-ticket items. Still, widespread usage of digital signatures may take another five or more years.[17]

Digital Certificates. Encryption using a public key provides confidentiality and privacy. It does not, however, provide authentication confirming that the sender of the message (or the receiver) is who he or she claims to be. If a stolen credit card is used online, there must be a way to detect that. **Digital IDs** or **certificates** are used for such authentication.

A third party called a certificate authority (CA) issues digital certificates (see Table 13-2). Businesses and individuals can acquire a digital certificate from a CA. A digital certificate is usually a small file containing the name and identification information of the certificate holder, the public key of the sender, the name of the CA, and the period of validity of the certificate. When a consumer and a merchant conduct a transaction through the Internet, the use of digital certificates allows both parties to verify each other's identity through a trusted third party.

An individual wishing to send an encrypted message must apply for a digital certificate from a CA. The CA issues an encrypted digital certificate containing identification information and the applicant's public key. In order for digital certificates to be used, the CA's own

---

Table 13-2 Digital Certification Authorities

Verisign (www.verisign.com)

Thwate Consulting (www.thwate.com)

Società per i Servizi Bancari—SSB S.p.A. (www.ssb.net)

Entrust (www.entrust.com)

Internet Publishing Services (www.ips.es)

BelSign (www.belsign.be)

public key must be widely available in different media, including the Internet. The sender attaches the digital certificate to the message (e-mail programs and Web browsers will do this automatically).

The recipient of the message will first use the CA's public key to decode the digital certificate. This will allow the recipient to verify that the certificate was indeed issued by the CA. The recipient can then retrieve the sender's public key and identification information, which is contained in the certificate.

Digital certificates are critical for the growth of E-commerce since they provide independent third-party authentication of messages on the Internet. Verisign is the best-known certification authority. Its certificates appear on virtually every E-commerce server on the Internet. Verisign and other CAs charge a fee for issuing certificates. Verisign charges $14.95 for a personal certificate for a year, and a much higher fee for business certificates. Other organizations, including Thwate, provide free personal certificates to individuals.

Secure Sockets Layer (SSL). SSL, which was developed by Netscape and incorporated into its popular Web browser, is the most commonly used method of implementing encryption. SSL establishes a secure connection between a browser (the consumer end) and the server (the merchant end), and it encrypts HTTP (hypertext transport protocol) transmissions, which are used in sending and downloading Web pages. SSL authenticates the browser and server, but it does not authenticate the two parties at either end.

When a consumer fills out personal information in an online order form, typically the connection between the browser (consumer) and the server (merchant) will be secured by SSL. This will be denoted by a closed "lock" in the Netscape browser (see the security icons in Exhibit 13-1).

Secure Electronic Transaction (SET). To overcome the main disadvantage of SSL, which is lack of authentication of parties, Visa and MasterCard joined forces to create a new protocol for securing online transactions. Several technology companies, including Microsoft and IBM, also collaborated in this effort. SSL makes it virtually impossible to intercept information travelling on the Internet by using encryption. SET, on the other hand, goes a step beyond and authenticates the identity of the parties.

Exhibit 13-1 Secure vs. Insecure Internet Connection

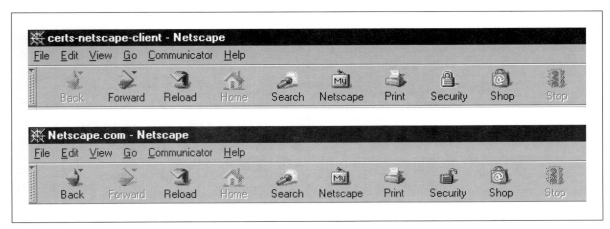

SET relies on cryptography and digital certificates to ensure message confidentiality and security. "Message data is encrypted using a randomly generated key that is further encrypted using the recipient's public key. This is referred to as the 'digital envelope' of the message and is sent to the recipient with the encrypted message. The recipient decrypts the digital envelope using a private key and then uses the symmetric key to unlock the original message."[18] SET requires merchants to install specific software. Several companies offer SET-compliant merchant software, including Cybercash, Entrust, Fujitsu, IBM, Verifone, and Verisign. SET allows merchants using their system to display a seal on the site, which it hopes will become a symbol of security in the minds of consumers.

SSL does not require any new technology or software installation, whereas SET is a technology-heavy solution. The additional cost and effort involved in establishing SET has limited its use so far.

Privacy

Security of computer networks and data are not enough to ensure high levels of consumer participation in E-commerce. Consumers are also deeply concerned about their personal privacy online. In areas such as online healthcare, consumers are fearful of sharing personal information.[19]

There are many legitimate uses of personal information, such as personalization of Web services, and consumers are not usually averse to providing personal information for such purposes. A study by Cyber Dialogue (www.cyberdialogue.com) found that more than 80 percent of consumers are willing to provide personal information in exchange for personalized products and services. Consumers also perceive other uses, such as providing personal information for online coupons or incentive programs, as legitimate and beneficial. They are, however, unsure and concerned about how personal information is being used by online companies.[20] Unauthorized of sharing of consumer information with other companies and unauthorized use of consumer information for purposes other than those agreed to by the consumer are the main sources of concern.[21]

Often consumers are unsure of their rights online. Many sites do not provide consumers with the choice of opting in or opting out of a membership or direct mail program. Some of the sites sell consumer e-mail and other personal information to companies that engage in bulk e-mail campaigns. The general consumer distrust with Web sites is exacerbated when reports about companies breaking their own privacy policies are reported.

Well-known companies like DoubleClick and Amazon have been in the news for controversial privacy policies. DoubleClick wanted to match online consumer-tracking data (obtained through cookies) with consumer demographic data from its sister company Abacus Direct (www.abacusdirect.com). Abacus is the largest direct marketing research company in the United States that provides demographic and purchase behaviour data at the household level. DoubleClick's move to link online tracking data (where individual anonymity is still maintained) with offline demographic data would have eliminated user privacy. Adverse negative reaction from consumers has stalled this move by DoubleClick.

Amazon also received some negative press coverage when it announced that it was changing its policy on revealing consumer information to third parties. Previously, Amazon had maintained that personal information and book-buying habits of its patrons would not be revealed to outside companies. On September 3, 2000, Amazon alerted 20 million of its consumers to a "clarification" of its privacy policy.[22] Privacy groups immediately reacted strongly. Amazon defended its policy change by saying that it has strengthened previous loopholes in its privacy policy and has truthfully disclosed the changes to consumers.[23]

Consumer Information as an Asset. There have been numerous high-profile cases involving companies like Amazon, More.com, Toysmart.com (where Disney had an investment), and Living.com. These cases raise an important issue. Is consumer information a corporate asset that can be bought, sold, or transferred to other parties? Who owns this information? Can the company use the information in new ways (beyond what the consumer agreed to), by simply changing its privacy policy, as Amazon did?

Companies that have filed for bankruptcy, such as Toysmart and Living.com, have attempted to sell customer data, as if it was a corporate asset. Many companies, including More.com, are fighting legal battles over alleged misuse of consumer data. Many US state attorneys general have taken pre-emptive measures to protect consumers from loss of privacy.

In the information-driven world of online commerce, marketers would argue that detailed knowledge of their consumers gives them the competitive advantage. It is, hence, an asset that enables them to differentiate themselves from their competitors. The plethora of legal battles suggest that consumer and privacy groups are not likely to buy such arguments easily.

Privacy Policy. These days E-commerce sites routinely display their privacy policies. The policy statements are often several pages long and filled with legal jargon. It is unlikely that many consumers actually read and understand the privacy policies of online stores where they make purchases.

A good privacy policy can offer a company legal protection, when required. If it is written in simple English, it can also help the consumer understand what personal information is being collected, how it is being collected, how it is being used, and what rights the consumer has with respect to the collection or dissemination of personal information.

TRUSTe. One organization that plays an external auditor's role in terms of privacy policy is TRUSTe (www.truste.com). TRUSTe prescribes minimum privacy standards (see Exhibit 13-2) for sites that wish to obtain its seal of approval. Companies that wish to join the TRUSTe program must first develop a privacy policy in line with TRUSTe's guidelines, sign the TRUSTe license agreement, and pay an annual fee. The fee ranges from $299 for companies with revenues below $1 million to $6999 for companies with revenues over $75 million.

The TRUSTe seal is now seen in some of the most popular sites, such as Drugstore.com, eBay, Yahoo!, and E*TRADE. Other leading sites like Amazon and Barnes&Noble.com have so far chosen not to participate in this privacy program.

The TRUSTe seal provides consumers with the assurance that the site adheres to well-accepted principles of privacy and that the site's policy has been vetted by an independent third party. As consumers see the TRUSTe symbol at several popular sites, they may come to expect it at other newer sites.

Better Business Bureau Online (BBBO). Another organization that plays a similar third-party watchdog role is the Better Business Bureau Online (www.bbbonline.com). BBBO operates through its local BBB offices and requires companies to become a member of the local BBB in the city where the company is headquartered. Most consumers are already familiar with the Better Business Bureau in the bricks-and-mortar world. BBBO has a reliability program, a general privacy program, and a special privacy program for children's sites.

Under the reliability program, companies are expected to have a good customer complaint handling record. The privacy program requires companies to spell out their policies

Exhibit 13-2 TRUSTe Minimum Privacy Requirements

- What personal information is being gathered by your site
- Who is collecting the information
- How the information will be used
- With whom the information will be shared with
- The choices available to users regarding collection, use, and distribution of their information: You must offer users an opportunity to opt-out of internal secondary uses as well as third-party distribution for secondary uses.
- The security procedures in place to protect users' collected information from loss misuse, or alteration: If your site collects, uses, or distributes personally identifiable information such as credit card or social security numbers, accepted transmission protocols (e.g. encryption) must be in place.
- How users can update or correct inaccuracies in their pertinent information: Appropriate measures shall be taken to ensure that personal information collected online is accurate, complete, and timely, and that easy-to-use mechanisms are in place for users to verify that inaccuracies have been corrected.

Source: TRUSTe (www.truste.com).

with respect to the collection of personal information, sharing of information with third parties, choice and consent of the consumer (ability to opt-in and opt-out), access and correction (ability of the consumer to correct or change personal information), and details of online security on the site. Details of the privacy seal requirements can be found at www.bbbonline.com/privacy/threshold.asp#2. The kids' privacy seal program goes further and specifies guidelines for companies that target children under the age of 13.

AMA and ESOMAR. Professional bodies, such as the American Marketing Association (AMA) and the worldwide association of market researchers ESOMAR, also provide guidelines to their members with respect to privacy (see Appendices D and E).

Consumer Efforts to Protect Privacy. Consumers must also take sensible measures to protect their privacy online. Giving out one's address or other personal information on bulletin boards or chat forums should be avoided. Parental supervision of children and their online surfing habits is also essential.

Cookies are used by sites to track Web surfing patterns and online shopping sessions to track items purchased (see Chapter 5 for a more detailed discussion). Consumers who do not want authorized sites to track them using cookies can turn off the cookies feature in their Web browser. They can also use other software applications such as Cookie Crusher,

Buzof, Cookie Pal, and PGPCookieCutter to manage or delete cookies, and thus prevent sites from tracking their online behaviour.

Consumers must also make an effort to read the privacy policies and understand how consumer tracking on the Web works. By becoming more knowledgeable, consumers can better protect their privacy.

Global Regulations. Companies that do business online must become aware of privacy policies in different countries. In Europe, governments take a much more proactive role in protecting consumer privacy than in North America. The European Union's Directive on Data Privacy, which came into effect in 1998, ensures uniformity in standards across countries. One of the provisions of the directive is that data about consumers from Europe cannot be sent to any country that has inadequate privacy protection laws. The United States, in particular, was found have inadequate privacy protection. This raises some interesting challenges for American companies that want to do business in Europe. What online data can they collect about consumers? To make online business between the United States and Europe easier, the EU and the American government have agreed to a "**safe harbor**" program. This is a voluntary program where US companies will follow privacy policies that are similar to the EU requirements.[24]

The safe harbor program requires participating companies to fully disclose their consumer data collection procedure and give control to the consumer to modify or delete their personal information maintained by Web sites. Further, if a company shares its consumer data with third parties, then the company must ensure that the third party also offers the same level of privacy protection.

In the United States, the government has encouraged self-regulation on the part of the industry, along with a role for private organizations like BBBOnline and TRUSTe. Meanwhile, European (and to a lesser extent, Asian and Latin American) countries are seeing a greater governmental role.[25]

The Challenges. While TRUSTe and BBBO provide consumers with some assurance that the companies they deal with are using personal information in accordance with stated policies, not every E-commerce site participates in these programs. These programs are voluntary. As we have seen in cases with DoubleClick and Amazon, companies may change their privacy policies, which can be confusing to consumers. Privacy policies are often difficult to comprehend and are written in a legalistic tone. Consumers may not fully understand what they are agreeing to. BBBO requires its members to display their privacy policies in simple English. Some see new legislation as the answer. There are several pending legislations that may provide some protection to consumers. Others argue that self-regulation and voluntary participation in trust-building programs such as TRUSTe and BBBO are the best answers.

Legal and Regulatory Issues

The Internet has tested several existing laws and is forcing lawmakers in many countries to consider new legislation. In this section, we will look at some of the legal and regulatory issues raised by E-commerce.

Contracts

The general rule under English law, followed in many countries, is that "a contract is formed when and where an acceptance of an offer is communicated and received by the offeror."[26]

The Internet offers different ways of communication that can lead to different legal outcomes and even raise doubts about whether a contract has been formed.

A contract has two parts—an offer and an acceptance. But there are still many subtler questions. Does the vendor's Web site constitute an offer? Does clicking on a "buy" button at an e-tail site constitute acceptance of an offer and an agreement to buy? Is a digital signature the equivalent of a handwritten signature for legal purposes? Is a contract signed digitally a legal contract? Courts have accepted e-mail communication as evidence (as in the US Justice Department's anti-trust case against Microsoft). Experts have argued that digital signatures can be forged. The Electronic Signature Act (ESA) passed in the United States defines an e-signature very loosely as any "sound, symbol or process." Thus, even clicking on a "yes" or "accept" button would be sufficient for a person to enter into a contract with another. Groups like the Consumer Project on Technology (<u>www.cptech.org</u>) have criticized the "lax standards" of what constitutes an electronic signature.[27]

Shrink-Wrap vs. Click-Wrap Licences. When a consumer buys a software product, the vendor gives the consumer a licence to use the product according to the prescribed terms of sale. When the consumer breaks the shrink-wrap package, the contract is said to take effect. On the Internet, when downloading software the user may simply be required to click on a button to accept the terms of agreement.

In the United States, the Uniform Computer Information Transactions Act (UCITA) has been adopted by a few states, and applies in the case of products or services that can be delivered electronically (such as software and online games).[28] According to the UCITA, clicking on a button to buy or accept the terms of sale is sufficient to establish a contract. Software companies routinely ask consumers to "accept" or "reject" the terms of sale before allowing them to download their products.

The UCITA has a consumer protection clause including the right to get out of an online contract in the event that the consumer accidentally clicked on a button, and the right to return a software product even if the package has been opened. The UCITA, however, does not require vendors to display their terms of sale and licence agreements before the purchase has been made. In the case of shrink-wrap licences, the consumer cannot even see the contract or the licence until the product is purchased and the package opened. This has led to the criticism that the UCITA is more favourable to vendors than consumers. Some courts have ruled that shrink-wrap licences are unfair to consumers. Recently, however, other courts have upheld shrink-wrap and click-wrap licence agreements.[29] Clearly, this law drastically changes the manner in which a contract is executed.

Jurisdiction

Typically, contracts specify a jurisdiction where the buyer and seller can settle any disputes. When there is a dispute between a buyer and seller, which court should have the jurisdiction to hear the case?

Software companies like Microsoft and Corel choose jurisdictions that are convenient to them or favourable to them. Consumers often have no choice in this matter because the terms of sale are presented in a "take it or leave it" manner. Online transactions can occur between buyers and sellers in different countries.

The Hague Convention on Jurisdiction and Foreign Judgments in Civil and Commercial Matters is in the process of establishing a global treaty that will provide guidance on jurisdiction for business-to-consumer transactions on the Internet (for details see the Hague Conference site at <u>www.hcch.net/e/workprog/jdgm.html</u>). While a draft version of the convention sought to make unilateral jurisdictional declarations by sellers invalid, it is unclear if such consumer protection will receive the support of all parties to the convention. The US government and many E-commerce firms have been supportive of letting sellers determine the jurisdiction. The US government is presently opposed to guaranteeing consumers the right to bring private legal action in their country of residence. For E-commerce to flourish globally, such a global agreement on contract law issues is vital.

International Regulations

We saw earlier that privacy laws vary in Europe and North America. Products or services that are legal in one country may be illegal elsewhere, and international laws regarding who owns or is responsible for content on the Internet can be murky (for example, should Internet service providers be held responsible for pornographic content on Web sites they host?). In Germany, the head of Compuserve's operation in that country was convicted in 1998 for not blocking pornographic content on the Internet.[30] The conviction alarmed many in the Internet community because it made the ISP, and not the individuals posting the offensive material, liable. Later, an appeals court in Germany overturned that verdict. Before companies decide to engage in online sales to foreign customers, they must be fully aware of the laws affecting such international sales. Before expanding operations to foreign countries, something that many "dot-coms" are trying to do, companies must be conversant with local laws.

The wide disparity in laws in different countries could deter the growth of worldwide E-commerce. There are several efforts underway to develop a set of globally acceptable laws and regulations. Organizations such as the Organization of Economic Cooperation and Development (OECD) and the United Nations Commission on International Trade Laws (UNICITRAL) have contributed to the development of global regulations and laws that can ensure the growth of E-commerce worldwide.

UNICITRAL's work has mainly focused on developing policies for cryptography and digital certification. UNICITRAL has also proposed a model law that supports the commercial use of international contracts in electronic commerce. This model law establishes rules for the validation and recognition of contracts established through the use of electronic means. It also "sets standards governing electronic contract performance, defines what constitutes a valid electronic writing and original document, provides for the acceptability of electronic signatures for legal and commercial purposes, and supports the admission of computer evidence in courts and arbitration proceedings."[31]

The OECD has put out policy papers on taxation and the vexing issue of jurisdiction and permanent establishment.[32] For instance, if an online company has Web servers in different countries from which its Web pages are downloaded, the issue of determining the permanent establishment becomes tricky. (Note that many companies do use multiple Web servers in different countries to ensure faster downloading of pages.) Permanent establishment is critical for determining taxation. In which country or countries should such a company pay taxes? Permanent establishment also becomes an issue with respect to ISPs who host the Web sites of many companies on their servers, but do not actually operate those businesses.

Businesses are not waiting for lawmakers in different countries to come to a consensus. The Global Business Dialogue on Electronic Commerce, or GBDe (www.gbde.org), a group made up representatives from over 200 of the leading global E-commerce companies, focuses on a self-regulatory approach that would make global E-commerce easier. The GBDe also lobbies governments to reach a consensus on issues such as consumer confidence, privacy protection, security, and intellectual property protection.

Intellectual Property and Copyright

Digital products, such as music, photographs, videos, digital art, software, and textual content, can be copied and distributed easily via the Internet. The Napster case (see iMarket Demo 13-1) is seen as a challenge to the copyright laws. Businesses and artists are concerned that unlawful reproduction and distribution of copyrighted material will result in a huge loss of revenue, and new legislation has been passed in some countries to combat this problem. This legislation, however, must not only define copyright in the digital world, but must also define liability. For instance, should ISPs be held liable for copyright violations of those using the ISPs?

In the United States, the Digital Millennium Copyright Act (DMCA), which was passed in 1998, imposes new safeguards for software, music, and written works on the Internet, and outlaws technologies that can crack copyright protection devices.[33] The Canadian government is considering modification of existing copyright laws and has also adopted the World Intellectual Property Organization or WIPO (www.wipo.org) treaties. The WIPO treaties, when adopted and ratified by governments in 175 member states, will provide a global framework for dealing with intellectual property protection. The WIPO treaties give copyright holders exclusive rights to make their creations available through interactive media on a demand basis.

Domain Names, Brand Names, and Cyber-Squatting. Companies and many celebrities whose names may have brand value must also ensure that their brand names and trademarks are protected online. Anyone wishing to register an Internet domain name (such as www.xyz.com) must register the name with a registry service approved by the Internet Corporation for Assigned Names and Numbers, or ICANN (www.icann.org). A ".com," ".net," or ".org" domain name can be registered with registry services such as Networksolutions or Dotster. Country-specific domain names (such as ".ca" for Canada and ".au" for Australia) must be registered with appropriate national registry services. In Canada, Domainpeople.com is one such registration service.

Registration services, however, do not verify if a person registering a name legally owns that name. They also allow bulk registrations of hundreds of Web site names. There are individuals (and even some companies) that register hundreds of names (including misspellings of brand names and potential future brand names).

Registration of a name that legally belongs to someone else is referred to as **cyber-squatting**. Courts have repeatedly ruled in favour of plaintiffs when it comes to brand names and cyber-squatting, which is nothing but misappropriation of someone's registered name. Famous people like Madonna and Gary Kasparov have also been able to gain control of Web sites registered in their names. Others (such as singer Sting) have not been so successful. Companies such as Wal-Mart have been able to gain control of Web site names such as Walmartsucks.com. By registering misspellings and names that opponents of a company may use, companies can prevent potential exploitation or abuse of their registered brand names. There is, however, a freedom of expression issue in some of these cases that so far does not seem to have been tested in the courts.

Taxation

The US government has established a moratorium on taxation of E-commerce until the end of October 2001, with a further five-year extension. The proponents of such a moratorium have argued that E-commerce is in its very early stages and any undue tax burden would

iMarket Demo 13-1 Napster: A Pioneer or a Pirate?

Napster (www.napster.com) has been at the centre of a lot of controversy and legal trouble. The company is still under the threat of being shut down by the courts. The company has made the music record industry and many recording artists angry. At the same time, millions of consumers, mostly teens and young adults, stand by this company.

Napster is among several peer-to-peer (P2P) applications, which allow consumers to share files. Gnutella (gnutella.wego.com), Badblue (www.badblue.com), Freenet (freenet.sourceforge.net/), and myplay (www.myplay.com) are some of the other players in the P2P space. Napster allows consumers to download music files and share the files with each other. Napster users can see the music files residing on the computers of other Napster users. They can choose the songs they wish to download. The files do not reside in a central server, but in the individual computers of users. Record companies charge that this is copyright violation. Unlike Napster, which has a centralized server, Gnutella and Freenet are decentralized without a central computer system, making it even harder to detect copyright violations.

Record companies have sued Napster for promoting copyright violation and piracy. While copyright laws permit consumers to make personal copies of CDs, Napster enables the creation of millions of free copies. Basically, Napster acts as a clearinghouse, directing users to the computers of other users, where music files are stored.

A lower court ruled against Napster, which was followed by an injunction against that ruling. At the time this is being written, the legal battles between the major record companies, represented by the Recording Industry Association of America, and Napster are far from over. Napster has recently agreed to charge its users a low monthly fee, with some of the proceeds presumably going to the record companies in the form of royalties. There is some evidence that Napster is adversely affecting sales in bricks-and-mortar music stores, even though some analysts predict that music will continue to be sold predominantly in the form of CDs for years to come.

Experts predict a rise in peer-to-peer file sharing that may go beyond music files and even the potential for peer-to-peer commerce. Salespeople can use the technology for finding reports on their colleagues' computers, and consumers can use it to buy or sell products. Badblue is targeting the corporate market with its product. If the same content is available on many computers and if the content of the files is static (such as music files, which do not change in content), P2P may be a viable solution. While Napster's fate is still unknown, it may prove to be a pioneer—or simply a pirate.

Sources: Benny Evangelista (2000), "The Napster Effect: Program May Have Started Something That No Court Can Stop," *San Francisco Chronicle* (www.sfgate.com), September 28, 2000; John Borland (2000), "Napster Trial Won't End Music Industry Headaches," *CNET News.com*, July 26, 2000; "Appeals Court Grants Napster Reprieve," *CNN.com*, July 28, 2000; Andy Oram (2000), "Peer-to-Peer Makes Internet Interesting Again," *O'Reilly Network* (www.oreillynetwork.com), September 22, 2000.

curb its growth.[34] They also argue that by not taxing E-commerce, a rapid growth in Internet-related businesses can be achieved, which can then lead to a vast number of high-paying jobs. Even without taxation of products sold online, there would a significant economic benefit. Given that sales taxation varies locally and Internet companies sell to consumers in many jurisdictions, collecting and remitting the tax to appropriate agencies is a complicated task. Of course, E-commerce companies that make a profit and individuals employed in this sector will have to pay their corporate and personal income taxes.

Opponents of this tax moratorium maintain that this policy creates an uneven playing field, where bricks-and-mortar firms selling the same product to the same consumer as an online firm must collect the appropriate sales taxes. This means products sold through bricks-and-mortar stores can be higher priced. Further, the moratorium could also result in a loss of tax revenue for local communities and governments.[35] In the case of catalogue companies in the US, sales tax must be levied in the state where the company is domiciled. Some argue that a similar strategy may work online.

While there are arguments on both sides of this issue, there are also ongoing congressional hearings on this issue. Clicks-and-mortar businesses, which operate online and offline, present an interesting challenge. While a book purchased in a physical Barnes & Noble store is taxable, the same book purchased over the Internet is not. There is no resolution yet to such anomalies. Many private groups have made representations and have prepared position papers. Different solutions are being proposed, including a National Sales Tax, which will be collected electronically by the federal government and remitted to the states.[36]

Each country must wrestle with this issue and reach a position based on national and local interests. In Canada, the private sector and the government seem to favour tax neutrality and equity, which means that regardless of the channel through which a transaction is conducted (online or offline), equivalent transactions will be taxed in the same manner, and no additional taxes will be levied on electronic transactions.[37] Products purchased online are not exempt from sales taxes (or the Goods and Services Tax), as in the United States.

Internationally, the World Trade Organization (WTO) and OECD have taken the position of not taxing or levying duties on global E-commerce. Their efforts have focused on developing a framework where local tax revenues are not adversely affected, while at the same time ensuring the development of global E-commerce.

As we saw earlier, determining a permanent presence and jurisdiction for online businesses is challenging. This makes it harder to collect direct taxes based on source of income or residency. The OECD Model Tax Convention's concept of permanent establishment suggests that computer servers or Web sites may have to be included in the notion of what constitutes a permanent establishment.[38]

WTO member countries have agreed not to levy customs duties on electronic products and services delivered electronically. This agreement applies only for electronically delivered items. If a Canadian consumer bought and downloaded a software product from an American company, there would be no duties or taxes levied. This is consistent with current law. For instance, if a software product is shipped overseas, the duty is levied on the value of the media (CD or diskette) and not on the value of the software itself. On the Internet, the medium is eliminated, since it is not a physical entity (such as a CD or diskette). The argument, therefore, is that there should be no taxation on products delivered via the Internet (which is a virtual or invisible medium).[39]

It is evident that taxation and duties will continue to be difficult issues for policy makers. On the one hand, as Internet companies struggle to establish a foothold, excessive tax and regulatory burdens can stunt their growth. On the other hand, there are issues of fairness (to bricks-and-mortar stores) and the ability of governments to raise needed revenues. The moratorium in the United States is a temporary measure, which means we have not heard the end of this issue by any means.

Consumer Protection

A study by Jupiter Communications found that 64 percent of consumers do not trust Web sites.[40] Frequent incidences of credit card fraud, e-mail spamming, and misuse of personal information without consumer consent are some of the reasons for this lack of trust (see Exhibit 13-3 for statistics on Internet fraud). Such mistrust translates to reluctance to adopt online shopping. Adding to the problem is the fact that many online vendors do not excel in service delivery. Very few have return and refund policies posted on their sites. A study by the Gartner Group revealed that among the top 50 sites, none got a rating of good or excellent for customer service.[41]

The Federal Trade Commission's (FTC) Web site refers to cyber frauds as "dot cons" and has listed different types of frauds, including credit card frauds, "free" Internet access scams (which trap consumers into high-priced long-term contracts), and pyramid schemes (see www.ftc.gov/bcp/conline/pubs/online/dotcons.htm). The consumer protection section of the FTC site has a special category for E-commerce, which includes many useful articles for consumers (see www.ftc.gov/bcp/menu-internet.htm).

Exhibit 13-3 Internet Fraud Statistics

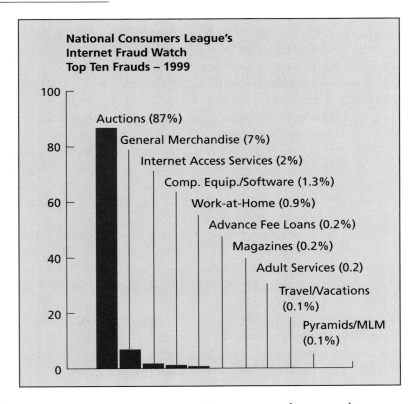

Source: www.natlconsumersleague.org.

The geographic distance that separates buyers and sellers on the Internet puts consumers in a more vulnerable position. Further, the use of foreign currencies in some cases and the lack of consumer familiarity with the purchasing process also contribute to confusion and an increased chance of fraud. By protecting consumers from scams and ensuring they have remedies when the service quality is poor, consumer trust and confidence in Internet shopping can be increased. Businesses must be aware that general principles of consumer protection on matters such as deceptive practices (e.g., misleading advertising), unfair practices (e.g., action that may cause damage to the consumer), product liability, and pricing will apply to online companies just as they do in the offline world.

Policy-makers and legislators have realized the importance of acting quickly on measures to protect consumers online, and so have businesses. In this section, we will examine some of the areas where consumer protection needs to be strengthened.

Consumer Privacy. As discussed earlier, consumers are most concerned with loss of privacy when the go online. In the United States and Canada, consumer privacy has been left in the hands of online companies. Through a set of voluntary codes and participation in voluntary programs (such as the TRUSTe program), consumer education, and privacy-protecting technologies and filters, companies in North America are expected to ensure consumer privacy protection. The FTC has also been a proponent of self-regulation.[42] It remains to be seen whether self-regulation will work or if eventually we may see direct legislation in this area.

E-mail, Spam, and Cyber-Stalking. E-mail has been called a "killer application" because it has revolutionized the way we communicate with each other, both socially and in business settings. E-mail, however, is also prone to a great deal of abuse.

Spamming or sending unsolicited commercial e-mail (UCE) has given direct marketing a bad name and causes consumers much frustration. Several states in the US have passed or are considering legislation to curb spamming. Some laws, such those passed in California and Washington, have been declared unconstitutional. The Washington law bans spam e-mail that has misleading information in the e-mail's subject line, disguises the path it took across the Internet, or contains an invalid reply address. These are all common practices used by spammers.[43] In the meantime, the US House of Representatives has passed the Unsolicited Commercial Electronic Mail Act of 2000, prohibiting the transmission of e-mail without a valid return e-mail address. This bill also forces e-mail marketers to provide a valid return address and use appropriate subject headings that describe the content of the e-mail accurately. There is, however, uncertainty over whether this bill will actually become law.

The FTC has encouraged industry self-regulation in this regard. Non-profit organizations like the Center for Technology and Democracy (www.cdt.org) and the Coalition Against Unsolicited Commercial Email, or CAUCE (www.cauce.org), have been vocal in representing consumer interests and have played a role in pushing for legislation. The current laws and proposals have been criticized for having certain loopholes. For instance, spam from overseas companies is not covered in any of this legislation.

E-mail marketers themselves have realized that consumer protection is good for businesses as well. An online marketers group called Responsible Electronic Communication Alliance (RECA) has proposed standards to limit spam and to give consumers greater control over the e-mail messages they receive by opting in or out. RECA includes well-known online marketing firms such as DoubleClick and 24/7 Media.[44] The Direct Marketing Association in the United States and the Canadian Marketing Association (CMA) offer an opt-out program, where consumers can sign up for deletion of their e-mail address from e-mail lists of companies that are members of the Direct Marketing Association or CMA. Consumers can do this by going to the e-mail preference service site (www.e-mps.org). This service will remove a consumer's e-mail address from participating direct market companies in the US, Canada, Australia, Belgium, Finland, Great Britain, Ireland, and the Netherlands.

Cyber-stalking is another nuisance or crime in which e-mail plays a big part. Cyber-stalking is simply any unwanted, obsessive pursuit of an individual by another through electronic means, including e-mail. Using false identities to lure children or defraud older people, and sending repeated, harassing, or offensive e-mail also fall under the category of cyber-stalking. The Web makes it easy to commit such crimes because people can hide their identities and it is often difficult to detect their location. Cyber-stalking happens on bulletin boards, newsgroups, and chat sites. It may then escalate to direct e-mail contact between the offender and the victim. Consumer education and taking proper precautions in online discussion forums can help guard against such attacks. Organizations like Cyberangels.org are trying to make the Internet safe for children and play an active role in educating consumers.

Credit Card Fraud. Businesses must take security measures necessary to protect the information they collect. Often, negligence or theft of information by employees tends to be the cause of such fraud. While credit card companies hold the consumer liable in most fraud cases for up to $50, some companies like Amazon give consumers a guarantee on their site saying they will even absolve the consumer of this $50 risk, if unauthorized use of the credit card occurs while shopping on that site. Such guarantees can help build consumer confidence.

As we saw earlier in the chapter, businesses pay a greater price in terms of penalties and increased discount rates and fees from the credit card issuer. Credit card transactions over the Internet fall under the **mail order/telephone order (MOTO)** or the "card not present" category. In such transactions, the vendor does not have a chance to verify the identity of the consumer or the authenticity of the card. As a result, these transactions pose a higher risk for both the merchant and the card-issuing bank. Businesses, while encouraging consumers to shop, must also take appropriate precautions. Investment in a secure server and the appropriate encryption systems such as SSL or SET are essential.

To help curtail fraud, some businesses do not ship to post box addresses or to an address that is different from the one on the credit card. Unusually large orders or unusual demands should be examined closely to ensure they are legitimate. Consumers also need to take precautionary steps such as giving credit card information only to trusted vendors who have proper security and privacy policies.

Child Protection. While regulators and legislators have been hesitant to call for new laws to combat some online problems, protection of children has received a different response. The Child Online Protection Act, which was passed in the United States in 1998, prescribes penalties for different offences, including directing adult material towards children. The Act requires schools and public libraries that receive government funding to install filters on their computers. The filters or "cyber-sitters" will simply block access to certain inappropriate Web sites.

The Commission on Online Child Protection, or COPA (www.copacommission.org), has issued a detailed report recommending filtering programs and calling for new technologies that empower parents and consumers (see iMarket Demo 13-2). Civil rights groups are worried that filtering will go beyond pornographic and other offensive or dangerous material and will act as a form of censorship.

The Internet Content Rating Association (www.icra.org) is a non-profit organization with operations in the United States and Europe that aims to empower parents by providing

iMarket Demo 13-2: Nannies on the Net

The Internet, just like the physical world, has both good and bad. The ease with which even small children can find information online makes the medium powerful and yet makes children vulnerable to harmful influences. Pornographic sites, bomb-making recipes, and hate literature are all available with a few mouse-clicks. While chat and bulletin boards allow social interaction, there have been a number of cases of pedophiles posing as children to lure small children. While the educational value of the Internet is unmistakable, how can parents protect their children from harmful influences?

Filtering programs, such as NetNanny (www.netnanny.com), Cyberpatrol (www.cyberpatrol.com), Bess (www.bess.net), and CyberSitter (www.solidoak.com), are among the many products that give parents the ability to restrict and monitor their children's Internet access. NetNanny (see Exhibit 13-4) allows parents to set a "can go" and "can't go" list of sites, restrict downloads of certain file types (such as MP3s), screen out known pedophile's pages or e-mail addresses, monitor Web sites visited through activity logs, and record and monitor chat room discussion.

Children who know more about the Internet and computers than their parents do may find ways to circumvent the filters. Web sites that illegally target children may also find ways to do this. Filters are not

Exhibit 13-4 NetNanny

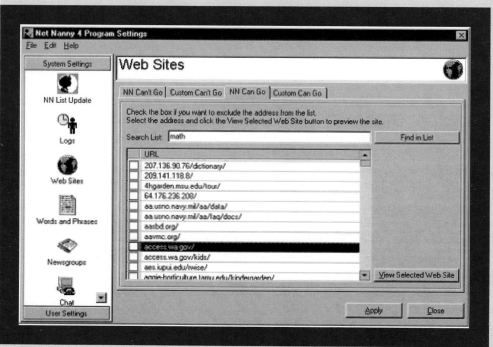

Source: www.netnanny.com.

fool-proof, but are a good defence against harmful influences on children.

Yet, filters are not without controversy. Civil rights groups such as the Center for Technology and Democracy (www.cdt.org) have voiced strong opposition to mandatory filtering in schools and libraries, as required by the Children Online Protection Act. Civil libertarians argue that filers go against the guarantee of freedom of speech.

These groups also argue that filters will create a false sense of security. Is there a middle ground here—where children are protected and free speech is still ensured?

Source: Letter from Senators Leahy, Jeffords, and Reeds, United States Senate Committee on the Judiciary Washington, DC 20510-6275 (www.cdt.org/speech/filtering/001020judiciary. shtml), October 20, 2000; Internet Child Protection Links (www.homeschoolcentral.com/prot.htm).

content ratings for Web sites. The "RSACi" rating symbol offered by this organization can be seen in many popular sites. This voluntary rating system provides consumers with information about the level of sex, nudity, violence, and offensive language (vulgar or hate-motivated) in software games and Web sites. Educational material about online child and family protection can be found at the FTC, COPA, and Disney Web sites.

Customer Service. Many e-tailers have not taken the need for customer service seriously. In the early days of online marketing, there was an erroneous belief among some marketers that consumers could be lured online simply by the "ease of online shopping" and that customer service was not important. A study by Forrester, however, found that 37 percent of consumers make greater use of online customer service because of ease of use.[45] According to a survey by BizRate.com, a company that rates customer satisfaction with e-tail sites, 89 percent of respondents said that return policies influence their decision to shop at particular sites. Still, there is evidence that marketers have yet to make the necessary investments in this area.

In a survey of 200 retail sites in 18 countries, the FTC found that although the companies usually provided general business information, very few provided adequate refund policies, cancellation terms, and warranties.[46] In this study, 100 US and 100 non-American English-text sites were studied. Only 9 percent provided cancellation information, 26 percent had refund policies, and 38 percent informed consumers about the currencies that could be used at the site. The US sites were often found to be laggards in this regard.

Timely delivery is another important issue in customer service. The United States has a regulation known as the Mail or Telephone Order Merchandise Rule, which is essentially a prompt delivery rule where a vendor cannot make false promises about delivery dates. The FTC has enforced penalties against some e-tailers for late delivery. Other commercial and consumer protection laws, not specifically drafted for the Internet, can also apply in the case of Internet transactions.

Most governments, including those in the United States and Canada, seem to be taking the view that consumer protection online should be achieved through a combination of existing or new legislations, voluntary codes for companies, consumer education, and enabling technologies.[47] Customer service and consumer protection are global issues because consumers can now shop at an overseas store without ever visiting that country. In this era of global E-commerce, there is a need for multilateral efforts to guarantee basic consumer protection on a global basis.

Building Trust Online

The discussion in the preceding section has focused on problems that lead to consumer mistrust of E-commerce sites, as well as potential remedies. Consumers' lack of trust in online companies is a major hindrance to the growth of E-commerce. Frequent news stories about various types of security breaches on the Internet do little to calm consumer fears. Security and privacy issues have emerged as the two major stumbling blocks to the growth of E-commerce. Low consumer confidence is also based on frequent reports of online fraud, security breaches, a lack of satisfactory complaint handling and refund policies in most sites, and the general state of confusion that seems to exist with respect to consumer privacy. Online vendors must individually and collectively address these issues to build consumer trust in E-commerce and e-tailers.

Consumer trust in E-commerce and e-tailers can be influenced by several factors, as depicted in Exhibit 13-5. Online companies must focus on all of these factors to build consumer trust.

If the company, brand, or store is well known, the reputation may influence consumers' trust. While established bricks-and-mortar companies that go online can take advantage of their reputations, newer online companies must build their reputation from scratch.

Having stringent security procedures and well-defined privacy policies (in accordance with the requirements of organizations such as BBBOnline and TRUSTe) are a good start. Posting Frequently Asked Questions (FAQs) and providing other help to guide consumers through the purchase process and answer questions on security, privacy, complaint handling, and return handling procedures are also essential.

Consumers are likely to use their prior experience with online vendors in forming a judgment about trust. Ensuring a high level of consumer satisfaction and establishing an effec-

Exhibit 13-5 Factors Affecting Trust in E-Commerce

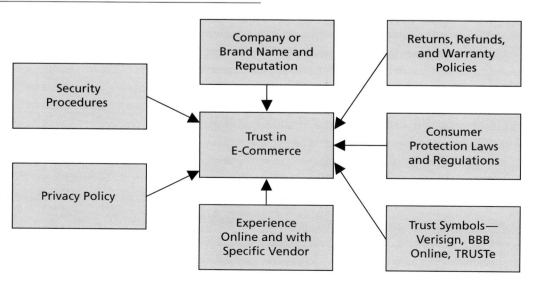

tive complaint handling mechanism are necessary. If the product, service, or online shopping experience is unsatisfactory, consumer trust in the vendor will be adversely affected. If the marketer is up-front about the policies and prices, without any hidden policies or costs, it will be easier to secure consumer trust.

Regulation is needed in Canada in the areas of privacy protection and spamming. Canadian privacy regulation leans towards industry self-regulation. While it is important not to go overboard with regulation, the efficacy of self-regulation must be studied. The Canadian Marketing Association (www.cdma.org/main.html) prescribes a code of ethics under the Privacy & Ethics section on their Web site. Specific standards of practice for the Internet are included. CMA members must abide by a non-spamming standard, where they agree to send e-mail only with consumer consent. While the CMA's efforts are important in creating awareness and some pressure among businesses, participation in the CMA is voluntary.

In the United States, as mentioned earlier, laws exist for the protection of children online. This is another area where the laws need to be strengthened in Canada. The key point here is that consumers will feel more confident about using the Internet for shopping and disclosing personal information to online firms, if the laws are clear and provide adequate consumer protection.

Lastly, by voluntarily signing up with some of the trust symbols like TRUSTe and BBBOnline (see Exhibit 13-6) and adhering to their standards, a marketer can win the consumer's confidence. Parents should also look for the RSACi rating (see www.icra.org). Sites that participate in BizRate.com's service must allow for consumer evaluation of the purchase experience immediately after the purchase is made. BizRate will request that consumers fill out a short, voluntary survey on participating sites, such as Buy.com, eToys.com, Outpost.com, or Amazon.com. The survey covers different service dimensions and the results are publicly posted at BizRate.com. A company that is seen as voluntarily complying with high standards is more likely to be trusted.

Other companies that also work toward improving trust in online commerce include escrow services, such as i-Escrow (www.i-escrow.com), and online dispute-settling firms, such as SquareTrade (www.squaretrade.com) and eResolution (www.eresolution.com), which is a Canadian firm.

It is evident that success in E-commerce is going to depend not just on attracting buyers once, but on ensuring that they are repeat customers. Online marketers who focus on providing high-quality products or services, while investing in trust-building mechanisms, will be the eventual winners.

Exhibit 13-6 Symbols to Promote Consumer Confidence

Sources: www.verisign.com, www.truste.com, www.bbbonline.com, www.bizrate.com.

Practices of Some Online Companies

By benchmarking against the best competitors, you can ensure that your trust-building practices are not just in conformity with the industry standards, but are the best in the industry.

Merely displaying the symbols of TRUSTe or BBBOnline is not sufficient. If a company wants to win the confidence of a potential customer and retain existing customers, proactive steps are required. Let's examine what some of the leading Internet companies do in the areas of security and privacy. These companies were chosen merely to provide a range of examples. It should also be noted that these firms may change their security or privacy policies periodically. The analysis presented here is based on the situation as of November 2000.

Amazon.com. Once the consumer selects an item, a box titled "Buy from Amazom.com" is presented in the product/buying information page. From here the consumer can access the details of Amazon's privacy and security policies. In addition to using SSL security, Amazon goes a step further to reassure consumers about safety of credit card transactions. Typically, credit card issuing banks make the consumer responsible for the first $50 in the case of credit card fraud. Amazon's security policy guarantees that if the fraud was committed when the customer was shopping at the site, Amazon will refund the amount that the credit card company does not cover.

Amazon displays its shipping and returns policies very clearly on the first page, and a link to the privacy policy is provided at the bottom of the main page. Information on security, privacy, and returns are in different locations. This means consumers have to make some effort to look for the information. Amazon's site does not display any of the trust symbols discussed in this chapter.

eBay. This company has been the recipient some negative publicity because of the nature of its business. Auction sites do not directly sell products, but they facilitate commerce between buyers and sellers. Unscrupulous sellers may exaggerate the quality of the products they offer. In some cases, sellers have failed to deliver products to buyers. eBay's fraud protection program pays up to $200 for items purchased and paid for, but not received. eBay has taken steps to curb fraud and auctioning of illegal products (such as body parts) by monitoring the products auctioned on the site, but the volume of transactions and traffic on the site makes such monitoring a challenge.

eBay also has a partnership with the online escrow service i-Escrow. This company will hold the buyer's payment in safe custody until the purchased item reaches the buyer in appropriate condition. Then i-Escrow will release the payment to the seller.

The practice of "shilling," where sellers bid on their own items to drive up the price, is another serious concern that auction sites face. On eBay, people can rate the quality of a particular seller or buyer through the "Feedback Forum." While this is supposed to act as "electronic word of mouth," there is potential for abuse here too. Sellers, for instance, can give themselves positive ratings using a different online identity.

eBay's service depends on both buyers and sellers behaving in an ethical and lawful manner. eBay polices the site and from time to time will ask a seller to withdraw an item if it is unlawful or if the product is distasteful. eBay's challenge is that it must be seen by consumers as providing an environment that is secure. At the same time, the company must encourage its clients (both buyers and sellers) to behave within legal and ethical bounds. eBay displays the TRUSTe symbol.

Buy.com. Buy.com's Canadian site (www.canada.buy.com) was examined. Its privacy policy is located in the main menu. Several other consumer-friendly features are provided, including an order-tracking system, where orders can be tracked from the moment they are placed online. The Customer Support option on the main menu takes the consumer to a section that displays information in a logical sequence—placing an order, tracking an order, managing your account, shipping, returns, and billing.

Buy.com also allows consumers to cancel an order within 30 minutes of placing it online. An automatic order confirmation e-mail is sent once an order has been placed, which provides some measure of security. The site uses 128-bit encryption. Buy.com's privacy statement is written in plain English, but this company does not offer the credit card fraud protection that Amazon provides.

JustWhiteShirts.com. This is a Canadian retail firm that started selling just white shirts, true to its name. Now the company has expanded its offerings to a range of men's professional and casual clothing. It has also gone global, expanding to the United States, Australia, and New Zealand. First, the consumer has to choose the country. Immediately after that choice has been made, the consumer is transferred to a secure server. Since regular members will log on before proceeding to shop on the site, security is important at this stage. The site has a "Best Practices Disclosure" section, where information on order fulfillment, customer service, delivery options, payment options, and returns are presented. The company offers free "live customer support" during specified hours of the week. This may provide some degree of assurance and comfort to customers.

One of the limitations of the site is that privacy and security information are not clearly displayed, even when an item is added to the shopping cart. The site does not display any trust seals.

Chapters. Chapters offers a credit card fraud safety program similar to what Amazon offers. On the main page, in the section "On Chapters.ca," consumers can find security and privacy information, along with shipping information. The help button at the top right corner takes the consumer to a page with links to shipping and returns information, privacy policy, opt-in policy, legal statement, and so on. Unless consumers know to look under Help, they may miss this section completely. The company does not display any trust seals.

Hsupply.com. This is a B2B company that brings buyers and suppliers in the hotel industry together. The company has a clearly displayed security and privacy policy, which can be accessed from the main page. It also offers a credit card protection plan that is similar to what Amazon has.

BizBuyer.com. This is a B2B firm that provides purchasing solutions by linking buyers and sellers and also allows firms to post RFQs. The privacy link on the main page leads to a detailed description of how the firm protects consumer privacy and security. The firm uses SSL encryption and also displays the TRUSTe symbol.

An Assessment of Practices Observed. Established companies like Amazon seem to march to their own drum. They may not gain as much from a trust seal program as an unknown start-up would. Some of the well-known e-tail names on the Internet are missing from the TRUSTe participants list, even though the list is growing and TRUSTe is gaining more recognition (see www.truste.com/users/users_lookup.html).

Often competing firms will match each other's features, as is the case with Amazon and Chapters. While most companies do an adequate job at ensuring security and privacy, eBay, Amazon, and Buy.com have some interesting additional features.

Perhaps due to bad experiences with some of their sellers or buyers, eBay has a comprehensive program to address trust. The program includes a secure server, escrow service, dispute resolution service, privacy protection, feedback forum where members can expose those engaged in unethical or unlawful activity, and a fraud protection program, where eBay will refund up to $200 for any item paid for but not received. This has to rank as being one of the best overall trust-building efforts.

Not all companies make it easy to find information on security, privacy, and business practices. In some cases, the information is presented in a technical language that may be difficult for the average consumer to comprehend. Some firms are woefully inadequate in their response to the trust challenge, so the evidence suggests a mixed report card.

Summary

Even after nearly five years of commerce online, the vast majority of consumers still have security concerns. Some high-profile online companies have yet to get serious enough about consumer privacy concerns. Businesses must invest in the security of their sites and ensure consumer protection measures. The Internet makes it easy to compare prices and switch from one vendor to another. This makes it all the more important for e-tailers to concentrate on measures that will build customer satisfaction and trust.

Security on the Internet must be addressed in multiple ways, including the use of firewalls and following SSL, or preferably SET, protocol with respect online transaction processing. Further, businesses must have a security policy for employees, prescribing rules for using the company's network and access to confidential information. Security breaches online can be very costly for businesses, ultimately increasing costs for both businesses and consumers.

While some laws have been enacted with respect to consumer privacy, this matter has largely be left to self-regulation. Participation in privacy programs of independent third parties, such as TRUSTe and BBBOnline, is a way to guarantee consumers that the company will not abuse personal data. This sort of assurance is crucial to building trust and consumer confidence.

There are several new legal challenges raised by the Internet and E-commerce in areas such as contract law, jurisdiction, taxation, copyright law, and consumer protection. The solutions differ from one country to another. While some new legislation has already been introduced in the United States, Canada, and Europe, some issues are likely to be left to voluntary compliance and self-regulation. The Internet has created a global marketplace. That means international consensus on issues such as taxation and consumer protection is necessary to ensure the growth of global E-commerce. Organizations such as the WTO, WIPO, and OECD are playing an active role in building such a consensus.

Key Terms

Click-wrap licence, 329
Consumer protection, 334
Cyber-squatting, 331
Cyber-stalking, 336
Digital certificate, 323
Digital signature, 323
Encryption, 323
Firewall, 321

Mail order/telephone
    order (MOTO), 336
Peer-to-peer (P2P), 332
Public-key encryption, 322
Safe harbor, 328
Secure electronic
    transaction (SET), 324

Secure sockets layer
    (SSL), 324
Shrink-wrap licence, 329
Spamming, 335
Symmetric-key
    encryption, 322

Questions and Exercises

Review Questions

1. Why are consumers concerned about online security?
2. What are some of the common crimes on the Internet?
3. What is a firewall? What are the common types of firewall systems?
4. Describe the differences between SET and SSL.
5. What measures can an e-tailer take to ensure consumer privacy on their site?
6. Name three areas where the Internet presents a legal challenge.
7. What new legal or regulatory challenges are present in the case of global E-commerce?
8. What are the arguments for and against child protection filters?
9. Describe at least three measures necessary to improve customer service online.

Discussion Questions

1. How does poor online security affect business? What arguments would you make to a small business to invest in adequate security measures online?
2. What role should governments play in ensuring consumer privacy online? Should privacy be self-regulated or should there be further legislation in this area?
3. Is making the Internet a "tax-free zone" a sensible approach to promoting E-commerce? What are the pros and cons of such a policy?
4. Do peer-to-peer (P2P) applications like Napster violate copyright laws in your opinion? What do you see as the future for P2P applications?
5. How should marketers go about building consumer trust? Discuss the specific steps you would take.

Internet Exercises

1. Visit the TRUSTe (www.truste.com) and BBBOnline (www.bbbonline.com) sites. Find out about the specific privacy programs they offer. What do you see as the strengths and limitations of each program?
2. Visit the following pairs of sites:
   i. Barnes&Noble.com (www.bn.com) and Amazon (www.amazon.com)
   ii. EToys (www.etoys.com) and SmartToys.com (www.smarttoys.com)
   Compare (a) the security policy and (b) the privacy policy on the competing sites. Describe your observations. Do the sites use any of the trust symbols described in this chapter? What specific trust-building mechanisms do each of the sites use?

Chapter 14

Social, Ethical, and Future Issues

Vignette 14 Internet in the Developing World

Only about 2 to 3 percent of the global population was online by the middle of the year 2000. While 50 percent of North Americans and a slightly lower percentage of Europeans enjoy the benefits of the Internet, over 90 percent of the world's population has no access to the Internet.

How can the benefits of the Internet spread to the developing world? Will the Internet remain a technology just for the wealthier nations? The developing world is keen to eliminate the so-called digital divide, or the gap between the "technology haves" and "technology have nots." The challenge, however, is of such magnitude that no single nation, company, or organization can address the issue on its own.

Consider these facts. China has one land-based telephone for each 60 citizens, while in neighbouring India the ratio is one in 200. Other developing countries in Asia and Africa are no better off in terms of access to technology for its citizens. Fifty percent of the world's population has never even made a phone call, and the number of PCs is 130 times higher in developed countries than in developing countries. In addition to poor infrastructure, low literacy levels and low incomes (and thus, the inability of the masses to afford the technology) are barriers in many nations.

Third world experts argue that for the technology to have a social benefit in these countries, other basic developmental issues, such as healthcare, education, poverty, clean water, and housing, must be addressed. At this point, it would not make sense to think of Internet access at the individual or household level in developing countries.

Solutions for the developing world may be different from what is feasible in the West. The best way to provide Internet access may be at the community level—in schools, community halls, and other places where public access can be provided. Even in parts of Europe, the community access model is being pursued effectively. The new technology may have to be integrated with the old. For instance, post offices can print e-mail and deliver it to individuals.

The efforts to bring the Internet and E-commerce to developing countries are being addressed at different levels. The US government has established a program with a funding of $20 million to increase Internet adoption in eight developing countries. Individual foundations (such as the one started by Bill Gates, Chairman of Microsoft) and businesses are also playing a role. The Kyushu-Okinawa G7 summit (held in Japan in 2000) led to the Charter on Global Information Society, which calls for ending the digital divide within and among nations. Some may argue that these are symbolic gestures, but they do suggest that global leaders are aware of the gap between developed and developing countries.

Businesses in North America have a vested interest in ensuring Internet growth in developing markets. Much of the growth for many North American companies will come in the future from developing economies such as China, India, and South America. Even if only 10 or 20 percent of the population in developing countries have access to the Internet and use it for commerce, the global impact could be enormous.

There are three areas, in particular, where the Internet can have an immediate impact on the developing world:

- *Health*. The use of telemedicine can help doctors and healthcare workers in remote areas become familiar with the latest medical techniques. Patients who need a specialist's opinion can have access to a specialist via the Internet at community health centres.
- *Education*. Schools in developing countries often do not have libraries. The Internet can open the door to libraries across the world. The cost of buying books and other physical resources can be avoided. Teachers can interact with their counterparts in other countries through sites such as School.Net. Technology can be useful, but it cannot address issues such as lack of resources, poorly trained teachers, or overcrowded classes.
- *Political process and government*. Many countries in the developing world are moving toward a democratic system of governance. The Internet ensures that information and news flow freely even in countries where freedom of the press is not guaranteed.

Experts like Nicholas Negroponte, of the MIT Media Lab, suggest that the developing world will leapfrog the West and go from no technology to the latest technology, whereas many developing countries must make the costly switch from older (analogue) technologies to newer (digital) technologies. Definitely, the wealthiest in the poorer nations can leapfrog into the modern world. The infrastructure cost for cellular phones, for example, is significantly lower than that for land-based telecommunication technology, and the use of cellular phones in developing countries such as India, Combodia, and Brazil is rapidly growing.

As the next generation of E-commerce focuses on mobile and hand-held devices, not just PCs, developing countries will be poised to take advantage of E-commerce. The growing middle class in the developing world is hungry for superior-quality products and more choice. North American firms that look beyond their national boundaries and have a global perspective can take advantage of the opportunities that will soon arise in developing economies. Unfortunately, with a few exceptions, most E-commerce companies (especially on the consumer side) seem to lack a global focus.

Sources: Okinawa Charter on Global Information Society (www.g8kyushu-okinawa.go.jp/e/documents/it1.html), G7 Summit, July 21–23, 2000, Japan; Maria Seminerio (1999), "E-Commerce in the Third World?" *ZDNet* (www.zdnet.com/zdnn/), March 24, 1999; Maria Seminerio (1998), "US to Spur Third World E-Commerce," *ZDNet* (www.zdnet.com/zdnn/), November 30, 1998; Paula Uimonen (1997), "The Internet as a Tool for Social Development," INET 97 Conference Proceedings, Kuala Lumpur (www.isoc.org/isoc/whatis/conferences/inet/97/proceedings/). Uwe Afemann (1997), "Internet for the Third World—Chance or Threat?" (www.uni-muenster.de/EthnologieHeute/eh1/afe.htm).

Introduction

As Vignette 14 outlines, there are challenges ahead in ensuring that the benefits of the Internet reach as wide an audience as possible. While E-commerce has been the focus of this book, in this chapter we will look at applications that go beyond E-commerce. The Internet has already transformed the way businesses operate. It is now beginning to transform the public sector and other areas, such as education and healthcare.

This chapter will also look at some emerging technologies that may change the face of E-commerce. Rapid changes in technology will continue to affect how marketers communicate with consumers. Then, as we conclude our discussion of Internet marketing, we will look ahead to see where future opportunities and challenges lie.

Beyond E-Commerce

E-commerce is only one of the applications of the Internet. We are already seeing the impact of the Internet on a variety of other areas, including government, education, and healthcare. Let's now examine the impact of the Internet in these areas.

E-Government

The government provides citizens and businesses with a variety of services. Many would argue that government agencies are seldom efficient in their operations. Dealing with government agencies can often be a frustrating experience for both businesses and ordinary citizens.

The Internet can become an important part of making democracy work for people. Citizens can use the Internet to keep informed about legislation and to voice their opinions to elected officials. Many of those in elected offices now have Web sites with e-mail access. For example, the US Congress's Web site provides complete access to legislative information. Governments in Canada and Europe similarly make the government accessible to ordinary citizens.

The US presidential primary elections in 1999 and 2000 saw the introduction of online voting. Election.com, a private company, was in charge of the online voting. Now the company has expanded to Australia, France, New Zealand, and the United Kingdom. Proponents of electronic voting say that it will make it easier for older, disabled, and younger people (who are less likely to vote) to participate in elections. Opponents say that marginalized sections of the society will continue to be excluded from the electoral process and the Internet does very little to change that. In spite of this opposition, online voting will likely become part of the democratic process in the future.

E-government is the transformation of government through the use of the Internet and information technology.[1] There are three specific areas where the Internet can have an impact on government and government services:

- Using the Internet, governments can provide more efficient services to businesses and citizens.
- Governments can become more accessible and open to citizens and give them a direct voice.
- Redundancy and unnecessary paperwork can be eliminated and processes made more efficient, which will ultimately result in cost savings.

For small businesses and citizens, finding government regulations, appropriate agencies to deal with, or even the appropriate forms to fill out can be an arduous task. The Canadian government has created a portal, which is a one-stop information site for businesses (see Exhibit 14-1). In the preceding chapters of this book, we saw how businesses can transform themselves and benefit from the Internet. Governments can do the same, and thus enhance the level of service they provide. E-government is simply the use of the Internet to make the functioning of government and government services more efficient.

B2G E-Commerce. Another area where the government is likely to play a key role is in business-to-government (B2G) E-commerce. Governments are among the largest buyers of goods and services, and their procurement processes have historically been inefficient. Online procurement can streamline processes and reduce transaction costs and inventory costs. Some B2G government initiatives in the United States include these:[2]

- FedBid is a reverse auction site where vendors bid on US government contracts. This is an online procurement marketplace for IT-related products that allows government purchasers to research products, specify the parameters of the bid, and review and evaluate offers from competing vendors.
- GSA Advantage! is another procurement Web site that allows US government employees to browse, search, order, and pay for items via the Internet. Over a million items from more than 2000 vendors are available to registered government buyers—everything from automobiles to paperclips are available.
- Nationtax Online allows businesses to use an efficient process for filing sales, income tax withholding, and other state and federal business taxes over the Internet. Ezgov and

Exhibit 14-1 Business-Friendly Government of Canada Online

Source: www.cbsc.org/english/.

govWorks are two private-sector initiatives in use at the local and state level. These portal applications, which are directed towards citizens, allow individuals to use a secure system for paying taxes and tickets and filing government forms online.

E-government can work if it goes beyond simply creating a Web site that replaces the tons of print material put out by governments. If e-government translates to an electronic brochure of government services, then it is a limited view of this concept. Just as the Internet challenges businesses to change their processes (as we saw in Chapters 2, 4, and 6), it also challenges governments to change their processes.

Allowing consumers to register their vehicles or renew their car or hunting licences online on a 24/7 basis does require a different approach to running government agencies. Whether e-government will just remain a buzzword without any real impact or will actually change how citizens and governments interact with each other remains to be seen. Just as business transformation due to the Internet requires leadership at the top, the same is needed if e-government is to succeed. For an interesting example of this sort of leadership in a state in India, see iMarket Demo 14-1.

iMarket Demo 14-1 E-Government in a Developing State

It's a state that is putting into practice the slogan, "anytime, anywhere government." It's a state that calls itself the smart state. This state is not in the US or anywhere in the developed world. It is the southern state of Andhra Pradesh in India. AP, as it is called, became the first government to offer its services via the WAP or wireless network. The use of cell phones is rapidly proliferating in India.

The e-governance initiative spearheaded by the state's dynamic chief minister, Mr. Chadra Babu Naidu, has three major components:

- To deliver convenient, transparent, uniform, reliable, and accessible services at better terms from a citizens perspective.

- Anytime, anywhere government, where citizens can transact with government departments at their convenience.

- Integrated services to cut through layers of bureaucracy and allow citizens and businesses to deal with government through a single window. In other words, one-stop government.

Farmers will now have access to Internet kiosks, enabling them to sell directly to food manufacturers, thus bypassing the intermediaries. Soon everything from driver's licences to building permits will be obtained online. One of the welcome by-products of e-governance is likely to be the diminished role of the state bureaucracy, which is known to be very corrupt.

The state is investing heavily in high-speed fibre-optic technology that will provide Internet access to every village. To ensure rapid growth of private-sector and public-sector initiatives, a huge investment in education has been made by tripling the number of engineering colleges. The number of telephone connec-

Exhibit 14-2 E-Governance in an Indian State

Source: www.andhrapradesh.com.

tions has risen four-fold from 600 000 to 2.4 million in a few short years.

Such efforts have drawn the interest of multinationals. Large companies like Microsoft and Oracle have set up operations in Hyderabad, the state capital. In addition, the Wharton School of Business and Kellogg at Northwestern have teamed up to set up a modern business school in this state. Foreign investment and software exports are dramatically rising.

The initiatives in this Indian state have drawn the attention of worldwide media, with reviews appearing in *The Wall Street Journal*, *Newsweek*, *Financial Times*, *Business 2.0*, and other major publications. But not all reviews have been positive. This poor state has very complex socio-economic problems, and investments in IT have to come at the cost of other priorities.

However, there are already signs that e-governance in this developing state has changed the face of the government, and people who were once used to their government repeatedly failing them are now beginning to expect more from the government.

Sources: Srivatsa Krishna (1999), "State of the Art as Art of the State," Proceedings of the Conference on Enabling E-Commerce in India, Global Information Infrastructure Commision (www.giic.org/events/ec990615agenda.html), June 15–16, 1999; Michelle Levander (2000), "By Its Bootstraps," *Special Report: World Business, The Wall Street Journal*, September 15, 2000.

E-Education

The nature of the student population today is vastly different from what it was a decade or two ago. The traditional approach to education was to complete your education before getting your first job. Now the emphasis is on continuous learning.

The Internet started and flourished in the universities and research centres before it was commercialized in the 1990s. Now, the Net is again playing a growing role in education. Today's economy requires most people to upgrade their skills on an ongoing basis, and the Internet is proving to be an ideal channel for training and education aimed at so-called "nontraditional" students.

It is estimated that over 2 million students will enroll in online courses by 2002. Net companies providing online education or educational products have raised over $1 billion in venture capital, which is an indication of the promise this sector holds. Universities and private companies offering e-training and online programs are expected to earn an estimated $11 billion by 2002.[3]

Currently, there are over 20 full-fledged MBA programs available completely online and innumerable diplomas and courses. In the United States, top business schools such as Duke and the University of North Carolina have entered the online MBA market. Other universities such as University of California, Berkeley, offer a variety of online courses. Even universities that do not offer complete programs are offering Web-enabled courses for students on campus. Such courses use a combination of classroom and online resources.

There are a variety of business models in the e-education space. In business education, as well as other higher education, there has been an increase in the number of organizations that have assumed degree-granting status—Jones International University in the United States (www.jonesinternational.edu) and Lansbridge University (www.lansbridge.com) in

New Brunswick are two examples. These are stand-alone for-profit universities. There are also a variety of partnerships between private-sector companies and universities. Columbia Business School, for instance, has a partnership with UNext. In this model, universities develop the content and courses, which are then delivered by the partner. Another business model focuses on online corporate training. There are over 5000 companies in this field, with none exceeding a 5 percent market share.[4] Some of the key players in this field include Cognitive Arts (www.cognitivearts.com), which focuses on management training, and LearningTree (www.learningtree.com), which focuses on IT training.

In addition to higher education and corporate training, the Internet has also had a significant impact at the primary and secondary school level. Virtually every school in North America is wired or will be wired soon. Sites such as School.Net (www.school.net/home.html) offer students and teachers online resources and allow them to connect with their counterparts in other places. This access to information through the Internet empowers students. Whether they're learning about a foreign culture or doing research for a paper, students can turn to the Internet as the first source of information. In a sense, the Internet has already left an indelible mark on our education system.

E-Health

A study by Cyber Dialogue predicts that by 2002, 39 percent of all online consumers in the United States will be e-health consumers, up from 25 percent in 1997.[5] E-health consumers are those who seek health-related information and services online, as well as purchase drugs online.

As we saw in Vignette 3, a growing number of seniors, women, and families online are fuelling the growth of the online health sector. E-health companies, which span a broad spectrum from B2B to B2C, had raised over $1 billion by the end of 1999.[6]

The cost of healthcare is a major concern in North America and in developed countries elsewhere. E-healthcare, the convergence of healthcare and information technology, promises to make healthcare delivery more efficient and cost-effective.

Telemedicine is an area of healthcare that has seen a dramatic growth in recent years. Since people in remote areas usually do not have access to the best healthcare and specialists, using telemedicine and the Internet can allow patients to receive treatment even when they are geographically separated from doctors. Telemedicine is the transfer of electronic medical data (such as high-resolution images, sounds, live video, and patient records) from one location to another.[7] This transfer of medical data may use a variety of telecommunications technology, including (but not limited to) ordinary telephone lines, ISDN, fractional to full T-1's, ATMs, the Internet, intranets, and satellites. Telemedicine is used in a number of areas such as dermatology, oncology, radiology, surgery, cardiology, psychiatry, and home healthcare.

In addition to such advances in patient care, there are numerous sites (both independent and sponsored by pharmaceutical companies) that target doctors. These sites aim to provide doctors with easy access to latest medical research, treatments, and advances. Examples of such sites include eMedicine (www.edmedicine.com) and Doctors.net.uk (www.doctors.net.uk).

E-health services, while holding a lot of promise, also raise some questions with respect to consumer protection. Consumers must surrender a lot of personal information in order to get some of these online services. There is also the concern that commercial motives might lead to advertising content being passed off as medical advice.

The American Medical Association, in order to protect consumers, has published guidelines for medical information Internet sites. These guidelines are designed to protect individual privacy and provide reassurance that the information is reliable. The guidelines suggest that authorship, including funding and sponsorship, must be disclosed; editorial commentary, advertising, and commercial sponsorship must be demarcated clearly; privacy must be respected; and E-commerce systems must be secure.

E-Charity

Charitable and volunteer organizations have played a key role in our society over the years. Fundraising has become increasingly challenging as charities compete for the same dollars. Corporations lend their names and donate money to high-profile causes. Smaller charities have had an increasingly difficult time providing services in an era of budget cuts and fiscal responsibility.

The Internet gives charities a new marketing tool. Charities can reach potential donors online at a lower cost, compared to telemarketing or direct mail campaigns. The Internet can also provide charities a venue for reaching out to their beneficiaries by providing information and some online services.

Netaid.org (www.netaid.org) is among the elite online charities, to which many celebrities are lending their support. This organization, which combats poverty and hunger in the developing world, holds live online concerts that attract large audiences. Singer Jewel is among those who have performed in such online concerts (a webcast of her concert is available on the Netaid site through RealPlayer). Other well-known organizations such as the Red Cross and the Cancer Society also have a significant online presence.

The Web can not only lead to innovative fundraising approaches (see iMarket Demo 14-2), but can also enable charities to build relationships with both donors and beneficiaries. Rather than approaching donors once a year for donations, charities can now use the Web to provide information to donors on how their dollars are being spent. There is room for more in-depth interaction with all stakeholders through the Web. At many charity sites, volunteers can sign up online. In particular, Netaid has a volunteer opportunity search section.

The Digital Divide

Digital divide is a term that refers to the gap between technology "haves" and "have nots." We have already seen that there is a vast digital divide between developed and developing countries. Developing countries are weighed down by a host of problems, including lack of telecommunication infrastructure, lack of financial resources, and lack of skilled human resources.[8] There is no magic bullet that will address these enormous difficulties.

In addition to the digital divide that exists between nations, there are also serious gaps within nations. A series of reports by the National Telecommunications and Information Administration (www.ntia.doc.gov) has raised concerns about Internet access in the United States. A report on digital divide in 1999 stated that urban households with incomes over $75 000 were 20 times more likely to have Internet access than rural households at the lowest income level. Blacks and Hispanics were one-third as likely as those of Asian/Pacific Islander descent and two-fifths as likely as whites to have Internet access.[9]

By October 2000, however, Internet access among African-American and Hispanic households had grown to nearly 24 percent, almost a hundred percent growth from 20 months before.[10] A study by Forrester Research also lends support to the notion of a declining digital divide. In 1999 alone, the number of African-American households online grew by 44 percent, and the study projects that this gap will continue to narrow.[11]

iMarket Demo 14-2 Charity Begins Online

As we have seen throughout this book, the Web is not just a medium for buying and selling products. It has applications in education, healthcare, and many other fields. One area that has received little attention is the use of the Web by charitable organizations.

Most charitable organizations are online. A growing number of sites accept donations online (through a credit card), and others use Web sites to promote their causes. There are also a growing number of independent sites that make it easier for charities to raise funds and for donors to give. High-profile charities such as Netaid.org have Hollywood stars and companies such as Cisco lending their names and support. Netaid has organized live online concerts to raise funds to alleviate poverty and hunger.

Not all charities have a strategy or the support necessary to succeed online. There are sites that offer assistance to charities. Sites such as helping.org and the National Charities Information Bureau (www.give.org) provide information and assistance to both donors and non-profit organizations. Others like causeLink.com encourage companies to participate in their online auctions, with the proceeds going to designated non-profit organizations.

Another model is to give a percentage of the price a consumer pays to the charity designated by the consumer. This approach, which is being pursued by iReach-Out.com, has attracted high-profile online stores such as Amazon, Pets.com, Ashford.com, and 1800flowers.com. Shopfor-Change.com and Shop2Give.com also follow a similar model. These sites attempt to make giving painless and convenient.

From a tax perspective, consumers must also consider whether the purchase (a portion of which goes to charity) is tax exempt. The existence of unscrupulous sites is a problem. At many sites there is no way of verifying whether the donation actually reached the designated charity. The Better Business Bureau Online has reports on the performance of charity Web sites called "Give… But Give Wisely" (www.bbb.org/pas/give.asp). Consumers must take some time to ensure that they are giving to reputable organizations.

Sources: Sandra Block (1999), "Shopping Online for a Good Cause," *USATODAY.com*, November 26, 1999; Stephanie Sandborn (2000), "Nonprofits reap rewards of Web," *CNN.com*, June 22, 2000.

Digital divide is not just an American problem. It exists in other developed countries too. In Canada, for instance, digital divide is along dimensions such as age (only 5.5 percent of those over 65 years have access) and income (those in the highest income quartile had four times the access rate as those in the bottom quartile).[12] At the same time, there is evidence that the digital divide in Canada is narrowing. In Europe, the results of the Pan European Internet Monitor revealed a similar income-based divide, with upper income consumers having a significantly higher Internet access and usage rate than lower income consumers.[13]

Implications of Digital Divide

While it is not surprising that people with lower incomes and those from disadvantaged backgrounds are less likely to own computers and have access to the Internet, society and businesses must face the implications of digital divide. Some see the digital divide as a civil rights issue.[14] Others argue that it is just a buzzword that politicians like to use. But whatever your views on the subject, the implications are quite clear.

If a large proportion of the population is not online, they will not have the skills required to compete and succeed in today's job market. An economy driven by knowledge workers cannot afford to have a large proportion of its population without computer skills or access to the Internet. Competitiveness of businesses depends on their ability to attract and retain skilled knowledge workers. In the United States, for instance, 60 percent of all jobs require some level of technology skill. There is a large shortage of computer professionals in North America, which, if not addressed adequately, can affect the growth of the new economy.

The solution should come from different fronts. In Canada, the government has taken an active role in ensuring that schools and communities across Canada have access to the Internet. A comprehensive program called Connecting Canadians (<u>connect.gc.ca</u>) was instituted to reach the goal of making Canada the most "connected" nation in the world. Many parts of this program involve private-sector participation. In Europe, there has been a discussion about a possible regulation mandating service providers such as British Telecom and Deutsche Telekom to provide universal access to the Internet.[15] It is not feasible for governments alone to address this issue. The private sector, which has a great deal to gain when all citizens are connected, must play a role too.

Impact on Psychological Well-Being

The Internet has changed how people communicate with each other. A growing number of people are using e-mail as their primary means of communicating with friends, colleagues, and associates. Online chat rooms and bulletin boards are also very popular (see <u>chat.chatroom.net/</u> for a list of the top chat sites). Online users are increasingly getting their news from Web sites, and shopping online is on the increase. Does increased Internet usage cause social isolation? Are there other negative psychological consequences of using the Internet? Psychologists and sociologists seem to have different perspectives on these issues.

Negative Psychological Impact

A longitudinal study on Internet use found that among those who used the Internet extensively for communication, there was a decline in their overall communication with their family members and a decline in the size of their social circle. In addition, among those using the Internet extensively, this study found increases in depression and loneliness.[16]

Studies on Internet addiction paint a similarly dismal picture. Excessive Internet usage can lead to Internet Addiction Disorder, or IAD, according to some psychologists.[17] Broken marriages, job loss, and failing school grades have also been cited as the consequences of this form of addiction. Such addiction leads to "decreased occupational, academic, social, work-related, family-related, financial, psychological, or physiological functioning."[18] People who frequent chat rooms and role-playing forums (such as Multi-user Domain, or MUD) seem to be the prime candidates for such addiction. Internet addiction is a contentious topic, and some experts do not subscribe to the existence of such an illness.

Positive Social Impact

A three-year study on the social consequences of living in a highly-wired neighbourhood had more encouraging news. A new suburban community, code-named "Netville," was wired with a no-cost, broadband (high-speed Internet access) technology. The key finding of this project was that a high-speed local network encourages greater community involvement, expands and strengthens local relationships with neighbours and family, and helps people maintain ties with friends and relatives in distant places.[19] Community e-mail was used for introductions of new community members, invitations to social events, and as a means of social support. Smaller discussion lists were created for discussing topics of specific interests. The study also found that such communication increased the community members' knowledge of each other.[20]

Netville, of course, is an online as well as offline community. People had access to each other face-to-face as well as through the Internet. As more studies are conducted on the impact of electronic networks on social communication, relations, and well-being, we will have a better understanding of the negative and positive implications of the technology.

The Future of E-Commerce and the Internet

The E-commerce sites we see in the year 2000 can be classified perhaps as the second-generation of sites. From simple flat Web pages, sites have evolved to become more interactive and engaging. The next generation of E-commerce sites will have greater interactive and multimedia capability. As broadband reaches more consumers, Web sites will come alive, and may even start to resemble television. E-commerce in the future is not going to be done just through personal computers. Wireless applications today offer us a glimpse of what we can expect in the future. In this section, we will explore some of the emerging technologies that may have a significant impact on commerce online.

Exhibit 14-3 Palm-Based Stock Quotes from Schwab

Source: www.internetworld.com.

Wireless and Handheld Devices

Many consumers are familiar and comfortable with Palms (see Exhibit 14-3), PocketPCs, cell phones, and other such devices. We are beginning to see Internet capability being added to these devices. It is now possible to get stock quotes, news, and weather reports from these devices, as well as do shopping online. Content providers like Britannica.com are now providing content for the wireless devices. **Wireless Application Protocol (WAP)** is poised to take over from the Internet Protocol (IP) that drives the Internet.

The possibilities for the wireless Internet are endless. Advertisers are trying to figure out how advertising can be done on such devices. In the future, it may even be possible to target ads to someone's cell phone based on that person's location. For example, a consumer who approaches a store may see an ad from that store on his or her mobile device.

E-tailers are getting ready for mobile commerce or **M-commerce**. While research companies predict a strong future for M-commerce, it remains to be seen if consumers who are just learning to shop via their PCs will start shopping through their Palms and cell phones. Snaz.com allows consumers to shop through a Palm VII device and offers access to vendors such as Dell, Borders, Barnes & Noble, and OfficeMax.

Other mobile applications include purchasing movie tickets using Palm (Encryptix), browsing city guides (Vindigo), and using a mobile telephone as a payment terminal for things like parking meters and vending machines (Qpass).

M-commerce seems to hold a lot of promise in developing countries. These countries cannot afford the huge investments needed for land-based telecommunications infrastructure. Cellular phones are easy and comparatively cheaper to deploy, and their use in developing countries like China, India, Vietnam, and Brazil is rapidly growing.

Voice and Speech Recognition

Another emerging technology that holds a lot of promise is **speech recognition**. Nuance.com and Speechworks.com are two of the companies developing technology in this area. While speech recognition has applications beyond the Internet, this technology makes the pages of a Web site come alive.

Voice browsers can enable users to access content and applications in voice-enabled Web sites through the use of standard voice devices such a telephone. Nuance has a product called *Nuance Verifier*, which uses a combination of speech recognition and voice authentication to provide an extremely high level of security. This technology has the potential to eliminate the need for passwords and personal identification numbers (PINs), but it remains to be seen if such technology will gain mass acceptance among businesses and consumers.

Several companies are developing applications for a voice-based Web. Tellme.com allows users to dial a 1-800 number and find out sports news and stock quotes, as well as search and find restaurants and other vendors. ShopTalk allows consumers to shop using the VoiceWeb technology. BeVocal can provide point-to-point driving instructions and real-time traffic reports. If the mobile and voice-based applications gain consumer acceptance, a computer may no longer be necessary to shop online.

Smart Appliances and Products

As we saw in Chapter 1, some cars now have Internet capability. Many Internet-enabled "smart" home appliances are also under development now. One example is an Internet-connected refrigerator that can "talk" to the local grocery store. The grocery store would automatically know when to home deliver routinely purchased grocery items. In the future, you may even be able to turn on or off a home appliance from a remote location.

Interactive TV

Forrester Research predicts a great future for interactive TV, which has implications for the Web. They predict TV-based impulse buying or "lazy commerce" (where the product can be ordered via interactive television) of $7 billion and interactive TV advertising revenues of $11 billion by 2004.[21] WebTV and Wink offer the Web via a TV set. These two platforms are expected to be dominant in the emerging interactive TV world.

Interactive TV (ITV) essentially allows the viewer to interact with the program, unlike the present technology, which is passive and one-way. For instance, a consumer who sees an advertisement can click a link and immediately place an order. It will become possible to view video-on-demand. Game shows and sitcoms can become interactive, allowing the audience to participate. Interactive TV essentially combines the interactivity of the Web with the emotive power of television.[22]

Implications of Emerging Technologies

The emerging technologies in handheld devices, voice-based browsers, and interactive TV have important implications for businesses.

The face of the Web is changing, even as this book is being written. The personal computer still remains the most dominant form of connecting to the Internet. Since 1994, content and commercial applications have been developed for delivery via computers. Now businesses face a new challenge. They must develop content and commercial applications for new types of devices, which may offer more or less flexibility.

Handheld devices have a small screen where only a very limited amount of information can be displayed. Product catalogues with pictures and multimedia content cannot be used. Marketers must learn to present information in a manner that is suitable for these devices. Use of cookies in this situation is not possible yet. That means some shopping cart applications or personalization applications based on cookies will not work. Security issues have to be addressed as well. Companies such as Baltimore Technologies (www.baltimore.com) are developing security solutions for wireless applications. Baltimore Telepathy is a product that addresses the security needs of companies that wish to engage in M-commerce.

Voice holds a great deal of promise because it can take many applications available on the Internet to people who do not own a computer. Interactive TV has the same potential of reaching consumers in the lower end of the market. There is usually no need to buy a new TV (a set top box is needed). Online shopping can be done via the consumer's television set.

The most significant issue emerging from the discussion in the preceding section is that several technologies are rapidly converging—Internet, telephone, and television. Consumers, even today, can reach the Internet in different ways. This also presents some interesting opportunities for marketers.

In Chapter 11, the concept of "contextual marketing" was presented. It simply means "anytime-anywhere" marketing. If the Internet can be accessed from anywhere through different channels (in a kiosk in a store, from a pay phone in the airport, or through a television) and if consumers can reach a company through these channels as well as land-based operations (bricks-and-mortar stores), marketers must do the following:

- *Manage channels.* Firms must address potential channel conflicts as well as the need for varied information presentation in these channels. Business hours are 24/7 today. Synergies must be developed across channels. Channels must be chosen strategically, not simply because the technology is available. Does M-commerce make sense for all products?
- *Manage customer relationships.* Customers will reach firms via different channels and expect the same high level of service. They may even expect to be greeted by their first names, no matter the channel. The challenge of dealing with diverse channels is not to be taken lightly. Firms that provide consistency across channels will hold on to their customers. Customer relationship management requires organization-wide coordination and commitment to serving the customer. While marketers may see M-commerce and other new forms of commerce as an opportunity, success will depend on developing and implementing an integrated strategy.
- *Understand the impact of technology on strategy.* As we saw in Chapter 6, strategic planning in this new era is more complex. Technology is not just a facilitator anymore. It is a driving strategy in most organizations and industries. The Internet has elevated the

importance of customer relationship management, and this has profound strategic implications. On the B2B side, online purchasing and supply chain management often call for significant business process re-engineering. Markets that were once not considered viable are now available. Organizations that understand the implications of technology for their markets, customers, and products will stand a better chance of succeeding.

- *Focus on the customer*. Technologies are evolving at a faster pace than either consumers or businesses can absorb. Eventually, consumer acceptance is important. Interesting technologies may never fulfill their promise if consumer acceptance is low. In the past, changes in technology were more predictable and took a longer time to reach the market. Now, when many new technologies are being developed at such a rapid pace, the challenge lies in figuring out what will succeed and what will not. Where should the organization lay its bets? This is not an easy question to answer. Should a company develop commerce applications for several technologies, such as mobile and voice? Being able to foresee changes in consumers' needs, attitudes, and behaviour is vital.

- *Manage knowledge*. The preceding discussion makes it clear that an in-depth understanding of technology, customers, and organizational processes is necessary to succeed in this new economy. It is not sufficient if this knowledge resides in the minds of a few senior executives or line managers. Knowledge must be captured on an ongoing basis and transferred or made available to the right people at the right time. Organizations that manage knowledge in all critical factors, including technology, will be able to foresee the changes in the future faster than their rivals who do not manage knowledge.

- *Manage organizational change*. Organizations will be rapidly evolving entities. In Chapter 6 we saw some of the challenges organizations face as they build structures conducive to competing in the new economy. Organizations that do not make a commitment to learning and changing will be left behind. Technology-driven change has positive as well as negative effects. It is vital that employees who are in charge of implementation have bought into the change. It is not just senior management's commitment that is required, but also employee acceptance and enthusiasm. As new technologies provide new ways of doing business, employees must be trained to handle the change. Rather than reacting to every new technology that may have some bearing on one's business, a proactive change management strategy must be developed.

- *Address social implications*. While mobile technology may make the Internet accessible to millions in the developing world, it will not do much for people in abject poverty. By some estimates, about half the world's population has never even made a phone call. While there is no easy global solution, businesses can play a constructive role. There are examples of how technology can help the poor. In Bangladesh, Internet access provided by an aid agency gives village farmers and craftsmen access to buyers in bigger markets, bypassing intermediaries who previously exploited them. There is a need for social marketing efforts that go beyond a simple profit motive.

Summary

The Internet has applications beyond E-commerce. In the fields of education, government, and healthcare, we are seeing important advances being made using the Internet. While the benefits of this technology are immense, there are concerns about sections of society not having access to the technology or being unable to take advantage of the emerging opportunities. While governments in some countries have taken proactive measures to ensure that all citizens have access to the Internet, there are no simple solutions here. The gap between rich and poor nations must be addressed as well, especially if global trade is to expand.

As businesses develop strategies for today's Internet, there are new applications emerging that threaten to change the face of the Web. The Internet is already accessible through mobile phones and other handheld devices. Even ordinary home appliances such as the refrigerator or the home security system may become Internet-enabled soon. Clearly, businesses must be forward-looking and prepare for the future today.

Managers must consider the social implications of the technology—the impact on consumers, workers, and the society at large. They must be aware of new technologies and able to take advantage of emerging online commerce applications. Some of the keys to success in online marketing include the following issues:

- *Integration.* As we have seen throughout this book, successful marketing on the Internet is not just about having a Web site. It requires an integrative approach, which blends offline and online marketing efforts.
- *Customer focus.* Customization will continue to gain importance. Consumers will soon come to expect customization for many products. Right now, this is a way for companies to differentiate themselves from the competition. Soon, everyone may offer some degree of customization.
- *Think next generation.* Managers who are building E-commerce applications for today are likely to miss the big picture. Even as we develop strategies for the current Internet, new technologies are emerging. These technologies will change the face of the Web.
- *Organizational changes.* Organizations must be quick to respond to changes and market needs. They have to work in an integrated fashion, where all functions of an organization are geared toward serving the customer. Many organizations are shedding unnecessary tasks and are outsourcing specialized functions to other companies. Businesses, using the Internet, are integrating themselves with their suppliers, customers, and business partners. Information flow and transactions happen more efficiently. It is not easy to accomplish these changes when organizations have done business the old-fashioned way for many years. Process re-engineering and organizational change will continue to be key areas that call for senior management's attention in the next few years.

Finally, the Internet demands that everyone—businesses, government, educational institutions, healthcare providers, and even consumers—learn to think in new ways. Organizations and governments that do not respond to the challenge will be in trouble. Companies not only have to master the present technology, but must prepare to embrace the emerging technologies. Businesses that miss the important trends will do so at their own peril.

Key Terms

Digital divide, 354
E-education, 352
E-government, 348
E-health, 353

Interactive TV (ITV), 358
M-commerce, 357
Smart appliances, 358

Speech recognition, 358
Wireless Application
    Protocol (WAP), 357

Questions and Exercises

Review Questions

1. What is digital divide? What are the reasons for the existence of digital divide?
2. What is e-government?
3. What is e-education?
4. What is e-health?
5. Name three emerging technologies that will have an impact on online commerce?
6. What psychological or emotional impact can extensive Internet use have on individuals?
7. How can the Internet benefit society?

Discussion Questions

1. How can digital divide be overcome within nations and between nations? Provide specific measures.
2. What are the pros and cons of online education? Do you think university education will increasingly be available online?
3. Which of the new emerging technologies do you think holds the most promise for commercial applications? Why?
4. Do you think governments will actually become more efficient due to the Internet? What are the pros and cons of delivering government services via the Internet?

Internet Exercises

1. Visit some online universities such as Jones International, Lansbridge, and so on. Go through the site carefully. Examine demos or sample courses, if available. Write a brief report on online education, its pros and cons, and whether such universities will become a threat to traditional universities. How should traditional universities respond?
2. Search for charity sites on a search engine. Visit at least three different charity sites. Review the sites and write a brief report on each site—its effectiveness, features, presentation, and user-friendliness.

Appendix A

Glossary of Internet Marketing Terms

Ad inventory Total ad impressions a Web site has for sale in a given period.

Ad or banner rotation Different ads from a list of ads may be shown on the same page at different times of the day or based on an ad targeting strategy.

Advertising networks One-stop shop for marketers to plan, serve, and track ad campaigns across many different Web sites; offers thousands of member sites where ads can be placed.

Affiliate networks or sites An arrangement between two companies where Company A's Web site places ads or links to Company B's site. Company A is compensated by Company B for sending the traffic (visitors) or for enquiries or sales resulting from such traffic.

Banner advertising A small image file (usually 468 × 60 pixels or smaller in size) that is placed in specific sites where the target market can be reached. Banner ads can be static or animated and they can also be interactive (e.g., allow consumer to enter purchase order directly from the ad).

Branding An integral part of product strategy that allows companies to differentiate their offerings from competitors' products by name, term, sign, symbol, or a combination of these.

Bricks-and-clicks A retailer that has a physical location and a Web presence.

Bricks-and-mortar A retailer that has only a physical location and no Web presence.

Brochureware A Web site in which it seems like a company has simply transferred its print brochure or catalogue to the Web without taking advantage of the Web's capabilities such as multimedia content and interactivity.

Broker An independent agent wholesaler that brings buyers and sellers together and provides market information to either party.

B2B (business-to-business) A site that facilitates buying and selling of products and services or exchange of information between businesses. All participants tend to be businesses. A single transaction on a B2B site can be worth tens of thousands of dollars. B2B sites can be company Web sites, horizontal or vertical hubs or B2B exchanges.

B2B exchanges Vertical markets that bring together buyers and sellers in a single industry to enable spot buying of manufacturing inputs

B2C (business-to-consumer) A site that facilitates buying and selling of products and services or dissemination of content aimed at consumers. Buyers tend to be individual or household consumers. B2C sites can directly sell products online, offer content services, or entertainment. They can also be portal sites.

B2E (business-to-employee) The focus is on the employee rather than the consumer. B2E encompasses everything an organization does to attract, hire and retain the best employees. Often B2E is implemented as a portal site within the organization allowing each employee to customize the site and include information that he or she desires (including stock quotes, news, sports updates and even online games). The emphasis is not just on efficiency but also on increased employee satisfaction. An Intranet consists of information that the company wants to provide its employees, whereas a B2E portal contains information employees want.

B2G (business-to-government) A site that caters to the informational and purchasing needs of government departments. Businesses and government agencies are brought together to facilitate buying and selling. A variation of B2B.

Broadband A high-speed, high-capacity transmission channel carried on coaxial or fiber-optic cables that allow high volumes of data and multiple channels of data to be carried over a single medium. Broadband transmission channels can simultaneously carry video, voice, and data at a rate much faster than a conventional telephone line.

Browser A software application that uses a graphical interface which allows Internet users to look at and interact with Web pages. Browser applications work in conjunction with other software applications called plug-ins and enable users to see animation and hear sound. Netscape and Internet Explorer are examples of browser software applications. The term "browser" is sometimes used to indicate the computer user who is browsing or visiting a Web site.

Business intelligence A systematic approach that allows organizations to monitor competition, consumers, and market trends on an ongoing basis.

Business model A description of how firms generate revenue and profits, and the methods of operation

Buy rate The rate at which browsers or visitors to a site are converted to buyers. Expressed as a percentage, it is the total numbers of unique buyers or customers divided by the total number of unique visitors.

Buyer-controlled sites Web sites set up by one or more buyers to source supplies online, to pool purchasing power.

B-webs Strategically aligned, multi-enterprise partner networks of producers, suppliers, service providers, infrastructure companies, and customers that conduct business communication and transactions via digital channels such as the Internet.

Certification Authority (CA) An organizing issuing and managing digital certificates and public as well as private keys.

Channel conflict A situation in which one channel member perceives another channel member to be acting in a way that prevents the first member from achieving its distribution objectives.

Click-through rate The measurement of how many times viewers click on a banner ad.

Click-wrap licence The licence agreement that takes effect once the consumer clicks on a button and downloads software from the Internet.

Clicks-and-mortar A retailer with a physical location and an online presence.

Clickstream The sequence of clicks or pages requested as a visitor explores a Web site. It is a record of the path that a visitor has takes while browsing through a Web site. Tracking the clickstream allows Web site designers and webmasters to study how the site is being used.

Co-branding Two brands jointly promoting a product or service, which carries the names of both brands.

Collaborative filtering The process that companies like Amazon use to make recommendations by filtering data based on evaluations, recommendations, or purchases made by other people.

Community A group of consumers who have shared professional or personal interests and feel the need to connect with other members of the same group.

Community commerce The congregating of many buyers and sellers on one site to support sales, bid/ask transactions, and source suppliers.

Competitive intelligence An ongoing process and a systematic approach to studying the competition.

Consumer profiling The tracking of consumer behaviour by marketers on the Web by studying their online surfing patterns, online purchase history, and demographic data.

Consumer protection The ensuring of the integrity, authenticity, privacy, and confidentiality of the consumer's data.

Contextual marketing An anytime-anywhere commerce strategy with multiple ways of reaching consumers (offline and online), including the use of cell phone or other mobile Internet-enabled devices.

Cookie A file on a Web user's hard drive that is used by Web sites to record data about the user. The file can contain information on user's preferences (if the site allows customization), products purchased, ad clicks and so on. The user can delete these files or set preferences in the browser software (such as Netscape or Internet Explorer) to block cookie files.

Corporate governance Rules and practices relating to how corporations are governed by management, directors, and shareholders.

Cost of customer acquisition The cost to the e-tailer to attract and maintain an online customer.

Cost-per-response (CPR) The media cost based on how many viewers click on a banner ad or actual sales on a designated Web site.

Cost-per-thousand impressions (CPM) The media cost of gaining exposure to one thousand persons with an ad on designated Web sites.

Cost transparency The ability of consumers to use the Internet to easily find the seller's cost, which impacts on the seller's ability to manipulate the price of the product.

Customer acquisition cost The marketing and advertising expenses needed to convert a prospective customer into an actual customer.

Customer experience The overall impression or experience that customers receive from visiting a Web site regarding quality of content, service, ease of navigation, ability to find information quickly, customizability and order fulfillment.

Customer Relationship Management (CRM) An organization-wide strategic effort to consistently unify customer interaction across all communication channels and all business functions, essential to satisfy and retain customers.

Cybermediary Internet-based intermediary who provides value-added services.

Cyber-squatting The registering of an Internet domain name that legally belongs to someone else.

Cyber-stalking Any unwanted, obsessive pursuit of an individual by another through electronic means, including e-mail.

Data mining Process of identifying patterns and meaningful relationships in huge volume of data. For example, use of statistical techniques to identify market segments based on data on purchase history of a store's patrons.

Digital cash Electronic cash that can be used to purchase products online. The buyer need not reveal his or her identity (as in the case of a credit card transaction). Usually cash credits are purchased in relatively small amounts and stored in the consumer's computer, and then spent when making online purchases over the Internet.

Digital certificate A method of ensuring security of information online. A certificate consists of a key made of very large numbers, which can contain information such as identity of the certificate holder, name of the certificate-issuing authority and the period of validity of the certificate.

Digital divide The gap in the adoption rate between the "haves" and "have-nots" of Internet access.

Digital signature Similar to a written signature, verifies the identity of the person sending a message or placing an order online, created by applying a hashing algorithm to the message.

Direct selling Basic E-commerce, where the products are sold directly from the seller's Web site to the buyer.

Disintermediation The elimination of some or all members in a distribution channel which allows the producer of the product or service to directly sell to the end-user.

Domain name A Web site address, which is unique to each site. The domain name identifies a Web server that hosts a particular Web site.

Dynamic pricing Price is determined in real time through buyer-seller negotiation and demand. Such pricing can result in a higher soft drink price on a hot day compared to a cool day. Using technology and by understanding demand and consumer behaviour, pricing can be adjusted minute-by-minute or transaction-by-transaction to ensure optimal pricing. Auctions are a form of dynamic pricing. Also called real-time pricing.

E-business The transformation of the business world through the use of the Internet and includes E-commerce, supply chain management, and customer relationship management.

E-commerce The buying and selling of goods and services over the Internet and other electronic networks.

E-Coupons or Online Coupons Similar to printed coupons, except they can be redeemed in online (and in some cases, offline) stores. They can be customized or delivered as a customer is browsing through a site.

E-education The transformation of the education system through the use of the Internet to offer students and teachers online resources and a channel for online training and education.

E-government The transformation of government through the use of the Internet and information technology.

E-health The transformation of the health industry through the use of the Internet by those who seek health-related information and services online, as well as purchase drugs online.

Electronic coupons A response-inducing sales promotion effort that can be redeemed in online or offline stores.

Electronic Data Interchange (EDI) Computer-to-computer transmission of orders, invoices, or other business information.

E-mail marketing A targeted or tailored message from a marketer to each recipient of the e-mail.

E-mail surveys Surveys sent to participants via e-mail.

Emoticons Small graphical expressions of emotion composed of characters which substitute for facial expressions and body language, e.g., a smile :).

Encryption A method of keeping networks, databases, and files private and secure by scrambling the data at the sender's end and descrambling the same data at the receiver's end.

E-tailer Seller of products or services online.

Extranets A password-protected Web site that links a company with other firms in the supply chain or with customers and partners.

Firewall The software and/or hardware that stands between a company's internal computer network and the external network that keeps unauthorized users or intruders outside the network.

Fulfillment The process of filling orders as they occur, for example, when a catalogue company selects the items from its inventory to be sent to a customer who has ordered them.

Horizontal hubs Online intermediaries who connect buyers and sellers across several industries (usually buying and selling MRO or maintenance, repair and operating supply items).

HTML (Hypertext Markup Language) The formatting language of the Web, the language humans use to talk to Web servers and browsers.

Hyperlinks The links that allow documents and other types of files within the same computer as well as between computers anywhere in the world to jump from one document or file to another.

Hypermedia An extension of coding text that includes audio, video, and graphical elements.

Infomediaries Online intermediaries who aggregate content and make it easier for buyers to find information on the Web.

Information goods Also called **digital goods.** Products or services which can be digitized and often delivered online.

Information Superhighway The term is widely used to mean the "Internet."

Instant messaging An online pager system that offers instant access to anyone as long as they are also online.

Integrated promotion A communication strategy that combines offline and online media, each with a specific objective, to produce the best results.

Interactive media Media that accept input from consumers and respond accordingly. The Web is an interactive medium, where customers can post messages or enter purchase orders in forms or play online games.

Interactive TV (ITV) The interaction of the TV viewer with the program, changing a passive viewer to an active, interactive viewer.

Internet marketing The offering of goods or services to customers over the Internet.

Internet Protocol (IP) A scheme that enables data or information to be sent from one computer to another or one network to another on the Internet.

Internet A world-wide system of linked computer networks that facilitates data communication services such as remote login, file transfer, electronic mail, and newsgroups. Computers connected to the Internet can transfer messages and files among each other.

Internet Marketing Plan A firm's Marketing Plan that is currently online or intends to go online. In addition to the usual components of a marketing plan (e.g., internal and external analysis, objectives, marketing mix and timelines), an Internet Marketing Plan also provides details of the Web site and online strategies in areas such as advertising, pricing, product customization and customer relationship management.

Internet Service Provider (ISP) a company that provides access to the Internet, typically for a monthly fee and in some cases free. An account must be set up with an ISP for Internet access. AOL, Netcom, Sprint and Sympatico are examples of ISPs. The user must have a modem and must dial a specific number to log on to the Internet. Many cable companies also provide access to the Internet through a special modem.

Internet time A system devised by Swatch, which divides the day into 1000 units and eliminates time zones. This term is also used to indicate the telescoping of normal phases of business development into shorter spans of time.

Internetworked organization A cluster of companies operating a cohesive whole, each with a specific expertise and each playing a specific role in the value chain. Internetworked organizations use the Internet to seamlessly integrate their activities. See also B-webs.

Interstitials An "in between" page that "pops up" in a new Window for the purpose of advertising or promotion. Interstitial ads are often displayed when a user exits one page or site and is waiting for another page or site to download. These ads are often timed to disappear from the screen after allowing enough time to register in the consumer's mind.

Intranet A private network inside a company or organization that uses the same kinds of software used on the Internet (such as Web browsers). Access to the network is usually restricted to employees through password protection. Intranets have been important in collaborative team-based projects and knowledge management within organizations.

Law of digital assets The concept that marginal costs will approach zero when a product is digitized and delivered online.

Lifetime customer value A relationship marketing perspective that suggests that a customer retained for many years or over a lifetime is more valuable and profitable to the firm than some one who does not exhibit such loyalty. LCV on the Web is computed by (a) multiplying the expected number of visits by a customer times the average amount of money spent per visit, then (b) deducting the cost of acquiring and servicing that customer, then (c) adding the value of new accounts referred to by the customer, and (d) discounting the sum by the appropriate period of the analysis.

Mail Order/Telephone Order (MOTO) The "card not present" category of credit card transactions that does not allow for face-to-face verification of the card holder's identity.

Many-to-many medium A medium, such as the Web, in which the sender of the message (such as an advertisement or an online promotion) can also be the recipient of the message. Online consumers communicate back to marketers, unlike in mass media (such as TV), where information flows in one direction only.

Market makers Independent Internet-based third parties or intermediaries that bring buyers and sellers together.

Marketing plan A detailed statement, usually in written form, detailing the firm's marketing objectives and strategy along with a schedule for implementation of the strategy.

Marketplace The physical "brick-and-mortar" market.

Marketspace The virtual or online market.

Mass customization The ability to create customized marketing messages, products or services for each customer or market segment without sacrificing the benefits derived from mass production or marketing (e.g., economies of scale).

M-commerce Mobile commerce that allows consumers to order products, purchase stocks, and receive news and targeted ads via cell phones or other hand-held devices.

Megamediary A megastore that sponsors other smaller stores and offers auction sales.

Meta search engines Search engine sites or programs that can simultaneously search several search engines and produce a search result with more relevant pages than possible by searching a single search engine. See Search Engines.

Micropayment Allows for marketers to sell products online for only a few cents or even a fraction of a cent.

Micro-pricing The selling of unbundled low-value items as separate units using micropayment methods.

Micro-site A mini online store site that runs during a specific ad or promotional campaign.

Multimedia Combining text, sound, graphics, and video.

Multiple channels The marketing to customers across a number of channels: catalogues, bricks-and-mortar stores, and online.

Navigation The ability to move around a Web site or from one site to another by clicking on hypertext links or images hyperlinked to other pages.

Networked organization An organization that is vertically disaggregated and knowledge-based. Networked organizational structure enables an organization to focus on its core competency and build strategic partnerships with other organizations that can provide expertise in other areas. The Internet links these various organizations.

Neutral sites Web sites run by independent third parties providing market-making functions, facilitating online auctions, and managing integrated supply chains.

One-to-many medium The publishing/broadcasting paradigm of mass media.

One-to-one marketing The publishing/broadcasting paradigm of the mass media, where information flows one-way (from the publisher/network or marketer to many consumers) and where all recipients get the same message without any customization.

Online brand community A brand-centred community of Internet-integrated consumers.

Online Focus Groups A market research technique where a group of pre-screened consumers are brought together online to provide information or feedback on any aspect of a firm's strategy. A "chat" software allows participants to log into a chat site from remote locations and have a group discussion without a face-to-face meeting. A moderator can ask questions and control the discussion. The chat software usually allows for product demonstrations through streaming video or for display of pictures or Web sites.

Peer-to-peer (P2P) The downloading and sharing of files with other consumers, e.g. Napster.

Permission marketing The sending of customized messages and e-mail flyers by marketers to consumers who have subscribed to this service.

Physical value chain The performance of a series of actions to improve efficiency and effectiveness of processes in each stage resulting in a final product or service, adding value at each step of the chain.

Plug-ins Software applications that run in conjunction with the browser and that allow users to experience video, audio, animation, and interactivity.

Portals Sites that act as entry points or gateways to the Web.

Positioning A company's strategy for favourably distinguishing its brand from other competing brands in the consumer's mind. Consumer's perception of the brand on important attributes in relation to competing brands.

Price discrimination The practice of selling a product at different prices to different buyers, even though the cost of the product is the same in each case.

Prosumption The blurring of the gap between producers and consumers, as in the case of "customization" where consumers participate in the production activity.

Public-key encryption A complex mathematical method to secure digital communications using a public key to encode the data and a private key to decode it.

Push Technologies Programs that deliver content from one or several sites to the user's desktop without the user having to visit or download information from any site. See also Webcast.

Random sample A sample that is selected in such a way that every unit in the defined universe has an equal chance of being selected.

Real-time pricing See Dynamic Pricing.

Reintermediation The reintroduction of an intermediary between the seller and the buyer or reincarnation of a disintermediated channel player, e.g., by refocusing on new value-added services.

Safe harbor A voluntary US program that requires participating companies to fully disclose their consumer data collection procedure and give control to the consumer to modify or delete their personal information maintained by Web sites.

Sales and marketing expense ratio (SMR) The percentage of total revenue that is spent on sales and marketing costs.

Sales force automation Strategy of equipping salespeople with laptop computers, cellular phones, fax machines, and pagers to give them access to databases, the Internet, and e-mail to help them manage accounts more effectively.

Search goods Products that do not require physical inspection or trial.

Search Engines Sites that use tools known as spiders or robots to index pages on the World Wide Web. Users can use key words to search the index and find sites that match their interests. Each search engine site has its own algorithm for determining the relevance and ranking of sites for a given key word search. Most search engines index only a fraction of the pages available on the World Wide Web. Some pages may be indexed in one search engine but not another.

Secure Electronic Transaction (SET) A protocol developed by Visa and Mastercard, and later supported by other credit card issuing companies, banks and software companies. SET ensures security of online transactions by authenticating the identity of the parties (buyer and seller).

Secure Sockets Layer (SSL) A protocol that delivers server authentication, data encryption, and message integrity. SSL allows for a "secure" connection between a browser (consumer-end) the server (merchant-end). SSL facilitates the encryption of messages and enables secure financial transactions online. While encryption offers some degree of security, unlike SET, SSL does not authenticate the parties.

Seller-controlled sites Web sites that are information-only (brochureware) or directly sell products online to end-users.

Shrink-wrap licence The licence agreement that takes effect once the consumer breaks the shrink-wrap packaging of a software product.

Smart appliances Internet-enabled appliances, such as smart refrigerators that can be linked to online grocery stores, which will trigger purchase orders resulting in automatic replenishment of the inventory as needed.

Spam Any unsolicited message that is usually sent to promote a product or service, mostly in the form of junk e-mail. Spam is also known as Unsolicited Commercial E-mail (UCE).

Speech recognition The ability of computers, wireless devices, etc., to recognize speech and authenticate voice.

Stickiness A Web site's ability to attract repeat customers and keep them on that site, allowing the measuring of time spent at that site.

Surfer (or Web Surfer) A consumer who seeks information or entertainment on the Web in an undirected manner or without a specific goal.

Symmetric-key encryption A complex mathematical method to secure digital communications using the same key to encode (sender) and decode (receiver) the data.

Total Consumer Experience (TCE) Every activity undertaken by the firm is designed from the customer perspective. Rather than focusing merely on selling the product, everything from how the customer will navigate the site, to the design of the site, the colours used, the customized features provided, the ordering process and customer care are taken into account.

Usenet newsgroups A global-spanning collection of informal bulletin boards distributed over the Internet.

Value exchange The concept whereby consumers give personal information to a marketer in exchange for something valuable from the marketer.

Vertical communities Participants within specific industries who participate in online communities.

Vertical hub Site used to facilitate B2B commerce within a specific industry by providing necessary technology and infrastructure.

Viral marketing A combination of e-mail marketing and word-of-mouth communication that propagates itself the way viruses do from one user to another via e-mail messages.

Virtual product development The tapping of globally-dispersed expertise to innovate and develop products using different team members working in different countries and across many time zones.

Virtual value chain In the virtual world, the creation of value at different stages of the value chain through the use of information. The virtual value chain, like its physical counterpart, includes several steps—from gathering, organizing, selecting, and synthesizing to distributing information. By capturing data at different stages of the value chain, an organization can convert the data into information and then knowledge, and can create additional value in the virtual world.

Vortals Vertical industry portals that specialize in a single industry or subject.

Web-based surveys Surveys posted on a Web site by market researchers and completed by participants.

Webcast The use of the Web to deliver live or delayed versions of sound or video broadcasts. Also referred to as "push technology." Viewing a webcast requires appropriate video viewing software applications such as NetShow, RealVideo, Windows Mediaplayer or Vxtreme.

Webmaster Someone who manages a Web site, monitors site traffic and performance, ensures reliability and acceptable download speed. A webmaster does not generally design the site.

Web site logs A file that keeps track of the activity on a Web site or server, intended to track consumer behaviour on a site. Information captured in the Log can include pages visited, files downloaded, time spent, repeat visits, the computer from which the visit took place, entry and exit pages, and more.

Wireless Application Protocol (WAP) The language that allows computers to communicate over the wireless Internet using devices such as cell phones and Palms.

WWW (World Wide Web) A global system where documents can be linked to each other (hyperlinks), where the user can click on a hyperlink and go from one document to another or one location to another within the same document or from one computer server to another. WWW uses the Internet as the transport system. Documents on the World Wide Web can include text, pictures, audio, video and animation. Users can interact with this medium, where user actions (such as a click on a hyperlink or the completion of an online form) can create a specific response. The Web allows consumers to browse through catalogues in online stores, purchase products and transfer credit card information securely.

XML (eXtensible Markup Language) A more advanced formatting language than HTML for designing Web sites that gives more control over formatting and presentation of information. It enables Web page designers to customize tags and to point links to multiple documents, which are features not available in HTML. XML has become the standard for B2B sites.

Appendix B

Internet Marketing Planning Guide

Introduction

In this appendix, we will look at a generic Internet marketing planning guide, which is presented as a series of questions. The nature of the product or service, objective of the Web site (selling versus advertising), and type of existence (pure-play versus clicks-and-mortar) are some of the variables that will affect the specifics of the marketing plan. Firms that distribute the product electronically (such as content and software sites) will have different issues to deal with compared to firms that sell tangible products online. Similarly, clicks-and-mortar firms will have to address certain issues (such as channel conflict) that pure-play firms will not face.

Every firm will not address all the issues or questions raised in this guide, and some firms may have to address issues or questions not raised here. The guide can be adapted for B2B or B2C firms that sell manufactured products or services. It can also be adapted to start-up firms and existing companies.

Internet Marketing Plan Guide

1. Overview of Company

This section should serve as an introduction to the company and provide an overview of the products, markets, and management.

- What is the history of the firm? When was it founded? Where is it located?
- Who are the founders and key management personnel?
- Provide a brief description of the products and markets.
- In the case of an existing firm, provide an overview of financial performance (such as return on investment, revenues, net income, and cash flow) and marketing performance (such as market share, customer acquisition, customer retention, and brand awareness) for the past three years.

2. Internal Analysis

This section should examine the operations of the organization critically. It should identify strengths and weaknesses of the organization.

- What is the business model?
  - How will the firm generate revenue? Describe the revenue sources.
  - Will the firm sell products or services online?
  - Will the firm's site accept advertising on its site?
  - In the case of an existing firm going online, how will the Internet affect the firm's business model?
- What is the firm's organizational structure?
  - In the case of an existing firm going online, what changes are needed in the firm's organizational structure to succeed online?
- What are the primary products/services offered by the firm?
- What are the key markets served or to be served?
- What competitive advantages does the firm possess?
  - How will the firm ensure its superiority over its competitors?
- What resources are available to the firm?
  - Discuss financial, human, and technological resources.
- What are the major strengths and weaknesses of the firm?

3. External Analysis

This section should critically examine target markets, competitors, and external factors. Market opportunities and threats should also be identified.

a. *Target Market*

- What is (are) the target market(s)? Why was this market chosen?
  - Is the target market local, national, or international?
- Market size and growth. What is the overall size of the market currently? How big is the potential market? What is the growth rate per annum?
- Are consumers in those markets currently online? If not, when can they be expected to become Internet users?
  - If the customers are online, how sophisticated are they in Internet usage? What is their usage pattern? (present hours of weekly use and place of use, if known).
- What is the profile of each market segment targeted?
- How can the target market be reached online?
  - Are they reachable via offline advertising, online advertising, e-mail, newsgroups, or community sites?
- What is the online decision process? What factors influence the buying decision?
- What factors will facilitate adoption of the products offered by this firm? What factors will act as barriers to adoption?
- Do consumers use the Web for information search and interaction with the company, or do they actually do the transactions online?
- How often do current customers visit the Web site?
- How is the frequency of purchase? What is the average purchase size?

b. *Competition*

- How intense is the competition in the industry?

- Who are the current competitors? Who are the potential competitors?
- Are there substitute products that can pose a threat as indirect competition?
- Are competitors online, offline, or both?
- What are the strengths and weaknesses of each major competitor?
- How is this firm's product/service superior to what the competitors offer?

c. *Social, Economic, Legal, and Technological Factors*

- What are social factors that affect this industry positively or negatively? Consider culture, changing demographics, lifestyles, and so on.
- Is the economy conducive to the growth of this market? Will interest rates, currency fluctuations, or other forces affect the market for the products?
- What regulatory and legal challenges are present online?
  - Consider taxation, copyrights, jurisdiction and contracts, privacy protection, and patents as some potential areas (see Chapter 13).
- What are the major technological trends in the industry?
  - Which of the newly emerging technologies are likely to have the greatest impact on this industry?
  - How is this firm prepared to deal with new technologies?

4. Marketing Objectives

- Describe the marketing objectives. These objectives should be consistent with the overall mission of the company and business strategy.
  - Provide quantifiable objectives such as market share, share of mind, revenues, and so on.
- Provide a timeline for achieving the objectives.

5. Strategic Overview

This section should provide insight into the strategy of the firm. The section should detail how the firm will differentiate its offerings from those of its competitors. (This section can be raised here and can be integrated into other sections. For instance, value creation can be addressed in internal analysis).

- In this section, describe the firm's overall business strategy.
- How would the firm gain a competitive advantage over its competitors? How is this firm's product differentiated from the competing offers in the market? How will this firm sustain or build on this advantage?
- How is the product or service going to be positioned? What attributes will be emphasized to present and potential customers?
- How does the firm create value for its customers? Describe the physical and virtual value chain. What are the value drivers?
- Will the company pursue a customization strategy? What level of customization (see Chapter 7) is appropriate?
- Will the firm pursue a customer relationship management (CRM) strategy (see Chapter 7)?
  - How will the firm attract, service, and retain customers over the long term?
  - How will customer service be implemented?
- How does the firm manage its costs?

6. Marketing Mix

This is, perhaps, the most detailed section of the plan. It deals with marketing tactics. Tactical elements should be linked to the marketing objectives outlined in the previous section, and be consistent with the strategic overview presented earlier.

a. *Product* (see Chapter 8)
  - What is the product or service? Is the product a purely digital product? Is there a digital or informational component to the product?
  - How do consumers use it? What benefits do they derive from it?
  - How is the product differentiated from competing firms' products?
  - What new innovations are forthcoming?
  - How will the Internet affect the development and delivery of the product (see Chapter 8)?
  - Is mass customization part of the strategy? How will customization be implemented? What level of customization is required?

b. *Pricing* (see Chapter 8)
  - What is the pricing objective (how does the firm generate market share or profits)?
  - What will the pricing strategy be? Is the pricing strategy one of market penetration (low price) or skimming?
  - Will there be geographical or other variations in price based on market segments?
  - Will the price be discounted? Will there be special offers or initial introductory prices?
  - How will the firm use the Internet in its pricing strategy? Will the firm adopt a dynamic or real-time pricing strategy (such as auctions) or a micro-pricing strategy (see Chapter 8)?

c. *Marketing Communications Mix* (see Chapters 9 and 10)
  - Objectives: What are the primary and secondary communication objectives?
  - Media mix: What will the role of the Web be in the communication mix? What role will mass media (such as print and television) play in achieving the communication objectives of the firm?
  - Will the Web be used in building customer relationships?
  - Advertising: What forms of online advertising will be used?
    - Will banner ads be used?
    - Will sponsorship of sites or live webcasts be done?
    - Will affiliate programs be used to drive traffic?
    - Will banner ad exchanges (such as LinkExchange) be used?
    - Will promotional sites be used to attract traffic and build brands?
  - Direct marketing: Will permission marketing be adopted?
    - What will the role of e-mail be in the online communication mix?
  - Promotion: What specific online promotional tools will be used?
    - Will online coupons, sweepstakes, or other promotional offers be used? If so, what will be the goal of such programs?
  - Personal selling: How will the Internet support personal-selling efforts (for example, integration with call centre)? Will online sales force automation tools (see Chapter 4) be used?
  - Public relations: How will news coverage regarding the product or service be managed?
  - Community: Will an online community of users or customers be built or exploited (if one currently exists)? If so, what will be the objective of such a community? (See Chapter 7.)

- Search engines: How will the firm register its site and Web pages in search engines? Will specific search engines be targeted to ensure a high ranking on certain keywords? Will the firm buy keywords on search engines? (See Chapter 10.)

d. *Channel Management* (see Chapters 11 and 12)
- Will the firm use the Internet as the only channel (direct selling) or will it use multiple channels? Which other channels will be used (such as retail, catalogues, and sales representatives)?
- Will the firm disintermediate existing channels?
- Is the firm a cybermediary?
- Is the product directly distributed online (such as a digital product like software) or will it be distributed offline, or both?
- How will the firm avoid/manage potential inter-channel conflicts?
- What specific synergies across channels are currently realized or can be realized in the future?
- How will the firm create value through its distribution strategy?
- Will the firm sell online?
- Will the online store be independently operated or located in an online mall? Describe the rationale for this decision.
- Describe the key features of the online store? How will the store be made attractive to customers?

e. *Integration of Offline and Online Marketing Efforts*
- How will online and offline marketing efforts be coordinated (this is a significant issue for firms with a physical presence)?
- In the case of a bricks-and-mortar firm going online, will the online and offline operations be run as independent entities or will the firm strive to provide a unified high-quality experience in all channels? How will synergies between the offline and online operations be achieved?

7. Web Site Management

This section should present the details of the Web site. The elements of the Web site should be linked to the objectives and strategy presented in the previous sections. Several issues raised in this section are addressed in different chapters of this book. The reader may have to refer to other sources for information on the technological issues.

- How will the Web site accomplish the objectives and strategy discussed in the previous sections?
- Will there be a single site or multiple brand sites?
- What will the key features of the site be?
- What will the image and theme of the site be?
  - How will the site convey the overall brand image and maintain consistency with other (perhaps offline) marketing efforts?
- What will the domain name be? Is the domain name easy to remember?
- User experience: How will the site be made user-friendly (discuss navigation, site search, site map, and other features)? What interactive or other features (such as streaming video) will be used to provide a rich online experience for the customer?
- Technology: What level of technology will be used in the site design (for example, cascading style sheets, Flash animation, Java, downloadable or streaming audio or video)? Will the pages be static HTML pages or dynamically created using ASP (active server

pages) and XML (eXtensible Markup Language)? Describe the catalogue and shopping cart technology used.

- Has the site been designed to reach the largest possible audience? Are plug-ins or features that work only on certain computers (such as PCs using Windows) used?
- Have the needs of the users and their level of Internet sophistication been considered in the site design?
- How do the technologies used in the site enhance the user experience on that site?

- Back-end integration: Will the site be integrated with back-end databases (such as an inventory system or customer management system) to add value to customers?
- Reliability: Has the site been designed to download quickly? A brief discussion of the type of server hosting the Web site, the nature of the Internet connection (TI or T3 lines), and back-up systems to ensure reliability would be appropriate. Where will the site be hosted (internally or through an ISP)?
- Security: How will security be assured for online transactions? Discuss the level of encryption (SET, SSL, or other security protocols) to be used (see Chapter 13).
- Payment: What forms of payment are acceptable online if it is an E-commerce site?
  - Discuss credit cards, cybercash, Net cheques, and other acceptable payment methods, including micropayments.
- Privacy: How will consumer privacy be guaranteed? Will the company share consumer data with other firms? Will the firm participate in the TRUSTe program? (See Chapter 13.)
- Consumer tracking (see Chapter 5): How will the site track consumer behaviour? Will cookies be used? If so, why? How will Web site log analysis be utilized? Will online surveys be used to gather feedback? What steps will be taken to protect consumer privacy and security of consumer data?
- Is the site scalable? As the number of users grows, will the site continue to have a fast download time, high reliability, and security?

8. Metrics and Evaluation (see Chapters 5 and 10)

This section should present conventional performance evaluation measures as well as measures that are specific to Internet firms. It is important to identify why a specific measure will be used and how it will help in the evaluation of performance.

- How will performance be evaluated? What are the measures of successful performance?
  - Metrics to evaluate Web site performance: Unique visitors, pages viewed, click-through rate, and time spent (stickiness).
  - Metrics to evaluate marketing performance: Customer acquisition cost, buyer conversion, customer satisfaction, customer attitude, and retention rates (loyalty).
  - Metrics to evaluate financial performance: Revenue, cash flows, cash on hand, ROI, ROE, EPS, and so on.
- Describe how these metrics would be used as a control system. For instance, what level of performance would be expected and accepted for each metric? When would corrective action be triggered?

9. Implementation and Budget/Financials

The plan should have an implementation timeline. Resources should be committed to ensure that the strategy could be implemented successfully. Details of implementation are as important as the strategy.

- Timelines for completion of specific tasks in launching the site or product. Include major milestones.
- Human resources required, including projections. Break-even analysis under different pricing and demand assumptions.
- Financial projection of sales, and cash flows for one year on a monthly basis. State assumptions used in making the projections.
- The budget should address all major categories discussed in the previous sections (for example, product, promotion, distribution, Web site, human resources, customer service, and CRM). Address both Web site start-up and maintenance costs.

10. Contingency Plan

- Address potential obstacles or external/internal events that may need a change in the course of action or strategy.
- Describe any alternative plans that could be adopted if the proposed strategy implementation does not meet expectations or if potential obstacles arise in the implementation of the strategy.

11. Conclusion

- Summarize the key advantages of the firm over its competitors. Why will this firm succeed? Briefly state the objectives again and explain how the firm will achieve these objectives.

Internet Marketing Plan Outline

This appendix is located online at www.mcgrawhill.ca/college/venkat so that the currency of information and the accuracy of the Web links can be maintained to your best advantage.

ESOMAR—European Society for Opinion and Marketing Research*

Conducting Marketing and Opinion Research Using the Internet

Basic Principles

Marketing and opinion research is the professional activity of collecting and interpreting consumer, business, and social data so that decision makers can make better and more efficient marketing and social decisions.

All research carried out on the Internet must conform to the rules and spirit of the main ICC/ESOMAR International Code of Marketing and Social Research Practice and also to Data Protection and other relevant legislation (both international and national).[1]

Such marketing and opinion research must always respect the rights of respondents and other Internet users. It must be carried out in ways which are acceptable to them, to the general public and in accordance with national and international self regulation. Researchers must avoid any actions which might bring Internet research into disrepute or reduce confidence in its findings.

Introduction

The rapid growth of the Internet has opened dramatic new opportunities for collecting and disseminating research information worldwide. At the same time it raises a number of ethical and technical issues which must be addressed if the medium is to be used effectively and responsibly for marketing and opinion research purposes.

The fact that the Internet is inexpensive to use and difficult to regulate means that it can be open to misuse by less experienced or less scrupulous organisations, often based outside the research industry. Any Internet surveys which fall seriously below the high standards promoted by ESOMAR and other leading professional bodies will make it more difficult to use the medium for research and could seriously damage the credibility of such research, as well as being an abuse of the goodwill of Internet users generally.

ESOMAR has issued this Guideline to protect the interests both of Internet respondents and of the users of Internet research findings. Because information technology and the Internet are evolving and changing so rapidly it is not practicable to discuss in detail all the technical features of Internet research in such a Guideline. This therefore concentrates on the main principles which must be followed in carrying out research on (or about) the Internet and in reporting the findings of such research.

Requirements

Co-operation is voluntary. Researchers must avoid intruding unnecessarily on the privacy of Internet respondents. Survey respondents' co-operation must at all times be voluntary. No personal information which is additional to that already available from other sources should be sought from, or about, respondents without their prior knowledge and agreement.

In obtaining the necessary agreement from respondents the researcher must not mislead them about the nature of the research or the uses which will be made of the findings. It is however recognised that there are occasions on which in order to prevent biased responses, the purpose of the research cannot be fully disclosed to respondents at the beginning of the interview. In particular, the researcher should avoid deceptive statements that would be harmful or create a nuisance to the respondent—for example, about the likely length of the interview or about the possibilities of being re-interviewed on a later occasion. Respondents should also be alerted when appropriate to any costs that they may incur (e.g., of on-line time) if they co-operate in the survey. They are entitled at any stage of the interview, or subsequently, to ask that part or all of the record of their interview be destroyed or deleted and the researcher must conform to any such request where reasonable.

The researcher's identity must be disclosed. Respondents must be told the identity of the researcher carrying out the project and the address at which they can without difficulty re-contact the latter should they wish to do so.

Respondents' rights to anonymity must be safeguarded. The anonymity of respondents must always be preserved unless they have given their informed consent to the contrary. If respondents have given permission for data to be passed on in a form which allows them to be personally identified, the researcher must ensure that the information will be used for research purposes only. No such personally identified information may be used for subsequent non-research purposes such as direct marketing, list-building, credit rating, fund-raising or other marketing activities relating to those individual respondents.

Privacy Policy Statements. Researchers are encouraged to post their privacy policy statement on their online site. When such privacy policy statements exist, they should be easy to find, easy to use and comprehensible.

Data security. Researchers should take adequate precautions to protect the security of sensitive data. Researchers must also reasonably ensure that any confidential information provided to them by clients or others is protected (e.g., by firewall) against unauthorised access.

Reliability and validity. Users of research and the general public must not be in any way misled about the reliability and validity of Internet research findings. It is therefore essential that the researcher:

(a) Follows scientifically sound sampling methods consistent with the purpose of the research.

(b) Publishes a clear statement of the sample universe definition used in a given survey, the research approach adopted, the response rate achieved and the method of calculating this where possible.

(c) Publishes any appropriate reservations about the possible lack of projectability or other limitations of the research findings, for instance, resulting from non-response and other factors.

It is equally important that any research *about* the Internet (e.g. to measure penetration, usership etc.) which employs other data collection methods, such as telephone or mail, also clearly refers to any sampling, or other, limitations on the data collected.

Interviewing Children and Young People

It is incumbent on the researcher to observe all relevant laws specifically relating to children and young people although it is recognised that the identification of children and young people is not possible with certainty on the Internet at this time. ESOMAR requirements about the precautions to be taken are set out in the ESOMAR Guideline on Interviewing Children and Young People. According to the ESOMAR Guideline, permission of a responsible adult must be obtained before interviewing children aged under 14 and asking questions on topics generally regarded as sensitive should be avoided wherever possible and in any case handled with extreme care. Researchers must use their best endeavours to ensure that they conform to the requirements of the Guideline referred to, for example by introducing special contacting procedures to secure the permission of a parent before carrying out an interview with children under 14. Where necessary researchers should consult ESOMAR or their national society for advice.

Unsolicited E-mail

Researchers should not send unsolicited messages on line to respondents who have indicated that they do not wish to receive such messages relating to a research project or to any follow-up research resulting directly from it. Researchers will reduce any inconvenience or irritation such E-mail might cause to the recipient by clearly stating its purpose in the subject heading and keeping the total message as brief as possible.

American Marketing Association Code of Ethics for Marketing on the Internet*

Preamble

The Internet, including online computer communications, has become increasingly important to marketers' activities, as they provide exchanges and access to markets worldwide. The ability to interact with stakeholders has created new marketing opportunities and risks that are not currently specifically addressed in the American Marketing Association Code of Ethics. The American Marketing Association Code of Ethics for Internet marketing provides additional guidance and direction for ethical responsibility in this dynamic area of marketing. The American Marketing Association is committed to ethical professional conduct and has adopted these principles for using the Internet, including on-line marketing activities utilizing network computers.

General Responsibilities

Internet marketers must assess the risks and take responsibility for the consequences of their activities. Internet marketers' professional conduct must be guided by:

- Support of professional ethics to avoid harm by protecting the rights of privacy, ownership and access.
- Adherence to all applicable laws and regulations with no use of Internet marketing that would be illegal, if conducted by mail, telephone, fax or other media.
- Awareness of changes in regulations related to Internet marketing.
- Effective communication to organizational members on risks and policies related to Internet marketing, when appropriate.
- Organizational commitment to ethical Internet practices communicated to employees, customers and relevant stakeholders.

---

* Copyright American Marketing Association.

Privacy

Information collected from customers should be confidential and used only for expressed purposes. All data, especially confidential customer data, should be safeguarded against unauthorized access. The expressed wishes of others should be respected with regard to the receipt of unsolicited e-mail messages.

Ownership

Information obtained from the Internet sources should be properly authorized and documented. Information ownership should be safeguarded and respected. Marketers should respect the integrity and ownership of computer and network systems.

Access

Marketers should treat access to accounts, passwords, and other information as confidential, and only examine or disclose content when authorized by a responsible party. The integrity of others' information systems should be respected with regard to placement of information, advertising or messages.

More information can be found at: http://www.ama.org/about/ama/ethcode.asp

Notes

Chapter 1

1. Andy Grove, Keynote Address, *Los Angeles Times 3rd Annual Investment Strategies Conference*, May 22, 1999 (www.andygrove.com).
2. Don Tapscott, *Digital Economy*, 1998, New York: McGraw-Hill.
3. Andy Grove, *Only the Paranoid Survive*, 1996, Bantam Doubleday Dell.
4. Barry M. Lemer, Vinton G. Cerf, David D. Clark, Robert F. Kahn, Leonard Kleinrock, David C. Lynch, Jon Postel, Larry G. Roberts and Stephen Wolff, "A Brief History of the Internet," *Internet Society*, April 14, 2000, (www.isoc.org/internet/history/brief.html).
5. Internet Domain Survey, January 2000 (www.isc.org/ds/WWW-200001/report.html).
6. Tim Berners-Lee, *Weaving the Web*, 1999, San Francisco, Harper.
7. "Face of the Web," Angus Reid Group (www.angusreid.com).
8. "The Case for Globalization," *Business 2.0*, May 2000, p. 178.
9. Ibid.
10. "Fast Forward: Accelerating Canada's Leadership in the Internet Economy," Report of the Canadian E-Business Opportunities Roundtable, Boston Consulting Group, January 2000.
11. Ravi Kalakota and Andrew B. Whinston, *Electronic Commerce: A Manager's Guide*, 1997, Reading, MA: Addison-Wesley.
12. "Fast Forward," Boston Consulting Group, January 2000.
13. "B2B E-Commerce: $403 Billion in 2000," *CyberAtlas* (cyberatlas.internet.com/big_picture/demographics/article/0,1323,5971_295831,00.html), January 26, 2000.
14. Kenneth Berryman, Lorraine Harrington, Dennis Layton-Rodin, and Vincent Rerolle, "E-Commerce: Three Emerging Strategies," *The McKinsey Quarterly*, 1998, No.1, 152–158.
15. "Fast Forward," Boston Consulting Group, January 2000.
16. "The Economic and Social Impact of Electronic Commerce," Organization for Economic Cooperation and Development (OECD), 1999.
17. Ibid.
18. Mary Meeker (1997), *Internet Retailing Report*, Morgan Stanley Dean Witter (www.msdw.com), May 18.
19. "B2B E-Commerce," *CyberAtlas*, January 26, 2000.
20. "Face of the Web," Angus Reid Group.
21. Hal R. Varian (1996), "Differential Pricing and Efficiency," *First Monday*, Vol. 1 (2), (www.firstmonday.dk/issues/issue2/different/index.html).
22. C. Shapiro and Hal R. Varian (1999), *Information Rules: A Strategic Guide to the Network Economy*, Boston, MA: Harvard Business School Press.
23. Jeffry F. Rayport and John J. Sviokla (1995), "Exploiting the Virtual Value Chain," *Harvard Business Review*, November-December, pp. 75–85.
24. Rashib Aiyer Ghosh (1998), "Cooking Pot Markets," *First Monday*, Vol. 3, (www.firstmonday.dk/issues/issue3_3/ghosh/index).
25. Rayport and Sviokla, op.cit.
26. "Users Pay for Niche Market Content," *CyberAtlas* (cyberatlas.internet.com/big_picture/demographics/article/0,1323,5931_152051,00.html), November 18, 1998.
27. OECD (1998), "Economic and Social Impacts of Electronic Commerce," (www.oecd.org).
28. Patrick Stähler, "The Myth of the Frictionless Economy," Institute for Media and Communications Management, (undated paper), University of St. Gallen, Switzerland (www.mcm.unisg.ch/people/pstaehler/content/research.htm).
29. "The Dot-Com Sky Is Falling," *CyberAtlas*, April 11, 2000, (cyberatlas.com/big_picture/demographics/article/0,1323,6061_338771,00.html).
30. Digital Divide Persists in the US," *CyberAtlas*, July 8, 1999, (cyberatlas.internet.com/big_picture/demographics/article/0,1323,5901_158701,00.html).
31. "Fast Forward," Boston Consulting Group, January 2000.

Chapter 2

1. Michael E. Porter (1998), *Competitive Advantage: Creating and Sustaining Superior Performance*, Free Press.
2. Michel E. Porter and V. E. Millar, "How Information Gives You Competitive Advantage," *Harvard Business Review*, July–August, 1985.
3. Jeffry F. Rayport and John J. Sviokla (1995), "Exploiting the Virtual Value Chain," *Harvard Business Review*, November–December, pp. 75–85.
4. Ibid, p. 3.
5. Timothy M. Laseter, Patrick W. Houston, Joshua L. Wright, and Juliana Y. Park (2000), "Amazon Your Industry: Extracting the Value from the Value Chain," *Journal of Strategy and Business* (www.strategy-business.com/strategy/00109/).
6. Lynn Margherio, Dave Henry, Sandra Cook, and Sabrina Montes (1998), "The Emerging Digital Economy," US Department of Commerce, Washington, DC (www.ecommerce.gov), April.
7. Saroja Girishankar (1997), "The Feds Get Down to Business with Latest E-commerce Push," TechWeb (www.techweb.com), November 3.
8. W. Michael Cox and Richard Alm (1999), "The Right Stuff: America's Move to Mass Customization," National Center for Policy Analysis, Policy Report 225, June.
9. James H. Gilmore, and B. Joseph Pine II, "The Four Faces of Customization," *Harvard Business Review*, January–February 1997, pp. 91–101.
10. Jeff Papows, Enterprise.com, Perseus Books, 1998.
11. Cox and Alm, op. cit.
12. Don Tapscott, *Digital Economy: Promise and Peril in the Age of Networked Intelligence*, McGraw-Hill, 1996.
13. Pankaj Ghemawat and Bret Baird (1998), "Leadership Online: Barnes & Noble vs. Amazon.com (A)," Harvard Business School Case, Reprint no. 9-789-063.
14. OECD (1998), "Economic and Social Impacts of Electronic Commerce," (www.oecd.org).
15. Louise Kehoe (1998), "High Street in Hyperspace," *Financial Times*, April 18.
16. Mary Meeker (1997), Internet Retailing Report, Morgan Stanley Dean Witter (www.msdw.com), May 28.

17. "Falling Through the Net," (1999) US Department of Commerce (www.ntia.doc.gov/ntiahome/net2/falling.htm), July 30.

18. Maria LaTour Kadison, Blane Erwin and Michael Putnam (1998), Middlemen on the Net, Forrester Research, Vol. 1, No. 7, January.

19. Sharon Machlis (1998), "Warning: Web Selling Isn't Cheap," *Computer World*, October 12, 1998 (www.computerworld.com/home/print.nsf/CWFlash/9810126EDA).

20. Rayport and Sviokla, op. cit.

21. Ibid.

22. Ibid.

23. Michael Rappa (1999), Business Models on the Web, (ecommerce.ncsu.edu/business_models).

24. Paul Timmers (1996) "Business Models for Electronic Markets," *Electronic Markets*, Vol. 8 (2), pp. 3–8.

25. "E-Tailers Cannibalize Offline Sales," *CyberAtlas* (cyberatlas.internet.com/big_picture/demographics/article/0,1323,6061_ 174851,00.html), August 4, 1999.

26. E. B. Baatz (1996), "Will Your Model Float?," *Webmaster Magazine*, October (webbusiness.cio.com).

27. "Hub Sites Will Drive E-Commerce," *CyberAtlas* (cyberatlas.internet.com/big_picture/demographics/article/0,1323,6061_ 153721,00.html), March 4, 1999.

28. "Better Than Clearance Sales: E-Tailing's Future Lies in Auctions," *CyberAtlas*, January 26, 1999 (cyberatlas.internet.com/big_picture/demographics/article/0,1323,6061_153431,00.html).

29. Gil McWilliam (2000), "Building Stronger Brands Through Online Communities," *Sloan Management Review*, Vol. 41(3), pp. 43–54.

30. John Hagel III and Arthur G. Armstrong (1997), *Net Gain: Expanding Markets Through Virtual Communities*, Harvard University Press.

31. Mitra Barun Sarkar, Brian Butler, and Charles Steinfield, "Intermediaries and Cybermediaries: A Continuing Role for Mediating Players in the Electronic Marketplace," *Journal of Computer Mediated Communication*, Vol. 1 (3), (www.ascusc.org/jcmc/vol1/issue3/sarkar.html).

32. Mohanbir Sawney and Steven Kaplan (1999), "Let's Get Vertical," *Business 2.0*, September, pp. 85–92.

33. Amir Hartman and John Sifonis (2000), *Net Ready: Strategies for Success in E-conomy*, New York: McGraw-Hill.

34. Rappa, op. cit.

35. Ibid.

36. C. Wilder. (1999). "E-Business: What's the Model?" (www.PlanetIT.com/docs/PIT19990808S0007).

37. Jeffry Rayport (1999), "The Truth About Internet Business Models," *Journal of Strategy and Business*, Third Quarter.

38. Mark A. Mowrey (2000), "Thank You, Please Come Again," The Industry Standard, March 20 (www.thestandard.com/article/display/1,1151,13016,00.html).

39. Machlis, op. cit.

40. "Customer Loyalty: Key to E-commerce Profitability," *CyberAtlas*, March 30, 2000 (cyberatlas.internet.com/big_picture/demographics/article/0,1323,6061_ 331431,00.html).

41. "Customer Relationship Management on the Web: Unlocking E-Commerce Profits," International Data Corporation (IDC.com), 1999.

Chapter 3

1. "Consumer Online Purchasing Climbs," *CyberAtlas*, September 14, 1999, (cyberatlas.internet.com/big_picture/demographics/article/0,1323,6061_201071,00.html).

2. "Business-to-Consumer E-Commerce: $380 Billion by 2003," *CyberAtlas*, October 13, 1999, (cyberatlas.internet.com/markets/retailing/article/0,1323,6061_217471,00.html).

3. "Online Retailing to Reach $36 Billion in 1999," *CyberAtlas*, July19, 1999, (cyberatlas.internet.com/markets/retailing/article/0,1323,6061_164011,00.html).

4. "US Internet Audience Growth Slowing," *CyberAtlas*, November 29, 1999, (cyberatlas.internet.com/big_picture/demographics/article/0,1323,5911_246241,00.html).

5. "Face of the Web,"Angus Reid Group, February 2000, (www.angusreid.com).

6. "The Emerging 20 Nations," *CyberAtlas*, June 1, 1999, (cyberatlas.internet.com/big_picture/demgraphics/article/0,1323,5911_150661,00.html).

7. "Net Continues Growth in Latin America," *CyberAtlas*, March 17, 2000, (cyberatlas.internet.com/big_picture/demographics/article/0,1323,5911,323391,00.html).

8. Hsiang Chen and Kevin Crowston, "Comparative Diffusion of the Telephone and the World Wide Web: An Analysis of Rates of Adoption," Syracuse University, 1997.

9. Everett M. Rogers, *Diffusion of Innovations*, 4th Edition, 1995, NY: The Free Press.

10. Craig S. Breitenbach and Doris C. Van Doren, "Value-added Marketing in the Digital Domain: Enhancing the Utility of the Internet," *Journal of Consumer Marketing*, 15 (6), 1998, pp. 558–575.

11. "Digital Divide Persists in the US," *CyberAtlas*, July 8, 1999, (cyberatlas.internet.com/big_picture/demographics/article/0,1323,5901_158701,00.html).

12. "Consumers Fear for Their Online Privacy," *CyberAtlas*, November 1, 1999, (cyberatlas.internet.com/markets/retailing/article/0,1323,6061_228341,00.html).

13. "Consumers Concerned with Reliability," *CyberAtlas*, January 27, 1999, (cyberatlas.internet.com/big_picture/demographics/article/0,1323,6061_153551,00.html).

14. GVU 10th WWW User Survey (www.gvu.gatech.edu/user_surveys/).

15. *Internet Fact Book*, 1999, A. C. Neilsen Canada (www.acneilsen.ca).

16. Ibid.

17. "Seniors Use Internet for Shopping," *CyberAtlas*, August 31, 1999, (cyberatlas.internet.com/big_picture/demographics/article/0,1323,5901_192461,00.html).

18. *Internet Fact Book*, 1999, A. C. Neilsen Canada.

19. "Kids and Teens to Spend More Online," *CyberAtlas*, June 7, 1999 (cybertatlas.internet.com/big_picture/demographics/article/0,1323,5901_150331,00.html).

20. "US Teens Increase Online Shopping," *CyberAtlas*, September 22, 1999, (cyberatlas.internet.com/big_picture/demographics/article/0,1323,5901_205961,00.html).

21. "Young Consumers Ignore Online Brands," *CyberAtlas*, July 8, 1999 (cyberatlas.internet.com/big_picture/demographics/article/0,1323,6061_158411,00.html).

22. Don Tapscott, *Growing Up Digital*, 1998, NY: McGraw-Hill.

23. "Online Habits of African-Americans Set Them Apart," *CyberAtlas*, December 16,1999, (cyberatlas.internet.com/

big_picture/demographics/article/0,1323,5901_261081,00.html).

24. Bill Guns, SRI International, Personal Communication with Author, April 2000.

25. Steven Bellman, Gerald L. Lohse, and Eric J. Johnson, "Predictors of Online Buying Behavior," *Communications of the ACM*, 42 (12), 1999, pp. 32–38.

26. Ibid.

27. "The Lifestyle of the Online Shoppers," *CyberAtlas*, December 8, 1999, (cyberatlas.internet.com/big_picture/demographics/article/0,1323,5901_256591,00.html).

28. Online Clothing Sales Continue Climbing E-Commerce Ladder," *CyberAtlas*, March 10, 2000, (cyberatlas.internet.com/big_picture/demographics/article/0,1323,6061_319041,00.html).

29. Eric Johnson and Naomi Mandel "Constructing Preferences Online: Can Web Pages Change What You Want?" February 1999, Wharton Electronic Commerce Forum (ecom.Wharton.upenn.edu).

30. Klein, L., "Evaluating the Potential of Interactive Media Through a New Lens: Search versus Experience Goods," *Journal of Business Research*, 41 (3), 1998, 195–203.

31. Bellman, Lohse, and Johnson, op. cit.

32. Hairlong Li, Cheng Kua, and Martha G. Russell, "The Impact of Perceived Channel Utilities, Shopping Orientations, and Demographics on the Consumer's Online Buying Behavior," *Journal of Computer Mediated Communications*, 5 (2), December 1999, (www.asusc.org.jcmc/issue2/hairlong.html).

33. "Brand Names Don't Stick Online," *CyberAtlas*, June 25, 1999, (cyberatlas.internet.com/markets/retailing/0,1323,6061_153691,00.html).

34. "40 Percent of Vehicle Shoppers Use Internet," *CyberAtlas*, August 26, 1999, (cyberatlas.com/markets/retailing/article/0,1323,6061_188331,00.html).

35. "Shop Before you Buy: Shoppers Do Homework on the Web," *CyberAtlas*, January 8, 1999, (cyberatlas.internet.com/big_picture/demographics/article/0,1323,6061_153821,00.html).

36. Cheryl Burke Jarvis, "An Exploratory Investigation of Consumers' Evaluations of External Information Sources in Prepurchase Search," *Advances in Consumer Research*, 25, 1998, 446–452.

37. Michelle L. Peterman, Harper A. Roehm Jr., and Curtis P. Haugtvedt, "An Exploratory Attribution Analysis of Attitudes Toward the World Wide Web as a Product Information Source," *Advances in Consumer Research*, 46, 1999, 75–79.

38. "E-tailers Cannibalize Offline Sales," *CyberAtlas*, August 4, 1999, (cyberatlas.internet.com/big_picture/demographics/article/0,1323,6061_174851,00.html).

39. Ibid, p. 32.

40. "Consumers Ready to Embrace Net Commerce and Marketing," *CyberAtlas*, November 11, 1999, (cyberatlas.internet.com/markets/retailing/article/0,1323,6061_237161,00.html).

41. "Digital Divide Persists in US," *CyberAtlas*, July 8, 1999.

42. Mary Hillebrand, "E-commerce Leaving Older Americans Behind," *E-Commerce Times*, March 31, 2000, (www.ecommercetimes.com).

43. "Consumers Fear for Their Online Privacy," *CyberAtlas*, Nov. 1, 1999.

44. Caroline Cartellieri, Andrew J. Parsons, Varsha Rao, and Michael P. Zeisser "The Real Impact of Internet Advertising," *The McKinsey Quarterly*, 1997, No. 3, pp. 44–62.

45. Li, Kua, and Russell, op. cit.

46. Greg Lindsay, "Selling in Three Dimensions," *Fortune*, Vol. 141, No. 8 April 17, 2000, (www.fortune.com/fortune/technology/2000/04/17/eco3.html).

47. "The Dot-Com Sky Is Falling," *CyberAtlas*, April 11, 2000, (cyberatlas.com/big_picture/demographics/article/0,1323,6061_338771,00.html).

Chapter 4

1. "B2B E-Commerce: $403 Billion in 2000," *CyberAtlas*, (cyberatlas.com/big_picture/demographics/article/0,1323,5971_295831,00.html), January 26, 2000.

2. "Higher Growth Rates Predicted for B2B E-Commerce," *CyberAtlas*, (cyberatlas.com/big_picture/demographics/article/0,1323,5971_267161,00.html), August 15, 2000.

3. "Global Survey of Chief Information Executives," Deloitte Research, New York, 1998, by S. Ford.

4. "Collaborative Commerce," Morgan Stanley Dean Witter (www.msdw.com), April 2000.

5. Ramesh Venkat (2000), "A Study on the Impact of Business-to-Business E-Commerce in Canada," Sponsored by Purchasing Management Association of Canada, August 2000.

6. "Collaborative Commerce," Morgan Stanley Dean Witter, April 2000.

7. Robert E. Spekman, John W. Kamauff Jr., and Niklas Myhr (1998), "An Empirical Investigation Into Supply Chain Management: A Perspective On Partnerships," *International Journal of Physical Distribution & Logistics Management*, Vol. 28 No. 8, 630–650.

8. "Collaborative Commerce," Morgan Stanley Dean Witter, April 2000.

9. Mohanbir Sawhney and Steven Kaplan (1999), "Let's Get Vertical," *Business 2.0*, September 1999, 85–92.

10. Ibid.

11. Kenneth Berryman, Lorraine Harrington, Dennis Layton-Rodin, and Vincent Rerolle, (1998), "Electronic Commerce: Three Emerging Strategies," *The McKinsey Quarterly*, 1998 (Number 1), 152–159.

12. "B2B: 2B or not 2B?" Goldman Sachs, November 12, 1999.

13. Berryman et al., op. cit.

14. Ibid.

15. "Collaborative Commerce," Morgan Stanley Dean Witter, April 2000.

16. Steven Kaplan and Mohanbir Sawhney, "E-hubs: The New B2B Marketplaces," *Harvard Business Review*, 78 (3) May/June 2000, pp. 97–103.

17. Ibid.

18. Ibid.

19. "eCommerce B2B Report," *eMarketer*, July 17, 2000.

20. "Small Biz Dissed by B2B," *eMarketer*, June 12, 2000.

21. "Web Ads Take a B2B Approach," *CyberAtlas* (cyberatlas.com/big_picture/demographics/article/0,1323,5941_324031,00.html), March 20, 2000.

22. Cliff Allen (2000), "B2B Selling Tools for Targeting Corporate Committees," *Clickz.com* (www.clickz.com/cgi-bin/gt/article.html?article=1501), March 28.

23. "The Use of World Wide Web for Business-to-Business Marketing," *Report of a Market Research Study Carried out in Western Europe* (www.prc.dk).

24. "NAM Poll Shows That Despite Tech Advances, Most Manufacturers Still Not Using E-Commerce," National Association of Manufacturers, Press Release, February 22, 2000.

25. "2nd Quarter NAM E-Commerce Survey," National Association of Manufacturers (www.nam.org), August 8, 2000.

26. Venkat, op. cit.

27. Ibid.

28. Ibid.

Chapter 5

1. Artemis March (supervised by David A. Garvin) "A Note on Knowledge Management," Harvard Business School, November 26, 1997.

2. Peter F. Drucker (1998), *Managing in a Time of Great Change*, Truman Talley Books.

3. Rudy Ruggles (1998), "The State of the Notion: Knowledge Management in Practice," *California Management Review*, Vol. 40 (3), Spring, pp. 80–89.

4. Larry Kahaner (1997), *Competitive Intelligence: How to Gather, Analyze and Use Information to Move Your Business to the Top*. Touchstone, Simon & Schuster, New York.

5. Maryann Jones Thompson (1999), "When Market Research Turns Into Marketing: A bitter legal spat between two leading firms highlights growing pains in the interactive market-research industry," *The Industry Standard*, August 23, (www.thestandard.com/article/display/1,1151,5995,00.html).

6. Leslie Marable (1997), "Online Market Research Begins to Catch On," *Web Week*, Volume 3 (8), March 31, (www.iworld.com).

7. Gilbert A. Churchill, Jr. (1995), *Marketing Research: Methodological Foundations*, 6th edition, The Dryden Press, Fort Worth, Texas.

8. Ibid.

9. Ibid.

10. Cyndee Miller (1994), "Anybody ever hear of global focus groups? International Video Focus Groups," *Marketing News*, Vol. 25 (27), May, p. 14.

11. Mary Beth Solomon, "Market Research in Cyberspace," *Cyber Dialogue* (www.cyberdialogue.com).

12. Churchill, op. cit.

13. Mitzi M. Montoya-Weiss, Anne P. Massey and Danial L. Clapper (1998), "Online Focus Groups: Conceptual Issues and a Research Tool," *European Journal of Marketing*, Vol. 32 (7/8), 713–723.

14. A. Massey and D. Clapper (1995), "Element Finding: The Impact of Group Support System on a Crucial Component of Sense Making," *Journal of Management Information Systems*, Vol. 11 (4), pp. 149–176.

15. Tom Greenbaum (1997), "Internet Focus Groups: An Oxymoron," *Marketing News*, March 3 (www.groupsplus.com/oxymoron.htm).

16. Michelle Tirado (1999), "Is There a Virtual Focus Group in Your Future," *Office.com*, August 24.

17. Churchill, op. cit.

18. Richard Kottler (1996), "Web Based Interviewing," *The Internet, Marketing and Research (December): A Seminar Organized by CM&R Consultant—Summary of Presentations*, pp. 114–126.

19. Raj Mehta and Eugene Sivadas (1995), "Comparing Response Rates and Response Content in Mail Versus Electronic Mail Surveys," *Journal of Marketing Research Society*, 37 (4), pp. 429–439.

20. Alan C. B. Tse (1995), "Comparing Two Methods of Sending Out Questionnaires," *Journal of Market Research Society*, 17 (4), pp. 441–446.

21. Ibid, p. 22.

22. Ibid, p. 5.

23. Arthur Kornhauser and Paul B. Sheatsley (1976), "Questionnaire Construction and Interview Procedure," in Claire Selltiz, Lawrence S. Wrightman and Stuart W. Cook, *Research Methods in Social Relations*, 3rd ed (NY: Holt, Rinehart and Winston), pp. 541–573.

24. Donald T. Campbell and Donald W. Fiske, Convergent and Discriminant Validation by the multitrait-multimethod matrix, psychological bulletin, 56 (1959), 81–105.

25. Thomas D. Cook and Donald T. Campbell (1979) Quasi-experimentation: Design and analysis issues for field settings (Chicago: Rand McNally College Publishing Co.) 37–94.

26. Thompson, op. cit.

27. Pete Comley (1997), "The Use of the Internet as a Data Collection Method," Simon Godfrey Associates (www.sga.co.uk/esomar.html).

28. Peter Krasilovsky (1996), "Surveys in Cyberspace," *Marketing Tools*, November/December, pp.18–22.

29. W. Frawley, G. Piatetsky-Shapiro, and C. Matheus (1992), "Knowledge Discovery in Databases: An Overview," *AI Magazine*, Fall, pp. 213–228.

30. Jim Rapoza (1997), "Tools Access Web Site Visitor Data," PCWeek.com, May 7.

31. "The Problem With Traditional Site Logs (Web Tracking)," Bellacoola.com (undated).

32. John Busch (1999), "How Well Do You Really Know Your E-Customer," *Insights and Incites*, www.cmpnet.com, April 19.

33. Kahaner, op. cit.

34. Helen P. Burwell (1999), "Online Competitive Intelligence: Increasing Your Profits Using Cyber-Intelligence," Facts on Demand Press, Tempe, AZ.

35. Will Rodger (1999), "Online Profiling Firms to Police Themselves," *USATODAY.com*, November 23.

Chapter 6

1. Evan I. Schwartz (1996), "Advertising Webonomics 101," *Wired* (www.wirednews.com/wired/archive//4.02/webonomics_pr.html), 4.02, February 1996.

2. "E-Tailers Still Lacking in Customer Service," *CyberAtlas* (cyberatlas.com/big_picture/demographics/article/0,1323,6061_435761,00.html), August 16, 2000.

3. "Wal-Mart Forming Internet Company," *USA Today* (www.usatoday.com/life/cyber/invest/in247.htm), January 7, 2000.

4. Ramesh Venkat (2000), "A Study on the Impact of Business-to-Business E-Commerce in Canada." Sponsored by the Purchasing Management Association of Canada.

5. D. Grant Freeland and Scott Stirton (2000), "The Organizational Challenge of E-Commerce," *Perspectives*, The Boston Consulting Group (www.bcg.com).

6. "General Electric: Business Summary," *SmartPortfolio.com* (www.freeshop.com/Advertising/largecapsample.htm).

7. Freeland and Stirton, op. cit.

8. Ibid.

9. "Wal-Mart Forming Internet Company," *USA Today*, January 7, 2000.

10. "Wal-Mart Expands European Web Presence," *The Standard* (www.thestandard.com/article/display/ 0,1151,17510,00.html), August 9, 2000.

11. Jill Albrinck, Gil Irwin, Gary Neilsen and Dianna Sasina (2000), "From Bricks to Clicks: The Four Stages of E-volution," Third Quarter, Issue 20, *Strategy + Business*, Booz, Allen & Hamilton (www.bah.com).

12. Ibid.

13. Ravi S. Achrol (1997), "Changes in The Theory of Interorganizational Relations in Marketing: Toward a Network Paradigm," *Academy of Marketing Science Journal*, 25 (1), 56–71.

14. Ravi S. Achrol (1991), "Evolution of The Marketing Organization: New Forms for Dynamic Environments," *Journal of Marketing*, 55 (October), 77–93.

15. Don Tapscott (1996), *Digital Economy: Promise and Peril in the Age of Networked Intelligence*, New York: McGraw-Hill.

16. Don Tapscott, David Ticoll, and Alex Lowy (2000), *Digital Capital: Harnessing the Power of the Business Webs*, Nicholas Brealey Publishing.

17. Donovan Gow and Bill Hills (2000), "Customer Relationship Portals—Managing Customers in an E-Business World," *CRMProject* (www.crmproject.com).

18. N. Venkatraman (2000), "Five Steps to a Dot-Com Strategy: How to Find Your Footing on the Web," *Sloan Management Review*, Spring, 15–28.

19. Amir Hartman and John Sifonis (2000), *Net Ready: Strategies for Success in the E-conomy*, New York: McGraw-Hill.

20. "The Case for Globalization," *Business 2.0*, May 2000, p. 178.

21. "US: Nearing Agreement With Europe on Privacy," Reuters, February 3, 2000.

22. Gow and Hills, op. cit.

Chapter 7

1. Arthur G. Armstrong and John Hagel III (1996), "The Real Value of Online Communities," *Harvard Business Review*, May–June, 134–141.

2. Ibid.

3. Douglas Rushkoff (1999), "How Business Is Killing the Net," *Shift* (www.shift.com), November, 48–50.

4. Katie Hafner (1997), "The Epic Saga of The Well," *Wired*, 5.04, March, p. 98.

5. Godwin, Mike (1994), "Electronic Frontier Justice and the 'Green Card' Ads," *Internet World*, September. Also see www.cybernothing.org/faqs/net-abuse-faq.html for more information on Net Abuse and the Canter and Seigel case.

6. "Internet Communities: Forget Surfers. A New Class of Netizen Is Settling Right In," *Business Week*, May 5, 1997.

7. This section is based on John Hagel III and Arthur G. Armstrong (1997), "Net Gain: Expanding Markets Through Virtual Communities." Harvard Business School Press.

8. Ibid.

9. Gil McWilliam (2000), "Building Stronger Brands Through Online Communities," *Sloan Management Review*, Spring, 43–54.

10. Connie Guglielmo (1998), "Web Communities Can Get Sticky," *Inter@ctive Week*, July 27, 1998.

11. David Futrelle (1998), "Downside: Community Missed," *UpsideToday*, August 2, 1998.

12. Kate Delhagen (1998), "Community Pipe Dreams," *Forreser Research*, May 1988.

13. "EBay Asks U.S. Court to Ban User for Bad Language," xone.network (www.xone.net/article.php?1423), July 13, 2000.

14. David Lake (2000), "WANTED: Loyal E-Shoppers," *TheStandard.com*, August 7, 2000.

15. Mark A. Mowrey (2000), "The Detail on E-Retail," *TheStandard.com*, May 1, 2000.

16. "EBay Asks U.S. Court to Ban User for Bad Language," xone.network, July 13, 2000.

17. Frederick F. Reichheld and Phil Schefter (2000), "E-Loyalty: Your Secret Weapon on The Web," *Harvard Business Review*, July–August, 105–113.

18. "EBay Asks U.S. Court to Ban User for Bad Language," xone.network, July 13, 2000.

19. Ibid.

20. Carl Klempner, George Lilly, Stephen C. Parowski, and John Steinhoff (2000), "Web-Driven Change," *The Journal of Customer Loyalty*, Issue 14 (www.eloyaltyco.com/ journal/index.htm).

21. Leonard Berry (1983), "Relationship Marketing," in *Emerging Perspectives on Services Marketing*, L. Berry, G.L. Schostack, and G.D. Upah, eds., Chicago, American Marketing Association, 25–28.

22. Barbara Bund Jackson (1985), *Winning and Keeping Industrial Customers*, Lexington, KY: Lexington Books.

23. Jagdish Sheth and Atul Parvatiyar (1995), "Relationship Marketing in Consumer Markets: Antecedents and Consequences," *Journal of Academy of Marketing Science*, 23 (Fall), 225–271.

24. Lois Geller (1998), "The Internet: The Ultimate Relationship Marketing Tool," *Direct Marketing*, 61 (September), 36–38.

25. Donovan Gow and Bill Hills (2000), "Customer Relationship Portals—Managing Customers in an E-Business World," *CRMProject* (www.crmproject.com).

26. John Calhoun (2000), "CRM: Driving Loyalty by Managing the Total Customer Experience," *CRMProject* (www.crmproject.com).

27. Gow and Hills, op. cit.

28. Ramesh Venkat (1999), "Relationship Marketing Online," Presented at the ASAC Conference, Saint John, New Brunswick, Canada.

29. "CRM Applications a $3 billion Market," *CyberAtlas* (cyberatlas.com/big_picture/demographics/article/ 0,1323,5921_443211,00.html).

30. Moosha Gulycz (2000), "Implementing CRM: The Need for Performance Alignment," *Customer Focus*, April, Vol. 4, Issue 3.

31. "A Crash Course in Customer Relationship Management," *Harvard Management Update*, March 2000, 3–5.

32. Susan Kuchinskas (2000), "More for Less," *Business 2.0*, September 12, 2000.

33. Chris Thomas (2000), "Putting Customers at the Center of CRM," *CRMProject* (www.crmproject.com).

34. Alex Lowy, David Ticoll, and Don Tapscott (2000), "Relationships Rule," *Business 2.0*, May 1, 2000.

35. Thomas, op. cit.

36. Christopher S. Rollyson (1999), "Using Websites to Create Electronic Enterprises that Transform Customer Relationships," PriceWaterhouseCoopers, May 27, 1999.

37. Andrew V. Abela and A. M. Sacconaghi, Jr. (1997), "Value Exchange: The Secret of Building Customer Relationships Online," *McKinsey Quarterly*, Number 2, 216–219.

38. James H. Gilmore and B. Joseph Pine II (1997), "The Four Faces of Mass Customization," *Harvard Business Review*, January–February, 91–101.

39. Richard Dean (2000), "Personalizing Your Web Site," CNET Builder.com (www.builder.com/Business/Personal/ss03.html), February 6.

40. B. Joseph Pine II, Bart Victor and Andrew C. Boynton (1993), "Making Mass Customization Work," *Harvard Business Review*, September–October, 108–116.

41. "How Much Are Customer Relationship Management Capabilities Really Worth," Thought Leadership, Anderson Consulting (www.ac.com).

42. Don Peppers and Martha Rogers, *The One to One Future: Building Relationships One Customer at a Time*, Currency/Doubleday, 1997.

43. Susan Kuchinskas (2000), "One-to-(N)one?" *Business 2.0*, September 12, 2000.

44. Susan Fournier, Susan Dobscha, and David Glen Mick (1998), "Preventing the Premature Death of Relationship Marketing," *Harvard Business Review*, January–February, 2–8.

45. Peppers and Rogers, op. cit.

Chapter 8

1. Marco Iansiti and Alan MacCormack (1997), "Developing Products on Internet Time," *Harvard Business Review*, September–October, pp.108–117.

2. Michael Cusumano and David Yoffee (1998), *Competing on Internet Time: Lessons from Netscape and Its Battle with Microsoft*, New York: Free Press.

3. Iansiti and MacCormack, op. cit.

4. Cusumano and Yoffee, op. cit.

5. Ibid.

6. J. Bradford DeLong (1998), "Internet Time," (econ161.berkeley.edu/Econ_Articles/Reviews/Internet_Time.html), December 16.

7. Kathy Chin Leong (1998), "Intranet Drives Ford's Efforts," *InternetWeek*, October 26 (www.internetwk.com/case/study/102698-2.htm).

8. Jeffrey F. Rayport and John J. Sviokla (1995), "Exploiting the Virtual Value Chain," *Harvard Business Review*, November–December, pp. 75–85.

9. "Ford Turns to Virtual Prototyping for Concurrent Engineering," *Intelligent Manufacturing*, October 1996, Vol. 2 (10), Lionheart Publishing Inc.

10. Rayport and Sviokla, op. cit.

11. Philip Kotler, Gary Armstrong, Peggy Cunnigham, and Robert Warren (1996), *Principles of Marketing*, Third Canadian Edition, Toronto, ON: Prentice Hall.

12. David A. Aaker (1996), *Building Strong Brands*, New York: Free Press.

13. "Internet Advertising Focused on E-Commerce, Not Brands," *CyberAtlas* (cyberatlas.internet.com/big_picture/article/0,1323,5941_192821,00.html), August 31, 1999.

14. Ibid.

15. "Web Promises Greater Price Transparency in Steel Mart," *Purchasing Online*, April 6, 2000.

16. Ellen Neuborne (1998), "Branding on the Net," *Business Week*, November 9.

17. Ibid.

18. Ibid.

19. Ibid.

20. Ibid.

21. Richard Lord, "What Are Web Brands Really Worth?" (www.marketing.haynet.com), undated paper.

22. "Offline Spending by Internet Brands Passes $1 billion," *CyberAtlas* (cyberatlas.internet.com/big_picture/demographics/article/0,1323,5941_259071,00.html), December 14, 1999.

23. Kevin Mabley, "Branding Matters, But Lesser Known Causes Can Prevail," (www.cyberdialogue.com), undated document.

24. "Marketing Commodities: Can You Brand Sand?" Booz, Allen & Hamilton, 1998.

25. Ibid.

26. "E-Commerce—The Promised Land: We've Landed. Where's the Promise?" NYMA Panel Discussion (www.nyma.org), October 22, 1998, New York.

27. Francesco Castelli, Tecla De Luca, and Claudio Leporelli (1998), "Cost-based vs. usage-based pricing and the Internet," Beyond Convergence ITS Conference, 21–24 June 1998, Stockholm.

28. Daniel Levy, Mark Bergen, Shantanu Dutta, and Robert Venable (1997), "The Magnitude of Menu Costs: Direct Evidence from Large Supermarket Chains," *The Quarterly Journal of Economics*, 112 (3), 791.

29. Scott Woolley (1998), "Mine Was Cheaper!" *Forbes Global*, November 2, 1998 (www.forbes.com/forbesglobal/98/1102/0116058a.htm).

30. Jakob Nielsen (1998), "The Case for Micropayments," *Alertbox*, January 25, (www.useit.com/alertbox/980125.html).

31. Indrajit Sinha (2000), "Cost Transparency: The Net's Real Threat to Prices and Brands," *Harvard Business Review*, March–April, p. 3–8.

32. Ibid.

33. Ibid.

Chapter 9

1. Netiquette, FAQs and Emoticons (www.webgate.net/services6.html).

2. Douglas Rushkoff (1999), "How Business Is Killing the Net," *Shift*, 48–50.

3. Katie Hafner (1997), "The Epic Saga of The Well," *Wired*, 5.04, March, p. 98.

4. "Study Says Web Is 500 Times Larger than Major Search Engines Now Show," *CNN.com*, July 27, 2000.

5. Computer Industry Almanac, February 1999 (www.cia.com).

6. "Internet Users Taking to Chat," Cyberatlas.internet.com, July 15, 1999.

7. Marshall McLuhan and Bruce R. Powers, *The Global Village: Transformations in World Life and Media in the 21st Century*, Oxford University Press, 1989.

8. GVU 10th WWW Survey, CommerceNet/Nielsen Survey of the Internet (www.commercenet.com) and A.C. Nielsen Canada (www.acnielsen.ca).

9. Maryann Jones Thompson (1999), "Net Ads to Break $7 Billion in 2002," *The Industry Standard*, March 22, 1999.

10. "Global Online Spending: $33 Billion by 2004," Cyberatlas.internet.com.

11. "Internet Advertising Survey," Internet Advertising Bureau of Canada (www.iabcanada.com/survey/index.shtml).

12. "Marketing Spotlight: Internet Ad Spending Keeps Climbing," *The Industry Standard* (www.thestandard.com), August 23, 1999.

13. "Average E-Commerce Web Site Costs $1 Million," *BizReport.Com*, September 22, 1999.

14. "Internet Users Taking to Chat," Cyberatlas.internet.com, July 15, 1999.

15. Donna L. Hoffman and Thomas P. Novak (1996), "Marketing in Hypermedia Computer-Mediated Environments: Conceptual Foundations," *Journal of Marketing*, July 1996.

16. "Non-U.S. Internet Commerce to Account for Almost Half of Worldwide Spending by 2003," International Data Corporation, August 25, 1999 (www.idc.com).

17. Erran Carmel (1999), *Global Software Teams: Collaborating Across Borders and Time Zones*, Prentice Hall, 1999.

18. "Internet Users Taking to Chat," Cyberatlas.internet.com, July 15, 1999.

19. John Hagel and Arthur Armstrong, "Net Gain: Expanding Markets Through Virtual Communities." McKinsey & Co., Harvard University School Press, 1997.

20. Hoffman and Novak, op. cit.

21. "Banner Ads Effective at Branding," *Cyberatlas.com*, February 17, 1999.

22. Courtney Macavinta (1998), "Playboy Wins Piracy Suit," CNET News.Com, April 1998 (news.cnet.com). Paul Ferris (1999), "Playboy Loses First Round of Advertising Battle," *eBusiness Journal*, September 1999, p. 3 (www.ebusiness.ca).

23. Joequim Menezes (1999), "Ad Cops Fighting Fake Clicks," *eBusiness Journal*, September 1999, p. 19.

24. James Careless (1999), "Internet Freedom Fighters," *eBusiness Journal*, September 1999, p. 13.

25. "$13 Billion Spent on Web Promotion," *CyberAtlas* (cyberatlas.com/big_picture/demographics/article/0,1323,5941_426701,00.html).

26. Mark Devaney (1999), "Full-Service or Lip Service," *ChannelSeven.com*, November, 9, 1999.

27. Alvin J. Silk, Lisa R. Klein, Ernst R. Berndt (1999), "Restructuring the U.S. Advertising Media Industry," Proceedings of Conference on Telecommunications and Information Markets (COTIM 99), September 1999, Rhode Island, USA.

28. Andrew V. Abela and A. M. Sacconoghi, Jr. (1997), "Value Exchange: The Secret of Building Customer Relationships Online," *The McKinsey Quarterly*, No. 2, 216–219.

29. Bruce Horow (1999), "Privacy concerns threaten P&G's Net plans," *USA Today*, January 26, 1999.

30. Privacy Partnership, TRUSTe (www.truste.org/partners/).

Chapter 10

1. "Best Micro-Site Ad of 1997," *ChannelSeven.com*.

2. "Pert Plus Shampoo Set to Clean Up with Email Marketing," *ChannelSeven.com*.

3. "NPD Electronic Coupon Study Highlights New Opportunities for Coupon Distributors," NPD Group (www.npd.com), May 2, 2000.

4. "The e-Marketing Report," Morgan Stanley Dean Witter (www.msdw.com), May 2000.

5. "Let the E-Mail Marketing Onslaught Begin," *CyberAtlas* (cyerbatlas.com/big_picture/demographics/articles/0,1323,5941_317871,00.html), March 8, 2000.

6. "The e-Marketing Report," Morgan Stanley Dean Witter, May 2000.

7. "Consumers Fear for Their Online Privacy," *CyberAtlas* (cyberatlas.com/big_picture/demgraphics/article/0,1323,6061_228341,00.html), November 1, 1999.

8. Seth Godin, *Permission Marketing*, Simon and Schuster, 1998.

9. Steve Markowitz, "E-Mail Marketing Done Right," Loves Me, Loves Me Not: An Overview of Email Marketing, Clickz.com.

10. Godin, op. cit.

11. "The E-mail Marketing Dialogue," Forrester Research, January 2000.

12. Heidi Anderson (2000), "Flooz-Your-Friends: Acquire Customers and Loyalty," Clickz.com, July 27.

13. Pamela Parker (2000), "Getting Viral with Rich Media," *ChannelSeven.com*, August 22.

14. Stacy Lawrence (2000), "Marketing Spotlight: Dot-Com Ad Spending Outpaces Ad Revenue," *The Industry Standard* (www.thestandard.com), March 6.

15. "NPD Electronic Coupon Study Highlights New Opportunities for Coupon Distributors," NPD Group, May 2, 2000.

16. Parker, op. cit.

17. Bill Doyle, Mary A. Modahl, Ben Abbott, "What Advertising Works?" Forrester Research, March 1997.

18. *Internet Advertising Report*, Morgan Stanley Dean Witter, 1997.

19. "Why You Shouldn't Hire an Ad Agency to Design Your Web Site," Bad Web Designer, No Cookie, (www.jaedworks.com/shoebox/no-cookie/ad-agency.html), June 1998.

20. "$13 Billion Spent on Web Promotion," *CyberAtlas* (cyberatlas.com/big_picture/demographics/article/0,1323,5941_426701,00.html).

21. "Global Online Ad Spending: $33 Billion by 2004," *CyberAltas*, (cyberatlas.com/big_picture/demographics/article/0,1323,5941_181901,00.html), August 12, 1999.

22. "IAB Online Effectiveness Study," Internet Advertising Bureau (www.iab.net), 1997.

23. "Ad Spending Doesn't Equal Brand Awareness," *CyberAtlas*, (cyberatlas.com/big_picture/demographics/article/0,1323,5941_405731,00.html), June 29, 2000.

24. Chang-Hoan Cho and John D. Leckenby (1997), "Copytesting of Advertising on the WWW: Click Motivation Profile," Working Paper, Department of Advertising, University of Texas, Austin.

25. Ramesh Venkat (1999), "Internet Advertising: Role of Involvement and Ad Characteristics," Proceedings of Conference on Telecommunications and Information Markets (COTIM 99), September 1999, Rhode Island, USA.

26. "Banners on the Decline," *CyberAtlas*, (cyberatlas.com/big_picture/demographics/article/0,1323,5941_154461,00.html), April 22, 1999.

27. "Banner Ads Effective at Branding," Cyberatlas.com, February 17, 1999.

28. Paul Ferriss (1999), "The Great Debate," *eBusiness Journal*, Vol. 1 (9), September, p. 13.

29. *Internet Advertising Report*, Morgan Stanley Dean Witter, 1997.

30. Venkat, op. cit.

31. Kim Doyle, Anastasia Minor, and Carolyn Weyrich (1997), "Banner Ad Placement Study," University of Michigan (www.webreference.com/dev/banners/). See also comments by Dr. Sunil Gupta (www.webreference.com/dev/banners/comments.html).

32. "Broadband Ads Are More Effective," *CyberAtlas*, (cyberatlas.com/big_picture/demographics/article/0,1323,5941_154651,00.html), March 1, 1999.

Chapter 11

1. Philip Kotler, Gary Armstrong, Peggy H. Cunningham, and Robert Warren (1997), *Principles of Marketing*, Third Canadian Edition, Prentice-Hall: Toronto.

2. Javier Solá (1996), "The Strategic Impact of the Internet in a Given Industry," Proceedings of Inet 96 Conference, University of Freiburg, Germany.

3. Don Tapscott (1996), *Digital Economy: Promise and Peril in the Age of Networked Intelligence*, McGraw-Hill, New York.

4. Mitra Barun Sarkar, Brian Butler, and Charles Steinfield (1995), "Intermediaries And Cybermediaries: A Continuing Role For Mediating Players In The Electronic Marketplace," *Journal of Computer-Mediated Communication* [On-line], 1 (3), (www.ascusc.org/jcmc/vol1/issue3/sarkar.html).

5. Benjamin, R., & Wigand, R. (1995), "Electronic Markets and Virtual Value Chains on the Information Highway," *Sloan Management Review*. Winter, 62–72.

6. "The Economic and Social Impact of Electronic Commerce: Preliminary Findings and Research Agenda," OECD, 1999.

7. "Are You Next: 20 Industries That Must Change," *Business 2.0*, March 1999.

8. "Death of the Salesmen" *The Economist*, April 22, 2000.

9. "Pull-Driven Order Management Helps You Fend Off Disintermediation," Prophet 21 (www.p21.com).

10. "The Economic and Social Impact of Electronic Commerce: Preliminary Findings and Research Agenda," OECD, 1999.

11. Alina M. Chircu and Robert J. Kauffman (1999), "Strategies for Internet Middlemen in Intermediation/Disintermediation/Reintermediation Cycle," *Electronic Markets*, Vol. 9 (1/2), 1–9, (www.electronicmarkets.org).

12. Don Chrusciel (2000), "The Internet Intermediary: Gateway to Internet Commerce Opportunities," *Journal of Internet Banking and Commerce*, June, Vol. 5 (1), (www.arraydev.com/commerce/JIBC/0001-09.htm).

13. Joseph P. Bailey and Yannis Yakos (1997), "An Exploratory Study of the Emerging Role of Electronic Intermediaries," *International Journal of Electronic Commerce*, Spring, Vol. 1 (3), 7–20.

14. Sarkar et al., op. cit.

15. Ibid.

16. Michael Rappa (2000), "Business Models on the Web," (ecommerce.ncsu.edu/business_models.html).

17. Ibid.

18. "Pure Plays Face Trouble in E-Commerce Shakeout," *CyberAtlas* (cyberatlas.com/big_picture/demographics/article/0,1323,6061_397301,00.html), April 20, 2000.

19. "Internet, Stores Work Together," *CyberAtlas* (cyberAtlas.com/big_picture/demgraphics/article/0,1323,6061_154001,00.html), May 19, 1999.

20. "Beyond the Boundaries: Enhancing Consumer Value in Multi-Channel Markets," Deloitte Consulting and Deloitte & Touche, 2000.

21. "Target spins off e-commerce group," CNET.com, February 1, 2000, (news.cnet.com/news/0-1007-200-1539508.html).

22. Greg Sandoval (2000), "Net Spinoffs a Risky Business for Old-line Retailers," *CNET.com*, February 4, (news.cnet.com/news/0-1007-202-1542735.html).

23. Megan Barnett (2000), "Citibank Kills Net-Only Project," *The Standard*, July 3, (www.thestandard.com/article/display/1,1151,16565,00.html).

24. Howard Wolinsky (2000), "Booming B2B: Brick-to-Click: Grainger's Huge Catalog Goes on Web," *Chicago Sun Times*, February 7, 2000.

25. Troy Wolverton (2000), "Toysrus.com Closes Site, Makes Way for Amazon," *CNET.com*, September 15 (news.cnet.com/news/0-1007-200-2785882.html).

26. David Kenny and John F. Marshall (2000), "Contextual Marketing: The Real Business of the Internet," *Harvard Business Review*, November–December, 119–125.

27. Gary A. Bolles (1999), "Channel Conflict and the Net: 'Everybody's Got a Gun'," *ZDNet.com*, March 9, 1999.

28. Andrew Mayer and Dawn Norris (2000), "Are You Affected by Channel Conflict?" *Digitrends*, June 30, (www.digitrends.net).

29. Ibid.

30. "E-Tailers Cannibalize Offline Sales," *CyberAtlas*, (cyberatlas.com/big_picture/demographics/article/0,1323,6061_174851,00.html).

31. "c-Discovery™: Approach to Customer-centric Insight," (www.digiarch.com).

Chapter 12

1. "Online Retail Spending to Soar," *CyberAtlas* (cyberatlas.com/big_picture/demographics/article/0,1323,6061_20881.00.html), September 29, 1999.

2. "Business-to-Consumer E-Commerce: $380 Billion by 2003," *CyberAtlas* (cyberatlas.com/big_picture/demographics/article/0,1323,6061_217471,00.html), October 13, 1999.

3. "Global Internet Retailing Report," Ernst & Young, LLP, 2000.

4. "Online Retail Spending to Soar," *CyberAtlas*, Sept. 29, 1999.

5. "120 Million Web Users Shop Online," *CyberAtlas* (cyberatlas.com/big_picture/demographics/article/0,1323,6061_338561,00.html), April 11, 2000.

6. "Demographics Influence Online Spending," *CyberAtlas* (cyberatlas.com/big_picture/demographics/article/ 0,1323,5901_344751,00.html), April 20, 2000.

7. "Holiday E-Commerce: More Shoppers, More Spending, More Problems," *CyberAtlas* (cyberatlas.com/big_picture/ demographics/article/0,1323,6061_ 266271,00.html), December 29, 1999.

8. Ibid.

9. "E-Commerce Faces Logistics Nightmare," *CyberAtlas* (cyberatlas.com/big_picture/demographics/article/ 0,1323,6061_190451,00.html), August 27, 1999.

10. "Customer Service Worries Online Shoppers," *CyberAtlas* (cyberatlas.com/big_picture/demographics/article/ 0,1323,6061_244341,00.html), November 24, 1999.

Chapter 13

1. "Security Keeps Women from Shopping Online," *CyberAtlas* (cyberatlas.com/big_picture/demographics/ article/0,1323,5901_278701,00.html), January 10, 2000.

2. "Concerns Don't Slow E-Commerce," *CyberAtlas* (cyberatlas.com/big_picture/demographics/article/ 0,1323,6061_153541,00.html), April 7, 1999.

3. "UK Consumers Wary of Online Security," *CyberAtlas* (cyberatlas.com/big_picture/demographics/article/ 0,1323,5911_429671,00.html), August 3, 2000.

4. "Canadian Shoppers Prefer Canadian Sites," *CyberAtlas* (cyberatlas.com/big_picture/demographics/article/ 0,1323,5911_260221,00.html), December 15, 1999.

5. "Security Keeps Women from Shopping Online," *CyberAtlas* (cyberatlas.com/big_picture/demographics/ article/0,1323,5901_278701,00.html), January 10, 2000.

6. "Internet Shopping Study: The Digital Channel Continues to Gather Steam," Ernst & Young, 1999.

7. Ibid.

8. David Legard (2000), "Net attacks to plague small and midsize firms," *Network World* (www.nwfusion.com/ archive/2000/109846_10-16-2000.html), October 16, 2000.

9. Ibid.

10. "Online Fraud: How Bad is It?," *CyberAtlas* (cyberatlas.com/big_picture/demographics/article/ 0,1323,6061_464841,00.html), September 20, 2000.

11. "Viruses and Hackers Costing Businesses Big Bucks," *CyberAtlas* (cyberatlas.com/big_picture/demographics/ article/0,1323,5921_410061,00.html), July 7, 2000.

12. Sally Katzen, Testimony by the Administrator, Office of Management and Budget, House Banking Domestic and International Monetary Policy, *Future of Money*, October 11, 1995; Ravi Kalakota and Andrew B. Whinston (1996), *Electronic Commerce: A Manager's Guide*, Addison-Wesley Longman, Inc.

13. "Vast Online Credit Card Theft Revealed," *I.T.* (www.it.fairfax.com.au/breaking/20000320/A19796- 2000Mar20.html), March 20, 2000.

14. Kalukota and Whinston, op. cit.

15. Matt Curtin and Marcus J. Ranum (1999), "Internet Firewalls: Frequently Asked Questions," (www.interhack. net/pubs/fwfaq/), November 15, 1999.

16. Ramesh Venkat (2000), "A Study on the Impact of Business-to-Business E-Commerce in Canada," Working Paper.

17. Dick Satran (2000), "Digital Signatures on the Way, Eventually," *Upside Today* (www.upsidetoday.com), July 4, 2000.

18. SET Secure Electronic Transaction LLC (www.setco.org).

19. "Privacy Fears Keep Consumers Off Health Sites," *CyberAtlas* (cyberatlas.com/big_picture/demographics/ article/0,1323,5971_425601,00.html), July 28, 2000.

20. "Privacy Issues Dividing Internet Consumers," *CyberAtlas* (cyberatlas.com/big_picture/demographics/article/ 0,1323,5941_346371,00.html), April 24, 2000.

21. "Consumers Fear for Their Online Privacy," *CyberAtlas* (cyberatlas.com/big_picture/demographics/article/ 0,1323,6061_228341,00.html), November 1, 1999.

22. Glen McDonald (2000), "Analysis: Who Cares About Amazon.com's Privacy Policy?" IDG.Net, October 2, 2000.

23. Miguel Helft (2000), "For Amazon, Honesty May Not Be the Best Policy," *The Standard* (www.thestandard.com), September 14, 2000.

24. Andy Walton (2000), "The U.S. and E.U. Have Agreed on 'Safe Harbor' Privacy Protection. But is it Really Safe?" *CNN.com*, June 9, 2000.

25. Ibid.

26. "Contract Law Has Still to Get to Grips with E-Commerce" (www.kmcoc.org.uk/contract-law.htm).

27. Brian Livingston (2000), "Beware: E-Signatures Can Be Easily Forged," *News.com* (www.news.com/Perspectives/ Column/0,176,463,00.html), July 14, 2000.

28. Trent Stinson (2000), "E-commerce Bill Aims To Revise Contract Law," *Sun-Sentinel.com* (www.sun-sentinel.com/ news/daily/detail/ 0,1136,30000000000119337,00.html), April 21, 2000.

29. "Are Shrinkwrap Licenses Legally Enforceable?" *Consumer Project on Technology* (www.cptech.org/ecom/ucita/ shrinkwraplegal.html).

30. Daniel Nathrath (1998), "Criminal Liability of Internet Providers in Germany: Conviction of a Compuserve Executive," *Journal of Internet Law* (www.gcwf.com/ articles/journal/jil_nov98_1.html), November 1998.

31. "A Framework for Global Electronic Commerce," *Information Infrastructure Task Force* (iitf.doc.gov/ eleccomm/glo_comm.htm#uniform), December 11, 1996.

32. "The Application of the Permanent Establishment Definition in the Context of Electronic Commerce: Proposed Clarification of the Commentary on Article 5 of the OECD Model Tax Convention, OECD (www.oecd.org/daf/fa/treaties/art5rev_3March.pdf), March 3, 2000.

33. Courtney Macavinta (1998), "Digital Copyright Bill Becomes Law," *CNET News.com* (news.cnet.com/news/ 0-1005-202-334727.html), October 28, 1998.

34. "Why an Internet-tax Moratorium is Needed," *SilliconValley.com* (www0.mercurycenter.com/svtech/ news/indepth/docs/qa042699.htm), April 25, 1999.

35. Michael Mazerov (2000), "Five-year Extension of the Internet Tax 'Moratorium' Would Further Erode the Tax Base of States and Localities," Center on Budget and Policy Priorities (www.cbpp.org/5-8-00tax.htm), May 12, 2000.

36. Philip Romero and James Wilburn, "E-Commerce & Taxation," *The Graziadio Business Report* (gbr.pepperdine. edu/993/ecommerce2.html), Pepperdine University, Summer 1999.

37. "The Canadian Electronic Commerce Strategy," *Electronic Commerce in Canada*, Industry Canada (e-com.ic.gc.ca/english/ecom_eng.pdf).

38. "Dismantling the Barriers to Global Electronic Commerce," OECD (www.oecd.org/dsti/sti/it/ec/prod/dismantl.htm), October 16, 1997.

39. Ibid.

40. "Consumers Don't Trust Web Sites," *CyberAtlas* (cyberatlas.com/big_picture/degmographics/article/0,1323,6061_185931,00.html), August 19, 1999.

41. "E-Tailers Still Lacking in Customer Service," *CyberAtlas* (cyberatlas.com/big_picture/demographics/article/0,1323,6061_435761,00.html), August 11, 2000

42. "Internet Privacy," FTC Statement Presented to the Subcommittee on Courts and Intellectual Property of the House Committee on the Judiciary, United States House of Representatives, Washington, D.C. (www.ftc.gov/os/1998/9803/privacy.htm), March 26, 1998.

43. Peter Lewis (2000), "Anti-Spam E-Mail Suit Tossed Out," *SeattleTimes.com*, March 14, 2000.

44. Linda Rosencrance (2000), "E-mail marketers announce anti-spam standards," *IDG.net*, September 26, 2000.

45. "Future of E-Commerce May Rest on Customer Service," *CyberAtlas* (cyberatlas.com/big_picture/demographics/article/0,1323,6061_274891,00.html), January 5, 2000.

46. Mary Mosquera (1999), "Consumers Need Global E-Commerce Protection," *TechWeb News* (www.techweb.com), June 8, 1999.

47. "The Canadian Electronic Commerce Strategy," *Electronic Commerce in Canada*, Industry Canada.

Chapter 14

1. Constantine Von Hoffman (1999), "The Making of E-Government," *CIO Magazine* (www2.cio.com), November 15, 1999.

2. "The State of the Internet, Report 2000," US Internet Council (www.usic.org), 2000.

3. "The ABCs of E-Learning," *The Industry Standard* (www.thestandard.com/grok) October 2000.

4. Ibid.

5. "Cybercitizen Health," *Cyber Dialogue* (www.cyberdialogue.com), 1999.

6. "The Emergence of the E-Health Consumer," Deloitte Research, Deloitte & Touche, 2000.

7. The Telemedicine Information Exchange (tie.telemed.org/).

8. "The State of the Internet," US Internet Council, 2000.

9. "Falling Through the Net: Defining the Digital Divide," National Telecommunications and Information Administration (www.ntia.doc.gov), November 1999.

10. "Falling Through the Net: Toward Digital Inclusion," National Telecommunications and Information Administration (www.ntia.doc.gov), October 2000.

11. John Cochran (2000), "The Digital Divide Narrows," *ABCNEWS.com*.

12. P. Dickinson and G. Sciadas (1999), "Canadians Connected: Household Computer Use," *Canadian Economic Observer*, February 1999, Catalog. No. 11-010-XPB.

13. "Digital Divide Persists in Europe," *Nua Internet Surveys* (www.nua.com/surveys), June 1, 2000.

14. Katie Hafner (2000), "A Credibility Gap in the Digital Divide," *LatinoLink.com* (www.latinolink.com/news/us/0309digi.php3), March 9, 2000.

15. Jane Wakefield (2000), "Europe May Regulate The Digital Divide," *ZDNet UK* (www.zdnet.co.uk/news/2000/18/ns-15301.html), May 10, 2000.

16. Robert Kraut, Vicki Lundmark, Michael Patterson, Sara Kiesler, Tridas Mukopadhyay, and William Scherlis (2000), "Internet Paradox: A Social Technology That Reduces Social Involvement and Psychological Well-Being?" *American Psychologist*, September 2000.

17. Storm A. King (1996), "Is the Internet Addictive, or Are Addicts Using the Internet?" (www.concentric.net/~Astorm/iad.html).

18. Ibid.

19. Keith N. Hampton and Barry Wellman (2000), "Examining Community in the Digital Neighborhood: Early Results from Canada's Wired Suburb," in Toru Ishida and Katherine Isbister (eds.), *Digital Cities: Technologies, Experiences and Future Perspectives*, 194–208.

20. Keith Hampton and Barry Wellman (1999), "Netville On-line and Off-line: Observing and Surveying a Wired Suburb," *American Behavioral Scientist*, 43 (3), November/December, 475–492.

21. Josh Bernoff (1999), "Interactive TV Cash Flows," Forrester Research (www.forrester.com), August 1999.

22. Ibid.

Appendix D

1. ICC/ESOMAR Codes and Guidelines are always subordinate to existing national law. There is currently no international unanimity as to whether country of origin or country of destination applies to research on the Internet. For More Information Please Visit: http://www.esomar.nl/guidelines/internet_guidelines.htm

Credits

Page 3, Autobytel.com. Used with Permission; Page 4, Mercedes Benz Canada, Inc. Used with Permission; Page 9, ActivMedia Research Inc.; Page 9, IPSOS-Reid. Used with Permission; Page 10, Permission granted by NUA http://www.nua.com/surveys; Page 10, IPSOS-Reid. Used with Permission; Page 19, Ananova Ltd. Used with Permission; Page 29, Bluelight.com. Used with Permission; Page 29, www.netzero.com. Used with Permission; Page 33, CDNOW. Used with Permission; 34, www.ic3d.com. Used with Permission; Page 43, www.mobshop.com. Used with Permission; Page 53, DrKoop.com. Used with Permission; Page 54, Drugstore.com. Used with Permission; Page 54, Medbroadcast.com animation. Used with Permission; 63, Rocketcash.com. Used with Permission; Page 74, www.selfcare.com. Used with Permission; Page 75, My Simon.com. Used with Permission; Page 81, www.globalnetxchange. Used with Permission; Page 93, Bidmix.com. Used with Permission; Page 99, ©2000 Dell Computer Corporation. Reprinted with permission. All rights reserved. Dell is a trademark of Dell Computer Corporation. Intel is a trademark of Intel Corporation; Page 99, www.office.com. Used with Permission; Page 99, Valassis. Used with Permission; Page 99, www.Nokia.com. Used with Permission; Page 99, Engage. Used with Permission; Page 113, Strategis Marketing Industry Canada. Used with Permission; Page 117, IPSOSReid. Used with Permission; Page 122, www.surveysite.com. Used with Permission; Page 124, Perseus Development Corporation. Used with Permission; 131, Deja.com. Used with Permission; Page 145, The Industry Standard. Used with Permission; Page 157, CDNOW. Used with Permission; Page 172, Blackvoices.com. Used with Permission; 178, Heineken Canada. Used with Permission; 193, Proctor and Gamble, Inc. Used with Permission; 194, ®Becel is a registered trademark of Unilever Canada; Page 197, Ceiva Logic, Inc. Used with Permission; Page 200, Swatch International. Used with Permission; Page 204, Casey Murartori, noa-mazon.com; Page 214, www.dotster.com. Used with Permission; Page 215, Indigo. Used with Permission; Page 226, Nielson/Netratings. Used with Permission; Page 231, Used with Permission; Page 231, Used with Permission; Page 240, © 2000 by Yahoo! Inc. Yahoo! And the Yahoo! Logos are trademarks of Yahoo! Inc.; Page 245, Nike, Inc. Used with Permission; Page 248, Reprinted with permission of General Motors of Canada; Page 248, BMW Canada. Used with Permission; Page 248, Ford Canada. Used with Permission; Page 248, Toyota Canada. Used with Permission; Page 248, Honda Canada. Used with Permission; Page 248, Mazda Canada. Used with Permission; Page 249, © 2000 by Yahoo! Inc. Yahoo! And the Yahoo! Logos are trademarks of Yahoo! Inc.; Page 252, Copyright © 2000, eCoupons Inc. All rights reserved; Page 265, Reprinted by permission of The Industry Standard www.thestandard.com; Page 268, ActivMedia Research. Used with Permission; Page 277, Courtesy of Mary Kay Inc.; Page 288, www.bluemercury.com. Used with Permission; Page 295, Circline, Inc. Used with Permission; Page 303, © Lands' End, Inc. Used with Permission; Page 306, www.Ashford.com. Used with Permission; Page 308, LivePerson.com. Used with Permission; Page 309, Etoys.com. Used with Permission; Page 327, Trust.e.com. Used with Permission; Page 340, Trust.e.com. Used with Permission; Page 340, BBBOnline. Used with Permission; Page 340, BizRate.com. Used with Permission; Page 350, Used with Permission; Page 351, www.andhrapradesh.com. Used with Permission; Page 357, *Internet World Magazine.* Used with Permission; Appendix D—ESOMAR guidelines Copyright © 2000 by ESOMAR, Amsterdam, The Netherlands. All rights reserved. No part of this publication may be reproduced or transmitted without the prior written permission of ESOMAR. Permission for using this material has been granted by ESOMAR. For further information, please visit the ESOMAR Website: www.esomar.nl; Appendix E—Copyright © by the American Marketing Association.

Index